C000113447

ENGLAND

IN THE REIGNS OF

JAMES II AND WILLIAM III

ENGLAND

IN THE REIGNS OF

JAMES II AND WILLIAM III

BY

DAVID OGG

Oxford New York
OXFORD UNIVERSITY PRESS
1984

Oxford University Press, Walton Street, Oxford OX2 6DP

London Glasgow New York Toronto
Delhi Bombay Calcutta Madras Karachi
Kuala Lumpur Singapore Hong Kong Tokyo
Nairobi Dar es Salaam Cape Town
Melbourne Auckland

and associated companies in
Beirut Berlin Ibadan Mexico City Nicosia

Oxford is a trade mark of Oxford University Press

First published by the Clarendon Press 1955
First issued as an Oxford University Press paperback 1969
Reissued 1984

British Library Cataloguing in Publication Data
Ogg, David
England in the reign of James II and
William III—(Oxford paperbacks)
1. Great Britain—History—1660–1714
I. Title
942.06'7 DA435
ISBN 0–19–881154–3

Library of Congress Cataloging in Publication Data
Ogg, David, 1887–1965.
England in the reigns of James II and William III.
Sequel to: England in the reign of Charles II.
Includes bibliographical references and index.
1. Great Britain—History—1660–1714. I. Title.
DA435.035 1984 941.06'7 84–908
ISBN 0–19–881154–3 (pbk.)

Printed in Great Britain by
The Guernsey Press Co. Ltd.
Guernsey, Channel Islands

PREFACE

THIS book is a sequel to the author's *England in the Reign of Charles II*, first published in 1934, and now available in a revised reprint; together, the three volumes[1] are intended to provide a continuous account of English history and institutions in the period 1660–1702. The title has been interpreted strictly, in the sense that the space allotted to Scotland, Ireland, and the Plantations bears no proportion to that allotted to the main theme—England—but, even with this limitation, it may be felt that the subject is a great, indeed an ambitious one. So, too, in the intermingling of narrative with descriptive or analytical chapters, the scheme of the earlier book has been partly followed, a scheme made clear by the list of chapter contents, from which it will be seen that the non-narrative material is placed at the beginning, or at the end, or is interposed at some point having special relevance to the stage reached in the sequence of events. To almost any such scheme there are objections, the best being that which has fewest; but at least this book has been built on a definite plan, and its use should be facilitated by the preliminary list of chapter contents, by numerous cross-references, and by an ample index.

Moreover, the long interval between the appearance of the two parts has enabled the author to mature and develop certain views about the English social structure which were tentatively suggested in the earlier volumes—these will be found mainly in chapters II, III, and IV of the present volume—in fairness, therefore, this work should be considered in relation to its predecessor. Nevertheless, the present book may claim to have a unity of its own for, in the space of seventeen years here described, England, from a Bourbon dependency, became a European power. A short period, but a great theme.

The author has been fortunate not only in the facilities afforded by our great libraries and archives, where the standard of efficiency and helpfulness is higher than ever, but also by the unstinted assistance of friends and colleagues. Dr. H. K. Andrews

[1] *Publishers note:* In the Oxford University Press paperback edition of *England in the Reign of Charles II* the two volumes are reprinted in one volume.

helped with music, Mr. H. V. D. Dyson with literature, and Mr. J. B. Butterworth with law. Professor Edward Hughes and Mr. K. G. Davies placed their very wide knowledge of commerce and finance at the author's disposal, as well as making many corrections and suggestions. Professor Andrew Browning repeated the noble service he had already performed for the earlier book by revising the whole of this one, and saving the author from many mistakes of fact and expression. To the criticism and interest of these distinguished scholars this book owes much. But no work of this kind can hope to be free from errors; for these, as for the opinions expressed, the author alone is responsible.

D. O.

January 1955

NOTE

I WISH to express my grateful thanks to Sir John Craig and Mr. M. W. Flinn for important corrections now embodied in this revised impression.

D. O.

May 1963

CONTENTS

ABBREVIATIONS

Add. MSS.	Additional Manuscripts, British Museum.
Aff. Étr.	Affaires Étrangères, Archives des, Paris.
Baschet	Baschet, Transcripts from reports by French ambassadors from originals in the Affaires Étrangères, Paris. (Record Office.)
B.M.	British Museum, London.
Bodl.	Bodleian Library, Oxford.
Burnet	Burnet, Gilbert, History of my Own Time, 6 vols., Oxford, 1833.
Cal. S.P. Amer.	Calendar of State Papers, America and West Indies.
Cal. S.P. Dom.	Calendar of State Papers, Domestic.
Cal. Tr. Bks.	Calendar of Treasury Books, ed. W. A. Shaw.
Cam. Hist. J.	Cambridge Historical Journal.
C.J.	Commons, Journals of the House of.
Cobbett	Parliamentary History of England, ed. W. Cobbett, 36 vols., 1808–20
Dalrymple	Dalrymple, sir J., Memoirs of Great Britain and Ireland, 2 vols. 1771–3.
D.N.B.	Dictionary of National Biography.
Documents	English Historical Documents, 1660–1714, ed. A. Browning.
Dumont	Dumont, J., Corps Universel Diplomatique, 8 vols., 1726–31.
Econ. Hist. Rev.	Economic History Review.
E.H.R.	English Historical Review.
Grey	Grey, Anchitel, Debates in the House of Commons, 1667–94, 10 vols, 1769.
Halifax	Halifax, George Savile, marquis of. Life and Letters, ed. Miss H. C. Foxcroft.
H.M.C. Rep.	Historical Manuscripts Commission Reports.
Instructions Données	Instructions données aux ambassadeurs de France depuis la traité de Westphalie, Recueil des.
L.J.	Lords, Journals of the House of.
Luttrell	Luttrell, N., A Brief Historical Relation . . ., 6 vols. Oxford, 1857.
P.C. Reg.	Registers of the Privy Council (Record Office).
P.R.O.	Public Record Office, London.
Ranke	Ranke, L., History of England . . ., 6 vols., 1875.
Rawl. MSS.	Rawlinson Manuscripts, Bodleian Library
S.P.	State Papers, Record Office.
State Trials	State Trials, ed. T. B. Howell, 21 vols., 1809–14.
Steele	Tudor and Stuart Proclamations, ed. R. Steele, 2 vols.
Trans. R.H.S.	Royal Historical Society, Transactions of the.

I

SCOTLAND; IRELAND; THE PLANTATIONS: A BRIEF SURVEY

In the later years of the seventeenth century the English-speaking peoples numbered about 8 millions, or little less than a seventieth part of the world's population, so far as that can now be estimated; in contrast, at the present time, about 200 millions, or nearly a tenth of the world's inhabitants, speak English as their mother tongue. Here is one of the greatest facts of modern history—the development and spread, not of English imperialism, but of British civilization. This is the more notable as England was a late arrival among the colonizing powers. Spaniards had long monopolized the gold and silver mines of the west; first the Portuguese and then the Dutch had seized the valuable spice islands of the east; the French were securely established in Canada, and threatened from the rear the thin strip of English settlements on the eastern seaboard of North America; hence, as we came late in the race for spices, furs, and precious metals, we had to content ourselves with territories which at first seemed second-best. But the future was to lie with men even more than with materials, and the English was not the only nation to take part in the building of Anglo-Saxon civilization, which, after all, embodies not merely racial character, but a distinctive way of life. Of that way of life, the English language is the symbol and bond.

This opening chapter is a brief survey of the peoples, predominantly English-speaking, in Scotland, Ireland, and the Plantations. It is followed by a short survey of England, with special reference to population and advantages, and then by two chapters devoted to analysis of some aspects of English society and institutions.

Estimates of the population of Scotland are conjectural, the figure most commonly accepted being a million, that is about half the population of Ireland, and less than a fifth that of

England. This was very unevenly distributed, as it was concentrated mainly in the central plain or waist of Scotland, and in the numerous small ports on the east coast, particularly those on both sides of the Forth estuary; moreover, the relative importance of the towns fluctuated considerably, because of economic changes and the Cromwellian conquest. Edinburgh, with its reputed total of 30,000 inhabitants, had nearly twice the population of Glasgow, followed by Aberdeen, Dundee, Perth, and Kirkcaldy; but it should be recalled that many parishes, now included in these cities, were then completely separate. Generally, the orientation of Scottish civilization was towards the eastern or continental side. This disposition is still attested by the fact that, of her four universities, three are on the east coast; a European outlook which for long had influenced both the culture and trade of the nation, so that her affinities were with France and Holland, rather than with England.

Four areas of Scotland may be roughly distinguished. First, the Highlands and the Isles of the west and north-west, where there were no towns in the modern sense, and where the grazing in the valleys provided for a cattle industry, supplemented by fishing on the coast and on the numerous salt-water lochs. Second, the north-east and east, in which are situated the cathedral and university cities of St. Andrews and Aberdeen; an area in which were located the majority of the ports, handling an export trade in wool, coarse cloth, hides, and salt, all comparatively bulky in proportion to value; in return for which there were imports of fine cloth from England, timber from the Baltic, and wine from Bordeaux. Third, the south and south-west, including Galloway, Dumfries-shire, Ayrshire, and the counties served by the Tweed; here arable was intermingled with grazing, and in these counties were to be found the small farms and crofts of a self-reliant peasantry, many of them Covenanters. The western shires of this area maintained some contact with the Presbyterians of Ulster. Fourth, and most important economically, was the midland belt connecting the estuaries of Clyde and Forth, a strip in which coal and shale deposits were abundant; here there were mining, distilling, sugar refining, cloth and paper making. Leith was Scotland's largest port, within two miles of the capital, Edinburgh, which, at that time, was distinguished, not for its spaciousness, but for the noisome congestion of its High Street. More picturesque, in the opinion of older travellers, was Glasgow, the second largest port, having a university, housed, at that time, in its fifteenth-century buildings, the only Scottish city on the mainland which still preserves its medieval cathedral. As the Clyde was shallow the Glasgow merchants conveyed their goods by lighter or road to Port Glasgow, about twenty miles down the river for shipment to the west; and the city was about to enter on the era of the tobacco magnates. In the period before the Union, Glasgow's trade with the Plantations was surreptitious.

Nevertheless, terms like 'industrial' or 'commercial' may be misleading when applied to such a country as seventeenth-century Scotland, where conditions were still rudimentary, and life had a harshness notable even on the standards of that age. Scottish trade had suffered from the three Anglo-Dutch wars, in which the northern kingdom had been obliged to take part; with the result that the old trade with Flanders diminished, and the staple at Veere fell into decay. Tariff barriers limited trade with England, and with her old ally France; moreover, as she was excluded from a legitimate part in the rich colonial trade, Scottish economy was mainly one of self-sufficiency, for there was little interchange of commodities; and, as the older crafts were limited to the royal or privileged boroughs, there was little expansion of industry. Enclosures were uncommon, except near the considerable towns; fences were rare, because of the shortage of timber; much of the land, notably in the north and west, was of moor or rock.

In such conditions one can well understand how, long before Dr. Johnson's time, the best roads in Scotland were those leading out of it. Traditionally, the most promising career for an ambitious young Scot was to be had in a continental army; if he were a scholar, he usually completed his education in France or Holland; if he were a small tradesman, he might join the large band of pedlars who toured England. Nevertheless, even before the Union, there were signs of awakening. Wherever arable was available it was well cultivated, oats, barley, and hemp being the main crops; and new devices, such as that of Jethro Tull, had a good reception in the north where, after all, some of the best farm land in Britain is to be found, notably in Morayshire, in parts of Aberdeenshire, and in the Lothians.

There was even some industrial progress, as new crafts came to be established in 'unfree' boroughs; there was also development of joint-stock enterprise. The Bank of Scotland was founded in 1695. Generally, the Scots, like their allies and co-religionaries the Dutch, were prepared to overcome by skill and hard effort, the natural difficulties with which they were confronted; but the contrast between the prosperity of their countries must have been galling to observant northerners.

These circumstances favoured the long survival of medieval institutions; indeed, at this time, Scotland had more in common with the continent than with England, and was saved from perversions of medievalism mainly by the common sense and independence of her inhabitants. The rights of baronial lords—long mitigated in the south—were applied in the north with rigour, and sometimes severity. Courts of Barony, which continued to be held until 1747, imposed many obligations on husbandmen and cottars,[1] one of the most oppressive being that of 'multure', whereby tenants had to have their corn ground at the lord's mill, which was generally let to a tacksman, or lessee. Farmers, usually holding from crop to crop, were liable to eviction at the lord's will, and leases of land were uncommon. As well as collecting his rents, the lord of the barony decreed, each half-year, the amount of the parish rates, sometimes including therein a levy for the village school, or for maimed soldiers; and wherever he held also a heritable jurisdiction, such as that of sheriff, he might raise an annual revenue from fines, in this respect contrasting with the English justice of the peace, who, however ignorant or oppressive, did not usually, at this time, have a pecuniary interest in his decisions. It was this absence of personal motive that helped to make local administration in England so much better than that in Scotland, where the selfish element was often unconcealed; and ingenuity might enable a hereditary sheriff to obtain his fine, whatever happened in the course of the proceedings.[2] Thus, if an assault could not be proved, there might be indirect evidence

[1] For examples of this jurisdiction, see D. G. Barron, *Baron Court Book of Urie*, and C. B. Gunn, *Records of the Baron Court of Stichill*. Both volumes have good introductions. Urie is in Kincardineshire; Stichill is near Kelso.

[2] For examples see W. Hector, *Selections from the Judicial Records of Renfrewshire*, 77–88.

of a brawl, and that would suffice. If such were the conditions in the local jurisdictions, it is not surprising that, in the supreme court, the Court of Session, justice was often perverted, especially in political cases, and men were convicted on evidence which, as Halifax said, would not have hanged a dog in England. Still more, Scottish juries might be imprisoned for their verdicts, and torture was used in order to extort confessions. In the administration of the law, Scotland resembled France rather than England.

The same was true of the legislative system. The Estates of the Realm[1] consisted of the lords of parliament, the bishops, the commissioners of shires, and the burgesses. In proportion to population, the Scottish peerage was more numerous and even more powerful than the English. The bishops sat with the lords in the Revolution parliament of 1689, but disappeared with the abolition of episcopacy in that year. The commissioners of shires, representing the thirty-three counties, were not unlike the English knights of the shire, but only a fraction of them were in the habit of attending the meetings of the Estates; the burgesses were returned by over sixty royal boroughs. In the old Parliament House of Edinburgh the Estates sat in the same chamber; their sessions were short; their proceedings, until the Revolution, were usually formal, mainly because parliament had so little to do with the initiation of legislation, this being the duty of a committee, known as the Lords of the Articles, which, in accordance with the royal instructions, drafted the business in advance. It is therefore significant that, with the end of Stuart rule, one of the first steps taken by parliament was the abolition of the Articles;[2] it is significant also that this was accomplished, not after debate in Parliament House, but as a result of preliminary negotiations in a nearby tavern.[3] At a time when the Irish legislature was little more than an annexe to Westminster, the Scottish Estates were a medieval body, showing few signs of development until the period just before their dissolution; but, on the other hand (in contrast with Ireland), Scotland was not content to copy the English statute

[1] The standard book is that by R. S. Rait, *The Parliaments of Scotland*. Much useful information will be found in the second volume of E. Porritt, *The Unreformed House of Commons*.

[2] *Documents*, no. 264.

[3] E. Porritt, op. cit. ii. 102–3.

book, for her legislation abounded in measures, mostly intended for national circumstances, some of them recalling the spirit of a bygone age, others anticipating reforms of modern times.

Several reasons account for the political backwardness of Scotland. Representative bodies in the north were of ancient origin, but they had not progressed as elsewhere, an example being the Convention of Royal Burghs, one of the oldest institutions[1] of its kind in Europe. In its constitution, this organization of merchants recalls the Cinque Ports[2] in England; but its functions were much wider, for these were extended to about sixty-five boroughs, whose domestic and foreign trade was controlled by the Convention, which, in this capacity, was acting like a great trading company. A revenue, raised from fines and levies, was applied to help decayed towns, or to repair harbours; so here we have a fraternity of a medieval type. More important, the Convention determined the proportion of national taxation to be paid by each of its constituent boroughs, and so was a parliament in miniature, with the result that a Scottish burgher served in a dual capacity—as a member of the Convention, and as one of the third estate in parliament; indeed, a meeting of parliament might have to be adjourned if the Convention happened to be in session elsewhere than in Edinburgh.[3] In this way, out of parliament, the attention of the Scottish third estate was focused on the regulation of trade; while, in parliament, it was not directed to the control of taxation, and so the third estate never played a part comparable with that of the Commons in the south, where the medieval conception of estates had faded, and where the House of Commons, whose province was steadily being enlarged, included a majority of landowners, with a sprinkling of lawyers and sons of peers. In contrast, the northern estates, as in many continental countries, were kept rigidly distinct, a separation which had been decreed by a parliamentary order of 1589 forbidding anyone to take upon himself the functions of more than one estate. Hence, like the third estate in France, that in

[1] J. D. Marwick, *Records of the Convention of Royal Burghs, 1597–1711*, and Mrs. T. Pagan (Theodora Keith), *The Convention of the Royal Burghs of Scotland.*

[2] This analogy is suggested by Mrs. Pagan, op. cit. 264.

[3] E. Porritt, op. cit. ii. 41.

Scotland was weak, because it was both normal and homogeneous; whereas, in England, it was strong, because so abnormal, and its composition so diversified. This is why Edinburgh could never have become a second Westminster.

The Scottish parliament was thus only one of the institutions through which public life was diffused. There was also the privy council, whose decrees were described as Acts, a body by means of which, prior to the Revolution, an absolute sovereign could sometimes obtain his ends, if parliament proved recalcitrant; and there was the General Assembly of the church of Scotland, restored in a somewhat attenuated form in 1689, but nevertheless an ecclesiastical parliament in which matters of secular import were often discussed. This diffusion of interest and activity helps to explain why Scotland could so easily be managed by such unscrupulous tools as Lauderdale and the earl of Perth, and how the real implications of Stuart rule were nowhere so fully realized as in the north. It also helps to account for the fact that, throughout the eighteenth century, the Scottish representatives at Westminster were no more than a reliable make-weight for the government. Emancipation came to Scotland, but too late for the development of a strong and organized political life.

Nevertheless, the northern kingdom was one of the best educated countries in Europe; and her peasantry, intelligent and independent, were not easily impressed by the externals of pomp and power. Calvinism endowed them with a strong sense of purpose and responsibility; poverty trained them in habits of thrift and self-reliance; persecution obliged many of them to prefer their faith to their lives; and the climate completed the process by inducing an intolerance of the frivolous and meretricious. The grim realities of existence sharpened insight into the grimmer realities of human character, expounded not only in the jeremiads of the pulpit, but in that more subtle irony with which the ploughman assuaged his lot. This quiet sarcasm of the Scottish peasant, seldom unkind, and often penetrating, had at times a genuine literary quality, because based on humanity and understanding; to this, an expression, universal in its appeal, was afterwards given by Burns. In the life of the older Scotland, poetry was as elemental as its soil.

But these things were barely perceptible in this turbulent

period when, in co-operation with her southern neighbour, Scotland at last cast off the yoke of her Stuart kings. It was an age of materialism, and so her poverty and backwardness ensured that, for the most part, Scotland was regarded by England with dislike and contempt.

Another neighbour regarded with dislike and contempt was Ireland. The population of Ireland, at the end of the century, has been estimated at just over two millions,[1] of whom probably about half a million were Protestants. In church and state, the country was ruled by a minority. The established or episcopal church of Ireland consisted of four archbishops—Armagh (the primate), Cashel, Dublin, and Tuam—with eighteen bishops and a clergy, many of whom were pluralist or non-resident. They had more detestation for the Presbyterians of Ulster than for the Roman Catholics. As representative of the sovereign, the lord lieutenant wielded executive authority in Dublin, with the help of a privy council and a parliament of two Houses, whose sessions were short, irregular, and usually placid. A revolutionary parliament, consisting mainly of Roman Catholics, sat in the summer months of 1689, but all its acts were annulled;[2] otherwise, there was no meeting of the regularly constituted parliament between 1666 and 1692; nor, in William's reign, was there any session after 1698. In Ireland, therefore, parliamentary government existed only in a very limited sense of the term.

The Irish peerage, consisting of about seventy-two Protestants and twenty-eight Catholics, did not play a part in the political or social life of the country comparable with that of the peers in England, partly because so many of them did not possess estates enabling them to maintain their dignity; some of them, indeed, but for pensions would have been destitute. Of the Protestant peers, between forty and fifty usually attended the sessions of the Upper Chamber, in which the lay peers were sometimes outnumbered by the bishops. In the House of Commons were 300 members, made up of sixty-four knights for thirty-two counties; 234 burgesses from boroughs each returning two members, and two from Trinity College, Dublin.

[1] K. H. Connell, *The Population of Ireland, 1750–1845*, which gives tables for the first years of the eighteenth century.

[2] *Infra*, 248–9, 260.

Procedure and legislation were modelled closely on the example of Westminster; so closely that a standing committee of the Commons studied English statute legislation in order to propose Bills; but, in spite of Poynings' Act, a slight element of autonomy had crept into the Irish legislature, and in 1692 the Commons went so far as to reject a money Bill because it had not originated in their House. This brought on them a sharp rebuke from the lord lieutenant;[1] but thereafter a compromise was adopted, whereby two kinds of Bill were recognized—government Bills, which came to the Commons from the privy council, and Bills promoted by the Commons in the form of 'heads'.[2]

Before the Revolution, Roman Catholics had not been excluded from the Commons, nor from voting at elections; but, after the English Act of 1691,[3] the imposition of the new oaths and the declaration against transubstantiation debarred them from both Houses, though they still voted at elections, until deprived of this right in 1727. Protestants married to Papists were disabled by an Irish Act[4] of 1697 from sitting in parliament. So far, therefore, as there was any political life in Ireland in this period, it was directed from London by the English legislature and privy council, acting through a subordinate privy council and parliament in Dublin. Against this, a protest came from William Molyneux, a member for Dublin, who wrote a book[5] to prove that, as Ireland was linked with England only through the crown, the English legislature had no jurisdiction in Irish affairs. The book was condemned by the English House of Commons.[6]

The land question in late seventeenth-century Ireland was not unlike that in the western states of North America in the early nineteenth century, except that in Ireland the dispossessed sometimes regained possession; moreover, English and Protestant interest in this matter was so strong as to explain the statement of a contemporary,[7] writing in 1682: 'Ireland is

[1] *Journals of the Irish House of Lords*, 1, 3 Nov. 1692.

[2] E. Porritt, op. cit., ch. 54.

[3] 3 W. and M., c. 2; also *infra*, 260.

[4] *Infra*, 263.

[5] *The Case of Ireland's being Bound by Acts of Parliament* (1698). Molyneux was the founder of a Philosophical Society in Dublin, on the model of the Royal Society.

[6] *C.J.* xii, 27 June 1698.

[7] R. Lawrence, *The Interest of Ireland*, 50.

become west England.' Before the rebellion of 1641 the Protestants were said to have had about four of the nine million cultivable acres; but, as a result of confiscations and the Cromwellian settlement, a great part of the remaining five millions was divided among the Protestants, most of them small, independent landlords. After the Restoration there was a complicated redistribution, mainly at the expense of the Cromwellians, to the advantage of Court favourites and, in some cases, Roman Catholics, a redistribution in accordance with the Act of Settlement passed by the Irish legislature in 1662, and modified by the Act of Explanation in 1665.[1] The result appears to have been that, by the time of the accession of James II, a proportion, estimated at between two-thirds and four-fifths of Irish land, was held in terms of the Act of Settlement; so it is not surprising that the revolutionary parliament of 1689 annulled that Act. Then followed the war, and the renewed subjugation of the country, accompanied by wholesale forfeitures, lavish royal grants, and some astute manœuvring by Protestant and Catholic alike, in which influence and guile, sometimes supplemented by perjury and forgery, appear to have determined the allocation of title deeds. Irish land, an investment for conquerors during the Commonwealth, provided a speculation for another set of investors after the Restoration, and a general scramble for all after the Revolution.

In the northern counties of the Pale, in Tipperary and Kilkenny and in the eastern counties of Ulster,[2] the level of agriculture was at least moderate; but elsewhere it was comparatively low. Bogs remained unreclaimed; woods, cut down by the English, were not renewed; mines were left derelict; commons were unenclosed. For this state of affairs the fertility and natural resources of the country were partly responsible. In western Ireland a salmon two feet long could be bought for a penny, 45 eggs might be had for the same price; a fat goose cost 3*d.*, a turkey 6*d.*[3] The diet of the poor consisted mainly of vegetables, with oatmeal, butter, and milk, commodities so

[1] These Acts are respectively 14 & 15 Car. II, c. 2 (Ireland) and 17 & 18 Car. II, c. 2 (Ireland). They will be found in *Statutes at Large Passed in the Parliaments of Ireland*, vols. ii and iii.

[2] See map no. 17 in *Documents* for apportionment of an assessment in 1698.

[3] *Ireland's Lamentations . . . by an English Protestant*, 1689.

plentiful and cheap that many were content with two days' work in the week; but contemporary evidence does not prove that the potato was the staple food—a dangerous stage not reached until late in the eighteenth century.[1] Tobacco was the only luxury enjoyed by the poor. Clay pipes were in universal use; one pipe might be passed round an assembled company, each member, as his turn came, holding the smoke in his mouth as long as possible,[2] a practice which may have promoted taciturnity. Ireland's cheap food, together with her comparative lack of industry, pointed this moral to the economists, that men will work only in order to avoid starvation.

Although English was the official language, Irish was still spoken in many districts, often mixed with English words;[3] it was expelled by the institution of national schools in the nineteenth century, and partly restored by a new set of schools in the twentieth. The urban population of Ireland was small, the second city, Cork, being credited, at the end of the century, with about 25,000 inhabitants, followed by Limerick (11,000) and Waterford and Galway with no more than 6,000 each.[4] Belfast was still only a small port, dependent mainly on coastal trade. Dublin, with its two cathedrals, St. Patrick's and Christ Church, and its seven parish churches, was reputed in 1681 to have a population of 58,000, probably an overestimate; but in 1706 the figure of 60,000 was considered an underestimate. In no other city were the extremes of hospitality and good conversation in such close proximity to squalor and destitution. With its resident viceroy, its parliament, its law courts, and its university, Dublin, set on one of the most magnificent bays in the British Isles, might claim to have at least the trappings of a national capital, and in the eighteenth century it was the centre of an intellectual and social life as brilliant as that of any city in Europe.[5]

Few Englishmen visited Ireland except on duty, and most of them appear to have been glad when that duty was fulfilled. But at least the strategic importance of the island was realized

[1] K. H. Connell, op. cit., ch. 5.

[2] *The Journals of John Stevens*, ed. R. H. Murray, 139.

[3] E. Maclysaght, *Irish Life in the Seventeenth Century*, 308–9.

[4] Ibid. 187.

[5] For an account of Dublin in this period, see M. Craig, *Dublin, 1660–1860*.

by some Englishmen. 'Set as a watch tower in the sea',[1] Ireland was essential for the maintenance of English maritime supremacy; some of her western inlets, notably Bantry Bay, might, it was thought, provide the best harbours in Europe.[2] But contemporary English opinion of Ireland was still influenced by memories of the Rebellion and the Cromwellian conquest. The Presbyterian element in Ulster was known to be frugal and industrious, but was suspected of republicanism; the Anglo-Irish, mainly in the Pale, though often improvident and degenerate, were preferred to Catholic landlords by the Irish themselves; as for the Catholic Celt, he was denied even the virtue of courage, being known to many Englishmen from the perjurers who had flocked across the Irish Sea at the time of the Popish Plot. The more conservative Catholics were in sympathy with Spain, with which some had family connexions, while the forward party favoured France;[3] in fact, many would have preferred allegiance to that country rather than to England. Like Scotland, Ireland in this period gave to the English language a new term of abuse—the word Tory. Here is a summary biography[4] of an aboriginal Tory by an officer of the army in Ireland:

> This is to let you know that last night I brought in the head of Cormick McCarrin who I shott myself; hee has binn a thife ever since hee was able to crale, and he robbed this 2 years paste.

But at least one contemporary considered the Irish Catholics to be 'a well natured people',[5] who might be made useful if freed from their priests.

Though not technically a plantation, Ireland was usually treated as one; alternatively, she was regarded as a conquered country, obliged to accept such laws as the crown might impose. Her value to England was mainly as a source of provisions, shipped to the colonies and to foreign countries; there was also a profitable export of fish to the Mediterranean, in

[1] *The Interest of England in the Preservation of Ireland*, by G. P., 19.

[2] For the proposed fortifying of Bantry Bay see *Rawl. MS.* A, 451, f. 8.

[3] T. Sheridan, *Historical Account*, in *H.M.C. Rep.*, *Stuart Papers*, vi.

[4] *H.M.C. Rep.* vii, app. 749. Lieut. W. Lucas to marquis of Ormond, 20 May 1680.

[5] *A Letter from the Duke of Schomberg's Camp* (1689) in *Bodl. Pamph.* 192.

which English merchants had an interest.[1] She was also a vent for English exports, such as hemp, paper, hops, lead, glass, harness, and coal; the Irish exports to England included malt, white herring, linen, tallow, hides, and timber; and in 1700 the interchange of such commodities between the two countries very nearly balanced at about £300,000 each way.[2] But these figures mean little, because the basic Irish exports of cattle, cloth, and wool were prohibited, lest their importation into England might lower English rents.

These prohibitions followed from the English Navigation Acts, which were extended to Ireland, and resulted in a number of economic changes. Under the later Stuarts, Ireland was, for a time, fairly prosperous,[3] because even the Acts prohibiting the export of cattle to England helped to create a large provision trade, which, in its turn, enabled the Irish to obtain more imports from abroad, and to increase their shipping. But this shipping was prejudiced by the Navigation Act of 1670–1 which required that colonial goods should be landed only in England; consequently, Ireland's overseas trade became more limited to foreign countries and their colonies. But it was with the Revolution that the period of full restriction began. Many sheep were pastured in Ireland, and a prosperous woollen industry was in the making. By 1698 England was adopting the policy of discouraging this new enterprise, and putting the manufacture of linen in its place; then, in the following year, the English legislature went farther, for it imposed additional restrictions even on Irish trade with foreign countries,[4] including the export of goods made or mixed with wool. The result was extensive smuggling of Irish wool and cloth, but this could not compensate for the loss of legitimate trade. Ireland, therefore, was forbidden to utilize fully the vast natural resources with which she was endowed.

So Irish commerce and shipping declined, with the result that there was stagnation and poverty throughout the eighteenth

[1] *The Interest of England in the Preservation of Ireland*, by G. P., 1689.

[2] See the tables for 1700–1 in sir C. Whitworth, *State of the Trade of Great Britain*, 1778.

[3] R. Bagwell, *Ireland under the Stuarts*, iii. 145.

[4] 10–11 Wm. III, c. 10. Miss A. E. Murray, *Commercial and Financial Relations between England and Ireland from the Restoration.*

century. There were other things. A cold, steady blast of social ostracism ensured that, beneath the embers, the ancient hatreds still glowed; and the imaginative were driven to seek refuge in that ancient dreamland of saints and kings, the more remote inspiration of Irish poetry and music. Politics and religion completed the tale. After the military conquest, thousands of Celts joined the French and continental armies; later, many Ulster Presbyterians, antagonized by the established Protestant Church, and hampered in their enterprise, emigrated to America, where their descendants were one day to play a great part in the War of Independence. Lost Irishmen and lost colonies still attest that older, illiberal attitude to those who were considered to be only on the fringe of English civilization.

Another fringe of that civilization was to be found on the eastern seaboard of North America, where English settlers were creating their distinctive institutions and traditions. On the 2,000 miles of coast between the sixtieth and the thirtieth parallels were to be found, articulated as it were in separate strata, the component elements of the English body politic; from the trappers of the Hudson's Bay territory and the migratory fishermen of the Newfoundland banks to the pioneers and frontiersmen of Maine; the shipmasters, publicists, and witch-hunters of New England; the small farmers and merchants of New York; the Quakers of Pennsylvania, scrupulous in morals and astute in business; the manorial lords of Maryland; the loyalist and Anglican squirearchy of Virginia tobacco planters; the 'mean whites' and smugglers who provided much of the scanty population in the malaria-infested swamps of the Carolinas. These, for the most part, were afterwards to be assimilated into the dynamic life of the United States, but they were largely English in origin nevertheless.

The old empire, however, was concerned more with materials than with men, and here a threefold distinction had been established by geography. The middle colonies, consisting of Pennsylvania, New York, and the New England group separated those northern and southern areas which could supply the raw material or the natural products in demand at home. Thus, in Newfoundland, which was not a settled plantation, and had no governor, there were only wooden huts round the harbours, where the fishermen remained for about two months in summer in order to cure and salt their catch. There the fleets, manned by men from Somerset and Devon, filled up with salted cod, which they took direct to Spanish and Portuguese ports, where, in exchange, they loaded up with wine, brandy, iron, salt, and Levant silks, which were then conveyed to England.[1] More than 10,000 tons of cod were carried annually in this trade, which, moreover, provided the most valued training ground for seamen. From the Hudson's Bay territory there were exports of pelts and furs. South of the middle colonies, that is in Maryland, Virginia, and the Carolinas, were the sources of the 'enumerated' goods, at this time mainly tobacco; towards the end of the century rice and indigo were being cultivated in the Carolinas. Thus, from the utilitarian point of view, the middle colonies did not comply with the demands of an empire which needed, mainly for re-export, the produce of north and south.

This factor, most clearly evidenced in the West Indies, can be illustrated by a reference to Jamaica and Barbados. Even more than Virginia, Barbados was noteworthy for the large proportion of Englishmen of aristocratic family among its planters; and during the second half of the century the island completely changed its character. From a settlement of comparatively small, mixed holdings and crops, in which the whites predominated, it had become, before 1700, a colony of large holdings, owned by substantial planters, devoted to one crop—sugar—and populated mainly by negroes. Her easterly position gave her an advantage over other West India islands, since the passage homeward was shorter, and was not impeded so much by adverse trade winds. Hence, in Barbados, exploitation of the slave and of an article of export became highly specialized, and was carried to its farthest limit; so that even in periods of low prices for sugar, as in many years of the later part of the century, the planters could hold out. In another respect Barbados was distinctive among the colonies. It was easier for the planter to retain his English connexions, or to visit his homeland, or even to retire there, when a fortune had been made. Many of them became not so much colonial settlers as Englishmen who had colonial plantations, and the degradation

[1] *Cal. S.P. Amer. 1697–8*, 130, and ibid. *1701*, 530. For a good modern account, see H. A. Innis, *The Cod Fisheries.*

of the slave seems almost to have emphasized the aristocratic character of the owner. This intimate connexion with England was facilitated by the development of a commission system, whereby the planters retained agents in London, whose duty it was to receive the cargoes, pay insurance and customs, and conduct a sale, either personally or through a broker.[1] In this way, a great West India interest was created, with important political ramifications;[2] and so Barbados became almost an integral part of the English economic and social system.

For a time, Jamaica was less fortunate. But she had at least one advantage. The trade winds which impeded the passage of her east-bound ships were the winds that blew the slave ships out to her; moreover, the position of the island, at the very heart of the Spanish Indies, made it the most convenient centre for the disposal of slaves. There they could be sold to best advantage among the Spaniards, who paid the highest prices, and paid promptly, either in gold or in produce. Hence the importance of the *Asiento* agency, which was leased by Spain to foreigners, and was located in Jamaica; by their contract, the *Asiento* agents had the monopoly of supplying the Spanish colonies with negroes. As these agents could afford to pay for the best specimens, the English West India planters often complained that they were left with the 'trash'. The slaves were imported into Jamaica mainly by the Royal African Company, whose ships, after disposing of their human cargo, filled up with sugar, usually in Barbados, which they exchanged in England for cloth and manufactured goods, intended for the trading ports of West Africa. Here was one of the triangular trades so much valued by contemporaries.

The home government alternately disavowed and encouraged the *Asiento*. The truth was that, in the last two decades of the century, England was doing all in her power to encourage trade with the Spanish colonies, even at the expense of prejudicing the English planters. So the governors of Jamaica were appointed from those who favoured the *Asiento*, including former agents of the African Company; H.M. ships were detached for protection of this trade against French privateers; even the

[1] K. G. Davies, 'The Origins of the Commission System in the West India Trade', in *Trans. R.H.S.*, 5th series, vol. ii.

[2] For this see R. Pares, *A West-India Fortune*.

Navigation Acts were suspended in its favour; and, during the war, two English regiments were stationed in Jamaica. One result was the steady flow of bullion to England, amounting in some years to as much as £200,000.[1] In this way, England wedged one foot firmly in the back door of the Spanish empire, and it was natural that this should arouse the jealousy of the many European nations engaged in the slave trade. Of these the most formidable was France. She wanted the *Asiento* for one of her West India islands; she was prepared to contest the steady English infiltration into the trade of the richest colonial empire in the world; still more, her effective acquisition of Spain in 1700 by the will of Charles II gave her full power to oust everyone else from that trade. This was one of the main causes of the War of the Spanish Succession.

The West Indies were therefore not only a source of valuable sub-tropical raw material, but also a spearhead for penetration into the Spanish empire; they were therefore regarded with special favour in the economic policy of the home country. It was otherwise with the mainland possessions, notably the New England group, which were not really 'plantations' at all; for, in these communities, there was a more developed economy, based not on the fields, but on the towns; using money instead of barter; having a population mainly of merchants and craftsmen, all endowed with strong traditions of independence and dissent. Already this was responsible for a certain sense of fragility in the mainland empire. Even more serious, as the Massachusetts shipowners were becoming carriers to many of the other plantations, English shipping interests seemed to be threatened by them as they had been threatened by the Dutch. Indeed the economy of these Puritan settlements appeared to be a microcosm of the English world, in so far as they had a woollen industry, which was the subject of complaint at Westminster;[2] and they based their export trade on a native commodity shipped in their own vessels. This was cod, caught off their own coast. Graded into three classes, merchantable, middling, and refuse, the first variety was sent to Spain and

[1] C. Nettels, 'England and the Spanish American Trade, 1680–1715' in *Journal of Modern History* (Chicago), March 1931.

[2] *C.J.* xii, 18 Jan. 1699. Report of commissioners of Trade and Plantations.

Portugal; the second to the Canaries and Madeira; the third—the refuse—to the West Indies, as the staple food of slaves.[1] This last branch of New England trade was particularly profitable, because the inferior cod was exchanged for molasses, which, when converted into rum, was sent to the west coast of Africa, where it was traded for negroes. Sharing of the spoils with pirates, who often fitted out in the western ports, and trading in goods smuggled into Newfoundland were among the other counts against this, the most Puritan of the colonies, which seemed, within the limits of the empire, to be beating us at our own game.

Whether from an instinct of precariousness, or because of a greater sense of responsibility, the home government in this period refused to accept additional colonial commitments. Thus, in 1687, when the captain of one of H.M. ships landed on the island of Dominica, then regarded as a French possession, but actually occupied only by cannibal Caribs, he gave his uncouth and probably bewildered hosts some kind of certificate that they had become voluntary subjects of the sovereign of England. A French protest to James II speedily annulled this peaceful addition to our empire,[2] but Dominica became British at the conclusion of the Seven Years War. Another neglected opportunity was in Tobago, consisting of two islands, valuable for their timber. The islands had originally been included in the grant of West Indian islands to the earl of Carlisle (1626); suzerainty was then claimed, in succession, by the duke of Courland, the Dutch, and the French, but the islands were left unoccupied, though the English claim was still considered valid. That claim was tacitly dropped, because it was thought that the settlement of more colonies in that region would prejudice our West India trade.[3] More remarkable was the case of Florida. With Carolina, this province had been granted in 1630 by Charles I to his attorney general, sir R. Heath, whose claims had descended to a Dr. Coxe. In 1699 Coxe applied to the committee of Trade and Plantations for leave to develop Florida with the help of a number of 'undertakers', including

[1] H. A. Innis, *The Cod Fisheries*, 133 sqq. Lord Bellomont's report of 28 Nov. 1700 in *Cal. S.P. Amer. 1700*, 674 sqq.

[2] Ibid. *1685–8*, 409, 20 July 1687. Memorial of Barrillon.

[3] Ibid. *1699*, 581, 30 Dec. 1699.

some French refugees.[1] In rejecting the application, the Board admitted that the proposed colony might provide some protection against the French in Louisiana, but on the other hand the claim might be contested by Spain (as she had already contested the Darien settlement), and an English colony in Florida would draw people from our other plantations in search of minerals. Moreover, the 'undertakers' might be influenced by the pernicious trade of stock jobbing. Most of all, the committee alleged, 'the multiplying of plantations tends to the encouragement of illegal trade'. So Florida was not added to those colonies which we were one day to lose.

At the time of the Revolution there were probably less than 270,000 European settlers in the English parts of the western hemisphere, of whom about 30,000 were dispersed in the West Indies. This sparseness of population over a wide area, so characteristic of the old empire, was strikingly revealed in contests with the French, when an extra thousand men might, at times, have made all the difference. In 1690, when sir William Phipps attacked Quebec, he had only about 2,500 men;[2] in the same year governor Codrington declared that, with the help of Barbados and 2,000 soldiers from England, he could master the French West Indian islands, which, between them, could not muster more than 5,000 defenders.[3] On the mainland there were larger populations, Virginia with its 58,000 whites and Massachusetts with about 45,000 being the most populous; the Carolinas (5,000) the least.[4] Of the towns, Boston, with 7,000, was the greatest, followed by New York with 5,000; and Charleston with just over 1,000; of these, only the first two, with their houses of brick, could be considered towns in any sense of the word. Jamestown, the capital of Virginia, was still only a village of wooden buildings, and even that had never been seen by many Virginians. In Maryland, where the manor served for purposes of local administration, it was found difficult to develop the two townships of Annapolis and

[1] *Cal. S.P. Amer. 1699*, 517, 579.

[2] Ibid. *1689–92*, 368, 12 Dec. 1690.

[3] Ibid. 225 sqq., 1 Mar. 1690.

[4] Ibid. *1693–6*, 171; also ibid. *1696–7*, 418 and 530. C. Bridenbaugh, in *The Colonial Craftsman*, 6, estimates the population of the mainland colonies in 1700 at 220,000.

Williamstad.[1] Not all the white settlers were of English stock. A strong Dutch element survived in New York; there were many Swedish and German immigrants into Pennsylvania; an Irish community in St. Kitts gave trouble during the war with the French; and the Scots were to be found in all the colonies. In Virginia, one of them, James Blair, became a member of the Council, and took the lead in establishing the College of William and Mary at Williamsburg.

In some cases there was a decrease of white population, notably in Jamaica and Barbados. In Jamaica the earthquake of 1692 was followed by plague and sickness, and many of the islanders were pressed into H.M. ships; but, on the other hand, the negroes increased from 9,000 in 1673 to about 45,000 in 1703.[2] This decrease in white population was most marked in Barbados, with the change in the character of the plantation from a collection of small holdings cultivating tobacco, ginger, and cotton to a highly capitalized sugar colony, worked by slaves. Some of the dispossessed found refuge in New Providence (Bahamas), where many of them joined mulattos, who lived mainly by searching for wrecks; 'if they miss any, they are sure to make one';[3] another resort for the unwanted was the Carolinas. In the province of New York such large holdings had been granted by Governor Fletcher that there was, at the end of the century, a shortage of land, which obliged many to migrate, usually to Pennsylvania and the Jerseys; a similar complaint came from Virginia and Maryland.[4] As in Barbados, this shifting of white population may have been occasioned also by the increase of negroes in the southern plantations, a factor which transformed the life and economy of a large part of our western empire.

The treatment accorded to the African slave varied considerably. In Virginia it was comparatively humane, because life there was patriarchal; in the Carolinas, on the other hand, with the development of rice cultivation at the close of the century, black labour was organized into large gangs by

[1] *Cal. S.P. Amer. 1696–7*, 418 sqq. Cf. also C. Bridenbaugh, *Cities in the Wilderness*.

[2] G. Guttridge, *Colonial Policy of William III*, appendix C.

[3] *Cal. S.P. Amer. 1701*, 367.

[4] Ibid. *1700*, 674, 20 Nov. 1700; also ibid. *1696–7*, 418.

bailiffs,[1] usually on behalf of absentee landlords; here, as in the West Indies, the negro was treated with brutality. In law, negroes were chattels, not persons. One of the very few protests against this iniquity came from a woman who could write from her early experience in Surinam, Mrs. Aphra Behn, known to Restoration England by her plays and novels. In her *Oroonoko, or the Royal Slave*[2] she pleaded for more humane treatment of the negro on the ground that he was a variety of 'natural man', having good instincts that might be developed by sympathy and patience.

A more immediate problem than that of the negro was the menace of the French, and to a lesser extent, that of the Indian. The French settlements could not muster more than about a twentieth part of the men available in the English mainland colonies, and were said to have only about 4,000 men fit for military service.[3] To the north-west they continued their contest with the Hudson's Bay Company for the fur trade, in spite of an Anglo-French agreement of 1686;[4] Maine and Nova Scotia were still disputed between the two races; to the south-west the St. Lawrence enabled them to menace New England and New York from the rear. Later, this threat was increased by French infiltration into the Ohio valley and by settlement of Louisiana. A small community of trappers and woodsmen, the French Canadians were well fitted for guerrilla warfare; moreover, their paucity of numbers obliged them to adopt a policy of active alliance with the Indians, a policy assisted by the fearless missionary work of the Jesuits, and by propaganda skilfully directed to inculcation in the savage breast of a firm conviction that the France of Louis XIV was the one great world power.[5] Selected tribesmen were sent to France in order that they might see for themselves the glories of Versailles as well as the size of French armies; while, in Canada, the 'praying Indians' conducted their forays with the enthusiasm of converts and the assurance of payment for each scalp. Our

[1] J. Fiske, *Old Virginia and her Neighbours*, II, 325.

[2] *Infra*, 535–7. A later protest against slavery was that by Rev. S. Sewall, *The Selling of Joseph* (1700). Defoe was also among those who condemned the system.

[3] *Cal. S.P. Amer. 1689–92*, 42 sqq., 29 May 1689.

[4] *Infra*, 190.

[5] *Cal. S.P. Amer. 1696–7*, 134.

policy was less effective, though the colonists knew the value of Indian alliance, and in some areas, notably in Connecticut, a system of native reserves was instituted.[1] At Albany, in New York territory, was our only considerable fort; but there we had the advantage of alliance with about 2,000 Indians of the Five Nations,[2] said to be the most warlike of all the aboriginal races in North America. These were nominally British subjects, and in 1696 an agent was appointed to look after them;[3] but many were withdrawn from their allegiance by presents of images and trinkets. They were the consistent enemies of the French and their Indian allies. 'We are now on our knees', declared their sachems at an interview in Albany with the governor of New York, 'but not quite down upon the ground. Let the king send his great canoes, and let the brethren of the other provinces awake, and we shall stand on our feet.'[4] Our Indian allies were the first and most zealous advocates of the conquest of French Canada.

This need for defence provided one of the main problems of colonial administration, particularly as the colonists were unwilling to contribute to its cost, and the soldiers sent out by the home country were so badly paid and equipped that many of them deserted. Nevertheless, as the old empire was to some extent held together by its realization of dependence on England for military and naval support, there may be some truth in the suggestion that, if we had succeeded in expelling the French from Canada, the New England provinces would have broken away altogether.[5] 'They seem to hate us that are English-born', wrote governor lord Bellomont[6] in 1699 of his subjects in Massachusetts and New York. It is notable that the only colonial governor of this period who advocated representation for the colonies at Westminster was the energetic Codrington,[7] governor of the Leeward Islands; but this measure, even had it been practicable, would not necessarily have preserved the mainland settlements, which, in different

[1] F. A. Mackenzie, *The Indian in Relation to the White Population of the U.S.A.*

[2] *Cal. S.P. Amer. 1685–8*, 326 sqq.

[3] Ibid. *1693–6*, 639. Order in Council of 16 Jan. 1696.

[4] Ibid. *1696–7*, 193, 9 Nov. 1696.

[5] Ibid. *1696–7*, xxiii.

[6] Ibid. *1699*, 430.

[7] Ibid. *1689–92*, 352 sqq., 26 Nov. 1690. For a good biography of Codrington, see that by V. T. Harlow.

degrees, resented what they considered exploitation by the mother country.

There was also resentment, varying in its intensity throughout the plantations, at the methods by which England recruited the population of the colonies. In cases of felony, the sentence of transportation was often substituted for the death penalty; and batches of reprieved felons were bought by dealers, who shipped them across the Atlantic, recouping themselves from the price paid by the importer. After Monmouth's rebellion, about 800 convicted rebels were dispatched to the west, mainly to Barbados, on terms profitable to speculators and beneficiaries;[1] at the same time, Argyll's defeat was the occasion of another enforced emigration, that of Presbyterian Scots, many of whom had sacrificed an ear to the executioner rather than admit the sovereignty of James.[2] Usually, such deportees acquired their liberty and a holding of land after four years' service (for the Monmouth rebels it was to be ten years); but the meaning of the term 'satisfactory' varied with the humanity of the master, so that while one ex-felon might achieve freedom and a distinguished place in the life of his colony, another might undergo an indefinite period of semi-slavery. Moreover, it should be recalled that, in this period, the term felony was applied to some offences which are now misdemeanours, and was denied to others which are now considered serious crimes; so the pickpockets and vagabonds were transported, while the forgers, the perjurers, and the large-scale embezzlers remained at home. Even thus, several colonies objected to this policy of the dumping ground; and in one case it was found difficult to induce a colony to accept a batch of female offenders, until Jamaica offered to take the risk, provided that a number of male convicts was added to the consignment.[3] Another type of involuntary emigrant was the victim of the kidnapper, usually a child, whose deportation provided a trade for which some ports, such as Bristol, were notorious. In the year 1670 alone, about 10,000 of these youthful unfortunates are said to have been shipped to America,[4] a profitable enterprise, which

[1] *Infra*, 153–4.

[2] *H.M.C. Rep.* xiii, app. pt. 8 (*MSS. of the duke of Buccleuch*), 105.

[3] *Cal. S.P. Amer. 1696–7*, 543, 8 July 1697.

[4] E. Channing, *History of the United States*, ii. 369.

remained unchecked because the penalties, a small fine and the pillory, were completely inadequate. It is to the credit of Jeffreys that he denounced this mean form of crime with his customary incisiveness.

An attempt was made to regulate free emigration to the colonies. An Order in Council[1] of December 1682 had prescribed rules for the emigration of indentured servants, whereby persons under twenty-one could be bound only by consent of their parents; and a register was to be kept of all such agreements, which could be signed only in the presence of a magistrate. Later, it was proposed to appoint commissioners for this purpose, with an office in London, and agents at the ports, the certificate from the registry to be a stop to legal proceedings in cases where one was unjustly accused of kidnapping. But even this very moderate reform does not appear to have been put into force; and so the peopling of the colonies continued to be the most haphazard element in English imperial policy. But the plantations were not seriously prejudiced by this lack of policy, for most of the Englishmen who went to the west were men of initiative, able to turn their hands to a great variety of occupations, and many of the early settlers had this merit, that they sacrificed convenience and comfort to principle. On her side, the home country sent out what she thought were the undesirables, never dreaming that the colonies often got the better of the bargain.

The voluntary emigrants were those able to pay their passage, usually costing £6–8, or those willing to undergo a period of servitude in lieu of the passage money. Some colonies, for a time, gave grants in aid for such emigrants.[2] Thus Jamaica undertook to pay £7 for the passage money of each manservant, with £1 to the master of the ship, the person imported to be entirely free; while in Barbados, so great was the shortage of white labour that in 1696 an Act was passed, to continue for three years, offering £6 for the fare of any Englishman or Scotsman between sixteen and forty, with £12 to the man on landing. But most of the voluntary emigrants were obliged to work their passage by four years of service, and many who prospered in the New World came of this stock. They were

[1] *Steele* i, no. 3737.

[2] *Cal. S.P. Amer. 1697–8*, 9 sqq., 4 Nov. 1697.

called 'redemptioners'. Defoe[1] thus described their prospects in Virginia:

> The meanest and most despicable creature, after his time of servitude is expired, if he will but apply himself to the business of the country is sure (life and health supposed) both of living well and growing rich. A transported felon is, in my opinion, a much happier man than the most prosperous, untaken thief; nor are those poor, young people so much in the wrong that go voluntarily over to these countries, and in order to get themselves carried over, freely bind themselves there.

Most of the colonists, now the second or third generation, were engaged in improvising a series of polities, each with some flaw or imperfection of its own, all reflecting in kaleidoscopic variety facets of that colourful civilization from which they had broken away. Not always law abiding, they specially valued the right, subject to the control of His Majesty in Council, to legislate for themselves. In exercising its power of review the privy council had no definite policy, except to forbid laws repugnant to English laws, or inconsistent with the laws of trade, or prejudicial to the prerogative. Review was sometimes as much in the interests of the colony as of the mother country.[2] After 1696 the new council of Trade and Plantations was almost always consulted, and the government sometimes acted as arbiter wherever it was thought that a law passed by one colony might injure another.[3] But the process of creating a uniform jurisprudence for the western empire was a slow one. At this period there was often the greatest confusion in regard to what law should be enforced; some holding that the laws of the colony had first place, and that only where these were silent should the English rule prevail; others alleged that only those English laws were valid that were in force at the first institution of the colony, or that they applied only where the plantations were specifically named.[4] This uncertainty led to many abuses. Thus, in the Leeward Islands, the law of England was some-

[1] *The Life of Colonel Jack* (Bohn ed.), 418. Cf. also J. C. Jeaffreson, *A Young Squire of the Seventeenth Century* (2 vols. 1878).

[2] E. B. Russell, *Review of American Colonial Legislation by King in Council*, ch. iv.

[3] Ibid. 199.

[4] J. H. Smith, *Appeals to the Privy Council from the American Plantations*, 473.

times accepted, and as often rejected;[1] in Massachusetts and Connecticut, laws were occasionally passed contrary to English law, or control was evaded by passing many temporary laws;[2] or their legislatures would accept a charter one day, and pass an Act contradicting it the next.[3] In Bermuda, where conditions were primitive, the laws were kept in the governor's custody, and nobody knew what they were;[4] in Rhode Island they were preserved in a smudged copy-book.[5] A new civilization of the legal-minded amateur was being evolved.

Less commendable was the actual administration of the law. In the early years of settlement, litigation had usually been limited to simple issues, such as could be determined by natural sagacity; but, by the close of the century, the courts were thronged with pettifoggers and 'small dealers in the law', who, knowing only the forms, confused judge and jury alike, with the result that litigation became more costly and dilatory. Appointment to responsible judicial office was often the result of jobbery; one, it was complained, had been a dancing master; another a glover; a third, a Scot, whose only qualification appeared to be that, at home, he had been sentenced to hanging for blasphemy.[6] All this was, of course, inevitable, since there were practically no opportunities for legal training, and those practitioners who emigrated from England usually did so in order to escape from their creditors. Nor was there yet an educated class from which the civil administration could be recruited; and, as so many patent offices could be filled by deputies, these were the days of the tapster and barber in high office.

The general result was that, while the letter of the law was insisted on, its spirit was often systematically evaded; for there is no lawlessness like that of those who have a knowledge of the law, and even some respect for it. Thus, in Virginia, members of the council were often appointed surveyors and collectors of Customs, their gains in these capacities, whether licit or illicit, being regarded as compensation for their trouble in attending council meetings.[7] Even a legislative grant of money might be

[1] *Cal. S.P. Amer. 1685–8*, 510. [2] Ibid. *1699*, 38.
[3] Ibid. *1696–7*, Preface, xxi. [4] Ibid. *1689–92*, 436.
[5] Ibid. *1697–8*, 129. [6] Ibid. *1699*, 81.
[7] For evidence see the interesting memorandum by H. Hartwell, J. Blair, and E. Chilton, ibid. *1696–7*, 641 sqq.

mingled with an element of self-interest, as when in 1687 the Assembly of Bermuda granted a tax on wine and rum for two years, having taken the precaution to stock up with these commodities beforehand.[1] This natural astuteness was sometimes reinforced by intimate knowledge of the text of the Bible. When the governor of New Hampshire complained to the Assembly that he had not received a penny for defence,[2] he incautiously quoted from Corinthians to the effect that no man goes to war at his own expense; whereupon the Assembly, giving chapter and verse, referred him to the passages in St. Luke[3] which condemn the folly of starting an enterprise without first sitting down and counting the cost. Reputation for these things may have somewhat prejudiced the planters, who found difficulty in raising credit in England because it was said to be almost impossible to obtain justice against debtors in the plantations; indeed there was a saying at home that if a man went to the New World ever so honest, 'the very air changes him in a short time'. 'But it is not the air', wrote a contemporary 'it is the universal corruption of justice.'[4] A less literate expression of the same opinion was that from a naval officer:[5]

> These parts of America are so much in combured by Governures and self intrist and imposinge upon His Majesty's subjects that no feasabell methudes are tackun to promote His Majesty's intrist and honure.

This condemnation of the 'governures' is probably too sweeping; for, in this period, they were a very mixed class. Within his colony, the governor had powers even more extensive than those of the king at home; he might call, prorogue, and dissolve the Assemblies; he commanded the forces; he made peace or war; he exercised a supreme prerogative in ecclesiastical, financial, and judicial affairs. His salary was always incommensurate with such numerous responsibilities, and he might experience great difficulty in obtaining its payment; in one colony, he had perquisites; in another, he had to

[1] *Cal. S.P. Amer. 1685–8*, 392, 1 July 1687. Governor sir R. Robinson to Blathwayt.

[2] Ibid. *1693–6*, 303. Lt.-Governor Usher to Lords of Trade, 1 July 1694.

[3] St. Luke, xv. 28, 29.

[4] *Cal. S.P. Amer. 1700*, 512. Pollexfen's memorandum.

[5] Ibid. *1696–7*, 224. Lieut. Roger Wright to duke of Bolton, 24 Nov. 1696.

limit himself to the annual grant from the home government, which was sometimes paid, not in cash, but in lottery tickets.[1] Or he might be entirely dependent on the grant made by the Assembly. It was in this last relationship that a colony could exercise pressure on its executive head; and so, in miniature, several of the plantations were able to apply the same lever as had proved so effective at Westminster, namely, refusal of supply. In these conditions, it is not surprising that many governors helped themselves. Harbouring of pirates was the simplest method of making a fortune; conniving at breaches of the laws of trade was another; straightforward extortion was a third. Of venal and corrupt governors examples are the duke of Albemarle (Jamaica) and Nicholas Trott (Bahamas). The commitments of the Royal African Company in the West Indies were reflected in the appointment of some of their agents to governorships, as Edwyn Stede (Barbados), Hender Molesworth (Jamaica), and sir William Beeston, an unusually efficient governor of Jamaica. Maryland and Virginia were comparatively fortunate in their governors, as these included the active sir Edmund Andros and sir Francis Nicholson, both of them arbitrary and tactless at times, but usually conscious of their responsibilities.

But the most notable governor of his period was Richard Coote, earl of Bellomont, an Irish peer who, after holding a number of Court offices, went to America in 1697 as governor of New York and New England. Impulsive, but just, his letters to the home government are probably the first colonial dispatches showing real knowledge of administrative problems, and ability to suggest reforms. He took an active part in the suppression of piracy, and he was one of the few governors of that age who did not enrich themselves; with such unusual qualities and in such circumstances, it is not surprising that in three years he wore himself out. He was a believer in empire as that term was then understood. With proper development, he thought, the colonists might well find their interest in being of a piece with England, for there is no bond like that of self-interest. The middle colonies might export more, if a silk industry were established, or if deposits of salt and potash were developed; farther south, there might be a wine industry.

[1] *Add. MS.* 40782, f. 232. Minutes of the Lords Justices, 1695–7.

Above all, he recommended that the granting of land should be reformed, in order to leave room for the smaller man. With good management, the plantations might be secured in 'a dependence on the crown'. Bellomont may have been deficient in vision, but at least he tried to ensure that an imperfect system would work. To the homeland of that imperfect system we must now turn.

II

ENGLAND: HER POPULATION AND ADVANTAGES

FOR the analysis of English population in the later seventeenth century we have the help of a band of contemporary writers who, if only for their ingenuity in reasoning from imperfect data were unique in Europe. As Boyle was the father of Chemistry, so Petty was the parent of Statistics. Petty's friend and collaborator John Graunt was the first to examine the Bills of Mortality in order to establish conclusions regarding the prospects of life in London; the astronomer Halley did the same for the city of Breslau, and with such skill as to provide the basis for life insurance tables; similarly, Charles Davenant applied statistical methods to his investigations into the balance of trade. All this may be connected with the strong mathematical element in seventeenth-century education, and serves to illustrate a characteristic of English genius, namely, the power to apply abstract principles to matters of everyday interest, in order to provide some guidance for the future.

Notable among these early statisticians was Gregory King, surveyor, architect, and herald, who estimated the population of England and Wales in 1688 at 5,318,100, or about five and a half millions, if allowance be made for vagrants.[1] Of this total, 540,000 were assigned to London, 876,000 to the other cities and towns, and 4,034,000 to villages and hamlets. These calculations were based on the Hearth Tax returns, which showed that, in 1690, there were 1,319,215 hearths or homes, about 100,000 being in the London area; and, on this basis, King applied a series of multipliers—5·4 for London houses; 4·4 for country towns, and 4·0 for villages—so that he deduced the total

[1] King's *State and Condition of England* will be found in G. Chalmers's *Estimate of the Comparative Strength of Great Britain*, 1804. A useful abstract showing incomes of different classes in 1688 will be found in *Documents*, no. 198. For analysis of King's estimate, see D. V. Glass, in *Population Studies*, iii, pt. iii, where the total is given as slightly less than that of King.

population from the number of families. His multipliers were derived from analysis of the information in parish registers, and on the returns to the assessments on births, deaths, and marriages, imposed by the statute of 1695.[1] It is of interest that by the beginning of the nineteenth century families had, on the average, become twice as large as they were in King's period.

Another source was provided by the weekly and annual Bills of Mortality, which first began to appear regularly in 1593, and survived until 1849. These were vital statistics for the parishes in the London and Westminster areas, from which source of information Graunt had already made some interesting deductions, as that the rate of mortality was higher in the country than in the towns, and that the excess of male over female births was neutralized by the higher post-natal mortality among males. But these statements might give an unduly favourable impression of the kind of material on which King and his contemporaries had to work. Thus, the Bills of Mortality were compiled, for publication by the Company of Parish Clerks, by a number of old women, most of them said to be venal and dissolute, who were usually put to this lugubrious employment in order to keep them off the rates.[2] They inspected the body, interviewed the relatives, and made their report. More informative than their classical prototypes, the Parcae, they intimated the reason for decease, favourite causes being: 'stopping of the stomach', 'convulsions', and 'griping in the guts'. So, for the London area at least, a definite cause of death was always given.

Gregory King's figure of 5½ millions for the population of England and Wales is the first reasonably accurate estimate before the days of the census. For periods before King's day we are dependent on conjecture—3 millions for the earlier years of the fifteenth century; 4 millions a century later; 5 millions in 1603, and 5½ in 1625.[3] This last figure, taken in conjunction with King's estimate, implies that between 1625 and 1685 the population was stationary, or nearly so; a conclusion supported by what is known of social conditions in that period. Of the

[1] 6–7 W. and M., c. 8.

[2] For this see *Epidemics and Crowd Diseases* and *Medical Statistics from Graunt to Farr*, both by M. Greenwood. Much useful information on this topic will also be found in N. G. Brett-James, *The Growth of Stuart London*.

[3] These are the figures in sir A. M. Carr Saunders, *Population*.

many factors having a bearing on this, we may conjecture that the civil wars, emigration, and plague accounted for little, but that malnutrition and tuberculosis counted for much. Also, the birth-rate was kept down by the fact that both in husbandry, where the workers often lived on the farm; and in those crafts still controlled by the apprenticeship system, early marriage was either discouraged, or made impossible. This brake on early marriage and the high death-rate were the two things which together helped to maintain static or very nearly static conditions in a great part of the population; and so provided what, for the circumstances may have been the 'optimum density' of population in the sense that it was in equilibrium with the area of cultivated land. Moreover, this was the state of things desired by contemporary opinion, which dreaded any change likely to upset a series of balances, such as that between the crafts and husbandry or that between town and country. In this way, the force of social inertia was much stronger in the past than today.

This fact may be better appreciated by comparing the population statistics of the seventeenth century, imperfect as they are, with the more reliable estimates for later times. Thus, in the eighteenth century the increase was only about 50 per cent.; whereas in the nineteenth century, when England became fully industrialized, the increase (from 8·9 to 32·5 millions) was over 260 per cent. This is one of the considerations which, especially in economic matters, should make one hesitate before applying modern terms, such as the word 'industrial' to the past. With this basic fact in mind, it is not difficult to understand how England, during the last decade of the seventeenth century, in the essentials of her social and economic life, had much more in common with the England of the last decade of the sixteenth century than with that of the last decade of the eighteenth. Nor was the resemblance of Tudor and Stuart England limited to externals; for in both periods there was the same rooted distrust of what we call progress. After all, wherever the population of a state is practically stationary, that provides at least a subconscious reason, not only for resisting change, but for accepting existing conditions as part of a divinely ordained order, in which the universe is regarded as something created solely for the benefit of our planet. Hence, it may be permissible to speak of an English *Ancien Régime*, having characteristics that were valued mainly for their supposed permanence.

Some of the implications latent in a static order of society were revealed in King's analysis of the constituent elements in the population. Having estimated that, in peace-time, the excess of national income over expenditure amounted to an average of £1,825,000, he then tried to assess the share of each class, whether negative or positive, in the creation of this surplus, for which purpose he divided men into groups, such as peers, gentlemen, office-holders, farmers, and traders, to each of which he assigned an average yearly income and expenditure. In all these groups, estimated to have a total of 2,700,000 persons, he claimed to find a surplus, so these were the 'profitable' classes. But it was otherwise with the lower, the 'unprofitable' classes, having a total of about 2,800,000. Among them he included the families (each, on his estimate, containing an average ranging from 2 to 4 persons) of 50,000 seamen, 35,000 soldiers, 364,000 labourers and out-servants, 400,000 cottagers and paupers, all of them showing a deficiency of income as compared with expenditure; and so, on King's figures, we have nearly three millions, made up not only of the destitute, the indigent, the itinerant, but also of the soldiers and sailors, the cottagers, the labourers, all of them, from the contemporary point of view, 'unprofitable' to the state—a vast margin of habitual mendicancy, casual labour, and permanent insecurity, distributed round the circumference which delimited those more privileged, more authenticated classes who constituted the hard core of the static state. A low birth-rate and a high death-rate in this 'fringe' population[1] helped to ensure almost stationary conditions; accordingly, so far as the upper and middle classes were concerned, English economy was prosperous, and the level of its civilization high, because based not on a submerged tenth, but on a submerged half.[2]

To only a fraction of this submerged half would the modern

[1] This may be inferred from the average number assigned by King to the families of the 'servantless' or lower classes—4 for an artisan, 3 for a common seaman, 2 for a soldier, 3½ for labourers and outservants, and 3¼ for cottagers and paupers.

[2] As has been well said by M. Dorothy George, in her *England in Transition* (1931 ed.), 11.

term 'poor' be applicable, since it included labourers, soldiers, and sailors; indeed, at this point King's classification reveals an attitude to society quite different from that which prevails to-day. There were, of course, as at all times, people who talked of the 'dignity' of labour; but the practice of the seventeenth century was to include among the legitimate social classes only those who had some stake in the country, whether land, or office, or profession, or regulated craft; all not so included were regarded, at best, as necessary evils. As a class, wage-earners were considered undesirable; indeed, the workers generally were thought of not as workers, but as the poor, for whom work was supposed to be available, otherwise they would be on the rates. Hence, in this period the word 'poor' has often to be translated as 'worker' or 'unemployed'. All this was a legacy of Tudor legislation which had imposed rigid rules and regulations in order to deal with social and economic changes that were imperfectly understood. Furthermore, this large portion of the population, indeterminate and voiceless, was supposed to be deficient in the ordinary standards of morality expected of those more fortunate classes who were restrained by landed responsibility, or corporate discipline; in contrast, the 'poor' were likely to be 'bad' because they were 'free'. Hence virtue and, even more, respectability were the monopolies of those who had an accredited place in the state, a fact which may have been in the mind of William III when, in a speech from the throne, he announced that an increase in the number of the 'poor' contributed to the increase of debauchery.[1]

According to the calculations of these early statisticians, the average expectation of life at birth was under thirty years, compared with over sixty today. Graunt[2] had estimated that 36 per cent. of living infants died before the age of six; but this rate compares not unfavourably with that of mid-nineteenth-century England, namely, 32 per cent., though it compares very unfavourably with that of the present time. This high rate of infantile mortality in the past was accounted for mainly by malnutrition, as well as by the infantile ailments; as there were more horses, so there were more flies to carry infection; there were also inherited causes, as from the luetic diseases, which at that time

[1] *L.J.* xvi, 16 Nov. 1699.

[2] M. Greenwood, *Medical Statistics from Graunt to Farr*, 31.

ran their full course, and often resulted in the death of the progeny. The enfeeblement of James II's mind in his later years was attributed by contemporaries to syphilis; her inheritance of this taint was regarded as the reason why queen Anne failed to produce a child capable of surviving infancy. On the other hand, the suicide rate in this period appears to have been less —for the year 1700 the estimate was 56 per million,[1] compared with about 100 per million in modern England.

But although, for the population generally, the expectation of life was short, this did not apply to the upper and middle classes, who could look forward to a span of life little shorter than that expected today. This was because they had more breathing space, and even more because they had enough food.[2] The great difference in this respect between the fortunate minority and the unfortunate majority is a clear expression of the fact, otherwise authenticated, that at least half the population of England was poised on, or just below, the level of subsistence. That half was specially susceptible to the 'deficiency' diseases, such as rickets (sometimes called the 'English disease'); there were also the 'killers', for example, smallpox, which carried away queen Mary, a scourge usually followed by complications, including blindness. Overcrowding, as in slums and gaols, was responsible for typhus, which today has practically disappeared, not so much from the skill of the physician as from that of the plumber; for eye diseases, the only practitioners were quacks. Overshadowing all these evils was tuberculosis, described by Bunyan as 'captain of all these men of death'.[3] Among the poor, especially among the young mothers, this was often the slow but certain solution of insoluble economic problems.[4] Such a high rate of wastage among the poor, in so far as it was known

[1] Dutch Reports (*Add. MS.* 17677), vol. ww, 7 Jan. 1701, which gives the figure for the London area.

[2] G. C. McGonigle and J. Kirby, *Poverty and Public Health*, a book of great importance for the social historian. This records the results of a social experiment at Stockton-on-Tees, when a number of slum dwellers were moved into a new housing estate, where they had to pay higher rents. The death-rate among them was higher than that in the slum which they had quitted, possibly because they were able to spend less of their earnings on food.

[3] *Works of John Bunyan*, ed. G. Offor, 1857, iii. 655.

[4] A. Clark, *Working Life of Women in the Seventeenth Century*, notably 86 sqq.

to contemporaries, may well have given cause for satisfaction, since otherwise more people would have fallen on the rates. In the seventeenth century it was the death-rate that kept down the poor rate.

One may well conjecture whether the mentality of civilizations is influenced by the death-rate. Where the expectation of life is short, where the gibbet provides a frequent and well-attended demonstration of the brevity of human existence, where disease and plague cause ravages apparently beyond the control of man, in such conditions life may well (on our standards) be more tense, more violent, more improvident, conditions which favour the poet and the man of action, both of them indifferent to the transitoriness of human affairs. From this point of view the Elizabethan age might be regarded as a grand and spontaneous youth movement, spontaneous, because not organized by grown-ups. But where there is a higher proportion of the middle-aged and the elderly, there one may expect to find more regard for the conventions, more solicitude for the future, both of the individual and of the race; and, as life becomes longer, it acquires a certain sacredness such as was unknown in the past. These conditions may favour the administrator and the planner of social reform. Probably the Welfare State was bound to come, if only because nowadays people live so long.

The Welfare State was preceded by a long period in which the function of government was mainly to repress or coerce, a fact of which the lower or submerged half of English humanity was made acutely conscious. Other and less radical classifications of society may be suggested. There were the professions and crafts, each of them playing a distinctive and regulated part; but these sections were cut across by others, less clearly defined, but nevertheless discernible. For example, there were the younger sons of the gentry and the sons of the clergy, two classes who had each this disability, that they had to make their way in life, and this advantage, that they usually had both the education and the social position which helped to ensure success. Our good fortune in this respect should be contrasted with that of other countries, where either the younger sons of the nobility were accounted noble, and so debarred from useful occupations, or where the clergy could produce no legitimate sons. In England it was not thought dishonourable for a man of good family to engage in trade, provided it was overseas or wholesale trade. Such a man might bring to his problems something of the sagacity and quiet assurance that pedigree often confers, a fact which may account for the high reputation abroad of English merchants, as compared with the traffickers of other lands.

England was fortunate also in another body of men, the inventors and projectors. These were to be found in every class of society, including peers and mechanics, most of them characterized by ingenuity and resource. The human element was there, ready for the stimulus applied by needs and circumstances. Among the circumstances was the encouragement given by the Royal Society; among the many needs were the problems created by the development of mining, and the uses to which coal[1] might be put. Improved pumps had to be designed; excavations had to be propped up, communications improved, and the problem of lighting had to be faced. Already, the air at the bottom of shafts was attracting the attention of the physicist,[2] as later of the physiologist; it was the necessity of drawing up water from pits which ultimately and indirectly gave us the steam engine. Of the 'projectors', a good example was Edward Somerset, second marquis of Worcester (1601–67). His *Century of Names and Scantlings of . . . Inventions* (1663) provided inspiration for generations of men of mechanical genius; indeed, his word 'scantlings' was well chosen, because it suggested ideas that might be worked out and applied by others. This marquis of Worcester is often included among the many 'inventors' of the steam-engine, his claim resting mainly on his 'water commanding engine', which appears really to have been a pump, intended primarily for irrigation, but possibly applicable to mines. The improved pumps of the later seventeenth and earlier eighteenth centuries did not result in the steam engine until the theory of latent heat had been enunciated and applied. A step forward was made in 1698 when Thomas Savery, a military

[1] For this see J. U. Nef, *The Rise of the English Coal Industry*, and T. S. Ashton and J. Sykes, *The Coal Industry in the Eighteenth Century*. See also *infra*, 44–47, 282–5.

[2] G. Sinclair, *Natural Philosophy Improved by New Experiments*. For Sinclair, see *infra*, 528.

engineer, obtained a patent for a pump, worked by steam; and, at about the same time, Thomas Newcomen, an ironmonger, who afterwards went into partnership with Savery, applied the principle of atmospheric pressure to drive a piston in a cylinder. The result was that, before the time of Watt, some forms of steam or atmospheric engines were actually in use, mainly in the mines. Savery, a man of great ingenuity, also designed a paddle boat, the paddles being driven by a capstan placed amidships; but the conservatism of men 'brought up in sail' prevented any application of this device; indeed, until an efficient steam-engine was evolved, there could be no revolution in transport.

It was natural that the traditional occupations of agriculture and cloth-making should attract the attention of the inventor. In 1701 Jethro Tull perfected and applied his mechanical drill for the more regular sowing of seed, a device derived from the mechanism of the church organ. Although this improvement was not widely used in the England of Tull's lifetime, it helped to inaugurate that period of 'scientific' farming which was to achieve such great results in the eighteenth century. Other national industries, weaving and spinning, were characterized by the same traditionalism, though there are references to improvements, such as Firmin's 'double wheel', which was used in his factory, where young children were employed, and was commended by a parliamentary committee.[1] Otherwise, there was little development in textile processes until 1733, when John Kay of Bury introduced the fly shuttle. But the inventors were interested in dyeing processes. Boyle's *Experimental History of Colours* resulted in the grant of several patents based mainly on his discovery that certain vegetable extracts change colour when made acid or alkaline, the earliest reference to what are called 'indicators'. Another scientist who, among many practical activities, experimented in dyeing was Robert Hooke. At a meeting of the Royal Society he produced a piece of calico dyed by a new process of his own devising.[2]

There were many other incentives helping to account for the great number and variety of inventions in the later seventeenth century. One of the most direct of these was the recovery of vast

[1] *C.J.* xii, 18 Jan. 1699.

[2] C. Singer, *The Earliest Chemical Industry*, ch. v.

treasure, in 1688, from the wreck of a Spanish galleon at Hispaniola; hence a crop of devices to facilitate deep-sea diving, one of them being a 'sea crab', or 'pair of lungs', intended for use at depths of as much as ten fathoms, for which a patent was issued in 1690.[1] Luttrell recorded how a man, fitted with such a contrivance, walked across the bed of the Thames at London Bridge. More generally, the war proved a great encouragement, and in this respect the official records[2] provide clear evidence of how ingenuity was stimulated. Thus, in the twenty-five years between 1660 and 1685, the number of patents granted was 114; but in the twelve years between 1685 and 1697 the number was 108, though obviously not all of them were put into practice. Of these, some were for war purposes, for instance, a musket-proof 'machine or chariot' of artillery, holding two field pieces and two hand grenades, to be used by 'the person sitting in the chariot', apparently a primitive form of 'tank'; a similar contraption may have been sir Richard Bulkeley's 'chariot on rollers', which had the advantage that it could not be overturned, but the disadvantage that it went on fire every ten miles.[3] As well as these, there were numerous patents for making salt water fresh, but these seem to have had limited success; the design of ships' hulls and means of propelling them mechanically provided another field of experiment. Less directly, the war, by the limitation or cessation of certain imports, caused manufacturers to utilize other materials, one of the many examples being the greater use of native vegetable oils in place of imported substances. Generally, the war was responsible for a great advance in technology.

It is probable that the distinctive genius of English inventors in this period was seen in the application of clock-work, which may be accounted for, not only by long habituation, but by the comparative backwardness in devising a new system of propulsion. At that time, the best clocks and watches were made in England; here our supremacy was unchallenged; in no other industry did the cost of material count for so little, nor the skill of the workman for so much. Hence the innumerable mechanisms based on clock-work. Examples were the 'Way Wizer',[4]

[1] *Cal. Tr. Bks.* ix, pt. ii, 835, Oct. 1690.

[2] *Titles of Patents and Inventions*, ed. B. Woodcock (1854).

[3] *Evelyn's Diary*, 8 Oct. 1685.

[4] *The Post Boy*, 19–22 June 1697.

which, by attachment to the axle of a carriage, recorded the distance travelled; another was a 'writing engine', which enabled one to make several copies of script, possibly a primitive duplicator, which had 'been brought to perfection by the skill of a clockmaker';[1] still another was a mechanical player, for attachment to an organ or harpsichord, whereby tunes might be played, with only half an hour interval for adjustment.[2] For those who were curious about the weather, there was a portable barometer.[3] In the absence of the modern steam-engine, and long before the era of electrical appliances, English ingenuity had exploited mechanical devices almost to their limit; and the skill of the craftsman, whether in wood or metal, must have been of a very high order indeed.

But it would be unfair to think of the inventive faculty only in relation to mechanical devices, for at this time native intelligence was applied to a vast field of enterprise, much of it related to social and national well-being. Of this intellectual awakening Defoe, always the most percipient of movements around him, was the greatest expositor. In his *Essay upon Projects* (1697), after alluding to the wonderful inventions used in the war, he traced the origin of 'projecting' to the influence of the Royal Society, the experiments of prince Rupert and the salvage of the Hispaniola treasure. He found evidence of a new spirit of progress in the establishment of banks, of new colonies, of the penny post (in London), of stock jobbing. His fertile imagination caused him to explore fresh possibilities, such as enclosing waste land by the wayside, improving the sea walls of Kent and Essex, forming friendly societies, instituting a scheme of accident insurance; also pensions for widows, contributory pensions for all except beggars and soldiers; a court merchant for determining mercantile causes; a British Academy on the model of the French Academy. Long before he wrote *Robinson Crusoe*, the inexhaustible fancy of Defoe had enabled him to picture in his mind many of our most advanced reforms; and it may be said that much of the better side of twentieth-century England had been anticipated, if only in imagination, before the end of the seventeenth.

[1] *The Athenian Mercury*, 9 Apr. 1695.

[2] No. 337 in vol. 1 of B. Woodcock, op. cit.

[3] Ibid., no. 342.

Another body of men who were contributing notably to the development of English civilization were the Huguenots, of whom about 70,000 are said to have settled in English-speaking lands at this time. They had begun to arrive a few years before the Revocation of the Edict of Nantes in October 1685; but, after the Revocation, it was very difficult for them to leave France, the death penalty being inflicted on those who were caught in the attempt. If James II did not welcome them, his subjects did; and letters of naturalization, issued as early as 1681, continued to be granted in large numbers until at least 1688, usually without fee. Large sums of money were raised for their relief, mainly by voluntary subscription. The result of this assimilation of part of a great Protestant population was speedily revealed; for, in all the essential elements of national life, the French refugees played an important and often a distinguished role. It is true that a small number acted as smugglers, and possibly as spies for France;[1] but many more were engaged in spying on behalf of their adopted country; indeed, our military and naval operations in the war were greatly helped by an elaborate system of espionage, manned chiefly by Huguenots, having its headquarters in Rotterdam. Our victory at La Hogue was said to have been aided by information supplied from this source.[2] There was also their public help in the war. They equipped regiments for service in Ireland and Flanders; they provided highly trained officers; they served in the navy, with the result that a Frenchman, in command of an English ship, might engage in combat with an English Jacobite in command of a French one.

But it was in the arts of peace that they excelled. Many settled in Bethnal Green, Spitalfields, and St. Giles as silk weavers;[3] others contributed to such industries as the making of linen, glass, paper, satins, velvets, clocks, toys, and surgical instruments; indeed, few of our industries were uninfluenced by this acquisition of French enterprise, skill, and, usually, taste. Ireland, the West Indies, and the Carolinas benefited by Huguenot immigration to such an extent that Louis XIV may justly be regarded as one of *our* empire-builders; moreover, the

[1] For impeachments on this score, see *L.J.* xvi, 16 May 1697.

[2] *Mémoires de Nicolas-Joseph Foucault*, ed. F. Baudry, 293.

[3] Sir F. Warner, *The Silk Industry*, ch. iii.

religious policy of that monarch was so clearly evidenced by the many proofs of atrocities brought by the refugees, that Englishmen were able to form their own conclusions about the likely results of a Bourbon-Stuart absolutism, conclusions which had some influence on the Revolution of 1688. Equally, the Huguenots not only brought something of French culture into England, but they served as intermediaries for the spread of English ideas on the continent, because it was mainly through their writers, such as Abel Boyer, that the works of Newton, Locke, and Addison were translated into French; and so was inaugurated that eighteenth-century tradition which attributed England's stability and felicity to her Protestant Revolution. As early as 1709 the following song[1] was popular in Dijon:

Le grand-père est un fanfaron,
Le fils un imbécile,
Le petit-fils un grand poltron,
Ah! la belle famille!

Que je vous plains, peuple français,
Soumis à cet' empire,
Faites ce qu'ont fait les Anglais,
C'est assez vous le dire.

Even more important than the Huguenots were the Protestant Dissenters, especially after the Toleration Act of 1689. Unlike the Roman Catholics they were not, after that Act, ostracized or subject to penalties; but, on the other hand, they were still excluded from a large part of public life, for they could not enter the universities, and the learned professions were, in effect, closed to them. Now, it has already been suggested that a disability, especially when allied to a social or educational opportunity, may account for a distinctive contribution to civilization on the part of a minority, a contribution often out of all proportion to that made by the completely privileged majority; indeed, much of our social history is a record of the success achieved, after great and sustained effort, by minorities, or by men who had to overcome some serious obstacle. This was true of the Dissenters. Many of them, endowed with intelligence and independence of character, most of them trained in their efficient Dissenting Academies, were driven into economic

[1] Quoted in P. Hazard, *La Crise de la Conscience Européenne*, i. 84.

enterprise, not so much from any (supposed) emphasis on usury and profit-making, such as writers nowadays attribute to Calvinist and Puritan ethics, as for a simpler and better reason, namely, because trade and industry provided practically the only outlet for their activities. Debar an active, educated man from the universities or professions and he is bound to take up something else; his success may more convincingly be explained by the opportunity which he has seized than by the 'theology' which he has inherited. To the English Dissenters was allotted a place not unlike that which had been assigned to the Huguenots in France; now that they were conjoined, the results were soon patent.

Of the many branches of Dissent, the Quakers[1] provide a good illustration of the consequences that may follow from partial disability. They had thriven on the persecution meted out to them, and were regarded by respectable Englishmen as lunatics. They had certain unusual principles and practices which were ultimately to have a profound influence on English life. Resolutely opposed to war, their ironmongers and ironfounders refused to make or sell armaments, preferring to supply a rapidly expanding market with cutlery, sickles, and domestic articles, an enterprise which, incidentally, proved to be very profitable. An even more important principle was that of paying their debts. This might seem irrelevant today, when there are so many effective means of enforcing a debt, and it is not fashionable to boast of eluding one's creditors. Now, paying one's debts is as much a social quality as a moral virtue, likely to be greatly influenced by the example of those to whom we naturally look for guidance, such as members of parliament. These responsible persons certainly set a clear example, because their parliamentary privilege enabled many of them to evade payment of debts altogether; and when in 1701 the Tory party passed an Act limiting parliamentary privilege, this was cited, in election propaganda, as a proof of self-sacrifice, since so many of our legislators would now be obliged to pay their debts.[2] Against such a background, the Quakers must indeed have seemed 'odd'. Another oddity was their objection to oaths;

[1] Isabel Grubb, *Quakerism and Industry before 1800*, and A. Raistrick, *Quakers in Science and Industry*. My illustrations of Quaker economic enterprise are derived from the latter book.

[2] *Infra*, 467, 473–4.

an objection explained by this, that among their contemporaries, never were there so many oath-takers nor so many perjurers. The Quakers proved, to the surprise of many, that honesty pays; and it is not too much to claim that their example greatly stimulated that steady improvement in commercial morality without which England would never have become a great nation. After all (so subtle is the distinction) the lunacy of yesterday often proves to be no more than the sanity of today, but the prudent and the successful leave to others the ungrateful task of effecting this evolution.

By 1690 the Quaker ironmaster was emerging, though he was still linked with the ironmongers. Most of them were conducting business in partnerships, using small furnaces for smelting iron, and forges for wire drawing and blacksmith's work. Certain families were beginning to establish a local connexion; for example, the Fell Robinson group in the southern Lake district; the Hanbury family in the South Wales ironworks; the Wilsons and Woodhouses at Barnsley and Sheffield; the Darby family at Bristol, and Coalbrookdale on the Severn, and the Lloyds, first in Merioneth, and later in Birmingham.[1] Of these, the last two are of special interest—the Darby family, because one of them, Abraham Darby, early in the eighteenth century, first successfully used coke for smelting; and the Lloyd family, because their name commemorates the close connexion afterwards established between the ironmaster and the banker. The Griffiths and Powells were actively associated with copper smelting in the Swansea district; but the most important mining enterprise of the Quakers, indeed the largest of its kind in England, was the London or Quakers' Lead Company, controlling many lead mines in the north of England.

In some of these enterprises, particularly where there were local supplies, coal was being used for fuel, either alone, or mixed with charcoal; but it will have been noticed that none of the above-mentioned areas is in the south-east of England, a district in which there was no production, but a great consumption of coal, amounting to as much as 700,000 tons annually, or little less than the total output of the whole of the midland area,[2] where the many metal industries readily account

[1] A. Raistrick, op. cit. 94 sqq; also in E. Hughes, *North Country Life in the Eighteenth Century*.

[2] J. U. Nef, op. cit. i. 80.

for the utilization of this fuel. In other words, we have this significant fact, that one of the greatest coal-consuming districts of England was London and the Thames valley, where, although there were many industries using coal, very few were of the 'heavy' or metallurgic type such as were coming into existence in other districts. This should be linked with another fact, that some of these 'heavy' industries were migrating in search, not of coal, but of wood. Thus, the Quaker ironmasters, anxious to conserve supplies, instead of using charcoal from virgin forests, were consuming coppice timber, about 15 years old, taking care to replant;[1] and there were instances of smelting and refining industries literally 'fleeing to the wilderness'[2] in order to obtain charcoal for fuel. Even late in the eighteenth century, furnaces were erected at such remote places as Invergarry and Inveraray in the West Highlands. These things, however they may be explained, should at least induce a sense of perspective, and may cause us to hesitate before accepting such a phrase as 'Industrial Revolution' for the England of this period. Neither in transport nor in the production of metal from ores was there such an advance as to warrant the use of this phrase,[3] the popularity of which may help to obscure some of the essential differences between modern, industrial England and the England of the past.

It is natural for the historian to assume that greater demand for coal meant greater industrialization, since the connexion between the two seems so obvious and direct. But it was neither obvious nor direct in the seventeenth century. The fleets of Newcastle colliers bringing 'sea cole' to London were valued mainly because they provided such good training for seamen; and there is reason to think that, in this period, the importance of coal was social and maritime, quite as much as industrial.[4]

[1] A. Raistrick, op. cit. 90.

[2] T. S. Ashton, *Iron and Steel in the Industrial Revolution*, 15.

[3] For confirmation of this view, see T. S. Ashton and J. Sykes, *The Coal Industry in the Eighteenth Century*, 13.

[4] This was implied in an Act of Anne's reign, intended to prevent combinations among coal owners and lightermen for enhancing the price. The preamble stated that cheap and reasonable prices of coal 'tend greatly to the improvement of the trade and manufactures of this kingdom *by breeding and employing many thousands of skilful mariners* for the service of Her Majesty and the defence of the realm, and to the relief of the poor' (9 Ann., c. 28).

Only thus indeed can we account for the fact that the second greatest coal-consuming area, the south-east, was using it largely for domestic purposes; while, in the 'industrial' areas of the midlands and the north, coal had by no means displaced wood. Coal brought with it, not a major revolution in the provinces, but a minor revolution of a social kind in London, where the smoke from this fuel ruined tapestries and hangings; and those venerable heirlooms, the family beds, became so stained that they had to be discarded, with great benefit to the health of the household. The result was, not that London gave up coal, but that she gave up tapestry; and panelling as well as wall-paper gradually took its place.[1] Now this continued preference of the metropolis for coal is an interesting and significant fact. It may have been caused either by shortage of timber, or by preference for a better method of heating, and ability to pay for it. That the latter was the true reason is supported by evidence of increasing wealth in the south-east, so marked as to bring with it a higher standard of comfort, and consequently, resort to a better type of fuel. Accordingly, London's greater consumption of coal may be evidence not so much of the increasing importance of coal as of the increasing importance of London.

Part of the evidence supporting this view is to be found in the Land Tax assessments,[2] which show that, in the later years of the century, the metropolis and the surrounding counties were gaining, in property values, in proportion to the rest of the country, a development attributable mainly to this, that money was then most commonly made not, as now, in industry, but in the intensive cultivation of land for large, local markets; in an expanding foreign trade; in profitable war-time contracts; in the perquisites of innumerable offices, created or expanded by the war. In this way, two Englands were coming to be more clearly distinguished—that of the south-east, the more eligible part—where new opportunities helped to fructify accumulated savings, as well as to develop social amenities that could best be enjoyed within easy reach of the metropolis; and, in contrast, the England of the midlands, the north, and the west, where there was more provincialism, a more sparse population, and

[1] 'An Essay on the Fuel of London.' Bound up with T. Nourse, *Campania Felix*, at p. 345 in the Bodleian copy.

[2] *Infra*, 402–5.

an older economy, gradually being disrupted by new and unaesthetic industries. In the one, men were making money without having to soil their hands in the process; in the other, a livelihood was coming to be associated with grime. Coal provided one of the earliest distinctions between these two Englands, for it ministered to the comforts of the one before it supplied the needs of the other.

This distinction, together with continued resort by the metal industries to timber, as well as to coal, was characteristic of a country which, though rapidly becoming a great maritime and trading state, was still essentially agricultural and pastoral, industrialized only here and there. The cottage, not the factory, was the unit; many enterprises, now kept separate, were then combined by a man and his family; and only in such highly capitalized activities as the cloth industry was the appearance of the middleman attracting attention.[1] It was not mass production but variety of product that impressed contemporaries, now becoming more acutely conscious of the distinctive qualities of their homeland. Thus, one of them noted how,[2] on the continent, vast areas might be devoted to one crop or industry, whether corn, or timber, or dairy farming; whereas, in England, there was always variety:

> There is rarely a farm of £50 per annum but has meadow and pasture ground belonging to it, together with some wood or coppice, as likewise with some arable land for corn, with sheep pasture, as also with trees for building . . . being yet further blessed with fresh and wholesome water, almost in every ground, so that a man enjoys all things within himself.

Now, this old order of things was in process of very gradual change by the free movement, mostly by the rivers, of corn, coal wool, and timber, and so the forces of specialization were already at work; indeed, the Tyneside, as an almost exclusively coal- and lead-producing area, was dependent on other districts for its corn.[3] But, nevertheless, economic development is often slow and halting. The England of the later seventeenth century still enjoyed a measure of self-sufficiency, accounted for mainly by soil and climate, a factor which caused men still to think in terms of the old separatism and localism.

[1] *Infra*, 289–90. [2] T. Nourse, *Campania Felix* (1700), 13.
[3] J. U. Nef, op. cit. i. 257.

England was thus thought of, not as a unity, but as a collection of separate areas, or 'countries' (the *pays* of seventeenth-century France), each having its own dialect and economic interests, a localism emphasized by the absence of transport and the Press as we know them today. Accordingly, the conviction that the welfare of one district would be prejudiced by the advantage of another was always given expression whenever an improvement, such as in river navigation,[1] was proposed. In William's reign, parliament enacted a number of measures for this purpose, on which occasions there were always protests by counties affected, or apparently affected, usually on the ground that, as land carriage would be diminished, there would be less consumption of oats by horses, to the prejudice of rents. In other cases, the rival interests not only of communities but of rivers themselves might be brought into conflict. Thus, when, in 1698, it was proposed to make the river Don navigable, the ship-masters of the Trent objected,[2] alleging that their river transport would be ruined; moreover, they claimed that, as the Trent was the third river of England, it was valuable as a nursery for seamen. In passing such Bills, parliament had to cut across areas of local self-interest, all of them convinced that any change in a static order of things would be their undoing.

But in contrast with this instinctive separatism, there was, among educated men, an acute awareness of the possibilities within reach of nation and empire, and it is from their expressions of opinion that we may deduce what intelligent men at that time thought of their country. 'Of all nations', wrote a pamphleteer in 1695,[3] 'we have least reason to fear the export of our bullion, because our native commodities are so valuable in most foreign markets, that they turn to more profit than the carrying of money would.' A similar optimism was revealed by the duke of Shrewsbury when, towards the end of the war, he expressed the opinion that free and trading peoples, like the English and Dutch, would, in one year, recover more strength than France in five.[4] These views were based on an assessment

[1] T. S. Willan, *River Navigation in England*, and the same author's *The English Coasting Trade, 1600–1750*.

[2] *C.J.* xii, 29 Jan. 1698.

[3] Simon Clement, *A Discourse on the General Nature of Money, Trade and Exchanges*, 1695.

[4] *Shrewsbury Correspondence*, ed. W. Coxe, 7 Aug. 1696.

of England's advantages as a maritime and trading state. She did not have the cheap water transport enjoyed by Holland, nor could she boast the low rate of interest, the land registries, the ready circulation of capital, the building of ships on almost mass-production principles which characterized Dutch civilization; but, on the other hand, she compared favourably with France in those matters which promoted maritime advantage. France, with a population of about eighteen millions, had a much shorter coast-line, and was not so well endowed with ports; moreover, her Mediterranean and oceanic trades were separated by the Iberian peninsula, a cleavage necessitating the maintenance of two navies. Of French Channel ports, Dunkirk was suitable only for shallow-draught vessels; Calais, Dieppe, Havre, and St. Malo were small, difficult of access, and poorly defended; Cherbourg was in ruins; Brest, a magnificent anchorage, was a naval base. The English ports, it is true, were still mainly on the south and east coasts, for the convenience of the Mediterranean and continental trades, but on the west and north-west there were almost limitless possibilities for handling the rapidly developing oceanic trade. In the newer orientation of European enterprise, England was geographically more favoured than France.

The distinction between these two rivals went even farther. With her fertility and comparatively large population, France was a storehouse of corn, cattle, wine, salt, linen, silk, and fruit —the essentials of an older, more self-sufficing civilization. She had less need for ships to import bulky commodities; and, as her main produce, wine, silk, linen, and fancy goods, were often conveyed in English or Dutch vessels, her mercantile marine was smaller than ours. Her colonies were subjected to a more rigid and unified control; moreover, the whole economy of the France of Louis XIV was devoted to the maintenance of the large armies necessitated by the policy of that monarch. By comparison, England appeared to be living in a different world. Her resources were more diversified; her internal communications, whether by river or road, were not impeded by the tolls and customs barriers so characteristic of France; her control was more adaptable to new circumstances, and so English economy was much more elastic and resilient than the French. In France the administrative machinery was so cumbersome and involved that only a superman could direct it, and (fortunately for England) that superman, Colbert, had died in 1683. In England, on the other hand, where we had no supermen, we made up for it by an efficient committee, the committee of Trade and Plantations, an ancestor of the Board of Trade. This was set up in 1696 in order to guide and co-ordinate both economic and colonial policy, so that full advantage might be extracted from English industrial and maritime resources.[1]

Contemporaries were well aware of our advantages and disadvantages in that long struggle with France which dates from the Revolution. In the essentials of food we were self-supporting; indeed, we could export provisions, and our supplies could be supplemented by imports of butter, beef, and fish from Scotland and Ireland. In our lead- and coal-mines we had commodities useful at home, and profitable for export; our cattle provided hides of the best quality, and English workmanship made possible the manufacture and export of high-class leather goods. Above all, in our wool we had abundant material, of almost infinite variety, for a cloth industry which gave employment to both highly skilled and semi-skilled labour. Cloth, adapted to some extent to climatic conditions, was our basic article of world export, in return for which we imported the 'enumerated' commodities from the west; saltpetre, silks, muslins, and luxury goods from the east; with cloth we paid for negroes from Africa, timber from the Baltic, wine from the Canaries and France, and later from Portugal; few parts of the civilized world were unfamiliar with the products of English looms. In Spain, monks perspired under our heavy broadcloth,[2] and stomached our veteran codfish, with no misgivings about the heretic source of these commodities; indeed, our chief competitor in supplying Catholics with material necessities was another Protestant nation, the Dutch. These things made possible a great re-export and multilateral trade, in which there was much 'superlucration'. By this, contemporaries meant that England enjoyed advantages in access to raw materials, in quality of native

[1] *Infra*, 305–6.

[2] J. O. Maclachlan, *Trade and Peace with Old Spain 1667–1750*, 6. Miss Maclachlan states that English heavy cloth was worn by Spanish monks and nuns.

workmanship, in abundance of shipping and skill in navigation, in number and accessibility of ports; advantages which, in combination, ensured a greater profit on capital outlay than was possible in less richly endowed countries, limited to fewer or more direct trades.

Then there were the disadvantages. In William's War—our first great European war—it was realized how a continental enemy can injure us most by attacking our shipping and communications; we were vulnerable because, in our ships, we presented so many targets.[1] In war we might become like a beleaguered fortress; hence the necessity for more shipbuilding and a stronger navy. There were other disadvantages. Our colonies were too far asunder; they were too diverse in constitution; some of them were even talking of separation. Even more, there was no real union between England, Scotland, and Ireland. At home, there were obvious impediments—the greater part of the taxes were levied not on expenditure, but on land; there was too great inequality between shires, dioceses, and parishes; important towns were either inadequately represented in parliament, or not represented at all; the power of raising money and deciding on war was not in the same hands; disputes about prerogative and religion, which had wasted the substance and intelligence of the nation, were now followed by equally futile wrangling about party politics. But it was thought that nearly all these defects could be remedied.

What were the qualities of Englishmen for the ordeals confronting them after the Revolution? On modern standards, it has to be confessed that, for the most part, they were noisy and dirty, brutal and quarrelsome. 'We are the most divided, quarrelsome nation under the sun.'[2] There was general agreement, at home and abroad, that Englishmen in this period were very quick tempered and violent;[3] indeed, this irascibility was such a noted characteristic that Dennis[4] defended the Stage on the ground that it provided a sedative. Of all humours, the splenetic was most in evidence; and, in the late seventeenth

[1] *Infra*, 296–8.

[2] *The Freeholders' Plea against Stock-jobbing Elections*, 1701.

[3] For a good general study of the period, from this point of view, see M. Beloff, *Public Order and Popular Disturbances, 1660–1714*.

[4] J. Dennis, *The Usefulness of the Stage*, 1698.

century, crimes of violence were probably of more than usual frequency.[1]

But some contemporaries took a more favourable view. Lord Ailesbury, a Jacobite, thought that Englishmen had some sense of moderation in their passions—they might welcome a few hangings as a deterrent—but they would not (after the Bloody Assizes) tolerate executions on a large and concerted scale.[2] At least one foreign observer noted the national love of fair play, for Englishmen would not allow two men to fight, except on equal terms.[3] Others claimed for their fellow countrymen a measure of magnanimity. They might resent paying taxes in a lump sum, but they would not object to paying by instalments; they were liberal, even lavish in expenditure, accustomed to contrasting their felicity with the plight of the poverty-stricken Scot, or that of the thrifty Dutchman, or the Frenchman with his wooden shoes. Earlier observers had maintained that the common people, by their part in parish gatherings, and their regular concourse at fairs and markets, had more solidarity and even more assurance than was possible in other countries.[4] Some observers made still larger claims. Writing in 1701 a pamphleteer emphasized the good nature of Englishmen; the comparative absence of sustained vindictiveness; their tolerance of iniquity up to a point—as witness their putting up with the Stuarts for so long. Even more, they had, it was claimed, a sense of fairness; the lower orders being more inclined to the spirit of justice than the same classes in other nations, a quality attributable to their semi-judicial training in borough or parish office, in juries, whether of the national or manorial courts. 'There is scarce a common man but is fit for an arbitration.'[5] An exaggeration concealing an important element of truth.

This capacity for arbitration, the temperamental ability in the public interest to set aside personal prejudice or predilection, was fostered in England and in New England not only by participation in the local administration of justice, but by long

[1] *Infra*, 107.

[2] *Memoirs of Thomas, earl of Ailesbury*, ii. 382–3.

[3] Henri Misson de Valbourg, *Mémoires et observations faites par un voyageur en Angleterre* (1698), 3–4.

[4] *The Jesuits' Memorial for the Intended Reformation of England*, 1690 (by Robert Parsons), pt. iii, ch. 5.

[5] *The Claims of the People of England* (1702), 14.

habituation to a jurisprudence which, though it may now seem harsh, was ancient, uniform, and even logical. Such a detached mentality, as it must often seem cold and phlegmatic to other, more forthright races, is a distinctive thing in our civilization, discernible, however faintly, at all times, though often overlaid or concealed by what, on modern standards, are considered abuses and injustices. This instinct for equity has provided a touchstone, to which there is steadily increasing resort, for the regulation of relations with our fellow men; it has also proved to be the mainspring of those social movements which posterity has rightly acclaimed. If national character is an amalgam of many elements, here perhaps we have a glint of the precious metal in Anglo-Saxon mentality.

III

FREEHOLD AND STATUS

THIS chapter, in continuance of the summary analysis of English society[1] contained in its predecessor, treats of two interrelated topics; first, freehold, with its appendages of corporation, office, and franchise; and, second, personal status, as determined by membership of a corporate body, or by human relationship, or by legislative enactment. Generally, an attempt is here made to link the conceptions of personality and full citizenship with property, or with some institution derived from property. For the purposes of the second of these two sections, the following have been selected as illustrations: (*a*) parent and child; (*b*) husband and wife; (*c*) master and apprentice; (*d*) stockbroker, scrivener, and banker; (*e*) physician and apothecary; and (*f*) Roman Catholic and Dissenter.

1. FREEHOLD

In trying to assess a civilization at any definite point, one is sometimes helped by examination of certain apparently simple words, the meaning of which may have changed in course of time. Examples are provided by the group of words denoting freedom and liberty. In an English law dictionary[2] published in 1729, liberty was defined as 'a privilege held by grant or prescription, by which men enjoy some benefit beyond the ordinary subject'; but it was noted that the word was coming to be used in a very different sense, namely, the power to do as one thinks fit, unless restrained by law. So too with the word 'freedom'. The freeman of a burgh might hope to exclude the 'unfree' from its privileges, for such freedom provided some protection against the intruder or amateur; to be 'free of all vices' meant, not the absence of these qualities, but complete initiation in them; and that to such a degree as to imply a

[1] For English society in this period, much valuable information will be found in the opening chapters of vol. i of G. M. Trevelyan's *England under Queen Anne*.

[2] G. Jacob, *The Law Dictionary*.

certain exclusiveness. Invariably, when examining the older conceptions of freedom or liberty, one is faced with privilege and exemption, the 'unfree' being those who do not fit into any of the recognized categories. This state of things lasted for a long time. Magna Carta and the first Reform Bill enclose a period in which liberty was closely associated with what we would now call exclusion; that this dualism—sometimes it was almost antagonism—aroused so little criticism or resentment, apart from that of such revolutionary theorists as the Levellers and Independents, is one of the most striking things in English history. It is sharply contrasted with the process of social evolution in France. There, many of the ancient privileges and exemptions, intensified and even commercialized, were brought into conflict with ideas of enlightenment and emancipation preached by the philosophers, with the consequence that the distortions of medieval survivals in eighteenth-century France were emphasized by the cold, harsh illumination which Voltaire brought to bear on them.

In both countries, so similar in their early institutions, so contrasted in the means whereby these were transformed or abandoned, society was fashioned from the interconnexion between the soil and the need for both subsistence and defence; into this structure, the trading boroughs were intruders. The system, as it achieved completion, might have taken for its motto the scriptural maxim: *In this service is perfect freedom*, because, on the land, the *liberi homines* were those who held by the service of a non-servile tenure; while, in the boroughs, the freemen were those who had completed a period of regulated servitude in a craft, carried on in a community which had received its *libertates* by grant from above. Now the freehold is the descendant of the fief, which was defined as 'the right which a vassal has in some lands, or some immovable thing of his lord's, to take the profits thereof, paying the feudal dues'. These feudal dues had been systematically enforced by Henry VIII's Court of Wards, and the greater part of English land continued to be held nominally by knight service, but actually by those personal and pecuniary obligations imposed by the Court of Wards, until (in the Civil Wars) that tribunal fell into desuetude. Its abolition by statute in 1660 was possibly the most important single event in the history of English land-holding;

for although manorial rights and tenure by copyhold still survived, all who held their lands by a noble tenure had now completely divested themselves, not only of their old obligations of service, but of those monetary payments which had been instituted as an equivalent. The emancipation of the fief was thus complete. This process of emancipation had been extended even to the villeins; for they were gradually freed from praedial services, and their status was abolished in the sixteenth century. They survived mostly as copyholders, having a recognized place in the territorial hierarchy, but not always a very secure place, for those who were ejected by enclosing landlords were obliged to join the large bands of cottagers and labourers, who were outside the pale.

Generally, therefore, 'liberty' was only one stage removed from the obligations of tenure, or the servitude of apprenticeship; and so 'freedom', having arisen from the performance of duty, and having been associated with emancipation, gradually came to be linked with privilege and exemption. This remained an assumption, so implicit that it was never formulated, throughout the seventeenth century, when the majority of the population did not fit into any of those classifications of the 'free' that had survived from medieval times. The newcomers, or outsiders, however we may describe them, as they had never qualified by service and had never been emancipated, provided an increasingly large element of non-initiates in a polity which was designed to be static, and for long remained nearly static; a state of affairs not disrupted until the time of the Industrial Revolution, with the great increase of population which it entailed. From this point of view, the real English revolution was not that of 1688, but the long series of social and economic changes which, between about 1780 and 1848, gradually ended our *Ancien Régime* and gave us the England of today. The French upheaval was contrasted with the English gradualness, but they were alike complete.

For this reason, it is possible to think of seventeenth-century England as an episode in a civilization so nearly stationary and self-contained that it can almost be studied *in vacuo*; a civilization having this dominating characteristic, that the freeholder on the land and the freeman in the town were, each in his sphere, the accredited elements in society, in comparison with which other men appeared, not as rival classes, but as adjuncts, or excrescences, or even social dangers. Like the citizens in Aristotle's city state, only the 'free' were endowed with complete virtue, the others being capable of no more than a secondary or reflected form, adapted to their subordinate function. But for Aristotle's word 'Nature we have to substitute the word 'God', and so the state, in the seventeenth century, had less to fear from the traitor than from the atheist; for, while the first endangered the government, the second undermined the theocratic foundation on which society was built. From this many consequences followed. One of the most obvious was the forcible imposition on the sailor of the duty of fighting for his country; and, as the same principle was extended, in Anne's reign, to the soldier, the effect was that the 'unfree' were obliged to fight for the 'free'. The privileged might often commit great crimes with impunity; for petty offences the unprivileged were hanged. It was selfish and unjust, but all great civilizations are selfish and unjust.

A community is seldom conscious of the 'evils' which posterity may condemn. Classification of men in the past was more elemental than modern class distinction; because, as it was unchallenged, it was not self-conscious; nor was it identical with economic advantage or educational opportunity, though either of these might facilitate passage from the unprivileged to the privileged class. Thus, the landed freeholders included not only peers, parsons, and squires, but some who were so poor that they had to apply for parish relief; equally, many men, not freeholders, made large fortunes which they usually applied to the purchase of freehold estates. Hence the landed proprietors were not, as in many continental countries, a closed caste, for their ranks might be joined, after at least one generation of training and approbation, by the ex-townsman; also, there was the younger son, who usually pursued a career away from the land. Even more, the landed classes were never without serious duties and responsibilities. They had to bear the greatest share of direct national taxation, as well as of the parish rates. Included in the latter was a portion of the fine levied on a hundred where a crime had been committed, and the offender had not been brought to justice; how serious this burden might be was shown in William's War when there was wholesale smuggling of wool from Romney Marsh, for which landowners in the neighbourhood were so heavily fined that many had to give up their estates.[1] As the landed freeholder had the most tangible and immovable stake in the country; as he filled the unpaid offices of lord or deputy lieutenant, or sheriff, or justice of the peace; as his land made possible the growing of the nation's food, as well as the production of the nation's cloth, can it be wondered at that he regarded himself not as one of several classes, but as the unit, in comparison with which the stature of other men might be assessed?

This attitude was revealed subconsciously. When complaining, in the House of Commons, about our shipping losses at the hands of the French, sir T. Clarges declared: 'If trade be lost, land will fall.'[2] Land was the standard of reference not only for trade, but for the law, as witness the question put to the Commons in 1693 by sir F. Winnington, when objecting to the estimates: 'What signify all our laws, if we have no estates?'.[3] A claim even wider had been urged in 1690 by sir H. Goodricke, when opposing an Abjuration Bill: 'When you abjure a government, you abjure your lands.'[4] So trade, law, and government itself were visualized as ministering, in different degrees, to the sanctity of landed property.

This monopoly of landed freehold might convincingly have been supported by the political theorist, since its influence can be demonstrated in the development of parliament itself. The House of Lords was still, to some extent, an assembly of *magnates*, the greater feudatories of the crown, their estates providing the most ample guarantee of their status, a principle not at first manifest in the Commons, where the core of knights of the shire was surrounded by the burgesses, i.e. townsmen resident in their boroughs, a class easily amenable to pressure from above, whether from the crown or the lords. In this way, some kind of balance between landed and civic elements had been maintained in late medieval times. But it was steadily being altered in the course of the sixteenth century, as more and

[1] *C.J.* xi, 23 Dec. 1696. Petition of gentry and freeholders now or lately inhabitants of the Cinque Ports and places adjacent in Kent and Sussex. Also ibid. xi, 18 Jan. 1697, statement of evidence by Customs officers.

[2] *Grey*, ix. 349.

[3] Ibid. x. 340.

[4] Ibid. x. 80.

more of the boroughs fell within the control of the landed gentry, and returned to parliament members of that class. As early as 1555 the crown had attempted to restore the old balance, by introducing a Bill[1] for enforcing the limitation of borough representation to resident burgesses. But to this, the Commons tacked a clause excluding office-holders from the House, a clause intended to deprive the crown of power to counterbalance opposition by the retention of a solid block of placemen in the House. As the Commons became more powerful, because of the greater landed element among them, more assiduous efforts were made by the sovereign to 'manage' them, by the bestowal of offices and pensions, the attempt being to neutralize one form of property by another. But the attempt failed. Freehold prevailed over office, the one symbolizing independence, the other subservience. This triumph was implied in the official title of the well-known Act[2] of 1711 imposing high *landed* qualifications on all members of the Commons, for that Act was described as one 'securing the *liberty* of parliament' by imposing these qualifications. In effect, therefore, parliamentary freedom was identified with landed freehold.

It was the same in juries, particularly grand juries, where it was thought that only freeholders would act with complete independence. Nor was independence the only virtue that could be claimed by the landed class, for they might have connected their freeholds with a sense of obligation, amounting almost to altruism, in so far as they showed willingness and capacity to serve the state, in the innumerable local offices, without being paid for it; indeed, this characteristic quality of Englishmen seemed, to many foreigners, so peculiar as to provide one more proof of Anglo-Saxon lunacy. So the freeholder was 'free' in a sense that could be applied to no other section of the community; and, after all, these were the men who built up our parliamentary institutions, and helped to make England a great European power. Accordingly, it was natural that these three things—law, trade, and government—were valued according as they promoted the interest and security of the landed proprietor. His freehold, even if small, guaranteed him a vote, described by Holt as 'a noble privilege which entitles the subject to a share

[1] J. E. Neale, *Elizabeth and Her Parliaments*, 26.

[2] 9 Ann., c. 5.

in the government and legislature; no law can be made to affect him or his property but by his own consent.'[1] So the freeholder's privilege, which we may now think narrow, was then considered as broad as the freedom of the nation.

This interplay of freedom and privilege can be seen also in corporations and offices, in both of which the conception of freehold was dominant. A corporation was defined as a body politic, or an assembly into a fellowship and brotherhood, of which one is chief and the others are the body, the whole being devoted to some useful or charitable object. It might be a corporation sole, as king or bishop; or aggregate, as a mayor and corporation, a dean and chapter, a warden and scholars. Corporations were created by prescription, by royal charter, or by Act of Parliament. All the commonwealth in respect of the king was said to be as one corporation, and all other corporations might be thought of as limbs of the greater body.[2] Within a corporation there might be created a fraternity, joined into a company for the purpose of exercising some mystery or business; London had many such fraternities or companies. A corporation could not commit treason, nor be outlawed, nor excommunicated, but in the opinion of some it might be dissolved, for it was a trust, and if that be broken, then the charter is forfeited.

In the seventeenth century there was great faith in the corporation as a means of securing good government within a certain sphere, or promoting some desirable object.[3] Hence, Englishmen might try to dislodge the Dutch from the North Sea fishing grounds by including exalted persons in a company created for that purpose, or the cause of science might be promoted by the foundation of the Royal Society. At a time when the scope of government was more limited, it was natural that many activities should be entrusted to bodies of men united into *personae fictae*, having privileges which distinguished them from ordinary men; activities which nowadays would be assigned to a department of state. It followed therefore that,

[1] L. C. J. Holt, in *Ashby* v. *White*. *English Reports*, xci. 19.

[2] G. Jacob, op. cit., *sub voce* 'Corporation'.

[3] See *Select Charters of Trading Companies*, ed. C. T. Carr (Selden Society). In the above paragraph, the author has drawn on Mr. Carr's brilliant introduction.

in the later years of the seventeenth century, when new industries were established at home, and new ventures were made in foreign trade, many features of the old gild system were retained; indeed, the commercial company is the child of corporation and gild.

But nomenclature reflected a change from the medieval to a more modern point of view; for, while the old corporations had been meticulously named so as to distinguish between the head and the body, and to indicate an abstract unity made from a plurality of human beings, the titles of the later corporations merely described the purposes for which they had been formed, as the English Copper Miners' Company or the Saltpetre Company. Corporate effort was now being directed not so much to ensure good government, or to promote pious objects, as to provide good dividends. But in England tradition dies hard. We still entrust the management of our pilots and lighthouses, not to a registered company, nor to a branch of the civil service, but to the Master and Brethren of the Blessed and Undivided Trinity.

The corporations[1] acquired a national importance in the period here considered. The crown had frequently limited or determined the franchise by which the parliamentary boroughs returned members to parliament, but the last instance of this was at Newark in 1673, and thereafter the right of the Commons to determine the franchise was for long unchallenged. It was in this link with the representative system that the parliamentary boroughs, about 200 in number, came to be of special interest at this time; for, while Charles II, after the Popish Plot, remodelled them in order to ensure the return of Anglicans and loyalists, James II reversed the process, in the hope that they would return Dissenters and supporters of the royal policy of toleration. The full significance of this was not revealed until the time of the Revolution settlement, when the Lords, in their consideration of a Bill[2] for restoring the charters which had thus been annulled or forfeited, called in the judges to answer the question whether corporations could be required to make a surrender. Holt thought that they might, because, as they were

[1] For James II's dealings with ecclesiastical and academic corporations, see *infra*, 183–5.

[2] *H.M.C. Rep.* xii, app. pt. 6, 422 sqq., 11 Jan. 1690 (*MSS. of House of Lords*).

franchises created by the crown, so they could be annulled by the same power. Mr. Justice Eyre said that, in this matter, they were all in the dark, because they had no precedents to guide them. Other judges maintained that a corporation cannot make a surrender, just as a man cannot resign his personality; and baron Lechmere put his finger on this cardinal point of later-Stuart policy when he declared that, if corporations which sent members to parliament could be dissolved at the mandate of the crown, then 'out of this leak may run all the government of England'. Here was a meeting-point between medieval and modern. The great majority of the House of Commons was returned by the boroughs, and the fictive eternity of these corporations was now cited as a reason why even an almost unlimited prerogative could not dissolve them.

Some of the attributes of freehold can be seen also in offices. An office, like land, might be granted in fee simple, fee tail, for life or for years; an office such as that of the wardenship of a prison could be granted in reversion; but, on the other hand, there could be no reversionary interest in a judicial office. The king could not grant an office to the prejudice of another man's freehold. Officers of justice and finance could (in theory) be fined or imprisoned for neglect of duty; and, by a statute[1] of Edward VI, any such officer selling his office was liable to suffer forfeiture of his estate in the office. But this Act contained so many exceptions that even in judicial offices there continued to be some trafficking, for the two chief justices might grant (i.e. sell) any of the numerous subordinate offices in the judicial administration that came within their province. By the end of the century the system was so organized that fees and perquisites arising from such transactions were managed by a farmer, who made equal payments to the judges from the pool.[2] When, in 1691, the judges were examined by the Lords regarding a Bill for remedying irregularities in the courts of justice, they insisted that they had a right, a freehold in the disposition of subordinate posts. Objection was taken to the same Bill by the philizers[3] of the court of Common Pleas on the ground that the

[1] 5–6 Ed. VI, c. 16.

[2] *H.M.C. Rep.* xii, app. pt. 6, *MSS. of House of Lords*, 193, 17 June 1689.

[3] The philizers or philacers were so called because they kept the files of judicial proceedings.

proposed simplification of process would greatly lessen the profits of their offices, 'which are their freeholds'.[1] The Bill[2] was dropped.

This sale and purchase of office extended to every branch of the administration. The post of messenger in a state department might be bought; for subordinate offices in the Customs, such as that of searcher in London docks, a sum of £1,000 was sometimes paid; indeed, as the patent offices in this department were regarded by the commissioners of Customs as bounties in the disposition of king or Treasury, the commissioners were concerned[3] only that a sufficient deputy was appointed. Within the control of the city of London were a number of prisons, including the two Counters and Newgate; the office of keeper of these prisons was sold, as much as £3,000 being paid for that of Newgate. The wardenship of the Fleet and of the Marshalsea, both of them debtors' prisons, were offices of inheritance, and so fetched much higher prices,[4] with the consequence that a larger revenue had to be raised from debtors than from malefactors. Now, it is characteristic of a freehold that from it one may hope to derive, during at least one's own lifetime, a rent or profit proportionate to the amount of the investment; this was made possible by the fact that the fees and perquisites might be much more valuable than the salary; so office holders often resorted to chicanery, oppression, and actual fraud in order to obtain money. Contemporaries were convinced that this was becoming a menace, particularly when informers were employed by the office holder to enable him to take action against anyone infringing his patent. An example is provided by garbling, or cleaning of spices. In London the garbler-in-chief paid a rent to the city of £300 a year and a fine of £276 for a lease of sixty-nine years.[5] He had seven assistants. He claimed the right to garble all spices and coffee imported, at so much a hogshead, and he brought suits in the Exchequer against all who evaded this imposition. Some merchants paid him *not* to garble, as it

[1] *C.J.* x, 9 Dec. 1690.

[2] *H.M.C. Rep.* xiii, app. pt. 5, *MSS. of House of Lords*, 17 sqq., 4 Apr. 1691.

[3] E. E. Hoon, *The Organization of the English Customs System, 1696–1786*, 203.

[4] For examples of extortion practised by office holders, including prison keepers, see J. Whiston, *England's Calamities Discovered*, 1696.

[5] *C.J.* xi, 2 Mar. 1696. Petition of West India merchants against the garbling of spices.

might do more harm than good; others, more astute, contrived to join their consignments with those imported by aldermen, and so escaped garbling altogether. It was alleged that the chief garbler made a considerable income, not so much from his fees as from the fines levied on those convicted of evasion by means of informers. The Commons, on hearing these complaints, could do no more than pass a resolution that the garbling of spices was a discouragement of trade.

The war necessitated the multiplication of offices and enhanced the importance of old ones. Among the old ones was that of Writer of Tallies in the Exchequer. In the reign of James I this official had received £91. 13*s*. 4*d*. per annum, with £9 for a clerk. In Charles I's reign the salary was more than trebled, and a house in the Cloisters was added. By 1691, when it was held by the hon. sir R. Howard, the office had expanded almost out of recognition. The salary, it is true, had been increased only slightly, but the fees amounted to £6,000 per annum, together with a pension of £1,500 paid by the Paymaster of the Army out of deductions from soldiers' pay.[1] It was this robbery of the poor to increase the wealth of the rich that aroused indignation even in an age of callous corruption. While the sailor was victimized by a new official—the slop seller, who made a commission on the clothing—the soldier was at the mercy of another new functionary—the regimental agent, who handled the money assigned to a regiment for pay and clothing, from both of which he took a profit. The House of Commons called upon some of them to produce accounts, but few did so; accordingly, several were taken into custody, and one of them was committed to the Tower for refusing to answer questions.[2] Technically, these men were protected by the freehold in their offices, a rampart in which the Commons could not make even a breach. Within a few weeks of their inquiry into these abuses, they had to expel their own Speaker, sir John Trevor, for taking bribes.

During the war, opportunities for making money were greatly increased, especially for those with some capital and astuteness. The most genteel method was to purchase an office. Agents

[1] *H.M.C. Rep.* xiii, app. pt. 5, *MSS of House of Lords*, 422–3, Jan. 1691. Evidence of excessive fees taken by officers.

[2] *Cobbett*, v. 884, 1695.

professed to supply the demand. An employment agency was set up in London which undertook to provide places in town or country, at from £50 to £1,200 per annum, most of them for life, the qualification being no more than ability to write a legible hand. 'Most of the great ones', it was candidly announced, 'need but small qualifications, and can be managed by deputies.'[1] Now, this craze for office was comparatively new in English life. It had been greatly encouraged by Danby, who used offices and pensions in order to secure a parliament amenable to Charles II's policy, as later he used the same method, in William's parliament of 1690–5, in order to ensure the grant of supplies for the war. Hence the attempts to pass a Place Bill, and hence also the drastic clause in the Act of Settlement excluding office holders from the House. But this was annulled, with some exceptions, by Acts of Anne's reign, a fact of great importance in the evolution of the Commons; for, while that body was still 'the grand inquest of the nation', experience was showing that it must have direct and personal contact with heads of departments. By eventually taking office holders into its membership, the House might now interrogate them, where formerly it would have impeached them; and, in this way, there was initiated not only that close co-ordination between legislature and administration, but also a sense of responsibility in the exercise of public employment, such as the old freehold office had never possessed. It may be added that in England neither the craze for offices nor the abuses in their exercise reached the same proportions as in France, where office holding, sheltered from public criticism, became increasingly important as a source of revenue. There also the creation of innumerable vested interests hastened that process of social ossification which preceded the French Revolution.

Closely connected with the freehold was the franchise, which was defined as a privilege or exemption from ordinary jurisdiction, a royal privilege vested in a subject or subjects. Included in this category were the Duchy of Lancaster and the Counties Palatine of Durham and Chester; also all manors and lordships. Every manor, it was said, is a kingdom in little. As these privileges were derived from the crown, so they might be forfeited to the crown by writ of *quo warranto*; in cases of abuse, remedy was

[1] *The Protestant Mercury*, 21–26 Jan. 1698.

provided by action in the King's Bench. Not all of these grants were necessarily for the sole benefit of the grantee; for example, the leet jurisdiction, exercised by many manors, was concerned with breaches of the peace, and offences of a public nature, except high treason, committed within its precincts. These courts could fine, but not imprison; for cases extending to life and limb, the jury merely found the indictment and committed the accused to the Justices of Assize.

But the lord of the manor might well benefit if the leet found in his favour in a matter involving forfeiture, for example, if a deodand were in question. This institution arose from the old fear of sudden death. Such a death gave no opportunity for confession or extreme unction; hence, in the interests of the unshriven soul, a vengeful deity must be placated—by a sacrifice. So, whatever had directly caused the death was forfeited to the king, who might (in theory) entrust to his almoner the duty of distributing the proceeds among the poor; but the king was more likely (in return for a valuable consideration) to have included this right in the grant of a franchise, the donee being expected (also in theory) to apply the forfeiture in almsgiving. It was evidence of its sanctity that a freehold, such as a mill, could not be a deodand; but if a part of it, for example the wheel, fell off, and in doing so killed someone, then that part could be a deodand. In William's reign, on an appeal to King's Bench, a decision was given in favour of the lord of the manor of Hampstead, whose claim to a deodand had been contested. It appears that a carrier, when trying to pass a carriage on the road, mounted his cart on a steep bank, causing it to overturn, and a wheel of the wagon passed over the head of the unfortunate carrier, causing his death. The judges of King's Bench[1] ruled that wagon, lading, and horses were all deodands, because they 'all moved to death'—the quotation was from Bracton. So here, in the late seventeenth century, was a specimen of medieval flora still, as it were, in full bloom. But the lawyers removed one petal after another. They distinguished between drowning in salt water and drowning in fresh, wherever the forfeiture of a ship was claimed; they argued that, if a man was drowned by falling from his horse into a stream, the horse was not a deodand, because the water, not the horse had caused

[1] *English Reports*, xci (King's Bench), 195.

the death; eventually, in road accidents, the opinion prevailed that only the wheel responsible for the casualty was a deodand. Extreme old age and the arrival of the railways account for the decease of this venerable institution in the year 1846; and so a privilege which, had it been retained in its medieval amplitude, might well have become an abuse, was allowed to die a death more leisured and natural than that which it avenged.

For the medieval peasant the church and the mill, the two permanent edifices on his horizon, had each embodied a form of service, the one spiritual, the other material. Servitude of the mill was much less common in seventeenth-century England than in France, but there were still cases where a franchise included the right to require the tenants of a manor to have their corn ground at the lord's mill. This led to complaint in 1687—one of the few instances of its kind. An innkeeper at Abergavenny was obliged to have his corn ground at the mill of his lord Charles Price. But the Herbert family, who were supreme in the district, had mills near Price's mill; so, as justices of the peace, they required the innkeeper to submit to the servitude of one of their mills. On his refusal he was denied a licence for his inn. In spite of this, the innkeeper brewed some beer for a fair at Abergavenny, and paid the Excise duty; whereupon the oppressive Herbert justices committed him to a house of correction. He petitioned the Treasury, urging shrewdly, not that he was a victim of 'feudalism', but that, by his incarceration, the Excise revenue would suffer, a plea accepted by the lords of the Treasury, who desired the Herberts to suspend their warrant and grant him a licence.[1] There was another instance in 1698, when the House of Lords, on appeal, confirmed the right of the lessees of the bailiffs and burgesses of Bridgnorth to compel the inhabitants of that borough to have their corn ground at the borough mill.[2] On the other hand, there are so few recorded cases of complaint against this medieval survival as to suggest that either the right was exceptional or that it was exercised with restraint. It was otherwise in France, where servitude of the mill, because of its profits, was more strictly enforced. This right, like so many, might easily become perverted, as in the recorded case of a seigneur who, not having a mill, imposed

[1] *Cal. Tr. Bks.* viii, pt. 3, 1396, 7 June 1697.

[2] *English Reports*, i (House of Lords), 174.

on his tenants a special tax, called *molinage*, as substitute for subjection to a mill that had never been there.[1] The garb of our *Ancien Régime* had, at first, been scarcely distinguishable from that of France, but there was a vast difference in the means and pace whereby the two countries divested themselves of their outworn garments.

The right to the estate of a convicted felon or *felo de se* was more valuable and more frequently enforced, whether the forfeiture accrued to the crown or to the manorial lord. Luttrell records how in 1696 the duke of Somerset as lord of the manor of Isleworth seized the house, valued at £1,000, of Moor the tripeman, who had been hanged for coining.[2] The miserably small estate of Alice Lisle, the first victim of the Bloody Assizes, was forfeited to James II, who bestowed it on Lord Feversham.[3] In some manors the lord could issue probate of wills of persons dying within the manor, a right confirmed by the House of Lords against the claim of a spiritual court;[4] in other manors the lord would have the right to hold a market, from which he would expect to derive some profit, and he might at least petition the king against another lord who set up a rival market in the neighbourhood. Sometimes the manorial jurisdiction was extended so far as to interfere with the ordinary course of justice. Thus in 1700 a man was committed to Newgate for subornation of perjury, bigamy, and assaulting a constable. He was fined £320 and sentenced to the pillory. He objected to payment of the fine on the ground that, as he lived in Bloomsbury, the fine belonged to Lady Russell, lady of that manor 'who had received satisfaction and given him his discharge'.[5] But there was a limit to the prerogative even of a Russell, and the lords of the Treasury expressed the opinion that her ladyship had no right to such fines. The same lady appealed against the establishment of a court of conscience or Poor Man's Court for Bloomsbury and St. Giles on the plea that it would prejudice the small-debt business of her franchise.[6]

[1] S. Herbert, *The Fall of Feudalism in France*, 21.
[2] *Luttrell*, iii. 499.
[3] *Cal. Tr. Bks.* viii, pt. 3, 1522, 15 Aug. 1687.
[4] *English Reports*, i (House of Lords), 43, *Oldis* v. *Donmille*, 1695.
[5] *Cal. Tr. Bks.* xvi. 130, 8 Oct. 1700.
[6] *C.J.* xi, 9 Jan. 1696.

A more serious impediment to the administration of justice was the sanctuary, or sanctified franchise. England abounded in such privileged places; the holiness diffused around them by church and king had, by an odd but very human perversion, come to denote those areas where criminals were free from arrest. Arrest for debt or a commission of bankruptcy might be evaded by removing oneself and one's possessions into such a place; indeed there were carriers who specialized in these moonlight flittings, accustomed to spiriting away the contents of a warehouse in one night.[1] Whitefriars was the favourite resort for this purpose. But the most notorious of all these *enclaves* was the Savoy, part of the duchy of Lancaster, and one instance of its lawlessness, as reported to the Commons in 1696, may serve to illustrate how grossly this exemption might be abused. A tailor, very rashly, went to a client in the Savoy in order to demand payment of a debt. He was set upon by a mob, which passed sentence. Having been stripped, tarred, and feathered, he was pulled by a rope round the streets and along the Strand, the crowd shouting, 'A Bailiff!' 'A Bailiff!' He then had to kneel and curse his parents.[2] This immunity was ended by the Act of 1697[3] which, characteristically, did not purport to end an abuse, but merely to facilitate the collecting of debts. The Mint[4] retained its right of sanctuary until 1722. Another favourite resort of persons fleeing from justice was Scotland Yard (from its proximity to the palace of Whitehall), where the noise and disorder were such as to cause complaint from the law-abiding citizens in the neighbourhood.[5]

Thus freehold, with its allied institutions of office, corporation, and franchise might be regarded as the residuary legacy from medieval times, a legacy often diverted by the beneficiaries from its original purpose. In many parts of England the skeleton at least of a manorial structure still survived, and, in other circumstances—such as long prevailed in France—the subject might have been vexed and burdened by the dead hand of seignorial jurisdiction. But already the skeleton was covered by the flesh and blood of new life—a life of enterprise and profit, in contrast with which, the old franchise revenues that might still have

[1] Defoe, *Essay on Projects*, 198.

[2] *C.J.* xi, 30 Dec. 1696.

[3] 8–9 Wm. III, c. 27.

[4] A district in Southwark.

[5] For an instance, see *P.C. Reg.* 71, 12 June 1685.

been squeezed from tenants must have seemed ludicrously small.[1] There was so much more to be gained from growing corn or wool, or from exploiting the minerals on one's estate, or from taking a share in industry, that there was no need for the landlord, even where he retained the power, to extract those profits of justice that had once been considered *magnum emolumentum*. The English landlord may well have been as rapacious as the French seigneur, but he could afford to be lax, and sometimes even generous; indeed, his comparatively high standard of wealth and well-being provides the main explanation of the contrast between the civilization of England and that of her neighbours. South of the border there may have been a few squires to whom could be applied the description which characterized so many lairds in the north: 'A puckle land, a load of debt, a doo-cot and a law plea', but it would have been hard to find in seventeenth-century England, as it would have been easy to find in France, a landed proprietor so penurious that he was obliged to stay in bed while his solitary pair of boots was being mended. This greater prosperity enjoyed by the English landed classes is one reason why 'feudal' survivals in England were far less oppressive than in Scotland or France. Nevertheless there still remained that mentality of freehold, which was at the basis of our representative system,[2] and had a profound influence on the conception of personal status. To this latter topic the next section is devoted.

2. Status

It may seem unusual to preface an account of personal status with a reference to property. But property always comes before the person, because the inanimate and tangible are so much more obvious than the subjective things that constitute personality. Two kinds of property are here in question. The law of medieval England distinguished between real and personal property, the distinction amounting roughly to this, that over the first, one had much less power of disposition than over the second. The personal property was one's own; from this idea of *own-ness* it was not a far step to *one-ness*, or individuality. This

[1] One of the few discussions of this important point will be found in R. H. Tawney's brilliant introduction to D. Brunton and D. H. Pennington, *The Long Parliament*.

[2] For this see *infra*, 130.

freedom of disposition of one's personalty, the earliest form of freedom to be protected by law, has exercised a profound influence on our words and institutions. Thus, when a woman married, she retained certain rights over her real property, but her personal property she surrendered completely to her husband; in giving up her personalty, she gave up her personality, two words which originally meant the same thing. Even today the woman has not, in theory at least, completely severed her old association with personal property, for the bride is still 'given away' in church, and always by one man to another man; a transfer which is at least consistent with the promise of obedience made by the subject of the transaction. This ancient association of animate with inanimate has led to a curious interplay of similar words among things now regarded as totally unconnected; for a term originally tied down to property may break away and cling to personality. Thus, the word 'propriety' originally meant no more than the right to one's property, and this in turn came to be limited to one form of rightness, namely, whatever is fitting or becoming in one's conduct. The word 'proper' still commemorates this progress from legal right to ethical rightfulness, and the moral justification of a man's claim to his personal possessions is thus deeply embedded in our language as in our law.

All this may help to explain why the word 'status', although a Latin term, appears never to have been used in the seventeenth century. It was unknown to the old law. Perhaps the earliest definition of what we call status is that in a statute[1] of Henry VIII making natural subjects of certain children born overseas, entitled 'to enjoy land by descent and purchase, to sue and be sued'. The same rights were conferred on those who had been ejected from religious houses.[2] The earliest recorded use of the word 'status' in our sense is by Boswell,[3] who may have derived it from his Civil Law studies in Scotland, where Roman Law terminology was in common use; indeed, the word does not appear to have been applied in its present meaning until about the time of Austin. So, in trying to describe status in the later seventeenth century, we are trying to describe something

[1] 33 Hen. VIII, c. 25. [2] 33 Hen. VIII, c. 29.

[3] In *Boswell's Johnson*, ed. Birkbeck Hill, iii. 204, where Boswell is referring to the negro slave. I owe this reference to the *Oxford Dictionary*.

which, strictly speaking, was not there. The person was just beginning to be disentangled from rights of property, a process helped by the fact that villeinage and wardship had both disappeared by 1660. But the villeins and the wards still continued to be cited in court as examples of chattels;[1] and for long there survived this intimate association of the person with property. 'God forbid', declared an eminent lawyer in the House of Lords, 'that there should be anything like a forcing of the master to abandon his property in the slave; once admit this principle, and there will be an end of all property.'[2] This was in 1830.

That property came before person was demonstrated in the law regarding abduction of a woman. To take her away against her will was no offence, unless she was a ward, or an heiress to landed property, in which case the offence was felony, punishable by death.[3] An example will make this clear. In 1702 a woman was indicted in King's Bench for taking away an heiress by force and procuring her marriage to an accomplice. At the trial[4] Mr. Justice Powell addressed the accused woman in these terms:

> Your offence hath been in a nation where property is better preserved than in any other government in the world. Here it is death for a man to take away anything, though never so small, by way of robbery; how much worse to take away the child of a man, and with her all that he hath gotten by his industry, a great offence against the public, being so great a violation of property.

On conviction, the abductress was sentenced to death; but, as she was with child, her execution was deferred until as soon as possible after her delivery. It is evidence of a slight increase of humanitarianism that eventually she was reprieved. This sanctity of property was bound to have influence on public events; or rather, these events might be interpreted according as they safeguarded property; here indeed we have one of the main justifications of the Revolution. The salvation of freehold in

[1] W. Salkeld, *Reports of Cases Adjudged in the Court of King's Bench* (1721), 666. For a recent and valuable study of the system of wardship, see H. E. Bell, *The Court of Wards and Liveries*. Mr. Bell notes (p. 125) the evil effects of selling the wardship and marriage of a minor.

[2] Cited in C. Grant Robertson, *Select Statutes, Cases and Documents* (4th ed.), 347.

[3] 3 Hen. VII, c. 2.

[4] *State Trials*, xiv. 632 sqq.

1688 does not appear to have been celebrated by any poet; but its salvation (again from the Stuarts) in 1714 was sung by Ambrose Philips:[1] 'O Property! O Goddess, English-born!' The poet's inclusion of investments, as well as freehold, in his enumeration of types of property thus salvaged for a second time suggests that his economics were stronger than his muse.

As property was a test applied to politics, so it was applied to the person. By the later seventeenth century the negro was the only surviving example of a human being who was still a chattel; and it was in the course of lawsuits about this article of merchandise that expression was given, for the first time, to a more modern conception of personality. These lawsuits arose mainly in actions of Trover and Trespass, of which the first provided a remedy against another who, having found any of one's goods, refused to deliver them up, an action which could be taken by the owner against a person detaining a negro slave. The second action, that of Trespass, was wide enough to include any wrong or damage done by one to the property of another; and applied to offences, such as taking away an heir apparent or an apprentice, whereby rights of property were invaded, a principle extended to claims arising against a third party from the beating of one's servant or apprentice, if to such an extent that the victim was unable to fulfil his functions. To the old law, the victim was not the servant, but the master, who, during the servant's disablement, was in a legal position similar to that of the modern car owner who is deprived of the use of his car in consequence of damage sustained through the negligent driving of another.

The hearing of evidence in cases arising from actions of Trover and Trespass resulted, within the space of a few years, in an extraordinary change of judicial opinion. Thus, in 1693 it was adjudged in King's Bench that Trover will lie for a negro in England, because 'they are heathens, and therefore a man may have property in them'.[2] Three years later, in an action of Trespass for taking away a negro, there were some momentous expressions of opinion, and even the reporter noted that 'a case

[1] This line (from an ode to the great Whig financier lord Halifax) is quoted in G. M. Trevelyan, *England under Queen Anne, Ramillies*, 84, footnote.

[2] *English Reports*, xci (King's Bench), 994, *Gally* v. *Cleve*.

like this never happened before'.[1] The negro, the subject of the action, appears to have been baptized; and it was contended that, if baptism amounted to manumission, then the whole plantation trade would be ruined; to which it was answered that, by baptism, the negro became a Christian, and Christianity is inconsistent with slavery. It was urged also that our laws are called *libertates Angliae*, because they make men free; moreover, it is against the law of nature for one man to be the slave of another. In the course of these proceedings Holt declared that 'Trover will not lie for a negro'; the judgement affirmed that neither would Trespass lie, technical statements which concealed the beginnings of a remarkable change in the conception of human life. Holt was more explicit in *Smith* v. *Browne and Others*,[2] an action of debt, when he declared: 'As soon as a negro comes into England, he is free.' This was one of the most revolutionary of all the judicial pronouncements of the century. It anticipated by many years the famous judgement of Mansfield in *Summersett's Case* (1771), and is probably the earliest expression of that modern conception of personal freedom which is so strikingly contrasted with the old.

This linking of personality with private property is very ancient, and had been clearly expounded by Aristotle in both his *Ethics* and *Politics*. It is possible that much of the early evolution of human status can be explained in terms of these vast and basic things—Christianity (including Canon Law), Land Law, and Aristotle; this indeed is one of the worthwhile historical subjects still awaiting research. Here only a small fraction of the subject can be attempted, by reference to a few examples. For this purpose the following will be briefly referred to: (*a*) parent and child; (*b*) husband and wife; (*c*) master and apprentice; (*d*) stockbroker, scrivener, and banker; (*e*) physician and apothecary; and, lastly (*f*) Roman Catholic and Dissenter.

[1] *Chamberlain* v. *Harvey*, 8–9 Wm. III. *Modern Reports* (1711), v. 182. I have followed this account because it is fuller than that in *English Reports*. From both accounts, it appears that the verdict was for the defendant, that is, against the owner of the slave, apparently on the ground that no action of Trespass will lie against a man for taking away a man generally, though there might be an action of Trespass for taking away a man's servant, or an heir apparent.

[2] n.d. Salkeld, op. cit. 666.

(a) Parent and child

It is because this is the most natural of human relationships that we hear so little about it. Men lived shorter lives; the children (of the upper and middle classes) married early (for a woman, the minimum age was twelve), and in poor families the children might be put to work at the age of three. As the father had the legal right to the profits of the children's labour so long as they were under age, and living with him, the family might be of economic importance, and in this respect might come into conflict with schemes, such as those of Thomas Firmin and John Cary, for the employment of young children in the factory or workhouse. Exploitation by parents of juvenile labour was usually a necessity, imposed by the low wages of labour. In such circumstances there could have been little or no family life.

Parents were considered to have such power as was given them by the Laws of Nature and the Divine Law. In accordance with these laws, they were required to maintain, educate, and defend their children, and in order to ensure this, the legislature sometimes intervened. A statute[1] enabled posthumous children to succeed to estates as if born within their fathers' lifetime; and in those cases where the child of a Roman Catholic[2] or of a Jew[3] became a Protestant Christian, the law required that the parents should make provision for him as if he had not changed his faith. On their side, the children were adjured 'to honour and obey parents, to be guided by them in the choice of a calling and of a spouse, to submit to their parents' reproofs and chastenings, to pray for them'.[4] In those families where economic conditions obviated the necessity of child labour, the parents often exercised a personal interest in the education of their young, because at that time there were fewer residential schools, whether 'public' or 'preparatory'; indeed Locke condemned residential schools, alleging that the pupils acquired 'a mixture of rudeness and ill-timed confidence'.[5] In consequence, education at home often began at a very early age. Although Gregory King was taken to the village school at the age of two, his father so carefully supervised him

[1] 10 Wm. III, c. 22.
[2] 11–12 Wm. III, c. 4.
[3] 1 Ann., c. 24.
[4] *The True Interest of Families . . .*, 1692.
[5] Locke, *Some Thoughts Concerning Education*, in *Works* (1823 ed.), ix, par. 70.

that at the age of three he could read the Psalter, but not till his seventh year did his father teach him to write.[1] 'The mother is the best teacher' declared Thomas Tryon,[2] a prolific writer on social reform, who claimed that women were at least as good teachers as men; like Locke, Tryon condemned the coddling of the young, and held up the example of the Scots, brought up on oatmeal. That the family was often a happy institution, wherever poverty did not break up its unity, is abundantly evident from the correspondence of the period.

Over the child, parental control was absolute; and, in a religious age, it was almost sacrilege to dispute it. For a girl, it ended only with marriage, when she exchanged one overlord for another, chosen by the father, who also had usually a say in the son's choice of a bride. In days when every well-to-do family had a large number of personal servants, there was a danger that a son or daughter might marry to the disparagement of his or her social class; and Locke was only one of the many who warned parents against too close contact between children and servants; 'you will have very good luck', he wrote,[3] 'if you never have a clownish or vicious servant.' That public opinion was alive to this danger is shown by the attempts of the legislature[4] to impose penalties, up to three years' imprisonment, on servants who married sons or daughters of their masters, while still minors, and without the parents' consent. At the same time, an attempt was made to raise the legal age of marriage from eighteen to twenty-one and from twelve to fourteen for male and female respectively. A Bill to this effect was passed by the Lords in 1689, but was lost in the Commons; and the same fate befell a Bill of 1690 intended to prevent clandestine marriages.[5] But, if parliament failed to alter the law in this matter, the courts ensured that, in arranging marriages, the monopoly of parents and relatives was maintained.[6]

[1] *Rawl. MS.* C. 154.

[2] T. Tryon, *A New Method of Educating Children*, 1695, 15.

[3] Locke, op. cit. ix, par. 69.

[4] These apparently began in 1677. *H.M.C. Rep.* ix, app. pt. 2, 90, 29 Mar. 1677 (*MSS. of House of Lords*).

[5] Ibid. xii, app. pt. 6, 267 sqq., and ibid. xiii, app. pt. 5, 253 (*MSS. of House of Lords*).

[6] There is a good illustration in *English Reports*, i, House of Lords, 52, *Hall et alii* v. *Jane Potter*.

(b) Husband and wife

The old law knew the married woman as the *feme covert*, and conferred on her a curious mixture of rights and disabilities.[1] A lunatic, that is one whose disability was intermittent, could not marry; but, on the other hand, an idiot, whose mental infirmity was congenital and permanent, could marry; and furthermore, if he or she begot a child, that in itself created a presumption of legal capacity. Marriage with a deceased wife's sister, or within the prohibited degrees, was incestuous and might be punished in the ecclesiastical courts by annulment of the marriage and bastardizing of the issue; marriage by a dissenting minister was irregular, but not void. The church courts might punish breach of promise by excommunication and (in theory at least) by imprisonment; but for monetary damages, either sex would have to go to a lay court, usually the Exchequer, which retained this type of business until the time of Gilbert and Sullivan's *Trial by Jury*. But, in the later seventeenth century, the claimant might well be the male, if he could produce evidence that his prospective father-in-law had promised him a sum of money with his daughter. This was not a sentimental age, and for many swains, marriage was an investment.

Marriage gave to the husband extensive control over the person and property of the wife, because by marriage the woman came *sub potestate viri*. The husband's rights were distinguished according as his wife brought real or personal property. Over the latter, which included money and clothes, his rights were absolute; but on his death, the widow was entitled to her necessary apparel, or *paraphernalia*, this being determined by her social rank. Over the former, the real property, there were limitations intended to ensure that, during their joint lifetime, neither party had full powers of disposition, but usually the husband took the rents and profits of land. On the other hand, the widow might have her right of Dower, usually a third part of her husband's land; but where this was regulated by the custom of a manor, she might succeed to a life-interest in all the land, so long as she remained *sola et casta*; she might also benefit, particularly where large estates were concerned, by the Jointure, a rent charge on the husband's

[1] For this, see *A Treatise of Feme Coverts, or the Lady's Law*, 1732.

lands, commonly secured to the widow for life through the agency of trustees. If the husband died intestate, the widow was entitled to a third part of his personal estate, the remaining two-thirds being divided among the children. Generally, the law regarded the status of the married woman as that of an infant, with the distinction that while an infant is capable of doing an act for his own advantage, a *feme covert* is not.[1]

Divorce was of two kinds, according as the causes preceded or succeeded matrimony. The first, *a vinculo matrimonii*, might be obtained in a church court by proving pre-contract, or frigidity, or consanguinity, or if one had been forced into marriage against his or her will. Divorce on any of these grounds, all precedent to the contract, sundered the marriage tie and made the children illegitimate. The parties so divorced could marry again. On the other hand, divorce *a mensa et thoro*, usually for adultery, did not dissolve the marriage, for this arose from a cause subsequent thereto, and the parties could not marry again. This disability in regard to second marriage led to a cleavage of opinion in the later seventeenth century, which was brought to a head in 1700 when the duke of Norfolk was granted a divorce by Act of Parliament, on the ground of the adultery of his wife, and express permission was given him to marry again, an event which marked the beginning of the long process whereby the state took over control of divorce from the church. Meanwhile, the view was being expressed that the ban on subsequent marriage of persons divorced *a mensa et thoro* was a relic of popish times, and some of William III's bishops[2] were said to favour relaxation of the disability in such cases, if only because there were so many good, Protestant precedents.

The status of women was thus defined by Halifax:[3]

> You must first lay it down for a foundation in general that there is inequality in the sexes, and that for the better economy of the world the men, who were to be the lawgivers, had the larger share of reason bestowed upon them, by which means your sex is the better

[1] An example is provided by a curious case where the wife of an improvident husband had, by her great frugality, saved a large sum for the benefit of the children. Chancery refused her permission to dispose of these savings, on the ground that it was dangerous to give a woman power over her husband's estate. *A Treatise of Feme Coverts*, 174.

[2] e.g. *Burnet*, iv. 228.

[3] *Advice to a Daughter* in *Halifax*, ii. 394.

prepared for the compliance that is necessary for the better performance of those duties which seem to be most properly assigned to it. . . . We are made of different tempers that our defects might be mutually supplied. Your sex wanteth our reason for your conduct, and our strength for your protection; ours wanteth your gentleness to soften and to entertain us.

Such was the theory. But the other sex did not always acquiesce in this subordination; indeed it was sometimes to their credit that they did not. A few led an active or adventurous life, though for this they had to don masculine garb; thus, one young Englishwoman, a Jacobite, served as a trooper in the French army; another, a cook maid, was said to function at night as a highway robber, armed with a black pudding which, in the dark, looked like a pistol.[1] More numerous were the women who used the most effective weapons in their armoury—their tongues—and indeed one of the stock themes of seventeenth-century comedy was the (vain) search for a silent woman. Scolding matches between teams of notorious viragos were sometimes held in London for a wager;[2] and many husbands realized the force of the scriptural injunction: 'better dwell on a house top than with a brawling wife'. This may be why some contemporaries held that the law allowed too much liberty to women; indeed, for the man, wedded life was sometimes depicted as a state of bondage, compensated for by a good marriage portion: 'better a fat sorrow than a lean one'. Much of the old literature about women was facetious or sarcastic, but there still survived traces of medieval invective, as when Bunyan personified the vanity of the world in a woman, Madame Bubble—'many that she brought to the halter, and ten thousand times more to hell'.[3] The versifiers added their quota:[4]

Oh Heavenly Powers; why did you bring to light,
That thing called Woman, Nature's oversight?
A wayward, a froward a constant evil,
A seeming saint, sole factor to the Devil.

There was an old proverb: 'women like linen look best by night'.

[1] *A Leicestershire Frolick or the Valiant Cook Maid*, in *Bodl. Don* B. 13, Broadside Ballads, f. 50.

[2] e.g. the advertisement in *The Protestant Mercury* for 9–14 June 1695.

[3] *Works of John Bunyan* (1857 ed.), iii. 239 (*Pilgrim's Progress*).

[4] F. Seymar, *Conjugium Conjurgium* (1684), 16.

This may well have been helped by candle light, so much more merciful than modern illumination to fragile charms.[1]

One class of married woman, the wives of the clergy, was still in a somewhat ambiguous position. Some of them had been lady's maids, or even cast-off mistresses of patrons of livings; and contemporary opinion was horrified when such persons, on the strength of a husband's doctorate of divinity (which conferred the status of esquire) claimed equality with the wife of the squire.[2] Moreover, as there lingered a certain objection to the marriage of the clergy, their wives were still to some extent on sufferance; indeed, even today, the wives of the lords spiritual do not enjoy the same social rank as that accorded to the wives of the lords temporal. As England was then nearer to the Reformation, many may have sympathized with the opinion said to have been expressed by queen Elizabeth who, when asked what place should be assigned to a clergyman's wife, is reported to have replied *Behind the door*.[3] Enforced celibacy had once enabled the clergy to maintain a certain apartness in the state; their marriage brought into society a new class of woman, for whom at first a definite status could not be formulated.

But, in regard to women generally, there was a gradual change of attitude as the patriarchal conception of the family, wherein the wife was little more than a chattel, was displaced by a more liberal conception of human relationship.[4] Some writers advocated greater recognition of their importance; for, though they are half in numbers, as wives and mothers they are at least two-thirds; furthermore, English women, it was held, were distinguished from those of other nations by their beauty; and, while it might be true that they had no souls (a medieval slander), yet they had 'a natural sagacity capable of very noble refinement'.[5] The author of this statement made the interesting observation that, since monastic days, no endowed provision had been made for the upbringing of women—all the endowments were for boys or young men. It was true that, in

[1] Cf. the remark of Angelica in Congreve, *All for Love*: 'I have seen fifty in a side-box by candle light outblossom five-and-twenty.' Act V, Scene 2.

[2] This is the theme of *Mrs. Abigail or a Female Skirmish*.

[3] Ibid. 13.

[4] For this see R. B. Schlatter, *The Social Ideas of Religious Leaders, 1660–1688*, 24–29.

[5] *Reflections on the Moral State of the Nation* (1701), 21–22.

some cathedral cities, such as Winchester and Salisbury, institutions had been founded for widows of the clergy; but these ladies, it was said, were condemned to 'an inactive and melancholy way of life', whereas they might be happier and more useful if engaged in teaching girls. But the rarity of such appeals serves to emphasize how, in the man-made society of the period, while women might play a great, though silent part in moulding the younger generation, they were denied a place in public life. If they were given to reading, printed sermons and 'good' books were thought specially suitable; if they were of the upper classes, their virtues provided inspiration, not for contemporary eulogy, but for funeral orations. A few pioneers, such as Mrs. Aphra Behn and Mrs. Manley, achieved a somewhat ambiguous reputation in letters; Celia Fiennes, who kept a fascinating diary of travel,[1] never aspired to authorship. Most of their female contemporaries were relegated to the kitchen or the nursery.

(*c*) *Master and apprentice*

An apprentice was defined as a young person bound by indentures to a tradesman or artificer, who was required to teach him his mystery or trade. He was 'a kind of bondman, a servant by covenant, usually for seven years'.[2] It was common for the master to enter into two obligations, one with the parent, relative, or friend of the apprentice, in consideration of a sum of money; the other with the apprentice himself. For purposes of poor relief apprenticeship constituted settlement in a place, and the justices were empowered to compel persons to take poor parish children as apprentices. Many boys were sent into sea service, and Trinity House appears to have exercised some supervision over them,[3] to ensure that they were given opportunities for learning their duties. Sometimes poor girls were forced on the clergy for training on the land,[4] a measure which shows how closely the parson was associated with agriculture; even more, it provides one reason for the decay of the appren-

[1] See *The Journeys of Celia Fiennes*, ed. C. Morris (1947). Mr. Morris's introduction is specially valuable.

[2] G. Jacob, *The Law Dictionary*, 1723, *sub voce* 'Apprentice'.

[3] This duty was included in the new charter which the attorney general was ordered to prepare in 1685, *S.P.*, James II, 5 June 1685.

[4] See the complaint of Rev. J. Ward, 15 Mar. 1689, in *H.M.C. Rep.* xii, app. pt. 2, 387 (*Coke MSS.*).

ticeship system, since that system was now linked with the stigma of pauperism.

Another reason for this decay is that the old system was based on the assumption of an unchangeable society, and was bound to disintegrate with the development of a more varied economy. In the course of this development there was continual trespass of one craft on another; also, with increasing specialization, one section of a craft might break away and form an independent body. Thus, as the grocers were obliged to part company with the apothecaries and distillers, so the blacksmiths failed to retain the allegiance of the watch- and clock-makers; indeed, this subdivision and specialization made nonsense of the old classifications.[1] Some London companies, such as the Carpenters, did succeed in maintaining a certain control over their apprentices, but it is significant that, on completion of their articles, very few took up their freedom of the Company.[2] This applies even more to craftsmen in the country, who complained of the expense involved in going to London for admission to their Company and of the heavy fees imposed;[3] hence the system decayed more speedily in the country than in the towns. Moreover, there was increasing cleavage between the trading and industrial elements, so that the latter gradually lost in bargaining power, and provided human material in later times for the trade unions.[4] Nevertheless, there still survived the personal link between master and apprentice; how sacred that was is manifest from the fact that the slaying of a master by his servant was the first offence to be deprived of benefit of clergy.[5]

As the century progressed there was more criticism of the system. It was being brought into discredit, some alleged, by the cupidity and harshness of masters. Premiums, it was said, had gone up from £80–100 to as much as £500; too many masters were using their apprentices as personal servants; for small faults, many were turned away, and so ruined in their trade. One harsh feature of the relationship was that all earn-

[1] S. Kramer, *The English Craft Gilds*, 122 sqq.

[2] *Records of the Worshipful Company of Carpenters*, ed. B. Marsh, 1. Apprentices' Entry Books, 1654–94.

[3] e.g. petition of the framework-knitters of Nottingham, Leicester, and Derby, in *C.J.* xii, 6 Apr. 1700.

[4] G. Unwin, *Industrial Organization in the XVIth and XVIIth Centuries*, 211.

[5] 12 Hen. VII, c. 7.

ings of the apprentice became the property of the master, a principle extended to include the wages of a waterman's apprentice who had been pressed into the navy.[1] The restriction on marriage was also capable of great abuse. But the necessities of war helped further to disintegrate the system; for by an Act of 1698[2] all disbanded soldiers were permitted to exercise their trades in those places where they had served an incomplete apprenticeship. A case decided in 1706 accelerated the process whereby the old civic monopolies were giving way to free enterprise. This case arose from an action brought by the corporation of Winchester against one exercising a trade in the city, in spite of the fact that he had not served an apprenticeship there; and it was argued, on behalf of the corporation, that only those could trade in the city who were free of the *gilda mercatoria*, the example of London being cited in support of this contention. But Holt, dismissing the suit, declared that the analogy of London did not apply to other towns; moreover, the action should have been brought by the *gilda mercatoria*, not the corporation, as the two were quite distinct. Here was one of Holt's many pronouncements in favour of the liberty of the subject.[3]

It may be said of the apprenticeship system that, by providing skilled training, it performed many of the functions now delegated to technical schools and colleges. It also helped to determine personal status, since the 'freedom' acquired by servitude brought with it a recognized position, and even a certain bargaining power. What this meant may be realized by comparison with new industries which, having never been subject to gild regulation, suffered from the evils of unorganized and sweated labour; accordingly, the new 'luxury' trades were those in which the poor, especially the women, were mercilessly exploited. Similar conditions prevailed among those male workers who had neither the protection of 'freedom' nor part-time occupations with which to supplement their earnings; as they did not fit into any of the recognized categories, they had to suffer, usually in wages, sometimes in social position. An example of this latter disability is seen in the coal miner, whose

[1] *English Reports*, xci (King's Bench), *Barber* v. *Dennis*, 1703.

[2] 10 Wm. III, c. 17.

[3] *English Reports*, xci (King's Bench), 181. *Mayor and Corporation of Winton* v. *Willis*, 1706.

position in English society was not unlike that of the sailor. Both lived strange, dangerous lives; they had their own vocabulary; their distinctive appearance marked them off from other men. The miner was further degraded by the black substance which he handled; moreover, he usually lived in a separate community, where he became one of a hereditary caste, the father usually training the son. He earned good wages, it is true, but he had to suffer ostracism. In Scotland, malefactors were sometimes sentenced to penal servitude in the collieries; in England, on occasion,[1] convicted felons had their sentences remitted on condition of completing five years' service in the mines. It was not until the time of Wesley and Whitefield that missionary enterprise penetrated so far as the pariahs of the pits.

The coal miner was, to some extent, protected from exploitation by his technical skill and intrepidity. In contrast, the occupation of coal heaver was comparatively new; it was unskilled, unregulated, and so was at the mercy of the middleman and the crimp. This unfortunate class appears to have emerged from the mass of casual labour employed in the rebuilding of London. With the increasing flow of 'sea cole' into London docks, unemployed men took to coal heaving; and they naturally sought to organize themselves into a fraternity, such as that of the Billingsgate Porters, who were 'free' of the city.[2] Repeatedly they petitioned the magistrates for such a privilege, in order that they might manage their own labour; but these petitions were in vain, partly because the heavers were not 'free', and partly because the material which they handled brought a social stigma. So the unfortunate coal heavers came to be the most mercilessly victimized of all forms of manual labour, and were soon at the absolute disposal of 'coal undertakers' and crimps, who hired their victims at public houses, where they obliged them to spend part of their wages; maintaining their hold by securing the sole right to purchase shovels from the makers.[3] In this way, wages were beaten down; disease and blindness from working in ships' holds full of dust added to the miseries of these new-comers into the world of labour.[4] In con-

[1] T. S. Ashton and J. Sykes, *The Coal Industry in the Eighteenth Century*, 216.

[2] *The Coal Heavers' Case*, in *Bodl. Firth* B. 16.

[3] J. U. Nef, *The Rise of the British Coal Industry*, i. 432–4.

[4] *The Coal Heavers' Case.*

trast, the Watermen, the Billingsgate Porters, and the Hackney Coachmen were all more fortunate because, as they were incorporated, they had a status, and it was status which ensured some guarantee against victimization.

(*d*) *Stockbroker, scrivener, and banker*

Tudor legislation had regulated many of the crafts and professions, a regulation based on a clear distinction between the secular and spiritual; and in this way were laid the foundations of the society which we know today. There was less of such legislation in the seventeenth century, but its enactment generally provides evidence that certain activities, either new or old, have become important enough to justify intervention by parliament. Thus William's war finance, based mainly on national loans, emphasized the importance of the stockbroker, whose alleged ill practices were, it was hoped, diminished by an Act of 1697,[1] the preamble to which recited that for many years the 'sworn brokers' had carried on the business of stock jobbing in London, but of late had been swamped by 'pretended brokers', who, in their trade of discounting tallies, Bank stock, and shares in joint-stock companies, had combined to raise or depress the value of securities. Accordingly, in future, stockbrokers were to be licensed by the lord mayor; and, on admission, were to take an oath against fraud, with a deposit of £500 as security. Their brokerage was limited to ten shillings per cent.; they were to wear a silver badge when conducting business; they were not to deal on their own account, and their number was limited to 100. Dealers in corn, coal, cattle, or provisions were not to be accounted brokers.

This Act is interesting as an example of how parliament might try to define an occupation and differentiate it from others. By limitation of numbers, by the imposition of an oath and the wearing of a badge, some kind of fraternity was created under the aegis of the lord mayor; but, on the other hand, the substantial monetary security raised stockbroking to the level of a profession, for it implied some public responsibility, and clearly distinguished that profession from ordinary trading activities in which, as tangible commodities were handled, the element of public trust was less in evidence. In other words, in

[1] 8–9 Wm. III, c. 32.

the increasingly commercial world of the later seventeenth century, money and trust intervene to amplify social and economic relationships, and a comparatively new class of men was accorded by statute a personal status commensurate in importance with that of the new national activities brought into prominence by the war.

There are other examples of this regulation of status by statute. The Poll Bills of the period levied a head tax on all persons according to the legislature's estimate of their function in the state, ranging from £50 levied on archbishops and dukes, £20 on barons, £5 on esquires, £1 on gentlemen, down to 6*d.* or 1*s.* on those who, though not in receipt of alms, had no status whatever. On this scale, the Law stood highest among the professions, a king's sergeant being equated with a baron, and a sergeant-at-law with a baronet: then came doctors of divinity, law, and physic, who, at £5 per head, were (actuarily) equivalent to esquires, and five times more valuable to the state than gentlemen. Very different was the status of the merchant. Those trading in London who were not free were penalized to the extent of £10; but those free, and also traders occupying a house in London valued at not less than £30 per annum, were charged only 10*s.* Many of these merchants and traders must have been much better off than some persons higher in the scale; and their light assessment shows how slow was the legislature to recognize the increasing consequence and financial resources of the mercantile community. In 1694, however, the Poll Bill brought a new set of occupations into the financial net, for cursitors, philisers, attorneys, solicitors, and scriveners were each charged £1. Of these the first two disappeared in the nineteenth century, their place being taken by the personnel of the courts of Justice; the second two later merged to become one of the most important branches of the legal profession; and the last, the scrivener, is one of the ancestors of the modern banker and financier. Another ancestor in this genealogy is the goldsmith, whose company was one of the twelve major companies of the City.

At this point the help of a philosopher and a poet may be enlisted in order to assist in the elucidation of an evolutionary process. In his *Essay on Riches*,[1] Bacon wrote: 'the scriveners

[1] Cited in the *Oxford Dictionary, sub voce* 'Scrivener'.

and broakers doe valew unsound men'. The scrivener, originally no more than a copyist, had come to draw up deeds and bonds, and his activities were regulated by the company of Scriveners. From that, he had proceeded to receive money, and place it out at interest; or he might arrange a mortgage[1] on behalf of an 'unsound' man, usually an impoverished landowner. An example of such an unsound man was the second duke of Buckingham, whose enormous wealth had been derived from lavish royal grants and at least one fortunate marriage. The process whereby the wealth of this dissolute but witty duke passed into the hands of brokers was summarized, as only a poet could do it, by Dryden, in his well-known line: 'He had his jest, and they had his estate.'

Among the many who had a share (a legitimate one) in the proceeds of these estates was the firm of Clayton and Morris, two scriveners in partnership, who had their office at the *Flying Horse* in Cornhill. They had an arrangement, as early as the years 1660–3, whereby they cashed notes to bearer, usually for £50–200 in favour of lord Loughborough, who, for this purpose, sent his boy or man with a written note of demand; on receiving the money, the messenger signed the note. In this way the scriveners were acting as bankers and were using a simple system of bearer cheques. They also supplied to their client a statement of account, similar to a modern pass book, which showed on his credit side a sum of £1,048, arising from a mortgage made by the duke of Buckingham—presumably interest or rent collected by the scriveners on behalf of their client.[2] This scrivener, afterwards sir Robert Clayton, accumulated a large fortune from banking and similar transactions; one of London's Whig magnates, he just escaped from the proscription following the Rye House Plot which brought disaster to so many of his colleagues. On several occasions he served as a burgess for the city; he was a governor of St. Thomas's and Christ's Hospitals. A munificent and public-spirited man, he provided the best example in his age of this evolution of scrivener into banker.

A less worthy person interested in the duke's affairs was sir

[1] D. C. Coleman, 'London Scriveners and the Estate Market in the later Seventeenth Century', in *Econ. Hist. Rev.*, 2nd series, iv, no. 1.

[2] *Bodl. MS., Eng. Letters*, c. 12.

Charles Duncombe,[1] who purchased Buckingham's great estate at Helmsley in Yorkshire for, it is said, £90,000. He illustrates another ancestral line in the banker's genealogy—that of goldsmith, for he began as apprentice to alderman Backwell, Charles II's goldsmith-banker, and died in 1711, by repute the wealthiest commoner in England. His career provides a good illustration of the new opportunities awaiting one who, a century earlier might well have lived and died a craftsman. In partnership with Richard Kent, he was one of the goldsmiths who kept 'running cashes' (at the *Grasshopper* in Lombard Street); and, as banker to lord Shaftesbury, he received timely notice of the impending Stop of the Exchequer, so escaping the losses that fell on many goldsmiths. As receiver of Customs and cashier of Excise he was closely connected with the financial administration of Charles II and James II; indeed, by 1685 Duncombe had claims on the revenues amounting to £390,000.[2] From a study of his commitments and investments, it is possible to deduce the course of national events. Thus, in the autumn of 1688, he refused an advance to the king, from whose revenues he had profited so much, obviously because he considered that James was no longer a good security; then, during the critical months of November and December, he withheld his Excise receipts, until the public position had been 'clarified'; but by 10 January 1689 he felt sufficiently sure of the investment situation to venture a loan of £20,000 to the new regime.[3] It was a clear signal that, so far as he was concerned, the Revolution might proceed.

But this loan was not an act of generosity, nor even a straightforward investment, for the commissioners of Excise claimed that it was caution money for his financial behaviour. That such security was badly needed in his case was shown when the issue of Exchequer Bills provided him with new opportunities for making illicit gains from the needs of the state, and again with impunity. In 1697 these Bills were at a considerable discount, but were accepted at par if paid into the Exchequer for taxes, the Bills so paid being always endorsed. Having cashed a large

[1] For the careers of Clayton and Duncombe, the author is partly indebted to the *D.N.B.*

[2] E. Hughes, *Studies in Administration and Finance, 1558–1825*, 165.

[3] Ibid. 173.

number of these Bills at a discount, Duncombe, in his capacity of cashier of Excise, then induced those who paid them in to endorse them with their own or fictitious signatures, and he then credited himself with the full face value of the Bills, as if he had received them for taxes.[1] For this he was acquitted in a court of law on a technicality;[2] and indeed, he had committed no indictable offence, but he was expelled from the House of Commons. The House passed a Bill against this 'Judas of the Age', as he was called, but the Lords rejected it by one vote, the majority having been influenced by the eloquence of three great lords, Nottingham, Rochester, and Leeds, whose views on financial matters could be described as latitudinarian.

It was nothing new for a man to acquire great fortune from the needs of the state. But Duncombe, whose composure and effrontery seemed new, achieved real eminence in the fine art of being always found out and never once convicted. As he left no male heir he did not found a noble family. Fortunately he was exceptional, even in his period, for better examples of great merchants and bankers were sir John Houblon and sir Michael Godfrey, who, as governors of the Bank of England, were notable for integrity and public spirit.

(*e*) *Physician and apothecary*

The physician was normally a fellow or licentiate of the Royal College of Physicians; the apothecary was free of his City Company; so both had a definite status, and this section is concerned with variations in that status which contributed to the evolution of a learned profession, that of medical practitioner. Like the clergyman and the school-teacher, the physician had to subscribe to a declaration affirming his belief in the royal supremacy, in the Thirty-nine Articles and the Book of Common Prayer. There were other links connecting physician and parson. They were both the creation of Tudor legislation, the Royal College having been founded by Henry VIII, largely through the munificence of Linacre; also, the bishops issued licences to qualified men; the fellows of the College, though not the licentiates, were drawn exclusively from the two universi-

[1] The procedure was explained in a letter from E. Southwell to Nottingham, 9 Feb. 1698. *Add. MS.* 29588, f. 9.

[2] *State Trials*, xiii. 1063 sqq.

ties; finally, as members of academic bodies, parson and physician had at least a tincture of classical learning. In remote districts, where practitioners were few or non-existent, the clergy sometimes acted in the capacity of amateur doctors, as did Baxter at Kidderminster.

By their charter and by statute the censors of the College were endowed with extraordinary powers. They could impose a fine of £5 per month on every unqualified person practising physic in London, or within seven miles thereof; over their own colleagues their powers were even wider, notably in those cases where members of the College were accused of *malpraxis*, as by administering *insalubres pillulae et noxia medicamenta*. For this offence they sent a Dr. Groenwelt to Newgate for twelve months; later, they discovered that they had made a mistake, and that the pills were harmless: but the unfortunate doctor obtained no damages from King's Bench, which affirmed the right of the censors to act judicially, though erroneously.[1] But the activities of the College were not limited to disciplinary matters. As its members might practise surgery, some teaching in anatomy was provided. In 1687, when the archbishop of Canterbury surrendered his right to license medical books, the censors appointed licensers; and in the same year they wrote to the bishops, asking them to license only those persons who had satisfied the College of their medical qualifications.[2] For the sick poor, the fellows showed some concern by appointing two of their number to attend, one at a time, in order to give free advice.[3] During William's War the College was invited to submit a schedule of such physic as was thought proper for the sick and wounded in the fleet; in the West Indies the state of the men's health was so serious that in 1696 the Admiralty asked the College to appoint a physician for service on that notorious station.[4] So, in these ways, the Royal College was playing a part of obvious importance in national life. The great development of the west end of London helped also to bring into prominence those physicians who had the requisite social

[1] *English Reports*, xci (King's Bench), 134, *Groenwelt* v. *Burnell* on a writ of *certiorari*, 1700.

[2] *H.M.C. Rep.* viii, app., 231 sqq., *MSS. of the Royal College of Physicians.*

[3] *Luttrell*, iv. 359–60, 26 Mar. 1698.

[4] Ibid. 18 Jan. 1696.

qualities; indeed, they might achieve fame, as did Dr. Radcliffe, who was a man of the world and a good bedside talker. Such was his eminence that he could choose his patients—the surest evidence of success at that time.[1]

Nevertheless, the modern general practitioner is descended not only from the physician, but also from the grocer. This genealogy may be thus explained. The grocers, one of the greatest of the city companies (Charles II and William III were both Grocers) originally included spices and drugs among their commodities; but in 1617 there was a break-away, when the specialists in drugs induced James I to grant them a charter as the Society of Apothecaries, a corporation which started life under the most favourable auspices, for the king regarded the new corporation as peculiarly his own. Their function was to prepare the numerous concoctions, purgatives, and drenches which so many of our ancestors managed to survive, some of the ingredients having been bought from herb women; and the vendors of these preparations were suspected of 'sophisticating' (i.e. adulterating) them, by the addition of cheap substances, such as honey. In order to check this abuse, the censors of the Royal College, with the wardens of the Society, were empowered to enter premises of apothecaries in order to examine such medicines and herbs which, if found defective or decayed, were to be destroyed; so in this way the knights of the pestle came within the disciplinary control of the physicians. Also, the latter wrote a prescription, the former made it up. But the apothecary often sold drugs on his own recommendation; and, before the end of the century, there were complaints that England was becoming a nation of drug-takers.[2]

Meanwhile, a third body of men (and women) was actively concerned in this work of keeping the nation fit. These were the herbalists, who were accorded some kind of status by an Act[3] of Henry VIII which (with the Tudor genius for compromise) authorized these unlicensed and usually quite uneducated persons to minister to outward sores and swellings, by the application of ointments and salves; also, to give drinks

[1] For a recent biography of Dr. Radcliffe, see that by bishop N. Hone.

[2] C. Merrett, *A Short View of the Frauds and Abuses Committed by the Apothecaries*, 1689. Merrett, a physician, complained that far too many drugs were in use.

[3] 34–35 Hen. VIII, c. 8.

for the stone, strangury, and ague, thus leaving to the physician all other ailments, and to the surgeon all the rest of the body. There was thus good precedent for amateur doctoring, and though a man might be held guilty of felony if his patient died from such unlicensed ministrations, the offence was clergiable, so at least one casualty was allowed. Another branch of the healing art developed rapidly in this period, recruited mainly from those apothecaries' apprentices who, instead of completing their articles, were astute enough to set up for themselves as quacks. This was the most profitable and least regulated of all medical activities; moreover, with the development of the newspapers, opportunity was provided for the advertisement on which quack medicines depend. The great popularity of these nostrums is one evidence that, by the end of the seventeenth century, the level of English civilization was very high indeed.

For those apprentices who completed their full term, there were increasing opportunities. They served as go-betweens, linking patient with physician; accordingly, many physicians gave a prescription, without even having seen the patient, merely on information supplied by relatives or an apothecary. With the help of a little medical jargon the vendors of drugs were usually able to impress their patients; there was also this in their favour, that during the Plague most of them remained at their posts, while many of the physicians fled. Moreover, the fact that the apothecary kept a shop helped to bring his trade into full public view; and, if he left it in charge of a handsome wife, he was likely to do all the more business by the concourse of gallants pretending to be ill.[1]

Thereafter, the apothecaries went through a very interesting process of social evolution. By 1690 they were powerful enough to petition the Commons against a Bill for enabling the surgeons to administer internal medicines;[2] five years later they were given statutory exemption from the onerous parish offices of scavenger and constable.[3] At this point the physicians naturally became alarmed, and the war of pamphlets which followed showed that the apothecaries were steadily gaining ground. In alliance with a minority of fellows of the Royal College, they succeeded in defeating a scheme for establishing, on behalf of

[1] *The World Bewitched . . . predictions for 1699*, 26.

[2] *C.J.* x, 1 Nov. 1690.

[3] 6–7 W. and M., c. 4.

the sick poor, a dispensary or out-patients' department, thus bringing down on their heads the ridicule of sir Samuel Garth's *Dispensary* (1699), which depicted a mock combat between what might now be described as the two main branches of the healing art. A few years later the College obtained a verdict against an apothecary who practised physic in the London area; but, on appeal, this was reversed by the House of Lords,[1] though this judgement did not give to apothecaries the right to charge fees for medical attendance. That right was eventually won for them by a favourable verdict in a lawsuit of the early nineteenth century, by which time many of them were acting as general practitioners. Today, the licence of the Society of Apothecaries is a full qualification for the practice of medicine and surgery, a fact which commemorates a long process whereby a craft has greatly contributed to the development of a profession, while still preserving its functions as a craft. The surgeons did not attain professional status until the foundation of their Royal College in 1800, an achievement attributable, not to the slow evolution of a craft, but to the increased opportunities for teaching provided by the London hospitals of the eighteenth century, and to the pioneer work of John Hunter, who transformed surgery into a science.

(*f*) *Roman Catholic and Dissenter*

There are no reliable statistics for the numbers of Roman Catholics and Dissenters in England during this period. An attempt was made for this purpose in 1676, based on the reputed number of freeholders in the province of Canterbury. To the figures thus obtained, was added a conjectural sixth part for the province of York; and, on the assumption that the proportion of denominations was the same in both provinces, it was deduced that altogether, of the freeholders, there were 2,477,154 conformists, 108,676 nonconformists, and 13,856 papists.[2] In the north of England the Roman Catholics and, throughout England, the Dissenters were probably much more numerous than these proportions suggest; moreover, it is

[1] *English Reports*, ii (House of Lords), 257–9, *W. Rose* v. *Royal College of Physicians*, 1703. See also Miss B. Hamilton, 'The Medical Professions in the Eighteenth Century' in *Econ. Hist. Rev.*, 2nd series iv, no. 2.

[2] A. Browning, *Thomas Osborne, Earl of Danby*, 197–8.

notorious that the denominational census is usually the most unreliable of all such estimates, since various considerations may influence a man's public acknowledgement of his faith.

But there is more certainty about the disabilities imposed on both these religious bodies. A series of statutes limited the power of a Roman Catholic to bring an action, or to claim part of a husband's estate; his right of presenting to benefices was taken away and vested in the two universities.[1] Personal restraints may well have been irksome, since Roman Catholics were forbidden to go more than five miles from their homes, or within ten miles of London; also, they could keep neither arms nor horses. They were liable to a fine of £100 for an unlawful marriage, that is, by a Roman Catholic priest; for some taxes they had to pay double if they refused the oaths; like the Protestant Dissenters, they were debarred from all public offices and from admission to either House of Parliament. There was some doubt, even in the reign of James II, whether they could be good witnesses, but Jeffreys said that they might, though he spoiled this liberal pronouncement by a vituperative attack on 'snivelling Presbyterians'. In fine, there had been accumulated in the statute book, mainly of Elizabeth's reign, measures intended to safeguard Protestant England against Catholic Europe, all based on the assumption that the most harmless papist might prove in reality to be a conspirator or traitor. These harsh laws long remained valid; but, by the end of the seventeenth century, they were either applied with lenience, or not at all. It says much for English common sense that public opinion was so far in advance of the legislation.

Proof of this assertion may be cited from an unexpected quarter. When Louis XIV sent count Tallard to England as his ambassador in 1698, he instructed him to do all in his power for English Roman Catholics.[2] The ambassador's representations on their behalf would, as Louis noted, be followed by English requests for similar mitigation in France on behalf of Protestants. But these, the French monarch insisted, must be refused, because the two cases, though apparently similar, were quite different. Protestantism was forbidden in France, whereas Roman Catholics in England had always enjoyed considerable

[1] 1 W. and M., c. 26.

[2] P. Grimblot, *Letters of William III and Louis XIV*, i. 281.

liberty. Thus, one of the most convincing tributes to the spirit of toleration in England came from Louis XIV.

It can well be understood that, even with this partial toleration, adherents of the old faith could play no part in the public or cultural life of the nation; in consequence, seventeenth-century English civilization was the poorer. The situation of the Protestant Dissenters was different. They had suffered from the disabilities imposed on them by the so-called Clarendon Code, until relieved by the Toleration Act of 1689, which did little more than absolve them from the penalties imposed by certain specified laws,[1] provided they took the oaths and made a declaration against transubstantiation and invocation of saints. Thus the Toleration Act permitted the sects to worship in their own way, but left them still excluded from the church, the universities, the corporations, and, in general, from the public life of the nation.

The attitude of conformist to nonconformist was influenced not only by religious disagreement, but also by social differences, and even by considerations of public policy. After all, the average Englishman is not interested in theology. But he is usually concerned about the maintenance of public order, and he regarded the church of England, with its hierarchy of courts and army of parochial and diocesan officials, as an institution designed for the maintenance of that public order. In his eyes, the offence of the Puritan was that he presumed to stand aside from his fellow men; for he rejected the authority of bishops, and refused to attend the parish church; in so doing, he was withdrawing himself from a system of discipline and control. Even more, he might try to evade some of the public duties imposed by the social order. For the holding of some of the unpaid and onerous offices, the legislature had laid down certain requirements, such as the taking of the sacrament according to the church of England, and there was nothing in the Toleration Act relieving Dissenters from such requirements in those cases where they were called upon to assume these offices. This complicated matter was illustrated in an important case decided in King's Bench in 1694. The defendant had been chosen sheriff (an expensive office) by the mayor and aldermen of Norwich. He was called upon to qualify himself for the office

[1] For the Toleration Act, see *infra*, 232–3.

by taking the oaths and the sacrament according to the Corporation Act of 1661. This he refused to do, on the ground that he was a Dissenter, and that he was covered by the Toleration Act. His plea was rejected by the court; because, it was held, the Toleration Act was not a public statute, since it concerned only a part of the nation, and because 'time out of mind there has been an established church of England, and an established discipline, which all were bound to observe before the Reformation'. The intention of the Corporation Act, declared the judges, was not to exempt a man from office but to qualify him for it, and moreover the king has the right to the service of all his subjects. No man can take advantage of his own disability; exemption from an onerous office could be obtained only by letters patent or by Act of Parliament. So the crown won its case.[1] This decision did not have serious consequences, but it clearly illustrates one of the non-theological reasons why objection was taken to the whole principle of nonconformity.

There were other reasons for objection. The Puritans, more especially the Independents, having staged a great revolution, and having destroyed much of the old order, not only made England respected, even feared abroad, but also inaugurated at home schemes of social, educational, and legal reform such as were not heard of again until the nineteenth century. They purged the naval and military administration of that corruption which seemed inseparable from Stuart rule, and they ousted the upper and governing classes from that control of the state which had come to be considered their sacred and vested right. All this was swept aside by the Restoration, which made little distinction between the Independents who had destroyed the monarchy and the Presbyterians who had restored it; indeed, the latter were consigned to perpetual obloquy by the supposed remark of Charles II that their religion was not fit for 'gentlemen'. So, most Anglicans regarded the 'Presbyterians' (to use the popular term) as small shopkeepers and tradesmen who, having once broken loose, had been brought back to their proper subordination.

Two consequences followed from this, one bad, the other good. The bad was that many changes, which we now consider

[1] *English Reports*, xci (King's Bench), 155. *Rex et Regina* v. *Larwood*, 1694. The Toleration Act was declared a public Act by 19 Geo. III, c. 44.

reforms, were indefinitely postponed, merely because they had been advocated by Puritans; and so Bentham had to begin where the Independents had left off. The other, the good one, was more indirect. Just as England was kept prosperous by the vent provided for export of her cloth, so she may have been kept healthy by the vent provided for ridding herself of spleen; or, to vary the metaphor, the constant vilification of Dissenters served, in the English body politic, to produce a counter-irritant which may have obviated more serious ailments. After all, the marvel is not that the Dissenters were so badly treated, but that they came off so lightly, an assertion which can be tested by comparison with the treatment accorded to religious minorities on the continent. Now, there was no question of England following the continental example, but she might have gone far in that direction had she chosen to interfere with the one institution through which a minority of laymen, whether Roman Catholic or Protestant, can be most effectively penalized. That institution is marriage. The marriages of Roman Catholics by their priests were punished by fine; those of Dissenters by their pastors were considered irregular; but neither was void; nor, in either case, did the courts of the church or of the state bastardize the issue. In consequence, the children of such irregular marriages were enabled, subject to certain restrictions, to succeed to property; for their parents were not regarded as living in concubinage. After all, to the average layman, these things are more important than abstruse points of theology; their importance was bitterly realized in those continental countries where an ecclesiastical faction might invoke the aid of the secular arm. England, the home of sects and heresies, was blessed with a hierarchy which, however hostile to minorities, had neither the power nor the inclination to penalize them in their most essential civil rights.

This is one of the respects in which England was more fortunate than France, where, as dissent was supposed to be nonexistent, it could have claimed no status. The English Dissenter occupied an intermediate position, such as accorded well with the English genius for compromise. On the one hand, there was a recognition, first admitted during the Popish Plot, and implied in the Toleration Act, that the Protestant Dissenters were not a political danger; but, on the other hand, the state for long refused to admit them to full citizenship. Denied complete status, placed as it were on the margin of society, they were able to view that society from a broad angle, enabling them to detect flaws and abuses in the institutions to which they were denied access. The Dissenter was a Protestant as no Anglican could be a Protestant; one of a minority, he had good reason to know that the majority is not always right; an individualist, he could contrast himself with the herd. It was this that helped to make Richard Baxter such a penetrating critic of his England; for, almost alone of his contemporaries, he perceived that poverty is not only an economic misfortune, but a spiritual evil.[1] The same instinct prompted Defoe,[2] but in his case there was the solitude of genius; ''tis hard for a man to say', he wrote, 'that all the world is wrong but himself; but, if it be so, who can help it?' So full status encouraged an attitude of acquiescence; dissent, with its imperfect status, inspired the spirit of criticism, and English social history has been built up from the interplay of these two things.

[1] For this see *Rev. Richard Baxter's Last Treatise*, ed. F. J. Powicke, with preface by George Unwin.

[3] *An Enquiry into Occasional Conformity.*

IV

AN ADOLESCENT SOCIETY

THE topics dealt with in this chapter are intended to illustrate further some of the characteristics of the English society briefly surveyed in preceding chapters. Four sections are devoted to these unrelated topics: (1) the law-breaker and the law; (2) the countryside; (3) the knights and burgesses; and (4) the place of London and Westminster in the national life. Here again the treatment is summary and selective.

1. THE LAW-BREAKER AND THE LAW

In these years England appeared to be passing through an unusually turbulent stage in her history, an adolescence even more stormy than the boyhood of Tudor times. Of this there is abundant evidence in the literature of the period, notably in Luttrell, that matter-of-fact collector and diarist, whose pages usually read like those of a police gazette. Crime and wrongdoing are of interest to the historian because they may throw light on the opportunities or temptations encountered by humanity in the past, and on the difference between the former attitude to these things and that which prevails today. From this point of view, social history might be regarded as a long process of readjustment, in which the statute book always lags behind; and so, to the student of history, as distinct from the student of law, the main interest of a national jurisprudence is that, by its gradation of penalties, it provides some assessment of social needs, an assessment often out of date. Hence, the seventeenth century is part of a long period in which offences against property were capital; while those against the person, other than murder or maiming, were deemed almost venial; a valuation which, to the layman of today, must seem anachronistic, unless he recalls two things; first, that in these matters, there is always a time-lag; and secondly, that in this period, property still preceded the person.

For this general tardiness of revaluation there were many

reasons, two of which may be suggested. The first was the abolition of the Star Chamber in 1641. During a period of about a century and a half, this high-handed tribunal had facilitated the passage of English society from medieval to comparatively modern conditions, mainly by dealing summarily with offences for which the Common Law was inadequate; and with persons who could not easily be reached by judicial process. Many of the misdeeds so penalized were of a kind which, in a rapidly changing world, were at last seen to have important social consequences; for example, perjury, which formerly had been punishable in the spiritual courts. So too with libel and slander. In the medieval world, these offences had prejudiced a man's soul; whereas, in the modern world, they might prejudice his livelihood, so a readjustment was necessary. One of the good services performed by the Star Chamber was the effecting of such a readjustment. In consequence of the abolition of that tribunal, England was left to carry on with a jurisprudence which had already proved inadequate for those newer forms of wrongdoing that were causing disquiet in later Lancastrian times. Another impediment placed in the way of this process of penal reassessment was the sustained antipathy to Hobbes and the Puritans[1]—those daring rebels against the existing order of things—who, from different points of view, had suggested fundamental reforms; indeed, it is possible that the former was the first English thinker to realize the social, as distinct from the moral or theological implications of crime. After 1660 the fact that a change had been advocated by either Hobbes or the Puritans was sufficient to ensure its repudiation; and here we have one of the many reasons for the rooted conservatism of the old criminal law.

The most common felonies in the seventeenth century were homicide (murder and manslaughter), rape, burglary, arson, robbery, theft, and mayhem. All of these, except mayhem and theft of goods under one shilling in value, were punishable by death, with confiscation of the felon's estate, except where he refused to plead, and suffered death by pressing—the *peine forte et dure*, the only form of torture recognized by the law. Originally all felonies had been clergiable; but, by the end of

[1] *Supra*, 96–97.

the century, benefit of clergy had been whittled down to a shadow of its former self; and, though it could still be pleaded for the theft of a sheep, it could not be pleaded for the theft of 1*s*. 6*d*. But in the latter case a compassionate jury might return a verdict of 'stealing to the value of 10*d*.', and so the pillory took the place of the gibbet. Sometimes also, a royal pardon might be pleaded, whereupon the culprit would be released on entering into recognizances; in other cases the sentence was commuted to transportation.[1] In the earlier part of the century Puritan reformers had protested against the frequency of death sentences, not on humanitarian grounds, but because of the wastage of human life; accordingly some form of forced labour was recommended instead;[2] so, too, objection might be taken to imprisonment or hanging for petty offences because the dependants were left on the parish.[3] Also punishable by death were high and petty treason (the latter included counterfeiting the coin). Piracy was a capital offence, but, until 1700, pirates indicted in the Plantations had to be sent to England for trial and execution. The law treated the woman more harshly than the man. She could not plead benefit of clergy, and until 1790 burning alive was the penalty imposed on her for either high or petty treason.

It is unlikely that, in the past, the death penalty provided a serious deterrent to crime; but on the other hand, it would be unwise to argue that therefore it is no deterrent today. There is really no analogy. In the seventeenth century men were so familiar with the sight of the gibbet (which might lawfully be put up by the executioner in one's private garden if there was no other convenient place)[4] that they treated it with familiarity; today the privacy of hanging, and its ignominy, may well provide deterrents. Even more, there is no large section of English society nowadays which can reasonably assume that most of its members are likely to die on the scaffold; whereas in the past this was considered, for some classes, not an assump-

[1] This is based on sir J. Fitzjames Stephen, *History of the Criminal Law of England*, i and ii.

[2] A notable example of Puritan ideas of law reform will be found in W. Sheppard, *England's balme* . . . (1657).

[3] *C.J.* xiii, 21 Feb. 1700. Petition of the governors of the workhouse at Crediton.

[4] *English Reports*, xci (King's Bench), *Sparks* v. *Spicer*, 1698.

tion, but almost a certainty. Among the preordained to such an end were vagabonds, journeymen wandering about the country, pedlars, fiddlers, cobblers, rope dancers, and rat catchers,[1] some of whom were even said to prefer the gibbet to the pillory. Furthermore, especially with political victims, public execution often provided welcome opportunity for last-moment propaganda, until Defoe demonstrated that, for this purpose, the pillory (with sympathetic onlookers) was much better. All this may help to account for the appearance in 1701 of a pamphlet entitled: *Hanging not punishment enough for Murtherers, Highway Men and House Breakers*, in which, as a substitute, perpetual labour with the negroes in the West Indies was recommended.

Criminal trials in this period often resolved themselves into contests between the accused and the court, with points to be scored on both sides. Thus, the accused was denied a copy of the indictment until it was read to him at the trial; and, as it was sometimes in Latin, he might not understand a word of it. One of the Seven Bishops courageously protested against having to follow the spoken Latin of the information, but this was overruled on the ground that 'all bishops are learned men'.[2] If the man in the dock could find a flaw in the indictment, no matter how trivial, that might result in quashing the proceedings; and so it was characteristic of this give-and-take that when, by the Trial of Treasons Act (1696), a person accused of treason was allowed a copy of the indictment before trial, and permitted to brief counsel for his defence, at the same time he was denied the old right to upset an indictment by proving a technical error. Judges often acted as counsel for the prosecution; evidence might be little better than hearsay, and the character of the witness was just beginning to influence the value of his testimony. Probably the earliest occasion when expert evidence was adduced in court was at the trial of Spencer Cowper[3] in 1699 for the murder of one Mary Stout; his acquittal followed the medical evidence, given by physicians, regarding death by drowning.

[1] T. Nourse, *Campania Felix*, 209–13.

[2] *State Trials*, xii. 230. The bishop was White, bishop of Peterborough. See also *infra*, 199.

[3] *State Trials*, xii. 1106–250.

Generally, in William's reign, the criminal law became more harsh, particularly in statutes intended to protect private property. Thus, an Act of 1691[1] made receiving a felony, as also the stealing of furniture by lodgers; a later Act[2] not only extended the category of theft to shoplifting, but included a provision whereby anyone securing the conviction of another should have a certificate (assignable once) relieving him from all parish offices in the place where the theft had been committed. At the same time, the old penalty of burning in the hand, in those cases where benefit of clergy had been successfully pleaded, was altered to the more conspicuous burning in the cheek.

There were three methods of accusation—indictment by a grand jury; information by a law officer of the crown; and appeal by a private person. In regard to the first method, it was open to anyone to appear before a grand jury with an accusation and witnesses to substantiate it; in this way, a prosecution might be started by one person having a grievance against another. This personal right, so easily abused, was not regulated until the nineteenth century. The second method, information by a law officer of the crown, was almost invariably adopted in political offences, then a very wide category, since it included the expression, in speech or writing, of opinions, many of which today would be considered harmless. The third method, appeal of murder or felony, serves to illustrate the partial dependence of judicial process on the co-operation of the public. It amounted to a declaration of another man's crime before a competent judge by a person, such as the widow or heir, whose interests were prejudiced by the crime; this accuser, the appellor, undertook to prove that the crime had been committed by a particular person, and he might claim the right to do so even after the acquittal of that person in a court of law. It was generally held that the crown could not pardon an appellee convicted on an appeal. In the case of *Ashford* v. *Thornton* (1818) an appellee demanded trial by battle (to which he was lawfully entitled); so the legislature, in face of this resurgent medievalism, abolished both battle and appeal.

[1] 3 W. and M., c. 2. See also Holdsworth, *History of English Law*, vi. 402 sqq.

[2] 10 Wm. III, c. 12. Cf. also 10–11 Wm. III, c. 23.

This share of the public in promoting the administration of justice is seen most clearly in the institution of the informer, an evil necessity at a time when there was no police force. Usually, those acts of parliament which imposed a monetary penalty provided that a portion should be paid to the informer, but these men often asked for the whole of the fine 'to cover their expenses'.[1] Or the informer might do better for himself by blackmailing one who, to his knowledge, had committed an indictable offence; or he might offer his services to a secretary of state, whenever it was proposed to proceed against a political offender. It was even suggested by the legislature that licensed paupers might inform against the unlicensed, on pain of forfeiting their licences.[2] No class was spared. In Bunyan's *Vanity Fair* the false swearers were of 'a blood red colour', because they brought men to their death; even in the sacred city of Mansoul there was an informer (for a godly purpose) a Mr. Diligence, who, by listening under the eaves of Mr. Evil Questioning's house, heard his discourse with such reprobates as Election Doubters and Salvation Doubters. On reporting this to the lord mayor, a conviction was obtained, with the satisfactory result that 'Old Evil Questioning was hanged at the top of Bad Street, over against his own door'.[3] But fact was even more extraordinary than fiction. After the Popish Plot many people realized that informers were being suborned to give perjured evidence. This introduced a curious complication, illustrated in a memorial submitted to the privy council by an official employed to prosecute the 'owlers' or smugglers of wool from Romney Marsh. This memorial[4] alleged that a syndicate of nine persons, including a justice of the peace, had been formed in order to obstruct prosecutions for smuggling. Their method was to bribe all the witnesses for the crown in such cases to swear that their own evidence was false, and that, as informers, they had been suborned to swear against innocent persons by officers of the revenue. Such a method of thwarting justice was possible only at a time when two different things

[1] An example will be found in *Cal. S.P. Dom. 1693*, 409, 27 Nov. 1693.

[2] *H.M.C. Rep.* xii, app. pt. 6 (*MSS. of House of Lords*), 448, 25 Jan. 1690. Proposed Poor Relief Bill.

[3] *Works of John Bunyan* (1857 ed.), iii. 369.

[4] *P.C. Reg.* 77, 23 Oct. 1699. Memorial of Mr. Baker.

happened to come together; namely, the fact that convictions could still be obtained by means of perjured informers, and the fact that their evidence was just beginning to be discredited.

That discredit was clearly evidenced at the trial of the Lancashire Jacobites in 1694, when the prosecution was dependent on the evidence of two informers, Taaffe and Lunt, of whom the first had brought his 'evidence' to secretary Trumbull. Equipped by the secretary of state with search warrants, Taaffe used them in order to burgle private houses, so Trumbull refused him the promised reward; whereupon Taaffe sold his evidence to the other side, and declared that the prosecution was an invention. The other, Lunt, was even more notorious; indeed his career inspired a contemporary biography, epitomizing the many and varied crimes that provided by-products in the informing industry, a biography[1] which serves the same purpose for its period as did Bunyan's *Life and Death of Mr. Badman* for an earlier and less sophisticated world. In July 1694 Lunt was in a house in Lancashire where he was 'coached' about the evidence which he was to give in the Jacobite trials, then impending; but the coaching proved inadequate, for in court he mistook the identity of the men against whom he was swearing, and so had to be withdrawn by the prosecution.[2] Thereafter, as there was a decrease in the amount of game for informers, Lunt had to make his living mainly by stealing and selling the horses owned (surreptitiously) by Roman Catholics.

Englishmen were gradually losing that gullibility which had accounted for the success of the Popish Plot. But though the danger from the informer showed signs of diminishing, there still remained the factor which made informing so easy and profitable—the law relating to perjury and forgery. Neither of these was a felony for a first offence; indeed, perjured evidence in court was not even punishable, if found to be unessential for the prosecution.[3] Forgery was at last seen to be a serious crime when, in the course of William's reign, paper currency was widely used. Now it was petty treason to conterfeit the coin of

[1] It will be found in *H.M.C. Rep.* xiv, app. pt. 4, 310 sqq. (*MSS. of lord Kenyon*).

[2] *MSS. of House of Lords*, new series, 1, 1693–5, Introduction xli.

[3] *English Reports*, xci (King's Bench), 1067. *Rex* v. *Griepe*, 9 Wm. III.

the realm, but no more than a misdemeanour to forge a promissory note. By a long series of piecemeal measures, starting from the statutory provision (in 1696) that the forging of an Exchequer Bill was felony,[1] opinion was gradually prepared for the enactments which, beginning in the reign of George II, eventually gave us the law of forgery as we know it today, an evolution attributable not to the fact that England became more moral, but that she became more commercial.

So too with perjury. Contemporaries had no doubt that this was the most serious social evil of the age.[2] It was a menace to trade; it poisoned human relationships; it might leave an innocent man so helpless before malicious accusers that he was obliged to petition the crown to pardon him for an offence that he had not committed.[3] Equally, when a royal pardon was being solicited by an influential cheat, his victims might petition the crown that perjury be omitted from the scope of the pardon, as otherwise they would have no remedy at law.[4] Long before, Hobbes had maintained that to accept money for giving false evidence resulting in an innocent man's death was a more heinous offence than to obtain the same sum by theft;[5] but Hobbes, as a reputed atheist, was discredited, and, moreover, he had propounded some strange doctrines, as that it is more wicked to rob the poor than to rob the rich.[6] Throughout the last decade of the seventeenth century attempts were made to include perjury among the felonies; indeed, these began in consequence of the notoriety of the Lancashire Trials; but all these attempts were in vain, although the perjury was limited to those cases where a man lost his life in consequence of the false evidence. In 1694 a Bill for this purpose was dropped, mainly because of opposition from the judges; the proposed measure, they said, would make it almost impossible to obtain convictions. 'It is very difficult to convict persons', declared chief justice Treby.[7] So perjury helped to make of the informer

[1] *Infra*, 432.

[2] e.g. T. Doolittle, *The Swearer Silenced . . .* and *Perjury the National Sin*, both 1689.

[3] *Cal. S.P. Dom. 1691–2*, 287–8. Petition of D. Jones, 19 May 1692.

[4] *P.C. Reg.* 71, 23 Mar. 1688. Petition of dame Stapleton.

[5] *Leviathan*, xxvii.

[6] Ibid., conclusion.

[7] *MSS. of House of Lords*, new series, i, 1693–5, 410. Bill to make perjury a felony in certain cases.

the equivalent, not of an efficient police force, but of a corrupt one.

The wrongdoing of the later seventeenth century ranged, in its scope, from the mean and sordid to the emotional and spectacular. Of the first type, an example was that of cheating a domestic servant of his or her wages, an offence which could not be entertained by the justices, because domestic servants did not come within the province of the Statute of Apprentices.[1] Another, that of cheating a sailor of his pay or pay ticket was, at most, punishable in the pillory; consigning a sane relative to the madhouse, in order to make free with his estate,[2] was another 'easy' crime, not eradicated until the nineteenth century. Most common of all were crimes of violence. Usually these occurred in the heat of a quarrel, by men in drink; sometimes, they did not even have this excuse, as when, in 1698 a man, presumably a Jacobite, pursued and murdered an apothecary's wife, for no other reason than that she reminded him of the late queen Mary.[3] Or the crimes might be multiple and speedy; thus, Luttrell[4] records how, in 1693, a man was convicted of sacrilege, rape, burglary, murder, and highway robbery, all committed within twelve hours. It was unfortunate that, in this unusually quarrelsome age, every man with any pretension to quality wore a sword; and so, especially in London, manslaughter was frequent. The homicide rate generally was high; among the peerage very high. Trial of a peer in the House of Lords for murder usually had an element of farce (which queen Mary deplored),[5] for it was attended almost as an entertainment, and the concourse of spectators was so great that sir Christopher Wren had sometimes to supervise the arrangements for extra accommodation. At these trials the verdict was usually taken for granted; and it seems certain that of the numerous peers convicted of murder in the years 1660–1702 not one suffered any penalty. Even in political trials there was sometimes the same partiality. On one occasion, lord

[1] In order to remedy this, the Commons in 1696 brought in a Bill for the more easy recovering of servants' wages, but it was not proceeded with. *C.J.* xi, 18 Mar. 1696.

[2] An example will be found in *Luttrell*, iii. 90, 4 May 1693.

[3] *The Protestant Mercury*, 1–3 June 1698.

[4] *Luttrell*, iii. 85, 27 Apr. 1693.

[5] *Memoirs of Mary* (ed. Doebner), 53.

Mordaunt (so indiscreet that he was considered mad), having stood up and solemnly pronounced his verdict of Not Guilty, turned to his fellow peers and remarked, in an audible whisper: 'Guilty, by God'.[1]

On another level in the realm of wrongdoing were abduction and duelling. Several men of fashion were executed for abduction of heiresses; but often the law could be evaded. Thus, a lieutenant took away a woman of property from her husband and 'married' her. When the aggrieved husband prosecuted the offender, the lieutenant first sheltered himself under his military rank; and when, at last, he was consigned to the law, he prevailed upon a member of parliament to give him protection as his menial servant.[2] For duelling, another fashionable offence, the favourite place was behind Montagu House, in Bloomsbury.

What appears to be a combination of abduction and duelling was performed, with both delicacy and decision, by a lady. The widow of a peer, lady Kingston, became enamoured of a young army officer; and, though completely unknown to him, she resolved to marry him. So she sent him an anonymous challenge to a duel behind Montagu House. The officer turned up at the appointed time; and, to his surprise, saw no one but a lady in a mask standing by a coach. Explaining to the bewildered duellist that she was the person he was looking for, the fair challenger bundled him into her carriage, and within a few hours the marriage took place. The abducted bridegroom was probably not inconsolable, as the lady had a considerable estate in land and money.[3]

In a class by themselves were prisoners for debt. In William's reign it was said that there were about 50,000 prisoners in the debtor's prisons of London and the provinces,[4] some of them knights and esquires, all of them confined in consequence of attachment for debt, or because of judgements entered against them, or from inability to pay costs or damages decreed in a court of equity; indeed there were innumerable processes of the

[1] *Memoirs of Thomas, earl of Ailesbury* (Roxburghe Club), i. 134–6.

[2] *Cal. S.P. Dom. 1693*, 166. Case of lieut. Francis Flood.

[3] *The Foreign Post*, 30 July–2 Aug. 1697.

[4] This is stated in an undated memorandum 'For enabling debtors to pay their debts' in *Bodl. Firth*, B. 16, no. 80.

law whereby a man might be held 'in execution'. The old law knew the word execution in two different degrees of the same sense. On the one hand was the taking in execution of enough money or property to satisfy the debt in full; on the other hand, there was the mitigated form, or *quousque*, where the body of the debtor was taken as a pledge for the debt. Confinement in a debtors' prison was not then thought of as a punishment, but as providing, by the safe custody of the debtor, some kind of guarantee to the creditor that the debt would be paid. Many creditors soon realized that this was a most unlikely method of obtaining payment; others, from sheer vindictiveness, might keep a man in prison indefinitely. So too, in a commission of bankruptcy, if even only one creditor refused to accept a composition, that was enough to consign the bankrupt to prison. That the imprisoned debtor was thought of not as a delinquent, but as a pledge can be seen in the numerous actions for Escape against gaolers; and also in the rule that if husband and wife were taken in execution for debt owing by the wife, she was discharged, because she had nothing liable to the execution, whereas the unfortunate husband was detained. Indeed, imprisonment was not then so common a punishment as it is today, since malefactors in gaol were usually either awaiting trial; or, after conviction, awaiting transportation, or a form of execution even more drastic than that above described. English society was passing through that long stage in which it was necessary to devise means for obliging people to pay their debts, and a financial deficit was made good by putting the body of the debtor into the gap in the balance sheet.

On behalf of the genuinely poor debtor, the legislation of Charles II's reign[1] had provided this amount of alleviation, that he might be discharged from custody if he swore before a magistrate that his entire estate was not worth more than £10. This was renewed by an Act of 1696[2] which, however, did not extend to those who owed more than £100, nor to anyone under forty unless he either enlisted in the army, or procured someone else to do so. But this left unprotected the comparatively poor man who, mainly because of his confinement, was either unable to realize his assets, or precluded from earning

[1] 22–23 Car. II, c. 20, and 30 Car. II, c. 4.
[2] 7–8 Wm. III., c. 12.

money with which to satisfy the debt; moreover, he might well be so victimized by the gaoler that any chance of satisfying his creditors disappeared.[1] There was an awareness of these injustices, and remedies were proposed in parliament which did not eventually become law. One would have limited process for debt under 40*s.* to reasonable distraint of debtor's goods; another would have enabled debtors to make compositions with their creditors.[2] Otherwise, so far as there was any demand for reform, it was directed to ensuring that custodians of debtors' prisons should be in a position to pay damages for an escape, and as they were mostly substantial persons, having an estate of inheritance in their office, it was reasonable to suppose that their property was available for that purpose. But this was not generally so, because, by mortgage or otherwise, they conveyed away their estates, and so evaded the consequences[3] of their own negligence. In other words, the legislature was concerned with prison reform mainly to ensure that the prisoner was kept in safe custody, and that damages were obtainable in the event of an escape.

All gaols were nominally within the custody of the crown, but this was effective only in the county gaols, controlled by the sheriffs; these might be subsidized by a local rate. In some debtors' prisons the inmates were allowed to beg at the gate for alms; in others, there were charitable trusts for the benefit of such unfortunates. But there were many gaols of inheritance, where the keepers, having bought or inherited their offices, were intent on securing a good income from fees, rents, and perquisites. It might well be asked how this was possible, since we generally think of the imprisoned debtor as a man without resources. There were many such in debtors' prisons. They might be assisted by doles from the prison poor box, or from

[1] *H.M.C. Rep.* xiii, app. pt. 5, 161, 11 Nov. 1690. Evidence on the proposed Creditors' and Poor Prisoners' Relief Bill.

[2] Ibid. xiii, app. pt. 5, 44. 1 May 1690. Small Debts Abolition Bill, and *MSS. of House of Lords*, new series, i. 512, 21 Feb. 1695. Creditors' Relief Bill. Both Bills were dropped.

[3] There were many such complaints. In 1699 the Commons resolved that the best means of preventing abuses in the King's Bench and Fleet prisons was by discharging the encumbrances, if necessary by the sale of the offices, and that for the future the wardenship of these prisons should not be liable to encumbrances, except on escapes. *C.J.* xii, 4 May 1699.

their relatives, but usually they languished in underground cellars, where their clothes rotted on their bodies; such places were described as 'vaults fit for nothing but corpses'.[1] A more numerous class consisted of those who, in order to evade their creditors, contrived to have themselves committed to the Fleet or the Marshalsea, or entered voluntarily into one of the London sponging houses, of which Defoe enumerated 119. Indeed, the seventeenth-century debtors' prison combined some of the characteristics of the torture chamber, the almshouse, the club, the boarding house, and the home of refuge. As boarding houses, they were considered dear[2]—30*s.* per week for a dog hole which elsewhere would have cost 2*s.*; as clubs they were exclusive in the sense that the charges and the privileges varied with status. In the Fleet[3] the tariff was hung up in the hall, archbishops, dukes, and duchesses being at the top of the scale of entrance fees; there were similar charges on 'dismission'. As well as payments for weekly commons, there were fees for the clerk, the porter, the gaoler, and the chamberlain, all of whom had bought their offices; and for permission to go out (with a keeper) the charge was 10*d.* for a half day and 1*s.* 8*d.* for a whole day. As the Fleet and Marshalsea were too small for the large number of guests, there were annexes, or 'Rules' in the neighbouring streets. From rents, fees, sub-letting of accommodation, and a commission on the sale of beer and tobacco, the keeper of the Marshalsea made over £5,000 a year.[4] So it appears that the custodians of such prisons had a good return on their investment.

It is as the home of refuge that the debtors' prison is of greatest interest to the social historian. It was said that the Fleet[5] took in annually between 200 and 300 persons who, for one reason or another, were seeking temporary seclusion, most of them able to pay a bribe for release, as soon as the coast was clear; or, when things became unpleasant, the bogus

[1] *H.M.C. Rep.* xii, app. pt. 6 (*MSS. of House of Lords*), 328. Evidence regarding the Marshalsea.

[2] J. F., *The Gaoler's Extortion Exposed or the Prisoner's Grievance*, 1690.

[3] *H.M.C. Rep.* xii, app. pt. 6, 325. The tariff was similar, in its enumeration of classes, to that adopted in the Poll Bills, the lowest being 'a poor man in the wards that hath his part in the box'.

[4] Ibid. 328, also *MSS. of House of Lords*, new series, ii. 396. 8 Feb. 1697.

[5] *C.J.* xi, 30 Dec. 1696.

prisoner might have himself transferred to another gaol, by suing out his habeas corpus. A delinquent might also evade the process of law by bribing a gaoler to swear that he was in his gaol, when in fact he was at liberty somewhere else. But the worst abuses followed from the enforcement of legal process. So complicated were these processes of law that a rich *debtor* might, by vexing a poor *creditor* with a frivolous suit, procure his consignment to a debtors' prison; hence it was said that many prisoners had more money owing to them than they owed.[1] The vindictiveness shown in many such cases was one of the harshest features of the age; 'if he dies, the debt's paid', summarized the attitude of the fraudulent debtor who, by taking advantage of the law, succeeded in consigning an unfortunate creditor to prison,[2] and keeping him there. In this way the prison system helped to facilitate wrong-doing; it might even provide a refuge for thieves, maintained in not unpleasant custody by the contributions of accomplices.[3] Generally, the debtors' prisons concealed from public view a great mass of humanity, some of them astute rogues, some the drifting wreckage of turbid seas, others the victims of hard circumstance, or of a harsh jurisprudence, or of callousness in the hearts of their fellow men.

Like the prison, the throne was an institution in the administration of justice. A royal pardon might be granted to a named person either before indictment or after conviction; so too, in an Act of Indemnity, a general pardon was granted to all persons, with exceptions for certain specified offences. The former secured immunity within the limits of the pardon; but the latter had wider effects, because by it a person might, in the words of Holt, be made a new man. Consider, for example, the case of a man convicted for libel, and sentenced to a number of penalties, including the pillory. Now, the offence, libel, was not then considered infamous, whereas the punishment of the pillory was so regarded, and the pilloried culprit could not thereafter be admitted as a witness, or as a juror. But even these disabilities were taken away by a general pardon, for such

[1] *H.M.C. Rep.* xiii, app. pt. 5, 162, 11 Nov. 1690.

[2] Cf. the interesting memorandum (dated 1690), 'Observations offered to parliament on behalf of creditors', in *Cal. S.P. Dom. 1701*, 561.

[3] This is stated in J. Whiston, *England's Calamities Discovered*, 1696.

an exercise of the prerogative had, as it were, a cleansing effect.[1] On the other hand, the granting of a pardon to a named person was often accompanied by grave abuses. Such a pardon, given in one reign, might be pleaded in the next; this personal immunity was permanent. In this way, many embezzlers of public money could not be brought to account; indeed, at one time, a large part of the proceeds of fines levied on recusants proved to be irrecoverable,[2] because so many of the trustees had taken the precaution of securing royal protection against their own malversation.

In this respect, some of the pardons granted by James II are of particular interest. In June 1687 he bestowed on his brother-in-law, lord Rochester, who had recently been dismissed from the office of lord high treasurer, a pardon extending to 'all debts and accounts'; in November of the same year he gave pardons to two officials, high in the financial administration, Richard Kent and Charles Duncombe, in respect of 'extortion and usurious contracts'. But the spate of pardons did not begin to flow until October 1688, when it was clear that nothing more could be made out of James, and that protection must be sought against his successor. Accordingly, pardons couched in the most ample terms and marked 'immediate' were issued to (among others) Sunderland, sir T. Jenner, Henry Guy, lord Dover, and Jeffreys.[3] Nor were these persons concerned merely with political offences; their wrongdoing was of a more straightforward kind. For example, Sunderland, during a period of years, had been assiduously pilfering plate from the Jewel House, to the amount of more than 8,000 ounces;[4] Jeffreys had committed several judicial murders, a fact which he well knew. These beneficiaries of the last male Stuarts were rats leaving a sinking ship, but with some guarantee of immunity in the next ship to be invaded. This exercise of the royal prerogative of pardon in favour of such persons was a direct encouragement

[1] *English Reports*, xci (King's Bench), 584, *Rex* v. *Crosby*, 1695.

[2] *Luttrell*, iii. 37, 16 Feb. 1693. Sir T. Jenner, one of the trustees for recusants' fines, when unable to account for £3,000, successfully pleaded James's pardon.

[3] A list of these will be found in *H.M.C. Rep.* xii, app. pt. 6, 303 sqq. (*MSS. of House of Lords*).

[4] He received a discharge in respect of this amount in March 1692. *Cal. Tr. Bks.* ix, 1522.

to crime among the ruling classes; it also provides an exposure of the rot behind the Stuart tinsel. If the Revolution settlement did not greatly limit what kings might do, it indirectly limited what they might forgive.

The last decade of the seventeenth century was not a period of great law reform, though Bills were introduced into parliament to amend the jurisdiction of the ecclesiastical courts, to reform Chancery, to take away imprisonment for small debts, to abolish the purchase and sale of office, whether civil, military, or ecclesiastical; and there were the usual attempts to diminish the numbers and malpractices of solicitors and attorneys.[1] Various reasons account for the failure of such measures to reach the statute book; one might be a prorogation, or one of the frequent quarrels between the two Houses, or the opposition of a vested interest. The law is the most conservative of all the professions, and even as late as Holt's day the practitioners in King's Bench wore mourning for the late Charles I. Moreover, the law, both civil and criminal, was still unbelievably intricate. The innumerable statutes were, many of them, either obsolete or inconsistent; the frontiers of common law and equity jurisdiction were not yet clearly established; there were constant prohibitions withdrawing suits from the church courts; many mercantile and maritime matters were still nominally within the jurisdiction of the Admiralty court, but were gradually being drawn within the province of the common law; and, presiding over this confused mass of principle and precedent was the grim genius of Coke. England, while rapidly developing into a great commercial state, was still regulated by a jurisprudence the letter and spirit of which were both, to a large extent, medieval. That serious dislocation did not ensue may be accounted for by the native spirit of compromise, the genius for improvization, the habitude of piecemeal legislation; all of which, working together, obviated the necessity for radical change. After all, the common law could boast a longer period

[1] *MSS. of House of Lords*, new series, iv. 62, 11 Jan. 1700. The other measures, most of them already cited in the text, will be found in the earlier volumes of the *MSS. of House of Lords*, published by the Historical Manuscripts Commission, in Reports xii–xiv. The new series of *House of Lords MSS.* began after Report xiv, app. pt. 6, the first volume covering the period 1693–5.

of continuity than could any other national institution; and this, together with its rough and homely logic, served to place it high in the esteem of Englishmen.

2. The Countryside

Of the total acreage of England and Wales (about 37 millions) at least 20 millions were in agricultural use, almost evenly divided between arable and pasture.[1] From the point of view of farming the richest counties were in the Midlands, notably Hertfordshire, Northamptonshire, and Leicestershire; the poorest were in the north, such as Durham, Northumberland, and Cumberland. Throughout, there was a sprinkling of what might be loosely called industrial areas; near London, in Essex and Kent; in Wiltshire and Somerset; in the West Riding, in Durham and Cumberland, where wool, iron, or coal provided the bases of specialized activity; but England was still a country predominantly of farm land, of commons, of moor, waste, and forest, wherein the climate encouraged outdoor exercise, and provided opportunities for sport. Sport helped to occupy the leisure of the upper classes, which otherwise might have been misapplied. The south and south-east were preferred as places of residence by those who could make a choice; and already the two Englands[2] were coming to be contrasted.

There was no great advance in agricultural science in the later seventeenth century. As about half the cultivable land remained unenclosed, much of English farming was wasteful because conducted by village communities which annually allotted in the open fields strips too narrow to be ploughed economically, and liable to be invaded by the small, skinny cattle which helped to provide the open-fielders with a precarious livelihood. Contemporaries noted some advantages in the open-field system.[3] There was not the trouble of making and repairing hedges; the land was more open to the sun, so that corn usually ripened well; there was less trouble from hedge birds. But the advantages of enclosure were now fully recognized, mainly because the private property in enclosed land encouraged experiment and improvement, such as were

[1] Lord Ernlé, *English Farming, Past and Present*, 5th ed., 145 sqq.

[2] *Supra*, 46–47.

[3] T. Nourse, *Campania Felix* (1700), ch. 2.

impossible in the older, hand-to-mouth system; moreover, the hedge, which often included walnut and fruit trees, was becoming a characteristic feature of the English landscape. Near towns, the fields could not be enclosed by hedges or fences, because in winter these were pulled up for firewood by the poor, who, at that time, usually lived not in the centre but on the outskirts of towns;[1] so walls or mounds of earth had to be erected instead. In contrast with the respectability and often prosperity of the large tenant farms, the commons were depicted as 'a naked theater of poverty, both as to man and beasts, where all things appear horrid and uncultivated'.[2] This contrast must have been a striking one, because the old and the new systems were so often found side by side.

Some advances in agriculture may be noted. In William's reign Jethro Tull was experimenting with turnips at his farm near Wallingford, where he invented his famous drill in 1701. More use was now being made of lime; there were tanks for water storage; silos were to be found on many farms, and there were tentative beginnings in drainage and in the analysis of soils. The new grasses, particularly clover and sanfoin, were grown in some areas, the turnip was being fed to sheep in winter, and Worlidge recommended the growing of buckwheat on sandy loams as a food for pigs and poultry.[3] The virtues of the rubbish heap were well known, and the burning of soil was frequently resorted to as a means of increasing its fertility.[4] All these improvements were to be found on enclosed lands, which were most commonly situated near to market towns, in the midlands, and the south-east. It is possible that the area of enclosures would have been considerably increased had parliament passed a Bill introduced for that purpose in 1697. This was rejected because, it was said, of the suspicion that out of the enclosed land the king would have carved large estates for his favourites.[5]

At the bottom of the agricultural hierarchy were the labourers and husbandmen, the latter usually having a holding, the yield

[1] T. Nourse, *Campania Felix*, ch. 4. [2] Ibid. 98.

[3] J. Worlidge, *Systema Agriculturae* (1669), in D. Macdonald, *Agricultural Writers 1200–1800*, 46. [4] T. Nourse, op. cit. 34–36.

[5] *H.M.C. Rep.* xiv, app. pt. 4. *MSS. of lord Kenyon*, 416. P. Shakerley to R. Kenyon, 6 Mar. 1697.

from which had to be supplemented by wage labour at harvest and other times. The wages of the agricultural labourer, as assessed by the justices, did not differ much from the maximum allowance to the adult pauper, namely, 4*s.* to 5*s.* per week; added to this was a housing shortage, attributable in part to the Elizabethan statute which forbade anyone to take a cottage, unless he could add four acres to it. But not all the workers on the land were dependent solely on wages; for there were many copyholders; and there was a large class, usually to be found in the open fields, loosely designated 'cottagers'. Their's was a self-sufficing economy, eked out by paid labour in harvest; in contrast, the enclosure supported fewer people, but gave a much larger yield. In a small way, many of these cottagers were enclosing on their own—a meadow on which they kept a cow and a few sheep; a small orchard, with 'a little rib of tillage' for corn; so that 'every cottage seems to be the epitome of a small farm'.[1] But the position of this class was very precarious. The manorial lord might give them a tree or two in order to build a wooden cabin; he would then induce them to accept a lease; and, on its expiration, 'the hungry landlord swallows the cottage, with all its dependencies which by sweat and labour were improved to a kind of competency'.[2] The cottager was one of the many who, having no status, was always liable to victimization.

Wherever the worker on the land was dependent solely on his earnings, his lot must have been indeed hard. As the greater part of his expenditure was on food, he suffered from bad harvests; so the price of corn provides some index to his well-being. In the reign of James II, the average price of wheat was 34*s.* 8*d.*; in William's reign, the average was about 46*s.*; in 1698 it rose to 62*s.*; and the last years of the century, in both Scotland and England, were years of almost famine conditions, when many families had to live on beans and water. In these years, bread had to be made of oats, beans, acorns, and turnips.[3] Resentment was felt that while there was rigid machinery for keeping down wages, there was none for keeping down the price of corn, and regret was expressed that, unlike the Dutch, we had not provided ourselves with a sufficient number of

[1] T. Nourse, op. cit. 103. [2] Ibid. 105.

[3] *The Poor Man's Plea Against the Extravagant Price of Corn*, 1699.

granaries.[1] Attempts are sometimes made to link the price of corn with the course of political events. Obviously, in periods of dearness and scarcity there will be discontent and even tumult, but in the past there were ready methods for restoring order; moreover, in regard to these economic influences in our history, it has to be recalled that there existed a deep and inarticulate substratum of society, obliged to endure, without a murmur, the stresses and strains of the organization over their heads. But with the coming of the eighteenth century conditions improved. Cheap corn brought adversity to the small farmer, but more abundant food to the labourer; and higher wages attracted many of the dispossessed, including cottagers, into the towns.[2]

The landowners have been classified by a distinguished authority[3] into three main groups: first, the great landlords, having a rent roll of about £3,000; second, the substantial squires, with rents of from £800 to £2,000, and thirdly, the smaller squires, having a rent roll of less than £800. In the first class were those who had benefited by munificent royal grants, notably from the Tudors and early Stuarts. In the second class were many, now in the second or third generation of descent from merchants who had bought land in the sixteenth or early seventeenth centuries, and were letting out enclosed land in large farms. The third class, the smaller squires, approximated to the smaller freeholder and even leasehold farmer, in so far as they cultivated a portion of their land directly; but on the other hand, the greater part of their income came from rents. In general, during the later part of the seventeenth century, there was an increase in the number of large estates and a decrease in the number of smallholders,[4] two processes which, working together, may have helped to accentuate the aristocratic character of landholding. Fewer landholders were dependent on land for their livelihood, as so many had supplementary sources of income, whether from a government office, or directorship of a trading company, or the profits made in a legal career; at the other end of the scale, more copyholders and lease-

[1] *Add. MS.*, 17, 767. Report of Charles Davenant.

[2] M. Dorothy George, *England in Transition* (1931 ed.), 11–18.

[3] H. J. Habakkuk, 'English Landownership 1680–1740', in *Econ. Hist. Rev.* x, 1939–40.

[4] For this see A. Johnson, *The Disappearance of the Small Landholder.*

holders were becoming tenant farmers or even wage labourers. It has been estimated that, in the period 1680–1740, many of the large-scale purchases of land were made by families which already had considerable estates, most of them having acquired fortunes in the two great wars of that period; while of the smaller purchases, that is, of 500–1,000 acres, the motive was usually the acquisition of a country seat for residential purposes.[1]

Neither prices nor rents rose considerably in the period 1685–1702, but on the other hand the increasing burden of the Land Tax prejudiced the position of the poorer landlords. Of this, a slender but significant piece of evidence was the institution, late in William's reign, of lotteries, ostensibly to help them out of their difficulties.[2] Nor could this class always retrieve the position by raising rents, since the good tenant farmer could usually make a better bargain with the large, enclosing landlord, who had the backing of capital. In this way enclosures and the Land Tax helped to increase the cleavage between the large landlords and the smaller squires, the former living on a scale of some amplitude, which extended to the Court and the Grand Tour, while the latter became more localized, more provincial in outlook, and, if Roger North is to be believed, more selfish.[3] The development of the fashionable west end of London served still further to deepen the distinction between these two types of landholder. Harassed by war taxation, jealous of their richer neighbours, antagonistic to the official and financial classes brought into prominence by the war, the small squires, with their fellows in misfortune, the lower clergy, made up the strength of the Tory party.

Nevertheless, land retained its attraction as the most stable article of property, the devolution of which to a line of heirs might be ensured by entails and the strict family settlement. That stability was enhanced by legislative measures designed

[1] Habakkuk, op. cit.

[2] *C.J.* xii, 18 Dec. 1699. Petition of the proposers of the Kentish Land Lottery and of the Norfolk Land Lottery. They urged that their scheme was to discharge debts, which could otherwise be done only by sale of estates, and they petitioned to be allowed to complete the drawings in spite of the recent Act (10 Wm. III, c. 23) abolishing lotteries. The petition was rejected.

[3] *Autobiography of Roger North*, ed. A. Jessop, 182.

to encourage the provision and cattle industries,[1] and most of all by the Corn Laws. Briefly these laws, which began in 1663, were intended to favour the producer by restricting imports and encouraging exports. The Act of 1689[2] restored the bounty on exported grain, a measure which, in the opinion of Arthur Young, was the reward given to the landed classes for their part in the Revolution; while, according to others, it was designed to induce the landlords to acquiesce more willingly in the Land Tax. Actually, the measure may have been dictated simply by the abundant harvest of 1689 and the exceptionally low price of wheat.[3] A few years later, however, with a sequence of poor harvests, the price of corn rose, and exports were, for a time, prohibited; nor did the amount of grain imported greatly alter the situation. But between 1715 and about 1750 exports of corn steadily increased, and throughout the eighteenth century, as the corn laws exercised a stabilizing influence on prices, the landowning interests benefited.

Such, in brief, were conditions in the English countryside. But it would be wrong to assume that the country was of interest only in so far as it brought increased rents or enhanced social influence, for there were men whose outlook was not limited to economic or personal advantage, men like Evelyn, or some members of the North and Coke families, for whom landowning was connected with interest in horticulture, or afforestation, or estate management. There were also the poets, always knowledgeable about flowers and trees and birds. By the end of the century much of the English countryside had become distinctive for its mingling of the charm of quiet landscape with the amenities of the country house, the well-kept estate, and the large, orderly farm; indeed, nowhere else were these things so fully developed. Among many Englishmen, not given to literary expression, there was often keen appreciation of nature when humanized by labour and skill; as witness the following

[1] e.g. the Act of 1691 (3 W. and M., c. 8) which removed export duties on beef, pork, butter, and cheese in order to encourage the cattle industry.

[2] 1 W. and M., c. 12. This allowed the export of wheat when it was at 48*s*. per quarter or under, and gave a bounty on export of 5*s*. per quarter if in English ships.

[3] D. G. Barnes, *A History of the English Corn Laws*, ch. 2, and N. S. B. Gras, *Evolution of the English Corn Market*, 253.

example,[1] which brings conviction by its simplicity and directness:

> The meadow, which to-day is green, two or three days hence appears in another livery, even that of flowers, one week white, anon yellow, anon purple, or perhaps in divers colours at once . . . Fruit-bearing trees are covered with spotless and sweet-smelling blossoms, such as perfume the air, and ravish our senses with surprising delights. Then, dropping off, the fruit begins to appear in its infancy, which every day grows more fair till it arrives at maturity, and then serves further to gratify our senses in yielding us food of delicacy, but more eminently by yielding us those excellent liquors, by which the heart of man is made glad.

Not yet was there love for the mountains, and the sea was not yet appreciated; but even in the towns it was still possible to maintain contact with nature, as evidenced by this description of the ideal existence in retirement:[2]

> In a country town, by a murmuring brook,
> With the ocean at distance, whereon I may look,
> With a spatious plain, without hedge or style,
> And an easy pad nagg to ride out a mile.

But of these charms the Londoner may have been more keenly appreciative than the countryman. Here is an early account[3] of a 'ramble' from Southwark into the fields of Kent:

> Who would not exchange the stench and foggs of a city for the open, balmy air? Or the noisy dinn of coaches and carts for the delicious whispers of Zephyrs, the charming russle of the leaves, the agreeable murmur of fountains, and the matchless harmony of the birds? Can anything be more transporting? Listen to these feathered quires. Their music is nothing else than a perpetual triumph in their liberty. Hear how they sing apart the high counter and mean. And then together they sing their parts, a trio of two trebles, one concordant and a bourdon, and after all everyone sings alone the four parts. . . . Who would not be a rambler, since it is a life so full of bliss?

This sensitiveness to music, always a national characteristic, was shared by all classes, including the Puritans. It was music[4]

[1] T. Nourse, op. cit. 3.

[2] 'The Wish' in *Bodl. Firth* B. 21, no. 34, 1691.

[3] 'A Ramble Round the World', no. 1, 1689 in *Bodl. Nicholls Newspapers*, 7 B, no. 434.

[4] *Works of John Bunyan*, ed. G. Offor, iii. 240.

that Bunyan kept as a special reward for his pilgrims when, having reached the land of Beulah, they were at last beyond the Valley of the Shadow of Death, and within sight of the Celestial City; 'the bells did so ring, and the trumpets continually sounded so melodiously that they could not sleep; and yet they received so much refreshing, as if they had slept their sleep ever so soundly'. These two things, music and love of nature were among the refining influences in English life.

3. The Knights and Burgesses

The English countryside can be considered from many points of view other than that of landlord and tenant. The grower of corn and wool was likely to serve in one of the offices of a local administration,[1] the most highly perfected of all such administrations; for the landowner, this was a duty as much as a privilege; indeed, if he were not chosen for such service, that usually implied some disability, whether of character or of religious profession. So too, in the absence of such disqualification, if he was denied a place in the local hierarchy, or removed from it, without good reason, that was tantamount to violation of his birthright. In this way the county was, not inappropriately, referred to as the 'country', for it was a microcosm of the nation, having its armed force, the militia; its judiciary, the justices in petty or quarter sessions; its local parliaments, such as the meetings of the lord lieutenant with the deputy lieutenants, where assessments for the upkeep of the militia might be determined; and the grand juries, which received their charge from the justice of assize, and often gave expression to opinion on some question of the hour. The men who served in these capacities were likely also to be among the local commissioners for administering national taxation, such as the Land Tax or the Poll Tax. Frequent meetings for these purposes ensured a local solidarity, based on personal acquaintance and often on marriage alliance; to this extent it is true that the history of England is the history of her local politics. So, too, their tenants were likely to fill some of the parish offices; or to serve on the jury of a leet, or in the militia; so far as they had

[1] For a good, recent (1953) bibliography of the subject, see *Documents*, 434–6.

any opinions about public events, these were likely to be the opinions of their landlords. Moreover, these communities were held together by a certain disciplinary element, exercised by the justice, the village constable, the manorial lord, the church-wardens, and the archdeacon; and, as people in the country are more spread out than in the towns, it was easier to keep an eye on them. The emblem of this vigilant supervision, to which the lower orders were subjected, was to be found in the village stocks. It was not a merry England, but an England disciplined, turbulent, and robust.

The county was also a unit in the system of parliamentary representation; not only because it returned two knights of the shire; but because, long before the end of the seventeenth century, a majority of the parliamentary boroughs were within the control of the landed gentry. Nevertheless, the knights of the shire still enjoyed a somewhat higher local prestige than the (parliamentary) burgesses; for, historically, they were the descendants of the lesser tenants-in-chief; and to be returned as number one of the two knights of a county was the highest tribute that could be paid by a man's neighbours. At the other end of the scale were the burgesses for such obscure boroughs as Gatton in Surrey, or one of the Cornish boroughs, where a nomination was usually to be had. This contrast between the reputable and the less reputable types of constituency may have been slightly accentuated at times, as in the political agitation of the year 1701, when, according to Burnet,[1] the great counties and chief towns returned men who were devoted to king and parliament, while the other electorates, 'the rotten part of the constitution', returned 'bad men', presumably Tories. A clearer distinction recognized by the House was that between those members who had ability and those who had estates. On one occasion, when a Place Bill was lost, it was contended that the decision should have been the other way, since, among them, the minority had greater landed possessions than the whole of the majority, and therefore were of more consideration.[2] But none of these distinctions was pushed very far. Prominence in parliament had little to do with repute of electorate; magnitude of estates did undoubtedly influence many voters, both inside

[1] *Burnet*, iv. 546.

[2] Report of F. Bonnet, 30 Jan.–9 Feb. 1694, in *Ranke*, vi.

and outside the House, but did not determine the method of voting, since it is easier to count heads than rent rolls.

As the knights had usually such a secure local standing in the counties, their return to parliament, often unopposed, provided a strong element of continuity, which exercised a stabilizing effect at such changes as the Restoration and Revolution. Thus, of the eighty English knights of the shire who sat in the Convention Parliament of 1689, at least forty had sat in one of the short Exclusion parliaments of 1679–81, but only seventeen had sat in James's packed parliament, figures which support the view that this last parliament was objected to, not so much because its institution violated freedom of election, as because it involved the exclusion of so many families whose seats in the Commons were nearly as secure as those of the Lords in their House. Indeed, we have a confirmation of this in the fact that Danby, when compiling a list of those who, in the Commons, opposed James, appended a list of those even more formidable persons, outside the House, who could be relied on to maintain that opposition—a significant hint, as has been noted by a distinguished authority[1] of the forces that could be marshalled for the Revolution. That Revolution was really a restoration, in so far as it renewed this continuity of family connexion, which was accentuated, in the last two parliaments of William, when over fifty knights were returned who had sat before. One finds among the county representatives such names as the Russells (Bedford), the Whartons and Lees (Buckingham), Boscawens (Cornwall), Courteneys (Devon), the Edens and Lambtons (Durham), the Strangeways (Dorset), the Lowthers and Musgraves (Westmorland), the Onslows and Evelyns (Surrey), the Pelhams (Sussex), and so on. These men, many of whom could trace a parliamentary ancestry at least as far back as the sixteenth century, provided a core of landed aristocracy in a House where, as party distinction became more clearly defined, there began that sensitiveness to changes in political opinion so characteristic of modern times.

A similar continuity is seen among the burgesses, of whom, in the Convention Parliament more than 130 (of a total of 421) had sat in previous parliaments for English or Welsh boroughs. As with the knights, this proportion steadily increased,

[1] A. Browning, *Thomas Osborne, earl of Danby*, iii, appendix 4.

until in 1701 it amounted to more than 275, so that, in William's last parliament, altogether about three-fifths of the Commons had sat before. Although the landed element preponderated, the composition of the Lower House was extremely varied, consisting of certain strata, such as these: men of great distinction in spheres other than politics, as Dryden, Wren, Newton, and Addison; judges and lawyers, as Maynard, Somers, and Holt; or men high up in what we would call the civil service, as sir Stephen Fox and William Lowndes; or great city merchants, as sir Robert Clayton; or generals and admirals, as Talmash, Cutts, Russell, and Rooke. These representatives of such varied interests and professions served to raise the level of intelligence and efficiency in a body consisting mainly of country squires; and in this sense, the old, 'unreformed' House of Commons was more representative than that of today, because it included a wider cross-section of national activities and achievement, as well as a smaller proportion of those who devote themselves to politics as a career.

The aristocratic character of the Commons was emphasized by the establishment of a connexion, sometimes of long standing between the younger members of a noble family and a borough or boroughs usually, though not always in the neighbourhood of 'the big house'. In this way the Grenville (earl of Bath) family are found in Cornish boroughs; the Cavendishes (duke of Devonshire) in Derbyshire boroughs; the Paulets (marquis of Winchester) in Hampshire, and the Russells in boroughs of Bedfordshire and Devon. Among other families there was a similar continuity, a few characteristic examples being the Bradshaighs and their long connexion with Wigan; the Blacketts, Liddels, and Carrs, who, among them, usually provided the two burgesses for Newcastle upon Tyne; the Slingsby family which, with intermissions, represented Knaresborough for two centuries; the Whartons in Beverley, the Harcourts in Abingdon, the Leveson-Gowers in Staffordshire boroughs; the Actons in Bridgnorth; the Foleys, Winningtons, and Harleys in the western counties; the Seymours in Devon; the Godolphins in Cornwall; the Hobarts and Walpoles in Norfolk; the Churchills in Dorset; the Temples and Whartons in Buckingham. The names of some of these families attest the long duration of this, one of the fundamental things in English political life.

The events of the seventeenth century created an intense national interest in parliament; hence a seat in the Commons came to be more highly prized, since it might lead to a career, an office, a pension, or a bribe. More men, outside the ranks of the parliamentary families, became candidates for seats, a class more likely to be accommodated in the boroughs than in the counties, and only in those boroughs where both seats were not already monopolized. Some of these constituencies were bought singly or in groups; a few might descend by marriage; or a relative might be recommended even in a will;[1] or a nomination might be had from a lord lieutenant or other local magnate. Or, especially where the franchise was narrow, bribery might be resorted to—this indeed was becoming more common by the end of the century—or a contest might be engaged, in which the strategy of the polling booth would decide the issue, which was often upset by a successful appeal on a false return. In contrast, where there were large electorates, as in Westminster and Southwark, there was often occasion for mob oratory. The great variety of franchise in the boroughs, and the small size of most of their electorates account for the ease with which they could be manipulated, in contrast with the counties, where the electorate consisted of the 40*s.* freeholders, whose numbers made it more difficult to bribe or buy or manage them. Hence, so many of the older schemes of parliamentary reform consisted of advocating an increase in the number of county representatives at the expense of the boroughs.

Other schemes of reform advocated the transfer of members from over-represented areas, such as Cumberland, Cornwall, and Wiltshire, to London and the greater centres of population, which were either inadequately represented, or not represented at all. So there were, even in the seventeenth century, a few pioneers who advocated the representation of numbers. But the majority had no sympathy with this view, for they were still thinking in terms of landed property and certain national interests which appeared to have greater claims than mere population. In this way, the four members for the city of London were thought to represent trade; the two members for each of the universities were supposed, however nominally, to speak

[1] This was reported of one of the Lowther family. *H.M.C. Rep.* x, app. pt. 4, 335. *Capt. Bagot's MSS.*

on behalf of learning; the burgesses for the Cinque Ports, the dockyard towns, and some of the coastal boroughs were regarded as qualified to represent the interests of the navy and shipping. In nearly all the counties and in many boroughs choice of the two members was limited usually to three families, with alternations among them at successive elections.

All the signposts therefore point to the political families; here indeed we have one of the major subjects of later-seventeenth-century history still awaiting research, such as has been so well done for the parliaments of Elizabeth;[1] the Long Parliament,[2] and the earlier parliaments of George III's reign.[3] A few tentative generalizations on this subject may be confirmed by such research. Such are that in the seventeenth century the Commons were not clearly divided between Whig and Tory; that these labels were repudiated by many to whom they were applied; and that, in contested elections, while opinion about some question of the hour might influence the result, this seldom took the form of a straightforward party contest. Men were more often returned to Westminster, not because of their opinions about politics, but because of local opinion about themselves. And even in the very few cases where a clear-cut issue was presented to the electorate, voters were often thinking in concrete rather than in abstract terms; for example, in the 'Exclusion' elections of 1679–81, many gave their vote not so much for the Whigs, as for Dr. Oates; just as in 1710, many went to the polling booth, not on behalf of the Tory party, but on behalf of another Doctor—Dr. Sacheverell.

When the necessary parliamentary biographies are available it should be possible to construct some kind of electoral seismograph recording details of the shock of 1679, when so many Whigs were returned; the tremor of 1698, when opponents of placemen and high taxation, i.e. Tories, were substituted for Whigs, and the earthquake of 1710, which, after the Whig resurgence of 1708, swept the Tories back into Westminster. The recordings of such an instrument will reveal not merely the returns and rejections at successive general elections, but also something more subtle and more characteristic, namely, the movements within the electoral hierarchy. As elections were

[1] By professor J. E. Neale. [2] By D. Brunton and D. H. Pennington.
[3] By sir Lewis Namier.

not all held on the same date, there was always a chance that a candidate, unsuccessful in one part of the country, might be returned somewhere else—usually in his own county, but sometimes, where the shock was severe, at a considerable distance from his headquarters. Hence, we may expect to obtain information about three categories, the rejected, the displaced, and the immovables. Many of the first class were uprooted because they had no secure hold in their constituencies; among them were the 'carpet baggers', whose number was increasing in this period. Of the second class, the displaced, an example was sir J. Trelawney who, having served in the Court interest in Charles II's Long Parliament, as a knight for Cornwall, was moved by the landslide of 1679 into the Cornish borough of East Looe, where he remained fixed; in the same county, the Whig Boscawen, a knight of the shire, was thrown into Truro by the convulsion of 1710. A more serious dislocation was that experienced by sir Richard Onslow, who for long had been almost hereditary knight for Surrey, until in 1710 he was obliged to transport himself to the 'rotten' borough of St. Mawes. In this way the numerous Cornish boroughs provided homes of refuge for displaced politicians. But most interesting of all were the immovables. Of Whigs, examples are the Russells in Bedford or Tavistock, the Whartons in Beverley, and the Pelhams in Sussex, all of whom retained their seats in the cataclysm of 1710, though sir Michael Wharton—that munificent benefactor of Beverley and its minster—experienced a jolt, for he had to yield first place (which he had long held) to a Tory. Among the Tories and those of doubtful party allegiance the number of fixtures was probably greater; so great, indeed, that in a general election one could have safely prophesied the names of a large number of those families which would retain their seats, *and in their own 'country'*.[1]

The word 'representation' is one of the most difficult of all the words used by the historian, because its meaning may reflect deep-seated historical changes. It is not enough to say that the old parliamentary system was 'unrepresentative';

[1] Among the many useful books dealing with these local connexions are W. W. Bean, *Parliamentary Representation of the Northern Counties*; G. R. Park, *Parliamentary Representation of Yorkshire*, and W. P. Courteney, *The Parliamentary Representation of Cornwall.*

rather it was representative in a sense hardly understandable today, when the member of parliament may be an almost impersonal link between a numerical majority in a constituency and party organization in the House. In the later seventeenth century members did not regard their return as the result of a local option between rival policies; nor were they always classed, either inside or outside the House, by party labels, for they were 'Patriots' or 'Churchmen' before they were Whigs or Tories. How then were they distinguished? By their reaction to certain important events—such as offering the crown to William and Mary; or voting for large subsidies in the war years 1690–5; or signing the declaration of loyalty to William in 1696; or deciding between disbanding and the retention of a large army in 1699.[1] Not all of these divisions of opinion quite coincided with party principles; and, moreover, in 1690–5 these principles, such as they were, had been obscured by lavish grants of pensions and offices. Independence and corruption were thus conjoined as in no other institution; and, as the incongruity deepened, the level of political oratory rose. What is certain is that in the House the member was free, either to act on his opinion as influenced by the debates, or in his interest as deflected by a reward.

Now, all this initiative had been superimposed on a medieval system of which one relic survived—the tradition that the burgesses merely personated the burghers who had elected them, and that they had no more than a power of attorney in respect of the borough. Their first concern was about local matters; the constituency controlled the mandate. This ancient conception of representation still occasionally found expression, as in the crises of 1679 and 1701 when boroughs gave printed 'directions' to their members. Accordingly, the old system was based on the assumption that there would be agreement within each pair of members, if only because their mandate had once been so local and limited. This principle had, of course, broken down long before; but, in a characteristic way, its apparatus still survived; for, with the exception of the Welsh counties and boroughs (each returning one member), and excepting also the five single-member[2] and the two

[1] For this, see the lists printed and edited by A. Browning, op. cit. iii.

[2] Monmouth, Bewdley, Abingdon, Banbury, and Higham Ferrers.

four-member[1] English boroughs, all the constituencies returned two members. As these representatives were now concerned, not with local petitions but with great national questions, many of them highly controversial, one might expect to find (as one does find) difference of opinion on important matters within pairs of representatives; and to this extent a constituency might at times, on our standards, be disfranchised. Even as late as 1710 there are instances of a constituency returning two members, one Whig the other Tory. Hence it is possible that the old parliaments were 'unrepresentative', not because of the absence of an electorate, as we understand the term, but because the two-member system with its occasional but inevitable disagreement between two colleagues must have created temporary gaps separating Westminster from opinion in the constituency.

Nor was this disagreement in the period here considered so simple as that which we connect with Whig versus Tory; on the contrary, the difference often divided a pair who, according to modern classification, were of the same party; and was usually not about abstract doctrine, but about the line to be adopted in the House regarding some concrete question. The fact that this difficulty caused no protest from members; the absence, in schemes of reform, of any proposal to amend it, and the circumstance that constituencies appear to have made no objection to what now looks like temporary disfranchisement, these are among the most striking things in our *Ancien Régime*, and they possibly provide a clue to the real difference between our idea of representation and that which prevailed in the past. The explanation may perhaps be found by reference to what inspired and directed that *Ancien Régime*, namely, the sanctity of freehold. A majority of the Commons consisted of freeholders—in this respect they had something of the status of the Lords, who represented themselves; but, unlike the Lords, the Commons 'represented' other freeholders—the straightforward freeholds of the counties, and those caricatures or perversions of freehold which often determined the franchise in the boroughs. Even more extraordinary, from the modern point of view, the Commons derived much of their strength from their 'repre-

[1] The city of London and the double constituency of Weymouth–Melcombe Regis.

sentative' character; for they were freeholders who personified, in some way, all the freeholders of the country—all, in fact, who had any claim to citizenship. They had begun as no more than the mouth-pieces of local areas; now, by slow adaptation of a medieval idea, they had acquired a collective personality, which transcended not only conflict of opinion among its members, but also those differences which might divide representatives of the same constituency. The medieval conception of incorporation, the *persona ficta*, thus found its highest expression in a legislature endowed with the greatest power and prestige in the world.

Nevertheless, there still survived traces of the old localism; and there were even attempts to adjust difference of opinion by reference back to the constituency. An instance of this occurred at what was probably the first party convention, when an attempt was made to secure joint action among two representatives supposed to be of the same party allegiance. The occasion arose in this way. In the 1690–5 parliament the two knights of the shire for Westmorland were (in this order) sir John Lowther of Lowther and sir Christopher Musgrave. Both are now designated Tories, if only in the sense that neither could be called a Whig. Both had opposed James II in parliament; but while Musgrave had busied himself with securing the forfeitures of charters of several northern boroughs, Lowther had done much to bring over the northern counties to the cause of William. The result was that, immediately after the Revolution, Lowther was given office, and Musgrave was not. The one represented the 'ins', the other the 'outs'. Hence, in the 1690–5 parliament, one knight for Westmorland advocated the grant of the large subsidies required for the war, while the other knight as resolutely opposed them. Here was an important difference, not to be settled at Westminster, but at one of the local parliaments of their 'country', namely, the meeting of general quarter sessions at Kendal.

Accordingly, sir John, accompanied by sir R. Sandford and escorted by sixty horsemen, arrived in Kendal, where he met sir Christopher, who was accompanied by the mayor. At the sessions in the town hall Musgrave delivered a 'learned address' to the grand jury; and was followed by Lowther, who frankly acquitted his brother knight of the charge that he was disaffected to the government. This was followed by 'three speeches apiece', and 'each appeared to take the other's part'—obviously they were manœuvring for the real business on hand. An attempt was then made in these very friendly circumstances to unite them, but in vain. Lowther proposed that Musgrave should, in the presence of the bishop of Carlisle, sir G. Fletcher, and sir D. Fleming declare that he would vote such a supply as might be necessary for carrying on the war in the following year. To this Musgrave gave a diplomatic reply. Beginning with a general declaration in favour of the church of England and of His Majesty, he announced that he was unwilling to bind himself in advance, as that would infringe his liberty as a member of the House, a sacrifice inconsistent with his duty to king and parliament. So this Tory convention ended indecisively.[1]

But more effective means eventually brought Musgrave over to the Court; and, in December 1697, it was he who moved that a Civil List of £700,000 should be granted to the king. The explanation of this sudden departure from high principle was revealed to the world by the accidental dropping and bursting of one of the bags of guineas with which he was hurrying away from the royal presence.

3. The Place of London and Westminster in the National Life

The city of London consisted of 110 administrative areas, ninety-seven parishes within the walls and thirteen outside. Population was estimated at 540,000, as compared with that of Paris, 488,000; Amsterdam, 187,000; Rome, 125,000; Dublin, 60,000; and Bristol 48,000.[2] London had unique privileges distinguishing it from other English cities; and, in the events of both Restoration and Revolution, it had acted almost as a fourth estate. Integrity in the handling of its finances was another element in the high reputation of the metropolis. The

[1] *H.M.C. Rep.* x, app. pt. 4, 231 sqq., *Capt. Bagot's MSS.*

[2] For this, see P. E. Jones and A. V. Judges, 'London Population in the Late Seventeenth Century' in *Econ. Hist. Rev.* vi. The figures for the other cities are very conjectural, and are based on those given by Petty in *Political Arithmetic* (1769 ed.), 185.

Chamber of London administered a fund for the orphans of freemen, the reputation of which was so high that, long before the age of government securities, it attracted the investments of persons wishing to make reliable provision for dependents.[1] The great city companies retained their importance as civic and charitable institutions, many of them maintaining schools in the city and elsewhere; in 1694 the Bank of England was founded; and, before the end of the century, the Exchange was thronged by 'stock jobbers', thus adding one more to the numerous occupations housed in the city.

In some industries, notably the cloth industry, there was an increase in the number of middlemen,[2] many of whom, such as the 'factors', made their headquarters in London. As occupations became more clearly differentiated, the number of such intermediaries increased, and so the city came to harbour a large population of those whose means of making a livelihood seemed, on the old standards, recondite and obscure. A similar process can be seen in the arts, notably in music. Whereas this had provided one of the amenities of the country house, it was now becoming more professional, and inevitably the centre was London. The metropolis was steadily gaining at the expense of the provinces. One of the many evidences of this was the practice whereby some of the country gentry retained the services of London solicitors or scriveners, who sent a regular account of the news;[3] as well as this, the visitor to London would learn a great deal about politics by visiting the innumerable taverns and coffee houses.

Increased size and population brought many improvements to the metropolis. The water supply was enlarged by building new reservoirs at Highgate; for the lighting of the streets, the householder could now dispense with the old lanthorn and candle by buying a lamp of new design, sufficient to illuminate the exteriors of twenty houses, and costing only 35*s*. a year for maintenance.[4] Meanwhile shops were displacing stalls and booths; with the rebuilding, Londoners became proud of the

[1] *C.J.* xi, 23 Jan. 1693.

[2] R. B. Westerfield, *Middlemen in English Business, 1660–1760.*

[3] For an example see *H.M.C. Rep.* v, app. 378 sqq. *MSS of J. B. Pine Coffin*; see also *The Portlege Papers*, ed. R. J. Kerr and I. C. Duncan.

[4] *The Protestant Mercury*, 11–16 Aug. 1699.

new and more spacious city gradually taking shape around them. Visitors marvelled at the innumerable diversions provided, such as bear-baiting, executions, or visits to Bridewell; for the more sophisticated there were the theatres where, after the Revolution, obscenity became less fashionable, and some of the actresses were women of virtue. There were also many social functions. Commemorative dinners in town brought together Yorkshiremen,[1] Wiltshiremen,[2] old Etonians,[3] old members of Merchant Taylors,[4] old members of St. John's College, Cambridge,[5] and the sons of the clergy.[6] London was becoming something more than a capital city, for already it was a microcosm of a nation, as later of an empire.

This development was unusually rapid after the conclusion of the war in 1697. More newspapers and magazines made their appearance; publishers found profit in the production of cheap, popular books, including 'sixpennies', from which one could learn the art of japanning, or 'limning in oil', or speaking in public.[7] There were schools of penmanship, of boxing, and of chemistry; there were employment agencies, the managers of which left their lists of vacancies in the coffee houses; a new bagnio in Chancery Lane supplemented the one in Long Acre; and in 1693, opposite the latter establishment, there was opened a beauty parlour by a 'gentlewoman who has attained to great perfection in preserving and improving of beauty'.[8] For the connoisseur there were the auction rooms, where paintings could be bought; the goldsmiths and silversmiths were selling wares of the highest standard of workmanship in Europe. Or in the concert rooms one could listen, often for the first time, to the music of Purcell, or to strains of military music specially composed for a time of war.[9] Outside, a medley of

[1] *London Gazette*, 2945, 22–23 May 1687.

[2] *The Protestant Mercury*, 18–23 Nov. 1698.

[3] *The Post Boy*, 19–22 Feb. 1698.

[4] *The Postman*, 30 Dec.–2 Jan. 1699–1700.

[5] *The Post Boy*, 19–21 Dec. 1695.

[6] *London Gazette*, 2397, 3 Nov. 1688. This was an annual meeting for relief of the poor orphans of the clergy.

[7] A list of these will be found in *The Protestant Mercury*, 4–6 May 1698. The publisher was G. Conyers at The Ring in Little Britain. See *infra*, 521.

[8] *Athenian Mercury*, no. 13, 9 May 1693.

[9] *The Flying Post*, 20–22 July 1697.

street calls and refrains, many of them tuneful, advertised the wares offered by hawkers, men and women; later, some of these calls were used for improvization by Handel. Within less than fifty years from Cromwell's death, London had changed from a medieval town, built mainly of wood, into a spacious and cosmopolitan city of brick and stone. It was Voltaire[1] who said that London did not become a great city until after it had been burnt down. Nor was this true only in a physical sense; for, while the old metropolis of wood might at any moment have been consumed by the fires of religious fanaticism, the new structures of stone might be expected to last as long as the constitution itself. Together with Westminster, London was indeed the august capital of an empire slowly emerging into consciousness.

The connexion between London and Westminster suggests a wide field of speculation about the consequences that may follow from the relative sites of the commercial and the legislative capitals of a state. Where, as in Paris, the one is superimposed on the other, we may expect a somewhat higher political temperature, arising from close contact between deputy and citizen; and one might even conjecture whether the French Revolution would have come earlier if the kings of France had lived in the Louvre, instead of at Versailles. Power exercised from a distance may have greater leverage, and, as it is likely to be more impersonal, it cannot so easily or so speedily be contested. The detachment in space of Washington and Canberra may have some influence on the politics of the United States and Australia respectively; since, by the creation of a legislative capital withdrawn from the main centres of population and trade, political life may become more specialized and even more professional, because isolated and concentrated. In contrast, the relations of London and Westminster have this unique quality that the two places are as close in space as they are distinct in spirit.

In later medieval times, it is likely that the Commons, who were still only on the fringe of parliament, may have acquired some cohesion by resort to London hostelries; later, the taverns and clubs of the metropolis provided informal meeting-places, where a plan of campaign might be discussed, afterwards to be

[1] *Dictionnaire philosophique*, *sub voce* 'Lois'.

carried out in the more formal chamber at Westminster;[1] it is even possible that, in moments of tension, such semi-social gatherings provided a better 'cushion' for withstanding strain than did the tennis court in the early days of the French Revolution. After all, the first fully organized opposition, that of the Whigs in the Exclusion controversy, was concerted in the London coffee houses, and some of its asperity may have been dissipated in such centres of relaxation. There were other consequences of this close proximity to the capital. Before the end of the seventeenth century, many who had made fortunes in trade or war contracts were crowding into the House, which, for them, was within easy reach of their place of business; at the same time, the movement of fashion from the neighbourhood of the Inns of Court to the rapidly developing west end brought the legislators into closer contact with social life. The location of these two cities is so close that they appeared to coincide; but they never quite coincided, and the intervening gap may have been of momentous consequence.

In contrast with London, the remoter associations of Westminster were sacred, royal, and legal. The abbey church of St. Peter has played a greater part in national life than its French counterpart the abbey of St. Denis; for, while the latter preserved only the tombs of kings and queens, Westminster Abbey has commemorated all who, by their achievements, were deemed worthy of commendation to posterity. In this way, the shrine of St. Edward is the shrine of the nation. So, too, in early Norman times, a great royal palace was erected, of which the hall accommodated the law courts until 1873; for long, therefore, Westminster was the venerable repository of the church, the crown, and the law. Our legislature was bound to be influenced by close proximity to such fundamental things. One obvious consequence was that the lawyers could combine practice in Westminster Hall with attendance in the Commons; moreover, they had easy access to another, less-known institution of Westminster, situated next door to St. Stephen's, namely, the great library of medieval manuscripts of sir Robert Cotton, ancient sources which provided ample, and apparently

[1] In 1585 queen Elizabeth complained that the business of parliament had become 'the talk of ordinaries'. J. E. Neale, *The Elizabethan House of Commons*, 416–17.

well-authenticated precedent for opposition to the early Stuarts. Can it be wondered at that we speak of a lawyer-made constitution? These associations have meant so much in English civilization because they are so ancient; they may be forgotten or obscured today because the two cities are now barely distinguishable.

This distinction can be more clearly elucidated by reference to the place assigned for the deliberations of the old House of Commons; at first in the chapter house of the Abbey, and later in the church of St. Stephen. Now, the nave of a church recalls in shape and etymology a ship; and as in a ship one naturally thinks in terms of two sides, so in a church this dualism is always somewhere in one's consciousness. The mere shape of their habitation may have prompted the Commons to take sides, usually two sides; and so the dual party system may have been made almost inevitable by enclosure within straight, parallel lines. A circular chamber, so characteristic of some continental legislatures, suggests, by its very rotundity, division into segments, for the accommodation of more numerous parties and affiliations.

But, as well as shape, the church suggests other and more important things, namely, ritual and sanctity; moreover, with many men, these things are accentuated by the dim light filtering through stained glass and gothic arches. It is noteworthy that the original architecture of Westminster was predominantly Norman; and, when the two Houses were rebuilt after 1840, the style known as Later Perpendicular was adopted. Habituated to such ecclesiastical surroundings, the two Houses have maintained, throughout their long history, a devotion to routine, one might almost say ritual; they have regulated their proceedings by standing orders as binding as canonical decrees; and, more than any other legislative body, they have elevated the course of their proceedings to the level of a liturgy. Even on men not very susceptible, these things may have had some subconscious influence. Lords and Commons included a number of men who were infamous; but even they may at times have been restrained, to some extent, by their surroundings; and their environment may account for the fact that, collectively, they were always superior in moral sense to the average of the individuals making up their number. However undignified or acrimonious might be the debates within the privacy of the two chambers, however mean and venal the private lives of some of their members, as aggregates they took upon themselves something of the dignity and order so manifest around them.

All this reached a climax when the king appeared in his full parliament, providing a reincarnation of that medieval sovereignty in which the sacred transcended the secular; surrounded by his Peers in their robes, and confronted by his Commons, hatless and reverent. On such occasions, when the royal approval of legislative measures was announced to the world, there was distinction of neither persons nor things; and Bills passed by the two Houses awaited the life-giving touch of the sceptre in an order as indifferent as that of souls attending their turn in the Day of Judgement. This brought together some strange bed-fellows who, in other legislatures, would have been kept apart; and so an Act altering the principles of the constitution might be placed next to one altering the bounds of a parish. When, in 1533, Henry VIII assented to the Bill annulling appeals to Rome, the clerk of the parliaments announced the royal consent in the same breath as had served him for approval of a Bill for paving the Strand and a Bill for destroying crows;[1] and when, in 1689, William III gave his royal sanction to the Bill of Rights, he did so at the same moment as he made valid a Bill for naturalizing one William Watts.[2] There was something of the omnipotence and detachment of providence itself when the crows, the cobbles in the Strand, and the nationality of William Watts were assigned places next in order to measures which broke the bonds of Rome, and brought us that constitutional government which we know today.

[1] *L.J.* i, 24 Hen. VIII, cc. 12, 11, and 10 respectively.

[2] Ibid. xiv, 1 W. and M., sess. 2, cc. 2 and 3.

V

JAMES AND JEFFREYS, 1685–6

THE death of Charles II on 6 February 1685 in his fifty-fifth year caused genuine concern and regret throughout his dominions. In spite of his failings, or because of them, the late king had not only won popularity among many of his subjects, but had strengthened the position of the throne in national life; for he had succeeded in creating a new kind of personal rule based, not on parliament, whose criticism he resented, but on the church of England, in the tenets of which he did not believe. On this secure foundation, his wit, intelligence, and charm account not only for contemporary, but even more for posthumous reputation; and explain why he has long been established, in popular literature, as the greatest and most deeply beloved of all kings. But this had been achieved at some cost. The Whitehall of Charles I had become a dissolute annexe to Versailles; the England of Elizabeth and Cromwell was now a dependency of France. During the last months of the reign, when retribution for the Rye House Plot was being exacted in blood, the tranquillity of the rapidly ageing king was ensured by the solicitude of a mistress, the vigilance of a brother, and the efficiency of the executioner. That brother, whom the Exclusionists had tried to debar from the succession, now ascended the throne.

James[1] was thus described by a contemporary:[2]

He was something above the middle stature, well-shaped, very nervous and strong; his face was rather long, his complexion fair, his countenance engaging; his outward carriage was a little stiff and constrained ... In his conversation and arguing, he endeavoured rather to convince with good reason than fine expressions; and, having something of a hesitation in his speech, his discourse was not so graceful as it was judicious and solid. [He was] all his life, a great enemy to drinking, gaming and all such pleasures as were

[1] For good accounts of James see those by Mrs F. M. G. Higham and Mr. F. C. Turner.

[2] *Life of James II*, ed. J. S. Clarke, ii. 604–6.

obstructive to business . . . or were but loss of time, which he always accounted precious. He was a kind husband, notwithstanding his infirmities. . . . He was the most indulgent father in the world.

This is by no means a solitary tribute. Contemporaries so contrasted as Burnet and Ailesbury, were impressed by the moral qualities of James. 'If it had not been for his popery', declared Burnet,[1] 'he would have been, if not a great, yet a good prince.' Ailesbury[2] was even more explicit: 'a prince that had all the moral virtues . . . the most honest and sincere man I ever knew . . . a great and good Englishman.' Already in contemporary correspondence, a constantly reiterated theme had been the contrast between the virtue and reliability of James and the fickleness and debauchery of his brother; indeed, if high purpose, consistency, and industry ensure success in the art of governing, then the new king had all the qualifications for a brilliant reign. It was natural therefore that misfortune should add to an already high reputation. In his exile, those who were most closely in touch with him regarded him as a saint, an impression confirmed by the numerous miracles performed just after his death, all of them vouched for by persons of unimpeachable integrity.[3] No other king of England was ever distinguished by so many virtues (if words mean anything), or by such sacrifices for the true faith. But James II has not yet been canonized by the church of Rome.

In spite of the king's religion, in spite of his well-known policy of 'thorough' as recently illustrated in Scotland, the nation was ready to welcome the new sovereign, and to accord him at least loyalty and obedience. Economy was the keynote of the new reign. The funeral of the late monarch was conducted with what some regarded as unseemly parsimony; a number of royal servants and officials were dismissed, including the man who showed visitors round the tombs in Westminster Abbey. The most expensive of the royal mistresses, Kate Sedley, was banished from the Court (to which she speedily returned); while the duchess of Portsmouth was packed off to Versailles

[1] *Burnet*, iv. 540.

[2] *Memoirs of Thomas, earl of Ailesbury*, i. 131.

[3] e.g. the bishop of Autun, a nephew of Bossuet, who was miraculously cured of a *fistula lachrymalis*. Other examples will be found in *Add. MS.* 20311, f. 8.

(where she lost so heavily at the gaming table that Louis talked of putting her in a nunnery). All this piety and economy contrasted favourably with the character of the preceding dispensation. The king's first speech to his council conveyed assurances that he would support and defend the church of England, that he would invade no man's property, and that he would maintain the government as by law established. The ministerial appointments helped to confirm the good impression. Rochester, the king's brother-in-law, instead of going to Ireland as lord deputy remained at home as lord high treasurer; his brother, Clarendon, became lord privy seal; even Halifax was left in office, as president of the council. Godolphin became chamberlain to the queen, Mary of Modena; and Sunderland remained in office as secretary of state. Such a ministry seemed likely to remain faithful to the principles of Clarendonian Anglicanism, then regarded as a bulwark against popery. Less reassuring was the proclamation[1] that Customs and Excise should continue to be paid as in Charles's lifetime; but this was not altogether irregular, since part of these revenues had been farmed out just before the late king's death, and, in the opinion of the judges, the farm was still good.

James was crowned with Anglican rites on 23 April 1685, but the sacrament was omitted, and the ceremony[2] was greatly curtailed. Writs were issued for a meeting of parliament in May. But already some disquiet had been caused by the ostentation with which James practised the rites of his faith. There might have been even more disquiet had people overheard the conversations between James and Barrillon, Louis's ambassador in England. On 8 February the king explained to the ambassador why he had decided to summon a parliament at once—if he delayed doing so, he would lose credit for the act; moreover, he hoped that the legislature would grant him his revenues for life.[3] It was true, he added, that he had taken this step without consulting Louis, but delay would have been dangerous, and might have obliged him to collect the revenue by force. Nevertheless, he would need financial help from Louis;

[1] Steele, i, no 3775, 9 Feb. 1685.

[2] L. G. W. Legg, *English Coronation Records*, no. xxvi.

[3] Barrillon to Louis, 9–19 Feb., in C. J. Fox, *A History of the Early Part of the Reign of James II* (1808), Appendix, xviii.

without it he could not do what he designed in favour of the Roman Catholics. Next day Rochester[1] called on Barrillon to amplify the justification, or apology already offered by his royal master for his summoning of parliament. That decision, he explained, was really a clever move, since it would 'dish' Halifax and the malcontents; moreover, it was in the interests of Louis himself, since without the parliamentary revenue James would have to make even heavier demands on French generosity. Indeed, without such help, James would be 'à la merci de son peuple'.[2] In response to these clear hints, Louis sent to Barrillon bills of exchange for half a million livres,[3] not to be paid out at once, but to be kept for use as occasion required. He also gave his approval of the summoning of parliament, knowing that, in his wisdom, James would prevent it doing anything inimical to the interests of France.[4]

The fund of half a million aroused the cupidity of king and ministers. James[5] wept with gratitude when he heard of it, and communicated the glad tidings to Rochester, Sunderland, and Godolphin, who, with eyes on the money, assured Barrillon (at that time somewhat concerned about English commitments with Spain) that, as regards the treaty of 1680,[6] there need be no anxiety at Versailles, because James would not keep it any more than his brother had done. On 15 February the English king made further protestations of gratitude. 'I am considering not my present situation', he assured Barrillon, 'but the situation that I can achieve. Everything is possible in England and Scotland; your master has succoured me at a time when he could not have known whether there was a rebellion in London, or whether I had been expelled from my kingdom.'[7] Thus early was James providing the best commentary on his own reign.

The direction taken by royal policy was also revealed in the king's choice of confidential advisers, and in preparations for the coming parliament. Within a few weeks of his accession he was assisted by a secret conclave of Roman Catholics con-

[1] Fox, op. cit. xx, 9-19 Feb. 1685.
[2] Ibid. xxi.
[3] Ibid. xxv.
[4] Ibid. xxvii.
[5] Ibid. xxix.
[6] *Dumont*, vii, pt. 2, 2-4; June 1680. A mutual assistance agreement between the two countries, limited to Europe.
[7] Fox, op. cit. xxxii.

sisting of Arundel, Belasyse, Talbot, and Jermyn. Sunderland occupied himself with the parliamentary elections, for which purpose he engaged in a campaign of unprecedented thoroughness.[1] Letters were sent to lords lieutenant and their deputies, to prominent noblemen, to mayors, indeed to everyone having any local influence in order to ensure that, if any malcontent did stand for election, a loyalist would be put up against him. Deputy lieutenants were asked to attend elections for this purpose. The response was encouraging; for, with few exceptions, the counties and boroughs showed a willingness amounting to subservience. The result was that, of the 513 knights and burgesses returned to the House, about 400 had never sat in parliament before, many of them being the creatures of remodelled corporations, whose new charters were of doubtful validity. Very few Whigs were returned, indeed James himself said that there were only about forty members of the Commons on whom he could not rely. But Barrillon[2] noted (and he had long experience) that it was impossible to prophesy what an English parliament might do. After the elections there was similar management to make sure that the hereditary revenues would be granted for life; and, at the king's request, lord Ailesbury convened a meeting at the Fountain tavern, attended by more than 250 members, 'prime lords that were Commons and the top gentry of each county', a body which sent to the king an assurance that his wishes would be carried out.[3]

James's one and only parliament met on 19 May. Sir John Trevor, a creature of Jeffreys, was elected Speaker; the unofficial managers in the Commons were two Scottish peers, lord Middleton (one of the secretaries of state) and Richard Graham, lord Preston. The unofficial chancellor of the Exchequer was the able but unscrupulous Dudley North. The king's speech,[4] delivered on 22 May, repeated the usual assurances about preserving the government in church and state, but a new note was struck when James passed on to the subject of his revenue, for he expressed disapproval of frequent parliaments and 'feeding me from time to time by such proportions as they shall

[1] The letters of Sunderland will be found in *S.P. James II*, 17 Feb.–25 Mar. 1685.

[2] Fox, op. cit. xcvii, 28 May–7 June.

[3] Ailesbury, *Memoirs*, i. 100–1.

[4] *L.J.* xiv, 22 May.

think convenient'. The best way was 'always to use me well'. At the same time he intimated that Argyll had landed in Scotland. The Commons promptly voted him for life the revenue which Charles II had enjoyed. To this there was only one dissentient—sir Edward Seymour, who moved that before a supply was granted the petitions against irregular returns should be examined, so that only qualified members should sit and vote in the House. His motion was not even seconded. The House, in a committee of religion, then accepted two resolutions, one expressing devotion to the church of England, the other calling on the king to put into execution the penal laws against recusants; but as soon as it was understood that the latter request would cause offence, it was withdrawn, and its place was taken by a resolution expressing entire confidence in the royal promise to protect the church of England. All this showed James how far he could go.

But the revenues granted to him did not provide for much more than the normal, peace-time administration. Moreover, they were heavily anticipated in advance; there were also Charles's debts; the naval and ordnance stores were exhausted. So on 30 May the king again asked for money, assuring the two Houses that 'he had a true English heart'.[1] Once more the Commons responded. Under the guidance of Dudley North they voted additional duties on wine and vinegar, and on sugar and tobacco for eight years, the two Bills[2] for this purpose receiving the royal assent on 16 June. Two days later, on the news that Monmouth had landed, there was another request for money, answered by the grant of a supply, to be raised by imposts on French linens, brandies, silks, and also East India goods for a period of five years.[3] As the three special grants of supply brought in over £400,000 per annum, and as the hereditary revenue averaged about £1,500,000, James started his reign with an income of nearly 2 million, or about twice that which had been granted to Charles II at his accession.

This strong position was to be further consolidated by the failure of two badly planned rebellions, both of them sequels of the anti-popish agitation of 1681, which, having been suppressed by Charles's government, had again raised its head in the Rye

[1] *L.J.* xiv, 30 May 1685.
[2] 1 Jac. II, cc. 3 and 4 respectively.
[3] 1 Jac. II, c. 5.

House Plot. That plot had provided a pretext for establishing a reign of terror. Notable among those who escaped to Holland was Archibald Campbell, ninth earl of Argyll, whose father had been executed in 1661 as a participant in Cromwellian rule. The son, having succeeded to the family Presbyterianism and the family estates, had been sentenced to death in 1681, nominally for treason, but actually because he was the most formidable opponent of Stuart rule in Scotland. Having escaped from prison, he took refuge in Holland, where he had an estate, and there he consorted with such men as Monmouth, Hume, Cochrane, Ayloffe, and Rumbold. But as he did not support Monmouth's claim to kingship he acted with some independence. A fatalist, he seems almost to have courted disaster by the inadequacy of his preparations. With £10,000 given him by a rich widow in Amsterdam, he fitted out three small vessels, as for a trading venture; and on 2 May he set sail, with about 300 men, for an invasion of Scotland, where he hoped to raise an army from his clansmen in Argyllshire, and from the Covenanters of the south-west. Arriving at Orkney four days later, two of his party imprudently went ashore, whereupon they were seized, and the plan discovered; so the royal troops under Athol and Dumbarton were in readiness by the time that the earl reached Campbeltown in the peninsula of Kintyre. There he set up his standard with a motto which would have meant little anywhere else, namely 'No Prelacy, No Erastianism'. At first, the response was poor; and, although he was joined by considerable numbers at Tarbert on Loch Fyne, divided counsels speedily ruined what little chance of success remained. While the earl was naturally anxious to raise his clansmen of Lorne, that was made difficult by Athol's occupation of the district; on the other hand, there was a strong party, headed by Hume and Cochrane, anxious to join with the Covenanters south of the Clyde. So against the leader's will a section of his troops was detached for what proved to be a purposeless raid on Greenock.

Meanwhile, on 11 June Monmouth landed at Lyme Regis. The 'Protestant Duke' had made somewhat more elaborate preparations than had Argyll; as well as this, he had a personal popularity to which the chief of the clan Campbell could never have laid claim. Instructed by Shaftesbury, Monmouth had taken part in the Rye House Plot, and had been one of the Council of Six;[1] but, as a plotter, he had shown some chivalry, together with a lack of resolution, qualities which did not favour success in the trade so assiduously pursued by his associates. Charles had pardoned his erring Absalom, but as he refused to give evidence against his fellows, Russell and Sidney, he was banished from the Court. Crossing to Holland in 1684, he was entertained by the prince of Orange, who advised him to serve the emperor in the Hungarian campaigns; but unfortunately, the death of his father caused the duke to reject this advice, and soon he was in active communication with Argyll, sir Patrick Hume, and Robert Ferguson for the purpose of a simultaneous rising in England and Scotland. The landing in Scotland was to precede that in England, so that James's troops would be drawn off to the north by the time Monmouth had disembarked. Lyme Regis was selected as the place for the landing probably because it was known that Monmouth was popular in the south-western counties; and the design was that the landing should be accompanied by risings in London and Cheshire. In order to prepare the way an agent, Christopher Battiscombe, had been sent in April to rally the duke's friends in the west, as well as to concert measures with Delamere in Cheshire, and Wildman in London. These schemes failed. Battiscombe found that the gentry of Somerset and Dorset were not enthusiastic; and Wildman failed to send a promised supply of money.[1]

Moreover, there was a serious cleavage in Monmouth's following. Some supported his claim to the throne; while others, fired by ardent republicanism, regarded the duke only as a means to an end. Wildman treated the whole enterprise as no more than an episode; and, as he failed to start a rising in London, he fled to Holland, from whence he returned at the Revolution. In Cheshire, Delamere (who was on bail from the Tower) does not seem to have attempted anything; and so it may be claimed that the rebellion had failed before Monmouth set sail. Extravagant optimism in moments of success and equally unwarrantable pessimism as soon as danger threatened were the two qualities of character which led Monmouth to his doom.

[1] A good recent account of Monmouth's rebellion is that by W. R. Emerson; a good biography of Wildman is that by M. P. Ashley.

The tragic story of Argyll and Monmouth has been told by Macaulay with a dramatic intensity unmatched in historical literature, and with an accuracy of detail which has withstood the scrutiny, often niggling, sometimes vituperative, of more than a century. Here one can record only a meagre summary. After failing to seize his capital of Inveraray, Argyll was obliged to seek refuge in the island of Bute, from whence he ventured on a desperate march to Glasgow. Deserted by most of his followers, he was a fugitive by the time he crossed the Clyde at Renfrew, and on 18 June—the same day as that on which Monmouth proclaimed himself king at Taunton—Argyll was captured. His execution followed twelve days later in accordance with the sentence of death passed on him nearly four years before. Monmouth's enterprise lasted longer, and had more chance of success. His landing at Lyme on 11 June was accompanied by the issue of a flamboyant declaration, penned by Ferguson, announcing that Monmouth was the true heir to the throne, that James had started the Fire of London and had poisoned his brother, assertions accompanied by the enumeration of a number of Whig principles, such as annual parliaments, security of tenure for judges, no standing army, and toleration for all Protestants. When the duke reached Taunton a week later, his army, consisting mainly of peasants of Somerset and Dorest, amounted to about 7,000 men; his cavalry were mounted on cart horses, which stampeded in action. Nevertheless, in skirmishes with the militia, the rebels usually had the best of it; had Monmouth pressed on to Bristol, he might at least have held out in that stronghold of Whigs and Dissenters.

But the duke's conduct showed hesitation, and his adjutant, Forde, lord Grey, gave evidence of cowardice. From Taunton the rebels marched[1] in a wide loop to Keynsham, five miles south-east of Bristol, which was reached on 24 June. At this, the critical point of the rebellion, Monmouth showed fatal indecision. He was troubled because he could not shake off the remorseless Churchill; he panicked when a small body of enemy troops blundered into his camp; trained in the formal school of military art, he could not improvise with the raw

[1] For a good modern account of the campaign and the battle of Sedgemoor, see sir W. S. Churchill, *Marlborough, his Life and Times*, i, ch. 12 (with plans).

recruits who flocked to his standard. He appears to have over-estimated the strength of the forces opposed to him; and already, by delay and much marching and counter-marching, he had sacrificed the one essential for success—surprise. Leaving Keynsham, he led a retreating army, constantly thinned by desertion, through the rain-soaked countryside, until (for the second time) he was in Bridgwater on 2 July, when his army now numbered only about 3,000 men. On the night of 5 July he set out from Bridgwater for a night attack on the enemy troops who were encamped on Sedgemoor, an attempt which might well have succeeded, for the royalist commander, Feversham, was notorious for his lack of discipline, and was himself in bed when the attack began. But ill luck pursued the duke to the end. Disobeying or misinterpreting his orders, lord Grey, posted on the duke's left, led the cavalry to the right, and so became entangled with the infantry, who were struggling in the mud of the Bussex rhine, a deep ditch protecting the front of the royal troops. The capture of his guns early in the morning of the 6th was the end of the battle; and by dawn Monmouth and Grey were in flight, leaving behind them their wretched supporters, now falling in masses under the fire of sixteen guns brought up against them, and revealing a fortitude of which their leaders were incapable. After capture, in conditions of extreme distress, Monmouth was executed on 15 July. Forde, lord Grey, was pardoned, on his giving a bond for £40,000, and undertaking to swear against his fellows. In the next reign he became a privy councillor and earl of Tankerville.

Such was the end of a rebellion, one might almost say an escapade, led by that favourite son of Charles, whose popularity and Protestantism had made him a serious rival to James in the succession. Six years earlier he had won a reputation for military prowess in his easy victory over the Scottish Covenanters at Bothwell Brig; but, more important, and more unusual, he had stirred many hearts by his clemency to the defeated, a clemency of which his father and uncle sternly disapproved. Monmouth's cause was a good one, because based on Protestantism and humanity; indeed, although he had shared in the debauchery of the Court, the duke was the only Stuart who understood the common man. It is probably in these simple, straightforward things, rather than in any economic motive, that the explanation may be found why so many flocked to his standard. There was undoubtedly some economic distress in the west of England, as there was in every part of the country in most years of the century; there were, it is true, a number of Somerset cloth workers and Mendip miners in Monmouth's army who were suffering from low and precarious wages. But these things are relative. It was the year 1686, not 1685, that was noted as a year of special hardship[1] in the clothing industry; and even thus, it has to be recalled that the majority of the rebels were peasants, not craftsmen. Notable also is the fact that, in the declaration of Lyme, sweeping as it is, there is not a word about economic matters, but a great deal about what in the seventeenth century caused men to take up arms, namely, the (alleged) right of Monmouth to the crown, his Protestantism, his crusade against Popery which, to many contemporaries of James and Louis, implied a régime of obscurantism and butchery. These things may well have provided adequate reasons for action among men so accustomed to economic hardship that they had come to regard it, like the weather, as part of a divine order of things. A suggested reason for historical events is not necessarily wrong because it is old.

Clemency was not a Stuart virtue. The rebels, now crowded into the gaols in such numbers that plague broke out among them, were soon to experience what 'firmness' meant. A suitable instrument was at hand—George Jeffreys, an ambitious and able man who had been called to the Bar in 1668 and who, in the business of the Old Bailey, had distinguished himself by astuteness and vehemence. Never learned in the law, he was formidable in cross-questioning, mercilessly bullying the witnesses on the other side—while outside the law court he cultivated only acquaintances likely to promote his career. In 1677, with the help of Chiffinch, he was appointed solicitor to the duke of York, and so began the close association between these two men; from that point his fortune was made. He appeared as counsel for the crown in several prosecutions following the Popish Plot, and as Recorder of London he

[1] One reason for this was that in 1686 the Levant Company, which drew most of its cloth from the west country, was in difficulties, and took up less than its usual amount of cloth. A. C. Wood, *The Levant Company*, 108.

signalized himself by obstructing and traducing petitioners for a parliament. The leading spirit in the campaign of the *quo warranto* confiscations, he presided at the trial of Algernon Sidney, a trial notable, even in that age, for its unfairness. Lord chief justice since 1683, he was created baron Jeffreys of Wem in May 1685. Two days after the battle of Sedgemoor he was appointed president of the commission to try the captured rebels, his fellow judges being sir William Montagu, sir Cresswell Levinz, sir Francis Wythens, and sir Robert Wright. A military escort was provided for the president, and on 27 August proceedings began at Winchester, where lady Alice Lisle was charged with high treason.

Lady Lisle was the widow of that John Lisle who, for a time, had acted as president of the court of justice erected to try Charles I. She was over seventy, and so deaf that a friend had to repeat to her what was said in court. She begged that the fact of her being the widow of a regicide should not prejudice her case, and it was known that she had always expressed regret at the execution of Charles. The charge was that of harbouring two rebels—Nelthorpe (who appears to have hidden himself in one of the chimneys), and a dissenting minister named Hickes, brother of the scholarly dean of Worcester. The hearing resolved itself into evidence regarding the harbouring of Hickes, and it was on this alone that a verdict was obtained. Now Hickes may have been in the rebel army, but the accused's case was that she had no reason to think so, because she knew Hickes only as a dissenting minister, 'used to preach and not to fight'. Moreover, it was not uncommon for Dissenters to flee from 'justice', and indeed at the time of the rebellion the local authorities had been ordered to arrest them.[1] Even more, Hickes had not been convicted as a rebel, an important point raised by one of the jurymen, when he asked the judge whether it was the same thing to harbour Hickes before conviction as after. 'It is all the same', replied Jeffreys,[2] 'for if Hickes had been wounded in the rebel army, and had died of wounds in

[1] On 20 June the lords lieutenant were ordered to seize all disaffected persons, especially dissenting ministers. *S.P. James II*, 30 June. This fact strengthens the plea of Alice Lisle that she thought Hickes was a fugitive, not from the rebel army, but from arrest as a Dissenter.

[2] *State Trials*, xi. 370.

her house, she would nevertheless be a traitor.' This really strengthened the case of the accused, which was based on the fact that there was nothing in Hickes's appearance or conduct to suggest that he had been engaged in hostilities, a perfectly sound defence, which was brushed aside by Jeffreys: 'I tell you that there is not one of those lying, snivelling Presbyterian rascals but one way or other had a hand in the late horrid conspiracy.' In other words, the only evidence for Hickes having been a rebel was that he was a 'Presbyterian', just as, a few years before, the only case against Algernon Sidney was that his academic theories of tyrannicide might conceivably be put into action.

The jury, obviously perplexed, took so long over their verdict as to try the patience of the judge, but at last they accepted Jeffreys' logic, though they may have been doubtful about his law. On their returning a verdict of Guilty, the president declared that the evidence was conclusive, and sentenced Alice Lisle to death by burning. 'Had she been my own mother', he shouted, 'I would have found her guilty'.[1] There is no reason to doubt the truth of this statement.

This case is of some interest because it is now generally assumed that Jeffreys has been completely exonerated from the serious charges brought against him by nineteenth-century historians; a vindication based mainly on the facts that this was a brutal age; that the law regarding the harbouring of rebels was inexorable, and that Jeffreys was obliged to carry out the letter of the law, no matter how distasteful. To condemn him, it is said, is to read modern ideas into the past, and to forget that, in earlier times, the crown was dependent, for the enforcement of order, on a code far more harsh than that required today. There is some truth in these arguments. But, on the other hand, however much we may wish to condone it, brutality is not necessarily justified merely by the fact that it was perpetrated in another country, or in another age; more important, these exculpations are based on the assumption that

[1] *State Trials*, xi. 373. Sir J. Stephen, in his *History of the Criminal Law in England*, i. 413, stated that the conviction of Alice Lisle was 'probably illegal' on the ground that Hickes had not been convicted before the trial. In the above account the author has tried to emphasize a different point, that there was no evidence to show that she knew Hickes to be a rebel.

there was then a clear distinction between what was law and what was not. On the contrary, there was often a wide margin between the two, to be filled in by the discretion or (even in that age) by the humanity of the judge. An example is provided by the state of the law regarding the harbouring of a traitor. There was considerable doubt whether or not this applied only to the harbouring of a convicted traitor; and Jeffreys must have known that, on this point, the law was by no means clear. Accordingly, quite apart from any question of humanity, it was his duty to have made sure, before directing the jury, that the evidence was conclusive of Alice Lisle having known Hickes to be a rebel; indeed, when the foreman of the jury objected that they had no clear evidence on this essential point, the judge cited as 'proof' that, at supper time, the conversation was about the recent battle. And as for Jeffreys being a man of his age, one has only to compare him with Hale before him, or Holt immediately after him. This comparison with Hale was made at the time; for Baxter, at his trial for sedition,[1] had the courage to draw the attention of the court to the glaring contrast between Jeffreys and his predecessor.

This marginal element in the law was illustrated in the later proceedings of the Bloody Assizes when the penalty of whipping was imposed in those cases where the death penalty did not seem justified. Now, the punishment of whipping, often at the cart's tail, was not regulated by any clear rule, save that, according to the thirteenth-century *Judicium Pillorie*, it was to be administered *sine periculo hominis*. It was therefore designed not as a form of torture, still less as a means of death; what is certain is that this penalty was painful and ignominious, but did not extend to life and limb. Nevertheless, Jeffreys deliberately used it as a means of ensuring that life and limb would be endangered, and that by a form of torture. This may well have been the intention of the sentences, passed on many rebels, of whipping through all the market towns of a county. Now, here again we cannot point to the actual letter of any law broken by Jeffreys and his colleagues. But no system of law is proof against abuses committed by its administrators; for in law, as in everything else, there are certain silences, to be filled in by common sense, or by discretion, or even by common humanity. These

[1] *State Trials*, xi. 501.

silences provided Jeffreys and his colleagues with their opportunity.

Silence has also provided opportunity for those who maintain that these things have been grossly exaggerated. There was practically no protest against them at the time; therefore, it is now argued, neither Jeffreys nor the Bloody Assizes were so bad as they have been painted. But this argument, popular because 'moderate', does a serious injustice to seventeenth-century England; for there are degrees even in brutality, and the general condemnation of Jeffreys and the Bloody Assizes immediately after the Revolution (when it was safer to express an opinion)[1] showed that public indignation had been roused. That there was so little protest at the time was because any criticism of the government was seditious libel; and, especially in James's reign, men might well hesitate before committing such an offence; so the silence of the nation was by no means the silence of consent. What Jeffreys himself thought about it may be deduced from the fact that, in October 1688, when the dynasty was tottering, he took the trouble to obtain a royal pardon for his crimes.

From Winchester the commission proceeded to Salisbury, Dorchester, Exeter, Taunton, Wells, and finally Bristol. The number of persons on whom the death penalty was inflicted cannot be determined with certainty; it may have been no more than 300 (some think even less); but the bloodiness of the Bloody Assizes is not to be assessed on such statistics; for there are many things worse than death. There was a great trade in selling pardons to delinquents, in which Jeffreys shared large sums with James; for a rich landowner, Edward Prideaux, a total of £15,000 was paid. The king caused Sunderland to write to the president expressing entire approval of his actions, particularly of his having respited those prisoners who undertook to give evidence against Prideaux.[2] Jeffreys priced the humbler prisoners at £10–15, and advised the king to be discriminate in his allotment of these to applicants; 'otherwise persons that have not suffered in your service will run away

[1] e.g. the statement of sir Robert Cotton in the Commons, 14 May 1689: 'Those in the west did see such a shambles as made them think they had a Turk rather than a Christian for their King'. *Grey*, ix. 246.

[2] Sunderland to Jeffreys, 14 Sept., in *S.P. James II.*

with the booty'.[1] It was indeed a profitable investment to secure consignments of prisoners sentenced to transportation, of whom there were about 800, a traffic in which the queen and her maids of 'honour' made considerable profit; as for the unfortunate transportees, it was provided that they should be sent to the notoriously unhealthy West Indies, and that their servitude should be, not for the usual four years, but for ten. In these arrangements for disposing of the bodies of those rebels who were allowed to live, James revealed his virtues of attention to detail and economy in money matters. In order to save the expense of their maintenance, he ordered those courtiers and others, to whom allotments had been made, to take them off his hands within ten days.[2] Whatever doubt there may be regarding the economic motives of Monmouth's rebellion, there can be no doubt regarding the economic motives of those who stamped it out.

In the summer and autumn of 1685 retribution was not limited to the Bloody Assizes. Early in May Titus Oates had been tried for perjury and convicted before Jeffreys. The charges related to false evidence given about a meeting in the White Horse tavern in April 1678 whereby Whitbread, Ireland, Grove and others had been convicted and executed. Oates conducted his defence with his usual skill and assurance, alleging that the universal credence given to his stories was itself a testimony to their truth; to which it was answered that 'at the time when these things were done, the nation was in a hurry'. Jeffreys, acidly polite, may have been carefully thinking out a punishment to which death would have been preferable. This included a dozen items, the last of which—imprisonment for life—was probably intended to be superfluous, for the semi-lethal preliminaries consisted of a scourging from Aldgate to Newgate, to be followed two days later by another from Newgate to Tyburn.[3] But Jeffreys, however much we may sympathize with his intentions, had underestimated the rhinoceros-like quality of the hide concealed by the robes of a less substantial doctorate of divinity, and the upshot was that not only

[1] Ibid., 19 Sept., Jeffreys to the king.

[2] Ibid., Sunderland to Jeffreys, 14 Sept.

[3] Accounts of the two trials of Oates (8 and 9 May) will be found in the *Complete Collection of State Trials* (1730–1), vol. iv.

did Oates live, but he enjoyed a comfortable retirement after the Revolution, when he was still held in veneration by the more academic Whigs. Unfortunately his wounds, after the first scourging, were dressed by Charles Bateman, whose other offence was that he had acted as Shaftesbury's surgeon. It was not difficult to frame an indictment against him, alleging complicity in the Rye House Plot; and, on this pretext he was hanged and quartered in December 1685.[1] The same pretext was used in order to remove Henry Cornish, the Whig alderman, who had distinguished himself by opposition to the *quo warranto* proceedings against the city of London; he proved easy game for two informers Rumsey and Goodenough, and he was executed in October 1685. Another unfortunate victim was Elizabeth Gaunt.[3] She had given hospitality to one Burton, a refugee from Monmouth's army. To save his life, Burton gave evidence against his protectress, and she was burned at the stake on 23 October. Ferneley, another man unlucky enough to have given succour to Burton, was convicted and hanged on the latter's evidence.

But this melancholy sequence was interrupted in January 1686, when Henry Booth, second lord Delamere, was tried before Jeffreys as lord high steward, with a panel of selected peers. In 1683 Delamere had been arrested on a charge of complicity in the Rye House Plot, and he was on bail, in Cheshire, at the time of Monmouth's rising. He accounted for his visit to Cheshire by his desire to visit his sick child. During the period of his bail, he appears to have sat in the Lords and voted against the Bill attainting Monmouth. Jeffreys, intent on procuring a conviction, hinted that this was unfortunate for the accused, the insinuation being that such a vote, given in parliament, provided presumptive evidence of complicity in Monmouth's rebellion.[4] But the thirty peers do not seem to have shared the chancellor's standards of what constituted evidence; nor were they overawed by his bluster; moreover, they had been impressed by the obvious contradictions in the stories of the informers, so they brought in a verdict of Not Guilty. It was the first serious rebuff experienced by Jeffreys in a court of law.

[1] *State Trials*, xi. 467 sqq.
[2] Ibid. xi. 382 sqq.
[3] Ibid. xi. 410 sqq.
[4] Ibid. xi. 527.

During these months, foreign policy was engaging the king's attention almost as much as domestic policy. Louis expressed approval of James's conduct; in particular, his attendance at mass in public showed a firmness that would instil a proper fear in the hearts of his subjects.[1] Soon the king of England would be asking the pope to appoint Roman Catholic bishops, but he must be careful to exclude Jansenists. Early in April 1685 James was able to assure Barrillon that in all respects he was conducting himself in the interests of Louis, but he must have some tangible proofs of French goodwill; on his side, the ambassador assured James that Louis asked no more of his cousin than that he should do two things—restore the Roman Catholic faith in England, and securely establish his authority, these two things being inseparable.[2] As for his own motives, Louis declared that these were his personal esteem for James, and his (Louis's) devotion to the church. At a time when England was almost negligible in Europe, it is likely that Louis was speaking the truth. Meanwhile, by the end of April,[3] the half-million in Barrillon's hands was increased to about two millions, and this was apportioned as follows: 470,000 livres was kept apart for the arrears of Charles's pension; 400,000 was allocated for pensions to ministers, and the balance, about a million, was to be kept in reserve for contingencies. Louis left some discretion to his ambassador, but he insisted on the need for economy, and made it clear that the whole fund should be spent only if James was forced by his religious policy to take up arms against his subjects.[4] With so much money dangled before them, the ministers were fruitful in suggestions of how it might be spent. Sunderland proposed a definite French alliance; Rochester, with unconscious prescience, suggested a subsidy for *three* years.[5]

The rebellions of Argyll and Monmouth provided new excuses for demanding a distribution of the balance in Barrillon's hands, but Louis replied that, as these rebellions had been crushed, and as parliament had made liberal grants, there was no case for a donation. But the begging was unabated. In July the king himself, intent on securing at least a trifle, assured his French

[1] The king to Barrillon, 28 Feb.–9 Mar. 1685, in Fox, op. cit., appendix, liv.
[2] Ibid. lvii, 6–16 Apr.
[3] Ibid. lxxi.
[4] Ibid. lxi, 14–24 Apr.
[5] Ibid. lvi, 6–16 Apr.

paymaster that he had 'a French heart';[1] but Louis, anxious to see the Test and Habeas Corpus Acts abolished at once, intimated that James's gratitude to Providence for the crushing of two rebellions should be sufficient warrant for him to proceed with the establishment of the true faith in England.[2]

But, instead of turning to Providence, James and his advisers turned to the Dutch. The king disliked William of Orange; so an alliance with the States General seemed a clever means of putting these two against each other; moreover, such a move savoured, in some kind of way, of patriotism. Even more, it was an old expedient, already fully worked by Charles, for proving to Louis that a good price must be paid for royal subservience to Versailles. So a commission, of which Halifax was one, after discussion with the Dutch ambassadors, entered into a renewal of the Anglo-Dutch alliances, including that of 1677/8, whereby the late king had acquired a short and spurious reputation as an English patriot. This was signed on 7–17 August,[3] and ratified in the following October.

It failed, however, to produce the required effect, in spite of Sunderland's assurance that this renewal of Anglo-Dutch amity would mean no more to James than it had meant to Charles.[4] With his penetrating logic, Louis brushed aside this reasoning. Charles, he wrote, had allied with the Dutch at a time when he was estranged from his French cousin, and so deprived of French help; but James had renewed this alliance at a time when the relations between the two monarchs were cordial. Consequently, while Charles had acted from necessity, James was acting from choice, and so might keep his word with the Dutch.[5] To such a transcendent level had Louis raised diplomacy that the mere suspicion of good faith served as a reason for withholding a subsidy; and James seemed likely to suffer as much for his virtues as his brother had benefited by his sins. So the balance of the money was returned to France, in spite of Barrillon's assurances that it might well be employed to retain those prominent members of Charles II's parliaments

[1] Ibid. cix, 6–16 July 1685.

[2] Ibid. cxv, 16–26 July.

[3] *Dumont*, vii. 110.

[4] Fox, op. cit., appendix, cxix, 20–30 Aug.

[5] Ibid. cxx, 20–30 Aug.

who were now coaching James's House of Commons in the tactics of opposition.[1]

The upshot appears to have been that 800,000 livres was paid to James, 470,000 being in respect of arrears of Charles's pension. For the difference, 330,000, the ambassador was called to account.[2] Later in the reign, James received French money for the maintenance of a naval squadron and of troops in England; and it has been estimated[3] that the total of Louis's payments to, or on behalf of, his royal cousin, in the whole course of this reign, did not amount to as much as £125,000, a sum which should be contrasted with the total of more than £6,000,000 granted by parliament for that period. James and his two ministers, Rochester and Godolphin, were prepared to barter the independence of England for a sum little more than a sixtieth part of that granted by the national legislature. As for Sunderland, he was in a class by himself. He assured Barrillon that only by a close alliance of the two crowns could James's plans be put into effect; and of that policy he, Sunderland, was the only consistent advocate. Rochester, he claimed, was secretly in the interests of Orange. So impressed was Louis by what he heard of Sunderland that, late in November 1685, he ordered the payment to the secretary of a sum of between 20,000 and 30,000 écus, or between £5,000 and £7,500.[4]

Parliament, which had been adjourned on 2 July, resumed its sessions on 9 November when, in his speech from the throne, the king alluded to the failure of the militia in the late rebellion. What he needed was 'a good force of well-disciplined troops in constant pay'. As for the Roman Catholics in the army, he would not risk the want of them 'if there should be another rebellion to make them necessary to me'.[5] These injudicious words were probably composed by the king himself. The reaction of both Houses served to reveal a phenomenon in our older parliamentary history, never understood by the Stuarts, or their ministers; namely, that even the most stunted and clipped of legislatures might put forth roots, and show signs

[1] Fox, op. cit. cxlii, 10–20 Nov. 1685. [2] Ibid. cxxvi, 22 Oct.–1 Nov.

[3] R. H. George, 'Financial Relations between Louis XIV and James II', in *Journal of Modern History*, Sept. 1931.

[4] Fox, op. cit., appendix, cxlviii, 26 Nov.–6 Dec.

[5] *L.J.* xiv, 9 Nov. 1685.

of growth.[1] With the Lords, this was understandable, since fewer were tied to the administration by office, and they had pride in their caste and their ancient traditions; but the appearance of some measure of independence in this House of Commons is more difficult to explain; for, by all the recognized rules, it ought to have been completely subservient. Many of its members were venal, and most of them so obscure that they had never sat in parliament before; a number held offices, a greater number expected such rewards, and all of them were subject to assiduous management. Never before had a House of Commons been so carefully selected. But a few 'strays' had contrived to get in.

Among these were three old parliamentarians, sir T. Clarges, sir T. Meres, and sir E. Seymour. Of these the first was a brother-in-law of Monck, who, having started life as an apothecary, and having participated in Cromwellian rule, was afterwards distinguished as a loyalist (of Presbyterian associations) and an anti-Exclusionist. The second, sir T. Meres, had proved one of the most effective and responsible of the old Country party, and was noted for his intimate knowledge of the moods and traditions of the House. Very different in character was the third, sir Edward Seymour, who also had figured in Charles's parliaments, and had served as Speaker. Descendant of another remarkable man, the Protector Somerset, Seymour was the most arrogant member of an arrogant caste; but he had two fine qualities—courage, and an unflinching zeal for the integrity of parliamentary institutions. These three men, otherwise so contrasted, but between them so representative of English loyalty and parliamentary experience, provided a leaven in this, the most sycophantic House of Commons in our history. They could not have transformed it into a body of patriots; but, on the other hand, the voting shows that, with each day, some kind of opposition was gradually taking shape round this triumvirate, even at the risk of sacrificing office or pension. The most unpromising of material showed signs of developing into a legislature worthy of Westminster. This is why James's House of Commons is one of the most remarkable in English history.

[1] A contemporary, though summary, account of the debates will be found in *The Several Debates of the House of Commons in the Reign of the Late James II*, 1697.

It was this royal demand for an army in which Roman Catholics would have commissions that created the nucleus of an opposition. Now, there was probably not one member of the House who had any sympathy with the recently defeated rebels; nor was objection taken to a standing army altogether on the ground that it might be used to oppress Englishmen; on the contrary, most members feared that it would debauch them. But, in the course of the debates, some of the more unsuspecting legislators must have realized the remoter implications of the royal demand. On 12 November a committee of the whole House was treated to a discourse by lord Preston, showing how the unsettled state of Europe, together with the proved inadequacy of the militia justified the maintenance of an army of 14–15,000 men on a permanent footing; whereupon sir Winston Churchill, a burgess for Lyme, moved that a supply be granted 'for the army'. This was followed by an animated debate. Some members vindicated the militia; Seymour declared that he would rather pay twice for that body than half for the army; Meres tried to divert the motion into one for a grant to the navy; Clarges reminded the House how, in the Exclusion Bill debates, it had been prophesied that a popish ruler would have a popish army; others expressed a fear that the Test Act was being thrown over. The result was that the original motion, with its objectionable phrase 'for the army', was rejected by 225 to 150,[1] a clear indication of increasing disquiet.

The deletion of Churchill's candid phrase 'for the army' was followed by great difference of opinion about the amount of the grant, some proposing as much as £1,200,000, while others suggested only £200,000. At this point, sir Winston again intervened: '£200,000 is much too little. Soldiers move not without their pay. *No penny, no paternoster.*' This last phrase, even more candid than the first, may have caused the loss of the motion for the larger sum, though by only one vote.[2] On even the most dense there must have dawned some idea of James's ultimate intentions. So a compromise was adopted—£700,000—and the House also agreed to bring in a Bill for

[1] Ibid. 8–10, and *Autobiography of sir John Bramston* (Camden Society), 221–3. Also *Grey*, viii. 355 sqq.

[2] *Rome Transcripts* (*P.R.O.*), 31–39, 100 A. 18 Nov. 1685.

remodelling the militia. As well as this, the Commons sent a respectful address to the king, requesting him to give such directions that no apprehensions or jealousies would remain in the hearts of his subjects.[1] Subservience was now tempered by alarm. But, although the Commons had offered this substantial extra supply, James was enraged at these symptoms of distrust in an assembly which, after all the trouble that he and Sunderland had taken, ought to have been absolutely obedient. The royal answer to the Commons' address showed bad temper: 'I had reason to hope that the reputation God has blessed me with would have created and confirmed a greater confidence in me.'[2] It was noted that his face flushed with anger as he spoke these words.[3] Having returned to their chamber in anxious silence, the Commons then heard the bold words of John Coke, a burgess for Derby: 'We are all Englishmen, and not to be frighted out of our duty by a few high words.' He was committed to the Tower—the last instance of interference with freedom of debate in the Stuart parliaments. It was an ominous reminder of the days of Charles I.

But there was more freedom in the Lords, where the opposition was led by William Cavendish, earl of Devonshire, and Henry Compton, bishop of London. The impetuous lord Mordaunt warned his listeners that a standing army, officered by Roman Catholics, would lead to the establishment of arbitrary power; while Compton declared that, if the Test Act was abandoned, the church of England would be defenceless. It seemed, indeed, that the Upper House would press for guarantees more tangible than any offered by the king; and, now that a lead had been given them by the Lords, a change can be detected in the attitude of the Commons, for they were being coached by opposition leaders of former parliaments,[4] and it seemed possible that, like the Cavalier Parliament, this parliament would grow up. So James resolved to cut it short. He would rather sacrifice the promised £700,000 than suffer the accredited representatives of the nation to criticize his acts. Accordingly, on 20 November, he prorogued parliament, and by successive prorogations he kept it in a state of suspended

[1] *C.J.* ix, 16 Nov. 1685. [2] *L.J.* xiv, 18 Nov.
[3] *Grey*, viii, 18 Nov.
[4] Barrillon to Louis, 10–20 Nov. in Fox, op. cit. cxl.

animation until 2 July 1687, when he dissolved it. Those members of the Commons who had voted against the Court were deprived of their offices, and Compton's name was erased from the register of the privy council.

Like his paternal grandfather, James had great faith in his ability to bring others to his way of thinking. His principles of government were so obviously right and good that dissentients must be convinced. Careful coaching and propaganda would bring round nation and parliament to the royal views. For this purpose, a beginning was made with ministerial changes. Jeffreys had been appointed lord chancellor on 28 September; on 21 October Halifax was dismissed from the presidency of the Council, and his name was removed from the roll of privy councillors. This gave great satisfaction at Versailles.[1] In December Sunderland was promoted to the vacant presidency, while retaining his secretaryship of state; thereafter he was, in effect, prime minister. By this time the position of the Hydes—Henry, earl of Clarendon and Laurence, earl of Rochester—was somewhat ambiguous. As the sons of the great Clarendon, and as James's brothers-in-law, as the almost official lay exponents of Anglicanism, these two men, while still in high office, served to give some confirmation to James's declarations that he would support the church of England, though as that support became less convincing, the Hydes stood more in the way. But as their instincts of self-preservation were as strong as their Anglicanism, they were unlikely to thwart the king's designs. So Clarendon was made lord lieutenant of Ireland, to be the unwilling tool of James's policy in that country, his powers being actually inferior to those of the commander of the army, Tyrconnel. Clarendon's rule in Ireland was inevitably one of pusillanimity and, for a churchman, of shame.

His brother, the lord high treasurer, also continued to hold office, but with a different kind of shame. His accounts were such as to suggest peculation; and at one time there was talk of sending him to the Tower. Now, in his genuine desire to preserve James for the church of England, he embarked on

[1] Louis to Barrillon, 27 Oct.–6 Nov. and 6–16 Nov. in Fox, op. cit. cxxix and cxxxiii. Louis thought that as Halifax was a man 'of no religion' he could not be trusted to maintain the royal authority. His removal was 'fort avantageux à mes intêrets'.

a scheme such as could have entered into the mind only of one brought up in the court of Charles II. Kate Sedley, the prospective mistress-in-chief, continued to haunt Whitehall; so the old relations with James were restored; and in January 1686 she was created countess of Dorchester, with an extra £5,000 a year. Rochester and his wife now planned to give her some kind of official position, comparable to the metropolitan status which had been enjoyed by the duchess of Portsmouth, but with an important difference, for the sultana-elect was a Protestant and a woman of intelligence. In this desperate way, therefore, it was hoped to save the Lord's Anointed from the Whore of Rome. Opposing the scheme was the Catholic party, headed by Sunderland, Tyrconnel, and Dover, who dreaded the danger of this royal contamination with heresy.[1] But both parties had reckoned without Mary of Modena. While she stormed, father Petre interceded, and the king scourged himself in penitence for what some would regard as his most pardonable failing. So eventually the lady was dispatched first to Flanders, then to Ireland, to renew relations with her royal lover in August 1686, but this time in secret. Although this incident served to discredit Rochester, James was still unwilling to part with him; nor did he despair of converting him. So, early in 1686, he ordered the publication of the two papers in which, it was alleged, Charles II had made clear his reasons for conversion to Rome, and copies of these somewhat insipid compositions were eagerly pressed on all at Court. Rochester professed willingness to know more about the points in controversy, and later in the year he sacrificed his Anglicanism so far as to serve in the Ecclesiastical Commission. But his position was being steadily undermined.

Throughout the winter of 1685–6 Englishmen were given an opportunity of learning at first hand the implications of religion as understood by James's French cousin. In October 1685 Louis revoked the Edict of Nantes; and, in a sermon afterwards available in an English translation, the bishop of Valence called on the French monarch to aid his English ally in the extirpation of heresy. The revocation was well timed. Europe was in one of its short periods of peace; for years, the privileges of French Protestants had been steadily withdrawn, and at

[1] *H.M.C. Rep.* xii, app. pt. 5. *MSS. of the duke of Portland*, 103.

Versailles it seemed reasonable to suppose that a similar measure of proscription would follow the annulment of the Test Act in England. Louis's only complaint of James was that he did not proceed fast enough in the restoration of the true faith.[1] But meanwhile the revocation had not worked quite as intended, and French ministers were dismayed by the enormous exodus of population, skill, and capital. So, late in 1685 Louis dispatched to England a special envoy, François d'Usson de Bonrepaux, who was instructed to find out about English arsenals and fleets, and also to send back as many Huguenots as possible.[2] In this latter task the envoy signally failed. But he proved to be much more perspicacious than his senior colleague Barrillon, who was one of that party which would have pressed James to extremes.

At this point one might well ask: what were the influences brought to bear on the English monarch? There was first a moderate Catholic party, led by William Herbert, marquis of Powys, and John, lord Belasyse, both of whom had suffered from Oates's accusations, and were held in high esteem by James. They would naturally have liked to see their co-religionaries freed from disabilities, but on the other hand they dreaded lest extreme measures might do their cause more harm than good. In this attitude they had the support of the pope, Innocent XI, and the Spanish ambassador, don Pedro de Ronquillo. Among the English bishops were two who counselled moderation. One of these was Thomas Ken, bishop of Bath and Wells, who, in his humanity, had pleaded for some mitigation in the excesses of the Bloody Assizes, and in his sermons before the Court had had the courage to warn his sovereign against the dangers of popery. Another prelate had counselled similar moderation, namely, Nathaniel, lord Crew, bishop of Durham. In May 1686 Crew sent a strong letter to James advising him to discontinue his romanizing policy, and to call a free parliament; at the same time he declined nomination to the long-vacant archbishopric of York.[3] In a different category were

[1] In March 1689 Louis was reported to have attributed James's downfall to the fact that he had been too merciful to the Protestants. *H.M.C. Rep.* vii, app. 758 *MSS. of marquis of Ormonde.*

[2] *Instructions Données* (*Angleterre*), ed. J. J. Jusserand, ii. 325 sqq.

[3] *S.P. James II*, May 1686 (placed at the end of the papers for May).

those in high office who preserved some neutrality in religious matters; namely, Godolphin,[1] from instinct, and Jeffreys, from self-interest.

Ranged against these moderates was a party of irresponsibles and adventurers. These included Roger Palmer, earl of Castlemaine, compliant husband of one of Charles II's mistresses, whom James rashly appointed envoy to one of the European courts where a measure of personal decency was insisted on, namely, the Vatican. There was also Henry Jermyn, lord Dover, a Caroline rake, now a Jacobean devotee; also Richard Talbot, earl of Tyrconnel, commander of the troops in Ireland, 'lying Dick Talbot', the loudest blusterer of a noisy age. More respectable, and probably more effectual, was the Jesuit John Warner, who acted as the royal confessor, and afterwards accompanied the king to France.

It is probable that the Jesuits, as distinct from the Roman Catholics—and at that time the distinction was a very substantial one—may have had considerable influence on James II. This was exercised mainly through one of their fathers, Edward Petre, clerk of the Royal Closet, whose activities were so recondite that he has escaped inclusion in the *Dictionary of National Biography*. Another indirect tribute to his reticence is that the letters printed over his name are almost certainly forgeries. On the other hand, it is possible that he was an unwilling tool in the hands of a society which demanded absolute obedience from all its members.[2] Or, as with some priests, his head may have been turned by such close proximity to the royal presence; and so he may have acquiesced in measures which, in his heart, he knew to be wrong. But it is important that, for this Jesuit influence, there was in existence a textbook, compiled in 1596 by the English Jesuit Robert Parsons, entitled, 'A memorial for the Reformation of England . . .', easily available in manuscript for James and Petre, and afterwards published (in 1690). The parallelism between the recommendations of the memorial and the policy of James is very striking. Thus, parliament was to be retained, but with safeguards to ensure the supremacy of Catholicism. The members of the Commons must, according to Parsons, be 'regulated', and their business was to be determined

[1] For a recent biography of Godolphin, see that by sir Tresham Lever.
[2] This is suggested in E. L. Taunton, *The Jesuits in England*, 444 sqq.

in advance by a committee similar to the Scottish Lords of the Articles.[1] It was well known that James regarded queen Elizabeth as an impostor, so he may have welcomed Parsons's suggestion that the proceedings of her reign should be investigated by parliament wiith a vew to their annulment. But James did not succeed in reaching so far as some of the other recommendations in this outspoken book; such, for instance, as that the knights of the shire should be nominated by the (Roman Catholic) bishop of the diocese, and that an Inquisition should be established, disguised under the title of 'council of Reformation'.[2] There was nothing in this book about using compulsion, but the author's views on this point may be deduced from the fact that he had constantly incited Philip of Spain to attack England, and restore the true faith by force. Here indeed was the reign of Elizabeth in reverse. A king was being encouraged to effect a revolution which a queen had succeeded in thwarting.

Petre was one of the most influential members of a shadow Roman Catholic cabinet which met regularly in Sunderland's lodgings. But among the Roman Catholics generally there was a division of opinion in regard to Louis XIV, and the amount of help that should be expected from him. Of those who were opposed to Louis, the leaders were Mary of Modena and the papal nuncio, D'Adda. The queen, ignorant and somewhat contemptuous of her adopted country, showed a haughtiness and even arrogance which appears to have overawed her consort. She was not a woman likely to counsel compromise or moderation.

Such were the direct, personal influences. But there was another of a more impersonal kind. In the time of Charles I a large body of the church of England had adopted the doctrine of Passive Obedience or Non Resistance, and the execution of the king had provided this cult with a martyr and saint. Now, it was a cardinal principle of this new divine right theory[3] that the king *can* do wrong; and that, as often as not, he is doing wrong; of this, there was abundant evidence in the Old Testament, the textbook of the new creed. The church had always regarded the king as sacred, but not necessarily as good; for, in respect of his office, a man may be very holy, but, in

[1] *The Jesuits' Memorial for the Intended Reformation of England*, ch. 10.

[2] Ibid. ch. 7.

[3] *Infra*, 506–7.

respect of his private life, very wicked. The personal piety of Charles I made the sin of his murderers all the blacker, and elevated the cult into a religion, the main tenet of which was that tyrants, provided they were hereditary and anointed, must be obeyed, even to the point of martyrdom. Resistance to the lawful king is both wicked and sacrilegious; obedience is due to his lawful commands, and submission to those that are otherwise. Criticism of the royal acts is heresy; rebellion is parricide. Such were the commonplaces of many hundreds of sermons preached in later Stuart times, all part of the legacy of that never-to-be-forgotten, never-forgiven crime, the execution of Charles I. Can it be wondered at that the serious-minded James drew the conclusion that, to whatever lengths he might go, he could depend on the absolute submission of the church of England?[1]

But the churchmen were not so foolish as James assumed; nor had they any need to provide a martyr from among themselves, since Charles had already died on their behalf. So, in Charles II's reign, royal support of the church of England, and limitation of persecution to Roman Catholics and Dissenters, proved that the doctrine of Non Resistance was of divine institution; but it was otherwise in the reign of his successor, when it appeared that the church might be endangered, and might even share the fate of Nonconformists. Almost at the first suspicion of this danger, the doctrine was thrown over; and that too, not by obscure clerics, but by seven bishops. Their protest against being required to order their subordinates to read the Declaration of Indulgence made nonsense of the doctrine of Non Resistance, and helped as much as anything to effect the Revolution.

With such encouragement and such advisers, James, in the spring of 1686, began a policy of infiltration. The judges were first consulted on the question whether the king could dispense with laws relating to religious disabilities; four of them were dismissed because they refused to acknowledge any such right, and the same fate befell the solicitor general, Heneage Finch. The attorney general, sir Robert Sawyer, was then ordered to

[1] Cf. the admission in the *Life of James II* (ed. Clarke), ii. 168: 'His Majesty wanted not abetters amongst the Church of England partie themselves.'

issue warrants authorizing Roman Catholics to hold benefices. He refused, but the new solicitor general, Thomas Powys, complied; and before the summer was ended the results of this relaxation were in evidence, for Obadiah Walker was celebrating mass in University College, Oxford, of which he was Master; and three Roman Catholics, or crypto-Catholics, John Massey, Samuel Parker, and Thomas Cartwright were given preferment, the first to the deanery of Christ Church, the second to the bishopric of Oxford, and the third to that of Chester. Sir Edward Hales, a convert, had served as a colonel without taking the oaths. He was given a dispensation by letters patent. By a collusive action he was convicted at Rochester assizes in March, whereupon he pleaded the dispensation, and the case came before King's Bench in June, when eleven of the twelve judges upheld the dispensing power, the single dissentient, baron Street, probably acting on orders from the Court. In announcing the judgement lord chief justice Herbert made this pronouncement on political theory: 'the laws of England', he said, 'are the king's laws. Therefore it is an inseparable prerogative in the kings of England to dispense with penal laws in particular cases and upon particular necessary reasons, of which the king himself is sole judge.' So the bench, purged of dissentients, must be numbered with these forces which urged on the last Stuart king.

The State Papers contain ample evidence of the unsparing use made by James of this power to retain in office or appoint to office persons of the Roman Catholic faith; and it may be conjectured that, had he been allowed to continue this policy, the majority of places in the church, the army, the navy, the universities, and the administration would have been filled by Roman Catholics. Another form of penetration was seen in the large number of new religious establishments set up in London, to the horror of the populace. The Franciscans had their headquarters in Lincoln's Inn Fields; the Carmelites had their convent in the city; the Benedictines were established in St. James's Palace; in the Savoy the Jesuits had a church and a school. From the king's London printing press, under the direction of Henry Hills, there poured forth a mass of Roman Catholic literature, which provided good game for such controversialists as Tillotson, Tenison, Stillingfleet, Sherlock, Wake, and Atterbury. In Oxford Obadiah Walker busied himself with the printing and publishing of books advocating the claims of his faith; in Holyrood a popish press supplied Scots Calvinists with material for refutation.

So deep was the attachment of the nation to monarchy, so averse were men to a change of dynasty, that they might have tolerated such a policy for years, since propaganda and proselytism may be actively pursued among forbearing Englishmen without necessarily causing upheaval. But it was a cardinal element in the mentality of James and his extremist advisers that force must intervene when persuasion failed. Had not this been signally demonstrated by Louis in the revocation of the Edict of Nantes? Now James was an admirer of Louis and of all things French, particularly the well-disciplined, highly organized army which Louvois had done so much to create; the same results, reasoned James, could be obtained in England. Accordingly, in June 1686 about 13,000 regular troops went into camp on Hounslow Heath, a site obviously chosen with an eye on the capital. But the fears of anxious Londoners must have been dispelled by visits to the camp, for they could see how unmartial was the bearing of many of the men. Samples are provided by summary descriptions in the *London Gazette* of those who deserted: 'a middle-aged man, by trade a shoemaker', 'a short thick man, age near 60', 'a short fellow, wears a periwig, his face all spotted with gunpowder', and 'a tall, well-set man, red-faced, a large red nose and a wide mouth, talks much, being a bricklayer by trade'.[1] Possibly the last-mentioned personage figured prominently in the debating societies which (with drinking and card playing) helped to dispel the monotony of camp life; indeed Barrillon, on visiting the troops, was amazed to find that the soldiers, in discussing politics, took sides, as if they were in the House of Commons. Every common soldier on Hounslow Heath prided himself on the fact that, in contrast with the Frenchman, he had the palladium of Magna Carta over his head; and, when the time came for action, most of them showed that they were citizens first, and soldiers afterwards. In this respect, their dependability contrasted with that of a pliant bench and an unyielding block.

[1] *London Gazette*, 2244, 2385, 2395, and 2402, May–November 1687.

VI

JAMES AND SUNDERLAND, 1686–7

A COMMENTARY on the first year of James's rule in England was provided by proceedings in Ireland and Scotland. In Ireland, the real ruler was Tyrconnel, who divided his time between London and Dublin. He made no secret of his desire to see the Act of Settlement annulled, and the Celtic landowners restored to their estates. Nor, outside Ulster, did Tyrconnel have to fear much opposition, since the established Protestant church of Ireland was a somewhat effete institution, and the Irish Parliament, though consisting almost entirely of Protestants, was not in session; in any case, its activities could easily be circumscribed. So the country lent itself readily to remodelling. Catholics were intruded into municipal corporations, into the bench, and, most of all, into the army. In this way, James would have at his disposal a considerable force, officered mainly by Roman Catholics, to supplement the motley array on Hounslow Heath. Meanwhile the position of lord lieutenant, Clarendon, was becoming every day more untenable. Though he and his brother clung desperately to office, they were being forced out by Sunderland and Tyrconnel. Rochester was dismissed from his lord treasurership and Clarendon from his viceroyalty in January 1687. That the removal of two such Anglicans should have caused intense dismay in England is proof of how even the flimsiest and most formal type of Protestantism was cherished by Englishmen as providing some sort of guarantee in the entourage of James. Tyrconnel succeeded Clarendon as lord deputy, and he now embarked on measures intended to ensure that, when a parliament was summoned, it would revoke the Act of Settlement, and legalize the dispossession of Protestant landlords.

In Scotland the Covenanters had recently (1679) been defeated at the battle of Bothwell Brig, a defeat followed (in spite of Monmouth) by a policy of revenge similar to that which, in England, succeeded the Rye House Plot, except that the victims included none of notable rank. That persecution merely hardened the temper of the lowland Scots is shown by the emergence in 1680 of an uncompromising sect, known from the name of one of its founders as the Cameronians, which, in the Declaration of Sanquhar (June 1680), renounced Charles as king. These new challengers acquitted themselves creditably in the fight with royalist troops at Airds Moss, in the same year, and thereafter they were in open arms against the government; their 'Apologetical Declaration' of 1684 was a warning that every agent of government who sought their lives in court of justice or in the field would do so at his own peril. On its side the government possessed in the lord advocate, sir George Mackenzie, a prosecutor not unworthy of comparison with Jeffreys, and in the chancellor, James Drummond, fourth earl of Perth, a worthy successor of Lauderdale. Indeed, Scotland provided a suitable field for Stuart experiment, a fact which may have been in the mind of the chancellor when he wrote to James:[1] 'Scotland is not England. Measures need not be too nicely kept with this people.' What that meant was clearly elucidated by the inscriptions on the muzzles of cannon supplied to the royal troops, cannon intended for use, not against foreigners, but against Scotsmen. These inscriptions, in letters so large as to detract from the appearance of the weapons, were:[2] *Haec est Vox Regia* and *Non Sine Fulmine Regnat*, principles which, when rammed home by explosive, were more convincing than a whole library of books on political science.

James VII of Scotland was proclaimed king in Edinburgh on 10 February 1685. He omitted to take the coronation oath obliging the kings of Scotland to defend the Protestant religion. The Scottish parliament met on 23 April, with William Douglas, duke of Queensberry, a moderate and a kinsman of Rochester, as commissioner to the Estates. Closely linked with Perth, the chancellor, were his younger brother lord Melfort and the earl of Moray. Just as in England Sunderland was scheming to remove Rochester, so the two Drummond brothers were actively engaged in discrediting Queensberry. Already James had communicated to the Lords of the Articles a list of the legislative measures which he wished the Estates to pass,[3] and his wishes were complied with. Of these measures, one was for imposing

[1] *H.M.C. Rep. Laing MSS.* i. 443.
[2] *H.M.C. Rep.* x. app. pt. 1, 135.
[3] *S.P. James II*, 28 Mar. 1685.

the penalty of death on all attending conventicles, and on all who harboured such persons; another provided that, in trials for treason, witnesses refusing to give evidence should themselves be held guilty of treason. These were accompanied by an Act absolving officers, civil and military, and everyone acting under His Majesty's commission, from all suits and complaints for what they had done in the royal service, as if they had a full pardon under the great seal. Most inclusive of all was an Act placing the lives and fortunes of all His Majesty's subjects in Scotland, between the ages of sixteen and sixty, at the absolute disposal of the crown.[1] All these laws were passed at James's request. As a code, they constituted the Nuremberg decrees of seventeenth-century Scotland; and it is not unfair to regard them as a hint of what James may have ultimately intended for England.

Two classes of Protestant Nonconformists were affected by these measures—those who failed to attend the parish, i.e. the episcopal, church, or who frequented conventicles; and the more extreme body, the Cameronians, who held by the Apologetical Declaration. The first, the larger class, when convicted in the courts, might be fined or transported; the second class was hanged or shot, after 'trial' by a military court. An efficient agent in this policy had for some time been available in John Graham of Claverhouse, afterwards viscount Dundee, of the same noble house as the great Montrose. He had played an active part in the removal of Monmouth from the Scottish command because of the duke's mercy to the defeated rebels after the battle of Bothwell Brig; and as sheriff of Dumfries and Annandale he inaugurated in 1679 a more active policy of repression. The heritors were made responsible for the fines imposed on their tenants, and in October 1684 Claverhouse reported that all his prisons were full, mostly of small heritors.[2] To the leaders no mercy was shown; 'that great villain McLorg, smith at Minnegaff. I am resolved to hang him, for it is necessary I make some example of severity, lest rebellion be thought cheap here.'[3] But Claverhouse was intelligent enough to realize

[1] These Acts will be found in *Acts of the Parliaments of Scotland* (1820), viii. 460–84. The above acts are numbered 31, 29, 41, and 2 respectively.

[2] *H.M.C. Rep.* xiii, app. pt. 8 (Claverhouse correspondence), 259.

[3] Ibid. 270.

that such measures were futile, and that without mass extermination Calvinism would not be eradicated from the south of Scotland.[1] Such was Scotland's 'killing time', when Claverhouse with his dragoons established a régime even worse than that which prevailed in Protestant France.

Continued resistance served to increase the severity and variety of the measures adopted. In August 1684 a new device was introduced into the torture chamber—the thumbscrew, imported by generals Dalzell and Drummond from Muscovy. This was considered superior to the 'boot', which did not serve its purpose adequately when applied to people with thin legs.[2] In May 1685 Dunottar Castle was taken over in order to supplement the accommodation provided by the Bass Rock; but even in the former so many prisoners had to be accommodated that in one vault 110 men and women were confined in semi-darkness.[3] For taking part in anti-Catholic demonstrations death was the penalty; even for expressing approval of such disturbances the same punishment was imposed, as on an Edinburgh fencing master[4] in February 1686. This man was offered his life on condition of giving perjured evidence implicating Queensberry in such disturbances, but he refused. No class was spared. In June 1686 James removed Robert Bruce from the bishopric of Dunkeld for no other reason than that he was opposed to the establishment of Roman Catholicism, and the same course was adopted with Alexander Cairncross, archbishop of Glasgow.

James's policy in Scotland was indeed well served by the two Drummond brothers, Perth and Melfort, whose sincerity of religious profession may be deduced from the fact that both had been 'converted' simultaneously by reading the papers extracted by James from his brother's box. Their administration was characterized by a dense and mechanical stupidity in prosecuting persons who, on any ordinary canons of justice, were innocent. Thus, a Mr. Hugh Maxwell, like many of his fellow Scots, was in the habit of jotting down notes on theo-

[1] *H.M.C. Rep.* xiii, app. pt. 8, 268.

[2] Sir John Lauder of Fountainhall, *Decisions of the Lords of Council and Session* (1678–1712), i. 300.

[3] *Register of the Privy Council of Scotland*, xi. 70, 18 June 1685.

[4] Sir John Lauder, op. cit. i. 407, 26 Feb. 1686.

logical points. Unfortunately, he used shorthand. As it was indecipherable by his accusers, it must be seditious, so he remained in prison for seventeen months until a committee of the privy council discovered that the notes were harmless. In another case, pipers had to give evidence in court that *The Deil stick the Minister* was the name of a tune, not a slander on the episcopalian clergy.[1]

The second session of James's Scottish parliament opened on 29 April 1686. Queensberry, who had refused to change his religion, was removed and his commissionership was given to Melfort. In return for a promise of free trade with England, James asked for an Act removing all disabilities on Roman Catholics in Scotland. This caused a division of opinion; some, like the duke of Hamilton, proposing that, if such indulgence were granted, it should be extended to Presbyterians also; while others, including a number of episcopal clergy, such as T. Burnet of Aberdeen, maintained that the king might abrogate any laws.[2] But by this time, the beginning of the second year of James's rule in Scotland, many Protestants in the Estates were taking alarm, and it was clear that they would be less compliant than they had been in the year before.

Various devices were used in order to obtain the Act. Office holders were turned out, and the sessions were prolonged so as to wear out the poorer lairds and burgesses. Impatient at this delay the king decided to act through the privy council, which had powers of legislation comparable with those of the Estates. So in a letter of August 1686 he required the Council to annul the laws against Roman Catholics, and to set apart the royal chapel at Holyrood for their exclusive use. As the privy council showed some unwillingness to comply, a number of Protestant members were removed, and their places were taken by Catholics. Faced with this unwillingness on the part of both Estates and privy council, James resorted to his prerogative. In a proclamation[3] of 12 February 1687 complete toleration was granted to Roman Catholics, and they were declared admissible to office. In order to promote this, James deemed it expedient to link the Presbyterians with the concession, but they were allowed to worship only in private, and the death penalty still

[1] Sir John Lauder, op. cit. i. 157. [2] Ibid. 415, 419.
[3] *Steele*, ii. 2684.

remained for those who expressed 'seditious' opinions at conventicles. Even thus, the relaxation was a relief after years of persecution, and Scottish Protestantism could now gather its forces for the Revolution so close at hand.

By the summer of 1686 it had thus been made clear to James that the legislatures of England and Scotland, the most subservient bodies in the history of Great Britain, were unprepared to go the whole way in the king's designs. But he was financially independent of parliaments, and in both countries he had already gone far in his policy of infiltration, which, with the backing of an army, would eventually enable him to emulate the methods of Louis XIV. In June 1686 Londoners had seen for themselves the first unfolding of his intentions in the establishment of the camp on Hounslow Heath; in the next month there was a further development when the Ecclesiastical Commission was set up. Such a project had been in the king's mind for some time, and an event of the early summer of 1686 may have decided him. In May, John Sharp, rector of St. Giles-in-the-Fields, preached two sermons intended to refute the more extreme claims of Romanist theologians, sermons for the benefit of parishioners disturbed by the intensive Roman Catholic propaganda being conducted around them. There was nothing in the sermons in any way reflecting on the king, but on 14 June Compton was ordered to suspend the rector. Compton refused.

This was the first challenge to James's policy, and the challenge was accepted. On 15 July James instituted a body of Ecclesiastical Commissioners to whom power was given to exercise all manner of jurisdiction in all cases touching any spiritual or ecclesiastical matter, and to reform and correct all abuses and contempts in order that the spiritual and ecclesiastical laws might be reformed or amended. Every ecclesiastical person of whatever degree might be summoned before the Commission, and might be suspended or deprived. The universities and colleges, with all collegiate churches and schools, were expressly included within the scope of the Commission, and it was declared that the statutes of these bodies might be amended, or new ones imposed. The Commission, headed by chancellor Jeffreys, included archbishop Sancroft (for a time), Crew, bishop of Durham, Sprat, bishop of Rochester, lord president

Sunderland, lord chief justice Herbert, and lord treasurer Rochester. Any three might act, but Jeffreys must always be one.[1]

These clauses have been rehearsed because they make it clear that the object of James's Commission was to exercise visitatorial jurisdiction over ecclesiastical or semi-ecclesiastical persons and institutions. The word 'court' is not even mentioned in the instrument creating the Commission; moreover, the commissioners never acted as a court, for they neither fined nor imprisoned; nor did they summon before them any but the personages, many of them exalted personages, for whom the visitatorial jurisdiction was designed. This tribunal was first described as the 'Court of High Commission' in the Bill of Rights, but there was nothing, either in its institution or its proceedings to warrant such a term.

If only in justice to James, and because some important matters are concerned, it is necessary to examine this matter more closely. Macaulay, who referred to this commission as a 'court', declared with emphasis that its institution was illegal; a view which has been generally adopted by serious historians. At first sight, Macaulay's arguments seem conclusive. The early Stuart Court of High Commission, acting on what was afterwards believed to be a misinterpretation of clause 18 of the Elizabethan Act of Supremacy, had fined and imprisoned many humble and secular persons, without having any legislative sanction to act as a court at all. Accordingly, in 1641, the Long Parliament abolished it,[2] on the ground that it was exercising an ecclesiastical jurisdiction of a type totally different from that which had been restored by the Act of Supremacy; and, to make assurance doubly sure, the essential clause of the statute was also annulled. Then came the Cavalier Parliament which restored[3] the jurisdiction of the church courts (this had been abolished by the Act of 1641), but reaffirmed the abolition of the old Court of High Commission, as well as of the clause on which its powers appear to have been based. This Act of Charles II, however, enacted that nothing therein contained was to diminish or abridge the royal supremacy in

[1] The original of James's first commission will be found enrolled in Chancery (*P.R.O.* C. 66. 3286).

[2] 16 Car. I, c. 11.

[3] 13 Car. II, c. 12.

ecclesiastical matters; in other words, except so far as concerned the Court, the powers conferred on the crown by the Act of Supremacy remained intact. Meanwhile, the position was that two parliaments so diverse as the Long Parliament of Charles I and the Cavalier Parliament of Charles II had abolished the Court of High Commission and that part of the statute on which its powers were presumed to rest. So in James II's reign, nothing could be more certain than that a revival of this old and arbitrary court was illegal.

But the matter is not so simple as this; and the point is important because the later Stuarts, who seldom violated the law outright, were working in a vast, marginal domain, where it was by no means certain what was law and what was not. It can even be argued that James was quite within his rights. This claim rests on three things: the distinction between a commission and a court; the limitation of a commission's power to a certain class of person, usually a highly placed person; and the difference in the kind of penalty imposed. As regards the first, it has already been seen that James's Commission was never a 'court'; as regards the second, whereas the Court of High Commission had dealt mainly with laymen, mostly humble men, James's Commission was concerned solely with persons of ecclesiastical or semi-ecclesiastical status, including such personages as the aristocratic bishop of London and the vice-chancellor and senate of the university of Cambridge; in regard to the third point, the old Court had locked people in, whereas James's Commission, by suspension and deprivation, merely locked them out. Accordingly, there is reason to think that a tribunal such as James's was not in the minds of either of the two legislatures which had abolished the old Court of High Commission. But a more positive argument can be adduced. A clause of the Elizabethan statute, after reciting the repeal of everything relating to papal jurisdiction in England, enacted that all visitatorial power over the ecclesiastical state and persons was now vested in the crown. This has never been repealed, and its confirmation was implied in the clause of the Act of the Cavalier Parliament which affirmed that the king's supremacy in ecclesiastical matters was unabridged. Indeed, this old visitatorial power is still exercised over universities and colleges, in some cases by the sovereign, in others by bishops, or laymen or committees; but today, its exercise is safeguarded by the right of appeal to King's Bench.

This exercise of visitatorial jurisdiction was closely connected with the use of the dispensing power, in both of which functions of the prerogative James had the backing of law and tradition. Here indeed we have one of the medieval survivals; but survivals have a habit of gradually dissociating themselves from their surroundings; and this one, which in the sixteenth century might have seemed normal, appeared sinister in the late seventeenth. It all arose from two characteristics of the medieval world—pious insistence on elaborate rules, and never-failing ingenuity in evading them. In this art, the universities and colleges naturally gave a lead; founders prescribed the regulations, beneficiaries spent much time and thought in circumventing them. Henry VIII usurped and even exceeded the dispensatory and visitatorial powers which the papacy had exercised; indeed, in his reign, the universities held by a very precarious tenure, and the wonder is that their lands were not confiscated. A succession of royal commissions served to emphasize the dependence of academic bodies on the crown, and it was natural for the sovereign to require these bodies to dispense with their statutes in favour of royal nominees; for, after all, these societies were not learned institutions as we understand the term today, but charitable trusts, in the disposition of which the crown might make an overriding claim. So James's royal predecessors constantly exercised this right,[1] and in Charles II's reign so many royal nominees were intruded that the universities, particularly Oxford, became institutions, not so much for the advancement of religion and learning, as for the reception of royal charity boys who could not conveniently be provided for otherwise. But as these presentees either conformed to the church of England or took the oaths prescribed by the universities and colleges, the system had worked smoothly, and the supreme power of the crown in these matters remained unquestioned.

Why then did James's exercise of this power cause such disquiet and opposition? Because what may be acquiesced in so long as it is haphazard and intermittent, may be resisted

[1] For this see E. F. Churchill, 'The Dispensing Power in Ecclesiastical Causes', in *Law Quarterly Review*, xxxviii (1922), 297 sqq.

when it becomes constant and purposeful. James, in contrast with his predecessors, was obviously working on a definite policy. His nominees were even more disreputable than their predecessors, but that did not matter, since the Stuarts were almost expected to have a preference for such persons; what did matter was that they were all Roman Catholics. Now, there was no Act of Parliament invalidating the Dispensing Power, though in 1673 the Commons had succeeded in persuading Charles to withdraw his Declaration of Indulgence; and as for the visitatorial power, that was authorized by clause 17 of the Elizabethan Act of Supremacy. With the help of these two weapons of the prerogative, the universities and colleges, like all other corporate bodies, would be brought within the absolute control of the crown; and so, as in a modern totalitarian state, every person and institution would be subject to this personal prerogative, however capricious. James proposed to strain a legal right, with the ultimate design of substituting Catholic for Protestant among the ruling classes, a design which, however pious or lawful, was clearly impolitic and dangerous. Such an intention had already been enunciated, though not yet fully applied, in Scotland. At the king's hand was Jeffreys, who had just enough law to assure his master that he was right, but neither enough courage nor common sense to suggest that he might be wrong.

This legality of institution is, of course, a very different matter from the justice of the Commission's proceedings; indeed, the mere fact that Jeffreys had always to be in attendance ensured that the most elementary principles of justice would be violated. The proceedings against Compton began on 4 August 1686; and, at the adjourned session on 23 August, the bishop claimed to be tried by his metropolitan and suffragans. This being rejected, it was pleaded on his behalf by counsel that he had not disobeyed the king, because on receiving the royal mandate, he had advised Sharp to desist from preaching. To suspend him would have been unlawful, and no man can be required to do an unlawful act. On 6 September sentence of suspension on the bishop of London was pronounced by the commissioners.[1] This was the first time James had challenged the church of England, hitherto the strongest support of his dynasty. In past

[1] An account of the proceedings will be found in *State Trials*, xi. 1123–65.

conflicts between church and state, the churchman had usually shown himself more than a match for the layman, a fact which was soon to find one more illustration, for Compton was to prove the most astute and effective of those who opposed James.

It was James's fate to be influenced by men who, like Sunderland, were very clever or, like Father Petre, very rash. In a different category was William Penn, the Quaker, the oddest person in the royal entourage. His father, the admiral, had been the king's intimate friend; and it was in return for a loan of £16,000 that the younger Penn had in 1681 been given proprietary rights over the territory known as Pennsylvania. An ardent believer in toleration, Penn, who had many interviews with James after his accession, was optimistic or dense enough to believe that his sovereign was at heart clement and tolerant. Such credulity is often found among men who otherwise are unusually astute; it is possible also that Penn saw James at too close quarters, and that their personal relations, amounting almost to those of guardian and ward, precluded a more just estimate by the younger man. Another factor influenced their relationship. Of all the sects the Quakers had been the most severely persecuted, and alone of all the Protestant sects they could be absolved from any part in the execution of Charles I. James, one of a hated minority, had enough imagination to sympathize with those under a similar disability; and from idealist Penn he heard much discourse about toleration for all men. So in March 1686 a royal proclamation[1] of general pardon led to the release of all who were in prison for conscience' sake, and in this way about 1,200 Quakers obtained their liberty. Up to this point, Penn's influence on James was good.

It is possible that Penn's influence may also be seen in the first Declaration of Indulgence,[2] which James issued on 4 April 1687. The preamble asserted: 'we cannot but heartily wish . . . that all the people of our dominions were members of the Catholic church'; and, as in the Scottish proclamation of the preceding February, emphasis was laid on the right of the sovereign to the services of his subjects, irrespective of their creed. The Declaration suspended all penal laws in matters ecclesiastical, and neither the Test Acts nor the oaths of allegiance and supremacy were thenceforth to be applied to

[1] *Steele*, i. 3828, 10 Mar. 1687.

[2] Ibid. 3843.

office holders. The document concluded with an expression of the hope that parliament, at its meeting in the following December, would approve of the measure. Here was something more than dispensing with the penal laws in particular cases, for all these laws were now suspended at one stroke.

The Declaration was no more than an incident in the campaign now being conducted to win over the Dissenters, and thenceforth James preached toleration—it was good for trade, it enabled him to secure the services of subjects who otherwise would be disqualified, and it would end the old futile attempts to obtain uniformity by force. So Baxter was released from prison to which he had been consigned by Jeffreys; prominent Nonconformists, such as William Kiffen, were personally solicited by the king, and even Bunyan was named as one who might promote the cause. Never was James more assiduous in this courting of men whom he had always declared to be rebels and regicides. In truth, a new plant had sprung up in the night, but those for whom its fruits were promised were naturally anxious about the roots; moreover, the Indulgence was dependent on confirmation by parliament, and in the past parliament had not favoured Stuart attempts at toleration. But it was the giver even more than the gift that excited suspicion. Was this apparently enlightened step a move in the plan to establish popery? These misgivings were clearly expressed in a short pamphlet, the *Letter to a Dissenter* by Halifax, the greatest master in that age of trenchant prose and solemn irony. This new alliance between liberty and infallibility, he wrote, was a bringing together of 'the two most contrary things that are in the world'. The church of Rome, he claimed, did not merely dislike liberty, but by its principles was incapable of offering it. 'You are therefore to be hugged now only that you may be the better squeezed at another time.' The skill of Rome, he declared, was not in applying plaisters, but in cutting off limbs: 'she is the worst at healing of any that ever pretended to it'. The many who read Halifax's pamphlet[1] had good reason to fear the truth of these words. So the Dissenters were advised by Halifax to wait until 'the next probable Revolution'.

Nevertheless, many of us today may hesitate before accepting Halifax's opinion, and may feel that, after all, James was

[1] It will be found in *Halifax*, ii. 367.

freely offering a priceless boon to his subjects. It may even be argued (as it has been argued) that he was far in advance of his time. But this attitude ignores the fact that toleration is something positive, not negative. It consists not merely in allowing freedom of worship, but in opening place and office in the state to all persons, irrespective of their faith. Already James had made it clear that his object was to fill as many places as possible with Roman Catholics; a few more years of this policy would have created an England wherein Protestants were no longer among the governing classes. They would still, it is true, be able to exercise their religion, but they would be helots. And even that religious freedom would soon become precarious because James, urged on by priests, in command of an army officered by Catholics, and having behind him the moral, the financial, and the military support of Louis, would be faced with a great temptation—the temptation to follow the example of his French cousin, and destroy heresy by force. From what we know of the king's passionate religious fervour, and of the methods then in vogue for giving expression to that fervour, can we say that this temptation would have been resisted? The Declaration of Indulgence might have proved no more than an English version of the Edict of Nantes. It will be said that these are only hypotheses, but to many Englishmen they appeared grim certainties.

Indirect evidence that James's character had not changed overnight was provided in the spring and summer of 1687. With good reason, he was concerned about the discipline of his army, and he was convinced that hanging would provide the best deterrent to desertion. The law on the subject was not clear, since the statutes of Henry VIII's reign had imposed the death penalty for desertion only in time of war, or when the army was abroad, neither of which situations could be pleaded in 1687; indeed, for long this offence had been treated by the courts as no more than a misdemeanour. James now ordered the courts to inflict the death penalty in such cases. Rather than comply, Herbert resigned from his chief justiceship of King's Bench, and Holt from the recordership of London. They were succeeded respectively by sir Robert Wright and sir Bartholomew Shower. With these adjustments the king was able to have his way. He insisted that deserters should be hanged in view of their regiments; and, with his invariable attention to detail, he provided that, wherever the regiment had gone, the convicted deserter should follow, so that the punishment would be an example. But the desertions continued nevertheless.

An even more direct commentary on the Declaration of Indulgence was provided when, in the months of April and May 1687, the High Commission directed its attention to the two universities. The vice-chancellor and senate of Cambridge had been ordered by the king to admit one Alban Francis, a Benedictine monk, to the degree of master of arts. The university authorities were willing to admit Francis provided he took the oaths, but this he refused to do, on the ground that he had a royal dispensation. On 7 May, at an adjourned hearing,[1] Jeffreys asked Peachell, the vice-chancellor, whether a royal mandate of this kind had ever before been set aside, to which it was answered that several had been refused, including one for a Nonconformist in Charles II's reign, who had declined to take the oaths. It became clear in the course of the proceedings that, since Elizabeth's reign, the university had required either the prescribed oaths, or evidence that the royal nominee professed adherence to the doctrines of the church of England, so the action of the university, in the case now before the Commission, was justified by both law and tradition. These things meant nothing to Jeffreys. The Commission deprived Peachell of both his vice-chancellorship and his college headship. A few days later the representatives of the university were summoned before the Commission to hear a speech by Jeffreys. Referring to the sentence passed on the vice-chancellor, he declared that the others shared his guilt. In future they must show a ready obedience to the royal commands. 'Go your ways and sin no more lest a worse thing come unto you.' Among those who had to listen in silence to this tirade was Isaac Newton.

The turn of Oxford came next. In March 1687 the president of Magdalen College died, and in the following month the college had to proceed to an election. For this purpose the field was limited by the college statutes, which confined the choice to those who were or had been fellows of New College or of Magdalen, the first-mentioned having been connected with the Founder, Waynflete. The king called on the college to

[1] *State Trials*, xi. 1315–38.

elect a young convert, Anthony Farmer, notable for debauchery even in that age, and disqualified by the college statutes. In spite of this mandate the college on 15 April elected a qualified person, John Hough. In June the president-elect and fellows were cited before the Commission; and, after a stern reprimand for their independent conduct, Hough's election was declared void. Meanwhile Farmer was dropped, as his presidency would have been preposterous, and in August the fellows were required to elect another royal nominee, Samuel Parker, the crypto-Catholic bishop of Oxford. They refused, on the ground that they had already made their election. For some weeks relations between the king and the fellows of Magdalen College were in a state of deadlock.

Several weeks in the late summer of 1687 were spent in a royal progress. The king expressly desired that the militia should not be drawn up to receive him, for he wished mainly to interview the lords-lieutenant and deputies, the sheriffs and the county gentlemen, confident that he would bring them round to his opinion about the Test Act.[1] With this in view he may have chosen the west and north-west as the least loyal part of the country. The tour included Bath, Badminton, Gloucester, Worcester, Ludlow, Shrewsbury, and Chester; on his way home he passed through the midlands and Warwick to Oxford. At Bath, where his queen took the waters, he deplored the quarrel between the pope and Louis XIV, and he expressed the fear that the prince of Orange was forming a league against him. He proclaimed also that the Catholic powers must unite.[2] On his arrival at St. Winifred's Well in Flintshire he was presented by the inhabitants with a purse containing £100 in gold. This he accepted, with an injunction that they would choose members for the next parliament who would take off the Tests. In honour of the royal visit the mayor and corporation of Holywell collected all the fish they could lay their hands on, for the purposes of a civic dinner, but the king escaped by a back door. Meanwhile he was joined by Penn, who preached to the crowds, but was howled down.[3] At Chester

[1] Sunderland to duke of Beaufort, 9 Aug. 1687, in *S.P. James II.*

[2] Barrillon to Louis XIV, 23 Aug.–2 Sept. 1687, in *Baschet*, 172.

[3] *H.M.C. Rep.* x, app. pt. 4, 376. *Mr. Stanley Leighton's MSS.* The account there given is dated 1686, but there is reason to think that 1687 is meant.

James interviewed Tyrconnel, who reported the great progress he was making in Ireland.

In September, on his way south, the king stayed in Oxford, where he called the recalcitrant fellows of Magdalen to his presence, and again they refused to abandon their president and admit Parker. The result was the appointment of a special commission to exercise visitatorial jurisdiction over the college, and for a time it seemed that the fellows were willing to compromise. But James demanded that they should humbly beg pardon for their offence, and admit the legality of the commission, which they refused to do; so they were deprived, and pronounced incapable of holding any church preferments, thus making it difficult for them to earn a living. Early in 1688 bishop Parker died; whereupon Bonaventure Giffard, bishop of Madaura, one of James's favourite priests, was intruded as president. Of the original fellows, there remained only Charnock, who was to prove a resolute Jacobite in the next reign. The fellowships and demyships were filled with Roman Catholics, so that Magdalen became a popish seminary, occupied by new-comers, not of high character, who were expressly freed from the traditional jurisdiction of their visitor, the bishop of Winchester.[1] It was fortunate that no other college headship in Oxford became vacant at this time.[2] Nor was James concerned only with Oxford and Cambridge. Already (1686) he had required the provost and fellows of Trinity College, Dublin, to appoint a young convert to a lectureship in Irish Studies. As there was no such lectureship, the college could not comply; later, however, it refused to admit to a fellowship an unqualified person who would not take the oaths.[3] No corporate body was safe from James and his advisers.

Parliament had been dissolved on 2 July 1687 within a few days of the admission of D'Adda, papal nuncio. James, with discretion, arranged that the ceremony took place at Windsor. Now convinced that nothing could be done with the old Anglican and loyalist parliament, he and Sunderland thought that much might be done with a parliament having a majority

[1] James to Bonaventure, bishop of Madaura, 4 June 1686, in *S.P. James II*.

[2] For the proceedings against Magdalen College, see J. R. Bloxam, *Magdalen College and James II* (Oxford Historical Society).

[3] J. W. Stubbs, *History of Trinity College, Dublin*, 119–21.

of Dissenters, the Upper House, if necessary, to be flooded with compliant Protestants. Such a body would, it seemed, be willing to annul the Test; but, ostensibly at least, Catholics were not to be admitted to its membership. His progress of the late summer, and the 'firm' line taken with the Anglicans of Oxford and Cambridge, encouraged the king still farther; though some would think that he might have been content with what he had already achieved; for his revenue was sufficient, so long as he did not engage in war; and, so far as a proclamation could do it, he had succeeded where his brother had failed. Moreover, he had got rid of his most prominent Protestant ministers; he had introduced papists into high office and into the privy council; while by dispensations he had brought into the administration a number of Catholics out of all proportion to their ratio of the population. He had broken through the Anglican barrier of the universities; he had restored the ancient relations with the Holy See, except that England was still under the old excommunication imposed on queen Elizabeth, but absolution would put that right.[1] He had encouraged the setting up of monastic communities and schools; with the help of the Press he was engaged on an intensive system of propaganda and proselytism. All this was unpopular, it is true, but public resentment still stopped short of the person of the sovereign. The régime, created in little more than two years, might have continued had James known where to stop. That point was reached late in 1687.

It is almost a maxim of human conduct that while a risky or irregular thing can often be done once with impunity, it cannot usually be done a second time. James was responsible for a repetition, within a few years, of two irregular things: a remodelling of the parliamentary boroughs, intended to reverse their remodelling of the later years of Charles II, and a repetition, within a year, of the Declaration of Indulgence. These two things, both superfluous, both unnecessary for the interests of English Roman Catholics, proved to be the undoing of James and the immediate causes of the Revolution.

[1] For an account of this, see a memorandum, written after the Revolution, entitled, 'How to Treat with the Pope', in *Carte MSS.* ccviii (Nairne Papers, vol. i), f. 222. According to this, James was not yet qualified to treat publicly with the Pope.

James was convinced—and in this conviction he appears to have been encouraged by Sunderland—that by assiduous management it would be possible to ensure the election of a parliament which would favour his designs. There were two historical precedents for this, neither of which had been accompanied by much success. The nearer one was that which had been set by Charles II's remodelling of the local administration, followed by the parliament of 1685; the more remote one had been set in 1555 by Philip of Spain, who had instructed his English privy council to see to it that only Roman Catholics were returned to parliament. The result of this was the return of an unusually obstreperous House of Commons.[1] But James may have thought that he would succeed where others had failed; so a committee, headed by Jeffreys, was set up for regulating corporations, on the information supplied by local bodies of 'regulators'. The campaign had begun in October 1687, when letters were sent to the lords-lieutenant, requiring them to obtain answers from their deputies, the sheriffs and the justices within their areas to three questions propounded to them. As well as this, the lords lieutenant were required to supply an account of all corporations within their jurisdiction, showing what persons had credit enough to be returned to parliament, and what Catholics and Dissenters might be added to the roll of deputy lieutenants.[2]

The list of noblemen who, at the cost of resignation, refused to comply is impressive, and was in striking contrast with the list of those who were put into their places, such as lords Dover and Preston, and (of course) Jeffreys. One cannot judge of the success or failure of this second remodelling,[3] since it was never put to the test of a parliament; but, if experience was any guide, Sunderland must have known that the earlier remodelling had produced a parliament which, as it grew up, became less amenable to 'management'; nor was there any reason to think that a packed body of Dissenters would prove more docile than a packed body of Loyalists. Indeed, as a man credited with intelligence, Sunderland must have known that these reiterated efforts were worse than useless; but he appears to have

[1] J. E. Neale, *The Elizabethan House of Commons*, 288.

[2] e.g. Sunderland to duke of Beaufort, 25 Oct. 1687, in *S.P. James II*.

[3] For a good account, see R. H. George, 'The Charters granted to English Parliamentary Corporations in 1688', in *E.H.R.* lv (1940), 47–56.

conveyed no hint of this to the confident and untiring James. Eventually, local ingenuity proved more than a match for king and minister; because, in spite of the fact that some corporations were changed three and even four times, many of the old members crept back. The guile of the provinces outwitted the laborious folly of Whitehall.

The questions propounded in this national referendum were these:[1]

1. Will you, if returned to parliament, vote for the repeal of the penal laws and the Test?
2. Will you support candidates who are in favour of such a measure?
3. Will you live neighbourly and friendly with those of a contrary religion?

These questions were to be presented by the lords lieutenant to their deputies, the sheriffs and the justices; the answers were to be returned to Whitehall. As well as putting the questions to members of corporations, the local 'regulators' were to verify, from lists supplied to them, that the candidates proposed by the Court for election were 'right' men; they were also to send the names of those favoured by the boroughs, and also whether they were 'right'. There was to be similar investigation of the opinions of revenue officers. Dissenters were to be solicited and, when won over, their interest in the neighbourhood was to be enlisted. Wherever Dissenters did not appear to be convinced, the regulators were to find out with what malcontents in London they were maintaining correspondence.

James's regulators obtained a majority of replies which, as they tried to avoid giving offence, left things exactly where they were. The first question produced a stereotyped answer—they would be guided by the reasons emerging from the debates in the House. The second was easy—they would vote for such members of parliament as would serve their king and country. The third was even easier—everyone in that quarrelsome age undertook to live peaceably with everyone else. Generally, what the returns showed was the absence of such classifications as 'Whig' and 'Tory', and how strongly entrenched were local or family interests in the old electoral system. A few did place

[1] The materials, from originals in the Rawlinson MSS., will be found in sir G. Duckett, *Penal Laws and the Test Act* (2 vols., 1882).

their opinions at the king's disposal, but their number was not large; evasion was more common. On the strength of the very dubious material supplied to them, James and Sunderland, throughout a period of nearly nine months, devoted themselves to wholesale ejections from the offices of the local administration, as well as from the city companies and the revenue establishments; accordingly the registers of the privy council are littered with the names of the many, great and small, who were so removed. All who showed unwillingness to follow out the royal wishes were summarily ejected by a prince who had just proclaimed, in its broadest terms, a policy of toleration.

Of those who took their places, whether Roman Catholics or Dissenters, some were disreputable, and very few had the confidence of their neighbours; indeed, they were dubbed 'factors for popery'.[1] The result of this was the creation of a certain national unity. Party distinction and even family rivalry were still subordinate to the ancient principle that the local defenders of the royal dignity and authority were to be found in the landed classes. That royal dignity and authority had now, for the first time, been brought into grave disrepute by wholesale eviction of men who assumed, without question, a vested and hereditary right to power and pre-eminence in those parts of England where they had their estates. There was the same resentment in the boroughs, particularly in the cathedral cities, where the intruded persons were considered 'impossible' on social and religious grounds. Thus, the earl of Bath, who had shown himself a devoted agent of the royal policy in Cornwall and Devon, afterwards found reason to be alarmed by the results, particularly in Exeter, which he described as 'miserably divided'. There, the most substantial citizens, ejected for no offence, were domineered over by 'a packed chamber of Dissenters'. On Sundays the sword was carried in state before the mayor and corporation in their march to a 'conventicle'. 'Gentlemen', lord Bath reported, were leaving the city in disgust, and His Majesty would soon need a garrison to keep order.[2] The earl completed his political evolution by going over to the prince of Orange.

[1] Earl of Nottingham to prince of Orange, 2 Sept. 1687, in *Dalrymple*, ii, pt. 1, app. 202.

[2] *S.P. James II*, Bath to Sunderland, 9 Oct. 1688.

These domestic events aroused such interest as to overshadow foreign affairs. Of James's commitments with Louis, only one could be regarded as public, namely, the treaty of peace and neutrality between the two crowns, which had been signed in November 1686 and ratified in December.[1] According to its terms, disputes between English and French in Hudson's Bay territory were to be settled locally; and, in the event of a war between England and France, the colonies were to remain neutral. The other commitment was the naval agreement of April 1688, which reflected the anxiety of Louis regarding the attitude of William of Orange, an anxiety not fully shared by James. By this secret arrangement[2] James was to fit out twenty warships and eight fireships for service in the Downs and the Channel, Louis to pay for their maintenance. At the same time the French king offered to add fourteen or sixteen ships to this squadron, but James declined, as he feared that such close naval co-operation with France would have a bad effect on English opinion. To this extent it can be asserted that James was a patriot.

Although the king had served with distinction as an admiral, he appears to have had more faith in troops than in ships. At this time there were several regiments of English and Scottish soldiers in Holland, in the pay of the States General, some of whom had already been sent over to assist in the crushing of Monmouth's rebellion. In October 1687 James formed the design of recalling all these troops, apparently fearing that they might be infected by the republicanism of the Dutch; moreover, these regiments, if returned to England, would help to maintain James's interests, or rather, as Barrillon hinted, the interests of Louis.[3] Later they might be augmented by fresh levies, and in this way the Catholics in England 'would be united under Your Majesty's protection'. The sovereign so addressed was Louis XIV. Sunderland and Tyrconnel were enthusiastic about the scheme. For a time James thought that the recalled troops should be trained in France, so that a staff of highly skilled officers might be available as the nucleus of a large standing army;[4] and by December 1687 news that the queen was with

[1] *Instructions Données* (*Angleterre*), ii. 345. [2] Ibid. 387–8.

[3] Barrillon to Louis, 13 Oct. 1687, in *Baschet*, 173.

[4] Ibid., 16 Oct. and 10 Nov.

child made it all the more imperative that the dynasty should, if necessary, be preserved by military force. By January 1688 the chief Catholics in the king's confidence thought that the troops should not be recalled until after the summoning of a parliament and the annulment of the Test, when they would be useful 'for keeping order'.[1]

At this point Sunderland approached Barrillon with more concrete proposals. The maintenance of these troops, he declared, would cost the king (i.e. Louis) £50,000 a year; and in return for this sum, modest in comparison with the annuity paid to Charles II, he (Sunderland) would guarantee an Anglo-French engagement as formal and strict as any that had been entered into, for much larger sums, by Charles.[2] The question whether James would show better faith than his brother had done was not raised, the tacit assumption being that the virtuous James would give more value for less money. In return for his services in this matter, the English secretary of state asked for no more than a renewal of his pension, and, in addition, a lump sum large enough to enable him to view with equanimity the revolutions 'which occur so frequently in England'. 'Every day', wrote Barrillon to his royal master, 'Sunderland puts himself more and more into my hands and yours.'[3] It was true, added the ambassador, that rumour credited the English secretary with secret overtures to the prince of Orange, but these rumours were 'disproved' by Sunderland's active advocacy of the French and Roman Catholic interest. Meanwhile, by February 1688 James had made up his mind to recall the troops, and already in the shadow cabinet he had spoken sternly about the conduct of William and the States General. The proclamation of recall was issued on 14 March and caused considerable alarm. Ronquillo, the Spanish ambassador, expressed the fear that this foreboded a close agreement between James and Louis, and might be the prelude to an attack on either Spain or Holland.[4] The alarm spread to Holland, where the shares of the East India Company fell by 13 per cent. But all parties had reckoned without William and the States General. They refused to return the troops.

[1] Barrillon to Louis, 22 Dec.–1 Jan. 1687–8, in *Baschet*, 175.

[2] Ibid., 26 Dec.–5 Jan. 1687–8.

[3] Ibid., 16–26 Jan. 1688.

[4] Ibid., 26 Jan.–5 Feb. 1688.

So far from being disconcerted, the effusive Sunderland now proposed that Louis should maintain three new regiments for service in England. But this time Barrillon was not impressed; for, obtuse as he was, he considered that James had no need for more troops, and that French money would be better spent in strengthening the English fleet.[1] But the king could not be shaken in his desire for more soldiers. He sent agents to Liége and Antwerp to offer money and employment to Englishmen in the garrisons of Maestricht and French Flanders; with these, and some Roman Catholic English officers who succeeded in getting out of Holland, he formed the nucleus of three new regiments. By July 1688, when they had been brought to full strength by the enrolment of English Catholics, Louis was paying for their maintenance at the rate of about £4,000 a month.[2] Moreover, James already had the assurance[3] of Barrillon that, if the necessity arose, Louis would send a sufficient body of French troops 'pour opprimer ses ennemis et se faire obéir de ses sujets'. But, in spite of these assurances, James, throughout the earlier part of 1688, was perplexed by indecision. He could not make up his mind about his navy, whether to send a squadron to help his potential ally Denmark[4] against Swedish attacks; or to the Downs, in order to overawe the Dutch; he hesitated, possibly through his wife's influence, to commit himself to a definite alliance with Louis. He was unwilling to summon a parliament, though some of his advisers counselled this step, so that it might appear whether or not extreme measures would have to be taken for the annulment of the Test. Nor, even as late as the summer of 1688, could he be convinced that William of Orange was engaged in designs against him.

The man who more than any other had brought about this state of impotence was Robert Spencer, second earl of Sunderland. Son of a moderate royalist, he had a strict upbringing, supplemented by residence at Christ Church and the Grand Tour. He married a lady related to the Russells, who brought

[1] *Baschet*, 175, 19–29 Mar. 1688.
[2] Ibid., 16–26 July.
[3] Ibid., 27 Oct.–6 Nov. 1687.
[4] In March 1686 James instructed his envoy in Denmark to negotiate a treaty of navigation and commerce to supplement the treaty of 1670. *Rawl. MS.* D. 749, f. 24.

him not only money, but astuteness nearly as great as his own. His sister was married to Halifax (who detested him); his eldest daughter married the duke of Hamilton; his maternal uncle was Henry Sidney, lord Romney, brother of Algernon Sidney; more distant relations were the Coventrys and the Ashley Coopers. Later his son married the daughter of the duke of Marlborough. No one more keenly appreciated the value of 'connexion'; his was mainly with the great Whig and Protestant families of England and Scotland, a fact remembered by those who accused him of having ruined James in order to benefit William. As an Exclusionist he had, in the previous reign, been dismissed from his secretaryship of state; but, with the help of the duchess of Portsmouth, he had been restored to office as one of the 'Chits'. From experience of the Court of Charles II Sunderland had learned to survive disgrace; to use female influence; to remove by patient attrition those who stood in his way, and (from the royal example) to profit by that delicate situation when one is seriously considering conversion to Roman Catholicism, and in need only of encouragement to take the plunge. This he kept as a trump card until, in the summer of 1688, the stakes were at their highest. Interested in neither wine nor women, he could devote himself to his career with the ardour and asceticism of a monk. But he had one failing—gaming—in which he lost heavily. It proved of consequence in English history that Sunderland clung to office, simply because he could not dispense with its salary and profits.

From long experience the secretary knew that James was a fool; but it is unlikely that he tried deliberately to ruin his royal master, because he perceived that in this matter James would need no help: and it was a matter of indifference to him which master he cheated. So he decided to make the best of both worlds. On the one hand, he retained his place by pandering to the king, and pretending to favour his religious policy; on the other hand, he ingratiated himself secretly with the prince of Orange. The greatest exponent in his century of what is now called 'double crossing', he impressed James by an appearance of intellectual brilliance—indeed the Stuarts were very susceptible to such flashy creatures—while other men, equally uncritical, were fascinated by Sunderland's assurance, his quickness, his bluster, his vehemently expressed contempt for better men, characteristics which they mistook for ability. He must have known that James's policy was suicidal; but he remained the sycophant in office, because he so desperately needed the money. As late as October 1688 he declared that he would be ruined if William's enterprise succeeded, and at the same time he applied for refuge in France; but, when the deluge came, he fled to Holland, and from there he wrote to William, in March 1689, reminding him of how he had contributed 'what lay in me towards the advancing of your glorious revolution'.[1] But that revolution meant the end of his public career; for, in spite of royal support, he was thereafter considered beneath even the low level requisite for politics.

[1] Sunderland to William, 8 Mar. 1689, in *Dalrymple*, ii, pt. i, appendix.

VII

JAMES AND WILLIAM OF ORANGE, 1687–8

JAMES corresponded regularly with William throughout his reign. The letters were usually formal, but the king soon had reason to complain about the number of escaped rebels who were given asylum in Holland.[1] He appears to have known little of the intrigues, conducted from the moment of his accession by insistent Dutchmen, intent on shaping English policy to suit the interests of their master, an enterprise in which they were assisted, not by their pertinacity, but by the uninterrupted folly of the two royal cousins. 'Conscience' provided the most obvious pretext for betrayal; and soon the zealous monarch was surrounded by courtiers, always servile and sycophantic, some of them committed to Louis, some to William, and one to both. For the maintenance of this deception, an ideal setting was provided by the royal example of devoutness, industry, and economy unparalleled in even the most edifying records of English kingship.

Meanwhile the European situation had been altered, in the summer of 1686, by the formation of the league of Augsburg,[2] which brought together the emperor Leopold, Charles II of Spain (as duke of Burgundy), Charles XI of Sweden, the elector of Bavaria, and several German princes, an association intended to maintain the peace of Europe against the continued threat from France. The league provided for an army of 60,000 men, to be drilled for a short period each year; but the States General were not among the signatories, and William, the only ruler capable, by his determination and endurance, of putting its objects into effect, was not enthusiastic for it. As the first of a series of more concrete alliances, the league has given its name, not unjustifiably, to a war against France which lasted for

[1] James to prince of Orange, in *Dalrymple*, ii, pt. 1, app. 166, 7 Mar. 1686.

[2] *Dumont*, vii, 29 June–9 July 1686, 131 sqq.

nearly nine years. For the purposes of that war, William needed resources greater than any that could be supplied by his native country, where central direction was impeded by the large measure of autonomy vested in the provinces, and by the hostility of Amsterdam to the House of Orange; accordingly, as his wife Mary was heiress presumptive to the English throne, the prince had long shown a keen, but seldom tactful interest in English affairs. The failure of Argyll and Monmouth had demonstrated that no invasion could succeed, unless backed by adequate military force, as well as by assurance of support in the invaded country. Such assurances were speedily forthcoming. Early in 1687, just after the dismissal of Rochester, William sent Dykveld to London on a special mission, with instructions drawn up mainly by Burnet, then the most prominent refugee at The Hague. Dykveld was to consort with both Anglicans and Nonconformists; to the Roman Catholics he was to give an assurance of toleration by parliamentary enactment.

In his last audience with James in May 1687, Dykveld was adjured to assure the prince that the king depended on his support in the royal campaign for the removal of the Test, a pathetic illustration of the monarch's complete unawareness of the forces of treachery steadily gathering force around him.[1] Dykveld returned to Holland with assurances very different from those expressed to him by James. Nor were these assurances all from Whigs. Churchill sent the significant message that he and princess Anne would stand by their religion; Sunderland, too cautious to commit himself on paper, referred to what the envoy would be able to say of him; Nottingham wrote that the prince could depend on the attachment of the Protestant interest: 'you are the person on whom they found their hopes'; Clarendon cautiously wrote that Dykveld would give an account of affairs in England, while Rochester, with equal prudence, intimated that the envoy had good reason for knowing everything. Danby, more forthcoming, suggested a personal interview with the prince; Halifax, indeterminate as usual, expressed the opinion that no parliament would be called in November, and that 'our affairs here depend so much on what may be done abroad, that our thoughts may be changed by what we hear by the next post'. England's Elder Statesman

[1] The letters will be found in *Dalrymple*, ii, pt. 1, app. 183 sqq.

was too cautious for William's purposes. The earl of Devonshire, then under a cloud for an assault, referred to what Dykveld would have to say; Shrewsbury sent an assurance of his service. But the model for such risky correspondence was set by Compton, the ablest diplomat of them all: 'if the king should have any trouble come upon him, which God forbid, we do not know any sure friend he has to rely on abroad besides yourself'. All these letters, carefully preserved by William, leave one with a certain feeling of sympathy for the unfortunate James. More important, the correspondence made it clear to William that, while he might have help in ousting the king, he would have to depend thereafter on men of somewhat fickle allegiance.

Dykveld's mission was soon followed by others—those of count Zuylestein, who came to England in August 1687, nominally to offer the prince's condolence on the death of Mary of Modena's mother; and in July 1688, when the pretext was even more nominal, namely, the birth of the prince of Wales, who, according to many whom the envoy consulted, was spurious. In the period between these two visits, the intermediaries who maintained this close association between Orange and the malcontents were admiral Russell, cousin of the Whig martyr lord Russell, and Henry Sidney, uncle of Sunderland. There was also circulated in England a declaration of William's religious policy. This was said to have been occasioned by the efforts of a Scottish refugee in Holland to induce Grand Pensionary Fagel to influence William in favour of James's intention to abrogate the Test. The real motives of this move are not clear, but the opportunity was too good to be missed; accordingly, in a letter, Fagel announced that the prince, while personally in favour of toleration, considered that the removal of religious disabilities was a matter for parliament. Burnet's translation of this letter was printed and circulated widely in the early months of 1688; the replies, drawn up on behalf of James, merely served to give the letter greater publicity. The importance of Fagel's letter was that it rightly interpreted the feelings of the majority of Englishmen, and so created some community of feeling between English and Dutch.[1] Thus, by the beginning of 1688 William was so assured of influential

[1] For the Dutch point of view regarding the letter, see *R. Fruin's Verspreide Geschriften*, ed. P. J. Blok and P. L. Muller, deel v. 161–2.

support in England that he was able to enunciate, for subjects not yet within his allegiance, his policy on the main question dividing king and nation. The crisis may have been delayed by the curious situation in which James and his son-in-law found themselves with regard to their respective peoples. On the one hand, James knew the publicity value of cordial relations with the prince; on his side, William appreciated how Amsterdam was less likely to give trouble if it were thought that he was on friendly terms with James. But this period of deception was soon ended by a rapid succession of events.

The earliest of these was the issue on 27 April 1688 of the second Declaration of Indulgence. As in the first, the hope was expressed that it would be confirmed by parliament when it met in November 'at farthest', a statement which contemporaries may have compared with the broken promise of the year before. More serious, the Declaration was ordered to be read on two successive Sundays in every cathedral and parish church. There was widespread disobedience to this order; and archbishop Sancroft with six bishops met at Lambeth, where the metropolitan drew up in his own handwriting a petition against the order, in which the dispensing power was impugned. This was presented on the evening of 18 May to the king, who received it with surprise and anger; royal resentment was increased by the fact that, because of some leakage, a copy of the petition was printed and circulated. The reverend petitioners might have been summoned before the High Commission, where their fate would have been a certainty; but James's advisers decided on a bolder course, for an information was served requiring the bishops to answer a charge of seditious libel in the King's Bench. The prosecution was entrusted mainly to the solicitor general, the renegade Whig sir William Williams, with the help of the attorney general, sir Thomas Powys. The defence was led by sir R. Sawyer, assisted by Pollexfen, Pemberton, and Somers.

The trial of the Seven Bishops, one of the best-known incidents of English history, is important because a verdict was given against a whole system of government. The bishops, Sancroft, Ken (Bath and Wells), White (Peterborough), Turner (Ely), Lloyd (St. Asaph), Trelawney (Bristol), and Lake (Chichester), after a first hearing, were given a fortnight in which to prepare their defence, and the trial began on 29 June. The case has some unusual features distinguishing it from other trials of the period. In opening the prosecution, Williams stated that His Majesty so far resented the 'ill usage' of his mercy revealed in the Indulgence that he had ordered a public vindication of his honour by this trial. In other words, the real prosecutor was not the crown, but James Stuart. Then, as regards the two opposing counsel, Williams and Sawyer both found themselves in the difficult position of having to refute arguments which, on many previous occasions, they had successfully urged; so that Williams had to forget his defence of Whigs, and Sawyer his arguments against them. These things may have prompted the great historian of English law to say that,[1] in this period, 'Westminster Hall was standing on its head'. Next, the conduct of one of the accused, White of Peterborough, was unusual. Not only did he object to the difficulty of following the spoken Latin of the information, but he had the courage, or the temerity, to ask the presiding judge, sir Robert Wright, not to be of counsel against the accused, nor to direct witnesses what evidence they should give.[2] The unfairness of the later-Stuart trials, to condemn which is now considered unhistorical, was thus criticized at the time by an intelligent and influential man as soon as he found himself in the dock. The silence of humbler men in similar circumstances has been accepted as proof that no one objected to the procedure at these trials.

Even the judges acted abnormally in this extraordinary trial. Justice Powell frequently intervened, almost as counsel for the bishops; and Wright, the president, went so far as to express satisfaction with the verdict. But most remarkable of all was the direction of the court to the jury, for it left them to decide, not only the fact of publication of the document, but also whether or not it was libellous. Such an exceptional course may have been prompted by the feeling of trepidation evidenced throughout the trial, intensified by the large number of peers who attended as spectators. But nevertheless this direction by the judge to the jury anticipated Fox's Libel Act by more than a century. So, by the end of the day, Westminster Hall appeared to be standing on its feet again.

[1] Sir W. S. Holdsworth, *History of English Law*, vi. 511.

[2] *State Trials*, xii. 289.

The dispensing power was not on trial in this case, but it kept cropping up. Much time was spent on the question whether the bishops as spiritual peers might lawfully be committed for a misdemeanour; whether the offence had been committed at Lambeth in Surrey, or at St. James's Palace in Middlesex, and whether it could be concluded that the handwriting of the petition was Sancroft's. The intensity with which these matters were contested showed the unwillingness of the court to come to the vital point—did the denial of the dispensing power constitute sedition? Sawyer had no difficulty in making clear the implications of the dispensing power, for by it 'not only the laws of the Reformation but all the laws for the preservation of the Christian religion are suspended'. Pollexfen followed with the argument that, though the king's will is what the law is, if the king's will is not consonant with the law, it does not oblige the subject. Generally, it was pleaded that the bishops had done no more than exercise the subject's right to petition.

To this it was answered by Williams that the subject can petition only through parliament—at which justices Powell and Holloway expressed their disagreement by audible asides—and moreover, argued the solicitor general, the bishops, with their well-known doctrine of passive obedience, might have waited until the meeting of parliament. This was the shrewdest thrust against the bishops. When, in support of his contention that the dispensing power in religious matters was illegal, defending counsel cited the two declarations of the House of Commons (1663 and 1673) in that sense, it was answered that such declarations were no more than expressions of opinion; and when Alibone, the Roman Catholic among the judges, declared that anything written or spoken against the actual exercise of government was libellous, he was correctly stating the law as it applied then and for some time afterwards. In his summing up, Wright properly ruled out of consideration the difficult problem of the dispensing power, and put two questions to the jury—was publication (i.e. presentation to the king) proved, and was the petition libellous, in the sense that it disturbed the government and made a stir among the people? The jury returned a verdict of Not Guilty. By none was the acquittal applauded more vociferously than by the martial politicians on Hounslow Heath.

Meanwhile on 10 June a son was born to James and Mary of Modena. Among the many congratulatory messages was one from the commissary general of the Irish Capuchins in France: 'May we not looke on this dear, darling of Heaven as the Messiah of Great Brittayne, whose cradle is the tombe of heresy and schism?'[1] That the same cradle would prove the tomb of English liberty and Protestantism was the fear which found vent in the absurd legend of the warming-pan, and induced men to turn to the prince of Orange as their deliverer.

Good people, I pray,
Throw the orange away,
'Tis a very sower fruit, and was brought in play,
When good Judith Wilk[2]
In her pocket brought milk,
And with cushings and warming pans laboured to bilk,
This same Orange.[3]

The popularity of such doggerel, and of catchy tunes like *Lillibulero*, attested the feelings of the London populace. Now the warming-pan story was grossly unfair to James and his queen, who, whatever may have been their faults, were incapable of such deception. In his understandable resentment at such an imputation, the king convened a special meeting of his privy council and produced depositions on oath from the persons who had witnessed the birth, including Jeffreys, who stood by the royal bedside when the unfortunate Chevalier was brought into the world.[4] But historical events have often been precipitated by the most elemental of emotions, and among these was fear—fear that a Roman Catholic dynasty in England was now assured. We profess inability to understand such a fear today, but it would be unwise to underestimate its force in the past. That fear was speedily accompanied by hope, the hope that followed on the acquittal of the Seven Bishops. These two together were the direct causes of the Revolution of 1688.

The birth of the prince prompted Zuylestein's second mission, ostensibly one of congratulation, but really to make final arrangements for an invitation to William, who did not conceal

[1] 22 June–2 July in *S.P. France*, 78/151.
[2] Judith Wilkes was the queen's midwife.
[3] 'The Orange' in *Bodl. Firth* B. 21, no. 18.
[4] *P.C. Reg.* 72, 22 Oct. 1688.

his opinion that the birth was a fraud. Of those who were approached, only two, Halifax and Nottingham, declined to be drawn from their sympathetic neutrality, and on the last day of this momentous month of June the invitation was taken over to Holland by admiral Russell, dressed as an ordinary seaman. The signatories were Devonshire, Danby, Shrewsbury, Lumley, Compton, Russell, and Henry Sidney. The document contained a pledge of association with the prince whenever he might effect a landing, and included an assurance that nineteen-twentieths of the kingdom desired a change, so apprehensive were they of their religion, liberty, and property.[1] If, it was declared, a force strong enough to defend itself could be disembarked, that force would soon be increased much beyond the strength of James's army. William now knew that his carefully meditated enterprise was likely to have a very different result from those of Argyll and Monmouth, for the invitation came from leaders of the great interests and parties in England. From this point of view, only one name, that of Lumley, could be considered obscure. Richard, lord Lumley, afterwards earl of Scarborough was a loyalist who had taken part in the operations against the western rebels, but later he had been alienated by James's conduct, and was now allied with rebels of a more formidable stature.

In the invitation, the signatories alleged that there was disaffection in James's army. They were right. The rot began in July, when James, through lieutenant-general lord Dumbarton conducted a census in order to find out which of the officers and men were Roman Catholics. This was the second occasion in the reign when public opinion was tested by a full-scale inquiry, and the results were equally disastrous; for, among the troops, it was suspected that the king intended to turn out the Protestants, or transfer them to Ireland, their places to be taken by Catholics. The inevitable result was that an association of Protestant officers was formed, led by colonel Langston of the duke of St. Albans's regiment. Langston made no secret of what he proclaimed to be the intentions of the king, namely, that every Protestant in England and Scotland would have his throat cut; that there was an alliance between James and Louis, written in the former's own hand, which the prince of

[1] The invitation will be found in *Dalrymple*, ii, pt. i, app. 228–9.

Orange, by bribery, had caused to be extracted from the royal pocket. There was also, announced the colonel, a plot, engineered by James, Sunderland, and Petre, to poison William; and as for the supposed prince of Wales, William had in his custody the true mother of that infant, with 'proofs' of his real origin.[1] Such were the stories eagerly swallowed by the martial wiseacres on Hounslow Heath. Frequent meetings at the Rose Tavern in Covent Garden, attended by lord Colchester, Thomas Wharton, and colonel Talmash, led to a concerted plan of desertion, which was carried into effect shortly after William, on his march from the west, had reached Hungerford. There was also unrest in the fleet. James's ultimate intentions may have been unwise, but the rumours about them were much worse.

Even at this late hour the king might, by a policy of moderation, have saved his dynasty. But, as he was convinced that firmness would have saved his father, so he was convinced that the same policy would save him. Accordingly, he removed two of the judges, Powell and Holloway, who had shown sympathy with the accused bishops; Wright would have been removed but for the difficulty of finding a successor. In Council, wholesale ejection from office continued to be made; and on 19 May the king had solemnly ordered the removal of the clerk of the company of Tallow Chandlers.[2] On 13 July a significant change was made in the oath of a privy councillor by the omission of the undertaking to defend His Majesty's rights 'against all foreign princes, prelates, states or potentates'.[3] Equally injudicious was the requirement imposed on archdeacons to send returns to the Ecclesiastical Commission of the names of all clergy who refused to read the Declaration of Indulgence. Nor did the business conducted in Council during the late summer of 1688 give any hint of the crisis through which the dynasty was passing; for the trial of the Seven Bishops coincided with the issue of a proclamation against profaneness and debauchery,[4] a proof that, in high places, things were considered normal. At the same time, the king actively concerned himself with drawing up an elaborate establishment 'touching salutes by guns'.[5]

On 24 August the king in Council ordered the chancellor to

[1] 'Letter about the revolution in the Army, 1688' in *Rawl. MS.* D. 148.

[2] *P.C. Reg.* 72, 19 May 1688.

[3] Ibid., 13 July 1688.

[4] *Steele*, i, no. 3867, 29 June.

[5] *P.C. Reg.* 72, 22 June.

issue writs for the meeting of a new parliament on 27 November, and so it might have seemed that, at last, James was taking a wise step. The king was determined to have a parliament; but it seemed more than ever necessary that it should be a willing tool for the royal designs. Accordingly, new and even more elaborate instructions[1] were drawn up for the regulators of corporations, so elaborate, indeed, that they 'were to be read by them often'. These new instructions were extremely clever; a reflection probably of the mentality of Sunderland. In their dealings with corporations and leading men of the provinces, the regulators were now to be more circumspect, especially when dealing with men of parts—these were to be encouraged to declare themselves first. If they favoured persons opposed to His Majesty's interest, the regulators were to pretend approval of such men, in the hope that commendation from such a quarter would ensure their rejection, a convincing tribute to the suspicion with which the whole campaign was now regarded. Every effort must be made to procure the return to parliament of those 'who are likely to come up to the king's measures'; for His Majesty was intent only on 'the universal happiness of all his people'. As for the Seven Bishops, so recently acquitted, their real design had been to obstruct the meeting of parliament; but this, so far from discouraging the king, had decided him to pursue 'this great work' with even more zeal. Meanwhile, these directions were supplemented by Sunderland, who, in September, let loose a flood of correspondence directed to the lords lieutenant, indicating the names of persons whose return to parliament was to be promoted. Right up to the last, the secretary convinced James that his designs could be accomplished by a legislature composed of Dissenters whom the nation detested, and of renegades whom it despised.

Not till 28 September did the king in Council appear to realize what everybody else already knew; for on that date he ordered publication of a proclamation intimating that an invasion was being planned, having for its object the total conquest of the country.[2] Accordingly, the writs for a new parliament

[1] 'Memorandum for those that go into the country to dispose the corporations to a good election for members of Parliament.' A copy will be found in *Bodl. Pamph.* 134. It was issued in July or August.

[2] *Steele*, i, no. 3876.

were recalled and (in view of the recent order about gun salutes) strict economy in the use of gunpowder was enjoined.

These details were soon to be obscured by greater matters. Throughout the summer of 1688 the initiative lay with Louis XIV, in whose interests and power it was to impede William's enterprise, of the preparations for which he was fully informed by D'Avaux, his agent at The Hague. Why did he not come to the help of his English cousin, when it was obvious that the success of Orange would be a serious blow not only to Louis himself, but to the Catholic faith? Now, it is easy to be wise after the event; and it is only fair to note that, until the end of August, William's naval preparations were not certainly intended for an invasion of England; moreover, such an attempt, so late in the season, seemed destined to failure, or likely to involve, at best, a long and costly campaign.[1] It is also fair to add that, as soon as there was a suspicion at Versailles of the prince's real intentions, Louis offered naval help to James.[2] But the draft treaty was never perfected. This unwillingness of the English king to join actively and publicly with France may have been prompted by a twinge of shame, or may have been owing to the opposition of Mary of Modena, who resented the predominance of French influence at St. James's, and disliked Sunderland as the representative of that influence. On the other hand, the offer of French ships was not pressed; indeed, it was soon withdrawn, because it was thought that the necessary units could not be brought back in time from Toulon, where the greater part of the French fleet was stationed.[3] In November Louis promised to give naval help in the following April, but meanwhile he was disturbed by rumours of disaffection in the English fleet.[4]

[1] On 29 Aug.–8 Sept. Seignelai, the French minister of Marine, wrote to Bonrepaux, in England, that William was unwilling to attempt an invasion that year, partly because of opposition from Amsterdam. The prince, however, would probably make the attempt in the following spring. P. Clément, *L'Italie en 1671*, 336.

[2] The maritime convention, dated 13–23 Sept., was drawn up at Windsor, and empowered Barrillon, Bonrepaux, Sunderland, and Dartmouth to complete the details of naval co-operation. The original is in *Aff. Étr.* (*Angleterre*), 166, f. 214.

[3] Seignelai to Bonrepaux, 29 Aug.–8 Sept., in P. Clément, op. cit. 337.

[4] Seignelai to Barrillon, 14–24 Nov., ibid. 338–9.

This fact—the whereabouts of the French fleet in the summer and autumn of 1688—was to prove of great consequence in the course of the English Revolution. In July of that year, the naval bombardments of Algiers had been ended;[1] so there was still time in which to bring at least a squadron to Brest, for intervention in the Channel and North Sea, which seemed likely to be the theatres of important events in the autumn. Why were the naval forces not brought from Toulon? Answer must be sought in matters of high policy, of which two may be tentatively suggested. One was the affair of the electorate of Cologne, which threatened, in the summer, to be a cause of war; in which event Louis may have intended an attack on the papal states; the other was the chance that, at the same time, the whole of the Spanish Succession would come into his grasp. Hence it is at least likely that, in this critical summer, Louis's interest was neither in the North Sea nor in the Channel, but in the Mediterranean.

These two preoccupations of the French monarch provided the international background against which the earlier scenes of the English Revolution were staged. In regard to the first—Cologne—Louis had for long been on such bad terms with the pope, Innocent XI, that at this time the French church was almost in a state of schism. Now Cologne had some strategic importance from its position on the Rhine, within easy reach of the Dutch frontier; and already the archbishop elector, Maximilian Henry of Bavaria, had been forced into the arms of France by his two ministers of the Furstenberg family, of whom one, cardinal Furstenberg, was named as successor-designate. This matter became of European moment when in June 1688 Maximilian Henry died, and the pope refused to confirm the election of Furstenberg, on the ground that he was a notorious pluralist and simoniac.[2] The papal nominee was Clement of Bavaria, who was supported by the emperor. No one has ever succeeded in explaining why this matter suddenly figured so prominently in European politics, or why the French king was willing to go to such extremes in order to establish his obscure and venal nominee in Cologne. Louis himself tried to account

[1] C. de la Roncière, *Histoire de la marine française*, vi. 15.

[2] *Instructions Données* (*Rome*). Instructions to marquis de Laverdin, 333.

for it, and the great length and vehemence of his explanation[1] suggest that the matter needed a lot of explaining; moreover, his contention that, by refusing to institute Furstenberg, and by favouring the Imperial-Bavarian candidate, the pope was instigating a European war, is difficult of acceptance. Louis, of course, was anxious for peace; but, on this matter alone, he was willing to create in western Europe a situation in which peace was impossible. His real motive was not to obtain any diplomatic or strategic advantage, as is commonly supposed, but to gratify a personal and unworthy motive, namely, to inflict public humiliation on the pope.[2] Even James, who deeply deplored this unfortunate division within the Catholic fold, thought that his royal cousin was becoming unbalanced.

The other matter, less public or notorious, was possibly more important. Early in June Louis received secret information that Charles of Spain was (at last) about to die.[3] So he caused a proclamation to be drafted in which he announced that, as it had pleased God to call to His mercy his dearly beloved cousin and uncle, no reasonable person could doubt that the whole of the Spanish empire devolved on the Dauphin, to whom all subjects of the crown of Spain were to swear allegiance in a prescribed form of oath.[4] So, in this momentous summer, Louis had acted with his customary foresight and cleverness; and he must have felt that the affairs of James and William of Orange were puny indeed, in comparison with the great dispensation of Providence about to be vouchsafed in his favour. The French king had, it is true, once agreed with the other claimant, the emperor, to divide the inheritance between them; but here, unknown to anyone else, was a chance of seizing the whole. With his fleet at Toulon, he would be able to take over all the Spanish possessions in the Mediterranean before the emperor could interfere.

But Charles of Spain persisted in living. This, with other worries, caused a heightening of righteous indignation at

[1] *Instructions Données* (*Bavière, Palatinat et Deux Ponts*). Instructions to marquis de Villars, 11–21 Sept. 1688, 93 sqq.

[2] 'Ludwig XIV hoffte in Rausche seines Machtbewustseins den Papst unstimmen zu machen.' L. Pastor, *Geschishte der Päpste*, xiv. 935–7.

[3] *Instructions Données* (*Espagne*), 382–411, 10–20 June.

[4] *Aff. Étr.* (*Espagne*), 75, f. 47.

Versailles; and, as summer passed into autumn, the increasing tension resulted in quarrels between Louvois and Colbert de Croissy, even in the royal presence.[1] Louvois, who at least kept his head, urged the importance of preventing William's expedition;[2] but, not unreasonably, Louis, until the end of August, assumed that the States General were unlikely to support an invasion of England. As for James, who had refused Louis's help (not very seriously offered), experience of facing his difficulties from his own resources would give him a more realistic appreciation of his duties as a satellite. Accordingly, it would be unfair to object that the French king should have taken measures to prevent or stop William's proposed enterprise.

So Louis turned away from England and Holland to a wider world, a world full of vexations. There was the league of Augsburg which, in however platonic a manner, seemed to augur alliance among his enemies; there were the successes in Hungary of the emperor against Louis's secret allies, the Turks, likely to be followed by the arrival of imperial troops on the Rhine; there was the refusal to admit his rights in the Lower Palatinate to certain articles of furniture and several towns which he claimed on behalf of his sister-in-law, a sister of the former elector. As the Palatinate had come into the possession of William of Neuburg, father-in-law of the emperor, it seemed that one more was added to the numerous enemies of France. Above all, there was the pope, who 'de gaieté de cœur' (he was seventy-eight) 'et d'un dessein prémédité' was stirring up 'a bloody war' among Christians, directed against a king who was sacrificing everything in order to destroy heresy.[3] All this boiled over in a royal Declaration[4] of 14/24 September in which Louis, having recounted his grievances, and how much he had endured for peace, announced that his armies were about to invest the imperial fortress of Philippsburg, which, after capture, would be restored as a proof of pacific intentions. As for his claims to furniture and towns in the Palatinate, he was willing to com-

[1] An interesting report on the situation at Versailles in this period will be found in a letter from baron Nils Lilierote to Trumbull, in *H.M.C. Rep.*, *MSS of marquis of Downshire*, i. 299.

[2] *Ranke*, iv. 413.

[3] These words occur in Louis's instructions to Rébenac, ambassador at Madrid, 10–22 Oct. *Aff. Étr.* (*Espagne*), 75, f. 131*b*.

[4] *Dumont*, vii. 170–3.

promise these for a monetary payment; as for Cologne, he would withdraw his troops as soon as the pope gave way; these matters settled, he would enter into a general pacification. Europe was given three months in which to accept this 'peace' offer. Even Louis's contemporaries were surprised and bewildered. For the moment, however, the threat to William had been averted; but only for the moment.

William, who had learned from long experience that one never knew where Louis would strike next, was anxious that the French king should not repeat his exploit of 1672 by an invasion of Holland. But before that anxiety was removed he had had to overcome many difficulties. As he could not be sure that the States General or Dutch opinion would support him in an invasion of England, he had been obliged, in the summer of 1688, to resort to subterfuge. He had to apply, for the purposes of the expedition, money intended for fortifications; he had to win over a number of burghers; and in these transactions he showed such skill that even the separatism of the provinces was turned to his advantage.[1] Thus, Amsterdam had long been hostile to the prince, especially when, as in the years 1683–5, it was thought that he was on good terms with James;[2] but meanwhile the city had filled up with English malcontents, who taught the citizens to believe that James's conduct at home made him harmless abroad. Intense commercial jealousy of Rotterdam served still further to mitigate the hostility of Amsterdam to the House of Orange; and meanwhile French prohibition of the import of herring from Holland helped to unite the Dutch.

The European situation also helped to promote William's plans, while concealing their real object. James's agreement of April 1688, whereby Louis contributed to the cost of maintaining an English squadron in the Downs, justified the fitting out of a Dutch fleet, which, it was professed, might have to be used in defence of Sweden, Holland's ally, against Denmark, the ally

[1] *Ranke*, iv. 405.

[2] G. H. Kurtz, *Willem III en Amsterdam*. This monograph shows the important part played by Nicolas Witsen, a leading deputy of Amsterdam, who was afterwards won over by William. For subsequent relations between William and Amsterdam, see P. J. Blok, *History of the people of the Netherlands*, iv. 477 sqq.

of France. The attempted recall of English troops from Holland provided an obvious reason for raising more men; and persistent rumours of an active alliance between James and Louis increased Dutch anxiety regarding their security, thus causing them to acquiesce more readily in William's plans. On 19–29 September the province of Holland took the lead by a resolution that the intention of the kings of France and England was to subvert the Protestant religion in Britain, and to destroy the United Provinces.[1] Meanwhile, with the help of Bentinck, William was busily transforming the league of Augsburg into a series of active and offensive alliances. In these, a leading part was played by his relative Frederick, elector of Brandenburg, who undertook to supply 9,000 men and a famous general, Schomberg. Hanover was later detached from the French side; the elector of Saxony and the dukes of Celle and Hesse were also brought within the orbit of the prince's allies. Not yet was there a public treaty, save for a renewal in June of existing agreements between the States General and Brandenburg.[2] As Ranke observed,[3] the princely houses of Germany, which had taken the lead in the Reformation were now combining, under the direction of William, in opposition to France. But there was a difference—the Protestant allies had the support of the emperor and the sympathy of the pope. The critical point in all this had come in September when, to the intense relief of both William and the Dutch, Louis dispatched his troops to the middle Rhine.

Late in September and early in October James was advised by Sancroft and a number of bishops to dissolve the Ecclesiastical Commission, to bestow office only on those qualified by law, to cancel dispensations, restore the universities and colleges, re-establish the boroughs, stop the writs of *quo warranto*, and summon a free parliament. In proposing what was not unlike a first draft of the Bill of Rights,[4] the church was playing a role comparable with that played by Langton in the reign of John; indeed, behind such a façade of Protestantism and constitution-

[1] *R. Fruin's Verspreide Geschrigten*, ed. P. J. Blok and P. L. Muller, pt. v. 183.

[2] 20–30 June, in *Dumont*, vii. 156.

[3] *Ranke*, iv. 416.

[4] A copy will be found in *A Collection of Papers Relating to the Present Juncture of Affairs*, 1689, no. 7.

alism, James might at least have tried to preserve the throne for his House. At first he showed a measure of compliance. On 5 October he announced the dissolution of the Ecclesiastical Commission, and next day he restored the charter of the city of London.[1] A proclamation of 17 October[2] ordered the restoration of their franchises to the corporations. But he would not give up the dispensing power. Moreover, his concessions were interpreted as resulting solely from the threat of invasion, and therefore likely to be recalled as soon as the threat was over. It was ominous also that, though an attempt was made to bring back to their posts those lords-lieutenant and deputies, sheriffs, and justices who had been evicted, very few returned to their posts. There was the same unwillingness of the gentry to accept commissions in the new regiments that were raised.[3] After the excitement of the summer, the general mood of the autumn was one of apathy, to be accounted for mainly by the fact that Englishmen were obliged to decide between two dislikes—of the Dutch and of the Papists. A certain elementary patriotism caused many to regard with disgust the prospect of submission to a foreigner, akin, it is true, in religion, but antagonistic in temperament; the other dislike, however, arose from something even stronger than personal repugnance, namely, knowledge of what treatment a Protestant community might expect from a strongly established Catholic dynasty. So the mood of England on the eve of the Revolution was not, as has sometimes been maintained, one of spiritual exaltation; on the contrary, it reflected that listlessness which comes from having to choose between two evils.

This proved to be important, since it helps to account for the absence of bloodshed. Many must have felt as did sir John Bramston, an old Clarendonian loyalist, who expressed his dislike for those who took the lead in the Revolution, but afterwards confessed that, once James had left the country, there was no alternative but submission to his successor.[4] Not perhaps a very consistent attitude. Other revolutions have been more consistent, and therefore more violent.

[1] *P.C. Reg.* 72, 5 Oct. 1688. [2] *Steele*, i. 3881.

[3] For example, the letter of the duke of Norfolk to Sunderland, in *S.P. James II*, 15 Oct.

[4] Sir John Bramston, *Autobiography* (Camden Society), 355–6.

James's concessions in domestic affairs were accompanied by what, for a time, looked like a change of heart in foreign policy. This resulted from French reaction to news of William's preparations. Louis instructed D'Avaux[1] at The Hague to inform the States that he would regard any active move against James as a move against himself. In helping to procure this manifesto, Skelton, the English ambassador in France, had taken a leading part, which he naturally regarded as in the interests of his royal master; but, to his surprise, he was recalled, and sent to the Tower[2] on 17 September. Once more James's foreign policy was vacillating. This move may well have been on account of the queen's influence; it may also have been helped by Sunderland and Jeffreys, who both perceived that a disavowal of the French connexion was a necessary accompaniment to concessions at home. So, on the recall of Skelton, Albeville at The Hague was instructed to offer the States General an alliance for the maintenance of the treaty of Nimeguen, a move by which James may have hoped to divide William from the Dutch, or even to give a more patriotic complexion to his foreign policy.

But the move failed, as the prince and the States were now working in harmony; and the preparations for invasion were far advanced. On the last day of September William published a Declaration,[3] giving his reasons for the proposed invasion of England; a few weeks later this was followed by a resolution of the States General, pledging their support.[4] So ended this short diversion. It involved the ruin of Sunderland, who was dismissed on 26 October. Shortly afterwards he fled, not to France, but to Holland, preferring to rely on the gratitude of William, rather than on the gullibility of Louis. This coincided with a renewal of the French connexion. In October James received about £25,000 from his French paymaster,[5] in spite of the fact that, only a few weeks before, he had talked of an active alliance with the Dutch; and even as late as November he suggested a verbal agreement with Louis. He thought French troops might be useful; but, most of all, he needed money to pay his own

[1] *Negociations de M. le comte d'Avaux en Hollande*, vi. 222.

[2] This was attributed to the influence of Sunderland. *Life of James II* (ed. J. S. Clarke), ii. 179–80.

[3] *Dumont*, vii. 198, 30 Sept.–10 Oct. 1688. [4] Ibid. vii. 205, 18–28 Oct.

[5] *Instructions Données* (*Angleterre*), ed. Jusserand, ii. 412.

soldiers, who might revolt if he left London in order to face the invader.[1] Even after William had set sail, there was a consignment of bullion, sent from Versailles, waiting in Calais for dispatch to James.

The monarch, who was thus prepared to subsidize his pensionary right up to the end, had not been idle during the three months ultimatum granted to Europe in September. It is possible that the march of French armies to the middle Rhine was intended as no more than a flamboyant demonstration, and that Louis had no wish to engage in another war. But he was never more dangerous than when he came forward as a lover of peace. In October Philippsburg was captured; Avignon was seized; an appeal was made for a general council against the pope, and the nuncio at Versailles had to consider himself either a prisoner or a hostage. Then, early in November, there came news that William had landed, so Louis declared war on the Dutch. His fury was steadily rising. He could still have retrieved an unfortunate situation by sending his armies north for an invasion of Holland, but (to their surprise) William and the Dutch were left alone. Meanwhile, the elector palatine had not answered the demand for monetary compensation; and, near at hand, was his province, predominantly Protestant, almost defenceless, an obvious object for that divine retribution of which Louis was the agent. The decision, in the winter of 1688–9, to wreak vengeance on that province, instead of interfering in the north, ensured the success of the English Revolution; a fact which must be accounted for in any assessment of the statesmanship of Louis XIV. That statesmanship was abundantly evidenced by a devastation of the twice-unfortunate Palatinate (it had been ravaged in 1674), accompanied by atrocities of such savagery as to make clear to the world the degree of irritation and frustration experienced by the Eldest Son of the Church. So Louis had his revenge, while the English had their revolution.

Delayed by westerly winds William's fleet, under the command of Herbert, had set sail on 19 October, only to be driven back by a storm; but by the 1st of November the 'Protestant' wind began to blow, and a second start was made. No one in

[1] *Instructions Données*, ii. 413. Also R. H. George, 'Financial Relations of Louis XIV and James II', in *Journal of Modern History*, Sept. 1931.

England appeared to know for what part of the coast it was bound. Some said the coast of Scotland, others favoured Essex; pilots 'in drink' said Sole Bay, the sober ones thought it would be Bridlington Bay. All this favoured the naval part of William's enterprise, and as there were twenty English pilots among the Dutch ships a landing might have been effected almost anywhere. The point had been reached when James's first line of defence, his navy would be tested.

The English ships, now commanded by the Protestant Dartmouth in place of the Catholic Strickland, were at anchor off the Gunfleet, on the northern side of the Thames estuary. There were 52 ships of the line, 3rd, 4th, and 5th rates, with 17 fireships, mounting a total of 1876 guns, very slightly inferior to the Dutch armament of 54 ships and 2,040 guns.[1] The loyalty of many of the officers and men was doubtful, and some may have been won over to William's cause by Herbert's letter from Goree, announcing that 'as the kingdom has always depended on the navy for its defence, so you will go farther by making it the protector of her religion and liberties'. Other influences were at work. It has been said that harbours corrupt men and ships. The sailors in Dartmouth's fleet were receiving pamphlets and newsletters from ashore, and were caballing among themselves;[2] indeed, the situation at the Gunfleet was not unlike that on Hounslow Heath. Nor could reliance be put on the equipment. 'There is not one ship behind you', wrote Pepys to Dartmouth on 20 October, 'from whose commander I do not daily hear of the want of guns, carriages, . . . or something relating thereto.'[3] On the same day James wrote to Dartmouth suggesting that, as the wind was again in the west, he should leave his anchorage and prevent the Dutch fleet from getting out;[4] to which reasonable request the admiral returned the answer: 'I am of opinion that the keeping of this fleet together and entire is essential to His Majesty's service',[5] adding that, in such a season of the year, the enemy would be safe in their harbours, while we 'would be knocked about'. This may be interpreted in one of three ways: it may have been an early

[1] *Rawl. MS.* A. 186, f. 438.

[2] *H.M.C. Rep.* xi, app. pt. 5, 259 (Dartmouth papers), Dartmouth to king, 17 Oct. 1688.

[3] Ibid. 169.

[4] Ibid. 169.

[5] *Rawl. MS.* A. 186, f. 368.

expression of the doctrine of the 'fleet in being', or it may be attributable to the commander's doubts regarding the dependability of his ships and men, or it may even reflect, in the mind of Dartmouth, a lack of enthusiasm for his master's cause. What seemed certain was that the English fleet would not oppose the invasion.[1]

Not till 30 October, when the wind was at south-south-east, did Dartmouth leave the Gunfleet, and next day the easterly wind obliged him to anchor off the Longsands Head, where he remained until 4 November, having already sighted the invading fleet sailing west in an easterly gale. Entering the Channel, Dartmouth was off Beachy Head on 5 November, when he reported to the king the unanimous decision of the flag officers and commanders not to attack, since there was no longer any chance of preventing the landing.[2] James, who had shown great consideration for the admiral, now felt undecided. On 9 November he advised him to use his discretion, but three days later he ordered him to attack the Dutch wherever he might find them.[3] Meanwhile, Dartmouth was obliged by stress of weather to shelter in the Downs; on 16 November, however, he again set sail for the west, apparently on a forlorn mission to Torbay; but heavy weather and the tide drove his fleet south-west as far as Alderney, by which time most of his ships had parted company, and many were leaking badly. Eventually, with only twenty-two ships he was off Torbay on 19 November, a fortnight after William's landing; and having learned that the whole Dutch fleet was still at anchor there, he turned east, and was at St. Helen's on the following day. So ended one of the most ambiguous episodes in the history of the Royal Navy. James had had the willing service of Pepys,[4] the ablest of all naval administrators, who since April 1686 had devoted himself to an ambitious programme of reform, after years of corruption and waste. But, whatever success may have been achieved in carrying out this programme (about which contemporary opinion was divided),

[1] For this subject generally see E. B. Powley, *The English Navy and the Revolution*, and J. Ehrman, *The Navy in the War of William III*, ch. viii.

[2] *Rawl. MS.* A 186, f. 374.

[3] *H.M.C. Rep.* xi, app. pt. 5, 190, 198.

[4] For this see J. Ehrman, op. cit., pt. 2, ch. 8, and A. Bryant, *Samuel Pepys, the Saviour of the Navy*.

there was the human factor, which probably explains best why the English fleet failed to offer any effective opposition to the landing. Illustration of this is provided by three messages sent in December 1688. The first was from lady Dartmouth to her husband:[1]

. . . I hope deare, you will be so wise to yourselfe and family as to doe what becomes a reasonable man, who I am sure is left in the most deplorable condition of any subject or servant whatsoever. I doe not find the prodistant interist disatisfied with you, and the other I look upon as quit exterpreted. . . .

The second and third,[2] dated 3 and 6 December, were from Dartmouth to the king:

Remember, I pray sir, how prophetically I have foretold you your misfortunes, and the courses you might have taken to avoid them. . . . I did not think seamen would have troubled themselves about parliaments.

On 17 December, Dartmouth again wrote:[3] 'Your Majesty knowes what condition you left the fleet in.' This must have been one of the most bitter reproaches ever received by a king from a subject.

William landed at Torbay on 5 November, the day which still commemorates English hatred of popery. Having assembled his forces at Exeter, the prince was at first disappointed with the response of the local gentry, who may well have had the fate of Monmouth in mind; but he was soon to receive substantial reinforcements from the other side. James had under his command about twice as many as the number in the service of William. Having sent his son to Portsmouth in order that he might be taken to France, the king was with his troops at Salisbury on 19 November, a few days after lord Cornbury, Clarendon's son, had deserted to William. The appointment of Feversham to command the royal troops ensured inaction and delay, conditions which favour desertion; and on 24 November a council of war decided that the troops should retreat to London. That night Churchill went over to the other side; his example

[1] *H.M.C. Rep.* xi, app. pt. 5, 232, 12 Dec.

[2] Ibid. 276, 278.

[3] Ibid. 282. In January 1688 Dr. Plot had scraped from the bore of guns at Chatham scales of rust 'as thick as a milled shilling' (*Rawl. MS.* A. 171, f. 76).

was soon followed by the duke of Grafton; and at Andover prince George of Denmark experienced those twinges of conscience which were almost epidemic at that time. Princess Anne, under the efficient protection of Compton, fled to Nottingham to join the earl of Devonshire, where a body of nobility and gentry issued a manifesto condemning the misdeeds of the king and calling for a free parliament.[1] The recent concessions of James were declared to be no more than 'plums for children'. Similar pronouncements came from other quarters.

Even thus, James's position was far from hopeless, since there had not been a word about putting William in his place, and in his public declarations the prince had always posed as a liberator, anxious only to restore the Protestant religion, and to ensure that James would rule with the help of a free parliament. To many of the peers it seemed that William's presence in England might serve a useful purpose, not for the overthrow of the dynasty, but in order to extract concessions and guarantees from the king. The high church loyalists were intent on playing off king against prince, with a strong preference for the former; and had James possessed the slightest political capacity he could have taken advantage of the situation. Thus a Jacobite party was already coming into existence. But the king gave no lead. On his side, the prince maintained strict silence about his intentions, so an attempt at compromise was made by a body of about fifty peers and bishops, including Halifax, Clarendon, and Nottingham, which met James on 27 November, the day after his return to London. Led by Clarendon, they demanded the summoning of parliament, the dismissal of Roman Catholic officers, a full amnesty, and the sending of commissioners to treat with the prince, then on his way from the west. To James, this attitude of his brother-in-law, formerly the most sycophantic of his ministers, must have been indeed humiliating, and he may well have felt that his worst enemies were of his own household. Almost as humiliating, though in a different way, was the fact that Halifax was the most sympathetic and conciliatory member of this conclave.[2] For the first time the bewildered king gave way. He ordered writs to be issued for a meeting of parliament on 15 January, and agreed that Halifax, Nottingham,

[1] *Declaration of the Nobility, Gentry, and Commonalty at Nottingham*, 22 Nov.
[2] *Halifax*, ii. 10–22.

and Godolphin should act as his intermediaries with the prince. But, on reflection, Clarendon appears to have reconsidered his position, for on 1 December he joined his son in William's camp. This marked a cleavage between the high church party and the moderates, the latter being led by Halifax. Already, by his able conduct in the Exclusion controversy, Halifax had saved the crown for James; he at least tried to render him this service a second time.

William, having now been joined by many of the west of England gentry, left Exeter on 21 November; and, apart from a skirmish at Wincanton, he met with little opposition on his march to London. Arriving at Hungerford on 7 December, he was interviewed by the three ambassadors. Their mission was a delicate one. They had to announce that James had summoned a parliament; to remind him that this had been one of the avowed objects of his mission; and they were empowered to assure the prince that James was willing to enter into a treaty for guaranteeing that the elections would be free. But the embassy had little success. William, after consultation with the English and Dutch leaders at his headquarters, announced what were tantamount to conditions—papists must be removed from office; proclamations reflecting on himself must be recalled; the Tower and Tilbury fort were to be entrusted to the city of London, and a part of the revenues must be assigned to him for the maintenance of his troops.[1] These conditions, acceptable for the most part to Whigs and moderates, including Halifax himself, seemed to James so humiliating that they confirmed him in the intention which he had recently formed, of quitting the country. Having received the report of the prince's conditions on 10 December, and announcing that he would give an answer next day, he burnt many of the writs for a parliament, ordered Feversham to disband the army, and left Whitehall early on the morning of the 11th. At Sheerness, he embarked on a vessel bound for France. The night of 11 December was noted as one of the stormiest in the history of the capital, when the sky was lit up by the fires consuming the property of papists, the mob having been instigated by the rumour that Irish soldiers were marching on London in order to destroy the Protestants. It was in this orgy that Jeffreys, disguised as a sea-

[1] *Halifax*, ii. 29.

man, was captured in Wapping and placed, for his own protection, in the Tower.

James's small vessel, delayed by the tide, was anchored off Faversham on the night of the 11th. News that the king had left London spread throughout the country, and a band of fishermen decided to board the suspicious-looking craft when it was about to get under way. As they burst into the cabin sir Edward Hales stood up with a pistol in each hand to protect the king, but James forbade violence, and offered the fishermen a sum of £50. Having searched and robbed the king, the boarders then lit a fire in a brazier on deck; whereupon, when Hales complained of the smoke, he was answered roughly: 'Damn you, if you can't endure smoke, how will you endure hell fire?' James long remembered that night, the only occasion in his life when he had been subjected to violence and insult; later, in one of his proclamations[1] he specifically exempted from pardon those rough men who had so handled him. Next day, James, having been taken ashore, was lodged at the Queen's Arms, Faversham, where a crowd, in respectful silence, saw this wreck of a king; and one of the callers, sir Edward Dering, recorded this impression in his diary:[2] 'I observed a smile on his face, of an extraordinary size and sort, so forced, awkward and unpleasant to look upon, that I can truly say I never saw anything like it.' Meanwhile, lord Feversham was dispatched by the Lords with a body of troops to release the king, whom he took to Rochester, from whence James wrote a letter to William, desiring an interview, and this he sent by Feversham. William, then at Windsor, received the envoy with an order for his arrest.

James returned to London on Sunday, 16 December. The mob now accorded to him a welcome which caused him to feel more like his old self, so on the following day, at the last meeting of his Council, he refused all the proposals made to him. But this flash of haughtiness was short-lived. Zuylestein brought from William a message rejecting the royal request for an interview; and, when James asked the city of London to provide him with defence against the prince, he was met with a refusal. The Lords, assembled at Westminster, now intervened between the contestants, suggesting that the king should take up his

[1] *Steele*, i. 408*b*; 10 Apr. 1692; also *infra*, 367.
[2] *Add. MS.* 33, 923.

residence at Ham, near Richmond, once the house of Lauderdale, where he might have improved his situation by negotiation; for, so long as he was in England, he was the sovereign, and to that extent the position of William remained ambiguous. But James had been completely unnerved by recent events, and on the morning of 23 December he finally left England. On Christmas Day he was carried ashore, on the backs of the seamen, at Ambleteuse, a fishing village near Calais, and from there he joined his wife and child at St. Germains, where Louis had provided a refuge.

It is probably idle to speculate on the reasons why James left England. He may have feared that he would be deposed; he may even have thought that his life was in danger; what is certain is that he was sick in body and mind, scarcely able to think coherently. Like his father, he was essentially a family man, and it was in his family affections that he had been most deeply wounded; more dimly he perceived that he had been forsaken by those in whom he had always had complete confidence. His best general had gone over to the enemy; his chief minister had some kind of nervous breakdown at the moment when firmness was most needed; his favourite priest was one of the first to leave the country. Neither his army nor his navy showed any enthusiasm for his cause; a nation, to which he had offered what seemed like a priceless gift, had stood aside in sullen refusal. A cast-iron system had cracked and broken, pierced by shafts that brought not understanding but bewilderment. For all this, his religious emotions supplied the explanation—he had offended God by his love of women; he had not been firm enough with doubters and opponents; he repented of his sins, but of the wrong ones. Having lost an earthly crown, there remained the martyr's crown; had James been a better or wiser man, he would have been content with his spiritual reward. In all this he had not changed, nor had his French cousin, the embodiment of stability and order in a world of heresy and rebellion. That cousin was also the embodiment of power; so James turned to Louis, hoping with his help to piece together again the mechanism which had so unaccountably broken in his hands.

In days when it was believed that some kind of standard should be applied in valuations of the past, historians took it upon themselves to condemn evil and folly in rulers or their ministers, condemnation based on the assumption that these undesirable qualities were neither universal nor inevitable, and that their manifestation, even by pious kings, might be evidence not so much of high purpose as of low mentality. All this has changed. With our depreciated literary currency, it is easy to pass off pieces like Sunderland and Jeffreys as genuine coin of the realm; and, in an age of reconditioned products, we can account for, and even justify, the aberrations of the great men of the past with the simple formula, that they were men of their times. On such a plea, James II and his ministers have a chance, if not of eulogy, at least of condonation; and, on the same comforting plea, we are all (provided of sufficient social standing) sure of an acquittal in the Day of Judgement. Or we might maintain that James's tragedy derived from this, that, so far from being a man of his age, he was much in advance of it. It is possible, however, that neither of these claims is valid. James's character, simple and immature, presents no 'problems'. With the blood of Stuarts, Bourbons, Guises, and Medici in his veins, he appears almost as a reversion to an earlier type, a type best represented by one who, though not an ancestor, was built on a similar, but somewhat larger and more dignified scale, namely, Philip II of Spain, whom James resembled in his piety, his industry, his deadly consistency, his total and permanent impenetrability; above all, in his bitter hatred of heresy as the greatest evil in the world.

But historical verdicts are relative, in regard to both place and time; and success, whether in king or subject, is accounted for not only by character, but by the conditions in which one's life is passed. Had James ruled in Spain, or even in seventeenth-century France, history might now be resounding with his praises, voiced not only by Spaniards or Frenchmen, but by Englishmen. But as he ruled in England, he still awaits his apologist.

VIII

THE REVOLUTION IN ENGLAND

ONE of the best sources for the study of the English Revolution is to be found in the proclamations and declarations put forth by the contestants; never before had the printed word played such a part in political events. On 17 October 1688 James issued a proclamation[1] for the restoration of the corporations, and the removal therefrom of those who had been intruded; three days later came his proclamation ordering a strict watch to be kept on the coasts, and forbidding the spread of false news. On 1 November, the eve of his embarkation, there was an announcement from the prince of Orange, giving his reasons for invading England; next day, James imposed a ban on all public announcements made by the prince. On 6 November the king, after referring to the invasion, promised redress of all grievances; on the 17th a third party—the Lords—intervened with a declaration announcing that war could be avoided only by the speedy summoning of parliament. Then, on 22 November, there were published announcements, from the nobility, gentry, and commonalty of York and Nottingham, declaring adhesion to the prince of Orange; and, at last, on 30 November, a royal proclamation intimated a meeting of parliament for the 15th of January. The conditions laid down by William at Hungerford were published on 9 December; two days later, James, announcing that he had been forced to send his queen and son to safety, confessed that, as he could not trust the army, he would offer no opposition to the prince. On the same day the lords spiritual and temporal, in and about the cities of London and Westminster, intimated that, as the king had withdrawn himself, they had applied to the prince to summon a free parliament, with liberty of conscience to Protestant Dissenters. This date, 11 December, marked the end of the reign of James II and the beginning of the interregnum.

[1] The proclamations in this and the two succeeding paragraphs will be found in *Steele*, i, nos. 3881–3943.

The literary duel continued throughout the interregnum. During his short stay at Rochester James, on 22 December, put forth a proclamation intimating that he had left Whitehall because of the discourteous conduct of the prince, but he would return at the call of the nation, whenever it agreed to have liberty of conscience. This coincided with an order from the Lords, assembled in their House, requiring all papists to leave London. Next day, 23 December, the prince of Orange summoned all persons who had served in any of Charles II's parliaments to meet at St. James's on the 26th, together with the lord mayor, aldermen, and fifty of the common council of the city of London. These informal assemblies of Lords, ex-Commons, and city magistrates asked William to summon a convention. On Christmas Day the lords spiritual and temporal requested the prince of Orange to take upon himself the direction of affairs until the meeting of the intended convention on 22 January, for which His Highness was asked to direct the issue of writs. His compliance with this request was announced on 29 December. Finally, on 4 January 1689, came a proclamation from James, in the form of a letter to the privy council, intimating the concessions which he had made, and announcing to the world that he had been obliged to leave his country because of his fear of death. The history of the Revolution can be little more than comment on these official pronouncements.

If it be granted that the model revolution is one that avoids bloodshed and maintains a fundamental continuity with the past, then the English Revolution was a model of its kind. Parliament was not in session, but a body of lords and bishops sat in their House, while old parliamentarians met at St. James's, each of which conclaves invited William to assume the administration. The ex-Commons sitting at St. James's had, of course, no official status, but the lords spiritual and temporal, though consisting only of 'those about London and Westminster', and though not summoned by a king, had a somewhat stronger position, because they were independent of election. Indeed, they acted in an executive capacity; that they should have done so is one of the many illustrations of the aristocratic character both of the English constitution and of the English revolution. On 20 December the prince had summoned this body of peers to meet him at St. James's, where he informed them that he would assume only the direction of military affairs, leaving to them the civil administration. For nearly a month, therefore, the only semblance of a government was a camarilla of lords and bishops, acting with a singularly uncommunicative generalissimo. It will be noticed also that the critical point in these events was reached in the three days between the king's second flight (22/23 December) and the meeting of ex-parliamentarians at St. James's on the 26th. As James had burnt many of the writs for a parliament, and had fled the country, the apostolic succession in both crown and parliament was broken. Rochester, lamenting this disaster to Dartmouth,[1] confessed his opinion that, if James had not withdrawn himself, the peers would have sent to him before they made any address to the prince. 'What can the most loyal and dutiful body in the world do without a head?' For most of the high church party that head was now over the water, and William's difficulties were about to begin.

Lastly, tribute must be paid to the part played in this crisis by the city of London. Just as, at the Restoration, representatives of the corporation had actively co-operated with the Commons, so now at the Revolution they were associated with a rump of Charles II's parliaments, and served to confer on that portion of parliamentary anatomy a certain decency and even dignity. On both these occasions the Guildhall was a national as much as a civic institution; and, as if to commemorate this fact, the lord mayor and aldermen gave a banquet on 29 January to William and Mary and members of both Houses. It was attended by sir Edward Dering, the diarist who had noted the extraordinary smile on James's face at Faversham. In his diary, Dering recorded of this feast: 'the entertainment was great and orderly, as the thing would admit. In the year 1660 I was likewise present, and the order of this was in most respects like that.'[2] Here is an illustration of what foreigners mean by English 'phlegm'.

The elections[3] of January 1689 resulted in the return of a House of Commons in which the majority consisted of old opponents of Stuart rule, anxious to see the crown conferred on

[1] *H.M.C. Rep.* xv, app. pt. 1, 141, 25 Dec. 1688.

[2] *Add. MS.* 33,923, Tuesday, 29 Jan. 1689.

[3] J. R. Plumb, 'Elections to the Convention Parliament' in *Camb. Hist. J.* v (1937), 235–52.

William; while, in both Lords and Commons were some who, though they had been alienated by the conduct of James, were not prepared to admit a break in the succession. One is obliged to refer to these as Whig and Tory respectively, but this is an over-simplification, since it assumes that these labels were generally accepted and applied at the time.[1] Henry Powle was Speaker of the Lower House, Halifax of the Upper. On 22 January, the first day of the session, a declaration of the Lords enunciated the genesis of the Convention, namely, the invitations extended by separate conclaves of Lords and Commons to William, requesting him to cause writs to be issued for its summoning. They then concurred with the Commons in an address of thanks to the prince, with a formal request that he would continue to direct the administration of affairs.

The Commons were the first to address themselves to the great constitutional questions raised by recent events; and, as there was a certain hesitancy on the part of new members, the lead was taken by such veterans as colonel Birch, sir T. Clarges, and sergeant Maynard, with the help of those experienced parliamentarians sir T. Lee, sir T. Littleton, and sir Edward Seymour. Birch, who had started life as a carter, had a habit of driving straight through the subtleties and fine distinctions of debate. 'These forty years', he declared,[2] 'we have been striving against anti-Christ, popery and tyranny.' Here was an echo of a far-off past; this link with the Puritan Revolution was evidenced by the passing, on 29 January, of a resolution that a Popish prince was inconsistent with a Protestant state. There was another reminiscence, this time of the Restoration, in lord Falkland's proposal[3] that, before they filled the throne, they should resolve what powers were to be conferred on the ruler, a proposal which started a hubbub of suggestions—frequent parliaments, independent judges, inviolability of corporations, and many more. That these demands were placed in the forefront may be attributed in part to the influence of Halifax, who was the reputed author of a broadsheet, distributed among the Commons, which counselled them to agree on their constitution before they decided on their governor.[4] So the House resolved that, before proceeding to fill the throne, it would secure the

[1] *Supra*, 127 and *infra*, 473–5.
[2] *Grey*, ix. 26, 29 Jan. 1689.
[3] Ibid. ix. 30.
[4] *Rawl. MS.* D. 1079, f. 4*b*.

religion, laws, and liberties of the nation.[1] The mistake of 1660 would not be made a second time.

The duty of formulating these constitutional guarantees was entrusted to a committee, in which John Somers played a notable part. This committee reported on 2 February with what proved to be the first draft of the Declaration of Rights,[2] a draft which included not only an assertion of the old Whig doctrine of the social contract, but also articles of reform, some of which did not appear in the Bill of Rights as it finally took shape. These proposals included provisions for uniting all Protestants in the matter of public worship, for making judges' tenure of office *quamdiu se bene gesserint*, for regulating Chancery and other courts of justice, for prohibiting the buying and selling of offices, for amending the procedure in trials of treason. Later proposals for inclusion in the Bill of Rights were that no pardon should be pleadable to an impeachment, and that, in default of heirs to either Mary, or Anne or William (in this order), the crown should go to the princess Sophia of Hanover.[3] This latter clause was dropped because the birth of the duke of Gloucester in the summer of 1689 made it possible that the line of princess Anne would be perpetuated. None of the clauses above enumerated appeared in the Bill of Rights as it was passed in the following December.

On 29 January the Lords went into committee, with Danby in the chair, in order to consider, item by item, the resolutions which had been sent them by the Commons. On the question of the social contract, and the assertion that James had abdicated the throne, the Lords' committee consulted the judges, who expressed the opinion that these matters pertained not to the common law, but to the law of parliament, on which they were unqualified to speak.[4] Accordingly, while the Lords accepted the social contract by a small majority, they substituted the word 'deserted' for abdicated, and they rejected by 55 to 41 the resolution that the throne was vacant. Conferences between the two Houses in the period 29 January–12 February revealed fundamental differences of opinion in regard to what the Revolution really implied. On the one hand the Whigs,

[1] *C.J.* x, 29 Jan. 1689. [2] Ibid. x, 2 Feb.

[3] *L.J.* xiv, 29 July, 22 and 23 Nov. 1689.

[4] *H.M.C. Rep.* xii, app. pt. 6 (*MSS. of House of Lords*), 16 sqq.

intent on declaring the throne elective, argued that the invitations to the prince to assume the administration presupposed a vacancy in the throne, an assumption challenged by the representatives of the Lords, who maintained that the throne was hereditary. From the part played by Rochester and Clarendon in the conferences, it is clear that they were anxious to preserve the crown solely for their niece Mary, with William as regent,[1] a view shared by the bishops and, at first, by Danby; but opposed by Halifax, who saw that the prince would rule only as king. The deadlock was broken by William himself. From the first he had made it clear that he would not be content with the position of regent, nor would he act as a mere consort to his wife; if he were not given full regal power he would return to Holland. The difficulty regarding Mary herself was removed when she wrote to Danby[2] that she would occupy the throne only with her husband as king.

So at last the way was clear, and the two Houses adopted a compromise. On the one hand, the social contract was thrown over; on the other, the clause was retained which declared that James had abdicated, and that the throne was therefore vacant. On 12 February the two Houses agreed on a joint Declaration of Rights, afterwards embodied in the Bill of Rights. Meanwhile, Mary arrived from Holland on 12 February, and on the following day the prince and princess were waited on in the palace of Whitehall by the Lords and Commons, headed by Halifax. The Declaration having been read, Halifax, in the name of the Convention, offered the crown to William and Mary; and with their acceptance, the first stage of the Revolution was complete.

So ended the interregnum which had begun on 11 December 1688 with the first flight of James; its termination on 12 February 1689 marked both the restoration of monarchy and the beginning of the Convention Parliament. The apostolic succession of crown and parliament was restored at the same point of time. Rejoicings in England and Holland showed genuine relief that at last the menace of a popish sovereignty was over, and that the two great Protestant powers were ranged with each

[1] There is a full account of the conference in *Bodl. MS. Eng. Hist.* C. 299.

[2] A. Browning, *Thomas Osborne, earl of Danby*, i. 420–1.

other against the threat from France. But already the debates in the Convention had revealed a deep cleavage of opinion, for while the Whigs regarded William as their personal champion, and expected him to rule with their help alone, they had been so long out of office that they could not have provided the personnel of an efficient administration; while bodies of old Stuart loyalists retained, in different degrees, their scruples about the sovereignty of William. These very diverse elements had combined to effect the Revolution; and, mainly by the fiction of a 'Pretender', a compromise had been reached; but how long would this uneasy alliance endure? Even more serious was the fact that, after twenty-eight years of Stuart rule, the departments of state were riddled by debt, corruption, and waste. Men were retained, indeed had to be retained in office, who purposely cheated and deceived in the hope of prejudicing the new régime, and favouring the cause of the exiled James; their secret depredations did far more harm than the public hostility of the Jacobites. 'The king should have new men about him', declared the junior Hampden;[1] adding that, when the Dutch had shaken off the Spanish yoke, they did not employ the duke of Alva's ministers. But here William was the victim of circumstance. He could not even command the best service of his supporters, nor could he always be sure who were his worst enemies. The trouble was that there were two kings; and, as the one in England alienated people by the coldness of his presence, the other made more friends by the glamour of his absence, with the result that obedience to a ruler was often tempered by loyalty to a cause. This dualism lasted until 1696, the turning-point of the reign.

The appointments to high offices of state revealed the king's desire to balance the two bodies of opinion that had been divided on the question of his kingship. For him, 'Whigs' meant old Exclusionists, whose principles he disliked, because these were supposed to be republican; while 'Tories', he was taught to believe, were loyalists, and therefore to be encouraged. With the first, he could not dispense; with the second, he assumed that their loyalty would be extended to him. So one can hardly speak of a coalition of 'parties', for William was really attempting to secure co-operation among several loosely distinguished

[1] *Grey*, ix. 487, 14 Dec. 1689.

bodies of men, about most of whom he was making unwarrantable assumptions.

Meanwhile, in the foreground were two men who had to be given high office. Danby (now marquis of Carmarthen) and Halifax had both rendered distinguished service in effecting the Revolution, the former by the weight which his name conferred on the invitation to William, the second by the skill with which he had conducted the negotiations after the abortive colloquy of Hungerford. So Danby, always ambitious, was made president of the Council—a great disappointment to him because he had hoped for the white staff of the lord high treasurership; accordingly, he showed his resentment by irregular attendances at the meetings of Council, and devoted himself to the task of scoring against his rival Halifax, who became lord privy seal. The king disliked the complaints of the one as much as the dissertations of the other. The two secretaryships of state were given to Nottingham and Shrewsbury, the one the most accredited exponent of Anglican loyalism, the other, a noted dilettante, assiduously cultivated by the Whigs. Halifax and Nottingham had both declined the chancellorship, on the ground that, for this post, a trained lawyer was required; but James's reign had so degraded and denuded the judicial bench that no lawyer of sufficient repute was available, so the great seal was entrusted to a commission headed by Maynard. The Treasury, which remained in commission throughout the reign, was presided over by Charles, viscount Mordaunt, created earl of Monmouth,[1] whose qualification was mainly that he had opposed James; a minister of James, Godolphin, was included among the commissioners, for the good reason that he alone had knowledge of the national finances. The addition of lord Delamere, sir Henry Capel, and the elder Hampden served to give this board a Whiggish complexion. Heading the commissioners of the Admiralty was Herbert, later lord Torrington, a Whig by reputation; conjoined with him were William Sacheverell, a Whig by conviction, sir T. Lee, an old leader of the Country party, and sir John Lowther of Whitehaven, who, like his kinsman, sir John Lowther of Lowther,[2] was regarded as a

[1] Later the famous earl of Peterborough.

[2] Appointed first commissioner of the Treasury in 1690. Afterwards viscount Lonsdale.

moderate Tory. Of the judges, the most notable were sir John Holt, who became lord chief justice of King's Bench, and sir Henry Pollexfen, lord chief justice of Common Pleas. Sir George Treby became attorney general and Somers solicitor general. Court offices were found for the king's Dutch friends, Bentinck, Zuylestein, and Auverquerque.

In a different category were John Wildman, the plotter, now postmaster general, an office which provided him with opportunities for opening letters; and Aaron Smith, who, as solicitor of the Treasury, hired informers for crown prosecutions. Such was the motley array which filled what, for want of a better term, must be called William's first administration. In practice, balance proved to be little better than oscillation. The intense rivalry between Danby and Halifax was matched by that between Nottingham and Shrewsbury, Mordaunt and Delamere. Personalities were more important than party allegiance. This is why we can hardly yet speak of a ministry, though the word 'minister' was in common use, not in any modern sense, but simply as distinguishing the holder of high civil office, responsible to the crown. William was his own first minister.

On 23 February William touched with the sceptre the first Bill of his reign—that for declaring the Convention a parliament.[1] This Act imposed two oaths, one of fidelity to William and Mary, the other a repudiation of the doctrines that princes might lawfully be deposed by foreign powers, and that foreign powers had authority or jurisdiction in England, both of these oaths being intended as substitutes for the old oaths of allegiance and supremacy, which, as they contained the phrase 'rightful and lawful sovereign' were deemed unsuitable for the new reign. At first, the new oaths were imposed only on members of both Houses, but, after prolonged debate, it was decided to impose them on all office holders, including the clergy.[2] The Mutiny Act[3] was passed on 28 March. This Act had an immediate as well as a more remote cause. The immediate cause was the mutiny of the Scottish soldiers of lord Dumbarton's regiment,

[1] 1 W. and M., c. 1.

[2] 1 W. and M., c. 8.

[3] 1 W. and M., c. 5; also *Documents*, no. 311. For the soldier and the army, see *infra*, 328–9. For the subject generally, see C. M. Clode, *The Military Forces of the Crown; their Administration and Government*, and C. Walton, *History of the British Standing Army*.

one of the re-formed units of James's army. Stationed at Ipswich in readiness for transport to the continent, these soldiers resented the appointment of a foreigner, Schomberg, as their colonel-in-chief, and attempted to march back to Scotland. But the mutiny was soon quelled, with the help of another foreigner, Ginkel, and only the ringleaders were punished. More remotely, the events of the last two reigns had illustrated the need for some special code of military law to regulate the conduct of the soldier, particularly in cases of mutiny and desertion, but distrust of the executive had prevented the legislature coming to its aid by such a measure. Hence the Mutiny Act, at first passed for only six months, which, with subsequent additions, provided a special code of discipline for the soldier, including the power to inflict the death penalty for desertion. This Act did not provide any guarantee, expressed or implied, for the regular summoning of parliament; indeed the first series of such Acts came to an end with the conclusion of hostilities in 1697.

As the Restoration had been followed by an attempt to grant toleration to Protestant Dissenters, so the Revolution raised again the great question of unity within the Protestant fold. Ever since 1679, and even more in the reign of James II, it had been realized that the Protestant Dissenters had been thrown, by the menace of popery, into the same camp as the Anglicans; and to many it seemed that, politically at least, the two had much in common; there was also the example of Scotland, where the Presbyterians had maintained the most consistent opposition to the later Stuarts. Not unnaturally, therefore, it was from the period of the Popish Plot that two abortive measures, a Toleration Bill and a Comprehension Bill were revived. Nottingham tried to secure the passage of both Bills. He had little difficulty with the first, but he failed with the second, the more ambitious of the two. This, the Comprehension Bill, would have relaxed the ritual and discipline of the church of England in such a manner that Nonconformists might attend the parish church without violation of their scruples against such practices as kneeling, and wearing the surplice. It would also have qualified for the cure of souls all Dissenters who took the oath against transubstantiation, and expressed approval of the doctrine, worship, and government of the church of England.[1] But the strong church party in the Commons successfully opposed the Bill, which was dropped on 8 April. The argument had prevailed that, as Convocation was about to be summoned, to that body should be referred the great questions raised by the problem of establishing unity in non-Catholic England.

Another abortive proposal at this time showed how a section, at least of the Convention, was anxious to mitigate the rigidity of the old religious distinctions, and to end the monopoly whereby office holding was limited to Anglicans. At the third reading in the Lords of the Bill for substituting new oaths for the old oaths of allegiance and supremacy (23 March), one of the peers offered as a rider a clause which would have qualified for office anyone who had taken the sacrament either according to the practice of the church of England, or according to that of any recognized Protestant communion. The rider was lost. Those who protested against this rejection gave reasons which show a remarkable advance on contemporary opinion. By the rejection of the proposal, maintained the protesting minority, a great part of the Protestant freemen of England were excluded from public employment 'from a mere scruple of conscience'; moreover, these men professed doctrines which were about to be publicly tolerated in a Bill then before the House (the Toleration Bill). This exclusion, contended the protesting peers, might have bad effects on Protestant and Reformed churches abroad, because it turned the edge of a law, intended to penalize Papists, against Protestants and friends of the government as settled by the Revolution. Lastly, in the words of this protest, 'mysteries of religion and divine worship are of divine original, and of a nature so wholly distinct from the secular affairs of politic society that they cannot be applied to these ends'.[2] In these words, the spirit of 1689 anticipated that of 1829.

It was very different with the Toleration Bill.[3] This did not abolish any of the penal statutes against Protestant Dissenters, but merely declared that they should not be enforced against

[1] The amended draft of the Comprehension Bill will be found in *H.M.C. Rep.* xii, app. pt. 6, 49.

[2] *L.J.* xiv, 23 Mar. 1689.

[3] 1 W. and M., c. 18; also *Documents*, no. 151. For the Dissenters generally, see *supra*, 95–98.

those who fulfilled certain conditions. These conditions included, for laymen, the new oaths of fidelity to William and Mary, and the standard oath against transubstantiation; for preachers there was added the requirement of subscription to the Thirty-nine Articles, except those relating to homilies, traditions of the church, and consecration of bishops. Some recognition of the status of dissenting ministers (qualified as above) was conceded by their exemption from parish offices and from serving on juries; but no exemption from tithe was given, and it was expressly declared that nothing in the Act was intended to give relief to Roman Catholics. No longer were dissenting meetings to be held behind closed doors; indeed, their places of worship were to be certified to the bishop or archdeacon of the diocese.

At the same time as the nation gained this additional asset of a Protestant nonconformity now officially recognized, the church of England lost a body of men, usually estimated at about 400 in number, many of them distinguished by character and learning, all of them prepared to sacrifice interest to conviction. The new oaths, in spite of the fact that the old phrase 'rightful and lawful' had been deleted, were abhorrent to all consistent believers in the doctrine of Non Resistance, for whom the Lord's Anointed was still James. All office holders, including the clergy, had to take the oaths by 1 September, and the king was authorized by statute[1] to grant to twelve ecclesiastics scrupling the oaths a portion of the emoluments of their benefices. This was the origin of the non jurors. It is notable that they included five of the Seven Bishops, the only conformists among them being Lloyd and Trelawney. Sancroft remained at Lambeth, after delegating to three suffragans the duty of consecrating bishops, a somewhat pusillanimous compromise which brought him discredit; in contrast, Turner, former bishop of Ely, became an active Jacobite. The remaining three of the non-juring Seven Bishops were deprived, with Frampton (Gloucester), Lloyd (Norwich), and Thomas (Worcester). Ken, the most notable of these men, lived in seclusion until his death in 1711; George Hickes, the deprived dean of Worcester, having been irregularly consecrated bishop of Thetford, remained the most active perpetuator of the schism. This misfortune might

[1] 1 W. and M., c. 8.

never have occurred if the practice had been retained of excusing from oaths, at a new accession, all already in office; but the Revolution settlement, with its change of dynasty, necessitated some public recognition of the new régime. The movement may be said to have ended with the death of 'bishop' Hickes in 1715. Its importance lies mainly in its association with learning and scholarship, encouraged by enforced leisure.[1] About 300 ejected Episcopalian clergy in Scotland maintained a similar separation, though, as the most uncompromising supporters of James, they had better excuse than their fellow sufferers in the south, who, after all, were asked to do no more than to admit that an absurd doctrine had been discredited by events.

William appointed to bishoprics only those on whose loyalty he could depend. He began with Gilbert Burnet, who was consecrated to the first vacant see, that of Salisbury. Few men have been more derided than this large-hearted, flat-footed Scot; indeed, he was the first Scotsman, after James I, to become well known to Englishmen, and their recorded impressions were mostly unfavourable. As her chaplain, he sorely taxed the Christian forbearance of Mary; as a zealot for the Reformation and a suspected Presbyterian he was detested by the churchmen; but nevertheless, in the administration of his diocese, he set a good example by the assiduity with which he maintained contact with his clergy, and by the charity, even generosity, with which he promoted endowments on their behalf. To him may be credited a large share of responsibility for the Toleration Act, and even a certain element of liberalism in the ecclesiastical policy of the reign. Burnet's consecration on 31 March was followed by that of Stillingfleet to the see of Worcester. Tillotson was elevated to the archbishopric of Canterbury in 1691, after Sancroft had been induced to leave Lambeth, to be succeeded on his death in 1694 by Tenison. Why Compton was passed over is one of the mysteries of the reign; as a haughty and independent English aristocrat, he may have been personally unacceptable to William and Mary, who were guided mainly by Burnet in their choice of bishops. Within three years, fifteen new bishops were consecrated, all of them latitudinarian in their sympathies, and in favour of the Revolution settlement. These included Simon Patrick (Ely), one of the founders of the

[1] *Infra*, 523–4.

S.P.C.K.; John Sharp, archbishop of York; Richard Cumberland (Peterborough), one of the many who 'refuted' Hobbes; and John Hough (Oxford), best known in his earlier capacity as president of Magdalen. They were, on the whole, more tolerant than their predecessors, because better educated; none of them very eminent, they possessed a quality which had been denied to many of their predecessors, that of ordinary Christian charity.

The coronation of William and Mary took place on 11 April with the customary pageantry. In the absence of Sancroft, Compton officiated, and Mary was crowned as queen regnant. In accordance with the Act[1] for establishing the coronation oath, the two sovereigns were obliged to swear that they would govern the people of England and the dominions thereto belonging according to 'the statutes in parliament agreed upon, and the laws and customs of the same'; that they would maintain the true profession of the Gospel, and 'the Protestant Reformed Religion established by law'.[2] Two new things had thus been introduced into the coronation oath, namely, the statutes of parliament, and the 'Protestant Reformed Religion'. In regard to the first, kings had formerly been obliged to swear observance of the laws and customs emanating from their royal predecessors, especially those granted to the clergy by St. Edward. These are now replaced by the laws and statutes of the realm.

Coronation oaths, though so few in number, are the most precious of all the materials on which the constitutional historian has to work, because they embody fundamental conceptions of the state; they are sensitive to deep-seated changes in these conceptions, and they are sworn in circumstances of the utmost solemnity. Conversely, their misinterpretation, as by George III, may prove of momentous consequence; indeed, if that monarch or his advisers had read the debates in the Commons[3] on the new oath, they would have seen that it was not intended to bind the king in his legislative capacity, for the legislature had in view the fact that important concessions in religious matters were being embodied in Bills, to which it was hoped that the crown would assent. Some of the essential

[1] 1 W. and M., c. 6.

[2] L. G. Wickham Legg, *English Coronation Records*, xxvii.

[3] *Grey*, ix. 190–9, 25–27 Mar. 1689.

principles of both the Revolution and the modern constitution were incorporated in the coronation oath, almost as much as in the Bill of Rights; but the former is much more difficult of interpretation, because so much shorter, and because, even within its brevity, there appears on modern standards to be redundance. About one new-comer we can be certain—the king is no longer the sole law-giver, for thenceforward he is only a part of the legislative body; here is an obvious and non-controversial change. But it is otherwise with the second new-comer—'the Protestant Reformed Religion established by law'. Here the main difficulty arises from its context, since it immediately precedes the obligation to defend the settlement of the church of England and Ireland, 'as by law established'. Does this imply that 'the Protestant Reformed Religion established by law' was something different from the doctrine and discipline of the church of England, also established by law? This question was in the mind of one parliamentarian[1] when he objected that the new phrase created another church in addition to the church of England; moreover, the amended formula 'Protestant Church of England' was rejected by the House. So the two apparently similar things were kept apart. Nor is this the end of the supposed redundance, for nowadays 'Protestant' and 'Reformed' are regarded as meaning exactly the same thing, and it has even been held that to distinguish between the two is mere pedantry.

But before we dismiss the new coronation oath as a piece of pedantry or redundance, we should bear in mind that tautology is often the resort of those who are striving desperately to be clear and emphatic; also, that words which mean the same thing today have not always meant the same thing. Nor was the coronation oath enunciated, as it were, *in vacuo*; on the contrary, it was closely related to historical events, and can be understood only in the light of these events. Unlike previous coronation oaths, this one was drafted by laymen, to be understood by laymen. The legislators provided a guarantee for the church of England; but, on the other hand, they kept in view the part played by that church in recent history, and how, by its insistence on Divine Right and Non Resistance, it had, in their opinion, done much to encourage the excesses of the Stuarts.

[1] *Grey*, ix. 196. The member was sir Henry Capel.

So long as the Stuarts had supported the established church, they were free to engage in a policy of crypto- or public Catholicism; and so it seemed to many intelligent laymen that the church of England had degenerated from the position of a national church into that of a political party. The Seven Bishops had for a time restored this lost prestige, but only for a time, because five of them refused to recognize William; it was also clear that the church was divided, or at best only lukewarm in the cause of the Revolution. Accordingly, guarantee of the church of England was preceded by guarantee of something else—the Protestant Reformed Religion. The legislators of 1689 were taking no risks.

This dual phrase also derived from the past. By 1689 the term 'Protestant' was coming to be used in its modern sense as an inclusive term for all the western churches opposed to Rome; but it was still distinguished from 'Reformed', that is, the more extreme Calvinist and Zwinglian movements of the later sixteenth century which had exercised such influence on the England of Elizabeth. Already the Whigs had emphasized the glories of Elizabeth's reign in contrast with the shame of the Stuarts; and, as that shame deepened, many Englishmen—not necessarily Whigs, for this was well above party distinction[1]—reverted to those great changes of the sixteenth century which, in their view, had created a 'Protestant' and 'Reformed' England. By 'Reformed' they meant the Elizabethan settlement, when some of the most characteristic doctrines of Calvinism had been embodied in the Thirty-nine Articles, where they still remain. Here was a 'Reformed' religion, 'established by law'; or, in other words, a reminder that if the church of England had thoughts of taking the path to Rome, it had not yet (so far as the law was concerned) retraced the steps already taken on the way to Geneva. To most churchmen this reminder was obnoxious in the extreme.

'Reformed' was preceded by 'Protestant'. Here there is great latitude of interpretation. The term may possibly have been used in order to exclude the casuist who could argue that, after

[1] The representative character of the large committee of the Commons which drafted the coronation oath may be inferred from the fact that it included Clarges, Birch, Garroway, Sacheverell, sir C. Musgrave, and sir E. Seymour. *C.J.* x, 25 Feb. 1689.

the Council of Trent, the church of Rome was a 'Reformed' church; or it may have been adopted simply as the widest possible expression to denote those churches of western Europe which were uncompromisingly opposed to Rome. The term, described in the debates as an 'honourable' one, may have included both these things; but it may also have had some reference to Henry VIII's Reformation, with its transference of enormous areas of church lands to secular proprietors, many of them among the ancestors of those who adopted the phrase; indeed, Henry's Reformation was distinctively 'Protestant' in the sense that the German or Lutheran reformers had used the word, since their original 'protest' was not merely against certain Roman Catholic practices, but against the threat of imperial interference with large-scale confiscations of land. Now Henry's confiscations had also been authorized by law; here was the security by which many members of parliament held their estates. So there was no redundance or pedantry in adding 'Protestant' to 'Reformed', for these words meant quite different things. Taking the Henrician with the Elizabethan settlement, the view of parliament was that the official religion of England, *as recognized by law*, was both Protestant and Reformed.

These technical matters should not conceal the national importance of what the Revolution government was trying, almost desperately, to do. It was emulating the example set in Elizabeth's reign, when the menace from Spain was countered by association with those Protestant and Reformed communities on the continent which shared our peril; now that we were confronted by a similar menace from France, parliament clearly implied a renewal of this alignment with foreign churches again threatened by militant Catholicism, churches with which Anglicans indignantly repudiated any connexion. Nor was this all; for, so long as there remained any doubt whether or not England was Protestant, there was always a loophole for the intervention of the clergy in secular matters; whereas Protestantism (as distinct from the old 'Reformed' doctrines) means erastianism, or the complete subordination of church to state. Archbishops and bishops would continue to sit in the Lords, as some of them sat for a time in the Cabinet; but in both capacities their position was public and responsible, not secret and irresponsible. Here indeed we have the central achievement of the Revolution; 'this coronation oath', declared a member of the House, 'is the very touchstone and symbol of your government';[1] because its dual phrase, so often misunderstood, or resented, or repudiated, has served to enunciate one of the essential characteristics of Anglo-Saxon civilization. The alternative was Bourbon-Stuart civilization, a totalitarian system, having as its agents the priest, the dragoon, and the hangman, a system to which many Englishmen were determined not to submit. It was in accordance with this determination that William III declared war on Louis XIV on 7 May 1689.

But to many the war seemed remote; and meanwhile, to those members of the Commons who had suffered proscription or exile under the later Stuarts, it appeared that the day of vengeance had at last come. Throughout a large part of its sessions the Convention concerned itself with investigation into misgovernment since the time of the Popish Plot; and in February a beginning had been made with two agents, Burton and Graham, solicitors to the Treasury, who were found to have spent more than £6,000 in payments to witnesses and jurors in cases where the crown was anxious to secure a conviction.[2] There was also investigation into the methods by which Jeffreys and others had extorted large sums of money from persons implicated in Monmouth's rebellion. In May the judges were summoned to give evidence regarding their dismissals, the Commons being specially anxious to find out who had advised or approved the exercise of the dispensing power;[3] and on several occasions there was a demand in the Commons for exemplary punishment of those who had taken part in Stuart misrule—'nothing washes away blood but blood', declared sir Robert Rich,[4] a principle which, had it been consistently applied, would have made the Revolution in England as bloody as the Restoration. In these proceedings, no one was spared; Danby was attacked for his part in Charles II's foreign policy, Halifax for his conduct in the Exclusion controversy, and for his

[1] *Grey*, ix. 193. Significantly the speaker was John Hampden, junior.
[2] *C.J.* x, 22 Feb. and 23 May.
[3] Ibid. x, 14 June, and *Grey*, ix. 246 sqq.
[4] *Grey*, ix. 313–15, 14 June.

more recent misfortunes in the direction of Irish affairs. Throughout the summer of 1689 the Commons, so far from concerning themselves with the pressing needs created by the war, were turning themselves into a tribunal for the punishment of past misdeeds. All this severely tried the patience of William.

There was a prolonged dispute between Commons and Lords arising from the refusal of the latter to reverse the sentence passed by King's Bench in 1685 on Titus Oates for perjury; but there was agreement in regard to certain other measures of retrospective justice, as when the attainders of lord Russell, Algernon Sidney, and Alice Lisle were made void. A sum of £5,000 was ordered to be paid to the widow and daughters of sir Thomas Armstrong, who in 1684 had had the misfortune to have Oates for a hostile witness and Jeffreys for a judge. In this attempt to settle old scores, it was only human that many legislators sought to punish those who had taken part in the reign of terror which followed the failure of the Rye House Plot. This and other business kept parliament in session throughout the summer, until it was adjourned on 20 August, to meet again on 19 October. Meanwhile, the external situation was steadily worsening. Events in Ireland, notably the long delay in coming to the relief of Londonderry, had caused national anxiety; in November came news that Schomberg had been obliged to quit his camp at Dundalk, leaving thousands of Englishmen dead, not from battle, but from disease and neglect. Increasing disquiet was reflected in an address to the king in December, alleging 'the ill state of public affairs' and 'the want of ability and integrity' in those who had the direction of them.[1] In this atmosphere of suspicion, the spirit of faction, steadily mounting, came to a head in January 1690, when a Bill was introduced into the Commons for restoring the franchises of those boroughs which had lost their charters in the two preceding reigns. To this Bill Sacheverell proposed the addition of a clause disqualifying from municipal office, during a period of seven years, all who had taken part in the surrender of the charters, a clause which would have penalized many loyalists who had suffered in the reign of James; and would, in effect, have limited municipal office to Whigs. William was so disgusted by this changed temper of the Convention that on

[1] *C.J.* x, 11 Dec. 1689.

27 January he prorogued parliament, and on 6 February he dissolved it.

It was not until May 1690, with the passing of a royal Act of Grace,[1] that this liquidation of the past was completed, and that in a manner which reflected both the king's dislike of revenge, and the wishes of those members of parliament who wanted bygones to be bygones. Even in the Convention there had been such men, for instance sir T. Lee, who in the previous January had declared: 'I would forget and forgive', a statement[2] in striking contrast with the spirit of 1660–1. Of the thirty-one persons exempted from the royal Act of Grace, Jeffreys had died in the Tower; sir Robert Wright in Newgate; Crew remained undisturbed in Durham; L'Estrange, after short periods of imprisonment, lived to be suspected of complicity in Fenwick's Plot. The others, including lord chief justice Herbert, Melfort, Castlemaine, and Father Petre had mostly fled to St. Germains. Sunderland returned to England in May 1690, and took the oaths in the Lords. No one was executed for his share in the conduct of the later Stuarts. A few suffered short periods of imprisonment, but the majority were in France, busily plotting for their return to power. To some it appeared that this mercy was criminal folly. But to William it seemed that the gibbet and the block are not the ultimate resources of statesmanship; and that to be merciful may be proof not of weakness, but of strength.

Parliament's desire to prevent a recurrence of recent events, already signalized in the new coronation oath, was more fully evidenced in the Bill of Rights,[3] the final and legislative form of the Declaration of Rights, to which the royal consent was given on 16 December 1689. The preamble declared that James, with the help of evil counsellors, had attempted to destroy the Protestant religion and the laws and liberties of the kingdom. The Act next recited the events which had led immediately to the summoning of the Convention, the purpose of which was to ensure that religion, laws, and liberties should not again be endangered. Then followed a list of those things which the two Houses declared to be illegal, namely: the exercise of the suspending power without consent of parliament; the

[1] 2 W. and M., c. 10.

[2] *Grey*, ix. 541.

[3] 1 W. and M., sess. 2, c. 2; also *Documents*, no. 40.

dispensing power 'as it hath been exercised of late'; the commission for erecting 'the late Court[1] of commissioners for ecclesiastical causes'; the levying of money without consent of parliament for longer time or in other manner than it had been granted; the raising of a standing army in time of peace without consent of parliament. This list was succeeded by enumeration of a number of 'freedoms', such as: that elections of members of parliament should be free; that freedom of speech and proceedings in parliament should not be impeached or questioned out of parliament; that excessive bail should not be demanded; that jurors in trials for high treason should be freeholders; that it is the right of the subject to petition; and, lastly, that for the redress of grievances, parliament should be summoned frequently.

The Act concluded with the statement that, as parliament had complete confidence that the prince and princess of Orange would perfect the deliverance so inaugurated, and would preserve them from violation of these rights, the Lords Spiritual and Temporal and the Commons had resolved that Their Highnesses should be declared king and queen of England, France, and Ireland and the dominions thereto belonging, and that the sole exercise of the royal power should be in the king, with succession to the heirs of Mary, in default of which to Anne and her heirs, failing which, to the heirs of the prince of Orange. The concluding part of the Act declared that, as it was inconsistent with the safety and welfare of this Protestant kingdom to be governed by a popish prince, no Roman Catholic, nor anyone marrying a Roman Catholic, should be capable of succeeding to the crown; and that every future sovereign, after coming to the throne, should subscribe the declaration[2] in the second Test Act of Charles II's reign.

The Bill of Rights is our greatest constitutional document since Magna Carta; and, like that document, it emanated from

[1] *Supra*, 176–8.

[2] The declaration in the first Test Act (1673) consisted only of a denial of the doctrine of transubstantiation. The declaration in the second Test Act (1678), which came to be a standard form, added, to the practices repudiated, invocation of saints and the sacrifice of the mass as they are used in the church of Rome. Also—and this was important at that time—the extended declaration had to be taken 'in the plain and ordinary sense of the words'. See *Documents*, nos. 143 and 144.

the misdeeds of a king. Both instruments were concerned, not to enunciate abstract principles of government, but to provide safeguards against royal wrongdoings, many of them specified. Some of the omissions from the Bill of Rights are of interest. Reference to the social contract had disappeared in the conferences between the two Houses in February; on the other hand, the whole measure implies some kind of contract between king and nation, based not on law, but on the 'complete confidence' which parliament professed in the two sovereigns. There is little about parliament, except that it should be held frequently, and that elections should be free; otherwise, certain executive acts are pronounced legal only if parliament concurs. The suspending power is ruled out altogether; the dispensing power disappeared in a more devious way. At first, it was declared invalid only 'as it hath been exercised of late'; but a later clause (II) of the Bill enacted that no dispensation to a statute could be allowed unless expressly provided for in the statute itself, or in any statute passed by that session of parliament. As no such statute was passed, the royal exercise of the dispensing power came to an end.

Otherwise, there was no attempt to define the extent of the royal powers. The prerogative of mercy, the king's right to choose his ministers, to declare war and make peace—all these are left untouched. The legislators of 1689 did not even try to make monarchy foolproof; all that they were concerned with was that certain evils within their own experience should not recur. It is mainly for this reason that recent historians have depreciated the value of the Bill of Rights, arguing that it left William, as later George III, with many powers denied to the sovereigns of today. But this is to read the present into the past, and to misunderstand the essentially English character of the document. The Bill of Rights reaffirmed what had been asserted by the great medieval jurists, that the king is subject to law; and that, for many of his most important acts, there must be the consent of those (whether *magnates* or parliament) who could claim to speak on behalf of the nation. True, the king was left with certain important rights; but, meanwhile, parliament had come to stay, and it was only a matter of time before the residual prerogative of the king in person would yield to the rule of king in parliament.

In one more respect modern historiography has done less than justice to the Bill of Rights. With the discredit into which parliamentary institutions have fallen in some quarters, accentuated by assiduous eulogy of the Stuarts, the Revolution has been hailed as a drab or 'bourgeois' episode in our history, ending a period of 'brilliant' court life, and ushering in an era of dull and not always intelligent kings. But, at least from the point of view of the common man, the advantage does not always lie with the country governed by a fascist ruler, however facetious or devout; indeed, it may be much more enjoyable to read about such kings than to live under them. It was just for these unspectacular, everyday conditions that the Bill of Rights provided. There was not a word about democracy, nor about the economic betterment of the people, nor about the extension of the franchise, but there was a great deal about those elementary legal rights of the subject, rights to which we are now so accustomed that we take them for granted, and therefore assume that they have never been threatened. It is in the guarantee of these rights that the value of the Revolution consists; nor does the fact that we have enjoyed them so long diminish the importance of their origin. 'The Bill of Rights is to be as long as we are a nation',[1] declared a member of the House of Commons, and he was not exaggerating.

Lastly, the Bill of Rights evoked from some contemporaries the opinion that it was only the beginning of far-reaching reform. There should, it was argued,[2] be more guarantees for the rights of the subject, particularly in treason trials; the remedy of habeas corpus should be extended, and made more easily available. Most notable was the change in the practice and theory of the prerogative. The clemency of William's rule proved that for all, except the Jacobites, a policy of mercy was perfectly safe, and even the Jacobites were treated with great lenity. Moreover, William's practice was backed by a gradual change in public opinion, whereby the doctrine was repudiated that, for effective government, brutality was necessary. Here are the words of a contemporary,[3] writing in 1692:

It is a great mistake to imagine that an easie and full power of

[1] Sir J. Tredenham, 14 Dec. 1689. *Grey*, ix. 477.

[2] *Reasons for a new Bill of Rights*, 1692, in *Bodl. Pamph.* 208.

[3] Ibid. 29.

chopping men in pieces upon a block, or confining them in Newgate or other gaols, can add any strength to the crown, for Englishmen, generally speaking, are fond of a king, not only for his, but for their own sakes. . . . No authority can be so lasting as that which is founded on love and esteem.

Stuart England, like so many continental countries, had found kingship and liberty incompatible; the Revolution of 1688 gave us a constitution in which the two are inseparable.

IX

THE REVOLUTION IN IRELAND AND SCOTLAND

THE Revolution of 1688 was bloodless only so far as England was concerned. Ireland and Scotland were less fortunate; the first, because of a nationalist revolution which had to be quelled by a war; the second, because the highlanders were among the most faithful of Stuart supporters, and their loyalty to that House long survived their defeat in the short war of the Revolution. These two things provide the themes of the sections into which this chapter is divided.

1. The Revolution in Ireland

Early in February 1685 James Butler, first duke of Ormonde, proclaimed James II in Dublin. It was his last act as lord lieutenant, for already he had been recalled; and so the rule of one of the best of Irish administrators came to an end.[1] Then followed, after a short interval, the humiliating vice-royalty of Clarendon, to be succeeded in the spring of 1687 by that of Tyrconnel, who filled the bench, the army, and the boroughs with Roman Catholics.[2] The chancellorship was conferred on Alexander Fitton, who was objectionable, not as a papist, but as a forger;[3] of nine judges, only three were Protestant, and it was notable that of those Protestants who remained in office, a number were Quakers. At the time of the Revolution there was a division of opinion among those who governed Ireland. The English advisers of James were mostly against repeal of the Act of Settlement, on the ground that this would make England and Ireland irreconcilable; but the more advanced party, led by Tyrconnel, and instigated by the hierarchy, pressed for repeal, in the hope of ending the connexion with England, even if that involved subjection to France. With the birth of his son

[1] For a good account see R. Bagwell, *Ireland under the Stuarts*, iii, ch. xlvii, 'The government of Ormonde 1677–1685'.

[2] Ibid. 170 sqq.

[3] Ibid. 175.

in June 1688, James lost sympathy with those who were willing to abandon Ireland to a Bourbon. Meanwhile, there was a steady migration of Protestants across the Irish Sea, and the stage was being set for one of the most tragic episodes in the history of Ireland.

Nevertheless, tragedy might have been averted had not perfidy intervened. With the flight of James, even Tyrconnel, now rapidly ageing, showed a willingness to negotiate. Richard Hamilton, then a brigadier-general in the Irish army, a friend and relative by marriage of the lord deputy, was in England with James's army; and in January 1689, by the influence of the Temple family, he was sent to Dublin to negotiate some kind of compromise. Tyrconnel, aware of the forces which he had unleashed, feared that negotiation at this stage would cost him his life at the hands of his compatriots; so he vehemently declared against William, and induced the peace envoy to join him. Hamilton, having changed overnight, deserted the cause which he had been sent to represent, and at the head of over 2,000 men he advanced against the Protestants of Ulster, afterwards taking part in the siege of Londonderry. At the same time an Irish embassy was sent by Tyrconnel to France. This consisted of William Stewart, lord Mountjoy, master of the ordnance, a Protestant supporter of James, the only check on the excesses of the lord deputy, accompanied by chief baron Rice, a Roman Catholic. The different instructions to these two envoys reflected the two impulses pulling Tyrconnel in opposite directions; for while Mountjoy was to inform James that Ireland was untenable, his colleague Rice had orders to say that James was eagerly awaited, and that Mountjoy was a traitor. Rice was successful. On 15 February James left St. Germains for Ireland, accompanied by D'Avaux, leaving Mountjoy locked in the Bastille. The chances of peace, slender as they were, had been destroyed by two evils which have often played a sinister part in the history of Ireland—panic and treachery.

By the end of February 1689 the Irish revolution was gathering force. About 100,000 Irish Catholics were in arms; the small Protestant communities in Kenmare, Bandon, Mallow, and Sligo were obliged to capitulate, and their co-religionaries in Munster, Connaught, and Leinster went about in fear of their lives. In anticipation of the repeal of the Act of Settlement, much Protestant property was stolen or destroyed. Even in Ulster the position of the non-Catholics was nearly as precarious. Londonderry had, in the previous December, been attacked by a force under the Catholic earl of Antrim; and, though the attack failed, the city, organized for defence by Lundy—afterwards proved a traitor—was crowded with refugees. Enniskillen was the other rallying point of the Protestants in Ireland. It needed only the arrival of James to complete the upheaval. Landing at Kinsale on 12 March, with a French force, he was in Dublin twelve days later, after a triumphal procession through a land that must have seemed bleak and barren, amid throngs of vociferously loyal peasants, for whom the king and his cortege could scarcely conceal their disgust. After all, to the Irish, James was their ruler and co-religionary who had suffered from persecution by the English; he was the liberator, come to redeem his kingdom from the oppression and misrule of centuries. But James was soon to prove unworthy of such a cause. To him, Ireland might be useful as a place of refuge, or as a stepping-stone to Scotland, and so back to England; but for Irish aspirations he had nothing but contempt.

The high-water mark of the Irish Revolution was reached in the session of parliament which met at King's Inns in the summer months of 1689. Of sixty-nine Protestant peers, only five took their seats; these were swamped by the Roman Catholic lords, many of them of very recent creation; the Lower House had an equally strong Catholic majority, and no representatives appeared for the Ulster boroughs. In a speech from the throne delivered on 7 May James reproduced his arguments for liberty of conscience which, as they had made no impression on English Protestants, were as little likely to impress Irish Catholics. In its session of ten weeks, this parliament passed thirty-five Acts,[1] none of them destined to remain long on the statute book, but not all of them so bad as many historians have represented. One Act[2] declared that the parliament of England could not bind Ireland; this Act also annulled the right of the English judicature to reverse Irish judgements. An Act for liberty of conscience was, ironically enough, con-

[1] For these, see T. Davis, *The Patriot Parliament of 1689*.

[2] *Documents*, no. 288.

demned by the Protestant church of Ireland, indignant that any concession should be made to the Presbyterians. Another measure assigned the tithe paid by Protestants to the churches of their denomination, and the tithe paid by Catholics to the maintenance of their priests—a much more equitable arrangement than that which prevailed before or after. There was less of equity in an Act[1] which, without trial, attainted about 2,000 persons, an unjust measure of wholesale proscription, recalling the temper of the later middle ages. Most important of all was the repeal of the Act of Settlement, by which the great majority of the Protestant landholders were completely dispossessed, without any compensation for money spent in purchase or improvements. In this way, for a short time, was Ireland restored to the Irish. But, except for some money brought by the French, the Treasury was empty; and the brass money forced into circulation emphasized the unreality of the new régime.

In spite of its excesses, it is impossible not to feel some sympathy with the Irish parliament of 1689, which thus attempted to throw off the shackles imposed by an alien and unsympathetic power. But although, with a happier turn of events, some concessions might have been made to Irish nationalism, the cause of Irish unity, even thus early, was beyond human power of achievement, because Ulster incarnated the essence of Calvinism, a creed as uncompromising as Roman Catholicism itself. The two were about to join issue in the field, and the result was to provide one more confirmation of the sixteenth-century Reformation.

The siege of Londonderry[2] has been commemorated for all time in the classic pages of Macaulay. Behind the ramparts of the city were crowded almost all the militant representatives of the Protestant faith in Ireland; its fall, at this, the moment of Irish resurgence and English impotence, might well have established a Stuart or, still worse, a Bourbon despotism in Ireland. It was inevitable therefore that James's first activities should have been directed against the city; and so, with his arrival, accompanied by Irish and French troops, the siege

[1] *Documents*, no. 289.

[2] The best and fullest modern account is that by C. D. Milligan, *History of the Siege of Londonderry*.

began on 19 April 1689, two days after the treacherous Lundy had made his escape from the town with most of the officers of the garrison. From the start, the besiegers were handicapped by lack of suitable equipment; their trenches were filled by the tides of Lough Foyle and by heavy rains; moreover, they were subject to frequent sallies from the besieged, who maintained a continual fire from the walls.[1] Meanwhile, the spirit of the besieged was kept up by the exhortations and example of the redoubtable George Walker. While their ammunition lasted, the townsmen fired from their cannon sixteen-pounders and twenty-four pounders; but in return came many enemy bombs, one of which, weighing nearly 300 pounds, killed seventeen people. Far worse were the slow starvation and disease from which thousands perished. All the children died.

The long delays in bringing relief to Londonderry revealed English weakness and ineptitude in this, the first year of the war. On 26 March admiral Herbert, then at Spithead, received orders from the Irish Committee (the council in London for Irish affairs) to ship soldiers and supplies on board some Dutch ships at Exmouth, and send them to Derry;[2] but, by the treachery of Lundy, these men and stores were sent back to England.[3] On 25 April Herbert was ordered by secretary Nottingham to stop all arrangements for relieving Derry because, according to his information, the city had already fallen. A few days later, when William was informed of the conduct of Lundy, and that the city still held out, he ordered four regiments to be fitted out under the command of colonel Kirke, of Tangier notoriety, who did not sail until late in May, and then wasted several weeks in Lough Foyle. Councils of war provided excuses for continued inaction; but, at last, on the orders of Schomberg, something had to be done; so, on 30 July, the storeships *Mountjoy* and *Phoenix*, escorted by H.M.S. *Dartmouth*, rammed the boom stretching across the lough; and men from the *Dartmouth* succeeded, after breaking the cables, in forcing a way through.[4] Next day supplies were landed for the

[1] *Carte MS.* 181, f. 227.

[2] *H.M.C. Rep., MSS. of A. G. Finch*, ii. 196 (Nottingham Correspondence).

[3] Ibid. 203, 25 Apr.; see also *Halifax*, ii. 115–17.

[4] *Life of sir John Leake*, ed. S. Martin Leake (Navy Records Society), i. 26–27.

half-dead survivors of the siege, which had lasted just over 100 days.

This event coincided with another triumph for the Protestant cause. During his long stay in Lough Foyle, Kirke had received a deputation from the hard-pressed levies of Fermanagh who were holding out at Enniskillen. He landed William Wolseley, to act as colonel of the Enniskillen Horse, with commissions for the chief irregulars. This was the genesis of one of the most famous regiments in the British Army. Wolseley, a man of exceptional military talent, organized the Protestant volunteers into an efficient force which, though outnumbered, signally defeated a detachment of James's army, led by Justin McCarthy, at Newton Butler (30 July), one of the most sanguinary battles of the Irish war. This success, with the collapse of the siege of Londonderry, forced James's general, Patrick Sarsfield to withdraw his troops from Sligo to Athlone, and so the north of Ireland was saved for the Protestant cause.

This was speedily followed by another prolonged test of British fortitude, attributable mainly to mismanagement and corruption, and devoid of the glory which rewarded the heroic defenders of Derry. In England there was increasing anxiety arising from the presence of James in Ireland, where events in the early summer of 1689 presaged disaster for the Revolution. England had no army on which she could depend, for the remnants of James's troops, amounting to about 10,000 men, many of them re-formed in new regiments, seemed as likely to be as unfaithful to William as they had been to his predecessor. The new levies were completely untrained, and there was difficulty in equipping them, for those of Feversham's men who had left the colours took their arms with them. Nor was it merely a question of men and supplies. The whole system of army administration was hopelessly incompetent and corrupt. The commissary general, Henry Shales, who had served in that capacity on Hounslow Heath, was responsible for equipping the Irish expeditionary force, which was set on foot in the summer, an enterprise in which his embezzlements were so systematic as to create a suspicion not merely of dishonesty, which was almost to be expected, but of a singularly profitable form of high treason. Stores, for which he received payment, were never even delivered; the muskets broke in the hands of the recruits; the horses, on their arrival at Chester, were hired out to farmers for the harvest, and so were left behind; for the men, there were neither boots nor clothing. William Harbord, a member of parliament, acting as paymaster in the army, reported to the king that Shales bought salt at 9*d.* per pound and sold it to the troops at 4*s.*; 'it is no fault of his if the army is destroyed'.[1] Harbord could speak as an expert in these matters, for he was drawing the pay of a regiment which did not exist, and whenever he defaulted, he absconded. William III was indeed *le mal servi.*

On 12 August 1689 Schomberg with 10,000 men sailed from Hoylake in Cheshire, and landed next day at Bangor, county Down. Except for a few good Huguenot and Dutch troops, his army consisted mainly of untrained levies. This was the first expeditionary force undertaken by the standing army, so recently recognized by law; its fate was to be a melancholy one. Schomberg marched by Lisburn and Newry to Dundalk, a town just south of the modern border between Ulster and the Free State. As James's army, a few miles to the south at Ardee, showed no disposition to attack, his opponent encamped on a site well chosen for defence, since it had a good harbour, was protected on the west by the hills of Newry, and had easy communication with Ulster. But the site was unhealthy because of its proximity to bogs. Schomberg's long stay at Dundalk was attributed by contemporaries to the overcaution of age; even more, it was difficult to understand this dispatch of an army, greatly inferior to the enemy in numbers, at the close of what was then regarded as the campaigning season. Disaffection among some of the Huguenot troops caused trouble, but far more serious were the autumn rains, which were exceptional, even in that humid countryside. As old campaigners the French and Dutch had built themselves good, warm hutments; but the English neglected doing so until there was neither timber nor straw to be had. 'Our men died like rotten sheep.'[2] There was no hospital, not even medical supplies, except bandages; the cavalry had at least the protection of their cloaks, but Shales had seen to it that the infantry were almost destitute

[1] *Cal. S.P. Dom. 1689–90*, 294. W. Harbord to the king, 16 Oct. See also, for a good contemporary account, R. Kane, *Campaigns of king William and queen Anne* (1745).

[2] R. Kane, op. cit. 2.

of adequate clothing. Corpses of comrades were placed outside tents in order to keep out the draughts, or were to be seen floating about the bay with the tides. Of an army of nearly 14,000 men (some had joined from Ulster) about one-half is said to have perished in this way.[1] In November Schomberg moved with the survivors to Belfast, where many died in hospital. So ended the second, the most melancholy stage in the English reconquest of Ireland.

Early in 1690 William decided that he must go in person to Ireland to retrieve a situation now doubly desperate—in Ireland, where Protestantism was again on the defensive, and in England, where disgust and discontent were steadily mounting. In the preceding November an account had been given to the Commons of the tragic fate of Schomberg's army and the malversations of Shales. 'In plain English', said a member, 'knaves and villains are employed.'[2] 'If you want this war carried on with honour, you must hang Shales.' Accordingly an address was sent to the king asking that the commissary general be taken into custody. The only body which had any responsibility in these matters was the committee of council for Irish affairs, and as Halifax had played an active part in this council, he was selected as the obvious scapegoat, particularly as he had many enemies, including Danby, Schomberg, and the more zealous Whigs. The adjournment of the Convention Parliament on 20 August had postponed attacks; but meanwhile he resigned his speakership of the House of Lords, and on 8 February 1690 he gave up the Privy Seal, after his enemies had failed to press home the accusation of complicity in the proceedings of 1683 against the Whigs.[3]

The truth appears to be that, if anyone was responsible for mistakes of general policy it was the king. His heart was in the continental campaigns which had now begun; and at first he may have depreciated the strategic importance of Ireland; or he may have concluded that as James, in Dublin, was formidable only as the recipient of French supplies, the source of these supplies must be stopped. There was something to be said for a policy which would have left Ireland to fight her own battles, while conserving the scanty English resources for attack on the

[1] C. Walton, *History of the British Standing Army*, 76–77.

[2] *Grey*, ix. 446–53, 26 Nov. 1689.

[3] *Halifax*, ii. 89.

root of all the trouble—Louis XIV.[1] But, on the other hand, the secure establishment of the Stuart king in Ireland, the tragic delays in bringing relief to Londonderry, and the even more tragic episode of Dundalk had inflamed public opinion at home, as well as bringing the administration into discredit. William had yielded to public opinion by a compromise, the dispatch of Schomberg to Ireland with an inadequate force, at the wrong time of year. The inevitable disaster attending such a compromise brought out the king's best qualities as a man of action. He would go to Ireland in person, with an army capable of obtaining a decision.

On 14 June 1690 William landed at Carrickfergus with an army which, when reinforced by the loyalists of Ulster, amounted to about 35,000 men. Of this, about half could be described as British, some of it consisting of notably good fighting material, such as the men of Derry, led by Mitchelburn, and the men of Enniskillen, led by Wolseley; but both the loyalty and the military competence of the English regiments were so dubious that in action they had mostly to be put in the second line. The other half of the army consisted of Danes, Dutch, Germans, Huguenots, and a contingent from Finland. It was this motley array, led by a Dutchman, that retrieved a nearly lost Ireland for an unsympathetic England, its cosmopolitanism providing an eloquent testimonial to the diverse forces called to action by the threat from Louis XIV, while its motto 'Westminster' provided a fitting tribute to the part played by that place in the destinies of mankind. Of those who served under the king, the most notable were the Schombergs, father and son; Ormonde, Henry Sidney, count Solms (a relative of William), prince George of Hesse, and the duke of Württemberg. On the other side was James, with an army slightly less in numbers, composed mainly of Irish and French, with English Jacobites; good in its cavalry, but weak in its infantry. Among its officers were Berwick, a natural son of James, Lauzun, the commander

[1] On 4 Feb. 1690 William wrote to Waldeck that he would have preferred a defensive war in Ireland, so that he could use his troops for a descent on France. But, he wrote, the constitution of England was such that, for the time, he had to conduct himself according to the humour of his subjects. For this letter, see P. L. Muller, *Wilhelm III von Oranien und Georg Friedrich von Waldeck*, ii. 210.

of the French, Sarsfield, the idol of the Irish, a man of impetuous bravery and generosity; and Tyrconnel, now sinking into dotage.

William's army advanced to the Boyne, which was both the northern boundary of the Pale and the only serious barrier on the coast road between Belfast and Dublin. Behind that river, above Drogheda, James's army was securely entrenched on rising ground, the vegetation of which provided good cover, his left wing fronting the bend of the river to the south, where Slane Bridge, about eight miles from Drogheda, provided the only means of crossing dryshod. As the road over Slane Bridge proceeded by Duleek to Dublin, it was the strategic point of the site, but both sides were late in realizing its importance. On its extreme right, the Irish army was covered by a ravine; and, a mile above this, at Oldbridge, its advance guard was posted.[1] Arriving at the Boyne on 30 June, William could see for himself the defensive strength of the enemy position; but, in spite of the remonstrances of Schomberg, he decided to ford the river and attack on the following day.

On 1 July 1690 was fought the battle of the Boyne, a contest almost insignificant from the military point of view, but memorable in the history of civilization as a decisive victory of one way of life over another. William's main body of infantry, ranged in two lines, faced the fords below Oldbridge, flanked on the left by Huguenots, Danes, Dutch and Enniskilleners. The untried English troops were mostly in the second line. The cavalry on his right had been sent under Schomberg's son to capture Slane Bridge; and, when he learned that this had been accomplished, William at 10 a.m. ordered Schomberg, with the infantry, to cross the fords at Oldbridge. In the assault, the Danes gave way. As they climbed the slopes, the English and Dutch infantry had to engage in hand-to-hand struggles with the enemy, as they sprang from their concealment; but the Irish, French, and Jacobites were steadily pressed back, to make a last but ineffective stand on the heights of Donore. There James, a spectator of the battle, as soon as he saw the turn of events, took the lead in flight; and, with the remnants of his army, he succeeded in reaching Dublin. His losses were about

[1] One of the best modern accounts of the battle is that by C. Walton, *History of the British Standing Army*, ch. vii.

1,600 killed, wounded, and prisoners; William's were about one-third of that total.[1] Some contemporaries attributed James's defeat to lack of ammunition, to the inferiority of his infantry, and even to treachery, because only a fraction of his troops was sent to face the main onslaught at Oldbridge.[2] Just before the battle, William had suffered a wound in the shoulder, and the elder Schomberg was killed. When it reached England, news of this victory helped to alleviate the shame of the naval defeat on 30 June at Beachy Head; and so disaster and triumph, coming within one day of each other, served still further to show how precarious was the Revolution settlement. On the continent, the allied armies had been defeated in June by Luxemburg at the battle of Fleurus.

The battle of the Boyne was followed by a general retreat of the Irish army and the return of James to St. Germains. Limerick, Cork, Galway, and Athlone remained the chief Irish strongholds. It was on the first of these that William decided to advance, because it was occupied by about 20,000 troops under Sarsfield and the French general Boisseleau. But in the siege of Limerick the king's recent good fortune deserted him. By a daring stratagem, which endeared him even more to his men, Sarsfield, on the night of 11 August, succeeded in blowing up the siege train which was being brought up by the besiegers, an exploit which impeded William's operations until late in August; when, as the rains set in, the king raised the siege and returned to England. Before leaving he appointed the Dutchman Ginkel to command the forces, leaving the civil administration in the hands of Henry, lord Sidney, sir T. Coningsby, and sir C. Porter as lords justices. Before his departure the king had given his consent to a daring enterprise, intended to disrupt French communications with Ireland. This was Marlborough's proposal to capture Cork and Kinsale, a proposal which had been vetoed by Danby and the Cabinet council. His expedition left England on 17 September 1690 and was joined outside Cork by about 5,000 Dutch, Danes, and Huguenots under the duke of Württemberg. The assault on the walls of the city began on 26 September,[3] when the town was

[1] C. Walton, op. cit. 122, and R. Bagwell, op. cit. iii. 295–9.

[2] 'A Light to the Blind', in *H.M.C. Rep.* x, app. pt. 5, *MSS. of the earl of Fingall.*

[3] Sir W. S. Churchill, *Marlborough*, i. 287–93.

speedily mastered, the duke of Grafton being killed in action. Within a few days Marlborough captured Kinsale; and so, in a short, brilliant campaign, with very few casualties on his side, he had brought the south-east of Ireland within English control. Inexorably, the Irish were being pressed to their last stand in Limerick, Galway, and Athlone.

There were no more military operations in Ireland until May 1691. If English policy in that country can be condemned on the ground of dilatoriness and inadequacy, the same accusation can be made against the Irish and French. There was acute division among the leaders. Tyrconnel and Berwick resented the popularity of Sarsfield, the only general who had any faith in his cause or his men; Berwick, a dashing youth of twenty, was not able to secure unity of direction; Tyrconnel was anxious to give up the struggle altogether. At Versailles, owing to persistent misrepresentation about Sarsfield, Louis insisted that a French general should be given supreme command, so St. Ruth was sent to Ireland for this purpose; and, in compensation, James conferred on Sarsfield the title of earl of Lucan. Meanwhile, the British and allied forces, headed by Ginkel, having assembled at Mullingar, west of Dublin, advanced to the Shannon; and, late in June, they captured Athlone from St. Ruth. The French general then retired to Aughrim, between Athlone and Limerick, where, on Sunday 12 July 1691, with about 25,000 men, he faced Ginkel, with about 20,000.

St. Ruth's right flank was covered by a bog which extended half-way across his front; on his left, he was protected by 'a parcel of old garden ditches' stretching to the castle of Aughrim.[1] Ginkel's position was not so well covered, and at first things went badly for him, his men being mown down by the artillery fire from 'the little ould ditches',[2] while his cavalry, having crossed a ford, found it impossible to manœuvre in the bogs. By evening, so confident was St. Ruth of victory, that he rallied his men with the call: 'Le jour est à nous'. At this point, noticing that his opponent's right wing of cavalry was attempting to get round by a ford near the castle, St. Ruth rushed with his cavalry to defend the place, and was shot down by a cannon

[1] R. Kane, op. cit. 9–13.

[2] 'A Light to the Blind', in *H.M.C. Rep.* x, app. pt. 5, 147–50.

ball. It was not until this crisis that Sarsfield could intervene, for hitherto he had been kept in reserve by a jealous commander. But by the time Sarsfield took command it was too late. The British infantry, in spite of its losses, preserved good order; and, with cavalry support on both flanks, Ginkel pressed at the enemy centre. Soon the unfortunate Irish were completely enveloped by cavalry; there was no escape from the slaughter that followed. This battle, the most hard fought of the Irish wars, was also the most sanguinary; in St. Ruth's army, 7,000 are said to have been killed and wounded, in Ginkel's, 4,000. But for St. Ruth's death, victory might well have been with the Irish.

The gates of Galway were now opened to the victors, while the remnants of the Irish army, about 15,000 men, fled with Tyrconnel to Limerick, where a last stand was made. As the war had begun with a siege, so it ended with a siege.[1] It was now a race against the rains and the French supplies then on their way; it was in order to obstruct the expected French intervention that Ginkel arrested the Irish pilots waiting expectantly at the mouth of the Shannon. On 22 September the besiegers took up position before Thomond Bridge, and with the capture of the fort dominating the bridge, the city capitulated. Meanwhile, a fleet of French ships, with provisions for Limerick, had arrived off the Shannon, but as they could not enter the river without pilots, they had to put into Dingle Bay. They were just a few days too late to be of service to the besieged city, in this way providing a contrast with the last-minute arrival of the relief ships at Derry. In few wars have the accidents of time, weather, and personality played such a decisive part as in this.

The surrender of the city on 3 October 1691 was followed, after the arrival of the lords justices, by the signing of the Articles of Limerick.[2] The exceptional generosity of the original terms reflects the anxiety of William to end the war, so as to be free for his continental commitments. Accordingly, he instructed Ginkel to offer the utmost that was likely to be accepted by parliament. The military part of the treaty[3] was

[1] The best account of the siege will be found in the letters of Ginkel, *H.M.C. Rep. IV*, app. *MSS. of lord de Ros*, 323 sqq.

[2] *Documents*, no. 293.

[3] For the ratification, see *Documents*, no. 294.

simple—those Irish soldiers who wished to go to France, in order to engage in French military service, were free to do so,[1] and arrangements were made for their embarkation at Cork. This was an extraordinary concession from one belligerent to another. The civil treaty, almost equally generous, was complicated by the fact that, in its final form, as signed by Ginkel and Sarsfield, it differed from the first draft by the omission of an important phrase. By the first clause the Irish Roman Catholics were to enjoy such privileges as were consistent with the laws of Ireland, or as they had enjoyed in the reign of Charles II. An Irish parliament was promised, in which it was hoped to provide further security for Roman Catholics. By the second clause, the inhabitants of Limerick, and of every other garrison town in possession of the Irish, together with the officers and soldiers in arms for James II in Limerick, Cork, Kerry, Clare, Sligo, and Mayo, and *all such as were under their protection in the said counties*, should retain those estates and privileges that had belonged to them in the reign of Charles II, subject only to taking the oaths of allegiance as modified by the English parliament.

The phrase above italicized was omitted in the final draft. Its effect would have been to secure the estates of many who, though not serving in James's army, had been compromised in the insurrection; indeed, a majority of the 'rebels' would have been covered by this inclusive phrase. It is possible that the lords justices, who arrived when the treaty was being negotiated, may have insisted that, as the phrase was too sweeping, it must be omitted; so, in this way, they limited the amount of conciliation which William wished to extend to Ireland. Nevertheless, even the attenuated concessions of the Articles of Limerick saved many Catholic landowners from forfeiture. On the other hand, as the terms extended to the whole of Ireland, including areas which had not been conquered, where some kind of guerrilla warfare might have been carried on, it could be argued, from the Irish point of view, that the Limerick settlement was a compromise, and not a surrender. To England, however, it appeared that the sister isle had once more been reduced to obedience, and two measures passed at Westminster made clear the implications of this obedience.

[1] About 11,000 went to France; 2,000 went home, and over 1,000 joined Ginkel's army. E. Curtis, *History of Ireland*, 273.

The first was an Act of 1690[1] which annulled all the proceedings of the revolutionary parliament of 1689, and restored the Irish corporations to their state in 1683. This was followed in 1691 by an Act[2] which abrogated the old oaths, and imposed new ones, to be taken by the clergy of the established church and members of the Irish legislature, as well as by all office holders, barristers, attorneys, and their clerks. These new oaths consisted of the two standard oaths already imposed in England, together with the declaration against transubstantiation and invocation of saints required by the Test Acts; but to this declaration were added clauses intended to exclude crypto-Catholics; for the subscriber had to declare that even the pope could not absolve him from this solemn abjuration of all that was essentially Catholic. In this way England applied to Ireland the principle of total exclusion of Roman Catholics from public and municipal life, so reducing the Irish Celts to the anomalous position of an ostracized majority, a policy speedily followed by the Irish legislature. All this was a violation of the spirit of the Articles of Limerick.

After 1690 Ireland was ruled for a time by alternate lords justices and lords lieutenant. Among the lords justices first to be appointed were Henry, lord Sidney, sir T. Coningsby, and sir C. Porter, of whom the last-mentioned became chancellor. For a few months after September 1692, Sidney acted as lord lieutenant; and then, after two years of rule by lords justices, Henry, lord Capel was appointed lord lieutenant in May 1695, an office which he exercised for a year. Others who held office for short periods were Henri de Ruvigny, earl of Galway, and the earl of Rochester. Some measure of continuity and efficiency was ensured by the fact that sir Robert Southwell acted as secretary for Ireland in this period.

Meanwhile there was increasing resentment among the Irish ruling classes against the scandals which marked the disposal of the forfeited lands, a fact which prompted both Houses of the legislature in Dublin to oppose any further confiscations. In this way, a certain sympathy with the Celtic element became manifest, even in parliament, especially in the Upper House, where the bishops were dominant. In 1697 this chamber confirmed

[1] 1 W. and M., sess. 2, c. 9.

[2] 3 W. and M., c. 2; *Documents*, no. 296.

the Articles of Limerick by only one vote,[1] because so many objected to omission of the phrase that would have given the widest indemnity to those who had been involved in the rebellion;[2] and, at the same time, the legislature refused to introduce a Bill of Security, on the English model, which might have provided some kind of security for the king's person. This sympathy with Jacobitism helped in some measure to alleviate the position of the Roman Catholics. The religious orders had to leave the country, but the secular clergy remained, and Catholic schools were not usually interfered with.[3] This sympathy of the established clergy for Roman Catholics was matched by their hatred of the Presbyterians; and so Ireland's religious problems were by no means so simple as the straightforward antagonism of Catholic and Protestant.

Outside Ulster there was a simple dualism; and so communities such as Quakers, Huguenots, and Baptists, all of them regarded as sects, were accorded a large measure of toleration by the church of Ireland. But it was otherwise with the Presbyterians of Ulster,[4] said to number about 100,000, who were not a sect but a church. This distinction, so important in the seventeenth century, meant that the Ulster Protestants had the organization and the temper of an establishment, for they had their own formularies; their synods met regularly; their clergy were educated and ordained; like all established churches of the period, they had little patience with any form of dissent. This was accentuated by two things, namely, the renewal, shortly after the Revolution, of the Regium Donum, an annual grant of £1,200, derived from the Customs of the port of Belfast, which provided £15 for each Presbyterian minister; and, secondly, by the English Act of 1691[5] imposing oaths which, as they were intended to exclude Roman Catholics, indirectly favoured the admission of all Protestants. Thus the English policy at the Revolution was indirectly in favour of the Ulster Presbyterians; moreover, by the grant of the Regium Donum,

[1] *Documents*, no. 295.

[2] *Journals of the Irish House of Lords*, i, 23 Sept. 1697.

[3] *History of the Church of Ireland*, ed. W. A. Phillips, iii, ch. 4, 'The Church of the Revolution', by R. H. Murray. Also E. MacLysaght, *Irish Life in the Seventeenth Century*, ch. 9, 'The Clergy and the People'.

[4] This is the subject of a very interesting monograph, J. C. Beckett, *Protestant Dissent in Ireland 1687–1740*.

[5] *Supra*, 260.

there was implied some kind of recognition of their claim to be an established church.

But the attitude of the Irish bishops and clergy was very different. They knew that the cause of Protestantism in Ireland had been saved mainly by the Presbyterians of the north, whom they valued as allies, when needed, against popery; equally, in a crisis, the Presbyterians were prepared to sink their differences with Episcopalians, in order to resist the common enemy. By 1692 the menace had, for the time, been removed; and the situation recalled that of 1661 in England, when the church, once more in possession, felt strong enough to repudiate and even to penalize the English Presbyterians who had done so much to effect the Restoration. By 1692, however, opinion had hardened even more by the fact that episcopacy had been abolished in Scotland; so in Ireland of the Revolution, as in England of the Restoration, there was no room for two established churches. One consequence was that, mainly through opposition by the Irish bishops, who insisted on a Test, no Toleration Act was passed for Ireland in William's reign, with the result that the Presbyterians, while not debarred from office, were still subject, however nominally, to the penal laws of 1664–5. More serious, some of the bishops in their church courts insisted that Presbyterian marriages were unlawful, and that therefore the children were bastards. Fortunately, this was not pressed to extremes, but the survivors of the siege of Londonderry must have thought that the Irish prelates were deficient, not merely in gratitude, but in charity.

These were among the disquieting elements in the civilization of Ireland at this time. This was reflected in the statute book, which gave evidence of attempts to transplant English civilization, with modifications to suit the national temper. Examples are a statute of limitation, enabling one to presume death in certain circumstances already prescribed in English statute law; there was also (as in the legislation of the revolutionary parliament of 1689) an almost literal reproduction of the Statute of Frauds; other Acts, on the English model, were those for preventing frivolous or vexatious suits at law; for preventing clandestine marriages; for limiting benefit of clergy; and for better preservation of game. Profaneness and debauchery provided good old stand-bys. Gaming proved a more difficult problem than game, if one may judge by the severity of the penalties imposed on the winner in a game of chance, for the lucky one had to forfeit treble his winnings, while the loser was not even bound to pay. In this way it was hoped that the sons of the nobility and gentry would cease to be debauched and cozened, but the hope proved a vain one. Such were the chief measures enacted by the gentlemen of Ireland, intended mainly for themselves and their dependents.[1]

For the others—the Celts—there were laws of a very different type. An Act of 1697 banished all the regular Roman Catholic clergy; another of the same year, designed to prevent the intermarriage of Protestant and Catholic, enacted that a Protestant woman would forfeit her estate in land or money if she married a man who failed to produce a certificate, signed by a minister or justice, that he was a Protestant; and equally a male Protestant might choose his bride only from those equipped with such a certificate. Another Act forbade papists to practise the profession of solicitor, a prohibition which suggests that a number of Catholics were acting in this capacity, and they probably continued to do so. By another statute, the return to Ireland of those who had gone to France was forbidden; also the sending of children abroad to be educated by Roman Catholics. In order to ensure that the Celts would remain disarmed, it was decreed that makers of fire-arms might take only Protestant apprentices. No papist might teach in school, but this prohibition does not seem to have been generally enforced. By such measures the Irish legislature sought to keep the Celts a race apart, free to exercise their religion, it is true, but always contrasted, by their disabilities, with the ruling class; while in the north were the Presbyterians, always at hand when danger threatened from Versailles or Rome, but ostracized as soon as security was restored. So the triangular situation in Ireland ensured that the conditions making unity impossible were always kept steadily at work.

2. The Revolution in Scotland

The passenger list of William's expedition to Torbay included the names of a number of Scotsmen who, having known

[1] For these statutes, see *The Statutes at Large Passed in the Parliaments of Ireland* (1786), iii.

the Stuarts at close quarters, had migrated to Holland; and in such numbers that, before his accession, William had probably more experience of the Scottish than of the English language. Foremost among these returning exiles was Gilbert Burnet, destined for a bishopric and much publicity; with him was William Carstares, the prince's chaplain, one of the few men who enjoyed William's confidence. Later, Carstares had such influence in Scottish affairs as to be dubbed 'the cardinal'. Of the noblemen on board, the chief was Archibald, tenth earl of Argyll, son of that earl who had been executed in 1685; with him was the young David Melville, afterwards second earl, who had already acted as the prince's confidential agent at the court of Brandenburg. His father, the first earl of Melville, later secretary of state and commissioner to the parliament, followed a few weeks later; he was one of the few members of the Scottish nobility who could be described as moderate. Among the soldiers was general Hugh Mackay, a brave highlander and leader of men; according to Burnet, 'the piousest man I ever knew in a military way', who was soon, as commander in Scotland, to suffer defeat at the hands of Dundee, and later to die a hero's death at Steenkirk. The statesmen included sir James Dalrymple, afterwards first viscount Stair, about to join forces with his son John Dalrymple, then maintaining a precarious hold on office in the Scotland of James II.

Among those who were now making their second trip across the North Sea for the purposes of revolution were Robert Ferguson the Plotter and Andrew Fletcher of Saltoun. For the first of these men plotting was a chronic disease. He must have been one of the embarrassments of the expedition; and afterwards when, in his opinion, inadequately rewarded, he changed easily from Republicanism to Jacobitism. The other, Fletcher of Saltoun, one of the ablest Scotsmen of the time, was possibly the only member of this motley band who could be described as a Scottish patriot. The earliest advocate of separatism for the northern kingdom, he later inspired that Act of Security which proved so awkward for queen Anne's government. Sailing in another vessel which followed William's expedition was young William Cleland, son of a gamekeeper; a scholar and poet, the best leader of guerrilla troops in the north. Already he had defeated Claverhouse at Drumclog (1679);

and, ten years later, he was to defeat the highlanders at Dunkeld, the decisive battle in the Scottish war of the Revolution. In a sense, the course of the Revolution in Scotland might have been augured from inspection of William's passenger list.

At home, the greater part of the nobility were concerned to secure their estates, or, as often, to preserve what they had recently acquired. They were not by nature more rapacious than the English nobility, but their methods were speedier, and often conducted out of doors. This insecurity may account for the fact that so often father and son took opposite sides, in order that, whatever happened, the family estates might be preserved. Thus, in the great Douglas dynasty, William, third duke of Hamilton, an old opponent of Lauderdale and later of Claverhouse, adhered to William from the start, and was commissioner of the Scottish Estates in 1689 and 1693; while his son, the earl of Arran, was closely connected with the Jacobites. In another branch of the same family there was a similar but less acute difference of allegiance between the duke of Queensberry and his son lord Drumlanrig; so, too, the Dalrymples were divided in their political ties during James's reign, but they joined forces after the Revolution. Allegiance also divided the Murray family. John, the first marquis of Atholl, like so many of his peers, had been alienated by the excesses of Lauderdale, but the Revolution found him unable to make up his mind. His clansmen decided on his behalf by declaring for James, while his son came out on the side of William. The family seat at Blair in Perthshire was one of the main objectives in the short Scottish war.

From the moment of the birth of the prince of Wales in the summer of 1688 the alarm felt in England was shared by a majority of the people of Scotland. In September James summoned the greater part of his forces in the north to come to his assistance in England; while William, in a proclamation, offered himself to the Scots as their deliverer.[1] Only by the Episcopalian clergy was the prospect regarded with dread, because they knew that their existence was dependent almost entirely on force. They were the first to experience the hostility of the mob, for by Christmas of 1688 about 200 curates had been 'rabbled' in the south-west, and driven with their families

[1] P. Hume Brown, *History of Scotland*, ii. 439 sqq.

from their manses. At the same time the Roman Catholic chapel in Holyrood was destroyed, and the Jesuits expelled. James's second flight (23 December) was the signal for a general rush to London of all the parties anxious to press their interest with the Deliverer; accordingly, an assembly of the Scottish nobility and gentry, held at Whitehall early in 1689, invited William to assume the administration of the kingdom, and to issue writs for a Scottish Convention. In order to ensure that this would not consist solely of Stuart nominees, the Scottish Test Act of 1681 was tacitly set aside, with the result that, of the commissioners of shires and burgesses who had sat in James's parliament, only a small minority were returned to the Convention which met in Edinburgh on 14 March 1689 under the presidency of the duke of Hamilton. During its sessions, the city was covered by the guns of the castle; but the governor, the duke of Gordon, was anxious not to precipitate matters, and, moreover, his opportunities for mischief were curtailed by embezzlement of his stores and ammunition. More important was the presence of Dundee, who, for a time, took part in the deliberations of the Convention, and then withdrew to Stirling in order to set up a rival assembly.

After a month of stormy debate, the Convention on 11 April agreed to a Claim of Right and an invitation to William and Mary to accept the crown.[1] The Scottish Claim of Right shows the influence of the English Declaration of Rights, but went somewhat farther. It asserted that James had attempted to alter the constitution from 'a legal, limited monarchy to an absolute despotic power'.[2] He had, it was noted, omitted to take the oath at his accession that he would maintain the Protestant faith; he had turned Protestant churches into mass houses; he had sent noblemen's children abroad to be educated in popery, and he had put papists in places of trust. Equally serious, he had employed army officers as judges in places where there were heritable jurisdictions, and on the royal burghs he had imposed not only magistrates, but whole town councils of his own nomination, so that the estate of the burgesses had, in effect, been nominated by him. He had ordered judges how to proceed

[1] R. S. Rait, *The Parliaments of Scotland*, 98–101.

[2] For the text of the Claim of Right, see *Acts of the Parliaments of Scotland*, ix. 38–40, and *Documents*, no. 248.

in cases before them, and had changed their tenure from *ad vitam aut culpam* to *ad beneplacitum*. The Estates then embodied in the Claim of Right a resolution that William and Mary be declared king and queen of Scotland, and the succession was regulated in exactly the same way as in England. A special coronation oath having been prescribed, a commission was appointed to offer the crown to the two sovereigns, and on 11 May 1689 the ceremony took place at Whitehall. At the same time William and Mary agreed to change the Convention into a parliament. In all this the bishops, though they had appeared in the Convention, had taken no part; indeed the royal acceptance of the Claim of Right, with its clause condemning prelacy, implied the doom of their order.

Then followed the appointments to high offices of state. It was characteristic of the precariousness of William's position in Scotland that there were very few of the older nobility on whom he could rely; indeed, that nobility, like the peerage of France, was not yet fully habituated to traditions of allegiance. The duke of Hamilton, the chief peer of the realm, was appointed commissioner to the Estates, in which capacity his alternations of imperiousness and moroseness alienated the king, who, however, could not afford to sacrifice him. Sir John Dalrymple became lord advocate, and in 1691 was appointed to join lord Melville as one of the two secretaries of state. William's most influential adviser in Scottish affairs continued to be William Carstares,[1] a man having shrewd knowledge of his countrymen, who made no secret of his opinion that the king would never succeed in conciliating the Episcopalian clergy, as he was anxious to do. Accordingly, just as in England the king had to rely more and more on Whigs, so in Scotland he had to rely on the Presbyterians because, though the Episcopalian laity were mostly indifferent, their clergy were committed without reserve to James. So, in his appointments, the hands of William were, to a large extent, tied.

Meanwhile, events were moving to a decision. When, in March 1689, Dundee left Edinburgh with a troop of dragoons, few had any doubt that his intention was to summon a rival

[1] Though published in 1874, R. H. Story's *William Carstares* is still one of the best biographies for Scottish history in this period. It is based partly on family papers.

convention in Stirling and rally the highlanders to the Stuart cause. This necessitated the dispatch of troops to hold Stirling for William, so the rival assembly there had to be abandoned. Prompt action was taken by the committee of Estates, sitting in Edinburgh, which acted as an executive body between the time of the meeting of the Convention in March and that of the parliament in June. Letters were sent to the northern counties calling out the 'fencible' men; Dundee was proclaimed a fugitive and rebel, and Mackay with the government troops was sent in pursuit. Then followed that marching and counter-marching in Badenoch and the eastern Highlands in which the rebel leader picked up a number of reinforcements, after receiving a commission from James to command his followers in Scotland. At last a decision was reached in the contest for Blair Castle, in the Atholl district of Perthshire, held by the clan for James, and fought for by the son of the earl of Atholl, lord Murray, on behalf of William. On the night of 26 July 1689 Mackay, with about 3,000 men, marched north from Dunkeld to intercept Dundee, who, with an army only slightly inferior was marching south from Badenoch. Battle was joined next day in the pass of Killiecrankie, where the highlanders, barefooted and armed with claymores, rushing down the steep gorge, swept the lowlanders before them. This sudden descent of wild clansmen would have tried the mettle of veteran troops, and Mackay's men were mostly untrained. But two things seriously discounted this highland victory. Dundee was killed in action; and his followers, devoid of all discipline, at once took to plundering.

The battle of Killiecrankie left things in much the same state as before, except that the highlanders were now without a leader. Accordingly, Mackay summoned the dispersed rebels to surrender, promising an indemnity, and urging that, as James was hard pressed in Ireland, he would be unable to spare troops for Scotland. To this demand the general received the following reply, compiled by a committee, consisting of Cameron of Lochiel, Maclean of Loch Buie, and a number of Macdonalds:

> You tell us in both your letters that His Majesty has hott wars in Ireland, and cannot in haste come to us, which, though it were as true as wee know it is not, is onely ane argument for safety and

intrist. And that you may know the sentiments of men of honor wee declare to you and all the world wee scorne your Usurper and the indemnities of his government. And to save you further trouble by yr frequent invitat'nes, wee answer you wee are satisfied our king will take his own time and way to manage his dominions and punish his rebels. And altho' he should send no assistance at all, wee will all dy with our swords in our hands before we faill in our loyaltie and sworn allegiance.[1]

These brave words were soon to be put to the test. On 21 August was fought, in the small cathedral city of Dunkeld, on the south-eastern fringe of the Highlands, the grim, decisive battle of this short war. William Cleland, the victor of Drumclog, had brought his Cameronians to the help of the government. His psalm-singing Presbyterians were peasants, not trained soldiers; but they had all the conviction and fortitude of the New Model Army; also they had many scores to wipe off—the Highland Host, the butcheries of Claverhouse, ten years of harrying, dragooning, and devastation. With little more than 1,000 of these men, Cleland found himself surrounded in Dunkeld by a much larger number of highlanders. For four hours a bitter contest was waged in which at last Cleland forced his way out, and drove off his assailants. He shared the same fate as that of Dundee at Killiecrankie; but his cause, unlike Dundee's, was victorious, for on the granite walls set up by the despised peasants of the south-west the proud clans had been shattered, and without the clans the Stuart cause in Scotland was lost. So the two Scotlands, having clashed in battle, again separated, the peasants to their crofts, the clans to their inaccessible glens, which were soon to resound with news of the tragedy of the Revolution in Scotland, the tragedy of Glencoe.

As in England, the Scottish Convention was succeeded by a duly constituted parliament, which began its first session on 5 June 1689. Among the recommendations made by the king to the commissioner, the duke of Hamilton, were two—that he would endeavour to secure an Act for retaining the Articles, and also an Act for establishing the form of church government that was most agreeable to the nation. In regard to the first of these, it seemed to the king that the retention of the Articles (the committee for arranging parliamentary business in advance)

[1] *Acts of the Parliaments of Scotland*, ix, appendix, 60, 17 Aug. 1689.

was essential if royal influence on the Scottish legislature was to be preserved; for this committee resembled, in some respects, a modern cabinet, except that it was responsible not to parliament but to the crown. It was probably for this reason that the institution was so distasteful to men now conscious of their powers. After long debate, parliament set aside the royal wish, and by an Act of 8 May 1690 abolished the Articles altogether.[1]

There was a similar absence of compromise in the matter of religion. The episcopal church of Scotland had little in common with either the church of England of the seventeenth century or with the episcopal church of Scotland of the twentieth. It had no liturgy or traditions of its own; it retained kirk sessions; save only in its government by bishops there was little to distinguish the Episcopalian from the Presbyterian. But it was the bishops, or 'tulchan'[2] bishops who gave cause for offence. They were the sixteenth-century offspring of simony and royal autocracy; very few were men of piety or learning, and for the most part they were regarded as the mean and servile tools of Stuart policy in Scotland. The northern kingdom was divided by many religious differences, but on this subject there was a large measure of agreement. By an Act of 22 July 1689[3] prelacy was abolished. An Act of 25 April 1690[4] restored all Presbyterian ministers who had been ejected since 1 January 1661; a later Act[5] of the same year abolished church patronage, substituting the heritors and elders for the patrons, and leaving to each congregation the right to accept or reject the nominee of heritors and elders. This measure caused some disquiet in the mind of William, as it seemed to him an invasion of the rights of property. His disquiet was shared by many Englishmen who regarded the abolition of episcopacy in Scotland as likely to have repercussions south of the border; hence, the English bishops could not help sympathizing with the northern prelates in their misfortunes, particularly as these were attributed to the

[1] *Acts of the Parliaments of Scotland*, ix. 113.

[2] A 'tulchan' was a dummy calf placed within sight of a cow in order to induce her to give more milk.

[3] *Acts of the Parliaments of Scotland*, ix. 104.

[4] Ibid. ix. 111; *Documents*, no. 250.

[5] *Acts of the Parliaments of Scotland*, ix, 19 July, 196–7; *Documents*, no. 252.

victorious but detested Presbyterians. So the willingness of the church of England to make concessions to the Dissenters in Revolutionary England may have been strengthened by an instinctive desire to avoid what was happening in the north.

The deprived Scottish bishops perpetuated a non-juring existence until well into the eighteenth century. Of their subordinates, the curates who had been forcibly intruded into the manses, about 300 were 'rabbled' in the south-west, and afterwards about as many more for refusing to pray for William and Mary. All this was a great disappointment to the king and his adviser Carstares, who both favoured a policy of conciliation, and were anxious to ensure that the Episcopalians would not be driven into the Jacobite camp. To this extent William did not succeed in carrying out his intentions for Scotland.

A Confession of Faith,[1] promulgated on 26 May 1690, completed the religious settlement. The catholic or universal church was defined as the whole number of the Elect; some churches, it was stated, had become so corrupt that they were now 'synagogues of Satan'. The pope was officially declared to be Antichrist. The doctrine of predestination was reaffirmed, freedom of the will being stigmatized as an obnoxious heresy. Synods and councils were restored for the purpose of determining controversies about the faith, as also church censures for reclaiming offending brethren. Only two sacraments were recognized—Baptism and the Lord's Supper. That marriage was not regarded as a sacrament may be the main reason for the difference between English and Scottish opinion in regard to remarriage after divorce. In England that permission was granted only by Act of Parliament, and then usually to persons of rank;[2] in Scotland it was expressly allowed by the Confession of Faith to every innocent party whose marriage had been broken by adultery.[3] This is one of the many instances of how Scotland was less conservative than England, and how her law anticipated some modern changes.

Otherwise, the legislation of post-Revolutionary Scotland shows a mingling of the reactionary and the progressive. An example of the former was the revival, in 1695, of an old Act

[1] *Acts of the Parliaments of Scotland*, ix. 117–31; 26 May 1690.

[2] *Supra*, 78.

[3] *Acts of the Parliaments of Scotland*, ix. 128.

making blasphemy a capital offence. That this had the approval of the clergy was shown in the trial and execution of Thomas Aikenhead, who had made a jest of the doctrine of the Trinity.[1] The statute authorizing this punishment was passed in the same year as an Act creating the Bank of Scotland. In the following year, 1696, an Act[2] was passed for the erection of a school in every parish where a school had not already been established, responsibility for the enforcement of this measure being imposed on the local heritors; but Scotland was not yet ready for such an ambitious measure, and a number of parishes remained without a school for a century thereafter. In 1701 an Act[3] gave to Scotsmen the remedy of habeas corpus—a much-needed reform.

Regular meetings of the General Assembly of the church were restored, thus providing clergy and laity with opportunities for discussion of religious subjects, which gradually broadened from the old theology into matters of social and national import. It was partly because of this share of the laity in ecclesiastical matters that Presbyterianism was so detested by more highly professionalized bodies; but it suited the genius of the Scottish nation nevertheless, and its restoration was the most important event in the Scottish Revolution. Just as in England the old common law tradition had become an essential, almost subconscious element in national mentality, so in Scotland, Calvinism had a profound influence on intellectual development; for long impeding it, by diverting men from secular interests, but eventually encouraging it, by habituating Scotsmen to the handling of abstract ideas. As the Jew was familiarized with intellectual speculation by his study of the Talmud, so the young Scot was first introduced to metaphysics by enforced attention to the enumerated sequence of profundities known as the sermon. This is one reason for the eminence of these two races in philosophical pursuits; and in the next century the names of David Hume and Adam Smith are alone sufficient to attest this Scottish characteristic.

Even before the end of the seventeenth century there was just a hint of the intellectual promise to be fulfilled in the next.

[1] P. Hume Brown, op. cit. iii. 40.

[2] *Acts of the Parliaments of Scotland*, x. 63; *Documents*, no. 256.

[3] *Acts of the Parliaments of Scotland*, x. 272.

It was characteristic of this gradual emancipation that achievement was limited to two groups of subjects—to mathematics or physics and to law or economics, in which spheres the educated Scot found opportunity for indulging his love of the speculative or of the concrete. Of the first, an example is the *Physiologia Nova Experimentalis* (1686), by sir J. Dalrymple, first lord Stair, a treatise not on physiology, but on physics, a product of the author's scientific studies at the university of Glasgow, which he addressed to the Royal Society.[1] At Edinburgh, mathematics and astronomy were ably represented by David Gregory, afterwards professor at Oxford. Gregory was the first scientist to devote a course of lectures to an exposition of the significance of Newton's *Principia*.

Of legal learning, by far the most attractive exponent was John Lauder, lord Fountainhall, whose accounts of historical events (his *Historical Observes*) and of cases decided in the court of Session reveal that mingling of shrewdness with erudition so characteristic of the older Scotland. An opponent of persecution of the Covenanters, and a critic of James II's administration in Scotland, he described that monarch summarily as 'a silly man'. Between 1665 and 1667 Lauder had studied on the continent; of the many who wrote accounts of travel in this period, he and Celia Fiennes are probably the only two who are now readable.[2] Among those Scots eminent in the study of trade and public finance, William Paterson was the most notable and the most unfortunate—the predecessor of another fantastic and tragic figure, John Law. A keener interest in the social and economic conditions at home was shown by Andrew Fletcher of Saltoun, whose *Discourses on the Affairs of Scotland*[3] exposed many of the evils which retarded the development of the northern kingdom, such as insecurity of tenure among the tenant farmers; their obligation to pay corn rents; the insufficiency of hay and fodder in those districts, such as the Highlands and Galloway where there was some kind of cattle industry; and, most of all, the idleness and pride of the smaller

[1] For an account of Dalrymple, see Aeneas Mackay, *Memoirs of sir J. Dalrymple*.

[2] His *Journal*, recording travels mainly in France and England, has been edited and published by D. Crawford (1900).

[3] Printed in *Political Writings of Andrew Fletcher of Saltoun* (1732).

lairds, who despised work and aped their social superiors. Thus Paterson and Fletcher, by their writings, and their active share in public life, helped to create among educated Scotsmen an awareness about defects at home and opportunities abroad; and so, in the years before the Union, there existed in the north an educated body of opinion, not all of it in favour of closer association with the more powerful neighbour.

Even in the looser association between the two countries which prevailed before the Union, Scotland was in effect governed from London, a fact which had some share of responsibility for the massacre with which the Revolution in the north was accompanied. After their defeat at Dunkeld in August 1689 the highlanders were no longer an enemy in the field, but they continued to be a danger. As trouble was anticipated from the Highlands and Isles (partly owing to their proximity to Ireland) Mackay established a fort at Inverlochy, at the head of Loch Linnhe, to which the name Fort William was given. In 1691 the policy of bribing the chieftains was attempted, for which purpose Breadalbane was entrusted with a sum, estimated by some at £12,000, by others at £20,000, for distribution among those chiefs who were willing to accept money as the price of their fidelity. At the same time the chieftains were ordered, under the sternest penalties, to take the oath of allegiance by 1 January 1692. Unfortunately the chief of the Glencoe Macdonalds delayed taking the oath until late in December 1691; and, when he offered to do so at Fort William, he was told that this could be done only in the presence of a sheriff. As the nearest sheriff was at Inverary, nearly forty miles away in the snow and mountains, Macdonald trudged to the capital of his enemies, the Campbells, and at Inverary on 6 January 1692 he took the oath.

But his delay had encouraged enemies to hope that here at last was a good pretext for exterminating a community which was regarded as a nest of thieves and outlaws. Among the many enemies of the Macdonalds were the earls of Argyll and Breadalbane, both astute and smooth-spoken; but even more serious was the enmity of sir John Dalrymple, the secretary of Scotland, whose hatred of all the clans was sustained and consistent. He knew them from experience, for the lands of his family in Glenluce and the south-west had been ravaged by the Highland

Host in 1678. His attitude, otherwise inexplicable, is accounted for by a lawyer's detestation of the lawless, and a desire for revenge on the devastators of his patrimony. Resident in London as official adviser in Scottish affairs, Dalrymple had no difficulty in obtaining William's signature on 11 January to a warrant ordering sir Robert Livingstone to march against those who had not sworn, but permitting him to give terms to those who had taken the oath after the prescribed date. On 16 January additional instructions, countersigned by Dalrymple, were sent to Livingstone, containing the order that those who had not taken the oath were to be obliged to surrender, and to this were added these significant words: 'If Mac Ian of Glen Co and that tribe can be separated from the rest, it will be a proper vindication of public justice to extirpate that set of thieves.' On 30 January Dalrymple wrote to Livingstone expressing his satisfaction that Macdonald had not come in within the prescribed time.[1]

None of the royal warrants contained any order for the destruction of the Macdonalds, indeed they clearly implied that mercy was to be shown to latecomers. The certificate of Macdonald's oath was sent from Inverary to Edinburgh, but there it was 'obliterated', and the privy council took no steps to inform the government of the chieftain's tardy compliance. At this point the mystery begins. Dalrymple's somewhat vindictive satisfaction, expressed so late as 30 January, may possibly be accounted for by the fact that he, in London, had no knowledge of Macdonald's having taken the oath; but contemporaries suspected that he really knew, and that he was determined nevertheless, by setting a savage example, to terrify the clans into submission. So the necessary measures were hurried on, their execution being entrusted to two Campbells —major Duncanson and Campbell of Glenlyon. Early in February Glenlyon with over 100 armed men, mostly highlanders, went to Glencoe, ostensibly to be quartered there, and for several days they enjoyed the hospitality of their unsuspecting victims. Early on the 13th the butchery began, and nearly forty persons, including women and children, were

[1] The evidence will be found in 'Proceedings of the Parliament of Scotland Regarding the Massacre of Glen Coe,' May 1695, in *State Trials*, xiii. 879 sqq. There is a good account in Hume Brown, op. cit. iii. 19 sqq.

slain. Some managed to escape, in spite of the fact that all the passes were guarded.

For some time little was known of the incident, but news leaked through from indirect sources, such as the *Paris Gazette* and one of James's proclamations;[1] indeed, the Jacobites made good propaganda use of the massacre. Gradually, as the facts became known, indignation increased; and in the summer of 1695 the Scottish parliament conducted an inquiry. This clearly established the fact that the two royal instructions of 11 and 16 January 1692 contained a warrant for mercy to all who offered to take the oath, even after 1 January. While exculpating the king, parliament voted that the affair was a murder; and, on inquiry, named the persons against whom action should be taken. These included Dalrymple, now lord Stair, who was held to have exceeded his duties, and also Glenlyon and major Duncanson, both of them at that time abroad on active service. The king was adjured to bring the culprits to justice, but he did not comply. Breadalbane was committed to Edinburgh Castle for a time, but no action was taken against Stair, who resigned, and did not re-enter public life until the next reign. Thus, while the king can be exonerated from having ordered the massacre, or of having connived at it, he showed indifference to the demand that the persons responsible should be punished.

William was soon to incur even more condemnation in the northern kingdom for his part, or alleged part, in the unfortunate Darien scheme, in which about 2,000 lives and £200,000 worth of capital were lost. It has already been noticed that, in the later seventeenth century, there was a development of joint-stock enterprise in Scotland, and the tonnage of shipping steadily increased after the Revolution. Debarred from a legitimate place in the English plantations, Scotland naturally turned to colonial enterprise as the best means of promoting national development. This was evidenced in an Act of 1693, whereby Scottish merchants were empowered to establish companies for trade with those countries with which their king was not at war. It was William Paterson, the first promoter of the Bank of England, a believer in Scotland's economic future, who proposed to apply this statute of the Scottish Estates; and

[1] *Steele*, ii, no 2933, Apr. 20, 1692.

it was mainly through his influence that the same Estates, in May 1695, passed an Act authorizing the creation of a company for trading to Africa and the Indies. Exceptional privileges were bestowed on the proposed company, which might establish settlements in any part of Asia, Africa, or America not already in the possession of a European power. Its subscribers were not limited to Scotsmen; indeed, half of its capital of £600,000 was provided by English merchants, mainly opponents of the 'old' East India Company, anxious to have a footing in the new venture, a fact which supplied some excuse for the intervention of the English legislature, late in 1695, when it resolved to impeach Paterson and others.[1] An address from both Houses of the English parliament caused William to exclaim: 'I have been ill served in Scotland.' These words may have been prompted by the fact that the royal assent to the Scottish Act of 1695 had been signified not directly, but through commissioner Tweedale, who had not complied with William's request that the Act should be submitted for his consideration before approval, the king at that time being abroad.[2]

As a result of this opposition, the English portion of the capital had to be withdrawn, and the directors in Scotland decided to raise £400,000, instead of the original £300,000. By August 1696 the whole sum had been raised. As there were no great financiers in Scotland, most of the subscriptions consisted of the life savings of the thrifty and provident.

It was at this point that Paterson acquired a fatal ascendancy in the counsels of the directors. Although a shrewd business man, he was influenced by two impulses which together often cause disaster—resentment, occasioned by his conviction that he had not been adequately rewarded for his services to English finance, and a romantic optimism, arising from his own ventures in the West Indies, which induced him to believe that, in the isthmus of Darien, the meeting-place of the wealth of two hemispheres, was to be found the ideal site for a settlement.

[1] *Infra*, 308, 310.

[2] For a good general account, see P. Hume Brown, op. cit. iii. 27 sqq. Among the most important studies of the Darien scheme are: G. P. Insh, *The Company of Scotland Trading to Africa and the Indies*; F. Cundall, *The Darien Venture* (which utilizes information derived from the archives at Seville), and F. R. Hart, *Disaster of Darien*.

But at first he concealed this design, alleging that the Scottish company was intended for the East India trade; on which pretext, he tried to obtain subscriptions in Hamburg and Holland. In his visits to Campvere and Hamburg he is said, when in drink, to have claimed that the Scottish Act would enable the company to issue commissions to merchants of any nationality whereby, under the Scottish colours, they would be free to engage in the East India trade; moreover, owing to freedom from Customs duties, they would be able to undersell the 'old' English East India Company.[1] As this caused the Dutch East and West Indies companies to take alarm, their opposition ended the chances of obtaining any Dutch capital. A similar device was tried in Hamburg, where merchants were first attracted by Paterson's promise that they could have East India goods from the Scottish company at cheaper rates than from either the English or Dutch companies. But, though about £30,000 was spent in Hamburg, the English agent there, sir P. Rycaut, was instructed to oppose Paterson's efforts; so no money was forthcoming. A larger sum was wasted in Holland in the purchase of ships that proved unserviceable.

Undeterred by these failures, Paterson, on his return to Scotland, revealed the Darien scheme, and on 17 July 1698 the first expedition of five ships set out from Leith. The only useful trading commodities taken out were a supply of linen cloth and 1,500 fuzees; the large stocks of bibles and periwigs did not create a similar demand. A Jew to act as interpreter was one of the most useful of those who embarked. Two ministers 'with a journeyman to take up the Psalm' were commissioned by the General Assembly to accompany the expedition, which, it was hoped, would establish the Calvinist discipline among the natives; but, as a fellow-passenger noted: 'they just looked on that dear land of promise, and were gathered to their fathers'.[2] They were lucky compared with some of the others. By 1 November the ships were anchored off the Darien coast where, 'for want of any air but what was sulphurous, our men fell down and died like rotten sheep'.[3] Shortage of provisions added to the difficulties of those who effected a landing; the prospective

[1] *A Defence of the Scots' abdicating Darien* (probably 1700), in *Bodl. Pamph.* 234.

[2] Ibid. 37.

[3] Ibid. 61.

settlers sold even their shirts to Indians for plantains and potatoes, having already exchanged their cloaks and swords at Madeira for supplies. Added to these privations was the bad water. In January 1699 the English government communicated to the governors of the West India colonies a letter forbidding them to provide supplies to the unfortunates in Darien.[1] Of more than 1,000 emigrants, about 300 died from pestilence and privation; so in June 1699 it was decided to abandon the colony. Shipwreck took a heavy toll of the returning emigrants.

Unaware of these events, the directors at home fitted out a second expedition which left in May 1699, to find on its arrival only a deserted settlement. A party from this expedition sought refuge in Jamaica, where many of them died from fever. By this time, news of the tragedy had reached Edinburgh; nevertheless a third expedition, which left in September, tried to restore the settlement, but this time mutiny was added to pestilence. Meanwhile, the Spaniards were gathering their forces for the extermination of the settlers, who, in spite of a heroic resistance, were obliged to capitulate on 30 March 1700. But, even thus, they were pursued by ill fortune. About 250 died in the passage to Jamaica; two ships perished in a storm, one of them losing all its ship's company. Paterson himself had been prostrated by fever, and his wife died. As the news of these disasters reached Scotland, a feeling of bitter resentment swept through the nation. It was directed not against Paterson, whose schemes from the start were rash; nor against those whose mismanagement had ruined what slender chances existed, but against William, whose government had callously forbidden the West India governors to give any assistance; and even more against England, whose jealousy and hostility, it seemed, had ruined a promising scheme. It was natural that the old hatred for the southern and more powerful neighbour should be revived.

That William was disliked in Scotland is explained by the incidents of Glencoe and Darien. In the first of these tragedies he may have thought that, so far as he was concerned, the Macdonalds of Glencoe were as remote as the tribes of central Africa; in the second, his conduct was more justifiable, and was

[1] A copy of the order will be found in *MSS. of House of Lords*, new series, iv, *1699–1702*, 68–69.

indeed unavoidable, if only from the necessity of maintaining peace with Spain. But, indirectly, the disaster of Darien was one of the things leading to the union of 1707, and the king himself was conscious of the fact that, only by such a solution, could Scotland's economic difficulties be solved. In personal matters he was impenetrable to the verge of callousness, but on broad matters of policy he was clear and consistent. Almost his first and last act as king of Great Britain was his advocacy of a legislative union between the two kingdoms which had called him to their thrones.

The Revolution settlement, so peaceably effected in England, had thus been completed, to the accompaniment of war and tragedy, in Scotland and Ireland. But that settlement had to be fought for by nearly nine years of European war, commonly known as the war of the league of Augsburg. England's resources for that contest, in materials, as well as in men and institutions, provide the subjects of the next two chapters.

X

MATERIAL RESOURCES FOR WAR: INDUSTRY AND TRADE

ALTHOUGH England engaged in war for reasons not obviously economic, namely, in order to maintain the Revolution settlement and a Protestant dynasty, nevertheless the course of the war was conditioned by economic factors; because, in the struggle with a more powerful enemy, there was necessitated a straining of every resource, and a scrutiny into these resources, in order that they might be more fully utilized. Moreover, the nation emerged from the conflict with a keener appreciation of her economic advantages, and a determination to realize them, even at the expense of war; accordingly, a certain economic awareness, even purposefulness, followed from the national awakening of this period. The present chapter is concerned with our chief economic assets as they were realized in the struggle with France. These included: (1) industries based on easy access to raw materials; (2) shipping and blockade; and (3) an expanding overseas trade, directed by a policy of full exploitation. This chapter is followed by one devoted to an account of the persons and institutions concerned in the direction and conduct of hostilities, these two chapters being intended as an introduction to the three consecutive chapters (XII, XIII, and XIV) which deal with England's part in the war of the league of Augsburg.

1. Raw Materials and Industries

Three of the natural advantages enjoyed by seventeenth-century England were these: the corn-growing districts were seldom more than two days' journey from a navigable river; there were great differences in soil and rainfall within comparatively short distances; and, thirdly, coal or timber was usually found in those districts where metals were mined. The first advantage was most clearly evidenced in the southern half of England, where the rivers Severn, Trent, and the lower reaches of the Thames served districts in which innumerable industries were located, and bounded an area where few parishes were without some occupation helping to supplement the earnings from agriculture.[1] In regard to the second advantage, the great differences in soil and rainfall obviated the limitation of vast areas to one type of product, and were among the factors accounting for the distribution and quality of pasture, forest, and corn-growing land. The third advantage, proximity of fuel to minerals, was in process of utilization, and was instanced by the development of metal industries in the midlands, the north, and the north-west, thus producing a wider distribution of enterprise. To these advantages should be added climate, which, by its mingling of oceanic and continental elements, not only encouraged bodily activity, but also, by its influence on temperament, may have fostered that variety and even individuality which contemporaries acclaimed in the products of English soil and English hands. Lastly, to these natural advantages should be added the great ingenuity of inventors,[2] as well as the high level of English workmanship.

In the legislation of the later years of the century, one can detect some kind of policy for raw materials and industries. An expression of this is to be found in two Acts[3] of William's reign which authorized owners of land, where deposits were found, to dig or mine for tin, lead, copper, and iron, subject only to the crown's right of pre-emption. In this way, private enterprise was stimulated, and many estates came to be of greatly increased value. An old prohibition was removed by an Act of 1694[4] which permitted export of iron and copper to any country except France, provided the metal was made from English ore. The export of fish, mainly salmon, pilchards, and herring was for some years encouraged by bounties,[5] which were intended as compensation for a tax on salt. But corn provided the most notable example of discrimination in favour of one type of raw material. In order to promote tillage, not only could grain be exported free of duty, but a bounty[6] was paid thereon; a policy

[1] For agriculture, see *supra*, 115–16. [2] *Supra*, 37–40.

[3] 1 W. and M., c. 30, and 5 W. and M., c. 6.

[4] 5 W. and M., c. 17.

[5] 5 W. and M., c. 7, cl. x.

[6] For a reference to the Corn Laws, see *supra*, 120.

which, however, was suspended in periods of bad harvests, as in the years 1698–1700, when export was forbidden.[1] This alternation of encouragement and prohibition was reflected in the attitude adopted to the distilling of spirits from grain, and the export of beer and ale; for these were promoted in years when corn was plentiful, but discouraged or prohibited in years of scarcity.[2]

More indirectly, the land and the landowner were favoured by freedom of export of leather, and of provisions. So, too, with wool and cloth. In 1689 an Act,[3] intended to restrict still further the export of wool, authorized anyone, in any part of England, to export cloth, a freedom which may have reacted unfavourably on the companies for overseas trade, whose monopoly had been opposed mainly by those clothing areas, as in the south-west,[4] which for long had been dependent on one or other of the companies for their foreign markets. This encouragement of woollen manufactures was advanced a stage further when, in 1700, exports of cloth were freed from Customs duties by an Act[5] which explicitly stated that the prosperity of the country depended mainly on its cloth exports; and in the same year all imported wrought silks and muslins had to be re-exported, so that they would not compete with our native textiles.[6]

Similarly, certain manufactures were favoured in our tariff policy. Before the war we had been dependent mainly on Brittany for sail cloth and canvas; these had now to be made at home. So the import of flax and hemp from Ireland was permitted; while, at the same time, the export of sail cloth was freed from Customs duties.[7] Similar relief was given to English bone-lace and needlework,[8] as well as to another manufacture in which our craftsmen enjoyed a high reputation, namely, watches and silver-ware.[9] It is of interest that exported clock parts had to have the name of the maker engraved thereon, since foreign manufacturers were adding famous English names, like Quare and Tompion, to their wares. English glass was also

[1] 10 Wm. III, c. 3 (1698), and 11 Wm. III, c. 1 (1699).

[2] 2 W. and M., sess. 2, c. 9, and 10 Wm. III, c. 4.

[3] 1 W. and M., sess. 1, c. 32, par. 12.

[4] W. G. Hoskins, *Industry, Trade and People in Exeter, 1688–1800*, 14–16.

[5] 11–12 Wm. III, c. 20.

[6] 11–12 Wm. III, c. 10.

[7] 7–8 Wm. III, c. 39.

[8] 11 Wm. III, c. 3.

[9] 9–10 Wm. III, c. 28.

coming to have a high reputation abroad, the duties on which were removed in 1699.[1]

Encouragement of export of certain native materials and manufactures was carried out even at the expense of the Customs revenue. This policy may be attributed to a general desire for increase of exports, preferably in English ships, and was linked with the principle of favouring certain interests and occupations; there was thus some correlation between industries at home and markets abroad. For the selection thus made, the explanation is usually obvious. Thus iron goods were exported to the colonies and elsewhere, although England continued to draw a part of her supplies from Sweden and Spain, and even tried to obtain the metal from Ireland, a most unlikely source; moreover, the fact that, in the great Crowley works at Winlaton, Swedish iron had to be used for the making of steel suggests some deficiency in the English product, which, moreover, was produced in no great quantity; for, even as late as 1720, the total national output of bar iron appears to have amounted to only 20,000 tons.[2] This industry, still in the semi-domestic era of the small forge, using mainly charcoal, was slowly being transformed into the system of the foundry, using coke, and providing castings for structural work, a stage not reached until the eighteenth century. In this intermediate period, iron was valued not only as a raw material for home industry, but for the export of manufactured articles. That bar iron continued to be brought from abroad was because it was cheaper than English iron and was better adapted for some processes such as making steel.[3]

This may have been reflected in the attitude adopted to coal.[4] Since the time of Elizabeth there had been a steady increase of output, so that in the last years of the century, the total for England, Scotland, and Wales amounted to about 3 million tons annually.[5] But, before we speak of this as an age of coal, we should compare the figure already given with the 240 million tons produced in most years early in the twentieth

[1] 10 Wm. III, c. 24.

[2] T. S. Ashton, *Iron and Steel in the Industrial Revolution*, 12–13.

[3] For this see M. W. Flinn, *Men of Iron: the Crowleys in the Early Iron Industry* (1962).

[4] For coal in relation to inventions, see *supra*, 37; for the social consequences of its use, *supra*, 46.

[5] J. U. Nef, *The Rise of the British Coal Industry*, i. 19–20.

century. A number of considerations may have influenced the policy adopted towards coal. It was not yet a satisfactory substitute for charcoal in the smelting of iron, because of the difficulty experienced in the 'charking' or coking process, until that problem was solved at the Coalbrookdale works by Abraham Darby early in the eighteenth century. In the previous century, it is possible that 'Dud' Dudley had discovered how to make and use coke, but he kept the process secret; and so there were serious limitations to the early use of coal in English industry. Nor was there yet any overseas demand, so there was no encouragement of export; it was mainly for revenue purposes that an Act[1] of 1695 imposed duties on coal shipped from Scotland, or from one English port to another. Three years later the revenue from the coal duties was increased by transfer of their management to the Customs;[2] later legislation reduced the duties on coal brought coastwise to English ports, and initiated encouragement of export to Ireland and the Plantations.[3] There was also maritime policy. The large fleets of Newcastle colliers supplying the south-east of England with 'sea cole' were of value as providing training for seamen, who, on this account, were given some protection from the press gang; and, for the escort of their ships, nine of the forty-three coastguard cruisers were detached.[4] English policy towards coal was still as much maritime as industrial.

The corollary to the encouragement of certain exports was seen in the discouragement of selected imports. Customs dues on incoming and outgoing goods had been regulated by the monetary values assigned to them in the Book of Rates[5] (1660) which, by William's reign, was considered to be out of date in regard to these values. The demand for a new tariff was partly met by Acts of 1690 and 1692[6] imposing additional levies on most imports, including all East India goods; iron; manufactured metal goods; brass and copper wire; salt; tar; rice; and Scottish coal. The inclusion of soap, olive oil, barilla, and

[1] 6–7 Wm. III, c. 18.

[2] 9–10 Wm. III, c. 13.

[3] e.g. 4 Ann., c. 6; 6 Ann., c. 22; and 9 Ann., c. 6. For export figures in the early eighteenth century, see J. U. Nef, op. cit. i. 84.

[4] 6–7 Wm. III, c. 18, cl. 23.

[5] For specimen rates, see *Documents*, no. 103.

[6] 2 W. and M., sess. 2, c. 4, and 4 W. and M., c. 5.

potash among these commodities provides evidence that, as a result of war-time restrictions, England may now have been making her soap and glass entirely from native materials. Generally, these two Acts reflect the policy of discouraging the import of those commodities which could either be produced at home, or were incapable of further manufacture here; so the desirability of providing work for the 'poor' was always kept in view.

Such were some of the more important materials from the point of view of national policy. Throughout the seventeenth century there is evidence of some changes in the distribution of occupations, but these did not involve any large-scale movements of population, and it is easy to magnify their extent. Policy changed more quickly than did the people. One of the many gradual changes was to be seen in the old Wealden iron industry, which had long suffered from shortage of fuel, on which the local hop kilns were making increased demands. Moreover, the Weald was prejudiced by an inadequate water supply;[1] accordingly, this district had to yield in importance to areas, mainly in the midlands and the north, where coal as well as timber was available. A similar displacement can be seen in regard to the Forest of Dean, where the deposits were being slowly worked out by communities of miners and iron workers, organized on an ancient fraternity basis; another of these decaying communities was that of the lead miners in the Peak district. In these movements of industry, which were spread over a great many years—for example, the Weald was still producing cannon in the eighteenth century—the two main considerations were the need of access to fresh supplies of fuel, whether coal or charcoal; and the gradual superseding of the old 'close', carefully regulated bodies of workers by capitalist enterprise, dependent on unlimited supplies of cheap labour.

Of this newer type of industrial organization, an example was provided by the ironworks at Swalwell and Winlaton in county Durham, organized after 1702 as a large and even benevolent industry by Ambrose Crowley,[2] the greatest iron-master of the period, who, having begun as an ironmonger in

[1] E. Straker, *Wealden Iron*, 66.

[2] E. Lipson, *Economic History of England*, ii. 178, and E. Hughes, *North Country Life in the Eighteenth Century*.

Greenwich, became alderman and sheriff of London, and was said to have accumulated £200,000 by the time of his death in 1713. This transition from ironmonger to ironmaster was also illustrated by a number of Quaker families.[1] In another 'black' country, namely, the districts round Birmingham, Wolverhampton, Walsall, Stourbridge, and Dudley, the local deposits of coal were extensively used in numerous metal industries, notably in Birmingham, where small wares, nails, and gun-making provided employment for a rapidly increasing population. Throughout the west-midland coalfield, the raw material was supplied by the capitalist; and, as nail-making was considered an 'easy' occupation, it attracted a large supply of unorganized, underpaid labour, including that of women and children, many of whom had migrated from the poorer farmhouses of the midlands.[2] Some great fortunes were made in this industry, notably by the Foleys and Dudleys. So, too, with lead-mining; Derbyshire, as a source of supply was being displaced by the Tyne valley and the district round Alston (in the hills east of Penrith), where deposits were worked by the Quaker Lead Company.[3] By the eighteenth century lead had become a valuable article of export.

In regard to other metals there were economic changes. Tin was steadily declining, mainly because of the change in fashion which preferred china, glass, and silver-ware to pewter;[4] moreover, the East India Company refused to export tin, because it was cheaper in India.[5] All this spelt disaster for the Cornish tin miner. On the other hand, copper was being more widely used. It was mined in several parts of the country; and it appears to have had this advantage that it needed less fuel for smelting than did iron; indeed, at Kendal, charcoal and peat were used for this purpose.[6] Much of the ore was shipped across the Severn

[1] *Supra*, 43–44.

[2] For this subject generally, see W. H. B. Court, *The Rise of the Midland Industries, 1600–1838.*

[3] A. Raistrick, *Two Centuries of Industrial welfare; the London (Quaker) Lead Company, 1692–1905.*

[4] A. K. H. Jenkin, *The Cornish Miner*, 127 sqq. For the tin-mines generally, see G. R. Lewis, *The Stannaries.*

[5] *Rawl. MS.* A. 303. Letter from Child directing that no more tin be brought into India, 2 Dec. 1692.

[6] H. Hamilton, *The English Brass and Copper Industries*, 88.

to be smelted at Neath and other places in South Wales, where there was abundant coal. The metal was worked by a number of companies which made brass wire and sheets, with the help of domestic workers and small-scale employers;[1] brass was used in the manufacture of ornamental and domestic goods, but its most important application was in the making of ordnance. The same reason helps to account for the greater utilization of lead, which served for the sheathing of ships' hulls and the making of bullets.

Another native commodity which became of enhanced value in the exports of eighteenth-century England was salt. This was made from brine, pumped out of pits, as in Staffordshire; or from sea water, as on the north-east coast; of rock salt, deposits were discovered in Cheshire in 1671, leading to a new branch of the industry.[2] Throughout the seventeenth century, English salt had compared unfavourably with that from Setubal, or that from the Biscay coast; but, in the early years of the next century, better methods of refining improved the quality and value of English salt, which also provided a fruitful source of taxation. Yet another native commodity in which quality counted was glass. This was made in the numerous 'glass houses' throughout England; and Defoe recorded how poor children slept at night on the warm ashes left as refuse. The chief district for its manufacture was Stourbridge, within easy reach of coal, a neighbourhood long associated with the high reputation of English glass, which was exported to Ireland, Holland, the East and West Indies, and even to Venice.[3] But it did not provide, as did salt, a valuable source of revenue, for a tax levied in 1693 caused such unemployment in the industry, that it had to be mitigated, and finally abolished.

Leather was a valuable raw material. Its export had been banned[4] shortly after the Restoration, but it was one of the first commodities to be freed from export restrictions, for an Act of 1668[5] released the ban on leather and hides, which could now

[1] H. Hamilton, op. cit. 82–85; also J. U. Nef, op. cit. i, pt. 2, ch. 2.

[2] For this, and for the fiscal importance of salt, see E. Hughes, *Studies in Administration and Finance, 1558–1825.*

[3] *C.J.* xi, 17 Feb. 1697. Report from committee on the petitions of the glass-makers.

[4] 13–14 Car. II, c. 7.

[5] 20 Car. II, c. 5.

be sent abroad. Equally important in overseas trade were manufactured leather goods, which were considered superior in quality and workmanship to those of any other nation. This industry, regulated by a code[1] enacted in the reign of James I, provided employment for butchers, tanners, curriers, shoemakers, cordwainers, girdlers, and saddlers, each having a status so minutely defined, that any legislative concession to one was immediately followed by protest from the others.[2] Confusion between what was 'made' wear and what was raw material resulted in so many lawsuits, that in 1689 an Act[3] was passed which not only decreed that tanned, curried leather was 'made' wear, but provided that all leather workers were free to buy and sell tanned leather, whether curried or not, as well as skins and hides. This intervention by the legislature in favour of more freedom from gild restriction in a large and prosperous industry provides one more example of how the state, while still retaining its general control, might encourage greater latitude of enterprise. One of the many illustrations of the high standard of well-being enjoyed by Englishmen was that so many of them wore boots or shoes.

But by far the most important of our raw materials was wool. It was specially valued for these two reasons, namely; the rise and fall of rents were officially declared to depend on its price, and labour accounted for nine-tenths of the value of cloth. Decline in prosperity, that is, in rents, was thought to arise mainly from the export of cloth unwrought.[4] Moreover, in the organization of this industry, specialization had gone very far, so that by the end of the century it was heavily capitalized. Among the capitalists were the wool staplers, who stored large consignments of the raw material in warehouses, for sale to manufacturers; the yarn merchants, who supplied wool to the spinners, and sold the yarn in districts where there were few or no spinners; other buyers of wool included the broggers, usually agents or brokers of manufacturers. There was also the wool jobber, who bought the whole clip, and sold in smaller lots.

[1] 1 Jac. I, c. 16.

[2] For examples, see *H.M.C. Rep.* xii, app. pt. 6, 111 sqq. (protests against the Act of 1689, May 1689).

[3] 1 W. and M., c. 33.

[4] *C.J.* xi, 25 Nov. 1696. Answers to queries by Commissioners of Trade and Plantations.

The increase in number of these middlemen,[1] coming between producer on the one hand, and manufacturer or worker on the other, attests the greater specialization made possible by capitalist enterprise.

Generally, three great areas of cloth production can be distinguished—East Anglia; the South-West, including Wiltshire, Somerset, and Devon; and the West Riding of Yorkshire. In 1696 it was claimed that, in the county of Norfolk alone, about £200,000 worth of wool was used annually,[2] giving employment to about 100,000 persons; in Suffolk and Cambridge more than 40,000 persons were working for the say-makers[3] and worsted yarn-makers; Colchester was almost entirely given over to the spinning, dyeing, and weaving of bayes.[4] In the south-west, several areas could be described as partly industrial; there, as well as the heavy broadcloth, the lighter serges and perpetuanas[5] were made. In Wiltshire, large-scale production and division of labour brought into existence the commercial or capitalist clothier, not personally engaged in the processes which provided him with his cloth; in Devon, long wool provided the material for serges and cloth of the best quality; this industry was centred in Exeter, where a comparatively small body of capitalists profited by the mass of cheap labour which had drifted in from the villages.[6] This development had not gone so far in the third main area, the West Riding of Yorkshire, where the short, coarse wool was manufactured into cheaper varieties of cloth. Here the capital holdings were not so large; there was less specialization, for many small clothiers, having purchased the wool, themselves supervised its manufacture, and sold the finished product.[7] Thus, while some form

[1] For this, see R. B. Westerfield, *Middlemen in English Business, 1660–1760* (Yale, 1915), ch. v.

[2] *C.J.* xi, 7 Mar. 1696. It was said that the Norfolk industry was partly dependent on the East India Company.

[3] Say was one of the finer varieties of cloth, not unlike serge.

[4] i.e. baize, a coarse, woollen cloth. For the workers in Colchester, see *The Journeys of Celia Fiennes*, ed. C. Morris, 142.

[5] So called for their durability.

[6] W. G. Hoskins, *Industry, Trade and People in Exeter, 1688–1800*, 12–14.

[7] For this, see an account, based mainly on Defoe, by M. Dorothy George, *England in Transition* (1931 ed.), 60–61; also H. Heaton, *The Yorkshire Woollen and Worsted Industries*.

of capitalism was to be found throughout the industry, the differences were in degree, rather than in kind, and varied in proportion as the employer withdrew himself from the actual practice of his craft.

Language often provides the most permanent evidence of the part played in the national life by a substance or an occupation, as witness the number of our metaphors and similes derived from the sheep, from wool, from weaving and spinning. The 'spinster' is still the name used to designate all unmarried women; the phrase 'the Cloth' still commemorates the respectability and, one might add, the durability both of the old broadcloth and of the profession which wore it. There could be no real anti-clericalism among men habituated to such an honourable association of ideas. Even the scientist owed something to his observation of the products of the loom, for some of the earliest theories of morphology were based on the analogy between the woven fabric and the cellular structure of plant tissue.[1] In contrast, the sea has provided us with popular phrases expressive of confusion, or danger or dislike, an attitude to be expected of an age when every Englishman had seen a sheep, and many had never seen the sea.

But already the monopoly of wool and cloth was being contested. Cotton,[2] originally called Cyprus Wool, was imported from the Levant and the West Indies, giving rise to a comparatively new industry, having its centre in Lancashire, mainly in the districts surrounding Manchester and Salford, where it was carried on by hand-loom weavers in villages and hamlets that still preserved an agrarian background. As a new-comer, this was one of the least regulated of crafts; but control of the raw material and distribution of the finished product were on a capitalist basis; hence the wealth of such families as the Chethams and the Wrigleys. By the end of the century a new class of middlemen-manufacturers, the Manchester linen drapers, had come into existence.[3] Cotton provided a supplement or alternative to cloth, its wider use having some social significance, since cotton goods might so easily be washed, thus inaugurating a more hygienic age, in which permanence ceased to be the

[1] *Infra*, 525.

[2] A. P. Wadsworth and J. de L. Mann, *The Cotton Trade and Industrial Lancashire*, ch. iii.

[3] Ibid. 72 sqq.

sole requirement; and a clean shirt came to be the characteristic of a gentleman.

The growing of flax, mainly in the midland counties, was the basis of a linen manufacture, but in England this did not make much progress, though there was a damask industry in the Darlington district;[1] and imports of flax and hemp from Ireland and Holland made possible the manufacture of rope. There were two objections to the encouragement of linen manufacture in England; first, that it employed fewer hands than did cloth, and so was not suitable for the 'poor'; and, secondly, like paper-making, it was controlled by a joint-stock company, and therefore suffered from the evils of stock jobbing. The result was that linen came to be developed mainly in Scotland and Ireland, where labour was cheaper and the cloth industry not so well established. More important was silk. The sources of supply were Spain, Italy, the Levant, and Persia, the East India and the Levant Companies being the main competitors for the raw material, until the former captured the market. Except for the beginnings of a silk manufacture at Macclesfield, this industry was to be found mainly in Spittalfields and Canterbury, where many Huguenot weavers settled; indeed, by 1696, about 10,000 persons were weaving silk in the latter city,[2] while in London about twice that number were occupied in making striped and figured stuffs from silk mixed with wool. As in all the luxury trades, the employees, usually victimized by employers, were also at the mercy of fashion; but, on the other hand, the great increase in the demand for silks is one of the surest evidences of the development both of national wealth and of public well-being.[3]

Such in brief were the main industries. What of the human element? Among the workers there were many intermediate grades between the extremes of highly skilled worker, as in the crafts of silversmith or cabinet-maker, workers who derived some bargaining power from their gild status; and, at the other end of the scale, the great mass of unskilled, casual labour, whose work appeared to be justified by the fact that it kept

[1] E. Hughes, *North Country Life in the Eighteenth Century*, 54.

[2] *C.J.* xi, 7 Mar. 1696. Petition of the weavers of Canterbury.

[3] For this industry generally, see sir F. Warner, *The Silk Industry*. For silk weaving in Canterbury see *The Journeys of Celia Fiennes*, ed. C. Morris, 123.

them off the rates. Generally, two principles were widely accepted; first, that cheap corn, i.e. cheap food, not only prejudices rents, but makes it more difficult to obtain labour, since men work only to avoid starvation; and, second, that the product of labour is increased by more specialization in tools and processes, as well as by inventions.[1] The ideal of the system was national wealth and power, based on abundant shipping and an unlimited supply of cheap workers, with safeguards to ensure that labour was excluded from the benefits of that wealth and power; 'the surest wealth', it was said 'consists in a multitude of laborious poor',[2] who, 'as they ought to be kept from starving, so they should receive nothing worth saving'.[3] Accordingly, few dissented from the policy of beating down wages to the lowest level consistent with existence. That these views were closely related to existing conditions is shown by this, that in prosperous Exeter, one-third of the cloth-workers were on the subsistence level, and another third below it;[4] similar conditions may well have prevailed in other clothing towns. It is for this reason that distress among the workers was not considered something exceptional, likely to find expression in rebellion; but something chronic, in which many thousands had to acquiesce in silence.

Moreover, these things are relative. The lot of the artisan in England compared favourably with that of the worker in Scotland and in many parts of the continent; even at home, it was often better than that of the small tenant farmer, subject to pressure from rack-renting landlords,[5] and so often obliged to migrate to the towns. Both the town and country worker were helped, however, by the fairly steady price level maintained in the later seventeenth century, as well as by the cheap food which prevailed in most years of the earlier eighteenth. Even more, the attitude adopted to the poor was not usually so callous as the words of such a cynic as Mandeville might imply; for, before the end of the century, the social reform movement

[1] E. Heckscher, *Mercantilism*, ii. 165–7.

[2] B. Mandeville, *Fable of the Bees*, ed. F. B. Kaye, 287.

[3] Ibid. 193.

[4] W. G. Hoskins, *Industry, Trade and People in Exeter 1688–1800*, 22.

[5] *Rev. Richard Baxter's Last Treatise*, ed. F. J. Powicke, with introduction by G. Unwin.

at least familiarized Englishmen with conditions prevailing among the poor, and by the beginning of the following century some facilities for their education were provided by numerous charity schools.[1]

2. Shipping and Blockade

The policy of full employment and low wages was closely related to that of maximum exports, preferably to those countries able to make a return in raw materials, or in commodities capable of further manufacture, or (ideally) to countries able to pay, in whole or in part, in bullion. Hence the vital connexion between English industry and overseas trade; the under-dog made the goods, the sea-dog transported them. Unlike the Dutch, the English had native as well as imported raw materials; unlike the French, they had a large mercantile marine; as much as either, they had access to the products of eastern and western hemispheres, except spices, which were declining in importance. In this way, national wealth was based on close inter-connexion between these things—native industries, a large volume of shipping and, in William's reign, an increasingly powerful navy. This might be described as a salt-water economy, in so far as the survival of the nation depended on sailors and ships, and on free entry to the oceans of the world. The bowsprit of the merchantman was a spearhead thrusting into every port that offered a market, having behind it all the impetus of a young, maritime empire, intent not on conquest, but on expansion. This expanding force was seen most clearly in the years following the peace of Ryswick, notably in penetration into the closed Spanish empire through the loopholes of Cadiz[2] and the *Asiento*.[3]

Our ships and seamen were among our best assets. The design of English merchant ships (most of them still under 100 tons) had for a time conformed to that of the warship, but by the later seventeenth century, possibly from the example which had long been set by the Dutch 'fly boat', English builders paid more attention to stowage and convenience of handling; moreover, cranes and blocks were now used for load-

[1] For the social reform movements, see *infra*, 532–3.

[2] *Infra*, 314–15.

[3] *Supra*, 16–17.

ing and unloading, with the result that freight charges were lessened.[1] At the same time, the cost of building was reduced from £8 to about £5 a ton, in spite of the fact that so much timber had to be brought from the Baltic, and in spite also of the wastage in the yards.[2] The number of common seamen had been estimated by Gregory King at 50,000, which may be taken as the standard complement of the mercantile marine in times of peace; but in William's war the number was greatly increased by the pressing of fishermen, watermen, and landsmen; in contrast, France's peace-time merchant service was said to employ only about 15,000 men.

Shipowning was not yet a specialized occupation; for vessels were commonly owned by syndicates, who chose the master, to whom the ship's company was responsible, while the master was accountable to the owners, and they to the merchants who provided the freight. It was common to limit the term merchant to those engaged in overseas trade, some of whom had shares in ships, as well as a distinct portion of their cargoes. Encouragement of the building of good ships was given by the great trading companies, notably the East India Company, which supervised the construction of those vessels that were hired, the owners being often shareholders in the company. The legislature also promoted the building of 'good and defensible ships' by an Act of 1694,[3] which encouraged owners of vessels of at least 450 tons, having three decks, by a remission of part of the Customs duties for the first three voyages. More indirectly, parliament came to the assistance of the mercantile community by an Act of 1698[4] which provided that an award by arbitrators should be made a rule of court, and therefore binding on the parties concerned. Moreover, one of the few arguments on behalf of Chancery in this period was that, as it

[1] J. Cary, *An Estimate of the State of England in Relation to its Trade* (1695), 146–7.

[2] For proposals to reduce the wastage in the royal yards, see G. Everett, *The Pathway to Peace and Profit* (1694). For a good modern account of the building of warships, see J. Ehrman, *The Navy in the War of William III*, ch. iii, 'Shipyards and Dockyards'.

[3] 5 W. and M., c. 24.

[4] 9 Wm. III, c. 15. For this see Miss L. Sutherland, 'The Law Merchant in the Seventeenth and Eighteenth Centuries', in *Trans. R.H.S.*, 4th series, xvii.

adjudicated in matters of account, its jurisdiction was of special value to merchants and traders.[1]

Among the many evidences of the enhanced importance of shipping was the publication, usually thrice weekly, of *Lloyds News*, which gave accounts of the capture of prizes, and the movements of ships, including, even in war-time, the movements of H.M. ships. It was the ancestor of the modern *Lloyds Loading List*. The name also recalls marine insurance, which developed rapidly in William's war, mainly because of the danger from privateers; indeed, a premium of as much as 30 per cent. was sometimes charged; but it is worth recording that the integrity of English insurers was comparatively high, a factor which later induced foreign shipowners to insure with English firms. Also, it is from this period that official marine statistics may be dated. The Custom House Ledger was begun in 1696—afterwards to provide the basis of the very useful abstracts published by sir Charles Whitworth in 1776; the shipping and trade returns from consuls and naval officers begin in 1697.[2] In 1703 Charles Davenant, son of the dramatist, a voluminous but lucid writer on economics and finance, was appointed inspector general of imports and exports, and his official reports add to the authentic material on which our knowledge of overseas trade in this period is based.

Estimates of the total tonnage of the English merchant navy are complicated by at least two factors; namely, the large amount of foreign-built shipping which was either hired, or came into English possession; and, secondly, the great losses of our mercantile tonnage at the hands of the French privateers. In regard to the first, in some trades, especially those of the Baltic and Eastland ports, a large number of foreign vessels had to be utilized; and, in the later years of the century, more Dutch-owned ships sailed under the English flag.[3] In regard to

[1] *H.M.C. Rep.* xiii, app. pt. 5, *MSS. of House of Lords*, 22 Oct. 1690. Evidence on a Bill for reform of Chancery.

[2] Sir G. N. Clark, *Guide to English Commercial Statistics, 1696–1782*, and M. S. Giuseppi, *Guide to the Records Preserved in the Public Record Office*, notably ii. 65–69 and 141.

[3] V. Barbour, 'Dutch and English merchant shipping', in *Econ. Hist. Rev.* ii (1929–30); L. A. Harper, *The English Navigation Laws*; W. R. Scott, *Joint Stock Companies*; and sir G. N. Clark, *The Dutch Alliance and the War against French Trade.*

the second factor—our losses of ships and cargoes—this proved to be one of the most serious problems of the war, a problem shared by the Dutch. As early as November 1689 the London merchants complained of losses in the Channel amounting in all to £600,000;[1] in 1693 the disaster of the Smyrna convoy accounted for about 100 ships, having valuable cargoes, but the Dutch share of this loss was greater than ours.[2] In December 1695 evidence was given, at a parliamentary inquiry, that, in the period September 1694–September 1695, our shipping casualties showed a total of more than 2 millions in value[3]—a figure which means nothing, until we place it alongside the figure of 7 millions as the estimated annual total of our imports and exports in the later part of the war.[4] In this war the French privateer played the same part as did the German submarine in the two wars of the twentieth century; indeed, the French devoted themselves to the *guerre de course*, almost as a national industry, with such success that English and Dutch prizes accounted for the wealth speedily acquired by the privateers of Dunkirk and St. Malo. Large sums were invested in this enterprise; Vauban who, among other offices, held that of lieutenant-general of Marine, designed a special type of bomb for this warfare, as well as encouraging improved design of privateers and light cruisers.[5] As we presented so many targets, the enemy policy is understandable; in consequence, we had to adapt ourselves, in concert with our Dutch allies, to the new menace by an elaborate system of escorted convoys.

Events proved that our margin was very narrow indeed. At the time, greatly conflicting estimates were made; later, the French over-estimated our total losses, but their figure of 4,200 ships lost was not so wide of the mark; for in 1708 the official Admiralty estimate, as presented to the Lords,[6] was of just under 4,000 ships. Now it is difficult even to conjecture what may have been the value of these ships and cargoes, because we do not know what was the proportion of small craft; but it

[1] *C.J.* x, 13 Nov. 1689.

[2] A. C. Wood, *The Levant Company*, 111.

[3] *MSS. of House of Lords*, new series, ii, *1695–7*, 64.

[4] W. R. Scott, op. cit. i. 328.

[5] C. de la Roncière, *Histoire de la marine francaise*, vi. 161 sqq.

[6] *L.J.* xviii, 9 Jan. 1708. This estimate may be unreliable.

is certain that we lost much more heavily than the enemy;[1] and the disquiet, expressed by so many contemporaries at the time, was fully justified. An illustration of that disquiet was given in the fierce debates in the Commons in January 1696 over the proposed institution of the commissioners of Trade and Plantations, when it was moved that the new Council be given power to investigate complaints against naval officers who had neglected their duty in the protection of commerce. In those cases where negligence or disloyalty was proved, the commissioners were to be authorized to require the Admiralty to prosecute. Owing to strong opposition from the Admiralty,[2] this was dropped. Most flagrant of all was the conduct of those naval officers who demanded money for the provision of an escort;[3] and, on refusal, so denuded the crew of the unfortunate merchant vessel by pressing that it sometimes fell an easy prey to the privateer, a practice which, however, seems to have diminished in the course of the war. But even thus, some contemporaries, as late as 1696, felt that the navy might play a more active part in the suppression of the privateers.[4]

Against our losses we have to offset our captures of enemy ships and cargoes. According to the official figures of the judgements of the prize courts, these appear to have amounted to about 700, about 400 of them French.[5] But there is good evidence that our captures of enemy ships, and of ships trading with the enemy, amounted to nearly twice that number,[6] a

[1] But cf. the figures given by sir G. N. Clark, op. cit. 61–62.

[2] The best account of the debates is in the report of F. Bonnet, in *Add. MS.* 30,000 A, 21–31 Jan. 1696. Cf. *C.J.* xi, 31 Jan. 1696.

[3] The notorious captain Churchill was committed to the Tower for this offence in November 1689. *Grey*, ix. 430.

[4] e.g. the letter of sir Miles Cook to sir G. Treby, 13 Aug. 1696, in *H.M.C. Rep.* xiii, app. pt. 6, 42, *MSS. of sir W. Fitzherbert.*

[5] Sir G. N. Clark, op. cit. 61–62. *Rawl. MS.* C. 148 gives a gross total for ships and cargoes of only £480,000.

[6] Altogether 1,293 ships. Of these, 180 were taken before the passing of the Privateer Act of 1693; about 200 did not come within the cognizance of the Commissioners, either because they were in ballast or not carrying contraband; others were seized in port, or by the Corunna packet boats, or by privateers not having commissions. These figures are given by one of the Commissioners who was committed to the Tower—*Mr. Paschall's letter to a friend* . . . (1703)—and are confirmed by the Admiralty figure of 1,296. *L.J.* xviii, 9 Jan. 1708.

discrepancy so great as to cause the committal to the Tower of two of the commissioners of Prizes. For both sides, the war against merchant shipping was much more intense than has commonly been assumed; a matter far more important to the Dutch and ourselves than to France, which was dependent to a much less extent on her sea-borne trade. Nevertheless, there was steady recovery from shipping losses after the conclusion of peace, attributable to replacements by the shipyards, and to the fact that more foreign vessels were naturalized.

This policy of war on the merchant service, which had come to stay, was bound to have great influence on the conduct of naval operations. A large number of warships had to be detached for escort duty, and convoys had to be arranged; as well as this, forty-three cruisers had to be assigned to coastal patrol.[1] The system did help to reduce our losses, and its working shows some parallels with experience of similar operations in the first two great wars of the twentieth century; for captures or losses were frequent when either our ships sailed independently, or lost touch with their escorts, as often happened when the naval officer in command was not an expert seaman. Another difficulty characteristic of the period was that, as practically all the owners had heavily insured their ships, they were either indifferent to their fate, or even welcomed their loss, and so did not willingly co-operate in safety measures. At times, the privy council imposed embargoes on the sailing of ships;[2] and (so great was the shortage of seamen) enforced a rigid system of rationing on the number of sailors allotted to each trade.[3] Overseas trade was also directly influenced by the course of the naval war; for, after the battle of Beachy Head, we lost command of the Channel, and in 1693 we were practically driven out of the Mediterranean.

There were other respects in which this campaign against merchant shipping anticipated that of the twentieth century. The greater part of the sinkings and captures occurred at the

[1] 5–6 W. and M., c. 1, cl. lxxii.

[2] Usually on the recommendation of the Treasury, which sometimes acted from motives of trade policy. Ehrman, op. cit. 113–15.

[3] There are numerous examples in the Privy Council Registers, e.g. vol. 73, 18 Aug. 1692, when 20 ships were allowed to sail to Italy. For a ship of 350 tons the ration was 30 English seamen and 30 foreigners and landsmen.

entrance to the Channel; the whole of the North Sea was also a danger area, because so readily reached by the fast French frigates based on Dunkirk, and from Norwegian ports (by the connivance of the mercenary king of Denmark).[1] This unprecedented state of affairs caused some naval experts, including Pepys, to conclude that the day of the great man-of-war was over, and that the future would lie with the small, fast ship, notably the frigate,[2] having a low freeboard, well gunned, and carrying a greater proportion of canvas than the ship of the line. This also led to the suggestion, early in the eighteenth century, that we should equip an auxiliary patrol for privateer hunting.[3] From this it may be deduced that the sailor of the mercantile marine shared the dangers experienced by his colleague of the navy; to these should be added those, not limited to war-time, which, for long, made the life of the seafaring man one of unusual peril and hardship. One was the uneven distribution of lighthouses round our coasts, a distribution which, in accordance with the older orientation of overseas trade, favoured the east and south-east at the expense of west and south-west, in particular Land's End, where there was no light. In order to avoid that danger-spot, Liverpool merchants had often to send their ships round by the North Channel.[4] For the seaman this was no formal matter since, if his ship were wrecked, he would be drowned if he remained on board, and had a good chance of being murdered if he reached the shore. 'The man who would go to sea for pastime would go to hell for pleasure'—such was the opinion of the older type of seaman about his occupation, which was traditionally regarded, by respectable Englishmen, as suitable only for the bad boys of the family.

William's war anticipated modern conditions in one more respect—the attempt to impose an effective blockade on the enemy. On 20 August 1689 an Act[5] was passed forbidding all trade with France for three years; in March 1692 this was renewed,[6] with arrangements for privateering, and directions

[1] Miss M. Lane, 'Relations between England and the Northern Powers, 1689–97' in *Trans. R.H.S.*, 3rd series, v. 157–85.

[2] This emerges from Evelyn's interview with Pepys and sir A. Deane on 7 May 1690.

[3] *A Proposal for Putting a Speedy End to the War*, 1703, in *Bodl. G.P.* 1139.

[4] *H.M.C. Rep.* xiv, app. pt. 4, 429.

[5] 1 W. and M., c. 34.

[6] 4 W. and M., c. 25.

for the commissioners of prizes. Meanwhile, the principles to be applied in the blockade had been agreed upon in the conventions with the Dutch of 1689,[1] our allies undertaking not only to stop their trade with the enemy, but to join with us in diverting the ships of allies or neutrals attempting to enter French ports, and in seizing all ships found leaving these ports. But it may well be doubted whether the allies ever intended to enforce a blockade, as we understand the term; for, in the past, when trade routes were more rigid, and voyages much longer, it was not thought that hostilities on land should be accompanied by complete disruption of sea-borne commerce, even commerce with the enemy. In this respect the Dutch were much more latitudinarian than the English; indeed, their principle, 'Free ships, free goods', often meant that unlimited supplies, even of contraband, could be conveyed to the enemy in Dutch or neutral ships. With increasing divergence in this matter, it was inevitable that the Anglo-Dutch agreements of 1689 were soon set aside, and each of the allies acted with a large measure of independence. This divergence was again to create difficulties in the Spanish Succession War; meanwhile, in William's war, it helped to ensure that the allied blockade was almost completely ineffective.

The fact that the Baltic was such a great source of naval stores enhanced the diplomatic importance of the two neutrals, Sweden and Denmark,[2] who naturally resented the interference with their trade which the war involved. On his side, William was anxious to avoid antagonizing either of these powers, and dreaded most of all that they might be won over by France. A crisis was staved off by a long series of negotiations and short-lived agreements; and, in the steadily increasing tension, Danes and Swedes engaged in an armed neutrality by a treaty of March 1693,[3] the preamble to which recited that the ships of both countries had been attacked by the belligerents, to the prejudice of trade and of the Customs revenue. Retaliation on allied shipping was threatened, and warships were allocated for commerce protection; indeed, there was a chance that Scandinavian overseas trade might be suspended altogether.

[1] Sir G. N. Clark, op. cit. ch. 2.

[2] Denmark supplied troops in return for subsidies, but was not one of the allies.

[3] *Dumont*, vii. 325.

This state of affairs was made even more delicate by the conduct of the privateers. They were commissioned by letters of marque to attack and seize enemy ships and cargoes, which had to be brought into port for judgement; but very few privateers strictly adhered to the regulations, and the distinction between privateering and piracy became more subtle as the war progressed. These men plundered the ships of their own countrymen and of their allies; they attacked enemy privateers and warships; they fought with the armed escorts of neutral fleets, and they were usually venal and corrupt in their disposal of the plunder. Their ships were manned by the desperadoes of the sea, all of them anxious to make a fortune as quickly as possible; but their numbers were at least controlled by the requirement imposed on them in 1693 that one-half of their complements should be taken into the fleet.

It needed only smuggling, conducted on a large scale, to counteract the blockade. At that time Romney Marsh was tenanted by great flocks of sheep, and it was said that, of every 3,000 packs of their wool, 2,000 were exported to France.[1] Transport was provided by the 'owlers', who kept up such a regular intercourse between the marsh and the Channel ports, exchanging wool for French silks, wine, and brandy, that this became a national concern, particularly as the almost regular service between the two coasts provided for the coming and going of Jacobites. It was said that even the erection of gibbets in Romney Marsh within a mile of each other would fail to stop this trade. Moreover, the ringleaders could obtain insurance against loss;[2] and so heavy were the fines imposed on neighbouring landlords, in the innumerable cases where a conviction could not be obtained, that many of them had to sell their estates.[3] Active intervention by naval and military forces merely served to open up an alternative route; for wool was smuggled across the Scottish border, and conveyed to Dutch ports, where French merchants arranged for its transport to France in Dutch or neutral ships.[4] Our ally Spain lent a hand in facilitating the

[1] *An Abstract of the Grievances of Trade* . . ., (1694), 2.

[2] This was prohibited, under a penalty of £500 on insurer and insured by an Act of 1693, 4 W. and M., c. 15.

[3] *Supra*, 57–58.

[4] R. M. Lees, 'Constitutional Importance of the Commissioners for Wool, 1689' in *Economica*, xiii (1933), 157.

sale of French textiles in Sicily and other Spanish possessions;[1] she also 'doctored' large quantities of French wine, which was then conveyed to England, mainly through Portuguese ports. So our Dutch and Spanish allies saw to it that the blockade did not press too heavily on the enemy; with the result that there was a minimum of dislocation in French trade; and Englishmen, though now becoming accustomed to port, were not denied their claret.

France herself contributed to the breaking of the blockade. She needed naval stores; so bribes were offered to English seamen, captives in her hands, to induce them to help in the manning of privateers;[2] and, with the help of some of our own sailors, supplies appear to have been obtained mainly through Newfoundland, the most notorious centre of smuggling in the empire. Moreover, Jean Bart and his privateers were not idle. In November 1692 they captured a fleet of Baltic timber ships, in spite of its Dutch escort;[3] two years later, they seized a large convoy of corn ships, escorted by eight Dutch men-of-war, and this they took into Dunkirk, a feat commemorated by the striking of a French medal, having the inscription: *Annona Augusta*.[4] So France, though inconvenienced by the blockade, was by no means incapacitated or even prejudiced by it; for, by intensive privateering or smuggling, she could always obtain supplies, including munitions of war. Of this, one indirect but significant piece of evidence may be quoted. In March 1694, when the Commons were considering a Bill for the free export of brass, copper, and bell metal, the braziers and founders petitioned against it, one of their reasons being that, if the Bill passed, the French would be able to make their guns from English material.[5] We speak of the allied war on French trade; but, in view of the ineffectiveness of that war, and the very serious inroads by French privateers on both English and Dutch commerce, it would be more relevant to speak of the French war on allied trade.

[1] Dispatch of Stanhope in Madrid, 31 Aug.–10 Sept. 1692. *S.P.* (*Spain*), 94/72.

[2] *Cal. S.P. Amer. 1689–92*, 4 Feb. 1690.

[3] C. de la Roncière, op. cit. vi. 136.

[4] Ibid. vi. 192.

[5] *MSS. of House of Lords*, new series, i. *1693–5*, 368, 22 Mar. 1694.

3. Trade Policy and Overseas Trade

The war and the blockade were among the circumstances which induced many educated Englishmen to focus attention on trade and trade policy. Already, interest in economics and statistics had been stimulated by sir William Petty, an interest well maintained by such men as Gregory King and Charles Davenant; indeed, some of the best brains in the country were enlisted in this cause; for, in the coinage difficulties of 1695–6, Newton and Locke played an active part in finding a solution. In discussions about overseas trade a certain liberal tradition can even be detected, notably in the writings of Dudley North and Josiah Child, who both, from their personal experience, maintained that no trade advantageous to the merchant could be detrimental to the state,[1] and that favour to one trade was an abuse, as well as a prejudice to the economy of the nation. Some kind of free trade theory was thus in the making long before the time of Adam Smith, just as in industrial processes, division of labour was becoming more generally established. For many, the Dutch provided the example to be followed, since their prosperity was attributed mainly to their practice of buying in one country to sell in another; and, according to Davenant,[2] our imports were enabling us to follow their example, since such a great proportion of them was re-exported.

Theory thus tended to be somewhat more enlightened than state policy. That policy divided our overseas trade into sections, each of which was supposed to be favourable or unfavourable to us in direct ratio to excess of exports over imports. Favourable areas were Spain and Portugal, with some of the Mediterranean states; the East India trade was unfavourable in so far as bullion was exported, but favourable in the amount of re-exports; most unfavourable of all was that of the Baltic, because here we were using only a small proportion of our own ships, and there were no re-exports. But the Baltic trade was a disagreeable necessity[3] in an older economy, because it was our main source of naval stores, at a time when the vast resources

[1] For Dudley North, see particularly his *Discourses upon Trade*; for Child, his *Discourse on Trade* and *A New Discourse on Trade*.

[2] C. Davenant, 'An Essay on the East India Trade', in *Works* (1771 ed.), i.

[3] E. Heckscher, 'Multilateralism, Baltic Trade and the Mercantilists', in *Econ. Hist. Rev.*, 2nd series, iii, no 2.

of the Plantations were still untapped; and so strategic necessity obliged us to pay for timber, pitch, tar, and hemp, brought to us mostly in foreign ships. In this way, as in modern times, there were 'hard currency' and 'soft currency' areas,[1] but the distinction was then even more rigid, since bullion played a more direct part in regulating international indebtedness. In a somewhat cruder form, therefore, the main objects and problems in what used to be criticized as the 'mercantilist' era, were not unlike those of today, except that, in the past, the state had no means of ensuring exchange control. There was a clear recognition of the need for direction of overseas trade; there was also insistence on the principles that we must produce more; we ought to cheapen our products by improved methods; we must have imperial preference; we must increase our gold reserves; and, finally, our economy should always be consistent with the needs of national defence.

An example of this community of principle in the mercantile policies of the late seventeenth and the mid-twentieth centuries is seen in the establishment, in 1696, of the commissioners of Trade and Plantations.[2] Its institution nearly provoked a constitutional crisis because, as its members were to be nominated by the Commons, and, as its powers were co-ordinated with those of the Treasury and the Admiralty, it appeared to be an infringement of the prerogative.[3] But the Commons at last gave way, and the king nominated the members of the commission. All this was evidence not only of the acute economic crisis through which the country was passing, but also of the realization that the planning of trade and commerce was essential for national survival. This had been the theme of a pamphlet by J. Whiston,[4] in which he advocated that our economic affairs should be managed by some kind of supplementary parliament, chosen from the trading companies, from masters of ships, and from representatives of certain counties where industries of special importance were established. The Board actually insti-

[1] For this, see C. Wilson, 'Treasure and Trade Balances: the Mercantilist Problem', in *Econ. Hist. Rev.*, 2nd series, ii, no. 2.

[2] *Cal. S.P. Dom. 1696*, 154, 30 Apr. 1696; also *Documents*, no. 207.

[3] R. M. Lees, 'Parliament and the proposal for a Council of Trade' in *E.H.R.* liv. Also *Burnet*, iv. 295.

[4] *Causes of the Present Calamities* . . . (1695).

tuted in May 1696 was not nearly so vocational as this; but it represented, in addition to high officers of state and heads of departments, an element of general intelligence and administrative experience, for it included Blathwayt, Pollexfen, Locke, and John Methuen. Its duties were to propose measures for promoting the trade of the kingdom, and for inspecting and developing the Plantations. Improvement of special trades, employment of the poor, and encouragement of fisheries also came within its province. In co-operation with other departments of state, this new council played an active part in the regulation of trade policy, its recommendations being often embodied in legislation; generally its institution may be regarded as an attempt to extract all the possible advantage from the economic system as then practised and understood. It was an ancestor of our Board of Trade; moreover, by its frequent intervention in all matters affecting the Plantations, it was also an ancestor of our Colonial Office.

The reports of the commissioners are of great value as evidence about commerce and contemporary opinion. In 1699 they presented a review of our overseas trade.[1] From Sweden we were importing £200,000 worth of goods, mainly iron and naval stores; in exchange, we were exporting only about £40,000 worth, and that, as to one-half only, in English ships. With our wool, Sweden was making cloth, and exporting it to us through Scotland. In regard to Denmark and Norway the position, in the view of the Council, was not much better; for these countries were drawing their imports from Holland and Hamburg, so that our adverse balance with them amounted to £150,000. As regards France, the commissioners could do no more than repeat the old story that our unfavourable balance with that country amounted to one million annually. From the East Indies, in peace-time, according to the report, we brought in about £1,000,000 worth of commodities, of which about one-half was re-exported. Our exported goods to the east were valued at £70,000, to which has to be added a considerable amount of bullion.

But there was more cheerful news about Spain, Portugal, Italy, Turkey, Barbary, and Guinea, for, in these areas, our balance was favourable, and many of the goods imported there-

[1] *C.J.* xii, 18 Jan. 1699.

from were improvable by a further manufacture here. As for the Plantations, the southern ones were much more advantageous than the others; generally, according to the commissioners, we imported more from the empire than we exported to it, but part of these imports provided valuable re-exports. A plentiful supply of negroes should, they thought, be encouraged. With Hamburg, the situation was said to be very favourable, for through this port of entry Germany was supplied with our woollens, and the return goods, such as linens, were not luxuries. With Holland and Flanders our trade had increased in the recent war, and the commissioners did not see how they could overbalance us if we enforced our Navigation Laws. Among the recommendations of the Board were these: that a greater number of ships should be naturalized for the Baltic trade, and manned by Englishmen; that a new Book of Rates[1] should be promulgated to take the place of the obsolete tariff of 1660, the new schedule to provide relief for commodities capable of further manufacture in England, and to be heavily loaded against luxuries. There should also be revision of the statutes of the realm and of the by-laws of corporations, so far as they related to trade. Finally, the petitions of disbanded seamen for their arrears of pay should be dealt with.

Here in brief we have the main tenets of the economic gospel of late-seventeenth-century England. Overseas trade must be directed, rather than regimented; efficient direction was possible only with full and accurate information; we must retain and improve our position in trades favourable to us, while minimizing, as far as possible, our disadvantages in those that were unfavourable; volume and variety must be increased. Another tenet of that gospel was to be found in the Navigation Acts, which were based on the principle of limiting the access of foreign shipping to our ports by excluding vessels carrying commodities that had not originated in the country to which the vessel belonged. This obviously was intended to hit the carrying trade of the Dutch, but in practice the principle was greatly modified, because goods from the German hinterland of Holland were treated as Dutch in origin, and so could be imported in Dutch ships. There were also numerous relaxations, and dispensations in respect of named ships; only thus, indeed,

[1] *Supra*, 285–6.

could we have obtained naval stores from the Baltic. But, in regard to the Plantation trade, in which stricter control was considered necessary, this was aimed at in the Navigation Act of 1696.[1] By this Act, it was provided that inter-colonial trade might be conducted only in English ships (this designation applied also to plantation-built ships), and revenue officers in the colonies were given the same powers of entry and search as those enjoyed by Customs officers at home. Plantation goods could not be landed in Scotland or Ireland; all colonial laws repugnant to the laws of trade were declared void, and property in the colonies could not be devised to foreigners. England would keep her empire for herself.

In this attempt to tighten control over the colonies, the Act reflects the concern caused by the law passed in the Scottish Parliament of 1695 authorizing the establishment of a company for trade with Africa and the Indies, destined later to be merged in the Darien Scheme. The Scottish Act provided for a joint stock, and conferred important privileges on the Company, including freedom from Customs dues. So great was the indignation of the English legislature at this attempt of the northern kingdom to engage in overseas enterprise, that a committee of the whole House conducted a full-scale inquiry into English trade,[2] based on evidence from companies and merchants.

The inquiry really resolved itself into a contest between the merits of the joint-stock and the regulated type of company, a distinction which emerged mainly in attacks—the climax of years of opposition—on the 'old' East India Company. Ever since 1689 a rival body of merchants, headed by Thomas Papillon, had been attempting to force a way into the East India trade. Papillon, who had been alienated by the autocratic rule of sir Josiah Child, found ready allies among the Whigs, who professed to favour a 'regulated' type of control, in place of what many regarded as a Stuart and Tory monopoly. But this argument may have been little more than a pretext, since the distinction between these two types often disappeared, when the joint stock admitted private traders, merely on

[1] 7–8 Wm. III. See also E. Channing, *History of the United States*, ii, ch. ix, and L. A. Harper, *The Navigation Laws*.

[2] The evidence will be found in *C.J.* xi. 399–407, Jan. 1696, and *MSS. of House of Lords*, new series, ii, *1695–7*, 3 Dec. 1695, pp. 3–62.

payment of a fee; and the regulated company, notably the Levant Company, provided, by its system of 'general ships', a quasi-monopoly on behalf of its more influential members.[1] Pressure of capital on investment facilities (which were greatly limited by the war) was probably the real incentive acting on the capitalist opponents of the 'old' Company.[2] They might have subscribed to the capital of that company had the stock been at par, instead of at a high premium; so, as there was no other outlet, they combined to organize a rival.

Hence, at the parliamentary inquiry of January 1696, the 'old' East India Company found itself on trial. The interlopers argued that its trade might be greatly expanded, if more freedom were allowed. Formerly, it was said, the Company had imported spices; now it brought home calicoes and wrought silks, for which it helped to pay by the annual export of about half a million in bullion; and so, by means of cheap native labour, the Company was making in the east what should be providing work at home. By a 'regulated' system, in place of a joint stock, the evils of both monopoly and 'stock jobbing' would be avoided; therefore, it was claimed, there should be a return to that freedom in the eastern trade which England had enjoyed in the years 1653–7. Nor were these the only arguments against the directors of the 'old' East India Company. They had, it was pointed out, engaged in a disastrous war against the Mughals; they 'rigged' their auctions in Leadenhall Street; they had been guilty of great cruelty in their suppression of a revolt at St. Helena. The Whigs objected to it as a Tory institution, a creature of the later Stuarts, and one implication of the Revolution settlement was the extension of the legislature's control over what had formerly been the preserve of the crown. The London merchants opposed the Company's monopoly of East India goods; and, after 1698, they played a prominent part in the foundation of the new Company; outside parliament, the weavers, whether of wool or silk, joined in the campaign, since their livelihood was threatened by imports of wrought silks and calicoes; the public generally was led to believe that the Company did not provide a sufficiently good 'vent' for English cloth.

[1] A. C. Wood, *The Levant Company*, ch. viii.

[2] K. G. Davies, 'Joint-Stock Investment in the Late Seventeenth Century', in *Econ. Hist. Rev.*, 2nd series, iv, no. 3.

In answer to these criticisms, the 'old' Company[1] replied that a joint-stock enterprise was necessary for unity of action in India, in support of which contention they made a very candid admission:[2]

> It is very well known, how moral soever the people of India are said to be, yet their forms of government do not admit those open ways to justice practised in Europe; and therefore the double arguments of force or money must . . . always be had ready.

Moreover, alleged the defenders of the Company, the joint-stock system made possible the handling of more trade than did such 'diffuse' organizations as the Muscovy, the Hamburg, and the Levant Companies, all of them 'regulated' institutions. The Company also maintained that as much as £2,000,000 might profitably be employed in their trade; and, as regards their export of bullion, this was counterbalanced by re-export of a great proportion of their imports. Such were the main arguments, at this inquiry, for and against the conduct of our East India trade by a monopolistic joint stock. Except for this airing of grievances, the only result of the inquiry was that the Commons resolved to impeach lord Belhaven, William Paterson, and others for 'high crimes and misdemeanours', because they were guilty of encouraging a Scottish scheme, authorized by the Scottish legislature. This helped to antagonize the two countries.

The 'old' East India Company had been somewhat unjustly treated. Child had not used its troops for aggression, but for the security of the factories; some of the interlopers were in league with the Mughals. The Company did provide some kind of vent for English goods; since, in accordance with the requirements of its new charter, granted in 1693, it exported annually about £100,000 worth of cloth, some of it from Wiltshire, some of it made up from the finer or luxury varieties of Suffolk. The cloth was intended mainly for the markets in China and Persia, much of it being disposed of by Armenian merchants, an export which may have been carried on at a loss. The Company also exported our lead, copper, and swords; moreover, it often granted licences to 'free' merchants, enabling them to trade

[1] For the East India trade generally in this period, see S. A. Khan, *The East India Trade in the Seventeenth Century.*

[2] *MSS. of House of Lords*, new series, ii, *1695–7*, 30.

independently.[1] Its imports of silk, saltpetre, and indigo were in demand at home; muslins became more fashionable after about 1698, but there was not yet a great demand for tea. Re-exported imports included cheap calicoes to the West Indies, to Spain and the Spanish colonies, as well as porcelain, lacquered and fancy goods to markets in Europe and elsewhere; moreover, the Customs paid by the Company averaged about £150,000 per annum.[2] Generally, the Company was not only contributing to the variety and volume of our trade, but was providing means whereby expression was given to the greater wealth and the higher standard of well-being enjoyed by England in the later seventeenth century.

As well as this, the stock of the Company provided an opportunity for investment. Compared with those of other companies, the holdings were fairly large,[3] averaging about £1,000, many of the investors being women; moreover, the bonds were considered a gilt-edged investment. But the weakness of the Company lay in its finance. Possibly in order to maintain a good front, dividends were sometimes paid out of capital; there was some juggling with the stock on the Exchange, and fresh subscriptions obtained in 1693 did not retrieve the situation. There were large debts; in 1698, in England alone, these amounted to £600,000;[4] and, in that year, it had to compete on unfavourable terms with the projected new Company in the offer of a large loan to the state. A solution was eventually found in a sharing of the monopoly between the two rivals; by 1709 the amalgamation had been effected.

The other two great trading companies, the Levant and the Royal African were almost equally unfortunate. Ever since about 1680, the Levant Company,[5] which seldom sent out more than a dozen ships a year, had suffered from increased imports of silk by the East India Company, a fact which caused a number of Turkey merchants to join in the opposition to the latter enterprise. Even more serious was the increasing competition

[1] *Rawl. MS.* D. 747. List of ships sailing to India, 1696–7.

[2] S. A. Khan, op. cit. 256.

[3] In *Rawl. MS.* A. 303 there is a list of holdings for Jan. 1693, where the smallest is given as £25, and the largest as £10,000. For the subject of investment in the companies, see K. G. Davies, op. cit.

[4] *C.J.* xii, 14 June 1698.

[5] For this, see A. C. Wood, op. cit.

from French traders in the Levant, who were subsidized by the state. Hence the Levant Company's exports of cloth showed a decline, which was mainly responsible for the crisis in the clothing industry in 1686. Then, in the summer of 1693, came the loss of the great Anglo-Dutch Smyrna convoy, in which the Company's losses[1] were estimated at £600,000; and, until Russell's fleet went to Cadiz in 1694, the Mediterranean was very unsafe for English merchantmen. Nevertheless, after the coming of peace, the Company was able, for a time, to increase its exports to the Levant; but, meanwhile, the French were steadily gaining ground, mainly because they sent out the light, brightly coloured materials required in the eastern Mediterranean.[2] Other competitors included the English merchants trading from their headquarters at Leghorn.

Another joint-stock enterprise was the African Company,[3] which, as reconstituted in 1672, had about 200 members, including prominent merchants of the city of London, reputed to be attached, in Stuart times, to the Court interest. These, usually contrasted with 'Whig' merchants, comprised sir Dudley North, sir John Banks, sir Samuel Dashwood, and sir William Turner, the only prominent 'Whig' among them being sir Robert Clayton. The average holding in the stock of the Company appears to have been about £400. Like the 'old' East India Company, the African Company had an unfortunate financial history; for dividends had sometimes to be paid from capital, even from borrowed money; there was also manipulation of the stock on the Exchange—all this in spite of the rich triangular trade in which the Company engaged. Like the Levant Company, it suffered also from the private or illicit trade of its employees. Its exports consisted partly of cloth—generally serges and perpetuanas from the south-west of England—and partly of re-exported goods, such as iron from Sweden, linen from Germany, brandy from France, and tallow from Ireland, together with the cheaper East India calicoes. In a good year, between 30 and 35 ships were dispatched from England; and the round trip—London, Gold Coast, West Indies, London—might take as long as 15–18 months. Of the cargoes

[1] A. C. Wood, op. cit. 110–11. [2] Ibid. 151.

[3] For much of what follows I am indebted mainly to the kindness of Mr. K. G. Davies.

sent out, a certain proportion was usually allotted to the purchase of negroes, for sale in the West Indies at a price determined by the cost of the triangular passage, the total freight per slave being usually £4–5 before the war, and £7–8 in war-time; but, as so many died on the passage, there was a speculative element about this traffic. Increased imports of sugar from Barbados helped to secure for the Company some measure of English esteem, since in this way it was contributing to that change whereby the home country was receiving a greater part of her imports from outside Europe, and was also providing a vent for English goods abroad.

The Company appears, however, to have suffered from lack of capital, as did the 'old' East India Company, and also from the diffusion of trade over too wide an area. In the African trade it failed to maintain its monopoly, because the demand for negroes was so great. Planters and merchants in the West Indies were convinced that their prosperity depended on the cheapness and plentifulness of the negro;[1] at home it was thought that the planter should be encouraged, if only because he was the source of valuable imports; while his slaves were, to however wretched an extent, consumers of English goods;[2] so it was for these reasons that an Act of 1698[3] opened up the African slave trade to all comers. With free trade, the planters were able to obtain a larger supply, but at dearer rates, and with fewer facilities for credit than the Company had provided.

Of English trading ventures which suffered heavily from the rivalry and enmity of the French, the chief was the Hudson's Bay Company.[4] In their petition to James II in May 1687 the Directors complained that, although for twenty years they had traded peaceably in northern Canada, and had spent £200,000 on forts and factories, the French had burned their buildings and destroyed their trade at Port Nelson.[5] The Company derived little benefit from James's treaty of Neutrality[6] of 1686 with Louis XIV, because, it was alleged, the Jesuits, who

[1] *C.J.* xii, 28 Feb. 1698. Petition from planters and merchants in Barbados.

[2] Ibid. xi, 28 Feb. 1696. Petition of traders to Jamaica.

[3] 9 Wm. III, c. 26. For the slave trade generally, see the four volumes of *Documents* edited by Miss E. Donnan.

[4] For this see Beckles Willson, *The Great Company*.

[5] *Cal. S.P. Amer. 1685–8*, 368, 18 May 1687.

[6] *Supra*, 190.

controlled the beaver trade, had succeeded in excluding the Company's traders from the benefits of the treaty. Then came the war. In 1694 the French took York Fort; of fifty-three English trappers there, only thirty survived the ill-treatment which they received.[1] Two years later, the Company regained possession of this fort, and the treaty of Ryswick imposed a vague and uneasy peace on English and French in Canada.

Such were the most important of the chartered companies for foreign and overseas trade. But there were many unregulated bodies of English merchants for this purpose, each of them specializing in some area or country. There were, for example, the Baltic merchants, who imported timber, iron, and copper from Scandinavia; the Eastland merchants, who traded our cloths for the linens of north Germany; the merchants trading to Italy, whose agents were to be found at many of the Mediterranean ports. There were also the traders who for many years had been exporting woollens to south Barbary, and importing copper, as well as a certain amount of bullion.[2] With northern Barbary there was a regular trade, thus described[3] by John Prideaux, a nephew of Dr. Prideaux, dean of Norwich:

> As to the condition of our trade, it is mostly to Barbary, at Tetuan and the adjacent places thereabouts. We furnish the people mostly with cloth, exported from England, at about 6 shillings a yard; we .... send mixt cloths, that is, of several dyes and colours, and also several species of cloths. . . . What we have exported from Barbary is chiefly wax, dates, cuchaneal, estridge feathers and hides; but the greatest thing we trade in is wax; and that, and most of the things I mention, we send to Cadix. . . . At Cadix, we have a correspondent that sells these commodities there, and makes us return home in wine or bills of exchange.

This provides an example of one of the lesser-known trades in which English shipping was employed; it also illustrates how Spain, mainly through the port of Cadiz, played an important part in our overseas commerce. Generally, Spain continued, in this period, to provide a good market for our fish, lead, tin, provisions, and leather goods; there was also a ready sale in Spain and her colonies for the lighter varieties of English cloth,

[1] *Cal. S.P. Amer. 1696–7*, 298. Memorial of Hudson's Bay Company.

[2] *C.J.* xi, 8 Dec. 1696.

[3] *H.M.C. Rep* v, app. 372, 18 Sept. 1698, *MSS. of J.R. Pine Coffin.*

though even the heavier sorts were favoured by ecclesiastics.[1] So great was the demand of the Spanish colonies for European products that the Cadiz merchants had to take all available supplies[2] from English and Dutch, even though, in return, a balance had to be paid in bullion. The nominal closure of the Spanish empire to foreigners was thus evaded by illicit trade, chiefly through the West Indies, and by the establishment of English factors and agents at Cadiz.

But trade relations are seldom static for long, and in the last decade of the century there were some changes in our commercial connexions with several European states, notably France, Portugal, and Holland. For long, English patriots had condemned the importation of French claret and luxury goods, and had deplored our unfavourable balance with France, usually estimated at £1,000,000. It was, of course, much less. But in 1686 the tonnage of imports from France exceeded twice that of our exports to France;[3] while, in peace-time, French alamodes and lustrings were so popular in this country that every servant maid was declared to be 'a standing revenue to the king of France'.[4] Other imports were druggets (made from English wool), paper, hats, and canvas, with many miscellaneous fancy goods; there was also wine. All this was changed, but not suppressed, by the war. Thanks mainly to the Huguenots, we learned to make many of the articles which formerly we had imported from across the Channel; moreover, the weaving and finishing of silk and of other textiles provided a new source of employment, which at least tried to keep pace with feminine fashion. Directly, through the help of the refugees, and indirectly through the cessation of legitimate trade with France, England made a great advance in technique, notably in the textiles; and in the next century her production of artistic goods, including furniture, rivalled that of any other country.

The change in our relations with Portugal was as important. Thanks to abundant labour and water-power, the planters in

[1] J. O. McLachlan, *Trade and Peace with old Spain, 1667–1750*, 6.

[2] Ibid. 13.

[3] L. A. Harper, *The English Navigation Laws*, 295.

[4] *A Dialogue . . . in a Walk to Newington* (1701), 28. For a good account of our trade with France, see Miss M. Priestley, 'Anglo-French Trade and the Unfavourable Balance Controversy 1660–1685' in *Econ. Hist. Rev.*, 2nd series, iv.

Brazil were able to make sugar very cheaply; but, in the later part of the century, our increased imports from the West Indies enabled us to cut down the intake of Brazilian sugar.[1] Nevertheless, our exports of fish, cloth, and manufactured goods to Lisbon remained at a steady average of about £300,000, and so our balance of trade with Portugal remained favourable; even more, the cargoes of sugar and tobacco taken up by our ships in the Tagus were not brought to England, but were traded in the Mediterranean for native commodities and bullion.[2] In contrast, therefore, with France, Portugal was fulfilling on our behalf many of the requirements enjoined by orthodox economic theory, because she provided a vent for our manufactures, a part of which was paid for in bullion; she also supplied materials for a carrying trade. Moreover, shortage of Portuguese shipping enabled English merchants to acquire an increasing share of the Brazil trade, in which we were more favoured than the Dutch, who had to content themselves mainly with the Setubal salt trade.

It was natural that Portugal did not willingly acquiesce in this situation. Between about 1670 and 1690 she embarked on a shipbuilding policy, and for a time encouraged a native cloth industry; but she still offered a market for our lighter fabrics, which the Portuguese could not make for themselves. At this point wine came to our assistance. There had been a steady decline of our imports from the Canaries, attributed to change of taste, and adulteration by the London Vintners;[3] then, with the war, and the nominal ban on claret, we took more port, and this wine became strongly established in English taste. This change proved of diplomatic as well as of social and economic importance, for it led to Portugal's abandonment of her French alliance of 1701, and to the signing of the Methuen treaty of 1703, whereby Portuguese harbours were opened to British ships in the war of the Spanish Succession. By about

[1] *H.M.C. Rep.* ix, app. pt. 2, *MSS. of House of Lords*, 11 sqq., 29 Mar. 1671.

[2] For much of what follows I am indebted to the researches of Miss M. Turner (Mrs. Ede), of Somerville College, Oxford, who has kindly allowed me to use some of her results as embodied in a D.Phil. thesis on Anglo-Portuguese relations.

[3] 'Present State of the Canary Trade', 1686, in *P.R.O.*, *S.P. Spain* 9/472, letters from lord Lansdowne, ambassador in Madrid, 1686–9.

1750 bullion was beginning to play a greater part in Anglo-Portuguese trading relations, one of the factors which led England to base her currency on gold.[1]

Lastly, there was our trade with the Dutch. Before the end of the century, European trade was being conducted on a multilateral basis, having its headquarters at Amsterdam,[2] which was becoming the clearing house of world trade, as it was already the chief market for precious metals. In spite of serious English inroads, the Dutch retained their supremacy in overseas trade until the early years of the eighteenth century. Their chief industries were closely linked with their transport of raw materials, for these industries consisted mainly of distilling from foreign grain, tobacco cutting, sugar boiling, tanning, dyeing, and bleaching, with salt-refining and the fisheries. By 1700 England was playing an important part in that system, because she was supplementing the Scandinavian countries as a source of grain, and was re-exporting to Holland a large proportion of her plantation goods.[3] For the year 1696–7 our exports to Holland were nearly 1½ millions, in return for half a million of imports; in 1700–1, for the same value in imports, our exports were more than 2 millions.[4] This favourable balance with the Dutch may have made it easier for us to obtain credits in Amsterdam for trades, such as that of the Baltic in naval stores, which to us were economically unfavourable, but strategically essential.

Thus the war of the league of Augsburg had some influence on the development of our industry and commerce. We had to do more business with allies than with a potential enemy, allies who helped to strengthen our trading links with central and northern Europe, and with the Mediterranean. At the same time, the produce of the Plantations was providing more of the raw material in demand; with greatly increased capital, a more efficient exploitation of the vast resources of India was

[1] For this, see Miss L. Sutherland, *A London Merchant, 1695–1774*, and C. R. Fay, 'Newton and the Gold Standard', in *Camb. Hist. J.* v (1935), 116.

[2] C. Wilson, *Anglo-Dutch Commerce and Finance in the Eighteenth Century*, 3 sqq.

[3] C. H. Wilson, 'Economic Decline of the Netherlands in the XVIIIth Century', in *Econ. Hist. Rev.* ix, no. 2.

[4] From the tables in sir C. Whitworth, *State of the Trade of Great Britain* (1776).

in sight. An even broader vista of wealth was opened up through peep-holes into the Spanish empire; and indeed it seemed that our maritime ambitions would be limited only by the circumference of the globe. To all this, the negro slave abroad and the English worker at home contributed a full share.

But another human element came into play. The reputation of English merchants was as high as that of their ships; to integrity they usually added intelligence and resourcefulness; for they were 'adventurers' in the older and more honourable sense of the term, always seeking fresh outlets, and prepared to take a risk. That risk was lessened by the skill and courage of the men of the mercantile marine. 'England gambled on an imperial future, and gambled successfully.'[1] It was an age of gamblers and speculators; but in our overseas enterprise there was a virility and sometimes even a spirit of self-sacrifice which greatly diminished the element of chance.

[1] C. Wilson, 'Treasure and Trade Balances; the Mercantilist Problem', in *Econ. Hist. Rev.*, 2nd series, no. 2.

XI

HUMAN RESOURCES FOR WAR: MEN AND INSTITUTIONS

THIS chapter is concerned with the men and the institutions, other than parliament,[1] directly involved in the conduct of William's war.

1. The Men

Of the men, the most important was the king. William had none of the qualities which account for royal popularity. He was not easy of access; he did not tolerate fools, and he was often surly and morose. As he never had any patience for the trivialities of life, the salary of £300 a year paid to his jester, Charles Killigrew, must have been well earned; or, more probably, not earned at all. In these respects he compared unfavourably with the Stuarts.

But there was still something to be said for the rule of one man, provided he had ability, integrity, and courage, and William had all these qualities. They were shown in his foreign policy, a sphere in which he was solitary, because he alone had the requisite knowledge of European affairs, and only he could secure any co-operation between English and Dutch. On the other hand, he was probably unwise in assuming supreme military command. His poor health interfered with his campaigning; he could devise a good plan, but could seldom follow it out; he lacked the resource and ingenuity for modifying tactics in suddenly-changed circumstances. As a commander-in-chief he showed doggedness and fortitude, but he experienced a minimum of good fortune;[2] and, throughout his campaigns, he was concerned less with the fatigues of war than with anxiety to earn a high national opinion of his conduct.[3] Had his personal

[1] For this, see *infra*, ch. XVII.

[2] For an appreciation of William as military leader, see J. W. Fortescue, *History of the British Army*, i. 358.

[3] For this, see the curious contemporary pamphlet, *The Last Hours of Count Solms*, ed. J. H. Cooke, 15.

relations with Marlborough been different; and had he given supreme command to that great soldier the war might have taken a very different course.

This retention of command, in spite of repeated reverses, reflected a certain rigidity in William's character, a quality which had already been revealed in the sustained tactlessness and obstinacy of his attempts to divert Charles II from his pro-French policy,[1] as later it was shown in the meddlings of his agents with the policy of James II. In another and much more reprehensible form the same characteristic was revealed in his refusal to bring to justice the murderers of the De Witt brothers, or the murderers of the Glencoe Macdonalds; conduct which, not unnaturally, brought on him the accusation of brutality, or at least callousness; on the same plane was his retention of Solms, his relative, in command of the infantry, a general whose incompetence was equalled only by his hatred of the English, whose lives he threw away at Steenkirk. These things showed grave defects of character, not to be lightly condoned.

Their explanation, though not their excuse, is probably to be found in the exceptional and even unnatural circumstances in which the prince had spent his early years;[2] unnatural, in the sense that he had never experienced the parental and family influences which may do so much to shape men's lives; in their place, he had been embittered by sombre intrigue, and exclusion from his birthright. While still in his teens, he was already a man with a mission; when only twenty-two he had witnessed the devastation brought on his country by an arrogant and powerful adversary; by the time he had achieved kingship, his character had been chiselled into a granite-like rigour by adversity and disillusionment. That character, almost devoid of the humanity and kindliness which we appreciate most of all in kings, seemed like a grim edifice or institution, divided into separate, independent compartments, connected by few corridors, and known to the world only from its cold, forbidding

[1] An account of these attempts will be found in K. H. D. Haley, *William of Orange and the English Opposition, 1672–4*.

[2] There is a short biography of William by G. J. Renier. The standard account is that by N. Japikse, *Prins Willem III*, 2 vols. See also Miss C. Trevelyan, *William III and the Defence of Holland*.

ante-chamber. Of these compartments, the largest and most active was that devoted to his life work—his unwearied resistance, not to the French people, but to their monarch, of whom neighbouring states, especially small states, must have felt a dread, such as they were not again to experience until the age of the Dictators. Most impenetrable of all was that recess wherein he cherished and concealed his affection for his wife. Personal inclination, often heated by strong and sustained resentment, provided another section of this edifice, but it was kept strictly subordinate to the department of public policy, the link between them being toleration, which was actuated by an alliance of personal preference with politic expediency. There was no interconnexion, however, in those chambers where he received either ministers, like Shrewsbury or Somers, or confidants and intimate friends, like Portland or Heinsius, or backstairs agents, like Sunderland, whose usefulness as a tool, not his infamies as a man, provided the passport to royal confidence. Throughout this carefully partitioned edifice, as in Bunyan's House of the Interpreter, the dust of passion was allayed and settled by the waters, not of the Gospel, but of that Book of Destiny wherein, as William conceived, the channels of men's lives were ordained by inexorable decree.

As a ruler, William was moral in the sense that neither his alliance nor his neutrality could be bought. His enmity was consistent, and even idealist, it was therefore unsullied by the petty or the vindictive; moreover, it was by his energy and personality that he achieved some degree of unity among incongruous allies, brushing aside all pious resolutions with his insistent demand for strong armies and concentration of effort in order to stop the aggressor. He was the first English king who was a good European. The least forthcoming and the most inscrutable of monarchs, he nevertheless familiarized men with a new type of kingship, detached, dignified, and, in all impersonal matters, essentially just.

His consort Mary was the most attractive of all the seventeenth-century Stuarts. Her tragedy arose from these things, that she was denied a child, and that she was married to the leader of her father's enemies; otherwise, she might well have acted as Cordelia to the Lear of St. Germains. During her eleven years' stay in Holland she appears to have been happy;

but in England she was distressed by 'the universal corruption of the nation', and by jealousies and incompetence among the ministers whom William appointed for her guidance during his absences. She acted as queen-regnant in the summer months of the years 1690–4, two of which summers could be described as critical—that of 1690, the year of Beachy Head and the Boyne, and that of 1692, when there was a danger of invasion. In spite of her opinion[1] that women should not meddle in government, her conduct on these two difficult occasions showed calmness and decision, together with a refusal to be dominated by any faction in her Cabinet. But, while making a bold front in public, she was gnawed by constant anxiety about her unfortunate parent, and by a morbid sense of her own unworthiness; attributing national misfortunes not only to the pride of the nation, but to her own worldly pursuits, such as drinking 'the Spaw waters', or eagerly desiring 'that some great thing should be done'. She lived in perpetual fear that even her simplest pleasures would be followed by celestial retribution. Her letters reveal a tenderness and consideration for others such as was not common in this period, a human quality that has helped to procure for her a permanent memorial in the life of the nation. Shocked, as were few of her contemporaries, by the plight of the sick and wounded sailors, she expressed a wish that the old royal palace at Greenwich might be rebuilt as a naval hospital; and, after her death, William, conscious at last of his affection, applied himself to the fulfilment of this wish. So Greenwich Hospital, which might have proved the finest architectural achievement of Wren, commemorates the devotion of a king and the humanity of a queen.[2]

Together, these two sovereigns exercised some influence over a nation which has always responded quickly to a lead from the throne. Mary was the first English queen since Elizabeth. In the interval, queens of England had appeared remote and unsympathetic; Mary's subjects, on the other hand, as they could understand their compatriot, were more ready to follow her example. This accounts for the greater popularity of music, gardening, and porcelain. The queen's interest in gardening was shared by her husband, and the model set by the formal

[1] *Memoirs of Mary, Queen of England*, ed. F. Doebner, 22.

[2] For a good biography see that of Hester W. Chapman (1953).

patterns of Hampton Court was followed by many noble families, so that England became a country not only of great houses, but of famous gardens. Even more, though it cannot be said that William was faithful to his wife, nevertheless he did not displace her in public by a favourite, and to that extent marital fidelity ceased to be ridiculed as a 'bourgeois' prejudice. The king was not interested in books, but he appreciated good paintings, and in 1698 it was reported[1] that he proposed to establish an academy of art in England. He may also be numbered with those who suggested the foundation of a university in London which, according to report,[2] was to be a modest establishment for forty 'sons of decayed gents', who were to be instructed in such subjects as mathematics, navigation, and modern languages; but the scheme was cut short by the king's death. In fine, these two sovereigns did something to initiate that long tradition whereby the royal family has come to be regarded as the embodiment of those virtues which, from time to time, are held in highest repute.

As William was his own first minister, there was less opportunity for the exercise of statesmanship as we understand the term; but William's reign is important as a stage in the evolution of the modern minister, since there was established a clearer distinction between the older type, holding a high household or conciliar office, responsible only to the crown; and the newer type of official, the head of an administrative department, responsible to the Commons actually, though still (even today) one of His Majesty's ministers. In other words, while there survived high personages such as Danby, Halifax, and Rochester, all associated with council or household, the heads of the Treasury and Admiralty were coming more clearly into the public eye, because of the enhanced importance of these departments in time of war; and, most striking illustration of this process, an old office, that of chancellor of the Exchequer, suddenly leaped into prominence, not only in the Commons, but in the nation, because public finance came to be the crucial thing in the strain through which William's England had to pass. There were obvious difficulties in securing co-operation between ministers of such different categories; these were

[1] *Luttrell*, iv. 343.
[2] Ibid. v. 145.

increased by William's practice of communicating matters of high policy only to Dutchmen, such as Portland and Heinsius.

As well as this, William introduced complications by his failure to recognize that party politics were becoming an essential element in public life, and that he could rule effectively only with ministers who enjoyed the confidence of a majority in the Commons. But, though slow to learn this lesson, he nevertheless appears to have profited from experience; for, in the last years of his reign, he was obliged to sacrifice his most eminent English minister, Somers; and the impeachments of 1701 demonstrated the danger of signing treaties without the participation of ministers. It was probably Sunderland who, in the period just after 1693, induced the king to give his confidence to Whigs; just as, after 1700, he may have prevailed upon him to turn to the Tories, as the party having a majority in the House. So William, in spite of his obstinacy, was one of the few monarchs who showed willingness to learn anything from events.

But these events did not include military episodes; for, in his appointments to the higher military commands, William showed his preference for Dutchmen, a preference which naturally aroused resentment, because good soldierly material was available among English, Scots, and Ulstermen. This quality was evidenced by the careers of Thomas Talmash, John, baron Cutts, Hugh Mackay, and William Wolseley. Talmash, who was Ginkel's ablest subordinate in the Irish campaigns, led the infantry at Aughrim; he took part in the battle of Steenkirk, and at Neerwinden he succeeded in bringing away a large body of infantry from disaster. He was killed at Camaret Bay. Another good infantry leader was John Cutts, who had learned his soldiering in the imperial service. After serving in Ireland and Flanders, he showed such ardour at the siege of Namur in 1695 as to earn for himself the epithet of 'The Salamander'. A man of literary taste, Cutts, who had some business ability, was appointed one of the commissioners who set up a branch of the Bank of England at Antwerp; later, he was employed in a diplomatic mission to Vienna. Yet another skilled commander was Hugh Mackay, the defeated general of Killiecrankie, who died at Steenkirk. Wolseley, the brilliant victor of Newton Butler, was not given command in Flanders.

The king preferred to rely only on those generals of whom he had had experience before coming to England. Of these, two were Huguenots—Schomberg, who was killed at the Boyne, and Henri de Massue de Ruvigny, later earl of Galway. As successor to Schomberg, Ruvigny for a time led the cavalry in Flanders, afterwards commanding an expeditionary force in Piedmont where, as a diplomatist, he was outmatched by the unscrupulous duke of Savoy. The foreign general who rendered William the best service in Ireland was the Dutchman Godert de Ginkel, commander-in-chief there after the king's departure. Created earl of Athlone, he continued his military career in Flanders, and later served under Marlborough. A very different type of leader was another Dutchman Heinrich, count Solms. His unskilful conduct of the first siege of Limerick in 1690 delayed the fall of that city; later, at the battle of Steenkirk, when in command of the infantry, he refused help to the hard-pressed Mackay, and is said to have jeered as five British regiments were cut to pieces. He was by far the worst of William's choices. In contrast with him was prince George of Waldeck, whose skilful handling of the situation had helped to prevent a French invasion of Dutch territory in the critical months following Louis's declaration of war on the States General in November 1688. Although William might have made more use of British military talent, nevertheless his wars helped to train a number of younger officers who were afterwards to prove their mettle under Marlborough.

The holding of a military or naval commission was not then a completely specialized function. Some subordinate officers held commissions in both services; many of them were also members of the House of Commons. Some senior officers combined service with a diplomatic career, or with an administrative post, or with a governorship, such as that of the Isle of Wight, which was held in succession by Talmash and Cutts, a position which ensured, on behalf of the Court, control over a few parliamentary boroughs. For the sea service there was available a number of highly trained men who had learned their craft in the later Anglo-Dutch wars or in the campaigns against the Moorish pirates in the Mediterranean. Many of these were 'tarpaulins' who, in peace-time, changed over to the merchant service; others, such as Carter, Delaval, Shovell, and

Rooke were members of what might be called middle-class families. Service under an influential admiral sometimes helped to initiate a distinguished naval career. Thus, Shovell and Benbow were helped by Herbert, lord Torrington; sir David Mitchell, a Scot, was a protegé of Russell's. Of these, Benbow and Mitchell were good examples of promotion from the lower deck; the first, son of a tanner of Shrewsbury, had run away to sea; the second began as a Scottish fisher boy, and was pressed into the English navy.

The fact that the navy had so easily changed its allegiance in 1688 led to the fear that, with equal facility, it would change about again. Russell's loyalty was suspected, though he seems to have compromised by qualifying it with tacit reservations; suspicions were entertained of Killigrew and Delaval, both of whom were dismissed after the affair of the Smyrna convoy; George Churchill, the first to desert James, was suspected of being the first who proposed to desert William.[1] Almost as serious was the difficulty created by the numerous 'gentlemen' officers, many of them inherited from the previous régime, just as that régime had benefited by the legacy from the Commonwealth of such capable leaders as Monck, Myngs, and Haddock. In the naval service therefore, as in the civil administration, William had to employ men who owed their start in life to the later Stuarts. The 'gentlemen' officers included one peer by birth, John, baron Berkeley of Stretton, an efficient admiral who, however, professed unwillingness to obey the orders of those superior officers who were his social inferiors; there were also Herbert and Russell. Most of these men had begun service as volunteers; they were, many of them, men of courage, but they were not amenable to the discipline imposed so rigorously on sailors and skippers pressed from a despised merchant service. Contemporaries were accustomed to drawing a sharp contrast between the two types—the 'tarpaulin', who had usually inherited the hard-fighting, 'pell mell' traditions of the Commonwealth navy; and the 'gentleman' who, having either bought his commission,[2] or having been appointed thereto by some influential person, was said to favour the tactics of 'keeping the

[1] Nottingham to Blathwayt, 10 May 1692. *Add. MS.* 37991, f. 69*b*.

[2] For interesting evidence about the trade of commission buying, see the minutes of the commission of Accounts, in *Harleian MS.* 1489, f. 24*b*.

line', so that (it was alleged) he might evade action.[1] Hence the conduct of William's naval officers was frequently contrasted with that of their Puritan predecessors, as witness the dialogue between Fudge,[2] of the Admiralty, and captain Steerwell, an old Oliverian commander:

> *Fudge.* In your time, when did you judge a commander had fought his ship well?
>
> *Steerwell.* When he had two thirds of the men killed and wounded, with his masts and standing rigging shot by the board, and six or eight feet of water in the hold.

An exaggeration, but not without some truth.

Unfortunately, the trouble about 'gentleman' commanders did not end here. Many of them brought aboard a large following of servants and 'decayed kindred', who were put on the ship's books, and for whom accommodation had to be found—always at the expense of the already cramped sailor.[3] Even more, the handling of a square-rigged ship is a technical matter, the details of which were seen to by the sailing master, usually recruited from the merchant service; but an overbearing commander might reject his opinion, with the hazarding or even the loss of the ship in consequence. Such may well be the explanation of the unusually large number of warships 'cast away' in this period—by December 1695 the number was twenty-three[4]—in a similar category may be placed the ten English warships captured by French privateers. Nor was this the end of it, for there was much convoy work to be done in William's war; and to maintain constant contact between escort and convoy, especially at night, is far more difficult with the sailing ship than with the steamship; accordingly, many of the losses among escorted merchantmen arose from lack of seamanship in the commander of the escort.[5] Pepys, who had long experience, deplored the ruin brought by the 'gentleman' officer;[6] a survivor from

[1] 'Extract from a Commissioner's Note Book' (Richard Gibson, a Commonwealth purser) in *The Naval Miscellany*, ii, ed. J. K. Laughton, 137 sqq. (Navy Records Society).

[2] *The Present Condition of the English Navy* . . ., (1701 or 1702).

[3] H. Maydman, *Naval Speculations and Maritime Politics* (1691), 157 and 208.

[4] *C.J.* xi, 4 Dec. 1695.

[5] *Naval Miscellany*, ii. 163.

[6] Evelyn's *Diary*, 7 May 1690.

Commonwealth days declared bluntly:[1] 'we act as if king Louis had the management of our naval affairs'.

Now, all this was probably inevitable; for in the English, as in the French navy, there still persisted the tradition that good birth (more often influence or even money) was superior to wind and weather. In this way a long time elapsed before a gentleman could, with propriety, reveal an ability to handle a ship; in William's reign such an ability still savoured of association with the merchant service. But that reign nevertheless marks an important stage in the evolution of a more rational attitude, since it was so obvious that the big ships and the big fleets were there, but not yet the men to command them. By the end of the century there was this improvement, that a minimum of three years' service was necessary for a lieutenant's commission, and some kind of examination was introduced.[2]

As for the ordinary soldier and sailor, they were still barely distinguishable from the criminal. Recruits for the army were sometimes obtained from Newgate; seamen pressed for the navy were commonly lodged in gaols when in transit to the ports. It was claimed of the large, indeterminate class known as the 'cottagers' that, as they were bred hardy, they were specially suitable for the army, which would make them 'fit to kill or be killed';[3] indeed there was this to be said for active service that it supplemented the gibbet as a means of keeping down the number of undesirables. A military camp, it was often thought, might debauch a whole neighbourhood; the sailor had at least this in his favour, that he was isolated on board ship. On the other hand there were some who commended the soldier and sailor on the ground that, as they speedily parted with what money they had, they helped to circulate the coin of the realm, and so were of more value to the state than misers.

Long before the Revolution the system of discipline imposed on the sailor had been regulated by statute, based on earlier Acts of War. For the soldier this came later, and was expanded by successive Mutiny Acts, of which the first, that of 1689,

[1] *Naval Miscellany*, ii. 164.

[2] *P.C. Reg.* 78, 31 July 1701; also J. Ehrman, *The Navy in the War of William III*, 138–42, 311–12 and 355–6.

[3] T. Nourse, *Campania Felix*, 100.

imposed the penalty of death for desertion.[1] The second Act (1689–90) penalized the offence of false musters; three years later the conditions of enlistment were better regulated by the requirement that the prospective soldier should declare his consent before a justice. Later Acts included clauses that army agents should give bonds as security; that officers of the same regiment as that of the president should not sit at a court martial, and that the marine regiments should be subjected to the Mutiny Acts. In 1695 the approval of the crown was required before the death sentence could be carried out. Death, which might be by beheading, hanging, or shooting was the penalty, not only for desertion and mutiny, but also for spying, stealing from a comrade, plundering without permission, and neglect of sentry duty. Sometimes, when a large number of men had been convicted of a capital offence, one man in ten might be executed, the choice being determined by a toss of the dice.

For the sick and wounded of both services emergency measures were devised early in the war, the duty of carrying them out being entrusted to commissioners, of whom Evelyn for a time was one. They were subjected to much criticism. Their difficulties really arose from the fact that a hospital service, already inadequate for the civilian population, was suddenly obliged to take the strain of thousands of war casualties, for which purpose a certain proportion of beds had to be reserved in St. Thomas's and St. Bartholomew's hospitals, and a number were accommodated in Chelsea Hospital. But all this proved inadequate. The consequence was that, in ports like Plymouth, Portsmouth, and Chatham sick and wounded were placed in private lodgings, which became more difficult to obtain, as payment was so long delayed, with the result that wounded men sometimes died in the streets.[2] It was even worse for the soldier abroad. After the slaughter of Steenkirk, a number of British wounded were conveyed to Brussels, where there were no arrangements for them; many would have perished, but for the charity of the princess of Vaudemont, who took as many as possible into her house.[3] As there were no field hospitals or ambulance service,

[1] There is a good account of army discipline in this period in C. Walton, *History of the British Standing Army*, ch. xxvi.

[2] For an instance at Rochester, see *Cal. S.P. Dom. 1690–1*, 169, 25 Nov. 1690.

[3] C. Walton, op. cit. 230.

the wounded were generally left to lie where they had fallen, in which state they were often murdered and robbed.

The soldier had this advantage over the sailor that, until Anne's reign, he could not be forced into the service. For the manning of the large fleets required by William's war, the system of pressing, in abeyance at first, was soon stretched to the utmost, and was organized with almost brutal efficiency. In order that men of the merchant service might be available, embargoes were often imposed on the sailings of ships; and, for the actual pressing, a certain quota was prescribed for each maritime county, the duty of raising this being entrusted to the lords lieutenant and the vice admiralties of these districts. The warrants for pressing were issued by the Admiralty on the instructions of the privy council.[1] Two officials, the 'prestmaster' and the conductor, acted in conjunction. The first, equipped with a list of sea-faring men, went to each house on his list, where he left a shilling, with instructions when and where each pressed man was to appear; the conductor then conveyed the men to the ports, being allowed 8*d.* per day each when travelling. At the ports were agents who, having received the men, kept them in custody at the rate of 6*d.* per day until they could be handed over to the ships. It does not appear that there was even the most cursory examination of the men to see whether they were fit or not; consequently many diseased men were taken aboard, spreading infection. In 1701, however, the Customs officers were required to conduct some kind of inspection.[2]

This system, cumbersome and expensive, compared unfavourably with the French method of registration, by which ships could usually be manned quickly; moreover the English method was accompanied by certain distinctive evils. Thus, the men had often to be imprisoned for long periods in hulks before being taken on board, confinement which resulted in a high rate of mortality from disease; of those who tried to escape, many were shot or drowned. Even while the ships were laid up during the winter, it was thought too risky to allow the men to go home; so they were kept on board, at great expense and with a further lowering of vitality. Breakdowns or treachery in

[1] The arrangements will be found detailed in the Registers of the Privy Council, e.g. vol. 73, 17 Mar. 1693.

[2] Ibid. 77, 26 Feb. 1701.

the victualling departments, as evidenced by the supply of bad food and poisoned beer, notably in the autumn of 1689; and the short rations of 1694, when three men had to live on the rations of two, were among the other circumstances which made the life of the sailor at this period one of exceptional hardship. It is probable that the cumulative effect of these things was to cause a steady decline in the health of British sailors, weakened as many of them were by scurvy. This may have been in the mind of admiral Rooke when, in the spring of 1696, the fleet was mobilized in the Downs in order to meet the threat of invasion. 'I do not know', he wrote to secretary Trumbull, 'what can hinder the enemy from prosecuting their late intentions of invading us, but my great hopes are that their fleet may be as ill-manned as ours.'[1]

These things were notorious. In the large pamphlet literature directed to criticism of these abuses, the health conditions were universally condemned, and it was stated that more men 'stewed to death' in ships than were killed in action. Captain George St. Lo made a number of interesting suggestions, including that of some provision for the maintenance and education of the male children of officers and men who died on active service. Convinced that, although the press was still necessary, more use could be made of the voluntary system, he advocated paying off the ships' companies at the end of each voyage at a saving of half a million a year. Old ships moored in rivers might, he suggested, be used as training ships for boys.[2] The miseries of the sailors were shared by their families, on behalf of whom a charitable fund was established in 1701, when an appeal was made for gifts and loans in order to relieve such families by giving or lending them money, and obtaining employment for those seeking it. The appeal, though probably not well planned, was supported by a large number of Anglican and Dissenting ministers; and so the most irreconcilable elements in seventeenth-century England were brought together by their bond of common humanity in face of obvious suffering and distress.[3]

[1] *H.M.C. Rep. MSS. of marquis of Downshire*, ii. 660.

[2] G. St. Lo, *England's safety . . .*, 1693. Cf. also *Great Britain's Groans . . .*, 1695.

[3] The advertisement for this charity will be found in *Bodl. Pamph.* 240.

2. The Institutions

Such were the personages and persons involved in William's war. Of the institutions which were actively concerned in its direction, as well as in the administration of the country, some were attributable to a special circumstance, namely, the absences of the king. During his reign of thirteen years, William was away from the country for a total period of about sixty-two months; only in 1689 did he spend a whole year in England. Until 1697 his absences were on account of the campaigns in Ireland and, later, in Flanders; but in each of the last four years of his reign, he spent about four months in Holland. This caused resentment, for the later absences were attributed to dislike of his adopted country. But this had some indirect importance. Until 1694, the year of her death, the queen, during these absences, acted as sole sovereign, with the assistance of a Cabinet; but all important matters were referred to the king for decision. After 1694 the nominal rule, in such periods, was entrusted to lords justices under the great seal, selected mainly from holders of high office. Throughout the period of their commission, the lords justices maintained constant communication with William through secretary Blathwayt, referring to him all matters of policy. They heard petitions, including petitions for reprieve; they summoned the commissioners of the Treasury and Admiralty to appear before them to give information on matters within their province, and they issued orders to flag officers, in this respect sometimes overlapping the province of the Admiralty. In the opinion of the judges, their excellencies might prorogue parliament by commission or in person. But they had nothing to do with foreign policy; indeed, as a body they were not even cognizant of the partition treaties.

In the exercise of their powers the lords justices were indirectly responsible for the enunciation of a principle of some importance. In 1695 one of their number, Tenison, archbishop of Canterbury, expressed concern at the increasing circulation of scandalous and seditious pamphlets. The attorney general and solicitor general agreed in the opinion that the authors of such pamphlets were still punishable, in spite of the lapse of the Licensing Act in that year, and they thought that convictions might be obtained by means of informers. This recommendation was adopted, but it was represented by counsel that a general warrant could not be granted to search houses, as such a step could be taken only after particular information on oath. So the control of the Press, after the lapse of the Licensing Act, led to the first enunciation of the illegality of general warrants.[1]

The privy council brought together in a large and somewhat formal body those who held household offices and all who were responsible for the great departments of state. The old theory had been that the king was supported by parliament while it was in session, and was advised by the council whether or not parliament was in session; but for long the effective work of the council had been delegated to committees, on the recommendations of which the formal body took action. Nevertheless, even in this period, the council retained something of its old importance. As an executive body, it could commit a person to custody, on the warrant of a secretary; it exercised a constant review over Irish and colonial legislation; heard appeals from Ireland and the Channel Islands, and considered submissions by individuals or departments, on which it either made a decision, or referred the matter to the appropriate authority. The only definition of its activities is this, that one can hardly conceive of any matter that might not eventually come before the council; in William's reign it was the central clearing house of the administration.

Thus, to enumerate some of these miscellaneous activities. The judges were regularly summoned in order that they might be informed 'what they are to give in charge' at the next Assizes; in some of the years after 1696 they were ordered to see that the Association[2] and the Test were tendered to all suspected persons.[3] They had also to impress on grand juries the necessity of bringing to justice the authors and publishers of seditious libels. Occasionally the council acted in a manner that seemed like interference with the ordinary course of justice, as when a mayor was ordered to attend in order to answer the

[1] *Add. MS.* 40782, Minutes of the Lords Justices, 28 and 30 May 1695. For censorship of the Press, see *infra*, 510–13.

[2] *Infra*, 427.

[3] e.g. *P.C. Reg.* 77, 13 July 1699.

charge that he had hindered an ensign from seizing a deserter;[1] equally, on the petition of a mayor, a military officer might be brought in custody to the Board on a charge of abusive conduct.[2] All this was a faint echo of the wide judicial powers which the council had once exercised. Other miscellaneous matters included consent to the appointment of a town clerk, approval of applications from towns for incorporation, and the formal confirmation given to the appointment of justices of the peace. Concern with matters of wider import was seen in July 1698 when the new council of Trade was ordered to conduct an inquiry into the high price of corn.[3]

So far as one can generalize in this matter, it may be said that there were two main branches of conciliar activity; namely, minute control over the local administration, by communication with the lords lieutenant; and the giving effect to recommendations made by departments. Such recommendations were usually embodied in proclamations. But much of its time was taken up by trivial matters, usually petitions from private persons, some of which might come from councillors themselves, as when the duke of Bolton complained that he had been beaten and abused by a commoner.[4] A certain number of council's activities were regulated according to a fixed calendar;[5] thus, in February, during the war years, arrangements were made for pressing seamen; in August it considered the settling of trade for the following year; in September the king declared in council what number of men the victualling departments should provide for, the slaughtering season being between Michaelmas and Christmas. In spite of all this formal business, there appear at times to have been debates, and there are notes of the arguments used on both sides.[6] But these did not usually relate to large questions of policy, as they were concerned with such matters as allowing East India interlopers to sail, or laying an embargo on sailings. Exceptionally, in April 1693 council debated whether the king should be advised to prorogue the

[1] *P.C. Reg.* 73, 6 Aug. 1690. [2] Ibid. 76, 20 June 1695.

[3] Ibid. 77, 11 July 1698.

[4] *Add. MS.* 34350, 12 Oct. 1693. Southwell's privy council Notes.

[5] *Add. MS.* 34349. Southwell's 'Kalendar showing what things come before the Council in their respective months'.

[6] *Add. MS.* 34350 *passim*.

parliament summoned for 2 May. It was decided to advise prorogation until September, and the reasons given for this advice are of some interest; namely, that, as the Commons had already granted large sums, they were not likely to be of any further use; also, as many of them were justices, they would be of more service in the country; and, lastly, that by a prorogation the subject would be less vexed by the oppression of parliamentary privilege.[1] So parliament was prorogued.

But as the privy council consisted of about sixty members, it was too large for the intimate discussion of policy. This difficulty had been met in previous reigns by resort to committees, such as those of Intelligence or Foreign Affairs, or to an informal Cabinet, such as Charles II's Cabal. In James II's reign there had been a camarilla which included Jeffreys, Sunderland, Middleton, Godolphin, and Dartmouth, with Bridgeman as secretary,[2] which usually met on Sundays, but it was displaced in importance by the secret conclaves of the king, Sunderland, and Petre. It was natural, therefore, that after the Revolution there should be serious objection to such unauthorized gatherings; indeed, to many even the name of Cabinet was odious, and in 1692 it was thought that this difficulty might be overcome if the name were dropped, its members being given commissions as lieutenants or regents, with defined powers.[3]

But already, the needs created by the war, together with the king's absences in the summer, necessitated the institution of a Cabinet. Even before these absences, in February 1689, an Order in Council had created a committee of affairs for Ireland, which, among others, included Danby, Halifax, Mordaunt, Churchill, and Schomberg, with Shrewsbury as secretary.[4] an example of a formal, *ad hoc* body, concerned with the co-ordination of policy. But William's Cabinets really began in the summer of 1690 when he went to Ireland. On that occasion Mary was left with full powers, assisted by a Cabinet of nine, headed by Danby, in whom the queen was instructed to place special confidence;[5] among its members were Devonshire, Nottingham,

[1] *Add. MS.* 34350, f. 4, 27 Apr. 1693; see also *infra*, 467–8.
[2] *Baschet*, 173, f. 139.
[3] *Cal. S.P. Dom. 1691–2*, 543. Memorandum by earl of Mulgrave.
[4] *H.M.C. Rep.* xii, app. pt. 6 *MSS. of House of Lords*.
[5] *Memoirs of Mary . . .*, ed. R. Doebner, 28.

Shrewsbury, and lord chief justice Holt. This body was divided about the command of the fleet; and, when the Admiralty commissioners were called in, they stood out against the Cabinet's nomination of Haddock as one of the joint commanders, insisting that, as they gave commissions to admirals, they should have some say in the choice. On this occasion sir T. Lee, on behalf of the Admiralty, made a resolute stand against the queen, who, like a true Stuart, argued that if the Cabinet, as representing the king, could not appoint an admiral who happened to be unacceptable to the Admiralty, then the king had surrendered his powers.[1] The queen had her way. Later additions to this Cabinet included the eccentric Charles Mordaunt, earl of Monmouth (afterwards earl of Peterborough), Marlborough, and Lowther. Of the first Mary noted (correctly) that he was mad; of the second that he could never be trusted, and of the third that he was weak but honest. 'I believe never any person was left in greater streights of all kinds' was the queen's complaint[2] about the councillors imposed upon her, perhaps the earliest recorded opinion of a British sovereign about the character of a Cabinet.

As the Commons, particularly those opposed to the Court, disliked the Cabinet, it was natural that they should hold it responsible for disasters, such as that of the Smyrna convoy in 1693. Inquiry into this showed that there was a complete lack of co-operation between Cabinet, secretary of state, and Admiralty. It appeared that secretary Nottingham had received a letter from Paris, dated 1 June (new style) and received on 30 May (old style), intimating that the French fleet had left Brest, which news, had it been sent off immediately to the admirals, would probably have saved the convoy. The evidence[3] communicated to the legislature showed that the letter was placed by Nottingham before the Cabinet, but there was no evidence that it was even read; nor was its information sent to the admirals, nor to the Admiralty. This omission may have arisen from negligence in the secretary's office, where messengers were sometimes heard disputing whose turn it was to go next. But in spite of such incidents, William continued to be

[1] *Dalrymple*, iii, app. to bk. v, 107. Mary to William, 24 July–3 Aug. 1690.

[2] *Memoirs of Mary* . . ., 30.

[3] *L.J.* xv, 15 Jan. and 15 Feb. 1694.

assisted by a Cabinet, in the choice of which he showed little preference, nominating its members from those holders of high office who were entrusted with the duty of co-ordinating information and acting in an advisory capacity. Its advice was not always taken.

Historians have used the word 'Junto' of a body of men who, during the later and critical stages of the war, were assuming a large part in the direction of national affairs. This name, which may well be misleading, is no more than a term of convenience to indicate a group of ministers, most of whom served more formally as lords justices, some of whom also held offices which brought them into direct contact with parliament and with departments of state. Normally, the avenue to public eminence was from above, through the royal household; now, a new avenue was opening up from beneath, through the administrative department; in William's reign, the two avenues were running side by side. The Junto kept no minutes; it was as unknown to the constitution as the Cabinet; it had little corporate sense; when it met, it did so fortuitously, sometimes at country houses, such as Winchendon, lord Wharton's seat in Buckinghamshire; one may even hesitate to speak of the 'members' of such a nebulous body. Nevertheless, the Junto was our first real Cabinet, because, between 1695 and 1698, it had the support of a Whig majority in the Commons; its 'members', with the exception of Wharton were the heads of departments of state; and, collectively, this body appears to have deliberated on matters of high policy, though its opinions might be set aside by the crown. The best evidence of this semi-corporate capacity is the fact that three 'members', Somers, Halifax, and Orford were impeached in 1701 as the persons supposed to be responsible for William's part in the partition treaties.

Of those associated with the Junto, the only holder of household office was Wharton, who was kept out of administrative office by the king, because of a reputation for libertinism. So Wharton served mainly as an electioneering expert, and was also valuable because of the large number of boroughs in his control; moreover, he was distinguished by one quality almost remarkable in that age, namely, loyalty to friends and colleagues. Another potential minister, who had been denied this quality—Sunderland—claimed to have a share in the destinies of the Junto; and, as he appears to have advised the king to place his confidence in the Whigs, so he seems to have regarded the ministers as his creatures, whom, as he had set up, he might at any moment pull down. With the help of his tools, such as Trevor and Duncombe, Sunderland made the life of the Junto an uneasy one. As he played the part of Mephistopheles, so Shrewsbury played the part of Ariel; hovering benevolently, though hesitatingly, over the heads of admiring and deferential statesmen, who felt that their position was more assured by the patronage of a duke; for, after all, the system of *clientage* was by no means extinct. In this sense, the elusive Shrewsbury might be regarded as the patron or honorary member of the nebulous Junto.

The effective ministers in the Junto were Russell (Orford), Montagu (Halifax), and Somers, all of whom were consistent Whigs. Russell, as first commissioner of the Admiralty could speak, however truculently, for the Admiralty. Montagu, as chancellor of the Exchequer and later (May 1697) as first commissioner of the Treasury, was responsible for the financing of the war, and might be described as our first real cabinet minister, because he headed a great department, and had to defend his conduct of that department in the Commons; he was also, like Harley after him, one of the most skilled parliamentary managers of his age. Somers, as lord chancellor, held an office which, in the past, had often been connected with leadership in the royal councils, but for some time the Chancery had been yielding in political importance to the Treasury, which was thenceforth to provide the prime ministers. Nevertheless, by his moderation and integrity, Somers did secure some measure of co-ordination among the ministers of the Junto, and was one of the few Englishmen who succeeded in winning the confidence of the king. Moreover, these ministers had at their disposal, for advice on specific points, the two greatest intellects in Europe. Locke had been included in the committee of Trade and Plantations by the influence of Somers, who also helped to secure for Isaac Newton the post of Warden of the Mint in 1696 and that of Master in 1697. The presidency of Somers and its association with Locke and Newton conferred on the Junto an intellectual prestige such as was unknown to earlier cabals and cabinets.

The difficulties created by the war helped to emphasize the necessity for some conciliar body to integrate the various branches of the administration, and to advise the crown on policy. All were agreed that this was imperfectly performed by the privy council, the lords justices, the informal Cabinet, and the even more informal Junto; so various alternatives were suggested, including that of a committee of both Houses.[1] Meanwhile, two things delayed the evolution of an efficient Cabinet—the absence of clear party allegiance, and the extent of the prerogative still vested in the crown. It was Sunderland, with his long experience of devices for giving effect to the royal wishes, who first realized the necessity for a compact, efficient Cabinet; which, in his view, should be limited to ten persons, each having a right to be included in virtue of his employment. His Cabinet, while consisting mainly of high officials of the household, such as the lord steward and the lord chamberlain, would have included also the first commissioners of the Treasury and of the Admiralty, with the master of the Ordnance, the lord lieutenant of Ireland, and the two secretaries.[2] All the king's affairs should, in his opinion, be debated in such a council, two members of which were to prepare the king's speeches—a precaution doubtless derived from experience of James. It is to Sunderland's credit that he was possibly the first to suggest practical means for securing co-operation between crown and ministers.

Privy council and Cabinet were dependent on the services of the two principal secretaries of state. The senior had the southern, the junior the northern department; and there was a theoretical division of duties, whereby domestic, foreign, Irish, and colonial affairs were distributed between them.[3] But in practice, this was not always adhered to, and was set aside altogether when there was only one secretary, as Nottingham (March 1692–March 1693), and Trenchard (November 1693–March 1694). Shrewsbury and Nottingham, in the earlier years of the reign, were acting almost as first ministers, and the latter's dismissal in November 1693 was connected not only

[1] In the session of 1692–3 Halifax and Mulgrave proposed that a standing committee of both Houses should act as a council of state. *Burnet*, iv. 187.

[2] *Hardwicke State Papers*, ii. 463.

[3] For this, see M. A. Thomson, *The Secretaries of State, 1681–1782*.

with royal, but with national, dissatisfaction at his conduct of naval affairs. In the middle years of the reign, Trenchard and Trumbull represented a different type, both being eminent civil lawyers, a profession which, in earlier days, had supplied officials and secretaries who, by their knowledge of an international jurisprudence, were specially qualified to handle diplomatic matters. Later in the reign, their place was taken by still another type—clerks like Vernon or Hedges, or unenterprising peers like Jersey and Manchester. These successive changes in secretarial status may be attributed mainly to the decline in importance of the privy council, and the institution of such bodies as the Cabinet and the lords justices, which needed secretaries distinguished by competence and regularity rather than by initiative.

Of the other departments, Treasury and Admiralty call for reference. That the Treasury was so little noticed by either parliament or Press may have been because of the efficiency of men like Godolphin, Montagu, and Lowndes, assisted by prominent parliamentarians who, though not financial experts, were enabled as commissioners to acquire practical experience of the country's financial administration. The fact that Treasury control was now more strongly exercised over both Customs and Excise departments made it more valuable as a school of statesmanship. Of those who served as commissioners, sir E. Seymour, R. Hampden, and sir T. Littleton had associations with an earlier age; Godolphin was to be first minister in the next reign; the names of Thomas Pelham, John Lowther, and Stephen Fox recall some of the great political families of the eighteenth century. The Treasury was primarily concerned with the royal revenue, deciding on many vexed questions, some of them sent by the privy council, leaving to the Exchequer[1] the duty of accountancy, together with business arising from payment of taxes and floating of loans. The king sat frequently with the Treasury commissioners, taking an active part in its business, and sometimes (as with the misdeeds of Duncombe) pressing for investigation into malversation and fraud. Over departmental estimates the Treasury exercised some influence; while, by their membership of committees of

[1] For a good contemporary account of the Exchequer, see *Add. MS.* 36107, f. 47 sqq.

the Commons, the commissioners were able to provide the legislature with first-hand information about the revenue.[1]

But there was another, very active, body to which the Commons made increasing reference for such information, namely, the commissioners for taking the Public Accounts, established in 1690.[2] The institution of such a commission may have implied suspicion, not so much of the Treasury, as of the Court; for it was through places and pensions that the crown maintained majorities in the House; and it was mainly through this commission that a minority in the Commons was able to direct its opposition to Court measures. Voluminous evidence[3] of widespread corruption in appointments helped to stimulate opposition to office-holders in the Commons; and the advocacy of greater purity in public life provided a new doctrine for the developing Tory party at this time.

The Admiralty (until 1702) was in commission, in which were included a number of seamen, as Herbert, Russell, and Rooke, associated with several notable civilians, such as sir T. Lee, sir Richard Onslow, sir John Houblon, and sir John Lowther of Whitehaven. By an Act of 1690 the powers of the lord high admiral, with some exceptions, were vested in the Board.[4] It was subject to the direction of king in council, communicated to it by one of the secretaries. To its executive functions were added that of co-ordinating the work of inferior boards, such as the Transport Office, the Navy Board, and the Victualling Board. In this there was much overlapping. It was characteristic also that, in broad matters of policy and in the higher naval appointments, the king often ignored the Admiralty altogether. Thus, late in April 1689, just before the outbreak of war, Herbert wrote to secretary Nottingham, asking him for instructions; his letter was opened by the king, who informed him what action he was to take.[5] In January 1696,

[1] D. M. Gill, 'The Treasury', in *E.H.R.* xlvi (1931), and *Cal. Tr. Bks.* ix, pt. 1, cxxxiii sqq.

[2] 2 W. and M., sess. 2, c. 11.

[3] Notably in *Cal. Tr. Bks.* xi–xvii, Dr. Shaw's introduction. Also *H.M.C. Rep.* xiii, app. pt. 5, *MSS. of House of Lords.* For 1692 there is much valuable evidence in *Harleian MS.* 1489, ff. 24–164. For the years after 1693, see the *MSS. of House of Lords*, new series.

[4] 2 W. and M., sess. 2, c. 2. J. Ehrman, op. cit., ch. 9.

[5] *H.M.C. Rep., MSS. of A. G. Finch*, ii. 203–4.

when it was known that James was planning an invasion, the king personally ordered the return of the Mediterranean fleet, an order not communicated to the Admiralty until two months later.[1] In 1693 Trenchard informed the Admiralty that the admirals were to take their commands from the king or queen, an instruction which created confusion two years later, when the lords justices asked the Admiralty whether they had given instructions to lord Berkeley, in accordance with the king's directions; to which the Admiralty replied that they had received the royal directions, but were assuming that it was for the lords justices to give the orders.[2] There were obvious elements of danger in this confusion. While the Admiralty had to acquiesce in this subordination, the admirals were not happy in a situation which left supreme control to either king or queen, with no certainty as to how the royal commands would be communicated. So, too, with the higher appointments. The House was so critical of these that in 1691 the suggestion was made that the Commons should appoint the admirals.[3] It was also thought that all orders to the fleet should come direct from the Admiralty.[4]

In conjunction with their subordinates of the Navy Board, the Admiralty directed the movements of H.M. ships, issued warrants for the examination of lieutenants, appointed captains (to specified ships), and also rear-admirals. In arrangements for the transport of troops the Admiralty acted in conjunction with Blathwayt, the secretary-at-war and William's mouthpiece; in its provision of escorts for convoys, the commissioners consulted with the committee of Trade and Plantations, the commissioners of Customs and, on occasion, with merchants concerned in particular trades.[5] They also issued warrants for the press gangs and granted protections in specified cases. In October 1692 they went to Greenwich, in order to inspect the site of the future hospital.

As the war provided opportunity for the training of a higher

[1] *MSS. of House of Lords*, new series, ii, *1695–7*, x–xi, 360.

[2] *P.R.O. Adm.* 3/8, 1 May 1693. *Add. MS.* 40782, Minutes of the lords justices, 6 June 1695.

[3] Reports of F. Bonnet, in *Ranke*, vi, 6–16 Nov. 1691.

[4] *Cobbett*, v. 725, Nov. 1692.

[5] Admiralty Minutes in *P.R.O. Adm. 3/1*, 1689–92.

administrative personnel, so it helped to inaugurate the civil service. Already there existed something like the higher branch of such a service, represented by Blathwayt, William's secretary, and Edward Southwell, a clerk of the privy council. At the Treasury, William Lowndes was probably the most notable of the permanent officials of the period; and the success of the new financial measures owed much to his skill, and to what was then more rare, namely, personal integrity. At the Admiralty, there was no one with either the prerogative or the personality of Pepys; but there was at least competence in such secretaries as William Bridgeman and Josiah Burchett. But it was in the revenue departments that the increase in civil service personnel can be most clearly noted. This was accounted for mainly by two things—the gradual abandonment of the farming system, in favour of management by the state, and the great increase of taxation. The results can be seen mainly in Customs and Excise, in both of which the substitution of government control inaugurated that long tradition whereby a post in either branch became the last refuge of the unemployables. In the higher posts, limited for the most part to persons appointed by influence, no qualifications were necessary, since their duties could be performed by deputies; but, for the lower posts, some educational training was required; accordingly, after 1696, the Customs commissioners instituted a scheme of training for all but the menial branches.[1] At the same time, examinations were introduced, usually in mathematics and mensuration, subjects taught in the Dissenting academies, which were the first educational establishments to provide training for a rapidly expanding civil service.

In conclusion, it may be asked: how far did the English administrative system ensure efficiency in the direction of the war? It was not so efficient as that of the French in the time of Colbert and Louvois; but, on the other hand, it compared favourably with that of their successors, such as Pontchartrain and Barbézieux. There were special difficulties on the English side; of these, the chief arose from the long absences of the king, who, while autocratic in temper, had to entrust some measure of responsibility to representatives or subordinates—to an anxious

[1] E. E. Hoon, *The Organisation of the English Customs Service 1696–1786*, 203 sqq.

woman; to a Cabinet unknown to the constitution and disliked by parliament; and to a body of lords justices, whose powers were not clearly defined. These things enabled Englishmen to deliberate in the king's name, in his absence; but, for the time, there was much confusion and overlapping. Mistakes were inevitable; the wonder is that there were not more. Over the army, whatever may be said of William's generalship, the administration was comparatively good, because the king was on the spot, accompanied by the capable Blathwayt; but with the navy it was otherwise, since it was not always clear whether directions should be taken from the king, the Cabinet, or the Admiralty. There were other defects. Sometimes instructions to an admiral were so badly worded that they had to be redrafted;[1] still more, in planning, there was often a complete lack of secrecy, so that the enemy could obtain information months ahead. Another difficulty was the absence of any regular correspondence with our Dutch allies, a lack of which the lords justices were acutely conscious.[2] In all these respects France had the advantage; for she had unity of direction; she was not embarrassed by allies, nor had she any parliament which might call ministers to account.

But, in some obscure way, England muddled through her first European war.

[1] *Add. MS.* 40782. Minutes of the lords justices, 3 Sept. 1695.

[2] Ibid., 23 May 1695.

XII

THE WAR AT SEA, 1689–92
BEACHY HEAD; LA HOGUE

IN the two preceding chapters reference has been made to the resources in materials, men, and institutions which influenced England's conduct in the war of the league of Augsburg. Until the end of 1691 England's share in the hostilities on land was limited mainly to the war in Ireland;[1] and it was not until 1692 that British troops could be used at full strength in Flanders. This chapter treats of the earlier incidents of the war at sea, as well as of events at home, notably the proceedings in parliament.

The war had begun on 14 September 1688, when Louis dispatched his armies to the middle Rhine before his numerous enemies had time to mobilize. These enemies had been loosely federated two years before by the league of Augsburg, a league which brought together the emperor, the kings of Spain and Sweden, the elector of Bavaria, the duke of Savoy, and several princes of the empire for the maintenance of the truce of Ratisbon and the peace of Europe. The signatories of the truce of Ratisbon (August 1684) had hoped to preserve peace by confirming to Louis all that he had acquired by force and chicanery; but this hope was speedily disappointed; and even the mildly defensive league of Augsburg was cited by the French king as a pretext for again resorting to arms. The initiative lay with him, and his opponents were left guessing. But, as he did not interfere with William's expedition, nor declare war on the Dutch until just after the prince of Orange landed in England, contemporaries found it more difficult than ever to fathom his intentions.

There then ensued several weeks in the winter of 1688–9 during which the English Revolution was in the balance. At any moment Louis's armies might march to the lower Rhine; and a hard frost would have enabled them to accomplish with

[1] *Supra*, 253–8.

ease an invasion of the United Provinces which had proved difficult in the late summer of 1672; for the water which had impeded the earlier enterprise might have provided a good surface for the later one. So William, in the uncertainties of his first winter in England, must have kept an anxious eye on the thermometer. Meanwhile his friends had not been idle. The league of Augsburg had provided for a total joint force of 60,000 men under the command of prince George of Waldeck. Their mobilization was slow, only 12,000 German troops having assembled by October 1688.[1] But Schomberg, with Brandenburg troops, occupied Cologne, and there were 8,000 Dutch soldiers defending Maestricht. By the end of December Louis's opportunity for a blow at Holland was passing, since by then Waldeck's army was established on the lower Rhine,[2] and by the early spring of 1689, more than 100,000 men were ranged against France.[3] So the league of Augsburg was not so ineffective as is now commonly assumed. Louis himself may have underestimated it, for it is possible that his march to the middle Rhine was no more than a demonstration, intended to overawe his enemies. Finding himself faced with the prospect of another long war, he extended his devastations in the unfortunate Palatinate.

By the end of February 1689 the Dutch[4] felt strong enough to declare war on Louis, alleging his interference with their trade, his prohibition of Dutch imports, and his persecution of Dutch nationals in France. The next move was taken in April, when Louis declared war on Spain, alleging that Spanish diplomacy had favoured the formation of the league of Augsburg and that the governor of the Spanish Low Countries had assisted William's enterprise. These declarations of war were followed by a sequence of alliances, intended to make concrete the implications of the league of Augsburg. A treaty was concluded (19/29 April) between William and the States General, in which it was agreed that England would provide fifty warships and the

[1] P. L. Muller, *Wilhelm III. von Oranien und Georg Friedrich von Waldeck*, ii. 42.

[2] Ibid. 47.

[3] Ibid. 55.

[4] For a good account of the Dutch share in the war and the consequences of William's absences from Holland, see P. J. Blok, *History of the People of the Netherlands*, iv, ch. 17.

Dutch thirty, the total fleet to be divided into three squadrons, the largest for the Mediterranean, another for the Channel and Irish Sea, and a third for the straits of Dover.[1] The stores for the Mediterranean fleet were to be either at Port Mahon (Minorca) or at Porto Ferraio (Elba). This alliance was supplemented by a treaty of August 1689 for the union of English and Dutch forces against France, a treaty which contained clauses providing for the disposal of captured French cargoes.[2] On 1–11 May was signed an offensive alliance between the emperor and the States General, intended to restore Europe to its state at the treaties of Westphalia and the Pyrenees. This was concluded at Vienna, and the kings of Spain and England, with the duke of Lorraine, were invited[3] to accede to it; this they did, together with the duke of Savoy, and so a grand alliance was formed.[4] In August Christian V of Denmark, though not one of the allies, agreed with William to provide 7,000 troops, for a subsidy.[5] The elector of Brandenburg was already enrolled with the allies by his treaties of May 1686 with the emperor and of June 1688 with the States General;[6] and the duke of Bavaria by his alliance with the emperor.[7] In contrast, the diplomatic achievements of Louis were meagre—a treaty of neutrality (which he had no intention of keeping) with the Swiss, and a treaty of peace 'for a hundred years' with the pasha and divan of Algiers (then just recovering from a series of French naval bombardments).

In 1689, therefore, the European situation was this: the defensive league of Augsburg had been extended into a heterogeneous network of alliances between Catholic and Protestant states, owing what unity it possessed to the drive and leadership of William. Generally, the motive was resistance to the aggressions of Louis, but behind this there were separate interests. The rulers of Brandenburg and Savoy, ambitious of converting their principalities into kingdoms, could not afford to be neutral,

[1] *Dumont*, vii. 222; also J. C. M. Warnsinck, *De Vloot van den Koning-Stadhouder, 1689–90*, ch. 3.

[2] *Dumont*, vii. 238. For the agreement between the two countries, see Sir G. N. Clark, *The Dutch Alliance and the War against French Trade*, ch. 2.

[3] *Dumont*, vii. 229.

[4] Ibid. 241, 10–20 Dec. 1689, and 265–6, May–June 1690.

[5] Ibid. 237, 5–15 Aug. 1689.

[6] Ibid. 127 and 156.

[7] Ibid. 227, 24 Apr.–4 May 1689.

but defeat in the field obliged the latter in 1696 to desert the allies for France. The Dutch were concerned about their trade as well as their independence; Spain had good cause for anxiety over the Low Countries; the emperor had in mind his claims to the Spanish Succession; the king of Denmark and some of the German princes were lending their troops in return for subsidies. Moreover, some of these very temporary alliances had been obtained at a price. Thus, by a secret article of the league[1] binding William and the States General with the duke of Savoy, the last-mentioned undertook to revoke his edict of 1686 (modelled on Louis's Revocation) against the Protestant Vaudois. When in 1696 he signed a separate peace with France, one condition was the total prohibition of the reformed faith in Savoyard territory, and the punishment of those Vaudois who gave help to French refugees.[2] So the toleration of the duke of Savoy was temporary, and was the price which he paid for his association with the allies. The price demanded by the emperor was heavier. In his treaty of 1–11 May 1689 with the States General there was a secret clause pledging the Dutch to support by arms the imperial claim to the whole of the Spanish Succession, a condition which was accepted for England when William acceded to the treaty in the following December. Fortunately the seriousness of this commitment was not realized in England.

At home, on 16 April 1689 the House of Lords unanimously resolved that if the king thought fit to enter into a war with France it would give him every assistance in a parliamentary way.[3] Three days later the Commons followed suit with a long address[4] reciting the misdeeds of the French king, including the corrupt influence he had exercised over Charles and James, and his violation of treaties. On 7 May William declared war on Louis, stating as his reasons that the latter had invaded the empire; he had encroached on the Newfoundland fisheries; he had invaded the Caribbean Islands and had seized New York and territory in Hudson's Bay; French privateers had attacked English ships; heavy duties had been imposed on English im-

[1] *Dumont*, vii. 272–3.

[2] Cl. vii of treaty of Turin, June 1696 in H. Vast, *Les grands traités du regne de Louis XIV*, ii. 178.

[3] *L.J.* xiv, 16 Apr. 1689.

[4] *C.J.* x, 19 Apr. 1689.

ports into France, and some imports had been prohibited altogether; the right of the flag had been disputed; English Protestant subjects had been persecuted in France.[1] Here was a mixture of accusations, some unreasonable, and one, the allegation about the seizure of New York, obviously based on misinformation. The old pretext of the flag was now somewhat outworn; that Louis had invaded the empire was true, but that was not a serious English concern; and as for French tariffs, England also had her discriminations against foreign imports. There was some truth in the other accusations but, even taken together, they would hardly have justified war. Yet men are often most in the right when least able to explain themselves. England's motive was to preserve the Revolution settlement and keep out James II.

While there was a clear understanding with the Dutch regarding our naval contribution,[2] there was no definite commitment with anyone about the number of British troops for a continental campaign, a fact which provided some justification for the Tory argument that the English share should be limited to the sea. But William never fully appreciated the importance of sea power, and, like all generals, he wanted men and more men. So, almost insensibly, England came to be ranged with the great military states; for, within a few years, her quota of soldiers, that is of British troops or troops in English pay, rose from about 8,000 to nearly 90,000, at an annual cost of about £2,700,000,[3] exclusive of the cost of the navy, a development which caused some disquiet, and anticipated the situation in 1914 when Britain was suddenly obliged to improvise large armies. As in 1914 also it was assumed that enemy resources would soon give out, and that the war would be a short one.[4] Hence the Convention Parliament can scarcely be blamed for its failure to foresee the unprecedented load of expenditure about to be imposed on the state.

[1] *Cal. S.P. Dom. 1689–90*, 93.

[2] There was also the more remote agreement of 1677 whereby England undertook to combine with the Dutch in an alliance against Louis. For this, see A. Browning, *Thomas Osborne, Earl of Danby*, i. 257–8.

[3] *C.J.* xi, 28 Oct. 1696.

[4] In December sir John Lowther stated that the French king was not so great as reported, and would not be able to maintain the war for a year. *Grey*, ix. 487.

Hostilities at sea had begun before the declaration of war. James's landing at Kinsale on 12 March was followed by the dispatch of French reinforcements and supplies to Ireland, and it was while engaged in this work that the French fleet first went into action with the English. On 1 May Chateau Renault, after landing his stores, was leaving Bantry Bay with thirty-nine ships and a convoy, when he was met by Herbert, with a fleet of twenty-two ships. Probably through mistaking a signal, captain Ashby opened fire, and the contest began. For about four hours there was a running fight, stretching over about twenty miles of open sea, the object of Herbert being to get to windward and destroy the convoy ships, while the French admiral, with his superior forces, was anxious to engage the English squadron. He was prevented from doing so by the lack of support from his rearward ships, so he broke off the fight, after losing about forty men, compared with about twice that number in Herbert's ships. It was no more than a skirmish, and Herbert was probably lucky in getting away.[1]

It was hailed as a victory on both sides. But among those in charge of affairs there was keen disappointment with the result of this, the first naval engagement of the war. Seignelai, the French minister of marine, wrote to Chateau Renault expressing the opinion that he might have done much better;[2] on his side, William thought exactly the same of Herbert's conduct, but he nevertheless professed belief in the popular view, if only to encourage the seamen. So he visited the fleet in person; created Herbert earl of Torrington, but did not make him lord high admiral.

Bantry Bay was the façade behind which was concealed the unsatisfactory state of the Navy in 1689. There were not enough ships; soon a considerable number had to be diverted to commerce protection; even more serious, it seemed that the naval commanders were not inspired by that dash and self-sacrifice which had distinguished their predecessors. Material inade-

[1] There is a good account of the battle in admiral sir Herbert Richmond's *The Navy as an Instrument of Policy, 1558–1727*, ch. 9.

[2] Seignelai to Chateau Renault, 29 May–8 June in P. Clément, *L'Italie en 1671*. This book, important for its inclusion of French naval correspondence, is rare; a copy will be found in Cambridge University Library (Acton Collection).

quacy was accounted for by financial stringency; indeed, at one time it was thought that the ships might have to be laid up; and this need for economy caused difficulty in manning, so at first it was thought inexpedient to resort to the press gang. Already the French privateers were at work, and much escort duty had to be done. These facts help to account for the inadequacy of naval co-operation in the Irish campaigns—for delays in bringing relief to Londonderry, as well as for failure to prevent the regular sailings of French ships into the Shannon. Torrington, after covering the passage of the unfortunate Dundalk expedition, was asked in September whether he could make an attack on Kinsale, with the help of three regiments which had been sent to Plymouth.[1] But, even had he been willing, he could not have attempted such an enterprise, for a great part of his fleet was incapacitated by sickness, caused by the food and beer. In his squadron alone there were 530 dead, and over 2,000 sick; similar casualties were reported in Russell's ships.[2] Even the boiling of the beer made no difference; and there were deaths among the dogs that could be induced to eat the sailors' food. On 4 September Russell announced that, as the season was so far advanced, there was no danger of the French coming out; hence, for the rest of the year, a squadron of thirty ships in the Channel would be enough. So ended the naval activities of the first year of war. Meanwhile, late in June, the Toulon squadron had succeeded in slipping into Brest.

In the later sessions of the Convention Parliament (Nov.–Dec. 1689), the defects of Admiralty administration, the criminal conduct of the victuallers, the negligence of the naval officers, the proceedings of the committee of council for Irish affairs, and even the supreme direction of the war were all subjected to criticism. Papers and minute books were investigated by committees; angry speeches were made, but the only scapegoat in high places proved to be Halifax. But if parliament could do little, the king succeeded in effecting one improvement; for he induced T. Papillon to take over direction of the victualling; and at least the integrity of this veteran Whig ensured that the sailors were not again poisoned by their food.[3]

[1] *H.M.C. Rep.*, *MSS. of A. G. Finch*, ii. 237, 3 Sept. 1689.

[2] Ibid. 238–40.

[3] J. Ehrman, *The Navy in the War of William III*, 316.

Thus the year 1689, the year of Bantry Bay, Londonderry, and Dundalk, ended as a year of muddle and treachery; in the early months of 1690 it seemed likely that England would fare no better. Long delays in fitting out the fleet led to some resignations from the board of Admiralty, and may have caused Russell to decline appointment as admiral of the Blue; even Torrington had talked of resigning. A critical point was reached in the summer, when, with William absent in Ireland, an ill-assorted Cabinet was advising the queen, a Cabinet which included at least two of Torrington's many enemies—Russell, a professional rival, and Nottingham, an amateur naval strategist. In the higher direction of the naval war there were thus some of the elements requisite for disaster; it needed only an inadequate number of ships to ensure the defeat of Beachy Head. On their side, the French were enjoying one of their few periods of energy and efficiency in naval affairs. Seignelai, son of the great Colbert, was in charge of *Marine*; Tourville, one of the ablest admirals of his day, though also one of the most cautious, commanded a fleet of record size; and Jean Bart, chief of the Dunkirk privateers, was making fortunes for himself, his men, and for those who invested in his enterprises. It was fortunate for England that this corsair was not in command of the French fleet. In May 1690 Bart suggested that French ships should be detached to blockade the Thames, in order to prevent the junction of the English and Dutch fleets,[1] but delays in the French arrangements enabled Torrington to leave the Nore for Spithead, where he was joined by the Dutch contingent. Killigrew, whose squadron had been detached for commerce protection, was escorting a large convoy from the Mediterranean and was expected to arrive some time in June; and Shovell with his ships was recalled from the Irish Sea. Neither of these squadrons arrived in time for the action.[2]

A factor of some importance was that the reports of enemy

[1] C. de la Roncière, *Histoire de la marine française*, vi. 64.

[2] Good modern accounts of the battle of Beachy Head will be found in J. Ehrman, op. cit., ch. 10; also admiral sir Herbert Richmond, op. cit. 211–21; and La Roncière, op. cit. 67 sqq. There is a good Dutch account by J. C. M. Warnsincke in ch. 15, 'De Seeslag van Bevesier', of his *De Vloot van den Koning-Stadhouder, 1689–90*. 'Bevesier' is the name given by French and Dutch writers to Beachy Head. It may really mean Pevensey.

strength reaching Nottingham underestimated it, while those reaching Torrington overestimated it.[1] So the battle was preceded by disagreement between Cabinet and secretary on one hand and the admiral on the other. On 13 June Tourville, with Chateau Renault and d'Estrées, sailed from Brest with seventy-five warships, six frigates, and twenty fireships; from such an armament great things were naturally expected. Tourville, whose orders were to seek out the English even into the Thames, was informed by Seignelai that a victory was absolutely essential, especially as the French armies were then on the defensive in Flanders;[2] so the admiral at once stood over to the English coast. On 21 June, when off Torbay, he learned that fifty-eight allied ships were at St. Helen's (Isle of Wight); accordingly, it was resolved to engage the inferior fleet. Meanwhile Torrington, having received news from Weymouth that enemy ships had been sighted, was proceeding to the eastward with the flood tides and anchoring on the ebb, apparently anxious to avoid combat with an enemy so superior in force; while Tourville, hampered in his pursuit by a light breeze from the east-north-east, tacked across to the French coast in the hope of picking up a more favourable wind that would put his fleet between the English and the Pas de Calais.[3] Disappointed in this, he was again off the English coast on 29 June.

Two days earlier the queen, acting on the advice of the Cabinet, sent orders to her commander-in-chief almost identical with those that had been sent by Seignelai to Tourville, namely, that he must fight at all costs; so it was in face of what was practically an ultimatum that the English admiral paused in his eastward drift and faced his opponent. He had fifty-eight warships to the French seventy-five. The combat began off Beachy Head on the morning of 30 June when Torrington, in command of the Red, was opposed to Tourville; while Delaval, commanding the Blue, was against d'Estrées; and Evertsen, leading the Dutch ships in the van, impetuously attacked Chateau Renault. For two hours the fight consisted of a duel between the Dutch and the French; and, as some of the latter obtained the weather

[1] J. Ehrman, op. cit. 344.

[2] Seignelai to Tourville, 23 June–3 July in P. Clément, op. cit. 353.

[3] *Lettres, instructions et mémoires de Colbert*, ed. P. Clément, 2nd series, III. xlviii.

gauge, an arc was formed round Evertsen and Callemburgh, so that they were caught between two fires. In consequence several Dutch ships were dismasted and put out of action. Although the light breeze from the north-east was in his favour, Torrington, in the *Royal Sovereign*, having engaged Tourville in the *Soleil Royal*, succeeded in keeping just out of range, and eventually withdrew from the action, thereby enabling the French to enter the gap among the allied ships, and inflict further damage on the Dutch. By 1 p.m. the English commander was retreating to the east, and at 3 p.m., when the ebb had set in, he ordered the ships to anchor. As the wind had dropped, this manœuvre caused an increasing gap between the opponents as the French drifted off to the west, and so the contest was broken off.[1] After burning some of the disabled ships, the allied fleet continued to sail east at the turn of the tide; while the French pursued the retreating enemy all night. But their system of night signalling was defective, and so their ships were dispersed in the dark.[2] Ten Dutch and seven English ships had been destroyed, either burned by their crews, or run ashore, and Torrington did not end his retreat until he was well within the Thames. Next day—1 July—the French were in command of the Channel.

The disaster of Beachy Head caused a national panic. William and James were both in Ireland; the country was denuded of troops; suspicions of Jacobitism in the fleet appeared to be fully confirmed; an anxious queen, in the hands of a distracted Cabinet, presided over the destinies of a nation which lay open to invasion. But for this the Cabinet, quite as much as Torrington, was responsible, for the admiral's hands had been tied by rigid orders. On the day before the fight, queen Mary had sent him this message:[3] 'we apprehend the consequences of your retiring to the Gunfleet to be so fatal, that we choose rather that you should, upon any advantage of the wind, give battle to the enemy'. The Cabinet dreaded lest Torrington should retreat into the Thames, since this would endanger the large convoy arriving from the Mediterranean, and also Shovell's fleet coming from the Irish Sea; so Nottingham accompanied

[1] J. Tramond, *Manuel d'histoire maritime de la France*, 253.
[2] Ibid. 253–4.
[3] *Egerton MS.* 2621 (Correspondence of Torrington), f. 91.

the queen's order with this comment;[1] 'should you avoid a battle, we must lose more than we can possibly [lose] by one', a most unusual conception of naval warfare, because the loss of a fleet is usually regarded as the most final of all verdicts. Not content with this, the Cabinet on the same day (29 June) instructed Russell to proceed at once to Dover, to go aboard the English flagship and, after having put Torrington under arrest, to take command of the fleet and fight the French.[2] The panic in the nation after the defeat was as nothing compared with the panic in the Cabinet before it.

For several weeks invasion was anxiously awaited. The militia was called away from the harvest; a number of suspected Jacobites were arrested, and even the news of the victory of the Boyne, following so speedily on Beachy Head, failed to relieve the national disquiet. But traditionally it is on such occasions that the Anglo-Saxon character appears at its best, and a contemporary, Charles Montagu, afterwards coined a happy phrase when he said in the House that Englishmen might be frightened not out of their wits but into them.[3] Soon there were signs that this was coming to pass. The city of London, always to the fore on such occasions, offered a loan of £100,000; and that benevolent connoisseur, the duke of Shrewsbury, emerged from one of his many retirements with an offer to command the fleet, an offer which fortunately was not accepted. As parliament was not in session, the voice of faction was stilled, and the nation experienced a unity which it had not known since the time of the Armada.

The French were naturally anxious to exploit their victory. Seignelai's plan was that Chateau Renault's fleet should go to the Irish Sea in order to destroy William's transports and isolate him in Ireland. But two events occurring in quick succession damped down enthusiasm for this plan—the battle of the Boyne and the flight of James. Thereafter, French naval policy appears to have been directed to two things—destruction of the Mediterranean convoy of about 200 merchantmen which, escorted by Killigrew's squadron, had taken refuge in Plymouth; and protection of French transports engaged in withdrawing troops from Ireland. In regard to the first enterprise, Louis, who had

[1] *H.M.C. Rep. MSS. of A. G. Finch*, ii. 322. [2] Ibid. ii. 322.
[3] *Grey*, x. 311, 13 Nov. 1693.

studied English maps of the western counties, had no doubt that the design was feasible, and that the burning of so many ships would be a magnificent demonstration of French naval power; but Tourville, who thought otherwise, compromised by bombarding the village of Teignmouth (26 July), setting a number of houses and small ships on fire, thereby providing a pyrotechnic display on a scale somewhat smaller than that which his royal master had designed. As for the second part of his orders—covering the French retreat from Ireland—he was hampered by the number of sick men on his ships, so he used this as an excuse for returning to Brest on 12 August, hoping that the naval season was over for that year. Louis and Seignelai were so enraged at this disregard for their orders that they promptly commanded him to go to sea again, with a threat of dismissal.[1] Here was clearly illustrated a characteristic of this war, namely, the English problem to keep Tourville in Brest, and the French problem to keep him out.

All this caused intense anger at the French Court, where it was said that Tourville was 'brave de cœur, mais poltron d'esprit'. Two years later, when the roles of English and French were almost exactly reversed, the same remark might have been applied to Russell, who, like his French opponent, failed to pursue the advantage of victory, and probably for the same good reason, namely, to preserve a high reputation while it was still intact, and expensive ships while they were still afloat. So what seemed poltroonery may really have been prudence, according to one's point of view.

Torrington's conduct was generally condemned, by the Dutch in particular, who accused him of cowardice. Both queen and Cabinet accepted the Dutch view of responsibility for the defeat, and tried to make amends by providing for the repair of their ships, and by accommodation of their wounded in hospital. Torrington was sent to the Tower, but the proposal to impeach him was set aside on the ground that the result would be influenced by party faction. Instead, he was court-martialled in December 1690, and unanimously acquitted. It cannot be said that this verdict was attributable to professional support by colleagues, for the admiral had many enemies in the fleet, including Delaval, who presided at the trial. The

[1] P. Clément, op. cit. 363, 367.

accused defended himself with some ability. Attributing the Dutch losses to the rash impetuosity of their attack, he accounted for his own inaction by his inferiority in strength, and the urgent necessity of preserving (to use his own famous phrase) 'a fleet in being'. Such a defence would probably not have been accepted by the seamen of the Elizabethan or Commonwealth navies, but that it should now be put forward and accepted was an illustration of the changed character of warfare, which, though not yet 'total' or 'absolute', was national in the sense that not only the fighting men but all the resources of the state had to be utilized. Some kind of army can be improvised in months; some kind of fleet could formerly have been put together by arming merchant ships; but a fleet such as Torrington's only in years. Another lesson of Beachy Head was a demonstration of the folly of directing from Whitehall the actions of a commander-in-chief against his considered opinion of the facts as he sees them on the spot. Nottingham had taken it upon himself to decide, in his office, whether or not a battle should be fought; and in so doing, he was acting on information which underestimated the enemy strength. But contemporaries, including the king, had no hesitation in condemning the admiral. He was dismissed from his command, and was not again employed.

William, accompanied by Nottingham, left England for Holland on 6 January 1691, the first visit to his native country since he had embarked on his expedition. His reception, both at the meeting of the States General and at the Congress which followed, gave evidence of the European eminence which he had achieved. At the Congress of The Hague, over which he presided, it was agreed that a total of 220,000 men should be provided by the allies. William's policy did not differ from that which he had communicated to the Congress in the previous year,[1] namely, to induce the emperor to send a considerable force, if necessary through Switzerland, in order to invade France; to encourage the Vaudois or the Swiss to make a diversion in favour of the allies, and to persuade the kings of Sweden and Denmark to join in the war as public allies. But while the confederates talked, Louis acted. Organized by Louvois, and commanded by Luxemburg, a French army of

[1] Instructions to Dursley at The Hague, 20 Feb. 1689–90, in *Add. MS.* 34340, f. 60. Also P. J. Blok, op. cit. iv. 482.

100,000 men was brought together, and the siege of Mons, the best defended fortress in the Spanish Netherlands, was directed by Vauban. Louis came in person to make the triumphal entry. Hastening from the Congress, William assembled an army of 60,000 men, but while he was advancing to its relief, the city surrendered (9/19 April). This was attributed by some, including Nottingham, to treachery.[1] William's vexation was extreme, and he returned at once to England.

The king was again in Flanders in May, but while there was much marching and countermarching, no important action took place in the summer campaign of 1691. The French, content for the time with the capture of Mons, were able to live off enemy territory, so in Flanders and on the Rhine the enemy armies succeeded in avoiding each other. Only in the south was there considerable military activity, where, with the support of d'Estrées's fleet, the armies of Catinat and Noailles captured the greater part of Cerdagne and the county of Nice. At sea the French were not active, their ships' companies being crippled by sickness, such as had incapacitated the English fleet in the autumn of 1689; moreover, Seignelai had died in October 1690, leaving Louvois supreme in the councils of Louis. The result was the sacrifice of the navy to the army. Few additions were made to the French fleet, and in Pontchartrain the navy had a minister who was primarily a courtier. These events were to have their consequences in 1692. Thanks to an active shipbuilding programme, the disparity between the English and French fleets was reversed, and the initiative was about to be restored to the nation dependent on the sea.

William's second parliament, sometimes called the 'Officers' Parliament' (because of its large number of civil-office holders), met on 20 March 1690, and lasted for five years. It is generally said that it was more Tory than its predecessor; but it might be more accurate to say that, as it included fewer who had been active opponents of the Stuarts, it had a larger proportion of members who were not whole-heartedly committed to William's War. This was clearly evidenced at its third session, which began on 22 October 1691, when the estimates for army and navy showed a slight increase, at over 4 millions. Paul Foley, an

[1] Nottingham to Trumbull, 9–19 Apr. 1691 in *H.M.C. Rep. MSS. of marquis of Downshire*, i, pt. 1, 370.

active associate of Harley's, objecting to the large armies, claimed that a smaller force would serve for a 'diversion';[1] similarly, sir Edward Seymour thought that, if there was to be no invasion of France, a smaller number would suffice. Clarges plaintively asked: 'if we are unsuccessful, what will become of us?' These misgivings may account for the inadequacy of the supplies. An assessment of £1,651,702—equivalent to a Land Tax of 3*s*. in the £, imposed in the previous year—was renewed, and was accompanied by a Poll Bill and an additional Excise. The policy of paying for the war by current taxation was being tacitly abandoned.

This session was notable for the passage by the Commons of the Trial of Treasons Bill,[2] and for the beginning of a campaign against the abuses of office holding. The first of these, intended to remedy defects in political trials, provided that, in cases of treason, the accused should have the assistance of counsel, and should have a copy of the indictment ten days before the trial. The Bill was sent to the Lords, who added an amendment whereby, during a recess of parliament, the peers should be tried, not by a panel selected by the lord high steward, but by all the peers, a provision intended to prevent the trial of a peer, in the intervals of parliamentary sessions, by a jury of the crown's selection. The amendment led to a fierce controversy between the two Houses, in which the privileges of the peers,[3] considered by many to be excessive, were impugned. So prolonged was this duel, that this Bill did not become law until 1696.

The other matter, abuses in office holding and the large number of officials in the Commons, was one in which the prerogative was directly concerned, because only thus could the requisite majorities be obtained; so the opposition concentrated their attacks on this, one of the chief props of the Court. An important incident in this campaign occurred at the end of the session, on 24 February 1692, when the king vetoed a public Bill embodying the first attempt of the legislature to reform an important office. This Bill enacted that a judge should hold his place 'so long as he shall behave himself therein',

[1] *Grey*, x. 175; 19 Nov. 1691.

[2] For a study of this measure as a stage in the 'humanisation' of law, see S. Rezneck, 'The Statute of 1696', in *Journal of Modern History*, ii. (1930.)

[3] *Infra*, 501–3.

his salary to be at the standard rate of £1,000 a year, with no fees or perquisites, in place of the old system of salary and fees. A provision of this kind had very nearly been included in the Bill of Rights, and on this matter there was a large measure of agreement. But unfortunately, the salaries were to be paid from the king's civil revenue, and, for the imposition of this extra burden, the royal consent had not even been asked. So William vetoed the measure. This aroused much criticism, and appeared to compare unfavourably with the conduct of Stuart predecessors, but there is much truth in Macaulay's contention that these predecessors did not need to disallow legislation which they had no scruple in violating. William's veto implied that, where he consented, he was bound.

Thus, by the early part of 1692 there was evidence of a critical and restive spirit in the Commons, and there was even a chance that William's mixed administration of Whig and Tory would break down. That it did not do so was probably attributable to the skilled management of Carmarthen, who was utilizing his long experience in applying devices for securing Court majorities in the House. Left to themselves, a majority in the Commons would probably have refused to vote the large war grants; but the lord president saw to it that those holding office or hoping to obtain office were not left to themselves, as witness these marginal comments appended in 1690 to a list of actual opponents of Court measures: 'not willing to loose his place'; 'I think hath a pension'; 'would at least be absent'; 'would not loose his lieutenancy which supports his popularity'. Such were a few of the many ways in which pressure could be brought to bear on doubtful legislators. Occasionally, some simplification was made possible by the fact that Carmarthen did not always have to deal with individuals, for he might exert pressure on a group through an agent. Thus, the earl of Bedford would answer for his three sons; the bishop of London (Compton) 'for most of the Whig party'; lord Sidney for the Cinque Ports; lord Oxford for the Essex members; lord Lindsey for the Lincolnshire boroughs; sir Henry Goodricke 'for the church party in generall', and lord Abingdon 'for many relations and friends'. These marginal comments[1] provide the clearest

[1] Reproduced in A. Browning, *Thomas Osborne, earl of Danby*, iii (appendix), 173–87.

evidence of the disparate and heterogeneous character of the House of Commons at this time, its members connected by family ties, or by the management of a territorial magnate; many of them held to a line of conduct not by patriotism (an ambiguous term in this period), nor by party doctrine, but by personal interest. Carmarthen's skill concealed the precarious character of the parliamentary support on which William depended, a fact about to be evidenced in the year 1692, when there was again quick alternation between success and disappointment.

The defeat at Beachy Head had given impetus to a new programme of shipbuilding and naval organization. In December 1690 the Commons had voted £570,000 for the building of twenty-seven men-of-war; a new yard was built at Plymouth, and a dry dock was installed at Portsmouth.[1] The health of the sailor was at last recognized to be essential for efficiency; and that he might need the care of the physician, as well as the knife of the surgeon, was one of the discoveries of this war. Dr. Lower of the Royal College of Physicians was commissioned to investigate the hospital facilities of the fleet,[2] which he found inadequate; but the Admiralty did little, possibly because it was felt that, when completed, the naval hospital at Greenwich would be sufficient. Naval tactics provided another matter of concern to the Admiralty, so in the summer of 1691 a scheme was promulgated, based on the duke of York's Instructions of 1673, with later changes, the main effect of which scheme was that less initiative was given to subordinate officers, and the manœuvre of breaking the enemy line was abandoned, unless a gap could be utilized. To this extent the new instructions were more defensive, and there was an attempt to eliminate the 'pell mell' tactics of the Anglo-Dutch wars; indeed article no. XX forbade units of the fleet to pursue any small number of enemy ships until their main body was disordered or in flight.[3] The chief intention of the new instructions was probably to ensure that the maximum of gun-power should be brought to bear on the enemy. In contrast with the French, whose ships were built almost as much for speed as for action, our ships were

[1] J. Ehrman, op. cit., ch. xi. [2] Ibid. 441.

[3] Sir. J. Corbett, *Fighting Instructions, William and Anne*, 188 sqq. (Navy Records Society).

overgunned and undercanvased;[1] hence, at close range, the English gunnery was deadly and, at a distance, our shot carried farther.[2] Generally, so far as any naval policy could be formulated, it was that we should engage the enemy only if there was a reasonable hope of superiority in ships and guns; and there may even have been a tacit recognition of the principle that, against a superior force, evasive action should be adopted. Here was the lesson of Beachy Head.

Thus, by the winter of 1691–2 we could reckon on two things: naval superiority over the French, and the completion of the Revolution settlement in Great Britain and Ireland. Accordingly, a descent on France was planned for the summer of 1692. Before leaving England for Flanders in March of that year, William communicated to the Cabinet a design for a landing at St. Malo or Brest, and made arrangements for the train of artillery to be used.[3] It was decided also that the expeditionary force should be led by Meinhard Schomberg, duke of Leinster, and Ruvigny, earl of Galway. So, in the early months of 1692, extraordinary preparations were on foot. In February, the public witnessed at Marylebone the performance of a newly designed mortar which fired a shell of 30 lb. forty times an hour;[4] and, in the following month, 1,000 gunners and bombardiers began an intensive six-weeks' course at Blackheath. At the same time the victuallers of the navy and the commissioners of transport were ordered to provide for a large expeditionary force. The Admiralty was said to have contracted for 1,500 tin boats or pontoons, about 20 feet long by 10 feet beam, probably for landings, all to be ready for service by 1 June;[5] there were also to be a number of flat-bottomed boats for disembarking men from ships, each having watertight compartments, and fitted with guns in the bows.[6] These, it appears, were to be towed by 350 London watermen.[7] In April queen Mary was shown charts of the French channel coast, and a committee of experts explained to a diffident young woman a scheme of invasion such as was not successfully achieved until the second World War.

[1] J. Ehrman, op. cit. 33.
[2] *Mémoires de Nicolas Joseph Foucault*, 290.
[3] *L.J.* xv. 153–7.
[4] *Luttrell*, ii. 372.
[5] Ibid. 394.
[6] Ibid. 396.
[7] Ibid. 483.

But the queen and her Cabinet were working in an atmosphere very different from that which preceded D-day; they were racing against time, since it was known that James also was planning an invasion. More serious, they scarcely knew whom to trust; and, to crown all, a disciple of Titus Oates named Young came forward with 'proof' of a plot for the assassination of William and the restoration of James, in which Marlborough, Sancroft, and Sprat, bishop of Rochester, were implicated.[1] With a stroke of genius worthy of his great preceptor Young 'planted' the evidence in one of the bishop's flower-pots. This provided one more distraction for the unfortunate queen, already in dread of her husband's displeasure, and always anxious about the safety of her parent. Marlborough and Sprat were committed to the Tower.

On his side James had not been idle since his precipitate flight from Ireland two years before. Late in 1690 he sent colonels Barclay and Sackville to England in order to test the opinion of those of his former ministers who were still in office. Godolphin, as might be expected, was neither unfriendly nor helpful. More was expected of Marlborough. He was known to be ambitious as well as discontented; he resented the preference shown by William for foreign generals, moreover, through Sarah he dominated Anne, who was on bad terms with her sister and royal brother-in-law. Considering his brilliant service at Walcourt in 1689 and at Cork and Kinsale in 1690 he had been inadequately rewarded. Another target for this campaign was Shrewsbury, related by marriage to Middleton, a Protestant and moderate, one of the least irresponsible of the Jacobites, and therefore likely to be effective. So Middleton was sent to England in order to win over the perpetually vacillating duke.

On the basis of Macpherson's *Original Papers* and *The Life of James II* (only in part by James) historians formerly accepted as genuine certain highly treasonable communications, direct or indirect, between English ministers and St. Germains; but it has long been known[2] that Macpherson tampered with his

[1] Sir W. S. Churchill, *Marlborough*, i. 352.

[2] For this, see *Dalrymple*, iii, app. to bk. v, 225 sqq., A. Parnell, 'Macpherson and the Nairne Papers' in *E.H.R.* xii (1897); a criticism of Parnell's conclusions by G. Davies, ibid. xxxv (1920); Sir W. S. Churchill, *Marlborough*, i, ch. xxi, 'King James's Memoirs', and ch. xxv, 'The Camaret Bay

originals, and that even some of these originals, as preserved by Nairne, James's secretary, are highly suspect. The evidence resolves itself mainly into reports by agents of conversations with ministers in England. It was the object of these reports to create at St. Germains and Versailles a favourable view of the attitude to a Stuart restoration not only of Marlborough and Shrewsbury, but also of Carmarthen and Russell, the one the actual head of the administration, the other in command of the fleet. Indeed, it was only by 'proof' of such willingness to resume their old allegiance that James could hope to obtain military support from Louis; and in that period, only a few years after the Popish Plot, 'proof' was usually forthcoming whenever wanted, since forgery was a hobby before it became a crime. On the other hand, there was always a chance of a Stuart Restoration, and most successful statesmen are endowed with a keen instinct for their own preservation. To serve William appeared to some not unlike 'collaboration'; to plot against him seemed like 'patriotism'; but the distinction was not rigid, since so many succeeded in combining the two; and for those who had most to lose, it was expedient to have a foot in both camps. William had no illusions in these matters. The period was one of treachery in high places, suspected, but usually concealed.

It was of some importance to England that Seignelai's death late in 1690 was followed, within a few months, by that of Louvois, who, in his brutal efficiency, had always insisted on factual knowledge before committing French forces to vast enterprises. With inferior successors to these two men, Louis had now more scope for his ability and initiative, a fact which may account for the more ready acceptance at Versailles of the increasingly optimistic reports from St. Germains. According to these reports, there was reason to believe that an invasion of England was bound to succeed. Marlborough (not yet in the Tower) would bring over the army; Russell, assisted by Killigrew and Delaval, could answer for the fleet; the non-juring bishops, as well as many of the conforming clergy would put themselves

Letter'. In regard to Mr. Churchill's vehement criticism of Macaulay on this matter, see Professor G. M. Trevelyan's letter to *The Times Literary Supplement* of 19 Oct. 1933, reproduced in the third volume of his *England under Queen Anne*, x.

under the wing of Anne, whose fury against William had been increased by one more humiliation on her completely inoffensive and incompetent husband, the refusal of a Garter. So James was encouraged to go ahead with the plans for invasion, to which he applied himself with his well-exercised genius for detail. Late in 1691 he proposed that about 30,000 men should embark at Ambleteuse (a most inconvenient place, but known to him, for he had been carried ashore there in December 1688), while the French fleet was to take station in the Downs to prevent the English and Dutch from joining. The landing was to be effected near Dover; the troops were then to march to Rochester, in order to seize naval stores and ships. There also the invaders would have control over the wives and families of the men of the Chatham fleet, and this, in James's opinion, would seriously limit the activities of the English navy against him. Then there was to be a march on London, and, once the capital was occupied, the whole of England would submit, because in London were to be found all the men of quality and the rich merchants. Historically, declared James, a landing in England, when accompanied by an army, has never been unsuccessful.[1]

The smaller details were filled in by Melfort.[2] He had failed to extract money from pope Alexander VIII on the pleas that the Catholic religion was endangered by the alliance of the emperor and the king of Spain with heretics, and that James was the secular defender of the true faith.[3] Now he busied himself with the invasion. As well as estimating for the needs of the artillery, he provided a plentiful supply of parchment (for commissions), and a printing press (for proclamations). James's secretary of state warned his royal master of the chief danger to be avoided once the enterprise was completed, namely, that of long converse with subjects newly restored to their proper allegiance, particularly the clergy, since promises might be made which afterwards would have to be retracted. Even in the excitement of invasion, one must not forget that 'firmness' would

[1] *Bodl. Carte MS.* 181 ff. 438–44, Dec. 1691 or Jan. 1692. This is in the Nairne Papers, but, as it does not purport to be a communication from England, it is not suspect; moreover, it has all the characteristics of James's way of thinking.

[2] Ibid. 181, 451–8, 7 Jan. 1692.

[3] Memoir of Melfort, Oct. 1689, ibid.; also *Add. MS.*, 38144, f. 6 and f. 25.

afterwards have to be exhibited. But Melfort showed that he was not well informed when he assured Louis that the allied fleet of 1692 would be smaller than that of 1691, that it would not be ready before June, and that all the British forces would be engaged in Flanders.

Rumours of these designs soon leaked out. In April 1692 William, then in Holland, wrote to Nottingham intimating that, on his information, James was about to go to Boulogne or Cherbourg, for some design at sea, or for a landing on the Channel Islands, in order to divert the proposed English descent on France. So he ordered the main fleet to be put in readiness. Nottingham replied, informing the king of the recent arrest of Marlborough, Sprat, and others, and adding that there were rumours of intended desertions in the fleet. His news from France was to the effect that an expedition of 40,000 men was being planned at Dunkirk for Scotland.[1] In this atmosphere of expectation and uncertainty, the queen took what proved to be a wise step—she ordered Russell, now in sole command of the fleet, to assure the officers and men of her absolute confidence in them. But we were obviously in the dark as to the French and Jacobite designs. Their revised plan was to invade in April, with an army of 20,000 men, who were to assemble on the Cotentin peninsula, and effect a landing at Torbay, a site probably selected for commemorative purposes.[2] With this end in view, a camp had been formed early in 1692 on the bay of La Hougue, where the remnants of James's army of Ireland arrived, in rags, and had to be provided with necessaries by the local *intendant*.[3] James himself arrived at this camp in April, accompanied by Bellefonds, the French general appointed to command the troops, and Bonrepaux, who, having spent a short period as extraordinary ambassador in England (in 1686), was rightly regarded as an expert in all matters relating to English defences and arsenals.[4] These three constituted the invasion committee, entrusted by the confident Louis with the supreme direction of operations. Persistent easterly winds delayed the embarkation.

[1] *Add. MS.* 37991, letters between Nottingham and Blathwayt, f. 34*b*, f. 69*b*, f. 71*b*.

[2] J. Tramond, op. cit. 263–5.

[3] *Mémoires de Nicolas Joseph de Foucault*, ed. F. Baudry, 275–80.

[4] *Supra*, 164.

James had not contented himself only with military and naval preparations. His old love for proclamations had not deserted him. On 23 March 1692 he summoned by proclamation[1] all the members of the English privy council to be present at his queen's approaching confinement, so that there should be no doubt about the result; and in a manifesto[2] of 10 April he commanded the help of his subjects against the usurper, and forbade them to pay his taxes. An indemnity was promised to all, except Sunderland, Danby, Nottingham, Marlborough, and the 'Faversham insulters'. Ten days later came a proclamation for Scotland,[3] intimating the intended invasion. In this, allusion was made to the brutality of William, as evidenced in the recent massacre of Glencoe, and two agents of that massacre, Campbell of Glenlyon and major Duncanson, were exempted from pardon, also the magistrates of Kirkcaldy who had seized chancellor the earl of Perth, when trying to escape from Scotland in woman's clothes. So, by the eve of James's prospective restoration, everything had been arranged.

The delay in the embarkation at La Hougue enabled the Anglo-Dutch fleet to assemble, and Russell at Spithead was in command of over ninety warships manned by about 40,000 men. This was unknown to the enemy, who were also given to understand that, in action, the greater part of the English fleet, led by Carter, would come over to the other side. This helps to account for the very definite orders given to Tourville, who, as he made no secret of his misgivings regarding the invasion project, was accused of cowardice; with the result that, when he did go into action, it was not so much in order to win a victory as to redeem his personal honour. There were delays in equipping his fleet. Attempts were made to fit out about eighty ships at Brest, but stores and men were lacking; moreover, the registration system broke down, and so foundlings and Customs officials had to be forced on board the ships. Even thus, twenty ships had to be left behind in Brest; the same shortages held up the ships at Rochefort; and d'Estrées, with the Toulon squadron, failed to arrive in time.[4] On 2 May Tourville left Brest with only

[1] *Steele*, i, no. 4082. [2] Ibid. no. 4086. [3] Ibid. ii, no. 2933.

[4] For French accounts, see C. de la Roncière, op. cit. vi. 96 sqq., and J. Tramond, op. cit. 261 sqq. For a good recent account, see J. Ehrman, op. cit. 395–8.

thirty-nine ships, having been instructed not to enter the Channel, where Delaval and Carter were cruising, until he had been reinforced by the laggards; of these, only five appear to have joined; and so, with inadequate forces, he went out to meet the enemy. On 12 May Pontchartrain received news that the Dutch had joined the English ships, thus creating a great superiority of force, so orders of recall were at once sent to Tourville. But fog delayed the bearing of the message, and when it reached the French admiral, the battle of La Hogue had already begun.

The forces ranged against each other at La Hogue show the serious miscalculations of the French. On the allied side were 63 English ships, 36 Dutch ships, 38 fireships, and 6,736 guns; on the enemy side 44 ships, 38 fireships, and 3,240 guns.[1] Battle would never have been joined had the French been more accurately informed. Russell, against the queen's express wishes, was patrolling the short distance, about 60 miles, between St. Helens and cape Barfleur, helped by an easterly wind, and it was fortunate that he ignored the queen's instructions to cover an English landing party. Early on Thursday morning, 19 May, when about 20 miles north-east of Barfleur, gunfire was reported from the west, and Russell received a signal from his scouting frigates that the enemy was sighted, heading north. The allied fleet was ordered into line of battle, the wind now a 'small gale' from south-south-west, which gave the French the weather gauge.[2] At 4 a.m. it was seen that the French, having put about, were standing to the south, on the same tack as Russell's fleet; and by 8 a.m. the allied fleet stretched from north-north-east to south-south-west, the Dutch (Almonde) in the van, the Red (with Russell in the *Britannia*) in the centre and the Blue (Ashby) in the rear. At 10 a.m. the French bore down on the allies, and Tourville gave the signal for battle. With his superiority in numbers Russell ordered Almonde to try to get to the west of the French, while the Blue, now some distance astern, was ordered to tack also in a westerly direction, so that van and rear would weather the enemy and encircle his fleet. But at this point the wind dropped, so the manœuvre could not be executed. Then from 11.30 to 1 p.m. there was a brisk duel between the two flagships, the

[1] J. Ehrman, op. cit. 395.

[2] This account is based on the printed *Admiral Russell's Letter to Nottingham*, 1692. See *Documents*, no. 329.

Soleil Royal and the *Britannia*, the Frenchman plying his guns warmly; but, as Russell noted, 'our men fired their guns faster'. Soon the damage on the *Soleil Royal* was so great that she had to be towed off. Meanwhile fresh enemy ships entered into this gun duel, which was ended by the descent of fog at 4 p.m. When it cleared, it was seen that the enemy was retreating to the west, Tourville having given the signal, *Sauve qui peut*. So a chase ensued which was kept up all night, in which many of the French ships succeeded in making their way through the dangerous passage between Alderney and Guernsey.

The situation on the morning of Friday 20 May was that no ship on either side had been sunk, and it looked as if the action had been inconclusive. But the French ships were scattered over a wide area, some having succeeded in getting into Brest or St. Malo; some had gone across to the English coast, where several were seen off the Isle of Wight, fitting up jury masts, and others got back to France by sailing right round Britain. Three, which had sought refuge in the ruined harbour of Cherbourg, were burned by Delaval; others were observed to take refuge in the bay of La Hougue. On Monday the 23rd Rooke, entering the bay with fireships, destroyed six; the remaining seven, with a few transports, were burned to the water line on the following day. The committee of three, standing on the shore, were spectators of these two displays of fireworks, when thirteen of the best units of the French navy were destroyed. The transports, though nearly intact, were now useless for their purpose. And so, rightly or wrongly, this combat has traditionally been known in England, not from the sea battle off cape Barfleur, but from the burning of the ships in the bay of La Hougue, misspelt La Hogue.[1] This is not unreasonable, since the destruction of the enemy fleet is the main object of naval warfare, and in this respect the battle at sea had decided little. Louis, who loved pyrotechnics, had at last been provided with a good display.

The battle of La Hogue was very like that of Beachy Head in reverse, but with certain variations. In the latter, Torrington, by prudence, had preserved the greater part of the English fleet,

[1] There is much criticism of English misspelling of foreign place-names. But this is as nothing to foreign misspelling of English names, e.g. Bevezier for our Beachy Head. 'La Hogue' is at least identifiable.

and had conducted an orderly retreat; in the former, Tourville had been obliged to sacrifice a considerable number of his best ships, and had seen the others scattered to the winds. Both admirals had engaged in combat against their own opinion, and because of stringent orders from ashore. There was the same parallelism in the results of the two actions. As Tourville had failed to pursue the advantage gained at Beachy Head, so Russell appears to have set himself against any attempt to follow up the advantages of his victory. All this proved how imponderable are the considerations that may influence the contests of large fleets of almost irreplaceable ships; moreover, the handling of these fleets, in such a way as to secure a decisive victory over an enemy of comparable strength, is one of the rarest forms of genius, of which there was no evidence at this period. The result was that, for the rest of William's war, the situation was not unlike that which, in the first World War, followed the battle of Jutland in May 1916. As Germany, unwilling again to risk her fleet, resorted to unlimited submarine warfare; so France, after La Hogue, confined her naval energies mainly to privateering; as in 1916 also, allied failures in the continental campaigns obliged the combatants to settle down to a war of endurance, each hoping that the other's resources would give out. It was the same in both wars with the allied blockade, for this was extensively evaded by neutrals. Thus, before the end of the seventeenth century, insular England had suddenly been obliged to face the problems of warfare conducted on a continental and oceanic scale, comparable with that of the earlier twentieth century.

But, meanwhile, La Hogue had saved England from invasion and, for a time at least, had destroyed France as a naval power. It also served to throw a douche of cold sea-water over the enthusiasm of hot-blooded Jacobites, and on the confidence of their French allies. On James, it appears to have made no impression whatever. Englishmen naturally hoped that the victory would be followed by the projected descent on the French coast. They were to be disappointed. So far as the later history of this project can be pieced together from scraps of literary evidence,[1] one is left with the impression of a queen and Cabinet not quite

[1] This, and what follows, are based on the collection of papers submitted to the Lords and then to the Commons by Nottingham (*L.J.* xv. 153–7; 19 Dec. 1692).

decided what to do, and not always able to express themselves when they had made up their minds; a secretary, Nottingham, arrogating to himself executive powers in matters of which he had no knowledge whatever; an Admiralty, unable to determine the borderline between its functions and those of the Cabinet; and, lastly, an extremely truculent admiral who, after his victory, seems to have judged that, for his own reputation, the less he did the better. In the circumstances, he was probably right. He proceeded to apply this principle in practice.[1] First of all, he and Ashby were suspected, with some reason, of dilatoriness in pursuing the French ships scattered in the battle. Next, Russell began a literary duel by conveying to the queen a gratuitous assurance that events had justified his strategy rather than hers. The bewildered and long-suffering Mary then ordered him, on 6 June, to seek out and destroy the ships, more than thirty in number, sheltering in St. Malo, an order of which he had to be reminded by Nottingham. But on 30 June the admiral announced that it was impossible to keep station west of St. Malo; and, while Rooke thought that a landing could be effected at the adjoining Cancale, Russell said that the project was too hazardous. Eventually, the St. Malo ships succeeded in getting out, and reaching Brest.

Meanwhile, queen and Cabinet were anxiously waiting to hear from the admiral when the transports should be sent out, as they were depending on his initiative. The intention appears to have been to land the men at St. Malo; though what they were to do there was by no means clear, a fact which Russell may well have had in mind. On 13 June the admiral wrote that 'the land army would be of great use'; but ten days later he declared that he could not judge whether it would be of any use or not. On 10 July he thought that a mere handful of 12,000 men could be of no service at St. Malo, though (in his opinion) they might have been able to do something a month earlier, a clear hint that the invasion season was coming to an end. He had already added a fresh complication by suggesting that, if a landing were really intended, it should be effected at La Hougue, where there would be this additional advantage,

[1] For an interpretation slightly more favourable to Russell, but more critical of the administration, see admiral sir Herbert Richmond, op. cit. 232–3.

that he could retrieve the guns which the French had fished up from their sunken ships. But queen and Cabinet, concerned not about rusty guns, but about effecting a combined operation on the French coast, begged Russell to appoint a rendezvous for the transports, to which he replied: 'really, I am not able to tell you; only, I think not in the sea. Either they should come to the fleet or the fleet to them'—a fair example of his verbiage. At long last the expeditionary force embarked on 28 July and joined company with the fleet, but when a council of war was held to arrange for an assault on St. Malo, the naval officers maintained that nothing could be effected until their military colleagues were in control of the town, to which the military men, not to be outdone, replied that they were helpless without the fleet.[1] Exactly the same applied to attacks on Brest or Rochefort; moreover, it was now late in the season. On 29 July the scripturiant Russell wrote 'a very long letter' to Nottingham, 'with reflections on the whole', one of his literary masterpieces that has not survived; and so the month of July slipped away. In desperation, the queen on 2 August sent several members of the Cabinet, including Carmarthen and Nottingham, to Portsmouth, in the hope that something might yet be done, but the admiral now imputed the delays to the fact that the Cabinet had not kept him fully informed of its plans.[2] The truth is that a Whig commander was unwilling to carry out the orders of a Tory administration. Thus Russell won two great victories in one summer—that of the guns and that of the pens. It was for his success in the latter that he was relieved of his command.

In November he was congratulated by the House of Commons, where he had a considerable following, and where Whig influence was increasing. The Lords, less easily satisfied, entrusted to a committee the duty of examining all the papers, including the communications between the Cabinet and Russell, but so many of these were mystifying in their ambiguity, because their writers had an imperfect command of the English language, that the committee could make no recommendation, so they sent the papers to the Commons, who likewise could make nothing of them. A 'gentleman' commander had had his way.

[1] *Naval Miscellany*, ii, ed. J. K. Laughton (Navy Records Society), 168–201.

[2] *H.M.C. Rep.* xiii, app. pt. 6, 32–33.

XIII

THE WAR ON LAND AND SEA, 1692–5

STEENKIRK; NEERWINDEN; NAMUR

DEFOE, who has never been accepted as an authority on military matters, once declared[1] that the two maxims of war were these: never fight without a manifest advantage, and never encamp in such a position that you may be forced to fight. Two generals properly observing these principles could avoid combat indefinitely. For William's war there was some truth in this exaggeration, though it did not apply to Ireland, where the leaders always sought out the enemy; but it applied in some measure to the campaigns in Flanders, where William was anxious to engage in combat, and even to invade France. But he was faced with conditions which almost drove him to desperation. The French, who had raised warfare to the level of a fine art, had their bases on a securely defended frontier, from which they could prepare in winter for the next year's campaign. Their king loved warfare, particularly siege warfare, since this gave opportunity for the triumphal *entrée*, to the accompaniment of fireworks and the music of violins; when Louis, dominating the scene with the help of high-heeled shoes and a lofty periwig, seemed to have stepped out of the tapestries of Versailles, the embodiment, in a more drab age, of that colourful and flamboyant heroism associated with the ancient past and the far east. Moreover, war, conducted always on enemy or occupied territory, was one of the agencies of French civilization; an annexe to Versailles, not always an expensive one, since supplies could be extorted from the inhabitants, and undefended towns were offered the alternatives of blackmail or bombardment. Accordingly, with the help of brilliant generals and skilled administrators, Louis could conduct war, not for any object worthy of national sacrifice, but in the same spirit as he might arrange a fête, or a theatrical performance, having for its object the enlarging of

[1] *An Essay upon Projects* (1697), 257.

his glory, regarded by many as identical with the glory of France.

In Flanders, this policy was made possible by the nature of the terrain and by the genius of Vauban and Luxemburg. The Low Countries constitute an area where, it has been said,[1] men can always fight without being starved. It consists roughly of a quadrilateral limited on three sides by natural features—the sea on the west; the Rhine delta on the north, the Meuse on the east and south-east, the whole intersected by the Scheldt, flowing approximately north-east by Ghent to Antwerp. Only the south and south-west were lacking in natural defences, but here the French were strongly established; for by 1692 they were in occupation of Mons and Namur, the first dominating a large area from its height above the Trouille; the second at the junction of Sambre and Meuse. Among the many obstacles to manœuvring were the canals, the wooded areas, and the tributaries of the Scheldt, namely (enumerating from west to east), the Lys, Dendre, Senne, Dyle, and the two Geetes. As well as Mons and Namur, important fortresses were Charleroi on the southern base; Courtrai, Ypres, and Nieuport in the north-west; Maestricht and Liége on the east. At this time, Liége was an independent state under its prince bishop, who, in this war, was one of the allies. As more fortified towns were occupied by the opponents, more troops had to be detached for garrison duty, with the result that, in the restricted area left for manœuvring, tactics approximated to those of the billiard table; and, in proportion as French arms captured enemy standards for the decoration of Notre Dame, and as the *fleur de lys* waved over fresh ramparts, the scene approximated more closely to the background of a play, until the surfeited Louis at last called down the curtain. It was Marlborough who, in the next war, first disturbed this order of things.

William, who possessed neither military genius nor aesthetic sense, was driven to distraction by these martial theatricals. He wanted a war of swift movement—of invasion of France, from the north or the south-east—he hoped for a landing on the French coast. The failure of Russell to cover such a landing in

[1] J. W. Fortescue, *History of the British Army*, i. 356 sqq. For good maps of the Flemish campaigns, see those in Sir W. S. Churchill, *Marlborough*, i, opposite pp. 263 and 366.

the summer of 1692 was a grievous disappointment; and, except perhaps for the policy of sending the fleet to the Mediterranean in 1694, there was no co-ordination of land and sea power in this war. The king, anxious to use all the forces at his command for a vigorous offensive, was badly served, most of all by himself; the great fleets and armies had arrived before the men who were able to lead them. Hence, after desperate efforts, William was obliged by 1695 to acquiesce in those conditions of warfare which French strategy imposed; because, until that year, he had provided little more than good game for Luxemburg, though his costly resistance prevented the enemy from reaching Ostend or Antwerp. Accordingly, after the death of Luxemburg the king left the north and west of Flanders to look after themselves, and achieved his solitary success in a siege, that of Namur. This amounted almost to a confession that he was unable to accomplish anything in open warfare.

The French had seen to it that William would be forced into such an exasperating position, for the disposition of their troops was such as to impede allied movement at almost every point. From Dunkirk to the Meuse they had a line of forts, each providing supplies and defence over a wide area; these included Aire and Menin on the Lys; Cambrai, Bouchain, and Valenciennes on the Scheldt; Maubeuge on the Sambre, and Dinant on the Meuse. Capture of Mons and Namur greatly increased this defensive strength, while their army on the Moselle made difficult the passage of German reinforcements; moreover, the frontier of France was securely defended against invasion. But most of all, for this type of warfare, Louis had the help of two men of genius—Vauban and Luxemburg—the two leaders who made possible the military achievements of France at this time. Vauban, the greatest siege engineer of his age, was also a man of humanity and intelligence, qualities which eventually caused him to be disgusted with the waste and purposelessness of these campaigns, and so he lost favour at Court. As important as siege warfare was manœuvring, and here William was no match for François Henri de Montmorency-Bouteville, marquis of Luxemburg, more than ten years older than his royal antagonist, whom he had already outwitted in the campaigns which followed the invasion of Holland in 1672. Luxemburg had the two qualifications necessary for success in the Flemish campaigns—an unruffled patience which enabled him (with the help of agreeable female society) to spend weeks in dodging a battle that he did not want, and extreme quickness of intelligence when either he was obliged to fight, or saw a chance of doing so with advantage. A hunchback, he extracted more pleasure from life than did his fellow valetudinarian William, who never relaxed, whereas the marshal might go into battle humming an air from the latest Paris opera.[1] Hence, in this hopeless contest of Teuton and Gaul, a frantic king was always outmatched by an opponent whose reputation for invincibility was such that Louis himself had no hesitation in taking the field, so long as Luxemburg's army was between him and the enemy. The marshal's death in 1695 caused the French king to become weary of the war since, in Flanders, he was succeeded by inferior leaders, whose successful application of Defoe's principles ensured that, after weeks of evasive action, 'there was not one bloody nose among 400,000 men'.[2]

It was the British quality of dogged resistance that helped to neutralize enemy superiority in generalship and organization. French unity of direction, in the Low Countries, on the Rhine, in Piedmont, and in Catalonia, contrasted with William's difficulties in securing concerted action among ill-assorted allies, most of whom had to be subsidized. Five races, British, Dutch, Spanish, German, and Danish supplied contingents, whether of their own or mercenary troops. Of these the British and the Dutch were the largest; the former, in some years, raising over 90,000 men, the latter over 100,000; so that the joint total actually put into the field in Flanders by these two allies was usually about 120,000 men. Of the German contributions, the chief was that from Brandenburg—over 30,000 men—followed by small contingents from each of the other electors, that from Saxony (12,000) being the largest. Spain maintained about 7,000 men in Flanders, and 12,000 in Piedmont; the emperor supplied only about 12,000 troops. Altogether, by 1694 the allied armies totalled more than 300,000.[3]

[1] *Mémoires de Saint Hilaire* (Société de l'histoire de France), ii. 127.

[2] *H.M.C. Rep.* xiii, app. pt. 6 *MSS. of sir W. Fitzherbert*, 42. Sir M. Cook to sir G. Treby, 4 Aug. 1696. The number 400,000 is an overestimate.

[3] Figures for the troops enrolled by England will usually be found in the estimates presented to the Commons early in the winter session, e.g. *C.J.*

Two of these allies had qualms about their unusual bedfellows. From the outset, the emperor Leopold was uneasy regarding his alliance with Calvinist William and the implied recognition of his kingship; so he referred both points to the theologians, who were able, for a time, to soothe the imperial conscience. As for the first worry, alliance with heretics, it was pointed out how, in war, one may use horses and beasts of burden: *ergo etiam hominum infidelium*; as regards recognition of William's kingship, even the pope had referred to Elizabeth as queen, though everyone knew that she was spurious; and the Old Testament abounded with examples of usurpers who, when successful, were styled kings.[1] But Leopold need not have worried, for he sent less than a tenth part of the total contingent supplied by the two chief heretic states, and at the price of their undertaking to support by arms his claim to the whole of the Spanish Succession.[2] So, too, with Spain, whose contribution was moderate. The officials of the Spanish Inquisition, when things were going badly, pointed the obvious lesson, namely, divine displeasure at association with heretics;[3] but they might have taken comfort from the fact that Spanish aid was almost negligible. At Nieuport and Ostend the Spanish authorities provided no help for the British soldiers quartered there;[4] in the West Indies, they were sometimes obstructive, refusing water on one occasion to the British fleet.[5] In the Mediterranean, the state of their navy was such that its modern historian draws a veil over it, attributing this calamity to the prostration of the nation.[6]

It was Victor Amadeus II, duke of Savoy, who provided clearest proof of the incongruous nature of William's alliances.

xi, 5 Dec. 1693. Sometimes there is added a list of the allied contingents, as ibid. xi, 26 Nov. 1694. Lists will also be found in the War Office papers at the Record Office, e.g. *W.O. 24/20*.

[1] O. Klopp, *Der Fall des Hauses Stuart*, iii. 512, Anlage vi.

[2] *Supra*, 348.

[3] *Aff. Etr.* (*Espagne*), 77, f. 4. Decree of the Spanish Inquisition (early in 1697).

[4] *H.M.C. Rep. MSS. of marquis of Downshire*, pt. ii, 513, col. Hamilton to Mr. Tollet, 20–30 July 1695.

[5] *Cal. S.P. Amer. 1697–8*, 31, protest by admiral Neville to governor of Havana.

[6] F. C. Mascaro, *La Marina militar española*, 240.

Strategically, Savoy was of special importance[1] in William's plans because her territory might serve as the base of an invasion of France through Dauphiné, where, even after the revocation, there still lingered a resentful Protestantism. Such a disaffected element might well have allied with its neighbours, the Protestant Swiss cantons, which, in spite of neutrality, would probably be willing to send mercenaries; and so, with the help of such forces, it was thought that the duke might intervene effectively in the south-eastern corner of France, particularly as, in joining the allies, he had surrendered, for the time being, his policy of dragooning heretics. But neither in Switzerland nor in Dauphiné did there appear to be much belief in the duke's (temporary) policy of toleration, for the cantons refused to supply troops, and the inhabitants of Dauphiné put up a stiff resistance to his invasion. Moreover, the French also realized the strategic importance of Savoy; still worse, Victor Amadeus proved no match for the French general Catinat, whose two victories of Staffarda (1690) and Marsaglia (1693) resulted in the conquest of the greater part of French Savoy. Consequently, William was obliged to seek a decision in Flanders, with the help mainly of British troops.

As she had never been engaged in continental warfare on a large scale, England was not regarded as a military nation; moreover, after the achievements of the New Model Army and of Commonwealth organization, a period of decline had set in. The state of military administration under the later Stuarts was such that, for a time, it was considered almost disreputable to hold a commission, even in the Guards. Nor did there exist any department responsible for the army, except the Board of Ordnance, which supplied the army and navy with arms and ammunition, and was supposed to provide barracks and fortifications; its record for incompetence was notable, even in that age. The master general of the ordnance, from his headquarters in the Tower, also commanded the artillery and the engineers, who, as they were not yet embodied in regiments, still retained some civilian characteristics. There was no secretary of state for war, but a secretary at war, an office not regulated by statute until 1783; this office was filled efficiently

[1] For this, see L. A. Robertson, 'Relations of William III with the Swiss Protestants, 1689–97', in *Trans. R.H.S.*, 4th series, xii (1929), 137–62.

in William's reign by Blathwayt. In the higher command of William's army, there was at least the nucleus of an organization, which included a quartermaster general, a surgeon general, a physician general, an apothecary general, two adjutants general, and a judge advocate.[1] The first two of these offices were held in 1691 by Dutchmen. In the executive branch the king exercised supreme command. The two generals were Solms (infantry) and Meinhard Schomberg, duke of Leinster (cavalry). Of the six lieutenant-generals, only two, Marlborough and the earl of Oxford, were English, the others being Portland, Auverquerque, Charles, duke of Schomberg, and the Scot Mackay. Of five major-generals only two, Trevelyan and Talmash, were Englishmen. This was in 1691. Later experience was to convince William that Britain had quite as much military talent as any other nation.

In pre-Revolutionary England, study of the science of warfare, such as it was, had always been pursued by men of quality, usually in conjunction with mathematics; and in 1673 sir James Moore, a fellow of the Royal Society, had published a standard work on fortification.[2] For military tactics there was no similar book, but in 1689 there appeared a translation of a French manual,[3] describing the 'postures in exercising pike and musket', and illustrating the various roles assigned to dragoons, grenadiers, and horse. But already the pike was becoming a thing of the past, its place being taken by the bayonet and flintlock. More attention was now being paid to the proper functions of cavalry. When an army had been routed, the cavalry had the best chance of getting away; but equally they might protect the retreat, a duty often performed with brilliance and sacrifice; moreover, it was in the co-ordination of the two branches of the service that opportunity was provided for good generalship, as afterwards exemplified in Marlborough's campaigns. But in William's war there was more spade-work. In such a terrain as the Low Countries, with the constant marching and countermarching, it was necessary to send out bodies of engineers, sappers, and pioneers, protected by cavalry, in order to fill in ditches, make or repair bridges, and build boats. Combat was

[1] *C.J.* xi, 18 Nov. 1691.

[2] Sir J. Moore, *Modern Fortification.*

[3] Captain J. S., *Military Discipline or the Art of War.*

defined as only one of the five principal objects of field service, the others being marching, encamping, obtaining intelligence, and securing fodder and provisions. In this last respect William was served by contractors; money for purchases had to be obtained from financial syndicates, supplemented, after 1694, by advances from the Bank of England.

There was increased use of artillery in this war, one result of which was the creation of a large body of trained English gunners, quite distinct from the personnel of the Ordnance. But it was not until 1716 that the Royal Regiment of Artillery came into existence. Long before that date many famous regiments had taken shape, some of them at first no more than private ventures; for, only by gradual stages did the state assume full responsibility for the soldier. Some regiments owed their institution to the quelling of popular risings or rebellions; thus, the Household Cavalry was raised just after Venner's rising in 1661, and Monmouth's rebellion led to the formation of many private or semi-private companies of Horse and Foot. Of the cavalry, the Life Guards and the Blues were new formations created after the Restoration; the Tangier Horse, after its return to England, became the First Royal Dragoons.[1] Some regiments trace their origin to James's army, others to that of William; the heroic defence maintained by the men of Enniskillen resulted in the creation of two regiments of Dragoons and three of Foot.[2] The Coldstream Guards had been in the public eye ever since Monck's famous march from Scotland in 1660, and it was colonel Farrington of that regiment who in 1694 raised a body of infantry, afterwards the Twenty-Ninth (Worcestershire) Foot.[3] Another example of a regiment raised by private initiative was that of the South Wales Borderers,[4] started in 1689 by the Kentish baronet, sir Edward Dering, whose diary recorded the appearance of James, when he landed at Faversham, after his first flight.[5]

[1] For this, see C. T. Atkinson, *History of the Royal Dragoons*. In ch. 5 will be found an account of the part played by the regiment at the Boyne and the sieges of Limerick.

[2] J. R. Harvey and H. A. Cape, *History of the Fifth* (*Royal Irish*) *Regiment of Dragoons*.

[3] H. Everard, *History of T. Farrington's Regiment*.

[4] C. T. Atkinson, *The South Wales Borderers*.

[5] *Supra*, 219.

Names of regiments alone are sufficient to attest the large Scottish and Ulster contingents in William's army. The Highlanders were in the habit of drinking James's health, but they fought for William as well as any, and that too alongside their old opponents, the Cameronians, the last regiment of the British army to combine personal piety with theological orthodoxy (enforced by a committee of elders) and martial valour.

The change in the course of English history effected by William's reign is nowhere more clearly reflected than in the changed character of the army, and the new traditions begun by its regiments; for the hooligans who had served Stuart purposes at home were succeeded by soldiers who served a national purpose abroad. The courage and conduct of these formations were now to be tested, not in unequal contests with the ill-armed peasants of Scotland or Somerset, but in grim combat with the best-trained soldiers in the world. Those are indeed proud regiments which can include among their lost battles the defeats of Steenkirk and Neerwinden, for these defeats were magnificent demonstrations of fortitude and endurance in adversity. In this way was created a strong sense of professional cohesion which, almost as much as personal courage, enabled these men to endure hardships and dangers such as the loosely organized companies could never have borne.[1]

These qualities had already been tested at the first of the continental battles, that at Walcourt (August 1689), when the allies, led by Waldeck, defeated the French under d'Humières and Villars. Much of this success may be attributed to Marlborough's skilful handling of a small British contingent, ably assisted by Talmash. But unfortunately for us, d'Humières was replaced by Luxemburg. The result was seen in June 1690 when Waldeck was defeated at Fleurus, but no British units appear to have been engaged in that battle.

The hostilities of the following year were opened by Boufflers' capture of Mons, which seriously impeded the allied campaign of 1691, for it gave to the French control of much of the territory between Scheldt and Sambre. The Allies, who had their main base at Anderlecht, now a suburb of Brussels, were scattered,

[1] For a good account of the early history of these regiments, see J. W. Fortescue, op. cit. i, bk. v, ch. i.

some in Bruges and Ghent, others in Liége and Namur. If these forces could be brought together, and if the contingents of Brandenburg and Hesse arrived in time, then it appeared possible to recover Mons; and, with the line of the Sambre restored, invasion of France was at least possible; indeed, some such project may have been in William's mind. But he did not take over command from Waldeck until June; and meanwhile, from his base at Mons, Luxemburg advanced on Brussels, while Boufflers, beyond the Meuse, held up the German reinforcements. William's speedy assembly of an army, and his advance to the Sambre obliged Luxemburg to abandon the attack on Brussels and devote himself to protection of Mons; but in the manœuvring for position that followed, the king dared not risk battle, as he had no fortified town on which to fall back; so, in disgust, he proceeded in August to lead his army into winter quarters near Brussels. This provided his opponent with a chance not to be missed. Suddenly pouncing on the rearguard of William's army, Luxemburg inflicted numerous casualties; and, when some kind of order had been restored, the enemy was out of reach. It was an illustration of how William's impatience provided Luxemburg's opportunity.

The French policy of securing the frontier by a line of fortresses within occupied territory was a good one, as the capture of Mons had shown. In 1692 came the turn of Namur. Its capture from the allies would endanger Charleroi which, with Maubeuge and Philippeville to the south, would give the French an almost impregnable quadrilateral of strongholds, whereby they hoped not only to break up the allied posts on the Sambre, but to disengage some of their own forces for service on the Rhine. Accordingly, the winter of 1691–2 had been spent in preparations for the siege, under the direction of Vauban. There were no British troops in Namur, but William rightly judged that it must be relieved; so in May 1692 he took up position on the eastern side of the Mehaigne, a tributary of the Meuse to the north-east of Namur, and across the stream his engineers proceeded to build temporary bridges. Between the Mehaigne and the besieged city Luxemburg had posted his army; so William hoped, by crossing the stream, to force an engagement. Then occurred an event such as may often happen in war, and for which no provision can be made. On the continent St. Médard enjoys the reputation of weather prophet assigned in England to St. Swithin, and on this occasion the saint proved to be right, for his day (29 May/8 June) ended with a deluge which lasted for more than a week. The narrow but deep Mehaigne flooded the countryside, washing away William's bridges, and bogging his army in a swamp.

Meanwhile, in Namur things were going badly. The garrison of Dutch, Spanish, and German was at loggerheads. As Coehorn had been wounded he could no longer direct operations; the lieutenant governor proved to be a traitor in the pay of France; and the inhabitants suffered from lack of water, as the French artillery had destroyed the wells. So, after a month's siege, Namur, the greatest stronghold in the Spanish Netherlands, capitulated; and, to the sound of trumpets, Louis made one more triumphal entrée. This was in June. So far, in the campaigns of this year, 1692, the fireworks had provided the chief display of artillery.

This semi-comedy was soon succeeded by tragedy. William took up station at Genappe, a few miles south of Waterloo, more than ever determined to seek battle with the enemy, whose forces were now somewhat dispersed to the west of William's position. From Genappe he advanced north-west to Halle on the Senne, while Luxemburg collected his main body and moved to Enghien, so that the gap between the two armies was narrowed to about nine miles. The road from Halle to Enghien, going west-by-south, is almost parallel to the Senne, and it was in the space between river and road that the battle of Steenkirk was fought on 24 July/3 August. With the help of a secretary in the allied camp who had been caught spying for the enemy, William attempted a stratagem. He dictated to the spy a letter intimating that a large foraging party would be out on the next day, and this letter was delivered to the French camp in the hope that the enemy would not suspect William's intention to attack.

On the morning of 24 July the king advanced his army along the narrow lanes connecting the two positions. For a time the ruse succeeded, the French having been put into disorder by a sudden and unexpected attack. The ground favoured an infantry battle, but by some mistake the allied cavalry on the left wing got in front, blocking up the narrow approaches, and producing chaos like that from which the enemy was now recovering. Another circumstance intervened. Solms, in command of the Foot, in spite of urgent requests from Mackay, made no attempt to bring up help to the British infantry, on whom the brunt of the fighting now fell. Under the gallant Mackay, English and Scottish infantry fought desperately against the restored formations of the French. Advancing up a slope under fire, they reached the thick hedges covering Luxemburg's vanguard; and so close was the fighting that the muzzles of the British muskets brushed against those of the enemy through the branches. For a time the British battalions succeeded in driving back their opponents from one line of hedges to another, a feat in which the Cameronians specially distinguished themselves, but at the cost of many of their lives, including that of their commander, lord Angus. Mackay and Lanier were killed; about one-half of their men were casualties, and the king in sorrow and desperation had to witness this, one of the most tragic episodes of his stormy life. It was desperate and brave, but futile, for thirteen British battalions were pitted against a great French army. Had they been supported by the main body of allied infantry, stationed about a mile from the action, the result might have been different. The carnage was ended only by retreat, under cover of the Coldstream Guards, and one more was added to the long list of William's military defeats. About 3,000 men were killed on each side, the French losing a high proportion of their officers, and it is said that Luxemburg considered himself lucky to have turned into a victory what might well have been a defeat.[1] Such was the miserable end of the campaign of 1692, the year of La Hogue.

The campaign of 1693 was as unfortunate. French strategy was to limit the war as far as possible to the Meuse, in order to keep it away from Lys and Scheldt, where elaborate earthworks, known as the lines of Espierre, provided the extreme northern defence of the French frontier. Accordingly Luxemburg's plan was to capture Huy and Liége, for which purpose elaborate preparations had been made in the previous winter. William, who arrived in May, took up position at the well-defended Parcq, near Brussels, with 23,000 cavalry and 38,000

[1] Fortescue, op. cit. i. 367–9; C. Walton, *History of the British Standing Army*, ch. xiv.

infantry, the latter still commanded by Solms, in spite of a recent address to the king by the Lords urging that the chief command of the British forces should be in the hands of a natural-born subject.[1] The first incident in the campaign was the surrender of Huy to the French early in July, a surrender attributed to treachery; and for the defence of the other fortress, Liége, William had to detach a considerable number of his troops. Luxemburg, with a large army, now covered Liége from the west, apparently intent on its capture, but ready to pounce on William as soon as he could be taken at a disadvantage. This happened when the king, having sent 20,000 men for the defence of the threatened city, advanced south and east from Brussels, and encamped at Neerwinden, near Landen, with the lesser Geete in his rear.[2] Here his long line had little depth; moreover, the few bridges on the river made a retreat difficult. Entrenched between mounds of cultivated soil, the allies faced a great onslaught on 19/29 July, which resulted in the battle known indifferently as that of Neerwinden or Landen. Although there were large contingents of Brandenburgers and Hanoverians, the brunt of the fighting, in intense heat, again fell on the British, who in spite of brilliant cavalry support, were routed. Of the total of about 130,000 allied and French engaged in this battle, it is estimated that nearly 25,000 were casualties, about 9,000 being French.[3] Solms was killed and, on the other side, the gallant Sarsfield; it was even more bloody than Aughrim. Here William's defeat can be attributed to inferiority of numbers, for he faced 80,000 French with about 50,000 men.[4] Afterwards, in this campaign, the French captured Charleroi, thus completing their control of the Sambre.

Late in October 1693 the king returned to an England as discontented as himself. As well as his own misfortunes on land, there was the recent disaster of the Smyrna convoy, and there still lingered resentment at the failure to follow up the victory of La Hogue. In his speech to both Houses on 7 November the king attributed his defeat at Neerwinden to the superior forces

[1] *L.J.* xv, 18 Feb. 1693.

[2] William's choice of this site has been adversely criticised. C. Walton, op. cit. 249 sqq.

[3] Ibid. 249.

[4] J. W. Fortescue, op. cit. i. 374.

of the enemy; as for the Smyrna convoy, that affair had brought disgrace to the nation, and would be strictly inquired into.[1]

The recent course of the war in Flanders had confirmed the misgivings of those members of the opposition who were averse to large-scale continental commitments; and already, the defeat at Steenkirk had caused some adverse criticism, based on the contention that the king had made a bad choice of site.[2] Most of all was the conduct of Solms condemned; but the demand for more British officers in the higher commands was tempered by recognition of the tradition that it takes a long time to train a general.[3] For long, the debates in the Commons had shown increasing disquiet and ill temper. Some deplored the giving of commissions in the army to 'trumpeters and corporals'; captain Churchill, incautiously complaining that naval commissions were given to 'brewers' clerks', had to be reminded of his own infamy in demanding money for providing escort.[4] There had been other causes for complaint. That of longest standing was the continued loss of shipping at the hands of the privateers. Clarges estimated our losses at 1,500 ships, having a total value of 3 millions, and complained of the diversion of so many men and so much treasure to Flanders where, he maintained, France was invincible;[5] to which it was answered that we had not enough cruisers for escort duty; that ships parted with their escorts in order to reach port sooner, and that, as they were heavily insured, the owners were not worried about their loss.[6] Most of all was the Cabinet condemned. It was regarded as a cabal, usurping the place of the privy council; if, it was urged, such an unconstitutional body must advise the crown, then each member should be obliged to give his advice in writing, duly signed, so that, if necessary, he could be impeached.[7] Such had been the main complaints in the last two months of 1692; they were renewed in the following year. The large civilian element in the board of Admiralty accounted for a motion of 10 January 1693 that the king should appoint thereto only persons having experience of maritime affairs, a motion lost by a small margin; but a resolution that

[1] *L.J.* xv, 7 Nov. 1693.
[2] *Grey*, x. 258, 11 Nov. 1692.
[3] Ibid. 252 sqq., Nov. 1692.
[4] Ibid. 273.
[5] Ibid. 264.
[6] Ibid. 272.
[7] Ibid. 276–7.

all orders for the fleet should pass through the Admiralty was carried.[1] Disaster was prompting the Commons to probe into the *arcana* of a fast-developing constitution.

One of the many imponderable elements in that constitution was the royal right to exercise the veto. On 14 March 1693, at the close of the fourth session of his second parliament, William had vetoed the Triennial Bill, a measure favoured by many Whigs as an alternative to the Tory Place Bill. In taking this step, William appears to have consulted with a number of persons, including sir William Temple; and, for a time, he was undecided; but eventually, he considered that the measure was a diminution of his prerogative, so he forbade its passage into law. A year later, however, when some kind of Whig ministry was coming into office,[2] he authorized a similar Bill. In the exercise of his powers, the king was never capricious; but these powers seemed to stand in the way of a House of Commons, now conscious of responsibility for the conduct of the war, but constantly thwarted in its attempts to press home that responsibility. There was acquiescence, though not without demur, in William's leadership of the land forces, but there was supreme distrust of his appointments, whether to army commands, or to membership of the informal Cabinet, or to the commissionerships of the Admiralty. It was realized that, so long as the king's will remained supreme, and so long as he retained the right of making high appointments, the frontier lines of the administrative departments must remain blurred, and the spearheads of criticism must be deflected by the impenetrable armour of the king himself. A great war of a modern type was being waged by a nation which, though assured of parliamentary government, still retained a sovereign whose executive powers were little less than those of his predecessors. The Cabinet was the link which made possible the working of a system of dual control, but it worked clumsily and inefficiently; moreover, its dependence on king, not on parliament, produced an increasing sense of frustration in the Commons.

These growing pains, perceptible in 1692, became acute in

[1] *Grey*, x. 294, 10 Jan. 1693.

[2] Shrewsbury had accepted a secretaryship of state in March 1694, and the king's consent to the Triennial Bill in the following December may have been through the duke's influence. (Feiling, *History of the Tory Party*, 290–1.)

1693. They were occasioned, not by the defeat of Neerwinden, which could be ascribed to the fortunes of war, but by the loss sustained by the great Smyrna convoy, which could be attributed to bad management. The facts briefly are these. As early as the winter of 1691–2 the English Levant Company had been assembling a fleet of ships for the Mediterranean, and it was hoped that the victory of La Hogue would ensure for them, as for a similar Dutch convoy, a sufficient escort.[1] With the dismissal of Russell from his post, the command of the fleet had been entrusted to Killigrew, Delaval, and Shovell, of whom the first two were considered Tories, even Jacobites; and in February 1693 it was arranged that Rooke, with about eighteen ships, should escort them all the way to the Mediterranean. But, in view of the fact that the total convoy consisted of about 400 ships, it was considered necessary to add to this escort a stronger force, to accompany Rooke and the convoy until they were well clear of any risk of French interference. It was here that difficulties began. The three admirals complained that, for the main fleet, they had only forty-eight ships, compared with sixty-three of the previous year; also, there were great difficulties in manning, in spite of the vigorous enforcement of the press; moreover, the breakdown in the victualling recalled that of the autumn of 1689. The situation was so desperate that, in March 1693, half the crews of the privateers were ordered to be pressed for the fleet; in May, five regiments of troops were put aboard the warships; and this dilemma had to be faced, that, while the unpaid seamen were clamouring for their pay, most of those who got it took the first opportunity of deserting. Food and beer were so scarce that four men's rations had to be divided among six; and so, by the summer of 1693, English seamen, assisted (or more probably hampered) by military amateurs, were required to perform the hard labour of a full-rigged ship on a diet suitable only for a life of contemplation.

Much of this was, of course, accounted for by increasing shortage of ready money, such as could scarcely have been even imagined at the outbreak of hostilities, and for which no administration could be blamed. But while such things caused delay, they did not directly account for the disaster. In the early

[1] The introduction to *MSS. of House of Lords*, new series, i, *1693–5*, contains an admirable account.

summer of 1693 it was known that Tourville with his fleet was in Brest, but there was no means of keeping him there, nor any certain means of knowing when he got out. On 15 May the three joint admirals resolved at a council of war that, until more certain news was received of the movements of the French fleet, the Levant ships should wait still longer, and that meanwhile Rooke should join them. Afterwards they argued, quite properly, that, had this resolution been accepted, the misfortune would not have occurred. Carmarthen and other members of the Cabinet visited Spithead, as they had done in the previous summer, in order to impress on the admirals the necessity for action; and, in these representations, they were now joined by the Admiralty, which, on 19 May, ordered the admirals to sail on the first opportunity. Later, the Admiralty defended itself by saying that, not until 30 June, was it informed of the admirals' resolution of 15 May.

On 30 May the convoy with its escorts set sail and, four days later, they were at the rendezvous thirty leagues west-south-west of Ushant. The admirals, concerned about leaving the English coast undefended, resolved that they could not accompany Rooke more than another twenty leagues; so, on 6 June, the Grand Fleet left the convoy. The admirals had made no attempt to ascertain whether or not the French fleet was out; actually, Tourville with his ships had already (26 May) left Brest for Lagos Bay, but there is no evidence that he knew anything about the Smyrna convoy.[1] He sighted the allied ships off Lagos on 17 June, and at first thought that they were escorted by the greater part of the fleet. An engagement followed in which, though Rooke, with his Dutch colleagues, put up a stiff fight, in the hope of enabling the merchantmen to escape, they could do little against such odds; so the convoy was broken up, some of the units being captured, others driven ashore, and others scattered to places as far off as Madeira. About 100 merchant ships, English and Dutch, were destroyed, their total value estimated at about a million.

Throughout the winter of 1693–4 a parliamentary committee investigated the conduct of secretary Nottingham and the admirals. In regard to the first an instance of gross mismanagement was revealed. A letter had been received from Paris on

[1] C. de la Roncière, *Histoire de la marine française*, vi. 139.

30 May announcing that the French fleet was out; had this news been sent by a fast frigate, the convoy might have been saved; but no action was taken by the secretary, who appears to have contented himself with merely placing the letter before the members of the Cabinet.[1] By a majority vote in the Lords Nottingham was exonerated from the imputation of negligence; and in both Houses a similar majority saved the admirals from censure. But the majorities were narrow, and there was evidence of serious disquiet about the admirals and the naval administration.

So, when William returned to England in October 1693, with his own disaster of Neerwinden in the background, he found a state of things in which the Revolution itself seemed to be imperilled. The fifth session of his second parliament proved the most critical of any that he had yet faced. On 28 November Clarges made a speech which enables one to appreciate how William's War must have appeared to a survivor of the Cromwellian age: 'it grieves my heart', declared this relic of better days, 'to see the king of England at the head of confederate armies.' The army, he declared, was really for the defence of the kingdom, not for campaigns abroad; by 'fundamental law' no man could be sent out of England but by his own consent; the Dutch, he claimed, were the only gainers by the war, for they supplied our army with butter and cheese. Worst of all was the expense. Cromwell's army had cost no more than £600,000 a year; William's army was costing nearly 3 millions. With all this money pouring out of the country, what would become of them?[2] On 4 December the presentation of the army estimates—93,000 men costing about £2,700,000—aroused another storm of criticism. Already, the Commons had demanded a sight of the treaties which obliged the nation to engage in war; and Clarges maintained that, excepting a treaty with the Dutch,[3] they were all defensive. Musgrave said that we were ruining England to save Flanders; sir Francis Winnington complained that the more they gave, the less success they had; and sir Charles Sedley, now somewhat recovered from Restoration days, but apparently under the impression that the war was being fought in Holland, solemnly declared that, if that

[1] *L.J.* xv, 10 and 15 Jan., also 15 Feb. 1694.

[2] *Grey*, x. 332, 28 Nov. 1693.

[3] *Supra*, 346–7.

country were destroyed, 'it will be our turn next'.[1] On behalf of the executive, secretary Trenchard reminded the chamber that the treaties had been laid before them in the previous year; and lord Colchester, a serving officer, hopefully declared that, if we could equal the French in numbers, we could beat them.

It was fortunate that both services were so well represented in the House; otherwise, the Commons might have refused supplies. The ablest defence of William's strategy was that made by general Talmash.[2] The king, he said, had to defend Flanders against the 80,000 foot and the 35,000 horse put into the field by Louis. The costly battle of Neerwinden, he declared, had been fought in order to defend Louvain and Mechlin; had these places been taken, the enemy would have pressed on to Nieuport and Ostend, ports which would serve them well for privateering attacks on our merchantmen. A peace might be had at any time, but only at the cost of another war. He was as weary of it as anyone. Within a few months Talmash was to die in one more disaster—that of Camaret Bay.

It needed only another exercise of the veto to raise the indignation of the Commons to fever heat. This occurred on 25 January 1694, when William withheld his assent to the Bill for free and impartial proceedings in parliament, generally known as the Place Bill, which would have disqualified office holders from sitting in the House. The king may have been influenced not so much by a premonition that the proposed measure would prove unworkable, as by the feeling that it trenched on his right to bestow offices. This, the third veto of the reign, raised a storm in the House. Clarges moved that the advisers of the rejection were enemies of king and kingdom; sir John Lowther, equally pessimistic, deplored the fact that the House was now coming to be divided into parties—two at least—and he proposed that the king should be guided by a council in which both he and the Commons could trust.[3] The House submitted to the king a protest against his veto of the Place Bill, which originally contained a clause attributing his action to ignorance of the constitution of parliament, but by resolution this was omitted.[4] To this protest William gave a conciliatory reply, expressing his high regard for parliament. This was one

[1] *Grey*, x. 341, 4 Dec. 1693.
[2] Ibid. 363, 11 Dec. 1693.
[3] Ibid. 375–7, 26 Jan. 1694.
[4] *C.J.* xi, 27 Jan. 1694.

of the occasions when the rift between crown and legislature might have widened into a gulf; that it did not do so may be attributed to the exercise of forbearance on both sides.

These events had already caused William in disgust to turn to the Whigs, just as, in the same mood, he had turned to the Tories in the early months of 1690. He was unwilling to part with Nottingham, but the share of the secretary in the naval miscarriages of two successive years was so patent, and had been so fiercely criticized, that he had to give up the seals in November 1693. He was succeeded by Trenchard, already secretary for the north since March 1693, a man of very different type, whose knowledge of the political underworld, derived from membership of the Green Ribbon Club, was now turned to good advantage in ferreting out Jacobite plots. In March 1694 he was joined by Shrewsbury, who took over the department of the south. At the same time the naval triumvirate of Killigrew, Delaval, and Shovell came to an end, and Russell the Whig was restored to the sole command. He also became first commissioner of the Admiralty and a member of the Cabinet. Charles Montagu, a Treasury commissioner, was made chancellor of the Exchequer and a privy councillor in April 1694. Already, in February 1693, Somers had been appointed lord keeper, and by the spring of 1694 there existed an administration predominantly Whig, in which the Junto provided the nucleus of a ministry. Carmarthen, now duke of Leeds, and sir John Lowther of Lowther were still in office; but the former had suffered such discredit from evidence of his acceptance of a bribe from the East India Company that he did not again play a notable part in the reign. Lowther, afterwards first viscount Lonsdale, was obsessed by neither party nor ambition. So the way was clear for Whig supremacy, which lasted until 1698.

These years of Whig ascendancy are important for the completion of two changes in naval strategy, namely, the recognition that a substantial portion of the fleet must be used for commerce protection, and the sending of a large fleet to the Mediterranean. The first change had been anticipated in the Land Tax Bill of 1693[1], which stipulated the number and strength of the warships to be detached for escort and patrol duties, and appropriated £1,000,000 for the navy—an unheard-

[1] 5 W. and M., c. 1.

of sum. The second change had been foreshadowed as early as 1689 in the Anglo-Dutch agreement,[1] and was part of William's policy of using the fleet in an area where diplomatic and military conditions were sensitive to the presence of a large, mobile force.[2] The loss to the Smyrna convoy had strengthened the argument for a strong British force in the Mediterranean; and the necessity of protecting the coast of Catalonia was now more urgent than ever, since Spain was too weak to do so. So in August 1693 William had urged, from his camp in Flanders, that a squadron should be sent to the coast of Portugal for the protection of English merchant ships passing through the Straits.[3] Meanwhile, there still remained the menace of sorties from Brest, and so the Cabinet, early in 1694, devised a combination of two things—an attack on Brest, and (if Tourville escaped) the pursuit of his ships, if necessary to the Mediterranean. The plans were not very clearly concerted, and their execution was entrusted to Russell.

Tourville left Brest late in April 1694, and Russell showed no hurry to take up the chase, in spite of William's injunction that he should do so.[4] At last he sailed with the main fleet on 2 June, bound for the Mediterranean, and accompanied by transports for the attack on Brest, these being under the protection of a naval squadron led by lord Berkeley. Talmash was in command of the troops, who were to be landed at Camaret Bay, situated on a promontory just south of the great harbour of Brest. For at least a month beforehand the French knew of our intentions, and already Vauban had erected defences at the spot; but it is not necessary to impute French foreknowledge of this plan to treachery, since the lack of the most elementary precautions ensured that many Cabinet secrets quickly became public knowledge. The situation, however, is complicated by the fact that it was realized on our side that the French knew our intentions, and so the Cabinet must have been aware that the landing

[1] *Supra*, 346–7.

[2] At Versailles it was believed that William's main object was to promote his cherished design of an invasion of France through Dauphiné. *Aff. Etr.* (*Angleterre*), 173, f. 3.

[3] J. Ehrman, *The Navy in the War of William III*, 503. J. S. Corbett's *England in the Mediterranean* is still a useful book, but should be supplemented by Mr. Ehrman's chapter 12.

[4] J. Ehrman, op. cit. 511.

would be hotly contested. Why was the original enterprise carried through in spite of the fact that the essential element of surprise had disappeared? There is no certain answer. The Cabinet which had proved so negligent in the matter of the Smyrna convoy may have been equally negligent in the matter of Camaret Bay, in the sense that it may have failed to modify a plan when that plan was obviously inadvisable. In view of the situation, Talmash may have been allowed a certain amount of discretion which he failed to exercise properly. Here is one of the many mysteries of the reign.

On 6 June the armada was off Ushant; on the 7th Berkeley's squadron, with the transports, was off Camaret Bay. Approaching the place in a yacht, Talmash could see no sign of troops or fortifications, so on the following day he went in with his landing party, while the ships battered the fort, in order to cover the landing. But, as soon as they reached the shore, the troops were confronted with batteries and trenches; and, as he advanced at the head of his men, Talmash was fatally wounded. There was nothing for it but to return to the ships, leaving behind about 500 dead and prisoners, besides many wounded carried away from the beach. One Dutch ship was sunk. So ended our attempt to effect a landing in France.[1] Thenceforward, the Channel served only for cruising and for the bombardment of French Channel ports. The chances of a major action at sea had now completely receded, and 'the fleet in being' was, until January 1696, in the Mediterranean, from whence admiral Russell kept up a steady flow of querulous correspondence.

Nevertheless, his presence there served a useful purpose, if only by immobilizing the Toulon fleet, and so relieving French pressure on Catalonia. On 23 July William communicated through Blathwayt his wishes that the fleet should remain in the Mediterranean for so long as was consistent with its safety, and that a squadron should be stationed there in the winter.[2] In face of some opposition from the Cabinet, and in spite of the fact that stores would have to be sent from England, William

[1] *Cal. S.P. Dom. 1694–5*, 168, Berkeley to Trenchard, and 183, relation of captain N. Green, 15 June. Also *Naval Miscellany*, ii, ed. J. K. Laughton (Navy Records Society), 202 sqq.

[2] J. Ehrman, op. cit. 519. Also ibid., ch. 12, for the administrative arrangements made for the fleet in the Mediterranean.

in the early autumn gave definite orders for the wintering of the fleet in the inland sea, with the injunction that it should pursue and engage the French fleet if it tried to slip out of the Straits. Unwillingly Russell obeyed these orders, and during the winter of 1694–5 he refitted at Cadiz. This provided a new and exacting duty for the administration at home, since supplies had to be sent out, and arrangements made for financing locally, difficulties which were eventually surmounted with the help of the Bank of England and of our ambassador and consuls in Spain. On the whole, British seamen fared better at Cadiz than at Portsmouth.

In another respect the naval strategy of 1694–5 anticipated later events, for it inaugurated the policy of 'breaking windows with guineas'. This had begun in November 1693 when Benbow, with a squadron of more than twenty ships, appeared off St. Malo, accompanied by a new infernal machine. This was the invention of a Dutchman, William Meesters, and appears to have been based on the principle of the old medical prescriptions, namely, that of including as many things as possible, in the hope that one of them would work. Meesters's contraption contained tar, sulphur, bitumen, nitre, and vitriol, with rows of grenades and barrels of powder. Its explosion broke some windows in St. Malo, and killed the crew of the vessel on which it was placed.[1] But gunfire proved more effective. In July 1694, when Dieppe and Havre were bombarded, considerable damage was done. This was followed by attacks on Calais and Dunkirk, but in neither case were the frigates able to destroy the defences. The same policy was repeated in the following year, and in this way the French Channel coast was kept in such a continual state of alarm that troops had to be diverted from Flanders. In July 1696 a naval force under Berkeley covered a landing of 800 men on the Ile de Groix, on the Atlantic coast of Brittany, where all the houses and the harvest were destroyed. This, our only uninterrupted landing on French soil, provided a somewhat ignominious ending to a naval offensive on which so much money had been spent, and from which so much had been expected. But there are many occasions when the importance of the navy must be judged, not from what happened, but from what did not happen. This was to be

[1] C. de la Roncière, op. cit. vi. 171–2.

shown in the spring of 1696, when the last attempt at a French-Jacobite invasion was foiled by British sea power.

On land, as at sea, a certain slackening of intensity had been evidenced as early as 1694, when, after nearly five years of war, there was a suggestion of stalemate. Even Louis, in spite of merciless extortion from the peasants of France and of occupied Flanders, was beginning to experience a shortage of money, and had difficulty in raising new regiments; moreover, a large proportion of his troops had to be detached for garrison duty in Mons, Namur, Huy, and Charleroi; while the allies, though they had fewer conquests to their credit, had to maintain garrisons in Ghent and Dixmude. For both sides supplies presented an increasingly difficult problem in 1694, because many farmers ceased to grow corn, and cut their grass early, so that it could not be taken by the troops. In so far as the campaigns of this year were dominated by any single purpose it was that the allies, barred by fortresses in the south, sought to push forward to the west, where the prizes were Furnes, Knocke, and Dunkirk. But here again William was anticipated by Luxemburg. In just over five days the French general marched the 120 miles from the Meuse to the Scheldt, a record achievement, which cost him a large number of his men, but prevented the allies from accomplishing anything in western Flanders. No general action was fought, but it was clear that at last the French were on the defensive. So, in his speech to both Houses on 12 November 1694, the king was able to give his assurance that a stop had at last been put to the progress of French arms.

William was soon to suffer the greatest bereavement of his life—the death of queen Mary from smallpox on 28 December of this year. The king's grief attested the genuine affection which, beneath his churlishness, had endeared him to his wife. Politically, the event was of some importance, for the mere fact of Mary sharing the throne with her husband had been enough to secure the allegiance of many who would never have recognized the sovereignty of William alone; so the queen's death revived hope at St. Germains, where it was thought that the nation would now be justified in forswearing its allegiance. But certain circumstances obviated that danger. By 1694, the year when the Bank of England was founded, England was beginning to acquiesce willingly in the Revolution settlement. There was still the Jacobite danger, which was to raise its head again in 1696, but many Tories were finding it in their interest to support the existing régime; and the general election of the autumn of 1695, held after William's solitary success, his capture of Namur,[1] provided a Whig majority, which ensured that England would be carried through the last and most difficult years of the war. Had Mary died a few years earlier, the consequences might have been very different, for William's crown was never securely balanced on his head.

The stalemate on the western front may have helped this difficult situation, for in such periods people usually wait to see what turns up. There was stalemate also in another theatre of war, the West Indies, where conditions provided a replica of those in Europe, except that disease took a much heavier toll. Some kind of campaign had begun in July 1689, when the French, with the help of the Irish, captured the English part of St. Kitts; but in the summer of the following year Codrington, with a comparatively small force, succeeded in recapturing it. Codrington was convinced that with a fleet, and help from Jamaica and Barbados, we could make ourselves masters of all the French island colonies, as we were greatly superior in numbers. Better than his word, he effected a landing in Guadeloupe in February 1691, and would have captured the island, but for the truculence and cowardice of captain Wright, in command of the supporting naval squadron, one of the worst of the 'gentleman commanders' of the period.[2] Early in the following year a squadron under sir Francis Wheler arrived at Barbados, and after three months delay attacked Martinique, without success; in this enterprise a large proportion of men was lost by disease. All the mistakes of our West India strategy were united in the combined operation of 1695, when admiral Wilmot and colonel Lillingston landed on Hispaniola, which for some years had been occupied by the French. The expedition arrived in the early summer, the worst time of the year; troops were marched across swamps when they might easily have been taken by sea; service jealousy was so acute that the naval and military commanders acted independently. The result was that, of 1,300

[1] *Infra*, 398.

[2] *Cal. S.P. Amer. 1689–92*, notably 484–95. For a summary account of the West India campaigns, see that in G. H. Guttridge, *Colonial Policy of William III.*

men Lillingston was left with only about 300, the remainder having died of sickness. Had he been supported by the admiral, Hispaniola might have been taken.

By this time it appeared that, both in Flanders and in the West Indies the allied record was one of monotonous failure. But, for William, the year 1695 was to prove the one year of definite military success. Luxemburg, who died in January 1695, was succeeded by Villeroi, a man of lesser mould; moreover, the allies now outnumbered the French, facts which may account for a change in the fortunes of war. When the king arrived in Flanders in May, he had reason to think that at last something might be accomplished, and for once he succeeded in taking the enemy unawares. Namur was occupied by Boufflers, with 14,000 troops; in June William proceeded to invest it. At that time French troops were massed mainly in western Flanders where, by the treachery of the Dane Ellenberg, they succeeded in taking Dixmude; while, in the opposite corner of the Low Countries, William was proceeding almost unmolested with the siege. On 20/30 August the assault on the walls was led by Cutts, at the head of his grenadiers, aided by Bavarians, Hanoverians, Prussians, and Hessians. In the first assault, Cutts was driven off, with considerable loss; but serious breaches had been made in the defences, and next day Boufflers had to hoist signals of distress over the castle.

Villeroi, arriving on the scene, decided that it was impossible to relieve the garrison, so on the 22nd he set fire to his camp and marched off. Thereupon, Boufflers beat the *chamade* and, after exchange of hostages, the French general led the withdrawal of his men, drums beating and colours flying, the procession passing between the lines formed by allied troops. William, who had watched the scene from rising ground behind Salzinnes Abbey, now came forward to order the arrest of Boufflers, as security for the garrison at Dixmude, which the French had detained, contrary to the articles of capitulation on the occasion of the betrayal of the town. For this betrayal of Dixmude, general Ellenberg was afterwards shot. It was unfortunate that the capture of the great fortress of Namur was marred by the failure or treachery of a subordinate; and indeed, this constant alternation of light and shade, even in his few hours of success, provided the chequered pattern of William's life.

XIV

THE WAR TO THE LAST GUINEA 1689–97

THE NATIONAL DEBT: THE BANK OF ENGLAND

As active service was limited to only a small proportion of the population, and as that proportion consisted mainly of those who were considered a good riddance, the majority of Englishmen were able, in war-time, to continue their normal pursuits, undisturbed by thought of danger to themselves or their relatives, save only on those occasions when there was talk of invasion. Of printed parliamentary proceedings, anyone could buy a copy; but of the debates, the public could obtain no information, save by indirect or surreptitious means; as for the newspapers, still innocent of sensationalism, their news was generally scrappy and belated. But the war was brought home to everyone by rising prices, since the poor had to pay more for their beer, salt, and tobacco, and the rich for their tea or coffee; there were also many new taxes—on windows, on marriage, on the birth of one's children, on the burial of one's self. Of the human element involved in the sacrifice made by the fighting men there was scarcely any indication. The plight of the disabled or sick sailor in the dockyard towns was so obvious as to prompt some sympathy, but that of the wounded soldier abroad was, mercifully perhaps, veiled in obscurity. By 1693, the year of Neerwinden, the increasing number of widows was being noticed.[1]

This chapter treats of England's surmounting of her financial difficulties as one of the major campaigns of the war, and tries to link this achievement with the course of hostilities. It is in three sections, of which the first is a short account of the fiscal system in William's reign, and the second is a summary of the main principles and achievements of Revolution finance. In this second section, the sequence approximates to the chronological,

[1] 'The Petition of the Widows', 1693, in *Harleian Miscellany* (1810 ed.), x. 170.

and takes the account down to 1695–6, the terminating point of the preceding chapter. From there, the third section resumes the political narrative, with an account of the Assassination Plot, the financial crisis, and the invasion scare of 1696, concluding with a reference to the treaty of Ryswick, which ended the war in 1697.

1. The Fiscal System

At this time, the sources of revenue consisted mainly of two indirect taxes—Customs and Excise; and two direct taxes—the Poll, and what came to be called the Land Tax. The Customs, managed by commissioners after 1671 (having previously been farmed), were raised by a subsidy on all woollen cloth exported,[1] and a levy of 5 per cent. on imports and exports, according to the table of their values in the Book of Rates (1660).[2] Later Acts made many changes,[3] whether by addition or diminution of duty, and brought a large number of miscellaneous levies within the control of the Customs commissioners, including those on coal and glass, as well as those imposed in 1685 on wine, vinegar, tobacco, and East India goods. In 1686–7 the yield exceeded £640,000, but the war caused a decline in the revenue received from some of the sources, followed by a steady rise after 1697, with the net result that the total yield from Customs dues[4] in William's reign amounted to over £13,000,000. In addition to their fiscal duties, the commissioners performed many administrative functions; for they maintained the preventive service against smuggling; they collected the money for lighthouses; they assisted the press gangs, supervised the registration of shipping, and administered the Navigation Acts.[5] Like the Excise, the Customs came more directly under the control of the Treasury after the fall of Danby in 1679.

The Excise was in three branches—the hereditary, or that which had been conferred in perpetuity on the crown on the abolition of the Court of Wards in 1660; the life Excise, or that granted to the king for life, in addition to his hereditary revenue;

[1] For the withdrawal of Customs dues on exported cloth, see *supra*, 283.

[2] Specimen rates will be found in *Documents*, no. 103.

[3] *Supra*, 285–6.

[4] *Documents*, no. 122.

[5] B. R. Leftwich, 'Later History and Administration of the Customs Revenue, 1671–1814', in *Trans. R.H.S.*, 4th series, xiii (1930).

and, thirdly, the temporary, or that granted from time to time by parliament. Though falling mainly on beer, ale, and vinegar, its scope was extended to include salt, 'low wines',[1] malt, and linen from Scotland; its yield, in the course of William's reign, amounted to slightly more than the Customs (over 13 millions), to be accounted for by numerous additional Excises granted by parliament, and also by the fact that (after 1683) it was collected directly, and not farmed. Its wide incidence, mainly on what were considered necessities, made Excise, in spite of much malversation by officials, a singularly dependable source of revenue; and, as this was an era of cheap food, it seemed that an increasing Excise could, up to a point, be borne without complaint. A third advantage of Excise was that, unlike the Customs, it was not 'saddled' with any traditional commitment, and so could be freely used in order to provide backing for new financial schemes.

In its frequent resort to this source of revenue, the English fiscal system resembled that of Holland and Prussia, in contrast with that of France, where the national drink, wine, was the subject not of one great national tax, but of innumerable local levies. Here, indeed, we have one of the reasons why English public finance developed very rapidly in this period of strain; whereas, in similar conditions, France raised more money by intensifying the injustices of what was already an outworn system. Excise was the key to English financial success, because of these three merits—dependability, resilience, and freedom from commitment; accordingly, our first long-term loans were based on this fund, which, in the public eye, meant permanence and security. With such success did the legislature exploit this source, that it tried to extract too much from it, with the result that there was a decline in yield during the last years of the reign, which some attributed to mismanagement by the commissioners, while others regarded it as the inevitable result of over-taxation.

On several occasions between 1689 and 1698 a Poll Tax was levied, the rates being in accordance with a scale of rank or profession; those having no rank, and not in receipt of parish relief, paid 6*d.* or 1*s.* By a charge, usually of 1*s.* in the £, on pensions and salaries of public offices, the Poll Taxes provided

[1] 'Low wines' were spirits from the first distillation.

one of those levies which anticipated our Income Tax, and so was one of the few burdens imposed on personalty; but it reflected an earlier age, because it fell on rank rather than on income or expenditure. Many condemned its administration, which was entrusted to commissioners, whose assessments usually favoured themselves and their friends. Another badly designed tax was that on windows, which was controlled by the Land Tax commissioners. From this, cottages were exempt; the basic charge on each house was 2*s.*; houses having 10–19 windows paid 4*s.* extra; above 19, 8*s.* This tax, introduced in 1696 in order to pay for the recoinage, proved nearly as unpopular as the old Hearth Tax, because it did not sufficiently differentiate between rich and poor.[1]

The Aid or Land Tax, like the Poll Bills, included in its scope the profits of office, other than naval or military, as well as shares in certain public companies. Stock, merchandise, and money were assessed, nominally at least, on their capital value, and the tax was levied on 6 per cent. of that value. So this, the most important of the direct taxes, was not limited to land, since it was intended to be a property tax; but effectively it came to be levied almost entirely on rents, possibly because, while land is incapable of concealment, the owner of personal property was not obliged, by any stringent form of return, to disclose it. Commissioners, appointed for each county or borough by the Act authorizing the Aid, delivered their precepts to property owners within their area, announcing the rates, and charging them to certify their property. They then authorized the assessors to inform themselves of the full yearly value of the property and charge accordingly. The assessors made their returns to the collectors, who levied the amount. Property owners might be summoned to appear before the commissioners only if it was thought that there had been an omission or undervaluation; the commissioners also heard appeals from the assessments, if lodged within twelve days. Tenants paid the rates and deducted from rent; for the discovery of personal estates householders had to give an account of their lodgers. Papists, not having taken the oaths, had to pay double; the

[1] 7–8 Wm. III, c. 18 and *Documents*, no. 111. On this subject, see R. W. Ward, 'The Administration of the Window and Assessed Taxes, 1696–1798', in *E.H.R.* lxvii (1952).

universities and colleges were exempt in respect of their sites and stipends, but not in respect of their lands. No one was liable whose lands did not exceed 20*s*. annual value. The only oaths that could be imposed by the commissioners were the standard oaths of allegiance and supremacy; so loyalty could be attested, but not honesty.

During the Commonwealth, this tax had superseded the old Subsidy, and had been levied according to an assessment made by a parliamentary committee, whereby a total, fixed amount was to be raised, usually by the month, a total which was divided among counties and boroughs, so that each district had its definite quota. This practice, which can be traced as far back, at least, as 1640, was frequently resorted to in Charles II's reign. But already an alternative method had crept in, that of the pound rate. Experience showed that, in order to raise half a million, the rate had to be 1*s*. in the £; effectively, however, the yield, on this system, was usually much less; indeed it was notorious that, especially in northern counties, the pound rate provided the landowners with opportunity for evasion. In the years immediately following the Revolution, both methods were applied, the rate varying from 1*s*. to 4*s*. in the £, but as the rate was more common than the quota, it was obvious that much parliamentary pressure was being applied in order to ensure that land did not bear its full burden. Not till 1698 was William's government sufficiently established to make the quota system a permanent one,[1] for in that year a return was made to the more certain method of determining a definite amount for each district, on the basis of the assessments of 1693, the total for the whole country being £1,414,985, or the equivalent of 3*s*. in the £. Early in Anne's reign it was standardized at about £2,000,000, approximately a 4*s*. rate, and in 1798 it was made redeemable by a capital payment.

In this way the so-called Land Tax remained the most important of the direct taxes, although at first it had been regarded as an alternative to Excise, or a war-time measure. The mere fact that it came to be officially named the Land Tax is a striking illustration of the failure of the state to make personal property pay its share. Curiously enough, in an age of oaths, there was an unwillingness to oblige the owner to make a sworn

[1] For this, see R. W. Ward, *The English Land Tax in the Eighteenth Century*.

statement about the value of his personalty; in effect, therefore, he might often assess himself, whereas the landlord had no opportunity for concealment, because he had to recoup the tenant who had paid tax on his rent, while those who farmed their own land paid direct. In consequence, many trading towns paid much less than their true proportion.

As the Land Tax assessments reflect contemporary opinion regarding the comparative value of property in counties and boroughs, they are of special interest. These assessments may reflect actual changes in local prosperity, or may result from parliamentary 'lobbying'—in what proportion we do not know—so the temptation to draw definite conclusions has to be resisted. Nevertheless, some tentative suggestions can be made from a comparison based on the statistics of more than fifty years[1], extending from 1640 to 1698. Taking 10,000 as the unit for the total assessment of England and Wales, the simplest case is probably that of Cornwall, which shows a steady decline from 250 in 1640 to about 160 in 1698, a change attributable to the fall in the price of tin, linked with the strong representation of the county in parliament. In contrast, Cheshire, which was poorly represented, rose from 70 in 1640 to 140 in 1698, but part of this may be attributable to the development of rock salt. Durham steadily rose from 32 to 50, and the latter figure should be compared with Rutland's 26, Oxfordshire's 107, and Lincolnshire's 360, figures which suggest that contemporaries still placed much more value on corn and wool than on coal. The great clothing districts show a relative decline—Wiltshire, from 290 to 240; Suffolk from 500 to 360, with varying decreases in Yorkshire, Norfolk, Somerset, and Devon. In contrast, the London area (including Westminster and Middlesex) rose from 1,370 to 1,470, after having dipped to just over 1,000 in the long period of the rebuilding; by 1707 the figure had risen to about 1,600, or 16 per cent. of the total. This advance of the metropolis was shared by neighbouring counties; for example, Hertfordshire, 180 to 213; Surrey, 260 to 330; Buckinghamshire, 170 to 226; and Bedfordshire, 107 to 140. As all these figures are relative, they do not prove any absolute decline or advance

[1] i.e. the assessments for 1640, 1665, 1677, 1689, and 1698. Adopting a different method, the author has reached conclusions similar to those of Mr. R. W. Ward, op. cit.

in a particular area, but merely local readjustments in comparison with the estimate of the country's total wealth.

The most striking thing to be deduced from these statistics is the steadily increasing predominance of London and the home counties in contrast with the comparative decline of those areas devoted for the most part to the traditional occupations of agriculture, grazing, and cloth-making. Here perhaps we have a partial explanation of the continual complaints about the decline of the cloth industry; it may be that the decline was not absolute, but only relative to progress in other spheres. What seems certain is that the provinces were losing, in proportion to the estimated wealth of the nation, in the same ratio as the capital and its neighbours were gaining, a fact which may be attributed not only to the greater diversity of industry in the south-east, and the prevalence of enclosures in those areas which supplied the large towns, but also to the location, in the metropolitan area, of a majority of those who were making money from the legal profession, from office or from war contracts.

Altogether, in William's reign the Land Tax gave the greatest yield of all the taxes, i.e. about 19 millions, as compared with 13 millions each from Customs and Excise. To these taxes new ones were added, and the following were subject to tax or increased tax: stamped paper, licences of hackney coaches, licences of hawkers; births, deaths, and marriages; salt, windows, and tobacco pipes. The total proceeds of taxation in the period 1689–1702 amounted to more than 58 millions,[1] of which about 40 millions was raised in the war years 1689–97, or little less than the cost of the war. Experiment provided good fiscal experience. The Poll Taxes, which yielded altogether about 2 millions, became discredited, and disappeared from the fiscal system; the new or 'fancy' taxes such as those on births, deaths, and marriages gave such disappointing results that for the time they were abandoned. More was derived from salt, on which the tax was permanent;[2] and a slowly increasing revenue was derived from coal. Otherwise, Customs, Excise, and Land Tax provided the basis of taxation policy.

The above summary may give an impression of fiscal uniformity and efficiency such as characterize modern times. But these qualities are achieved only after long administrative evolution,

[1] *Documents*, no. 122.

[2] Except for the years 1730–2.

an evolution in which the events of the later seventeenth century played an important part. One obvious weakness in the finance of William's reign was that reliance could not be placed on those who handled public money; indeed, in the five years after the Revolution, only a fifth part of the Excise personnel had taken the oath of allegiance;[1] and it was notorious that many Jacobites, whether in office or not, were anxious to help their cause by obstruction, or even embezzlement; accordingly clipping the coin, an activity conducted with such assiduity as to threaten the stability of the kingdom, had with some a 'patriotic' element. As for the personal honesty of officials, that was a relative term. Members of parliament, in respect of their offices, could shield themselves behind parliamentary privilege,[2] which at least prolonged the period in which they could not be brought to account; another form of delayed action was to lend part of the proceeds of a tax to friends on short-term loans, or even to use the ready cash in order to bribe electors at an election.[3] When, at last, the collector did send the money to London, it might be stolen or lost on the way, though loss from this source was diminished by greater use of inland bills of exchange and paper money. Generally, leakage was considerable, not always from clear-cut dishonesty, but from ambiguous or dilatory methods of accounting, in which private profit could usually be combined with some regard to conscience. Then, as always, cheating the state was considered the most venial of all offences, its impunity usually varying in proportion to its magnitude.

So, too, with uniformity. England was not an administrative unit in the modern sense, but a collection of competing interests, for which parliament often provided a clearing house. Some districts, notably in the north, appear to have had considerable success in keeping down their Land Tax assessments, but failed with the Poll Taxes; whereas the south and south-west used the salt tax as a lever for raising the fish bounties, by which these areas particularly benefited. Even within the salt industry, there was a conflict of the brine and the new rock-salt elements, a conflict carried to Westminster.[4] Only in regard to the corn

[1] E. Hughes, *Studies in Administration and Finance, 1558–1825*, 188.

[2] *Infra*, 501–2.

[3] *Infra*, 505.

[4] E. Hughes, op. cit. 178 and 225–31.

bounties and cloth exports was there general agreement. A fall in wages meant little, except to the poor; a fall in rents was considered a national calamity. Geographically and socially, England was a bundle of conflicting interests, some vocal, the others silent.

2. Revolution Finance. The National Debt: the Bank of England: the Recoinage

William's war lasted for nearly nine years, at an average cost of under 5 millions per annum. It might have been possible, during the war years, to pay the cost from current taxation, but for a number of factors, including the necessity of allocating a sum, usually estimated at £1,200,000 for the annual charge of the civil administration; also, the Revolution government had to take over a debt of about 2 millions from its predecessor; more serious, the ordinary revenue was heavily pledged for perpetuities, pensions, and interest on departmental debts. Still more, as revenue had to be anticipated in order to raise ready money by loans, there were high and cumulative interest charges, which eventually amounted to nearly a third part of the capital value; there was also loss—direct and indirect—on the depreciated currency, with the result that by 1697 the financial deficiency on the funds amounted to 14–15 millions, which was reduced by 1702 to about 12 millions. This, in a strict sense of the term, might be called the National Debt; but there were also obligations of a more normal character, such as floating debt and the departmental debts, which may have brought the total amount of national indebtedness, by the end of the war, up to nearly 20 millions. At no time in William's reign, nor for many years thereafter, was this debt regarded as permanent; for, as it had been created by an emergency, so it would be ended by a period of peace. But, meanwhile, a system had been initiated whereby large sums could be raised on credit, credit ultimately guaranteed by fuller exploitation of the enormous resources of the country.

Such a system could not have sprung into existence overnight; it must have been linked with earlier developments. The discontinuity in politics created by the Revolution was not matched by discontinuity in finance; indeed, as a shrewd critic[1]

[1] E. Hughes, op. cit. 152–4.

has pointed out, there was a certain amount of regression. This was seen in the Excise, the administration of which had been taken from the farmers in 1683 and entrusted to commissioners, a change which, like the abandonment of farming in the Customs (1671), was intended to substitute state management for private control. The experience of Charles II's finance had pointed to some obvious conclusions, including this, that the state should take the benefit which formerly had been monopolized by financial syndicates. By stricter control, Danby had caused the farm to approximate to what was called a 'management'; hence, in 1677, when the Dashwood group of farmers accepted these stricter conditions in exchange for a guaranteed salary of £10,000 a year, the lesson was clear, namely, that this salary should go to the state. It was recognized also that the large sum advanced at the beginning of a farm, amounting at times to a quarter of a million, was not 'fresh' money, but the accumulated profits of earlier farms, so here was another argument for direct collection. In effect, therefore, if it had been possible to apply these object lessons, the farming system might have been eliminated altogether, and the administration of the finances might have been entrusted to government officials, dependent solely on fixed emoluments.

But this promising development was thwarted by the unprecedented demands for money following immediately on the Revolution, with the result that, in the Excise, where farming had nominally been abandoned, the commissioners had to be chosen from those who advanced large sums, as if they were farmers, intent, as of old, on profiting from the necessities of the state. These men naturally resented the addition to their number of commissioners who had made no advances of money, because such officials, in receipt only of their salaries, represented something new and even alien—the civil servant who has no vested interest in the proceeds of a tax. It was from this mingling of two different types of official that the modern administrator was gradually evolved; meanwhile, in William's reign, opportunities for 'snip' were greater in those cases where there was departmental co-operation; indeed a certain *esprit de corps* held together the old gang from which Charles II had tried to escape. Another inherited abuse was sir Charles Duncombe,[1]

[1] *Supra*, 88–89.

cashier of the Excise. As former banker to Charles he represented the alternative to the Bank of England, the foundation of which he naturally opposed.

English financial history after the Revolution is understandable only against the background of earlier attempts to dissociate public interest from private profit; indeed it may be said that William's ministers succeeded, where Charles's ministers had failed. An example had been provided as early as 1665 when the Act for an Additional Aid authorized the acceptance of loans from the public on the security of the fund to be raised by the Act. But this early experiment was not maintained, though it was resumed on an unexpected occasion in 1685 when, to the Act[1] for raising duties on imported linens, wrought silks, and brandy, there was added a clause inviting loans at not more than 8 per cent., to be repaid 'in course', that is, in strict sequence. The response[2] was a loan of about £350,000, in sums of £50 and upwards, an illustration not only of the large amount of money clamouring for investment, but of the financial support that would have been accorded to James II, had he chosen to rule in a parliamentary way. When it is added that the principle of appropriation of supplies was commonly applied, and that the Commons had obtained effective control over taxation, it will be seen that the financial administration of the later Stuarts, in spite of much malversation, marked a considerable advance. As well as this, in 1688 the country was able to bear increased taxation; for Gregory King had estimated[3] the annual income of that year at £41,000,000, and the annual increase of capital at about £2,000,000.

But in spite of this progress, it may be doubted whether a financial system responsible to a Stuart could have withstood the strain of a great war. An example was provided by the aftermath of the only military enterprise on the continent in which Charles II's government engaged—the expedition to Ostend in February 1678, designed as a public demonstration of 'good faith' in carrying out the recent Anglo-Dutch treaty, an expedition recruited from enthusiasts, many of whom, anxious to serve their 'patriot king', sold their estates in order to buy commissions, assuming in their guilelessness that at least

[1] 1 Jac. II, c. 5. [2] *Cal. Tr. Bks.* viii, pt. 4, 2176–81.

[3] In his 'State and Condition of England'.

they would receive their pay. For this purpose parliament, in 1679, granted a supply of £206,462 for disbanding. The orders registered on this Act, for loans, quartering, and clothing amounted to £230,980, of which £176,590 was paid off, leaving a deficit of £54,390. The men appear to have been paid, but not the officers. Six years later the commissioners for disbanding discovered that there was still due, for pay and clothing, the sum of £25,397, so the outstanding debt was £79,787. In July 1689, when the officers, clothiers, and inn-keepers petitioned the House of Commons for payment, it was represented that many of the petitioners, mostly officers and small traders, had been ruined.[1] This would seem inconceivable today, but it was not inconceivable in an age of debtors' prisons.

The committee of the House of Commons to which this petition was referred appears to have been sympathetic, and accepted the figures. But it could do little except suggest payment from a tax of 5 per cent. on bullion exports, or an extra duty on imported calicoes.[2] It is possible that payment may have been made from the latter source. This example has been cited not to suggest greater humanitarianism in 1690 than in 1679, still less to imply that, after 1690, creditors of the government were regularly or promptly paid; on the contrary, large pensions were paid promptly to favourites, male and female, new or superannuated; while sailors, soldiers, and small tradesmen had often to go without their money for years. The difference was that they got their money in the end, not from any increase of goodwill, nor even from any higher standard of integrity, but from a fundamental change in financial principle. The petitioners of 1689 suffered because the assessment of 1679, from which they were to have been paid, had not provided enough. So far as the Stuart system was concerned, that was the end of it. But it was not the end in the system as developed in William's reign, because, for the first time, a deficient fund might be supplemented from another,[3] and only by this approach to a consolidation of funds could the creditor of the state be sure of payment. And only thus would the investor be willing to lend his money to the state for long periods.

[1] *C.J.* x, 15 July 1689.

[2] Ibid. 15 May 1690.

[3] *Infra*, 413.

Opposed as we were to a much richer country, we were obliged, in our fiscal as in our commercial policy, to take a risk. English fiscal policy was a gamble, expensive but successful. In addition to greatly increased taxation, recourse was made to two devices, namely, linking revenue with public loans, and encouraging the potential lender by appealing to his desire for both security and a gamble. The first device, that of joining revenue with loans, was applied in practically every Money Bill of William's reign, but the results varied. With such well-established funds as Customs, Excise, and Land Tax, the Treasury could usually foresee, with some accuracy, the amount of the yield, and so could adjust the loan with confidence; though usually, even in these cases, the loan greatly exceeded the yield. In contrast, it was very different with some of the newer or more experimental taxes, such as that imposed in 1695 on births, deaths, and marriages. On this, the public lent £650,000; but, in its first year, the levy produced only about £54,000. The lenders were naturally alarmed, and in 1698 they petitioned the House.[1] Here was illustrated a defect in what was otherwise a virtue. Each of these public loans was tied to a definite fund, that to be raised by the revenue Act which invited the loan. The lender knew what security was offered, and he also knew that his loan would not be transferred to another source of revenue. So he would follow the fortune or fate of the fund on which his stake had been placed, having regard not only to the yield of the tax, but to the burden of debt placed upon it. As that fund was not an undifferentiated part of the national revenue, but something isolated, its deficiencies would not, at first, be made good from another and more prosperous source.

But this 'sectionalism', as it may be called, went even farther; for the same fund, if a large one, might be divided into a series of priorities, a higher rate of interest being paid in proportion to remoteness of redemption. Thus, in April 1695, the directors

[1] *C.J.* xii, 28 Apr. 1698. The committee of the House attributed this failure to the lack and inefficiency of the J.P.'s; to frequent removals; to absence of power to levy penalties on defaulters; to irregularities of the collectors, who were not obliged to give their accounts on oath; and, lastly, to absence of power to farm the duties. This last is à curious admission of the weakness of the financial administration. For the Act, see *Documents*, no. 117.

of the Bank of England refused to accept as security for an advance to the army a portion of the yield from Customs placed *after* a commitment of £700,000, but they helped in a critical situation by advancing money on their personal security.[1] In this way, not only the revenues, but the place assigned thereon as security for repayment caused the lender to the state to think in the modern terms of ordinary, preference, and debenture issues.

This borrowing on funds is accounted for mainly by the fact that a loan would come in much sooner than the total yield of the tax; and in all wars, ready money must be available at once. With high-interest charges and overestimates of yield, the inevitable result was the accumulation of debt on all the revenues, many of which had been granted for a limited number of years. On 1 December 1696 Montagu, the chancellor of the Exchequer, presented to the Commons what was probably the first Budget.[2] But it was not called a Budget, nor was it a review of the financial situation, for it ignored departmental debts and unfunded loans. It was styled simply: 'An account of tallies struck on particular funds, the payments made thereon, and the principal remaining due.' The tally,[3] or notched piece of wood, was still the device used by the Exchequer for accounting; and in this period the tally of loan was accompanied by an order of repayment from a specified fund. The discount on a tally, sometimes as much as 40 per cent., reflected Stock Exchange opinion, not so much whether the Exchequer would redeem its obligation, as when? According to Montagu's figures, nearly 13 millions had been borrowed on funds, of which about 10 millions remained to be repaid. The average yield of these funds for the years 1694–6 had been just over 1 million annually. The chancellor was thus debiting himself with the greater part of the national debt, and he seems to have implied that, if the war-time taxation were continued, he would pay off that debt in a reasonable number of years. His optimism was justified by the conclusion of peace within less than a year, but he

[1] *B.M. Lansdowne MS.*, 1215, 26 Mar. and 9 Apr. 1695.

[2] *C.J.* xi, 1 Dec. 1696.

[3] A contemporary account of tallies and Exchequer procedure will be found in *Add. MS.* 36107, f. 47 sqq. A good recent account is by sir Hilary Jenkinson, in *Archaeologia*, lxii.

could not have foreseen that another war would break out in 1702.

Accordingly, what we now call the national debt was then thought of, not as an aggregate, but as a series of deficiencies, of greatly varying amounts, in the funds—deficiencies which, it was thought, could eventually be made good by taxation. Acting on the lead given by Montagu, the House then passed one of the most important Acts of the century—an Act[1] for making good the deficiencies of several funds, and for enlarging the stock of the Bank of England. The Customs, which had been granted until 1699, and most of the temporary taxes were renewed until 1706; and these, together with the proceeds of additional rates on salt, were to constitute a general fund for making good the particular deficiencies, a sinking fund not to be used for any other purpose, until the whole debt had been cleared off. The contributions paid into this sinking fund were at first ludicrously small,[2] but nevertheless concrete expression had been given to a new conception of solidarity or consolidation in the national finances, so strikingly contrasted with the separatism and isolation of the old 'sectional' system. Thenceforth the investor knew that, in lending money on a specified tax, he had parliamentary guarantee for the security of his investment, based not only on the particular fund, but on the whole of the national revenue. This was one of the most notable financial achievements of seventeenth-century England. Its spirit was expressed by the king in one of his last messages to the House of Commons: 'Take care of the public credit, which cannot be preserved but by keeping sacred that maxim, that they shall never be losers who trust to a parliamentary security.'[3]

Such was one of the two main principles applied in Revolution finance, namely, the backing of public loans by allocating revenues for payment of interest thereon. The other device was a fairly well-planned appeal to the investing public by a combination of two things usually kept apart, namely, security and a gamble. Security is, of course, a relative term; and a government, even if more firmly established than that of William, can

[1] 8–9 Wm. III, c. 20.

[2] For an example, see *Cal. Tr. Bks.*, xiv. 157, 18 Oct. 1698, where £22,126 is distributed among funds having a total deficiency of about £5,000,000.

[3] *C.J.* xii, 2 Jan. 1702.

provide it only up to a point; it was provided in this period by the facts that the yield from most of the taxes could be relied on, and that after 1697 there was some consolidation of the funds. Tallies were usually at a great discount, but the interest on them was paid more regularly than the wages of soldiers, sailors, or dockyard hands; so the investor could feel some confidence; and, on the basis of that confidence, he could also engage in a speculation. For this purpose the chancellor of the Exchequer selected two old 'ventures', the tontine and the lottery; of which the first, as the winnings went to the last survivor, was very slow, while the second, as the result depended on the drawing of a ticket, was very fast; hence the two provided for a wide range of temperament. From the tontine, Montagu extracted the principle of 'survivorship', embodied in a scheme of tontine annuities, whereby subscribers to a loan of a million would have 10 per cent. until 1700, and thereafter a share in a fund, augmented as annuitants died off, until only seven were left; so that those who lived longest benefited most. The subscriptions, whether for one's own life, or for that of a nominee, were to be in units of £100; as an alternative, one could elect for a straightforward life annuity of 14 per cent. These were the two options offered by the Act of January 1693[1] imposing extra Excise duties for ninety-nine years, in order to raise a million. As it was our first long-term loan, it is sometimes regarded as the origin of the National Debt.

There was a deficiency of about £118,000. Of the subscribers, only a small number appear to have ventured on 'survivorship', of whom the last lived until 1783, when he was in receipt of a pension of over £1,000 a year,[2] presumably in return for an investment of £100 on his behalf. But, as so few people were prepared to wait for nearly a century, the great majority chose the 14 per cent. life annuities, the number of which was increased when the amount of the deficiency on the original Act was offered for subscription on the 14 per cent. life basis.[3] The scheme was amended by an Act of 1695[4] which invited annuitants to convert their life estates into estates for ninety-six years,

[1] 4 W. and M., c. 3.
[2] E. L. Hargreaves, *The National Debt*, 6.
[3] 5 W. and M., c. 5.
[4] 6–7 W. and M., c. 5.

on paying £63 in addition to each £100 already subscribed; later Acts[1] still further facilitated this conversion operation; and already, the annuities were declared by statute[2] to be tax-free. In this way the tontine element practically disappeared; the annuity was free from the heavy taxation which fell on rents, and one could provide, by accepting the conversion terms, not only for one's self, but for dependents. Also, here was that portion of our borrowings which would be repaid over a long period, in contrast with other loans which, it was thought, could be redeemed in a few years.

In this way, as the speculative element receded, the annuity became completely respectable; and the raising of money in this manner caused people to take interest in providing for themselves and others. For fire and shipping losses insurance was already available; but, just as the person lags a long way behind his property, so the principle of life insurance—to which the annuity schemes obviously pointed—came late. An approach to it, however, is seen in a scheme[3] (not a state scheme) for 'survivorship' started in 1699, which provided that any married man, 'qualified according to the articles of settlement', might subscribe for himself and wife, paying 5*s.* entry money and 4*s.* per annum, terms which do not suggest financial stability. The sum of £250 was payable on the death of husband or wife; so a tontine of husband and wife provided the link between an old gamble and the new life insurance. Still more, the trustees of this venture announced that, as soon as 1,000 married couples had joined, they would deposit a sum with the Bank of England as security for claims.[4] Thus one of the most important features of modern life insurance was anticipated; and English society made a step forward to a practice common only in very advanced civilizations, that of making financial provision for dependents after one's death. Hitherto that had been possible only for the owner of land.

It was very different with the other device used by Montagu—the lottery.[5] The Million Lottery of 1693–4,[6] based on salt

[1] e.g. 9 Wm. III, c. 24.

[2] 5 W. and M., c. 5.

[3] *The Postman*, 10–12 May 1699.

[4] Ibid., 6–8 Sept. 1699.

[5] For the lottery generally, see R. D. Richards, 'The Lottery in the History of English Government Finance', in *Economic Journal*, iii (1934), 57–76.

[6] 5 W. and M., c. 7.

duties and on an additional Excise granted for sixteen years, provided an annual fund of £140,000. £10 or units of £10 might be lent for a share in the fund. There were 100,000 numbered tickets, of which 2,500 were 'fortune tickets', one being worth £1,000 per annum and nine worth £500 per annum; for these, drawings were made as in a sweepstake. Most of this loan was contributed, possibly because there was a good rate of interest on the tickets. Lowering of this rate to about 4 per cent. may account for the failure of the Malt Lottery of 1697, to which only about £17,000 was subscribed,[1] a failure which, for the time being, discredited this method of raising money.

Another reason for this failure may have been that the state had too many private competitors; indeed, in this period, numerous enterprises were instituted for the purpose of dealing in government stocks, particularly annuities or lottery tickets. The most popular example was the Million Bank, which had for its capital a large number of annuities purchased from the Exchequer and from private persons. An annuitant could have his life rent of £14 converted into £83. 10*s*. 'Bank Stock', with the addition of £17 in cash; and for each £1 per annum on a lottery ticket, £7. 5*s*. would be paid for an eleven-years' interest, and £6. 5*s*. for a ten-years' interest.[2] In this way, investors in certain government securities could convert their holdings into cash, or into investments in a private bank. This Million Bank proved to be a sound institution.[3] More numerous were the lotteries established in imitation of the state example. Of these, some were for desirable, even national objects—as to provide funds for building Greenwich Hospital,[4] or for settling Huguenots[5]—others, more limited, were for setting up a workhouse, or for helping impoverished landlords;[6] but the great majority were speculations for the benefit of the promoters. In some cases, a ticket could be bought for a penny; and how great was the appeal of these privately organized lotteries can be

[1] *Cal. Tr. Bks. 1695–1702*, xi–xvii, Dr. Shaw's Introduction.

[2] *The Postman*, 1–4 June and 11–13 July 1700.

[3] It survived until 1796. See *Select Charters of Trading Companies* (Selden Society), cxvi.

[4] *The Postman*, 2–4 Jan. 1700.

[5] Ibid., 22–24 June 1699.

[6] *C.J.* xii, 14 Dec. 1699.

deduced from the fact that even prince George of Denmark ventured in one.[1] Their life appeared to be extinguished in 1699 when an Act[2] declared them illegal; but their continued existence is proved by an Act[3] of Anne's reign which again abolished the private gambles and (characteristically) provided for the raising of a large loan by a state lottery.

All this shows how deeply English life was affected by the parliamentary devices for raising money. Finance and investment were now threatening the old monopoly of land; indeed, concern was expressed in some quarters that landed proprietors, by investing large sums in life annuities, were withdrawing themselves from their estates.[4] Another expression of this movement was seen in the numerous flotations of joint-stock companies, which were encouraged by two things—fertility of invention,[5] and pressure of capital on investment.[6] As the war seriously interfered with foreign trade much capital was available; and, for its absorption, opportunity was provided by invitation to exploit new devices, or processes, while other incentives were the desire to produce at home what had formerly been imported from abroad. For the investor, one motive was escape from the heavy taxes falling on land. Consequently, joint-stock enterprise was applied to the production of armaments and powder; to smelting and water-supply undertakings; to the making of linen, paper, glass, and silk. The mining of coal, copper, lead, alum, tin, and antimony provided the business of other companies; a fishery company was revived, and there were joint-stocks for whaling and colonization. It has been estimated that by 1695 about 150 such bodies were in existence in England, having a total capital of about £4,000,000.[7] Thus the devices adopted by William's government not only enabled the country to survive a European war, but helped to inaugurate

1 *The Protestant Mercury*, 19–21 Oct. 1698.

2 10–11 Wm. III, c. 17. The Greenwich Hospital lottery was excepted.

3 9 Ann., c. 6.

4 For instance, this confession by a former landowner: 'I choose to keep my estate in money rather than in land, for I can make twice as much of it that way, considering what taxes are on land.' *H.M.C. Rep. V*, app. *MSS. of J.R.B. Pine Coffin*, 375.

5 *Supra*, 37–40.

6 For this, see K. G. Davies, 'Joint-stock Investment in the later Seventeenth Century', in *Econ. Hist. Rev.*, 2nd series, iv, no. 3.

7 W. R. Scott, op. cit. 1, ch. xvii.

those financial and trading institutions so characteristic of modern times.

Of these institutions the most important was the Bank of England. Its more remote origin may be found not in a fund of capital, but in a debt, the debt due to the goldsmiths and bankers, in consequence of the Stop of the Exchequer in 1672. By 1692 the principal outstanding was £1,340,000, with arrears of interest of about £700,000. Now the state had never repudiated this Stuart liability, for the steadily mounting load of debt continued to appear in official balance-sheets; but on the other hand no fund had been allocated for payment of capital or interest, so the chances of the creditors receiving anything appeared remote. Although one of the larger bankers, sir Robert Vyner, had been forced into bankruptcy, the debt was widely spread among their private creditors, and no one seemed interested until that fantastic and unfortunate Scot, William Paterson, appeared on the scene. It was known that he, with other financial projectors, had on foot some schemes, both for discharging the goldsmiths' debt and for raising a national loan, but their plans were not quite ready when they were examined by a committee of the House of Commons in January 1692.

There appear to have been two proposals from Paterson and his associates, but the connexion between them is not clear. One was that those who had a share in the goldsmiths' debt should forgo their claims to arrears of interest, and advance a sum equal to their outstanding principal, provided a perpetual yearly interest of 6 per cent. for the former and the newly-advanced principal was established by Act of Parliament. The projectors, who appear to have had shares in the goldsmiths' debt, were hopeful that they could induce the other creditors to accept these terms, but they had failed to bring in the goldsmiths themselves, who feared that, by acceptance of such a composition, they would prejudice their case, which was then pending in the Exchequer.[1] In this way, one debt was to be the father of another; the child, however, would represent 'fresh' money advanced directly to the state, while the creditors would

[1] *C.J.* x, 18 Jan. 1692. Cf. also the anonymous memorandum in *Lansdowne MS.* 1215, ff. 51 sqq., possibly the work of Paterson, where the scheme of a bank is further developed. For the legislative settlement of the bankers' claims in 1701 see *Documents*, no. 132.

be advantaged by receipt of perpetual interest on their share of the old debt, and on their new advance of an equal amount.

The other scheme was that parliament should assign a yearly rent of £65,000 for an advance of one million, £60,000 for interest, and £5,000 for payment to the trustees. This appears to have been designed as a national loan, administered by a body of trustees, who were to have authority to issue 'bills of property', for the guarantee of which an additional fund of £200,000 was to be subscribed. Here, in what was probably Paterson's scheme, we have the Bank of England in embryo, except that, when the Bank was later established, there was no separate fund for the guarantee of its notes. Curiously enough, it was this proposal for an issue of paper money to be made current which caused the committee to reject the scheme, though willingness was professed to consider any proposal for advancing a loan of a million on a perpetual fund, in the nature of a 'purchase', so that holdings therein would be assignable. Such a perpetual 'fund of credit', guaranteed by parliament appeared to offer a means for raising the large supply of capital so urgently needed by the state. In these suggestions it is possible to detect a certain change of mentality. On the one hand, the state would receive a large loan, with no clear obligations about its redemption; on the other hand, the lender was assured of a regular return on his capital, in which he could assign his interest to another in return for a cash payment. A committee of the Commons, stimulated by William Paterson, was thus formulating for English public finance the essential principles of modern investment.

The upshot was that, for the time, neither Paterson nor the goldsmiths' creditors had succeeded in persuading the government to raise money in this way. But these things appear to have roused the interest of Montagu, who was guided by shrewd judgement in his selection of those schemes of other men which he put into effect. He lost little time. Within a year he had launched his scheme for raising a million by the sale of life annuities,[1] the success of which encouraged him to go farther; and in April 1694 he succeeded in piloting through the Commons an ingenious Bill, which was intended both to raise a loan of £1,500,000 and to establish a national bank.

[1] *Supra*, 414–15.

The Bill was strenuously opposed in the Lords, the opposition being led by Halifax, Rochester, and Nottingham, who objected, not to the loan, but to the creation of a privileged corporation as incompatible with a constitutional monarchy. All the bishops, except the archbishop of Canterbury, were against it. Eventually the measure passed by 43 to 31, and received the royal assent on 25 April 1694. This Act,[1] known as the Tonnage Act, imposed certain duties for four years on incoming cargoes, together with additional duties on beer, ale, and vinegar, from the proceeds of which an annual fund of £100,000 was to be appropriated by the Exchequer for payment of interest, at just over 8 per cent. to those who advanced a sum of £1,200,000. The crown was authorized to incorporate the subscribers, and the corporation might terminate at any time after 1705 on a year's notice; but it was not to come into existence unless one-half of the £1,200,000 was subscribed by 1 August 1694. The new institution was empowered to borrow money beyond that amount on parliamentary security; it was forbidden to trade, but was authorized to deal in bullion and bills of exchange. As for the remaining £300,000 of the £1,500,000, that was to be raised by annuities, at the rate of 14 per cent. for one life, 12 per cent. for two, and 10 per cent. for three. The position was that the large sum required for the Bank might never be subscribed; on the other hand, Montagu could be sure of a moderate sum from the sale of annuities.

The mingling of such different things in one measure is characteristic, not only of the legislation of the period, but also of its urgent financial necessities. There was probably no thought that the institution envisaged by the Act would be permanent, and it seemed likely that the life annuities tacked on at the end would last longer than the Bank. But the success of the project was almost spectacular, for by 1 July the first half of the loan had been raised; by December £720,000 had been paid in cash, the subscribers including most of the Whig magnates of the city, such as the three Houblon brothers, sir Michael Godfrey, T. Papillon, and sir Gilbert Heathcote. The directors, who conducted their business first in Mercers' Hall, and later in Grocers' Hall, had advanced by the end of the year the whole of the £1,200,000 to the state, in spite of the fact that the

[1] 5 W. and M., c. 20. *Documents*, no. 116.

capital of the Bank was not yet fully paid up.[1] This was achieved by making the greater part of the loan in sealed bills, in exchange for tallies. The sealed bills, which at first bore interest, were taken by the Exchequer as cash, and were paid out to creditors, who, in turn, might cash them at the Bank, or leave them there as deposits, on which, from time to time, they could take 'running cash' notes.[2] As well as this, the Bank derived a modest revenue from discounting the bills and tallies of private persons, and acting as a pawnbroking establishment.[3]

As the Bank had parted with all its subscribed capital, its assets consisted of the £100,000 per annum promised by the state, and an issue of paper money, up to £1,200,000 in face value, for which the security consisted of an equivalent amount of tallies, mostly at a discount. The Treasury could not at first pay all of the £100,000 directly; for, in the half-yearly payment of July 1695, the Bank was promised the money from a loan to be made by one John Gee, on the credit of the Post Office revenues.[4] 'Interest on a loan comes from another loan', a good example of the risks incurred in this financial whirligig, in which the paper promise, chasing the elusive guinea, which it threatens to overwhelm, is restrained only by confidence that the guinea will eventually be caught by the paper, and knowledge that meanwhile the paper is earning a good rate of interest. Many contemporaries were amazed that, with its tenuous resources, the Bank remained solvent. They had good reason to wonder because, in the first two years of its history, the Bank circulated over £1¾ million worth of paper, and cashed about £1 million, so that for the remaining £¾ million it was dependent on its reputation and the forbearance of its creditors.[5] Still more, its manipulation of a 'fund of credit' conferred a mystic significance on that term, afterwards to prove so disastrous in the South Sea Bubble; indeed, of all the gambles in this reign of gamblers, the Bank of England was the most risky.

Although the financing of the army in Flanders continued to

[1] R. D. Richards, *The Early History of Banking in England*, 149.

[2] Sir J. Clapham, *The Bank of England*, i. 22 sqq.

[3] *Rules, Orders and By-laws for . . . the Bank of England* (1700).

[4] Sir J. Clapham, op. cit. i. 25–26.

[5] *Cal. Tr. Bks.* xi–xvii, Introduction, cxl.

be conducted mainly by private syndicates, such as that of Hearne and Evance, the Treasury transferred a part of this business to the Bank, which in March 1695 arranged to advance about £100,000 a month for three months at an agreed rate of exchange. But, owing to the increasingly bad state of the English coinage, the exchange went steadily against us, and Bank bills in Holland were protested.[1] So desperate was the position in the summer that the Bank had to borrow £200,000 in Holland, probably from the Bank of Amsterdam, and in May it was decided to set up a branch at Antwerp mainly for coining bullion, sent from England, into Flemish money. It was in this matter of helping to finance the army that, almost from its foundation, the Bank was performing a national service; but it was a hand-to-mouth business, with constant objections by king and Treasury regarding the high exchange rates, and protests by the Bank at the remoteness of the funds offered as security.[2] Only the public spirit of the directors prevented a breakdown.

The state of the English silver coin was at the root of these difficulties. For years our mint price had undervalued silver in relation to gold, with the result that it was profitable to export the former, and import the latter; from this imported gold, guineas were coined, which, in their turn were applied to the purchase of scrap silver, and so the trade was kept going. The coin was on a bimetallic basis, the silver being coined at the Mint for 5*s.* 2*d.* per ounce. But abroad it fetched at least 5*s.* 3½*d.* per ounce, so there was a regular exchange of silver for gold, conducted chiefly with Holland and the east, a traffic which had attracted the attention of the government as early as 1690, and accounts for the privy council's order that masters of the packet boats should search passengers' luggage for the precious metals.[3] This exported silver consisted mainly of clippings from the unmilled edges of old silver coins, many of them irregular in weight and shape; accordingly, in spite of the fact that it was petty treason to deface the coin of the realm, clipping and melting down were becoming almost a minor industry. It was estimated that between 1672 and 1696 about £2 million

[1] *Cal. Tr. Bks.* xi. 37.

[2] *Harleian MS.* 7421. Ranelagh's report of demands made by the Bank of England for its losses by remittances to the army in Flanders.

[3] *P.C. Reg.* 76, 18 July 1695.

had been lost to the state in this way,[1] and so the silver coinage suffered a depreciation of nearly 40 per cent. Already, the desperate state of the coin had been seen in the necessity of coining bullion into Flemish money, for payment of the troops in Flanders; and, when the market price of silver at home rose to more than 6*s*., and the guinea fetched 30*s*., it was clear that the English exchange abroad was seriously prejudiced, while at home there was the threat of inflation.

Early in 1695 the Commons adopted certain resolutions for the suppression of these evils; and a Bill of 1695,[2] imposing restrictions on the export of bullion, forbade bankers, not free of the Goldsmiths Company, to trade in it. The only result appears to have been that clipping increased, as the clippers saw that their time was short; so the clink of hammer and metal resounded more loudly than ever in the basements and garrets of Soho. Montagu resolved that there should be a recoinage, but he knew that the proposal would be strenuously contested by opponents of the Court.

The supporters of the Court, or Whigs, as most of them may be called, had usually some kind of majority in William's third parliament, which, under the speakership of Paul Foley, began its sessions in November 1695; and, in accordance with the Triennial Act of the preceding year, lasted until 1698. It was this parliament which surmounted the most difficult problems of the war, and saw the restoration of peace. In spite of strong opposition, the Commons, on 10 December 1695, accepted the recommendation of a committee that there should be a complete recoinage of the silver money, according to the established standard of the Mint, a policy which had been adopted after prolonged discussion between Montagu, Somers, Locke, and Lowndes, of whom only the last was in favour of lowering the intrinsic standard of the coin.[3] As there was great urgency, Montagu quickly obtained the consent of the House to his proposal that the cost of the recoinage should be borne by a tax on windows. His Bill,[4] hurried through both Houses, was

[1] This is the estimate of Hopton Haynes, in *Lansdowne MS*. 801, f. 71.

[2] 6–7 Wm. III, c. 17.

[3] For this, see C. R. Fay, 'Locke *versus* Lowndes', in *Camb. Hist. J*. iv, no. 3 (1933); also J. H. Craig, *Newton at the Mint*.

[4] 7–8 Wm. III, c. 1. Also 7–8 Wm. III. c. 18 (the Window Tax).

assented to by the king on 21 January 1696. This enacted that clipped money was to be accepted only in payment of taxes, and that only until 3 May. It also provided that, of the unclipped, hammered money (which was most likely to be tampered with, because it was unmilled), all the pieces having both rings and most of the letters were to be marked with a punch, after which, if they were clipped, they ceased to be legal tender. Such punched pieces, together with sixpences and gold coins, formed the greater part of the current cash of the kingdom during the next six months.

Meanwhile, with the help of Lowndes, secretary of the Treasury, the chancellor of the Exchequer was reorganizing the Mint, which began to issue the new, milled coins at an unprecedented rate, the clipped coins, as they came in, being melted down in the ten furnaces set up in the garden behind the Treasury. In June Montagu arranged for the erection of Mints in the chief provincial towns because it was there that the want of coin was most keenly felt.[1] For this purpose the cities of York, Exeter, Bristol, Chester, and Norwich were chosen, the coins made there being each stamped with the initial letter of the city's name; and by the end of the year these provincial Mints were producing in all about £20,000 worth per week, while the Mint on Tower Hill produced about £80,000 per week.[2] Inevitably there was much hoarding of the new coins; indeed some were not seen for more than a day, and therefore many observers assumed that the principles of Locke, as adopted by Montagu, had been discredited. It was not until 1699 that the state of English coinage could be described as no longer catastrophic, by which time paper money had become established in circulation, a fact of importance not only to the state, since it helped to abate some of its difficulties, but also to the public, since it added an element of security not to be found in a currency limited to coin. In 1700 this was made clear in one of many judgements of Holt that have had permanent influence on English law, for in that year he ruled that, if banknotes, exchequer bills, or lottery tickets were stolen or lost, then the owner could bring an action against the person into whose

[1] Lake, 'Historical Account of English Money', in *Lansdowne MS.* 850.

[2] Lake estimated that between 1691 and 1697 more than £8 million's worth of clipped money was brought to the various Mints.

hands they had come, for such notes or bills are clearly distinguishable, whereas coin is not.[1] As this provided some protection against the thief or the receiver, so the statutes,[2] at the same time, provided some protection against the forger; and accordingly the currency acquired a reasonable measure of stability and security, without which England would never have become a great trading state. It is one of the most significant things in the evolution of English civilization that measures, introduced as no more than emergency measures for the raising of money, were so devised and developed that they provided the foundations of national economy.

In this respect, the contrast provided by French finance is illuminating. In France the Customs, though not so uniform nor so well organized as in England, yielded about three times as much as ours in 1690, but they soon showed a steady decline. Fresh money was raised by capitation taxes, falling mainly on those least able to bear them—the *taillables*; much revenue was also obtained by the creation and sale of offices, so that a great 'black coat' hierarchy came into existence. Although the population of France was nearly four times that of England, the proportion, in respect of revenue, was about two to one, a fact which suggests a somewhat higher standard of living in the more sparsely populated country. France had no bank; indeed, it was said that Louis XIV would not tolerate one; nor, in view of his dislike of the *bourgeoisie*, would the French middle-classes have willingly lent to him; with the result that French economy remained dependent mainly on specie, and credit did not play an important part. But the contrast was more fundamental. In France, increasing need for money led to a certain hardening of the administrative system, notably in the greater power given to the *intendants*; and the royal prerogative was extended by the king's control in council over the financial edicts; in England, on the other hand, the Revolution had secured for parliament a permanent place in the constitution, and the exigencies of war ensured that the initiative lay with Westminster in every sphere of national effort, except foreign policy. For the subjects of Louis XIV, the war intensified the poverty

[1] W. Salkeld, *Report of Cases Adjudged in the Court of King's Bench* (1731), 283–4, *Ford* v. *Hopkins*, 12 Wm. III.

[2] *Supra*, 105–6, and *infra*, 432, 434.

and degradation of the poor; for Englishmen, it provided new opportunities for the middle-classes and the rich. Generally, as a distinguished French authority[1] has pointed out, the war of the league of Augsburg helped to make France more totalitarian, and England more liberal. The Revolution settlement was saved not only by the courage and self-sacrifice of the soldiers and sailors, but also by the ingenuity and boldness of men who were prepared to take a risk.

3. The Assassination Plot: the Crisis of 1696: the Treaty of Ryswick, 1696–7

Ever since the failure of the invasion plans of 1692, events in England had been eagerly followed by James and Louis, both of them well supplied with information distinguished for volume rather than for accuracy. Both monarchs were amazed that England continued to remain in the war against such a rich and powerful adversary. Obviously, a collapse or revolution must be imminent; and, as the years passed, all the evidence seemed to point in these directions. For example, there was the news of Scotland's indignation at the onslaught by the English House of Commons on her cherished scheme of a colonial company;[2] then there was the passing of the Trial of Treasons Act[3] (21 January 1696), which encouraged plotters to assume that the crown would thenceforth have more difficulty in obtaining a conviction; there was also the financial wizardry by which money seemed to be raised, not from resources, but from debts; and, already, late in 1695, the anarchy of the silver coinage appeared to augur the speedy downfall of the whole ramshackle edifice. So the Jacobite plotters, with the encouragement of St. Germains, had a new lease of life. Among them was sir George Barclay, an elderly Scot, who, having served under Dundee, and having acted as agent among the highland clans, arrived in England early in 1696 with a commission from James to raise troops for a rebellion, which was to be headed by sir John Fenwick, the most forthcoming of all who opposed William.

The impetuous Barclay anticipated the rising by engaging in a plot to assassinate the king, the plan being to seize him at a place near Turnham Green, as he was returning from Rich-

[1] M. Mousnier, in *Revue historique*, ccv (1931).

[2] *Supra*, 308, 310.

[3] *Supra*, 359.

mond. The date agreed on was 15 February. But news of the plan leaked out, so the conspirators were arrested, with the exception of Barclay, who escaped to France, and Fenwick, who remained in hiding, until his arrest a few months later. Another agent escaped the clutches of the government, the duke of Berwick, who was then in England in order to sound opinion regarding the prospects of an invasion, which was being planned by Louis and James, both of them convinced that the time for action had come, and that Englishmen themselves would give the lead.

This frustrated plot to assassinate the king had great influence on English opinion, and may have proved the turning-point in the reign. Rightly or wrongly, James was regarded as its instigator, a fact which caused, in some quarters, a certain cooling of enthusiasm for the exiled House, and even led to a revulsion in favour of William, for whom it evoked the first expression of loyalty in the reign. This, which was embodied in an Act[1] for the better security of His Majesty's person (passed on 27 April 1696), took the form of a declaration to the following effect:

> Whereas there has been a conspiracy . . . we declare that His Majesty is rightful and lawful king . . . and we engage to assist each other in the defence of His Majesty and his government.

The Act imposed the penalties of praemunire on all persons declaring that His Majesty was not rightful king, and required that the above Declaration or Association should be tendered to all office-holders, as well as to all members of parliament after the end of the existing parliament. It was also declared to be high treason for any English subject to come to England from France without leave. As the Association came to be a test of fidelity to the existing régime, it helped to make more clear-cut the distinction between Williamite and Jacobite, and to that extent more difficult for the latter to hamper the administration by serving in parliament or in office.

These events coincided with the last serious attempt to destroy the Revolution settlement and restore James, an attempt which failed because, though neither Louis nor James had changed, England had. After nearly seven years of war, the nation was now more conscious of the European implications of the

[1] 7–8 Wm. III, c. 27.

Revolution, and how the return of the exiled king would mean subordination to France. It was realized also that the overthrow of William would involve the repudiation of the millions of pounds that had been lent to the state; indeed, these investments probably constituted the strongest barrier to successful invasion, a factor which we today can hardly appreciate, since we take the financial integrity of the state for granted; whereas, by this point in William's reign, Englishmen were both surprised and gratified by the fact that the state was paying them substantial and regular interest on their loans. This entirely new development had occurred in little more than four years. Had the threatened invasion of 1692 succeeded, England might well have acquiesced in the restoration of the old dynasty; but even if the invasion of four years later had succeeded, it is by no means likely that the nation would have submitted, for its mood had greatly altered, and the political education of Englishmen had considerably advanced; factors which had no meaning whatever at Versailles or St. Germains, where it was assumed that military conquest is the final arbiter of human destiny. So, once more, two opposed conceptions of civilization were brought into conflict, and in the spring of 1696 the war was transferred from Flanders to the home front.

The best evidence of this change in national spirit is to be found, not in parliamentary debates, nor in official documents, but in something which was then entirely new, namely, a leading article in a popular newspaper. Now, the leading article, though not necessarily based on accurate information, usually purports to analyse a situation by enumerating the factors having a bearing thereon, and makes its appeal to an interested and intelligent public. Such a leading article appeared on 3 March 1696 in *The Flying Post*, a newspaper so well informed as to incur the censure of the House of Commons, and to cause a member to bring in a Bill for preventing the publication of news without licence.[1] Having referred to Louis's approval of the invasion plans, the writer then enumerated the circumstances which appeared to favour these plans, such as the coinage crisis, the resentment of Scotland, the small number of troops in England, and the fact that the Channel would be left bare owing to the need of providing escort for a large convoy

[1] *Cobbett*, v. 1164, 28 Jan. 1697.

coming from the Mediterranean. The duke of Berwick, according to this leader writer, had been sent to England in order to make preparations. The French fleet was to be commanded by Gabaret, Nesmond, and Jean Bart; the English plan was to station Berkeley's squadron off Dunkirk, while Shovell's was to patrol off Boulogne. Calais, in the words of this newspaper, was so crowded with masts that, from the sea, it looked like a wood in winter. Up to this point, the leading article was accurate; but some items, possibly apocryphal, were added. James, it was said, had arranged to accompany the expedition in person; and, in return for only £10,000, had pawned the crowns of England, France, and Scotland; moreover, as the enterprise was not unlike a crusade, the religious houses in Paris had invested heavily in its success; while the Jesuits, as their contribution, had supplied a large consignment of relics. So, in the spring of 1696, some of the increasingly large number of newspaper readers in England were supplied with a fairly reliable resumé of the external dangers confronting their country; in no other European state was such a reasoned exposition of a critical situation available for the public.

Willlam's government acted quickly. On 1 March the king in council, after calling in the Admiralty commissioners, ordered that bomb vessels and fireships should be fitted out, and that the great ships should be made ready at once.[1] At the same time frigates were sent to look into Brest and the Channel ports. A few days later Russell, then off Gravelines, ordered Shovell, with thirty-one ships, to patrol between Calais and Dunkirk in order to prevent any sortie by the French transports. Meanwhile Rooke, who had succeeded Russell in the Mediterranean command, had to be recalled, thereby releasing Tourville's squadron; with the consequent likelihood, anticipated by king and council, that the Toulon fleet, in conjunction with that of Chateau Renault in the Channel, would cover an invading force from either Brest or Calais. The French plan was that Chateau Renault should engage Rooke as he entered the Channel, while Nesmond and Jean Bart covered a landing of 16,000 men at a point near Dover.[2] In March it seemed that the fate

[1] *H.M.C. Rep., MSS. of duke of Buccleuch at Montagu House*, ii. 307, 1 Mar. 1696.

[2] C. de la Roncière, op. cit. vi. 214 sqq.

of the invasion depended on the race between Rooke and Tourville from the Mediterranean; but the French admiral's ships were foul, and experience had taught him caution, with the result that, perhaps not unwillingly, he was left a long way behind. So Rooke, who had managed to evade contact with Chateau Renault, joined Russell in the Downs early in April; but, even thus, the danger was not over, for the equipment of the English ships was poor, and their crews, weakened by scurvy and years of hard, unhealthy conditions, seemed unlikely to be fit for combat.[1] Fortunately for us, conditions on the French ships were just as bad.

Meanwhile James, having left St. Germains, took over supreme command. Having appointed the marquis d'Harcourt to conduct the military part of the operations, he proceeded to Boulogne, that seaside boarding-house of lost causes, having already received news from his son Berwick of the 'hopeful' conditions in England. From about the middle of March the king and Middleton spent what must have been a miserable time in the port, trying to persuade each other that what news came from across the Channel was in their favour. England, as the secretary reminded his royal master (who had had some experience of these things), was the home of rebellions, as witness that of Essex in Elizabeth's time, then that of Cromwell, beyond which point it was not thought tactful to proceed; moreover, in the present exhaustion of her finances, reasoned James's Protestant secretary, she would be likely to stage another rebellion. The situation was that the plotters in England were waiting for the invading army, while James and Middleton were waiting for news of the rising; and as no such news arrived, Middleton was obliged to write reassuring letters to Louis, who, after all, had paid the expenses, and had been assured of success. Then it was found at Boulogne that the larger transports would be able to leave harbour only at spring tides; and meanwhile the blockade kept up by Russell, Shovell, and Berkeley prevented any ships getting out.[2]

So the invasion scheme was quietly abandoned, the officers being the first to leave, followed by James, who returned to his

[1] *Rawl. MS.* A. 450, f. 33.

[2] Middleton's letters at this time will be found in *Carte MS.* 208, f. 277 sqq.

sombre and overcrowded retreat at St. Germains, after this, the last bid for recovery of his crown. One more threat had been warded off by the precautions of the Whig administration of 1696. But the cost had been heavy. The necessary withdrawal of Rooke's squadron ended for the time our Mediterranean policy, thus enabling the French to take Barcelona, and causing the duke of Savoy to end his vacillations by deserting the allies to France. Meanwhile events at home were leading to a financial crisis.

The coinage, the Assassination Plot, and the invasion scare all contributed to the mounting difficulties of the nation in the early months of 1696; they were intensified in the summer by a gigantic financial fiasco, that of the projected Land Bank. The Bank of England did not yet have a monopoly of lending money to the state; it had many enemies, notably the goldsmiths and the Tories generally; indeed, it seemed that it must be overturned by the first gale of wind. A strong point in the Tory argument against this Whig institution was that it served only the interests of the city's financial magnates, and did nothing for the landowner. Already a number of land banks had come into existence, which lent money on the security of land, and also advanced money for the purchase of land or property, in this respect fulfilling one of the functions of a modern building society. Generally, it was held that land, as the securest of all investments, was likely to provide the best guarantee of a bank, an argument strengthened by what was known of the very precarious assets with which the Bank of England had started business.

None of the land banks succeeded in acquiring parliamentary status except one—that promoted by Robert Harley, the rising parliamentarian; and Hugh Chamberlayne, popularly known as 'the man-midwife', who is known for his achievements in two unconnected spheres, finance and obstetrics. These two projectors proposed to the Commons a scheme similar to that which had preceded the foundation of the Bank of England, namely, the raising of a large public loan, to be advanced to the state, which in its turn would assign to the bank a yearly revenue from specified taxes. Their offer was attractive, for they undertook to raise £2½ million, or more than twice that raised by the earlier bank; and they proposed to do business by lending money on land and property. Montagu, who was in desperate need of such a large sum of ready money, in spite of his misgivings about the scheme, was obliged to obtain for it the same parliamentary sanction as had been accorded to the Whig financiers in 1694. As finally arranged, the promoters undertook to raise £2,564,000, all of which was to be lent to the state, in return for a yearly payment of £179,480, to be raised from a perpetual tax on salt, glass, earthenware, and tobacco pipes. The Land Bank would thus receive 7 per cent. on its capital, somewhat less than that charged by the financial syndicates; and, by the Act[1] authorizing the scheme, the promoters were given power to buy land, and to lend money on land and its produce.

The Bill received the royal assent on 27 April 1696. It contained a curious clause, probably added by Montagu, to the effect that, in order to further the prospects of raising such a large sum, the Exchequer was empowered to borrow from persons or corporations, on the credit of repayment by registered orders or indented bills, which were to bear interest at 7 per cent. It was declared to be felony to forge such bills, or Exchequer Bills, as they came to be called. But so dubious was the financial position, and so slender seemed the chances of such paper currency being widely accepted, that the Bill concluded with this provision and admission that, in case there should be a failure of cash coming into the Exchequer, then the purchasers of the bills, in lieu of repayment, might surrender their rights in return for a perpetual annuity of 7 per cent. In effect, therefore, the Land Bank Act authorized a loan which the chancellor of the Exchequer did not think would be raised; and, as an alternative, a scheme of bills which he did not think the Exchequer would be able to cash. Both surmises proved to be correct.

On the appointed day for the completion of the subscriptions, it was found that the total amounted to just over £7,000,[2] a ludicrous fraction of the sum invited. Various reasons have been suggested for this failure. The most obvious is that the great city merchants were unlikely to support a scheme intended not only to rival, but to ruin the Bank of England. Portland, after interviews with the Land Bank promoters, concluded that even the

[1] 7–8 Wm. III, c. 31.

[2] *C.J.* xi. 25 Nov. 1696.

professional, non-party syndicates had held aloof, lest the success of the scheme might enable the government to obtain advances at a lower rate than that which they charged;[1] and in a letter to the king of 21 July he referred to a sum of £20,000 which a Jewish syndicate had undertaken to send to Flanders 'on ordinary terms'. Increasing financial stringency may also account for the failure, a stringency best expressed in the letters of William himself. On 4 June he had written to Shrewsbury from Breda: 'in the name of God determine quickly to find some credit for the troops here';[2] six weeks later he wrote thus:[3]

> I know not where I am, since I see no resource which can prevent the army from mutiny or total desertion; for it is more impossible to find here than in England money sufficient for their subsistence; so that if you cannot devise expedients to send contributions, or procure credit, all is lost, and I must go to the Indies.

From a man like William, these words are eloquent. Here was the crisis of the war: it was financial.

As he had not got the promised loan, Montagu resorted to the second expedient—the issue of Exchequer Bills. As he had conjectured, these did not at first prove a success. In spite of the interest on them, they were soon at a discount, because of doubts whether the Exchequer could redeem them; indeed, they were accepted at par only when paid in for taxes. So the chancellor had to force them into circulation by a very expensive method. This was by recourse to a group of capitalists who, as trustees, subscribed a fund for the encashment of the bills, the high interest on this fund being guaranteed by a Land Tax. So a tax was assigned, in part, to pay 10 per cent. interest to a body of capitalists who undertook to redeem government paper which, in its turn, bore interest. For the first £2 million of Exchequer Bills, the cost[4] of interest and management amounted to over 20 per cent. But although at such a great cost, the Bills were eventually a success; and, like the Bank of England, they became a permanent element in our financial system.

By the autumn the situation was slightly easier, and in

[1] Portland's letters to the king on this subject will be found in *Cal. S.P. Dom. 1696*, 298 sqq.

[2] *Shrewsbury Correspondence*, ed. W. Coxe, 119.

[3] Ibid. 129, 20–30 July.

[4] *Cal. Tr. Bks.* xi–xvii, Introduction, cxlix.

October Montagu's schemes were endorsed by the Commons in their more generous resolutions to provide supplies for the war. Even William so far committed himself as to express to Heinsius the opinion[1] that the affairs of England 'might yet be put right'. By the early summer of 1697, when the new coinage was coming into circulation, the greater part of the floating debt was being discharged by Exchequer Bills, which also helped to pay the interest on loans; and it was then that Montagu decided to transfer some of the weight oppressing the funds to the institution best able to bear it, namely, the Bank of England. Accordingly, the Act[2] passed in April 1697 incorporated the governor and directors of the Bank as a body politic, with power to purchase and sell land, the corporation to be dissolved at any time after 1710 on repayment by the state of its borrowings therefrom. During its continuance no other bank was to be recognized by parliament, and it was declared that the forging of its notes was felony. It was this Act which provided for the supplementing of deficient funds.[3] But of more immediate importance was the clause in terms of which bank stock was enlarged by the grafting thereon of additional capital (actually it proved to be just over a million), which might be subscribed, as to four-fifths, in tallies, to be accepted by the Bank at their face value. As the tallies were standing at a great discount, the state was thus transferring to the Bank, at a par valuation, a load of securities, the ultimate redemption of which might have to be postponed to a remote date. Here, within the first three years of its existence, the Bank was playing a part of national importance. Today, it is customary to minimize this early importance, on the ground that the Bank was only one of the agencies resorted to by the government, and that it was not always the most efficient of these agencies. But financial confidence often arises as much from potential as from actual achievement. Thus early, the Bank had become an institution; its credit was applied to support government credit; the burden of Westminster was shared by London. In this way the Bank first embodied that vast, imponderable power which, today, we describe as 'the city'.

[1] Quoted in Sirtema de Grovestins, *Guillaume III et Louis XIV*, vi. 579, 20–30 Oct. 1696.

[2] 8–9 Wm. III, c. 19.

[3] *Supra*, 413.

But the immediate result for the Bank was a steep, though temporary, decline in the price of its stock, which, by delayed action, registered the strain from which the nation was emerging. For the first time in English history it is possible to express in commercial figures and stock-exchange quotations the severity of a national crisis. Early in 1696 Bank stock (then partly paid) was at 148; at the end of the year it had fallen to 93; in the early summer of 1697, with its load of engrafted tallies, it dropped to 51, its lowest point.[1] From that, there was a steady rise: 60–72 in July 1697,[2] until in June 1700 it stood at 130.[3] There were similar movements in the shares of joint-stock companies. Other figures tell the same tale. Thus, the exchange for the pound at Amsterdam in 1689 was 35 Flemish shillings, a discount of just over 5 per cent.; in August 1695 the discount was 37 per cent.[4] Total imports and exports in 1688 had amounted to more than £10 million; in 1696–7 they had dropped to about £7 million.[5] In 1688 it had cost about £5 to import a ton of sugar from the West Indies; in 1696, £25—the peak price.[6] Captures and sinkings of English merchant ships by French privateers were mounting, not to hundreds, but to thousands, a rate of wastage which brought the prospect of national collapse within measurable distance. Before the war ended, financial stringency was acute, but this helped to limit the inflation caused by bad coinage and unprecedented government borrowing. These things, and a debt on the funds of more than 14 millions, were the monetary price for securing the Revolution settlement.

The permanence of that settlement was further ensured by the removal of the most assiduous of the Jacobite plotters, sir John Fenwick, member of an old Northumberland family, the most consistent enemy of William. His offensive bearing in Hyde Park to queen Mary may account for the fact that William returned his dislike. Fenwick was one of those plotters who took advantage of the lenience shown by the government; for, in the intervals of scheming, he was engaged in Jacobite brawls; indeed, he was a fair representative of those who helped to

[1] W. R. Scott, op. cit. i. 350.
[2] *The Post Boy*, 29–31 July 1697.
[3] *The Post Man*, 25–27 Jan. 1700.
[4] W. R. Scott, op. cit. i. 347.
[5] Ibid. i. 328.
[6] Figures supplied by Mr. K. G. Davies.

discredit the Stuart cause by violence and bluster. He had been appointed by James to command the rising in England early in 1696 which was to coincide with invasion from France; but, the assassination plot led by sir George Barclay having failed, Fenwick was obliged to go into hiding.

Before his arrest in June 1696 he had tried to induce the two informers likely to swear against him, namely, Goodman and Porter, to leave the country. With Goodman he succeeded; the other accepted his money, and afterwards gave evidence against him. After he had been lodged in Newgate, a true Bill was found against him; but he then offered, as a condition of pardon, to give a full account of the Jacobite conspiracies. His confession, so far from revealing such details, consisted of serious allegations against Shrewsbury, Godolphin, Russell, and Marlborough, who were named as the chief friends of James in England; but, after examination by the House of Commons, this confession was voted false and scandalous. Although he was in prison and the subject of indictment, the two Houses, by narrow majorities, resolved to bring in a Bill of Attainder against him, and the debates in the Commons on this measure were among the most prolonged and acrimonious of the whole reign. The reason for this is that, while most of the Whigs were against him as a dangerous Jacobite, many of the Tories were said to be anxious for his death, because they might be compromised by his disclosures. Moreover, the method adopted for his removal was unusual and even suspicious, since a Bill of Attainder was the method adopted for disposing of great and dangerous persons; and, though Fenwick might be dangerous, he was not great. Were those who voted against him seeking to remove an enemy or an accomplice? The truth will probably never be known. Late in November the Bill passed the Commons; and, after a stormy passage in the Lords, it received the royal assent on 11 January 1697. On 28 January he was beheaded on Tower Hill. Thus, one of the most active of the menaces to the Revolution settlement was at last removed.

In the year 1697, therefore, the situation was one of stalemate in the campaigns; of financial exhaustion among the combatants, and of willingness in England to accept the new order of things. As in all his great wars, Louis XIV was becoming increasingly anxious for peace. Even with the pope he was now more conciliatory, for he gave up Avignon; and with another opponent, the duke of Savoy, he scored a success. Victor Amadeus by the year 1695 was neutral in all but name; and in the following year he was detached by the treaty of Turin, whereby he received Nice and Pignerol from France, together with the promise of a marriage alliance. The year of this separate peace was a year of renewed efforts to obtain a general settlement, at first conducted secretly in Holland by a French agent, named Caillières; and early in 1697 the allies, with the exception of the king of Spain, accepted the mediation of the king of Sweden. When Louis expressed willingness to surrender Strasburg and to recognize William, it seemed at last that negotiations might be successful. But the emperor, his hopes again raised by the latest bulletins about the king of Spain's health, was anxious that the confederation should not be dissolved before the death of that monarch, for the good reason that the two principal allies, Britain and Holland, had undertaken, as the price of meagre imperial help, to support by arms his claim to the whole inheritance. So he impeded the negotiations, and gave up his opposition only when it was made clear by the allies that they would not be diverted from their purpose by any attempt to settle the question of the Spanish Succession.

At last, early in May 1697, the peace congress opened its sessions in the castle of Ryswick, near The Hague. The States General were represented by Heinsius and Dykveld; Great Britain by the earl of Pembroke, lord Villiers, and the veteran diplomatist sir Joseph Williamson, the baron Lillieroot acting as mediator on behalf of the king of Sweden. For weeks the plenipotentiaries engaged in sterile and pedantic controversy, such as was almost to be expected of a seventeenth-century congress; but eventually William intervened. Passing over the heads of the congress he sent Portland to engage in private discussion with Boufflers, then at his camp near Brussels. William's demands were mainly these three: that Louis would cease to harbour James in his dominions; that he would not demand any amnesty for James's agents and supporters, and that he would allow French Protestants to settle in his principality of Orange. On the first point, Louis refused to abandon James, but undertook not to assist him openly; to the second point he agreed; to the third he gave a definite refusal, on the ground that a Protestant community, settled in an *enclave* of French territory, would be a source of sedition and rebellion. By 10 July some kind of agreement had been reached on the first two questions, on the general principle that Louis would not assist William's enemies; but the third stipulation had to be surrendered.

Nevertheless, a stage of conciliation had been reached between England and France; and when, in August, Louis offered to remit the heavy duties on imports from Holland, the way was opened for the conclusion of peace. The commercial concessions to the Dutch were afterwards embodied in a separate treaty; and on 10–20 September the agreements of France with the States General, England, and Spain were signed. The emperor still held out, hoping to secure a renunciation by Louis of his claim to the Spanish Succession, even at the expense of a Hapsburg-Bourbon marriage, but the allies resolutely refused to complicate the settlement by these family matters; moreover, even had they embodied in the treaty a satisfactory solution of the Succession question, how long would that have been observed by Louis? The same question-mark applies to the treaty of Ryswick itself, a fact of which William may have been conscious. On 20 October Leopold gave way, and so both the war and the league of Augsburg came to an end.

The preamble to the treaty[1] between Louis and William began with a great concession to the latter, who was styled king of Great Britain *par la grâce de Dieu*. After the usual assurances of perpetual peace and friendship, Louis undertook, by article IV, not to molest the king of Great Britain in his possessions, and gave *sa parole royale* not to aid, directly or indirectly, the enemies of William, nor to give any countenance to cabals or revolts in England, nor to assist anyone, without exception or reserve, who might design to trouble William in the possession of his kingdoms. James[2] was not named, but he was clearly implied; indeed, this clause was as definite and inclusive as language could make it. The treaty then provided that trade

[1] For text and commentary, see H. Vast, op. cit. 11.

[2] According to the *Life of James II* (ed. J. S. Clarke), ii. 574, William offered to grant £50,000 a year to Mary of Modena from his Civil List, and to bring up the prince of Wales as his (Protestant) successor, but this proposal was rejected by James.

and navigation between the two countries were to be restored to their former footing; conquests made by either power were to be returned to the other within six months. France retained Strasburg, which she had appropriated in 1681. Commissioners, representing both sides, were to examine the disputed territories of Hudson's Bay; all letters of marque and reprisal were to be cancelled. The territory of Orange was to be restored to its state at the time of the treaty of Nimeguen, a clause which, in effect, meant that the entry of French subjects into that province would be controlled by the king of France. A similar clause (VI) in the treaty with the emperor, ensured that, in those places restored by France, the supremacy of the Roman Catholics, established by conquest, should be retained, to the prejudice of those Protestant churches which had formerly been tolerated. Had he been assured of support from England and Holland, William would have held out against this surrender, which expressly subjected Protestant communities to intolerance and persecution.

Although it proved to be no more than a truce, the treaty of Ryswick was the first serious check to the aggressions of Louis XIV. If only on paper, it recognized William as king of Great Britain, and to that extent it was an admission of the failure of James and the success of the English Revolution. But the French king made it clear that, in view of his war-time triumphs, he was consenting to the treaty, not because obliged to, but because only thus could he show his genuine desire for peace. Thus the raging lion of September 1688 was now emitting lamb-like bleats, accepted by many as proof of a new order of things in the animal world. There then followed a few years of uneasy peace, to be broken when the greatest prize of all—the Spanish Succession—fell into Louis's grasp, the fulfilment, not of long-drawn-out diplomacy, but of a long-awaited death.

XV

THE PARTITION TREATIES, 1698–1700

'I ESTEEM it one of the greatest advantages of the Peace that I shall now have leisure to rectify such corruptions and abuses as may have crept into the administration . . . and to discourage profaneness and debauchery.' These were the concluding words of the king's address to both Houses at the opening of the third session of his third parliament on 3 December 1697. William, concerned about the low standard of public integrity, regarded with sympathy those attempts to effect a reformation in morals and manners which were arousing such interest in the later years of his reign;[1] had there been any reasonable prospect that the menace from France was ended, the king might well have tried to carry out his programme for peace. In the earlier part of his speech, he had referred to the debts with which the navy and army were encumbered, and complained that he was without a civil list. He therefore recommended, as a measure necessary for the security of the country, the maintenance of adequate forces by land and sea, possibly assuming that his audience was convinced, as he was, of the precarious character of the peace.

He was soon disillusioned. His subjects, as they had less experience of Louis, assumed that a peace treaty with a dictator ended a war. The Commons concerned themselves with the estimates, which showed that over £2 million was due to the land forces, £2½ million to the navy, including over £1,800,000 for seamen's wages; £300,000 transport debt incurred in reducing Ireland, with £90,000 still owing to the officers and men who had served there. These sums, with about £200,000 due for ordnance and £425,000 arrears of subsidies due to our German allies and Denmark, made a total of about £5½ million, all of it a personal obligation, to be paid in cash. Accordingly, on considering the king's speech (11 December) the first resolution of the Commons, proposed by Harley, was that all land

[1] *Infra*, 530–2.

forces raised since 29 September 1680 should be paid off and disbanded. The effect of this would be to reduce the army in England to about 8,000 men, with garrisons in Scotland and Ireland, in place of the 30,000 which William regarded as the absolute minimum. To make their demand more palatable, the Commons recommended the payment of a gratuity to all disbanded officers and men, and that a Bill should be brought in to enable them to exercise their trades. It was proposed also that legislation should be introduced for making the militia more useful. On 21 December a civil list of £700,000 for life was granted to the king, the first step in distinguishing between that part of the royal revenue which was used for defence or war, and that part used for civil government and upkeep of the royal estate. But meanwhile, in the opinion of a majority of the Commons, the necessity for a standing army had come to an end, and so no Mutiny Act was introduced this session.

Even more, William's Whig ministers did not have the support of the Commons; and one of them, Shrewsbury, had suffered some discredit from Fenwick's revelations. His sensitiveness caused him to withdraw from political activity, though he retained his secretaryship for the south until December 1698, and in October 1699 he accepted office as lord chamberlain, which he held for only a few months. He had been preceded in that office by Sunderland, appointed in April 1697. William may have hoped that this former minister of James, now brought out of his seclusion, would co-operate with the Whig ministers, helped by Shrewsbury as mediator. But for Sunderland there could be effective co-operation only with dupes or knaves; so the scheme failed; and, however unwillingly, the king had to acquiesce in a system which provided him with a ministry, just beginning to think in terms of parliamentary responsibility, rather than with a 'manager', the paymaster of agents such as Trevor, Guy, and Duncombe. So a public administration, however ineffective, had to take the place of secret manipulation, however efficient. Thus even William failed to obstruct one of the most characteristic developments in our constitution; even more significant, a House of Commons, not distinguished for idealism, nor even probity, showed such open objection to Sunderland, that in December 1697 he resigned.

These things show how difficult was the position of the Junto in 1697–8. Even had the Whig ministers shared the king's views on disbandment, they could not have carried these views against a hostile House of Commons, where they were now represented only by Montagu; for Somers as lord chancellor, Wharton as marquis of Wharton, and Russell as earl of Orford all now sat in the Lords. In this absence of direction, the Commons, left to themselves, selected from the King's Speech of 3 December 1697 only those items to which they were well disposed. So they refused to adopt the view that a large land force was still necessary, but they willingly followed the royal lead in regard to profaneness and debauchery, for the punishment of which they brought in a Bill, and invited the king to issue a proclamation for the suppression of these evils.[1] More ominous, when they introduced a Bill for making void all grants of forfeitures by Charles II and James II, attention was directed, in the debates, to William's lavish bestowal of forfeited estates in Ireland. Montagu himself was severely criticized on the ground that he had recently accepted such an estate, but so strong was his prestige in the Commons, that an intended vote of censure was turned into a vote of confidence.[2] The chancellor of the Exchequer was the ablest parliamentary manager of his time.

He soon followed this with another success. Ever since the Revolution the position of the East India Company had been precarious. Bodies of interlopers and city merchants had for long been scheming to usurp its place in the profitable East India trade, and by 1698 it was clear that the 'old' Company would have to pay heavily for the retention of its monopoly. Early in that year it came forward with an offer of £700,000 at 5 per cent., but a committee of investigation reported adversely on its finances, alleging that it was in debt, and that its dividends had been paid without any regard to valuation of assets or profits.[3] Soon there was another bid in the loan market. A body of London merchants, headed by one Samuel Shepherd and encouraged by Montagu, came forward with a proposal to lend £2 million at 8 per cent., in return for exclusive trade

[1] *Cobbett*, v. 1172, 9 Feb. 1698.

[2] 27 Feb. 1698. Sunderland had already used Duncombe to attack Montagu on the allegation that the latter had been guilty of irregularity in his handling of Exchequer Bills. The inquiry showed that Duncombe, not Montagu, was the culprit.

[3] *C.J.* xii, 14 June 1698.

to the East Indies. Opinion in the House was almost evenly divided, some Whigs joining with the Tories in opposition to the scheme; but a speech[1] delivered by the chancellor of the Exchequer late in May seems to have turned the scale, for a Bill promoting a new company passed through both Houses, receiving the royal assent at the end of the session on 5 July 1698. It had met with some opposition in the Lords[2] mainly because it was tacked to a Bill of Supply.

The Act[3] provided for an additional duty on imported salt, to be managed by the Excise commissioners, and a tax on exported pilchards, herring, and salmon. From these, and from the duties already imposed on stamped paper,[4] a fund of £160,000 per annum was to be reserved for the payment of annuities at 8 per cent. to subscribers to a loan of £2 million. Each subscriber might trade on his own account to the amount of his subscription; those who desired might apply to be incorporated in a general society. The 'old' East India Company was given until 29 September 1701 to wind up its affairs; later, in 1708, its members amalgamated with the new company. The subscription of £2 million was speedily completed, the greater part of the proceeds being applied to the payment of the land and sea forces. This was the last important financial measure of the reign, and the last parliamentary achievement of Montagu. But, for some years, there was bitter antagonism between the 'old' and the 'new' companies, which provided one more element in party distinction.

The third of William's parliaments came to an end on 5 July 1698, in accordance with the Triennial Act. Except for its refusal to maintain a large standing army in time of peace, and its threat to investigate William's grants of forfeitures in Ireland, this parliament had given great support to the king and his ministers. It had launched important financial measures for enabling the country to continue at war; it had removed the most prominent of Jacobite plotters; it had cleared up one of the ambiguities which confused royal with national revenue. One might even claim that it had ensured the permanence of the Revolution settlement. For the first time, some kind of

[1] Its substance is given in the Dutch Reports, vol. SS, f. 267.
[2] See the Protest, *L.J.* xvi, 26 June 1698.
[3] 9 Wm. III, c. 44. [4] 9 Wm. III, c. 25.

harmony had prevailed between king, ministers, and parliament, working together not because of any constitutional convention, but because the threat to stability and even existence impelled such unity. The conclusion of peace brought this state of things to an end.

Thereafter, until the end of the reign, the parliamentary situation recalled that of the later years of Charles II; for, just as the dissolution of the Cavalier parliament early in 1679 had been followed by a succession of three short-lived Whig parliaments, all hostile to the prerogative, so William's parliament of 1695–8 was succeeded by three parliaments, in each of which there was a strong Tory element, critical of William and his Whig ministers, in spite of the fact that these ministers had mostly left office by 1699. Thus, in these years between two wars, there came into prominence a 'new' Tory party, though its members preferred almost any other name; for, of these two terms of abuse, 'Tory' and 'Whig', the first retained its discredit longer than the second. This new party, which included 'old' Whigs who had gone into opposition and Jacobites who had forsaken the cause of James, derived strength from its criticism of the war, in which so much had been sacrificed, and in which, it appeared, so little had been gained; moreover, as a composite party, which included Harley and Clarges, it had learned much from the tactics of previous oppositions, and had even assimilated certain doctrines hitherto regarded as characteristically Whig. Hence, in the middle years of the reign, although the simplest expression of party distinction was that 'while the Tories sacrificed our liberties, the Whigs sacrificed our purses', the 'new' Tories were now professing a zeal for those liberties which hitherto had been regarded as Whig monopolies. Of this development the clearest illustration was provided in the law courts where, by the year 1702, a Tory could have an action for slander if referred to as a Jacobite.[1] So the 'new' Tories steadily gained at the expense of the 'old' Whigs. In spite of their borrowings, they had one definite principle of their own —that there must be an avoidance of large-scale military commitments, and that in continental entanglements we must depend mainly on the navy.

It was in these continental entanglements that William was

[1] *English Reports*, xci (King's Bench), 912 *How* v. *Prinn*, 1702.

busily preparing trouble for himself and the Whigs. The peace of Ryswick had been made possible only by avoiding altogether what everyone knew to be the most important question of European politics, namely, the Spanish Succession. The world empire of Charles V had been divided before his death into the Spanish and Austrian branches; and by a policy of in-breeding, maintained for more than a century, it was hoped that, on the failure of one line the other would succeed. This sacrifice of physiology to diplomacy resulted in the creation of Charles II of Spain, whose life was a living death. Married first to a French and later to an Austrian princess, neither prayer, drugs, nor incantations had enabled him to procure an heir; and for over a generation his decease had been the most eagerly expected event in the chancelleries of Europe. Unfortunately, the Habsburgs had not succeeded in limiting this matter to their family circle, for another set of cousins had been introduced by the marriage of Louis XIII with Anne of Austria, elder daughter of Philip III, and of Louis XIV with Maria Theresa, elder daughter of Philip IV. The imperial marriages had conformed to the same pattern, for Ferdinand III had married Maria, younger daughter of Philip III, while his son Leopold had married, as his first wife Margaret, younger daughter of Philip IV. The weakness in the French claim was that, on their marriages, Anne of Austria and Maria Theresa had successively renounced all claim to the Spanish Succession; but, in the case of the latter marriage, the condition of the renunciation, namely, payment of a large dowry, had never been fulfilled. Accordingly, the French king claimed on behalf of the Dauphin. On the imperial side, there were two lines on behalf of which a claim could be made. By his first wife, Leopold had a daughter, Maria Antonia, married to the elector of Bavaria, whose son, the electoral prince, born in 1692, might be regarded as the heir of both Philip III and Philip IV. But meanwhile, Leopold had married, as his third wife, a princess of Neuburg, by whom he had two sons, Joseph and Charles; and as Joseph was designed for the empire, Charles was selected, by his father, for the Spanish inheritance. For this reason, Leopold induced his daughter to renounce her rights in favour of her half-brother. This she did; and just before the birth of her child she renewed this renunciation; and so an obstacle to the imperial plans appeared to be removed. But as the Spanish Court refused to recognize either of these gratuitous renunciations, it appeared that the infant electoral prince had the best claim.

Diplomatic relations between England and France were resumed early in 1698, Portland being sent to Paris and count Tallard to London as ambassadors of their respective Courts. At Versailles, Portland had to submit to the humiliation of witnessing the ostentatious respect in which James and his entourage were still held; he had also to complain of the long delays in restoring the places which Louis had promised to return. From the start, William's ambassador had to report his conviction[1] that the peace would not be a long one. News as disquieting was received by the king from Heinsius;[2] and so, as early as the spring of 1698, there was reason to fear that Louis would not keep faith. On his side, Louis explained to Tallard the ambiguous circumstances in which England now found herself.[3] Like Holland, she was financially exhausted, a situation which had obliged her to make peace; she no longer wanted war, as she had experienced the cost of it. He (Louis) had shown his zeal for peace by his concessions made at Ryswick; he might easily have continued the war with advantage. Also England dreaded the authority of her king, who had reduced his secretaries to the status of mere clerks, and held councils merely for form's sake. William, according to Louis, gave his confidence only to Portland and Albemarle; he had to abandon Sunderland because parliament would not tolerate him; hence a growing cleavage between king and nation. War makes kings masters; 'it is only by means of war that arbitrary power can be established'. So Louis was assuming, from his intimate knowledge of our affairs, that England would be unwilling to go to war again, either over the Spanish Succession, or over anything else, an unwillingness which appeared to be proved by the disbandment of the land forces. He was still intent on securing the whole succession, and his agent in Madrid, d'Harcourt, was busily engaged in directing Spanish opinion to that object.

Of the three claimants, the newest arrival, the electoral prince

[1] *Cal. S.P. Dom. 1698*, 75, Portland to William, 27 Jan.–6 Feb. 1698.

[2] P. Grimblot, *Letters of William III and Louis XIV*, i. 218.

[3] Ibid. 243 sqq., 20 Feb.–2 Mar. 1698.

of Bavaria, had this advantage, that to him, as a Wittelsbach, the objections to the Bourbon and Habsburg candidates did not apply; and so, as ruler of the Low Countries he would be less embarrassing to England and Holland than a prince of either of the great dynasties. As Spain had refused to recognize the renunciation made by his mother, the claim of this six-year-old child seemed the best of all; and accordingly, it appeared that a solution might be reached by conferring the greater part of the inheritance on him, to be held if necessary in trust by his father, while dividing the remainder between the French and Austrian claimants. William, now deprived of a large army, was obliged to seek peace by compromise; and it was in the hope of reaching a settlement that, in the spring of 1698, he conducted negotiations through Portland and Tallard. He even suggested that, in the division of the spoils, England should be given bases in the Mediterranean, such as Ceuta, or Oran, or Port Mahon, with possibly a port in the West Indies,[1] the Spanish possessions in Italy to go to the emperor, a scheme which would satisfy English maritime ambitions and restrict French influence in the Mediterranean. In making these suggestions (through Portland) William appears to have had qualms about dividing up possessions before the owner was dead, particularly as one of the chief claimants, the emperor, was not even consulted. But Louis brushed aside these scruples by recalling how, as far back as 1668, the emperor himself had made such a partition with him; and as this was now a relic of some antiquarian interest, the French king offered to provide Portland with a copy of the treaty. Thus Louis lived so long that, within his own lifetime, his earlier commitments became matters of importance only to historical researchers. But indifference to past obligations did not impede his zeal for present advantage; and so, when Portland broached his master's suggestions about Mediterranean bases, Louis suddenly experienced qualms, protesting that England had no right to any concessions at all.[2] These details are not in themselves of importance, but they are important as indications of the foundations on which William was attempting to build a lasting settlement.

[1] William to Portland, 28 Mar.–7 Apr. 1698, in *Correspondentie van Willem III en van Hans Willem Bentinck*, ed. N. Japikse, pt. i, vol. i, 278.

[2] Ibid. 306, Portland to William, 7/17 May 1698.

The proposal that England should have a share in the spoils was complicated by this question: to whom should be assigned the major portion, that is Spain and the Indies? To the Dauphin or to the electoral prince? If to the Dauphin, then England might hope for some compensation in the Mediterranean and the West Indies, if only as a counterbalance to the French influence that would be established in these areas; if to the electoral prince, then there would be no question of compensation or balance, since the House of Bavaria was not one of England's rivals. Such at least appears to have been the reasoning.[1] In the interests of peace, William chose the latter plan which, though it involved sacrifice, diverted the lion's share away from the Bourbons. But meanwhile, the king was concerned about one thing: would Louis keep his word? Heinsius was convinced that he would not.[2] So there was a certain element of unreality about these prolonged negotiations, which ultimately were to have no result, except that they focused English opinion on this question: what overseas possessions and concessions were most essential for the development of her commercial interests and her colonial empire—a question to which an answer was first given in the treaty of Utrecht. Indeed, it is at this point that one can clearly distinguish two contrasted conceptions of power; the one dynastic and territorial, thinking in terms of areas and populations; the other maritime and commercial, based on the newer conceptions of markets, trade routes, and zones of influence. Britain eventually obtained these advantages, not by treaty, but by war.

Meanwhile the first Partition treaty[3] was signed in October 1698 between William, Louis, and the States General, whereby the electoral prince Joseph Ferdinand was to have Spain, the Indies, the Low Countries, and Sardinia; the Dauphin's share was to be Naples and Sicily, with Finale and Guiposcoa and several Tuscan ports, while the archduke Charles was to have Milan and the Milanese. This arrangement provided a fairly satisfactory solution so far as the Low Countries were con-

[1] A. Legrelle, *La diplomatie française et la succession d'Espagne*, i. 308–22.

[2] *Correspondentie van Willem III . . .*, ed. N. Japikse, 279.

[3] The text of the treaty, signed 1/11 Oct. will be found in Legrelle, op. cit. ii. 664–80. There are extracts from it in H. Vast, *Les Grands traités du regne de Louis XIV*, iii. 4 sqq.

cerned; but, on the other hand, it would have ensured French predominance in the Mediterranean. Moreover, it was unsatisfactory to the emperor, who held that his former allies were bound, by the treaty of 1689, to help him obtain the whole succession, and it was unacceptable in Madrid, where the idea of partition was distasteful. Indeed, in November, Charles in Council declared the electoral prince heir to all his possessions, and so discredited the Partition treaty altogether.

The treaty secured no advantage to England; but at least it can be maintained that the king, however sceptical about the outcome, was acting in the interests of European peace. Unfortunately, he took only Portland and Albemarle into his confidence, the Whig ministers being apprised of it when it was too late to do anything. Portland had communicated the details to Vernon; then Somers, on holiday at Tunbridge Wells, was informed; afterwards, Montagu, Orford, and Shrewsbury were brought into the secret. In the last week of August, these ministers agreed on a submission to the king, drawn up by Somers, which expressed serious doubts about the proposed treaty:[1]

> A proposal of this nature seems to be attended with many ill consequences if the French did not act a sincere part. . . . So far as relates to England, it would be want of duty not to give Your Majesty this clear account, that there is a deadness and want of spirit in the nation universally, so as not at all to be disposed to the thought of entering into a new war, and that they seem to be tired out with taxes to a degree beyond what was discerned till it appeared upon the occasion of the late elections.

In spite of this unfavourable opinion, the king ordered secretary Vernon to draw up a blank commission authorizing the conclusion of the treaty by plenipotentiaries afterwards to be named, and to this curious document Somers affixed the great seal. Portland and sir Joseph Williamson were the plenipotentiaries. The life of this treaty was to prove even shorter than that of the electoral prince, who died in January 1699 at the age of seven.

The first session of William's fourth parliament opened on 6 December 1698, when the king again urged the necessity of maintaining a large army, and providing for the discharge of debt incurred by the war. After electing the Whig sir T. Littleton

[1] Grimblot, op. cit. ii. 143–6.

as Speaker, and adjudicating on about forty disputed elections, the Commons turned to the army estimates, and voted that the land forces be reduced to 7,000, of whom all were to be natural-born subjects. This meant the dismissal of the Dutch Guards, and was taken by the king as an affront. 'Seeing that you have so little regard to my advice, that you take no manner or care of your own security, and expose yourselves to evident ruin, by divesting yourselves of the only means for your defence, it would not be just or reasonable that I should be witness of your ruin.' These words,[1] in the draft of a King's Speech, were intended as the royal farewell to England, with a promise to return if again invited to save the kingdom from peril. It was one of Somers's most notable achievements that he induced the king to give up his intention of returning to Holland.

William's position in England was becoming steadily more uncomfortable. He had been disappointed by the Whigs, since they seemed as anxious for disbandment as the Tories; and the nation generally was assuming, from what was public knowledge, that the Spanish king's recognition of the electoral prince as his universal heir had finally settled the succession question. Like Charles II, William did not dare to reveal his secret treaties—his pledge of 1689 to support the imperial claim, and the recent partition treaty which gave the French such predominance in the Mediterranean. So, as he could not explain, he could not hope to be understood. Even the Junto was failing him. Orford at the Admiralty was more truculent than ever, and at last in May 1699 he resigned; at the same time Montagu gave up the chancellorship of the Exchequer, and left the Treasury in the following November. Shrewsbury could not be induced to retain office, so in May 1699 he was succeeded as secretary for the south by the Tory earl of Jersey. Wharton, as a candidate for office, had finally to be dropped, in return for the king's temporary abandonment of Sunderland. In April 1700 Somers was obliged to give up the seals to the Tory sir Nathan Wright; and even Portland, who had steadily been losing the royal favour, was displaced by a new Dutch favourite, Arnold Joost van Keppel, created earl of Albemarle. Leeds was at last removed from his presidency of the Council in May 1699 in favour of the earl of Pembroke, and the privy seal was given

[1] W. Coxe, *Shrewsbury Correspondence*, 574.

to a moderate Tory, sir John Lowther of Lowther, now lord Lonsdale. John Egerton, third earl of Bridgewater, a commissioner of Trade and Plantations, was placed at the head of the Admiralty. Lonsdale, Bridgewater, and Jersey appeared among the new lords justices to administer the country during the king's absence in Holland in the summer of 1699. The effect of these changes was that in his last years William, with scarcely the semblance of a ministry, was confronted with a House of Commons consistently critical and even hostile.

The second session of this parliament, which had been prorogued on 4 May, commenced on 16 November 1699. William could not very well explain how the death of the electoral prince, by destroying the secret partition treaty, had caused a worsening in the European situation, a fact which made it all the more necessary that Britain should be well-armed. But he made one more appeal for liberal supplies to maintain adequate military and naval forces, and to discharge the debts on the funds. To this appeal the Commons were even less sympathetic than before. They presented to the king a remonstrance, expressing regret that, after providing so amply for national security, jealousy and distrust had arisen; and they complained of those who sowed such distrust in the mind of His Majesty.[1] Then, having received a report from the commissioners for taking account of forfeited estates in Ireland, they resolved on 15 December to bring in a Bill for applying all Irish forfeitures since February 1688 to the use of the public. A few months later they took an unusual step which implied an appeal to the nation against the crown, for in April they ordered the report of the Irish commissioners to be printed and published, together with those speeches of the king and resolutions of the Commons having a bearing thereon.[2] They then passed a Bill for granting an Aid to the crown by the sale of such forfeited estates, which they tacked to a Land Tax Bill. This had a stormy passage in the Lords, where the king's adherents tried to wreck it by a crop of amendments, which were objected to by the Commons as infringements of their control over taxation, and upheld by the Lords on the ground that, as forfeitures were involved, they had the right to safeguard the interests of possibly innocent

[1] *Cobbett*, v. 1199–1200, 16 Nov. 1699.
[2] *C.J.* xiii, 8 Apr. 1700.

persons.[1] One more of the many disputes between the two Houses was ended only when the king made it known that he wished the Bill to pass. The climax to these proceedings came on 10 April, when the Commons resolved on an address submitting that no person not a native of His Majesty's dominions, except prince George of Denmark, should be admitted to royal councils in England or Ireland.[2] In order to obviate the humiliation of receiving such an address, the king on 11 April 1700 prorogued parliament; and, after keeping it prorogued for eight months, he dissolved it on 10 December. The next, the fifth parliament, did not begin its sessions until 6 February 1701, ten months after the last meeting of its predecessor.

William was within his rights in conducting his foreign policy without reference to parliament, or even to his ministers, but such conduct was no longer politic, since recent events had introduced this change that, whereas war had formerly been limited, affecting mainly that portion of the population which otherwise would be on the rates, it had now assumed European dimensions, calling forth nation-wide activities, and imposing sacrifice (such as the Land Tax) on that large and influential proportion of the nation which previously could regard these things with indifference. Even more, it was clearly realized that English overseas trade, particularly in the Mediterranean and the West Indies, might have to be defended by war. The parliament, which had provided means for carrying on great campaigns, naturally assumed that it should, in spite of any constitutional rule to the contrary, be at least informed of negotiations that might determine peace or war. Though unappreciated at first by William, this was realized abroad, for in May 1699 the Spanish envoy in the Low Countries wrote to Cannales, the Spanish ambassador in London, asserting that, without the participation of parliament, the king's partition treaties were no more than scraps of paper.[3] This fact, together with Madrid's well-known objection to partition, caused Cannales early in September 1699 to deliver a strongly worded protest[4] to the lords justices, with a threat of denouncing such partition treaties to parliament. The ambassador was promptly expelled from England.

[1] *C.J.* xiii, 10 Apr. and *L.J.* xvi, 10 Apr. 1700. [2] *C.J.* xiii, 10 Apr.
[3] A. Legrelle, op. cit. iii. 97, footnote. [4] Ibid. iii. 149.

By that time William had agreed with Heinsius and Louis on the terms of a second partition treaty necessitated by the death of the electoral prince. An attempt was made to obtain the emperor's consent to the new scheme. But opinion at Vienna had hardened by what was known of opinion at Madrid, and so once again the three contracting parties had to divide the inheritance without reference to one of the two principal powers concerned. In January 1700 the terms of the treaty were communicated to Somers, the last of the Whig ministers still in office, and in February it was signed by Portland and Jersey. Briefly, the second partition treaty (3/13 March) assigned to the archduke Charles the share, namely Spain, the Indies, and the Low Countries, previously allocated to the electoral prince, while the Dauphin was to have the Italian possessions, together with Lorraine. The duke of Lorraine was to take Milan in exchange.

No attempt was made to keep this treaty secret. It satisfied no one, least of all Charles II's Court, and it may well be doubted whether Louis would have honoured a treaty which gave such a large share to a rival dynasty. The terms of this new partition may also have alienated the Bavarian Wittelsbachs from their recent association with the empire, and so have restored them to their old alliance with France. Moreover, European events in the summer of 1700 helped to provide Louis with a pretext for regarding lightly the obligations which he had recently undertaken. These events concerned the Scandinavian kingdoms, where the situation was completely altered by the death of the peace-loving Charles XI of Sweden in 1697, and the accession of his young and bellicose son Charles XII. Two years later Christian V of Denmark was succeeded by Frederick IV, who seemed likely to be a more dependable nominee of Louis than his predecessor had been, particularly as he needed help against his aggressive neighbour Charles. As Sweden was the traditional ally of England and Holland, the stage appeared to be set for another war in the north, especially as, in January 1700, a secret engagement was signed[1] between Sweden, England, and the States General, which committed the

[1] *Dumont*, vii, 11/21 Jan. 1700; also *Diplomatic Instructions 1689–1727* (Sweden, ed. J. F. Chance), xiii, and Legrelle, op. cit. iv. 149–50. The treaty was defensive, and was based on the Ryswick settlement.

two latter powers to come to the aid of Charles against Frederick. The Danish king was soon engaged in hostilities; accordingly, in June 1700 Rooke, in command of a large Anglo-Dutch fleet, appeared off Copenhagen, thereby obliging Frederick to make peace with his enemy at Travendal in the following August. This ill-advised Anglo-Dutch demonstration was a disturbing element in a precarious situation, as it appeared to foreshadow the grouping of European states into two hostile camps.

Nominally, therefore, Sweden was added to the allies or potential allies of England and Holland, while Denmark was well within the orbit of French influence. But Louis was not likely to engage in war for the support of fickle Denmark against bellicose Sweden; indeed, throughout the summer of 1700 he was genuinely anxious for peace in the north, so as to be free for his designs in Italy, as soon as the king of Spain died.[1] It was mainly for this reason that Rooke's intervention at Copenhagen was not followed by war; and so, while Charles of Spain continued to live, Louis (except in his propaganda) observed some degree of moderation.

Another factor in a complicated situation was provided by Spain itself. That country has always been distinguished by dislike of foreigners; and even d'Harcourt, Louis's envoy at Madrid, assisted as he was by French priests, had failed to make much impression on Charles's Court, which retained its rooted objection to any division of the empire. But French influence in the peninsula may have been fostered, not directly by an ambassador, but indirectly by a woman, the Austrian-born second wife of the king, whom Charles detested as much as he had loved his first wife, the vivacious Frenchwoman, Marie Louise, who had been removed by poison in 1689. Visits to her tomb, where he could still gaze on her features, their beauty preserved by the art of the embalmer, served to increase the misery experienced by the unfortunate monarch, and to heighten the contrast with her brawling successor, Maria Anna of Neuburg, who, in her tantrums, had to be locked in her apartments, where she broke everything within reach. D'Harcourt reported that she and her German women quarrelled like fishwives; some of them, more impatient than the expectant European powers, helped them-

[1] This at least was the opinion at The Hague. Stanhope to Vernon, 22 June/2 July 1700, in *B.M. Stowe MS.* 243, f. 225.

selves to movables of the Spanish Succession without waiting for the death. All this helps to explain why one of the few recorded utterances of this Charles II was: *Questos Alemanos me enfadan*;[1] it may also help to explain why, in his last will, drawn up in September 1700, the Spanish king showed such clear preference for France.

By this will, the Spanish empire in its entirety was bequeathed to the duke of Anjou, second grandson of Louis. Failing him, the order of priority for the succession was to be Anjou's younger brother, the duke of Berry; then the archduke Charles; and finally the duke of Savoy. It was a condition of the will that the crowns of France and Spain should always be kept separate; and (such is the irony of human conduct) it was recommended in the will that the duke of Anjou should marry an Austrian princess, presumably in order to keep the inheritance within the Habsburg family circle. Late in the following October Charles of Spain died.

After a few days of deliberation, Louis put aside the partition treaty and accepted the will. He had to choose in circumstances of extreme difficulty.[2] Fulfilment of the treaty would have added several Tuscan ports to French territory; by the projected exchange of Milan, Lorraine would have been incorporated on the eastern frontier, and a similar exchange of Naples with the duke of Savoy would have rounded off the south-eastern corner by the addition to France of Savoy, Nice and Piedmont. Such an enlargement of territory would have consolidated the position of France in Europe, and would have achieved the ambitions of Henry IV and Richelieu. But the objections to this course of action were at least as strong, because European opinion was not in favour of partition, and Spanish opinion was uncompromisingly against it; hence it is possible that the enforcement of the treaty would have necessitated a war. There was probably more to be said for acceptance of the will. Quite apart from any calculation of material advantages, the will had a certain sanctity such as no treaty could ever possess; and in days of indefeasible hereditary right, this counted for much with Louis and his contemporaries.

[1] C. Hippeau, *Avènement des Bourbons au trône d'Espagne*, xcvi.

[2] For this, see M. A. Thomson, 'Louis XIV and the origins of the War of the Spanish Succession', in *Trans. R.H.S.*, 5th series, vol. iv (1954).

Moreover, the orientation of Europe had altered since the days of Henry IV and Richelieu, because it now looked more to the west; and France, as much as England, was aware of the enormous resources of the Spanish empire; still more, war-weary Europe considered that peace could be preserved only if this empire remained intact. So Louis's decision was in accord with the opinion of the greater part of Europe, including England; nor did that decision necessarily imply that the crowns of France and Spain would one day be united, since the (contingent) succession of Philip of Anjou to the French throne would be followed by the accession of another prince to the Spanish throne, a contingency for which the will itself had provided. Up to this point, therefore, there need have been no war.

But success often provides a more real test of human character than failure; the king who had been roused to frenzy by the disappointments of 1688–9 was not likely to adopt wise counsels in 1700–1, when success was sudden and complete, particularly as that success was to be attributed, not to the industry or even intelligence of his diplomatic service, but to divine purpose, as clearly evidenced in the will. Louis had that unshakeable conviction of rightness which is both the strength and the weakness of the fervidly religious; hence he could not have been expected to make any concession to a Europe, now apprehensive after nearly forty years experience of chicanery and violence. Moreover, he was fortified in this attitude by the belief that his recent enemies, now exhausted by war, would not again resort to arms, however great the provocation; he knew this, because he controlled the greatest intelligence service in the world. It is true that, now on the threshold of old age, he was losing his earlier enthusiasm for war; but all the information at his disposal suggested that Britain and Holland would maintain peace at almost any price; so he could, it appeared, risk a course of conduct which, in other circumstances, would have led to war; he would have peace, but it must be his peace. Even after hostilities began, he believed that England could still be detached; and the reasons suggested for this hope provide a significant revelation of the kind of information on which he based decisions of momentous consequence to millions of men. The English people, according to this information,[1] were

[1] *Aff. Étr.* (*Angleterre*), 211, ff. 347–52.

now concerned solely about Stock Exchange quotations; when these were high, Englishmen were arrogant and bellicose; on their fall, the same people panicked for peace. Hence the obvious device—the sending to England of a *contre mineur*, who, with a little jugglery, would play havoc with the Exchange quotations. Equally important, on the same recommendation, was propaganda. Make up your mind what you want the enemy to believe, and then form a party among them which will adopt and spread these beliefs; such skilful infiltration will eventually ruin the war effort of any nation. Not till 1704, the year of Blenheim, was any illumination accorded to Louis XIV.

William, whose attempts at partition had thus met with such disaster, knew that there could be no satisfying his enemy, and he was convinced that the danger from France was greater than ever;[1] but neither he nor Heinsius found much support for this view, because the more conciliatory conduct of Louis after the treaty of Ryswick had induced a general feeling of security in England and in Europe. Nor was there even any strong anti-French feeling in 1700; on the contrary, it was insisted by Rochester, speaking in the House of Lords, that the name of the French king must be mentioned only with respect.[2] Hence the task of William in his last years was not unlike that undertaken in 1688–9, when he had to unite two nations against a monarch who had not yet opened hostilities on either of them. His sense of the extreme difficulty of such a task may account for the uncertainty of his conduct in the weeks immediately following publication of the will, thus explaining his breach of the parliamentary calendar in dispensing with an autumn and winter session, and delaying for ten months the summoning of parliament until February 1701; indeed, it is possible that he regarded the approaching session with dread. Using Henry Guy as intermediary, he maintained active negotiations with Sunderland, who, in the autumn of 1700, may well have advised him to make such ministerial changes as would be acceptable to a House of Commons in which Tories and high churchmen were likely

[1] Cf. the king's confession to Heinsius in November 1700: 'We must confess that we are dupes. . . . It grieves me to the soul that almost everyone rejoices that France has preferred the will to the treaty.' *Hardwicke State Papers*, ii. 393–6.

[2] *Cobbett*, v. 1239, 14 Mar. 1701.

to preponderate. For this purpose Rochester and Godolphin were available. The first, leader of the high church party, had opposed the Attainder of Fenwick; and, though untroubled by the vacillations and scruples of his brother, Clarendon, he had made it clear that he regarded William not as his lawful king, but as the widower of his niece Mary. So it was his ancestry and churchmanship, rather than his competence or loyalty, that induced William in December 1700 to appoint him lord lieutenant of Ireland, the nominal head of a ministry that scarcely even existed. In contrast, Godolphin was both efficient and unobtrusive, so he was brought back to office as first commissioner of the Treasury. With these two in the foreground and Sunderland in the background, William proposed to face a critical parliament and an unsympathetic nation.

In twenty years' time, history had thus completed a full circle, for these three personages were the 'Chits' who had served the purposes of Charles II after 1680. The trio had presided over an England subjugated by Stuart absolutism and shamed by dependence on a Bourbon; they were now resurrected in time to witness the resurgence of a nation, about to emerge as a great European power.

XVI

THE ACT OF SETTLEMENT AND THE SECOND GRAND ALLIANCE, 1701–2

In the general election of January 1701 there were said to have been about 3,000 candidates, or nearly six for each seat, evidence of how the European situation caused a heightening of political temperature in England; but the metal of which the old electoral structure was built did not quickly respond to changes of temperature, and it was noted that a majority of the former members was returned.[1] Those who were considered Tories still had a preponderance.

At the opening of this, his fifth parliament, on 6 February 1701 the king alluded to two deaths—that of the king of Spain, and that of the duke of Gloucester. With the death of the duke in the preceding summer the chances of Anne having an heir seemed to be extinguished; and, as the same was true of William, it was necessary to regulate the succession. There was also the situation created by Louis's acceptance of Charles's will. The Commons began with a resolution that they would support His Majesty and his government; and, after considering a memorial from the States General, communicated to them by the king, they requested William to enter into such negotiations with the Dutch as would conduce to the safety of the kingdom. Encouraged by this attitude, William next placed before both Houses a letter from Melfort to his brother the earl of Perth, intimating that a scheme was on foot for another attempt at invasion; a letter which, though it may have been a forgery, at least helped to diminish the feeling of security into which England had, for some time, been lulled. The peers responded by asking that copies of all treaties made since the conclusion of peace be laid before them.

This unexpectedly favourable attitude of the Commons may be attributed to one or both of two causes. It was a contemporary opinion that the mood of a House of Commons usually

[1] *Add. MS.* 17677 (Dutch Reports), vol. WW, 18 Jan. 1701.

differed in its opening and concluding sessions. At its opening, before affiliations had been formed, and before there was time to attack anyone, the House was thought to be more amenable to management by the Court; towards its end, the chamber was often a tumultuous assembly, divided by faction and personal strife, each member thinking of the next election, and resolved on anti-Court measures as the best means of securing a reputation for patriotism. The other cause may have been equally potent, namely, the beginnings of English disquiet at the doings of Louis. Late in January 1701 he had obtained from the Paris Parlement a decree confirming the right of the young Philip V to the French throne, in the event of failure of his elder brother in the succession. Nobody had ever questioned such a right; indeed the will had expressly provided for such a contingency; nor did the decree of Parlement support any assumption that the two crowns would necessarily be united. But this was just the assumption made by contemporaries. Louis, who could never leave well alone, took a superfluous step which was interpreted to mean that, thus early, the most important stipulation in the will had been violated. All this appeared to confirm the conviction of William and Heinsius that there could be no faith in Versailles.

Louis himself speedily supplied confirmation of this view. Ruling Spain and its provinces on behalf of his grandson, he sent French troops into the Netherlands, who expelled the Dutch from the frontier garrisons, and established themselves, with willing Spanish help, in the cities and fortresses of Belgium. Antwerp, Mons, and Namur were occupied; Ostend and Nieuport shared the same fate; Liége was filled with French troops through the defection to France of its prince bishop. All that had been fought for in the nine years of the war of the league of Augsburg was swept away in as many weeks. Determined to exploit to the full the enormous economic opportunities placed within his reach, Louis encouraged the formation of a French company designed to monopolize the *Asiento*; another company was set up to trade with South America, and the importation of Spanish wool was limited to French merchants. The conduct of the French king in the year immediately following acceptance of the will was as immoderate as it had previously been moderate; and this situation emerged, that, while the likelihood of war had, it seemed, been averted by a settlement, the will, which gave everything to the one power threatening European peace, and nothing to anyone else, it now appeared that Louis would so ruthlessly exploit his advantages as to make the continuance of peace impossible. In accordance with a policy of appeasement, and in spite of great provocation, the Dutch in February 1701 recognized Philip as king of Spain, a gesture followed by British recognition on 17 April. But both peoples were becoming increasingly alarmed, and the opening session of William's parliament reflected that alarm.

These ominous rumblings were scarcely audible in the din of party strife in the Commons which, after the deceptive quiet of February, was reaching its crescendo in March. On the 24th of that month, the Commons expressed condemnation of the partition treaty[1] (the second), which had been passed under the great seal during the sitting of parliament, without any reference to the legislature. By mid-April, when they were in full cry, the Commons resolved to impeach Portland, Somers, Orford, and Halifax, mainly for their parts in the partition treaties; and in the debates there were long duels between the young marquis of Hartington, the duke of Devonshire's heir, and the veteran Tory sir C. Musgrave, debates in which the vehement Hartington used such strong language as to risk being sent to the Tower.[2] Here, to the intense annoyance of the king, was a steadily widening diversion from the path of national security to the jungle of party faction. It was this party spirit that caused the Commons to omit from the impeachments the Tory lord Jersey, who had taken part in the second partition treaty, and to concentrate on Somers, who had been the means of authenticating both. Vernon's name was omitted, possibly on the ground that his status was that of a clerk; Portland's impeachment had been voted, but, possibly in deference to the king, it was not proceeded with. Somers was the chief culprit. He had opposed the Bill for resumption of Irish forfeitures; he had commissioned captain Kidd to suppress piracy, whereupon that notorious buccaneer had hoisted the black flag; most serious of all, he had issued commissions in blank for the partition

[1] *C.J.* xiii, 24 Mar. 1701.

[2] Tallard to Louis XIV, 29 Apr. 1701, in *Baschet*, 188.

treaties, and had affixed the great seal to the ratifications, without enrolling them in Chancery. In his defence (by royal permission) before the Commons on 14 April, he urged (as on the whole was true) that he had merely carried out the royal instructions; the defence of Orford and Halifax was that they were not fully cognizant of the treaties.

When copies of the treaties were supplied to both Houses, the Lords expressed regret that the emperor had not been brought into the negotiations, and showed disquiet at the preponderance in the Mediterranean which the treaties assured to France.[1] They resolved to beg the king, in his future negotiations with Louis, 'to proceed with such caution as to carry along with it a real security', a resolution against which Nottingham protested, on the ground that the phrase 'real security' was too vague.[2] The Lords then debated whether to invite the Commons to join with them in this resolution, but the proposal was negatived, an instance of unwillingness to co-operate with the Lower House in a matter of national emergency.[3] On 2 April the Commons, having been invited by the king to express an opinion, advised William to continue his negotiations with the Dutch, and to carry out the terms of existing Anglo-Dutch alliances.[4]

But, if the legislature was still somewhat undecided in its reaction to events abroad, evidence was soon provided that, outside Westminster, many people had made up their minds; for the wranglings of the Commons over the impeachments were suddenly interrupted by an event, rare in the history of parliament, which hitherto had retained a certain immunity from public tumult or solicitation. On 29 April the gentlemen, grand jury, the justices, and the freeholders of Kent met in general quarter sessions at Maidstone. This was just the kind of occasion when opinions about public events were freely expressed; this time, however, these opinions were embodied in a petition to the Commons, which was presented on 8 May. The five who presented the petition implored the House to have regard to 'the voice of the people', to provide for the religion and safety of the nation, that loyal addresses might be turned into bills of supply, in order that the king might be

[1] *L.J.* xvi, 15 March 1701.
[2] Ibid., 20 Mar.
[3] Ibid.
[4] *C.J.* xiii, 2 Apr.

enabled to assist his allies before it was too late. The gentlemen who presented this very moderate petition were at once committed to custody by an indignant House.

'The voice of the people' was not long in making itself heard, and this time it was the voice of Daniel Defoe. Adopting the style of the Kentish petition, he drew up a memorial purporting to express the opinion not only of the freeholders, but of 'many thousands of the good people of England', and this he signed 'Legion—for we are many'. One tradition is that Defoe presented this memorial (on 14 May) dressed in woman's clothes; another story is that he did so surrounded by a considerable number of persons of quality; in either case, the effects on the Speaker and the Commons must have been overwhelming. The Legion Memorial is notable for its frankness. First it condemned the committing of the Kentish petitioners to custody; then it rehearsed a long list of the Commons's shortcomings, including these: deserting the Dutch when the French were at their doors; failure to make good the deficiencies in the funds; addressing the king to remove ministers on bare surmises of their guilt; allowing 'saucy, indecent reproaches' on His Majesty's person to be made in the House, particularly by Jack Howe; neglecting reformation of manners, and 'being scandalously vicious in manners themselves'. Then followed certain claims: the right of Englishmen, in case their representatives in parliament did not proceed according to their duty and the people's interest, to inform them of their dislike, disown their actions, and direct them by petition or memorial; that the House of Commons had no power to imprison persons other than its own members; that if the Commons betrayed their trust, it was the right of the people to call them to account, and proceed against them as traitors. The Memorial ended with the request that the French king be obliged to quit Flanders, and that His Majesty be addressed to declare war on him, for which purpose supplies should be granted. The Commons, probably too surprised to order Defoe's arrest, had to content themselves with the appointment of a committee to lay before the king an account of the attempts of evil-disposed persons to raise tumult and sedition.

One accusation was made in the Memorial—that the members were bribed by French gold, distributed by Tallard.

This was widely believed, and was expressed at a dinner given in Mercers' Hall to the Kentish petitioners on their release, a function attended by Defoe. The menu was reported to have consisted mainly of calves' head (out of disrespect to the memory of Charles I); and the Kentish guests were presented with engraved portraits of themselves, having the legend: *Non auro patriam* (out of disrespect to the Tory House of Commons).[1] All this shows that a new force had entered into public life. It was styled 'the voice of the people', but it was really journalism, and its chief exponent was Defoe. As the only English man of letters who was honoured with the king's recognition, Defoe devoted himself to advertisement of what he knew to be the main principle of William's foreign policy, namely, dealing with Louis 'sword in hand'. In two pamphlets he warned the reading public of the dangers of departing from this policy. As early as 1697 he had maintained that England's changed circumstances necessitated a standing army;[2] in 1700 he showed in his *The Two Great Questions Considered* how dangerous to our commerce would be a French monopoly of the West Indies.

It has always been difficult to account for the fact that peace-loving England, still groaning under the debts of a war, should within a few years have taken the lead in promoting another and a greater war. The answer may be that nation and parliament were educated by the conduct of Louis XIV and by the pens of such men as Defoe. Never conspicuous for tact, the king at this time showed restraint, and allowed these two forces to do the work for him.

By this time—May 1701—the cleavage between the two Houses was becoming acute. Early in that month the king conveyed to parliament copies of a memorial received from the States General expressing fears that a French invasion was imminent. To this the Lords responded with a request that the king would not only implement all existing treaties with the Dutch, but that he would enter into a strict alliance with them and with the emperor.[3] This was afterwards brought to pass

[1] For an account of the Calves' Head Club see *Secret History of the Calves' Head Club or the Republican Unmasked*, in *Bodl. Pamph.* 226.

[2] *Reflections on a Pamphlet upon a Standing Army*, 1697.

[3] *L.J.* xvi, 10 May 1701.

in the second Grand Alliance of The Hague. The reaction of the Commons was very different. So far from responding to the ominous news from the continent, they proceeded to the completion of their articles of impeachment against Somers, the most important accusation being that he had affixed the great seal to the partition treaties without having communicated with either the privy council or the lords justices. Articles of impeachment against Orford and Halifax were also drawn up. There then followed weeks of quarrelling between the two Houses on questions of procedure, the Lords insisting on their right to appoint a day for the trial, without previous notice from the Commons of their readiness to proceed. As the Commons protested against the shortness of the time allowed them for preparing the prosecution, the peers delayed the trial until 17 June, when they retired to Westminster Hall, where the articles against Somers were read. As no representative from the Commons appeared to conduct the prosecution the Lords returned to their chamber and passed a motion acquitting the former Whig minister. They might, in the absence of prosecution by the Commons, have declared that the impeachment lapsed; but they went farther, for they pronounced a definite acquittal and so made impassable their breach with the Lower House. On 23 June, in the same circumstances, they acquitted Orford; and, on the following day, they dismissed the impeachment of Halifax. The general opinion was that the Lords had acted rightly, and that the Commons had discredited themselves by excess of party spirit.

This was the most bitter of the many disputes between the two Houses. Moreover, by ordering that all the proceedings be printed and published, the Commons, for the second time,[1] made an appeal to public opinion, this time against the Lords. On 20 June they resolved that the peers had refused them justice in the impeachment of Somers by denying them a committee of both Houses, and afterwards proceeding to a 'pretended' trial. To this the Lords replied with a resolution that the deferring of supplies for the services was attributable to the fatal counsel of delaying the meeting of parliament for so long, a delay extended by the unreasonable conduct of the Commons. On 24 June parliament was prorogued, but not till

[1] *Supra*, 451.

11 November was it dissolved. To such a deadlock had the two Houses been reduced that some contemporaries doubted whether William would again summon a parliament.[1]

Among the few Acts passed by this parliament was one for renewing Exchequer Bills;[2] another was for limiting privilege of parliament.[3] There were two measures of supply—a Land Tax[4] of 2*s.* in the £ for defraying current expenses in navy, guards, and garrisons, in which were clauses incapacitating members of parliament (mostly Whigs) from serving as commissioners of Customs, and imposing a penalty of £100 on Customs officers who tried to influence elections. The other grant of supply[5] was an additional levy on spirits, tea, coffee, and imported pictures. This last was regarded as creating a particularly good 'fund'; so, in spite of its animosity to the ex-ministers, it cannot be said that this House of Commons was niggardly in the financial support accorded to the crown. But all these measures were surpassed in importance by the Act of Settlement.

The Act for further limitation of the crown and for better securing the rights and liberties of the subject[6] began with a rehearsal of the clause in the Bill of Rights disabling Roman Catholics from the succession, and transferring it to the next heir, being Protestant. In accordance with this provision the electress Sophia, granddaughter of James I, was declared to be next heir after Anne and William. In this way were excluded the Catholic heirs of the Palatinate and Orleanist Houses, both of them claiming from marriage with Stuart princesses. It was enacted also that any person succeeding under the above limitation who held communion with the church of Rome, or married a Roman Catholic was declared to be incapacitated; and whoever came into possession of the crown was obliged to join in communion with the church of England. This exclusion of Roman Catholics from the throne is one of the few clearly-enunciated principles in the British constitution, and is one of the most obvious legacies of the seventeenth century to modern

[1] *Burnet*, iv. 518.
[2] 12–13 Wm. III, c. 1.
[3] 12–13 Wm. III, c. 3.
[4] 12–13 Wm. III, c. 10.
[5] 12–13 Wm. III, c. 11.
[6] 12–13 Wm. III, c. 2. This, the Act of Settlement, received the royal assent on 12 June 1701.

times. To this extent the Act of Settlement was not a party measure. On the other hand, the requirement that the sovereign should join in communion with the church of England reflects a somewhat more favourable attitude to that church than had prevailed at the time of the Revolution,[1] and here it is possible to detect Tory influence.

That influence is apparent also in the limitations which the Commons sought to impose on the crown when, on failure of heirs to Anne and William, the Act would come into force, and a foreigner would succeed. In that event the nation was not obliged to engage in war for defence of dominions or territories not belonging to the crown of England without consent of parliament. No successor to the crown was to go out of England, Scotland, or Ireland without that consent. All matters cognizable by the privy council—that is, all important matters of state—were to be transacted there, not in an informal Cabinet; and all resolutions taken were to be signed by the councillors advising or consenting thereto. No one born out of England, Scotland, or Ireland, or the Dominions, even if naturalized,[2] was capable of becoming a privy councillor, or a member of parliament, or of holding any office, civil or military, or of having lands from the crown. This ostracism of foreigners was followed by ostracism of office holders, for these, as well as pensioners, were declared incapable of serving as members of the House of Commons. Judges were to hold office *quamdiu se bene gesserint*; their salaries were to be 'established', that is, detached from fees and perquisites, and placed on the civil list. They were to be removed only on an address from both Houses. No pardon under the great seal could thenceforth be pleaded in bar of an impeachment. All the laws for the religion, rights and liberties of the subject were confirmed.

The Act of Settlement was immediately followed by a measure which may be regarded as its appendix—an Act for limiting parliamentary privilege. This provided that suits might be brought against members of either House during intervals of parliamentary sessions, and that statutes of limitation could no longer be pleaded in actions of debt, whereby the creditor's claim might lapse in consequence of such privilege. Here was one of the most popular measures of the new Toryism. That it

[1] *Supra*, 235–9.

[2] Unless of English parentage.

was gratefully accepted by the nation is evidenced by the statement of a contemporary;[1] 'no tongue can express the benefit of this Act to the trading part of the nation'.

Taken together, these two Acts present an interpretation of the constitution by a purged and revived Tory party, now led by Harley. According to this view, we have a somewhat idealist distribution of powers, for the Commons are separated altogether from the administration, by exclusion of office holders, and they are deprived of some of their immunities that had become social abuses; to this extent the Commons are restored to their primary function of national representatives, detached from departments of state, and entrusted with the duty of advising and petitioning the crown. Here there is just a hint of reversion to the medieval conception of Estates. With some consistency, therefore, certain recent innovations, such as the informal Cabinet, are ruled out, and the privy council is restored to its old place as the supreme advisory body, responsible for its advice to the crown, its members obliged, by the signing of their written opinion, to provide the best evidence for their own impeachment. Had these clauses come into effect, they would soon have proved unworkable; but one restriction—exclusion of placemen from the Commons—is now applied in a modified form, and our permanent civil service, altogether detached from parliament, provides an illustration of what the framers of the Act of Settlement may have had in mind. Also, in the force of public opinion, we have now something even more effective than the old impeachment, which the Act sought to safeguard. As the Act of Settlement was a tentative approach to future practice, so it included condemnation of past procedure. William's conduct, his long absences abroad, his foreign favourites, are criticized by implication; there is also a guarantee that the nation will not be drawn, by a king not a natural-born Englishman, into a war where English interests are not concerned, except by consent of parliament—the first statutory encroachment on royal control of foreign policy, afterwards to be constantly urged against the foreign policy of the first two Hanoverian kings.

Up to this point, the Act might be regarded as a repudiation

[1] *A Justification of the Proceedings of the House of Commons* . . . 1701, in *Bodl. Pamph.* 238.

of those innovations, introduced since the Revolution, which, in the future, might be abused by a Hanoverian; here, indeed, are evidences of some kind of party spirit. But, on the other hand, this measure develops and completes the Bill of Rights; it removes the last obstacle to ministerial responsibility by the provision that no royal pardon shall be pleadable to an impeachment; once more, it asserts the uncompromising Protestantism of seventeenth-century England. Such were the broad lines on which the nation was to proceed.

The settlement at home was contrasted with the uncertainty abroad; indeed, the year 1701, like the years 1688 and 1696, was one of national emergency. Once more, William had to build up a coalition against Louis, and once more Britain would have to take the lead. Again the king resorted to negotiation, even to a proposed partition, a desperate attempt, in which he was served by a great Englishman, Marlborough, whom he took with him to The Hague, early in July, where there were discussions at the Mauritshuis with Heinsius, and with representatives of other powers, including D'Avaux.[1] Marlborough, who went in the capacity of plenipotentiary and commander-in-chief of the forces, showed singular astuteness as a diplomatist; for he kept in close touch with the lords justices at home, in order to avoid the fate of Somers; and he refused to commit himself, in the talks with Heinsius and the imperial envoy, in regard to the number of troops to be provided by England for a continental campaign. He was authorized to demand a guarantee for the separation of the French and Spanish crowns, as well as the withdrawal of French garrison troops from the Dutch frontier, and adequate satisfaction of the imperial claims. This, in effect, would have meant a partition; but the proposal failed, mainly because the emperor demanded too much and the French would yield nothing at all. In August D'Avaux was recalled from The Hague, and so the attempt to negotiate with Louis had broken down. But otherwise, the talks proved a success. Marlborough managed to detach Charles XII of Sweden from the French interest; and he succeeded in obtaining, from the Dutch and imperial agents, adequate guarantees for English trade in the West Indies.

[1] For good accounts of these negotiations, see G. M. Trevelyan, *England under Queen Anne, Blenheim*, ch. 7; and sir W. S. Churchill, *Marlborough*, i, ch. 32.

Meanwhile French troops had entered Lombardy, where they were successfully opposed by the imperialist general, prince Eugene of Savoy, a fact which helped to encourage the formation of a new Grand Alliance of The Hague. This was signed on 27 August/7 September between the emperor Leopold, the king of England, and the States General for procuring 'equitable satisfaction' of the emperor's rights, and for the security of Britain and Holland. The 'equitable satisfaction' consisted of Milan, Naples, Sicily, and the Spanish Netherlands for the emperor, the Spanish Netherlands to constitute a barrier for the Dutch. The allies also undertook to ensure, by joint action, that the crowns of France and Spain would never be united, and that the French should not be allowed to possess themselves of the Spanish Indies; we would fight for the blessings of freedom at home and the profits of slavery abroad. Two months were given for negotiation with France on these terms. Later, a clause was added, on the initiative of Seymour, pledging the allies to support the Protestant succession in England.[1] This Grand Alliance was accompanied by a renewal of existing treaties with the Dutch, their co-operation at sea to be based on the treaty of April 1689;[2] and it was agreed that, in making peace, particular regard should be paid to the commerce and traffic of the two maritime powers.[3] Princes concerned in the maintenance of peace were invited to join the league, and the possibility of negotiation still remained.

Louis, who refused to negotiate, was never more amicable than when tired of a war, nor ever more formidable than when tired of a peace. Throughout the year 1701 he insisted that the allies, not he, were the disturbers of the peace; and, as always, he could give his evidence. Among the facts were the large subscriptions raised in England for the new East India Company, and the renewal of the privileges of the Dutch East India Company; there was also Rooke's enterprise at Copenhagen in the previous year. Among the many rumours were the alleged intention of the English to oust the Portuguese from the slave trade by seizing their Cacheo Company;[4] their intention (this

[1] G. M. Trevelyan, op. cit. 151.

[2] *Supra*, 301.

[3] The treaties were communicated in translation to both Houses, and can be read in *C.J.* xiii, 657–64, 2 Jan. 1702.

[4] A company for the slave trade.

he got from Tallard) to seize Gibraltar, Minorca, and the Canaries—and here he was not far wrong. But there was less substance in the story that William, concerned about his unpopularity, designed to unite the Catholic provinces of the Netherlands with Holland, so as to make the new state a place of refuge for himself, a design for which the Dutch were said to be preparing by removing foreign soldiers from some of the frontier garrisons, and substituting troops of their own.[1] This alone appeared to justify Louis's intervention in these frontier garrisons.

More effective than rumours was the grouping of forces that speedily followed the formation of the Grand Alliance. Pope Clement XI was, on the whole, friendly to Louis; the duke of Savoy adhered to France on the promise of a subsidy and a marriage alliance; more important, the duke of Bavaria and the elector of Cologne, as well as the bishop of Liége, declared for Versailles. Most of the Italian states were hesitant or neutral, but the majority of the German princes rallied to the emperor, headed by the elector of Brandenburg, whose price was the crown of Prussia; while the king of Denmark, open to offers, agreed, in return for subsidies, to supply troops to the allies. Later (1703) Portugal deserted France and joined the allies, thereby putting her harbours at their disposal, a factor to prove of great advantage to the maritime powers, now that Spain was under French control. Generally, however, the situation of France in Europe, in the autumn of 1701, was immensely stronger than that in the autumn of 1688, since there was the accession of power in the Mediterranean, and throughout a great part of the western hemisphere. A world empire, controlled from Versailles, was within measurable distance. It is in reference to this fact that both the difficulties and the achievements of Marlborough and Godolphin must be assessed.

In the midst of all these manœuvres for position, there occurred an event which brought matters to a head. On 5/16 September 1701 James II died at St. Germains, whereupon Louis recognized his son, the 'Old Pretender' as king of Great Britain. It was a chivalrous act on Louis's part, characteristic of his effusive generosity to an unfortunate dynasty; but it was

[1] For these rumours, see A. Legrelle, op. cit. i. 268; ii. 444; iii. 450–51; and H. Vast, *Les Grands Traités* . . . iii. 26.

a gross violation of the most important clause in the treaty of Ryswick; and to Englishmen it implied that the choice of their king rested with Versailles. Rulers cannot afford to be generous or even chivalrous if by such conduct they violate their public promises, for it is on such promises that peace ultimately depends. So the English and Dutch envoys were recalled from France, and the stage was rapidly being set for another European war.

During periods of acute tension, human beings often take stock of their situation, and sometimes modify their conduct or opinion in accordance with that valuation. It may be the same with nations. Already, the Popish Plot, the climax of increasing disquiet and suspicion, had been followed by a certain emotionalism, which resulted in a keener political sense, and a quickening of the imaginative faculty. One evidence of that change had been the enormous increase of party and popular literature. The Revolution was not accompanied by any such awakening; indeed, it was associated with a certain apathy, and very few thought of it as the beginning of radical change. But the years 1700–1702 recall the years 1679–81, for in both periods the temperature of the body politic was heightened, and the pulse of the nation beat faster. A characteristic shared by both periods was the practice whereby electors provided instructions for the guidance of their members in the House. In 1679 the instructions had insisted on the exclusion policy; in December 1701 electors implored members to concur with His Majesty in the Grand Alliance; that deficiencies in the funds should be made good; that soldiers and sailors should be paid their arrears; that trade should be protected by strong fleets; above all, that no more faith be placed in Versailles:

> We beseech you, gentlemen, not to be amused with the offers of any treaties from the French king; or, for the sake thereof, to defer any supplies that shall be convenient, before he has given entire satisfaction to the emperor for his right to the Spanish monarchy, and to His Majesty for the affront put upon him and his people by recognising the title of the pretended prince of Wales.

Such were the instructions given to the burgesses elected for Southwark.[1] Another illustration of the similar spirit inspiring these two critical periods is the reappearance of the great

[1] *The Elector's Right Asserted* . . ., 1701.

name of Shaftesbury. The grandson of the first earl, soon to be noted as a philosopher,[1] published in 1702 his *Paradoxes of State*, in which he maintained that, whatever names might formerly have been used in order to distinguish parties, there were now neither Whigs nor Tories, neither Williamites nor Jacobites, but only those who were for a French or for an English interest. So the heat engendered in this tense period of English history helped to fuse the old parties and factions into two clear-cut, contrasted moulds.

Some confirmation of Shaftesbury's opinion is provided by the fact that, in the enormous pamphlet literature of the years 1699–1702, the names Whig and Tory do not often occur. After all, these words had scarcely ceased to be nicknames, so they were not willingly professed; even more, there was still a feeling that party distinction in the House was to be deplored; moreover, though the House constantly divided, there was no clear recognition of a party element in the divisions. Nor are these the only complications. A man might profess one set of principles when in office, and another when out of it; or he might join a group advocating doctrines that had become fashionable, even though he himself had opposed these doctrines before they became popular; or he might arrive at Westminster with no party convictions, intent on declaring himself as soon as one faction or interest had won ascendancy. Hence politicians were not grouped as Whig or Tory, but according as they reacted to certain events.[2] As these events often produced a shifting of allegiance, there were continual cross-currents in the stream of party development.

An illustration of this was provided by the frequent printing and circulation of a list of members of the Commons who, according to different points of view, could be regarded as 'safe' or 'dangerous' men. As 'safe' men, they had promoted the Place Bill in order to diminish parliamentary corruption; they had pressed their investigations into embezzlement, mainly through the commission for taking public accounts; they had impeached those persons responsible for treaties which dishonoured the nation; they had asserted the rights of the Commons against the Kentish petitioners; they had conferred great benefits on the nation by limiting privilege of parliament,

[1] *Infra*, 540–3.

[2] *Supra*, 129.

even at personal sacrifice, since they could no longer evade payment of their debts by pleading such privilege.[1] They had promoted the Act of Settlement; they were true to the church of England; above all, they were of the best account, in the House, 'for estates, quality and principles'. From the other point of view, as 'dangerous' men, they had voted in 1689 against the motion that James had abdicated; they had mostly refused to sign the Loyal Association of 1696; they had voted against the Attainder of Fenwick; they had committed the Kentish petitioners to prison; they had decided all election petitions in favour of their party; they kept company with ambassador Tallard, from whom, it was alleged, they accepted French gold. Such, according to two different points of view, and in respect of different events, was the contemporary opinion of what was then sometimes called the Flying Squadron and is now called the Tory party. From the above list also, we can deduce some of the principles attributed to the Whigs.

The list, circulated by some as an advertisement and by others as a black list, included the names of many of the best-known political families of England. It does these men rather less than justice to describe them as Tories, for as yet they were not all of them thinking in party terms; indeed, they regarded themselves, not unreasonably, as the accredited and responsible representatives of the nation. Many of them had, in fact, signed the Loyal Association of 1696; and it was they, as much as the Whigs, who brought England into the War of the Spanish Succession.

In contrast, the Whigs in this period were less forthcoming; and, after their eclipse in 1698, they failed to produce younger men able to take the place of their seniors. Shrewsbury died without an heir; the only member of the Junto who had a son was Wharton, a son who eventually became a Jacobite. Of the magnates, Devonshire's heir, the marquis of Hartington, was an effective and vehement speaker in the last parliaments of the reign; the Russells were not again to be prominent in politics until a much later date. On the other hand, there were the great city merchants, who constituted the strength of the Whig party at this period; and there were also the office holders, some of them the ancestors of great landed and political

[1] *Supra*, 43.

families. Of the latter class, an example was sir Stephen Fox, father of lord Holland and grandfather of C. J. Fox. But, among the substantial squirearchy, the Whigs were not at this time so well represented, though there were some good examples, as the Onslows (Surrey), the Pelhams (Sussex), and the Walpoles (Norfolk). Moreover, the Whigs, before the Revolution, had had a much more chequered career than the Tories. Those of them who succeeded in surviving the reign of terror which followed the Rye House Plot had been in hiding or in exile until 1689, when they may have presumed too much on their share in the liberation. Thereafter, except for their direction of affairs in the critical years 1694–7, they produced few good administrators, and they were known to have profited financially from the war. Of abstract principle they had enough and to spare; indeed, at least one of their cardinal principles was adopted by the Tories[1], who, after the creeds of Divine Right and Passive Obedience had become somewhat discredited among the more influential of the laity, were in desperate need of a more up-to-date gospel. This the Tories brought from the wilderness of opposition. With a certain consistency, the party which had insisted on removing all limitations from a hereditary sovereign was intent on imposing them on a parliamentary sovereign; it demanded the exclusion of pensioners and placemen from the Commons, as well as limitation of parliamentary privilege; it was generally opposed to a standing army and continental commitments; hence the association of the new Toryism with constitutional scruple and popular measures, while the Whigs laboured under the imputation of influence and corruption.

Whatever were the party doctrines, it can be said that the interplay of the two parties provided, for long, the pattern of English political life. A body of men, willing to be called Whigs, formulated, in opposition, those principles on which our parliamentary constitution is based; but, once in office, they inevitably adopted the methods inseparable from monopoly and exclusiveness; while another body of men, unwilling at first to be called Tories, and discredited, for a time, by their association with Stuart absolutism, maintained in opposition much of that devotion to high principle which had originally been the

[1] *Infra*, 506–8.

strength of the Whigs. The one party had the backing of past achievement; the other had the incentive to live down past failings; the two together, constantly joined in a combat from which the mean and vindictive were usually absent, contributed to that vigour, diversity, and richness so characteristic of our public life in the eighteenth century.

But meanwhile, the situation was that for a period of about ten years after 1698 the Whigs were engaged in trying to retrieve lost ground; while, in the last years of William's reign, interest centres in the development of the Tory party, and its identification with the Protestant Succession.

One reason for this resurgence of the Tories is that, after all, they were the church of England party, and the old hatred of Dissenters was easily revived, especially as it was thought by many that the Toleration Act had given them far more than they deserved. By 1702 the High Church party was again raising its head, and in that year there was heard a whisper from one who was afterwards to make a great noise. This was the famous Dr. Sacheverell, whose sermons, accepted as commonplace by Tory Oxford, were afterwards to cause such consternation in Whig London. In his *Discourse Showing the Dependence of Government on Religion* (at that time a most ominous title) he held up, as a model to be followed, the rule of king David, 'who had no less than God himself for his privy council'. That such a sanctified government would indulge in persecution and injustice was almost to be expected, but this was easily accounted for by the fact that God often puts the sword into the hands of tyrants 'to chastise an insolent and rebellious nation'. The chastisement was likely to fall most heavily on Protestant Dissenters and Whig profiteers, so the application of the sermon to current events was obvious; but on the other hand the divine privy council advocated by the preacher was inconsistent not only with that which had recently figured in the Act of Settlement, but with the principles of the Revolution itself. So here was the doctrine of Non Resistance again in full blast.

But the important thing in this development of Toryism is that so many prominent men gradually gave up their opposition, not only to William, but to the Revolution settlement; and came to acquiesce in a policy that could be described as national, even patriotic. For illustration, one example may be cited, that of sir Edward Seymour. The most influential magnate in Devon and the south-west, Seymour had opposed James in the Commons;[1] he was so unwilling to see the crown conferred on William, that he had been classed as a Jacobite; he was unsparing in his criticism of the conduct of the war; he refused to sign the Loyal Association of 1696. Formidable because of his 'estates, quality and principles', he was distinguished by his zeal for the integrity and prestige of parliament. This may well have eventually induced him to moderate his opposition and support William's policy; in this way he was the most notable of those Englishmen who, in spite of their dislike of both William and the Revolution, gradually committed themselves to the causes of the Protestant succession and the independence of parliament, the two things which together outweighed the devotion of many fervid loyalists to the Stuart cause.

Some characteristics of this new Toryism were evidenced in a speech made by Seymour after his election to parliament in December 1701.[2] He began by commending the practice whereby electors gave instructions to their deputies, thus enabling them to convey to the House only the 'sense of their country'. Even during a session Seymour professed willingness to receive such directions; and the free postage enjoyed by members of parliament would enable voters to send their letters free of charge. 'I suppose you will agree with me', declared sir Edward, 'that it is absolutely necessary to put a stop to the imposing genius of France.' For this purpose, it was essential to bring Spain within obedience to her rightful ruler, namely, the emperor. We must help the emperor with men or money or both. If with both, difficulties would arise, because if we raised money for an army of our own, much of it would be embezzled. Great estates had been raised out of the last war; surplus wealth gained in this way should, according to Seymour, be confiscated by the state. Moreover, if we raised an army, what about disbandment? If an army should be kept upon us in time of peace, we are, from that moment, 'in French shoos'. On the whole, thought the successful candidate, it would be better to

[1] *Supra*, 159.

[2] 'Minutes taken from a speech of sir Edward Seymour at his election, December 1701' in *Bodl.*, *The Growth of Deism* (1419, e. 3378).

supply the emperor with money, especially as he could raise men much more cheaply than we. Sir Edward then admitted that, in the past, he had paid more respect to crowned heads than was their due, but the conduct of Louis had diminished that respect. War against France he considered honourable, if only to restore the liberty of Europe; and he thought that an English squadron before Naples would reduce Bourbon pretensions in that area.

At home, according to the speech, some changes were overdue. Parliament, not the crown, should appoint to important public offices; in particular, the Treasury officials should be kept under close parliamentary supervision. Then there was the grievance of prisoners for debt. Here sir Edward was thinking, not of the abuses of debtors' prisons, but of measures for securing better protection to creditors. As regards the admission of all Protestants to office he was non-commital; but at least he regarded it as an open question. He was against the private sale and purchase of offices; these, he thought, should be sold by public auction and the proceeds applied to the revenues. He next referred to an elector who confessed that he had given his vote for Seymour so as to avoid incurring that great man's displeasure. Sir Edward deplored such conduct, and professed himself in favour of vote by ballot. If anything else occurred to his constituents, the Post Office was at their disposal.

Seymour's election speech shows a commendable caution; but, coming from such an uncompromising opponent[1] of the Loyal Association of 1696, it suggests some development in himself and in his party. Contemporaries might have classed him with the 'State' or 'King William' Tories, in contrast with the 'Church' or 'King James's' Tories, who were little distinguishable from Jacobites, while the first two were approximating more closely to the Whigs. The 'Church' Tories, now raising their heads, were to prove a disconcerting element in the next reign, but meanwhile it was noted that the moderate churchmen, now enemies of Jacobitism, were showing more sympathy for the Whigs.[2] Moreover, the lines drawn across the Tories were also drawn across the Whigs; for there were

[1] A. Browning, *Thomas Osborne, earl of Danby*, iii. 198, note 4.

[2] For Sunderland's note on this, in the autumn of 1701, see *Hardwicke State Papers*, ii. 444.

'State' Whigs and 'Church' Whigs, 'Court' Whigs and 'Country' Whigs, while divisions such as 'New Company Men' and 'Old Company Men' provide variations roughly identical with the distinction of Whig and Tory. Consistency or simplicity are the last things to be looked for, but of this we may be certain, that, in the winter of 1701–2, a warlike policy was not dependent on a Whig majority in parliament.[1] After all, in the summer of 1914, when Britain declared war on Germany, the Liberal or peace-loving party was in power, just as in May 1702 there was a strong Tory element in the government which declared war on France. In both cases this was fortunate, as otherwise the progress of both wars might have been impeded by a greater amount of party strife.

But if it is difficult to draw clear-cut conclusions from the contemporary literature devoted to party politics, it is possible to be more certain about the even larger literature devoted to foreign policy. The pamphlets concerned with foreign affairs show, in many cases, not only wide information, but even a spirit of reasonableness, such as may well have proved an educative factor; indeed, the patriotic Englishman, knowledgeable about Europe, and conscious of the importance of his country in Europe, was being evolved. Only a small number of these pamphlets advocated isolation; more numerous were those which recommended intervention, and even more numerous those which presented their readers with a statement of the arguments on both sides.[2] People no longer, as in 1689, underestimated the French menace; also, it was maintained, too much must not be expected from our allies.[3] The emperor, as some alleged, was in the hands of priests; he had no naval force; his Jesuit advisers were really in the interests of France. As for the Dutch, because of their dependence on overseas trade, they were particularly sensitive to attack, and they had been greatly weakened by the late war. Moreover, as they were divided by factions, they could not be expected to play their

[1] e.g. 'Let the majority fall as it will, the present temper will force them (the parliament) to do what the king will desire'. Heads of Somers's argument to induce the king to call a new parliament, October 1701, ibid. 453.

[2] For example, article no. ix in *State Tracts* (1701), vol. i, no. 1.

[3] *The Dangers of Europe from the Growing Power of France* (1702).

full part in the coming contest. Of other continental states, there was Hanover, whose elector, George, now that he was assured of the succession, should be induced to come to England, so that he might learn English ways and the English language.[1] With management, this Hanoverian connexion should strengthen our position in northern Europe. In effect, therefore, England would have to depend on her own resources against a France now immensely stronger than in 1689.

Nearer hand was Scotland, embittered by the Darien tragedy, and so a promising field for Jacobite intervention. At least one writer deplored the English attitude of contempt for the Scots, and recommended a union.[2] So, too, with Ireland. Protestant grievances there should be redressed, and an attempt made to convert the Roman Catholics, not by dragooning nor by penal laws. In the West Indies our interests would have to be protected by a strong fleet against the combined forces of France and Spain. Such in general was the external situation. At home, we must avoid the evils of the previous war by ensuring that our military and naval leaders were loyal, that soldiers and sailors were paid, and that parliament exercised a closer supervision over financial administration.

Other writers[3] pointed to the fact that, by concluding a peace, Louis had induced England and Holland to disarm; the peace which he offered was as dangerous as war, but more deceptive. He had been apparently conciliatory after Ryswick so that the emperor would have no pretext for establishing the archduke in Spain, and he had entered into the partition treaties in order to embroil the emperor with his former allies. By a 'dictatorial way of proceeding' the second partition treaty had been presented to the emperor and king of Spain almost as an ultimatum, intended to force their hand. A favourite topic of this popular literature was the bad faith of Louis. Under the title of *Anguis in Herba* a writer maintained that Louis's principles would allow him to maintain a treaty only so long as it suited his interests. The newspapers echoed the

[1] This is recommended in a tract bound up with the volume of State Tracts above referred to (*Bodl. State Tracts*, 1124). It appears also in *Bodl. Pamph.* 242, no. 21.

[2] *Bodl. Pamph.* 242, no. 26.

[3] *The Fable of the Lion's share Verified* (1701), in *Bodl. G. Pamph.* 1142.

same theme. 'In short, the French king must and will have war, somewhere or other.'[1] Peace, for him, was merely the breathing space between wars. The newspaper expressing this opinion indulged in sarcasm:

> Why should we question the good intentions of Louis XIV? He was always so generous that he would scorn to surprise any of his neighbours. Was he ever guilty of any unfair action? No, sure. He always aimed at nothing but what was good, as the peace of Europe, and his neighbour's welfare.

The title of Defoe's book, *Reasons Against a War with France* (1701), probably ensured that it was read by those who still needed conversion.

It may thus be claimed that the public conduct of Louis XIV not only determined England's entry into the war of the Spanish Succession, but also proved a factor in the political education of Englishmen. So far as we can speak of the 'mood' of the nation, it was for war; a mood reflecting the opinion not only of what we call the electorate, but of the far greater number who had no votes. Of the political parties, while most of the Whigs were prepared to embark on full-scale hostilities, many of the Tories believed that, either there would be no war at all; or that, if things came to the worst, England should participate only as a naval auxiliary; or even that she should remain neutral (with all the trading advantages of neutrality), and placate her conscience by subsidies to the Dutch and the emperor. Other Tories, anticipating that war was inevitable, were said to profess warlike sympathies in the hope that they would retain or obtain office if hostilities broke out.[2] At the head of those who were definitely against war was Rochester, nominally the chief of the administration; actually the only Tory who, by his rank, his churchmanship, and his relation to the princess Anne, was the unavoidable choice for high office. But he may have presumed too much on these qualifications, high as they were. Those who heard his fulsome eulogies of Louis XIV could hardly have guessed that he had done much to encourage the venal and shameful relations of that monarch with James II; by his assiduous preaching of peace, this

[1] *A New Observator on the Present Times*, no. 2, 1–8 Jan. 1701.

[2] Tallard to Louis XIV, 22 Mar.–2 Apr. 1701, in *Baschet*, 188.

eminently respectable relic of a corrupt age may have done the cause more harm than good. In the absence of effective direction, Rochester's party was led by two men who inspired somewhat more confidence in parliament, namely, Harley and Seymour, the first as Speaker of the House of Commons, the second as one of the most influential advocates of the Protestant succession.

Outside the field of party manœuvres there was a general feeling, probably stronger than any political conviction, that war in its now almost 'total' form not only involved the straining of every human and material resource, but ensured the enrichment of the many who battened on the nation's difficulties. Embezzlement and profiteering would be inevitable. Added to this was the fear that we might fare as badly in the new Armageddon as in the last; and that we would continue to be 'the Fight Alls, the Pay Alls and the Lose Alls' of Europe.[1] So far therefore from being bellicose, England was in a reflective and even chastened mood. Characteristic of this sense of responsibility, amounting to a patriotism devoid of jingoism, was the proposal to institute some kind of Home Guard, independent of the militia; so, in February 1702, a Bill[2] was introduced into parliament for the arming of all freeholders, in defence of their religion, property, and the Protestant succession. More important for the future was the fact that on 31 May 1701 William had appointed Marlborough as commander of the troops then assembling in Holland, and so at last there seemed some likelihood that British valour would be matched by its leadership. In May 1689 a king had declared war on Louis XIV; in May 1702 a nation went to war with France. Therein is the measure of England's advance in the reign of William III.

The king returned in November from Holland, where he had completed preparations for defence. Though the emperor pressed for war at once, William chose his own time, so that English and Dutch ships in foreign ports might be recalled, and the legislature given full opportunity for deciding whether or not peace could be kept with France. There was increasing evidence of wider support of royal policy, so William was in

[1] *The Present Condition of the English Navy* (1702).

[2] *H.M.C. Rep.* xv, app. pt. 4, 16, F. Lloyd to E. Harley, 15 Apr. 1701; also *MSS. of House of Lords*, new series, iv. 487, 26 Feb. 1702.

hopes that his sixth and last parliament, summoned for December, would prove more amicable, and would vote liberal supplies for the coming war. The keenly contested general election of the early winter of 1701–2 resulted in a considerable number of boroughs changing their representatives, many of the changes being in favour of the Whigs, who were said[1] to have obtained a majority of about thirty. But, against Littleton, the Whig candidate for the Speakership, the Tory Harley won, though by only a few votes. In spite, however, of the difficulty of classifying the members of the Commons into two definite parties, it may be said that, in this parliament, the Whigs were stronger than they had been at any time since 1698. More important the parties and factions were, for the time, joined in some kind of unison.

The king's speech of 31 December, penned by Somers, clearly revealed the dangers to European states arising from the establishment of French power in Spain and the Spanish possessions. 'Though the name of peace may be said to continue', he said, 'yet they are put to the expense and inconvenience of war', an early definition of what is now called 'cold war'. After an eloquent plea for the putting aside of party strife, the king reduced the divisions among his subjects to two: those who were for the Protestant religion and the present establishment, and those who wanted a popish prince and a French government. The speech concluded with this message to both Houses, the last he was to deliver in person.

The eyes of all Europe are upon this parliament; all matters are at a stand till your resolutions are known. . . . If you do in good earnest desire to see England hold the balance of Europe, and to be indeed at the head of the Protestant interest, it will appear by your right improving the present opportunity.

The reply of both Houses was prompt. On 2 January 1702 the address of the Lords contained these words:

All true Englishmen, since the decay of the Spanish monarchy have taken it for granted that the security of their religion, liberty and property, that their honour, their wealth and their trade, depend

[1] *Add. MS.* 17677 (Dutch Reports), vol. WW, 16–27 Dec. 1701. The Whigs boasted that they had this majority, 'without counting those who afterwards declare themselves for the winning party'.

chiefly on the measures to be taken from time to time against the growing power of France.

On the same day the Commons resolved unanimously that, to the utmost of their power, they would enable His Majesty to make effective all his alliances for preserving the liberties of Europe and reducing the exorbitant power of France. There were then communicated to both Houses copies of the treaties which showed how assiduously the king had built up the new Grand Alliance, from the terms of which it was abundantly clear that England was intent not merely on securing his rights for the emperor, but on maintaining her own interests in the Mediterranean and in the West Indies. For these purposes, the Commons, on the 10th of January, resolved that the English proportion of land forces should be 40,000 men and the same number of seamen. It is true that, in the war which followed, Britain did not succeed in excluding the Bourbons from Spain; but, otherwise, she obtained most of the objects for which she fought, because these included Gibraltar and Minorca; still more, she obtained the Hudson's Bay territory, Acadia, and Newfoundland, thereby laying the foundation of the great dominion of Canada. So, indirectly, and at great cost, the old, exclusive empire of Charles V provided for the evolution of a new and greater British Empire, destined ultimately to combine freedom and loyalty, the two things incompatible with each other in the dynastic state.

This parliament passed two Acts which showed how the nation had been united by Louis's recognition of the Pretender. One was an Act of Attainder[1] of the 'pretended' prince of Wales. The other was an Act[2] imposing on all members of parliament and office holders an oath whereby they recognized William as 'lawful and rightful' king and repudiated the claims of the Pretender. Here, as in 1696, was a recognition of William as king *de jure* as well as *de facto*; here was a test, so far as it could be applied by an oath, of loyalty to the Revolution settlement, and denial of the king 'over the water'.

But this matter was soon overshadowed by a more important event. For more than a year it had been obvious that the king's health was failing; indeed, at the Mauritshuis in the late

[1] 13–14 Wm. III, c. 3.

[2] 13–14 Wm. III, c. 6.

summer of 1701, he had sometimes been unable to see foreign ministers because of illness.[1] On 21 February 1702, as he was riding from Kensington to Hampton Court, his horse stumbled on a molehill, throwing its rider, whose collar bone was broken. A week later he sent from his sick bed his last recommendation to parliament—that of a union between England and Scotland; and the Bills which had passed the two Houses received the royal assent at the hands of commissioners. At first it appeared that the king might recover, but the physical shock proved too much for his emaciated frame, and on 8 March he died, in the fifty-second year of his age. In an era when the symbolic often outweighed the actual, the molehill on which the king's horse had stumbled acquired, among the Jacobites, a mystical significance; and numerous toasts to 'the little gentleman in black velvet' attested their rejoicing that one, whom neither the enemy nor the assassin could destroy, had at last gone to his account. To a superficial observer, it might appear that his reign was a failure; because as he had arrived in England when a war with France was about to begin, so he left it when a still greater conflict was to be engaged with the same enemy. It looked as if all his work would have to be done over again. But, in history, two such situations are seldom identical. The French menace, it is true, was more serious than ever, but England was now a much more formidable antagonist, because, from a community of divided and quarrelsome adolescents, she had developed into the unity and maturity of a nation. A great king had died when his mission was fulfilled.

[1] This was stated in his dispatch of 16–27 Dec. 1701 by the French chargé d'affaires in London. *Baschet*, 189.

XVII

THE BEGINNINGS OF PARLIAMENTARY SOVEREIGNTY

SOVEREIGNTY is one of the most obscure and debated of all political subjects, for hardly any two people can agree in defining either its source or its extent. But in the progress of English civilization one aspect of the problem, namely, legal or parliamentary sovereignty, has steadily acquired clarity of definition and latitude of application, so that today it is almost outside the realm of controversy.

As early as the thirteenth century Bracton had thought in terms of some kind of association for the purposes of government, composed of king and *magnates*; then Magna Carta had formulated the principle of no taxation without the consent of the *commune consilium regni*. A more advanced stage was that represented by Coke who, in his Fourth Institute, claimed that the power of parliament was 'absolute and transcendent'; but his examples show that he had in mind the High Court of Parliament, concerned with the making of laws, rather than with the direction of policy. Next came Hobbes, whose theory of an unlimited, undivided sovereignty, though postulated of a single, hereditary personality, was easily applicable to a body of men, such as king in parliament, a theory so challenging and absolute as to repel all who thought in terms of balance or compromise, and all who resented the idea that government is ultimately dependent on force. Nevertheless, it was Hobbes's theory, the most logical and the most misunderstood of the century, that ultimately prevailed, though the achievement was indirect and long delayed. In the course of that process the Revolution of 1688 is the dividing line between two periods in the history of sovereignty—an earlier one, in which there was no guarantee for the summoning of parliament; and a later one, in which, though both Houses had an assured and permanent place, the king was still endowed with certain personal prerogatives which limited the scope of parliamentary sovereignty. Hence, in this later stage, it was natural for Locke to popularize at home, and even more abroad, the idea of division of powers, a cordial much more palatable than the distasteful medicine prescribed by Hobbes. But, even then, the formula of Hobbes was in process of application; for there was gradually emerging that omnipotent and indivisible trinity of King, Lords, and Commons in which supreme power and direction are vested today.

Accordingly, in any estimate of the progress made by parliamentary sovereignty in the later seventeenth century, a beginning must be made with those personal rights still exercised by the crown. These rights were legacies from a long and sacred past. The prerogative of the Stuarts had owed much to the sacerdotal element in kingship; and, whatever may be thought of Charles II's virtues, there can be no doubt that, in his exercise of one element in that prerogative—the healing touch—he was (therapeutically) by far the most efficacious of English kings. This literal contact with the body of the subject, never attempted by William, was practised for the last time by queen Anne. In spite of the Bill of Rights, there still survived, in English kingship, many powers and exemptions, some of them relics of an older, mystic conception of sovereignty; for the prerogative was thought of as something essentially good, since it did not extend to anything that might injure the subject, or deprive him of his just rights. The king, it was conceived, had an interest in all his subjects, and a claim to their service; he had supreme patronage, appointing bishops by his nomination; as the fountain of honour, he created peers; as the supreme repository of mercy, he granted pardons. He could incorporate a town; and, in the opinion of some, he could revoke a grant of incorporation; he could make an alien free-born; he could put a value on the coin of the realm; he had a right to the lands of convicted felons. His prerogative was an essential part of the common law of England. Such were among the commonplaces of those lawyers who attempted to define this, the most elusive element in the constitution.

As James II had taken the Non Resistance divines too seriously, so he may have been encouraged, in his course of conduct, by the cloudy amplitude of rights and privileges with which the lawyers surrounded the throne. That cloudiness had been clarified in the Revolution settlement only by dispersal of the fog surrounding the dispensing power; otherwise, most of the old rights remained, including those of summoning, proroguing, and dissolving parliament; dismissing judges (before the Act of Settlement); appointing to high offices of state; vetoing legislation; declaring war and making peace. These were substantial rights. It is one of the paradoxes of English history that the parliamentary constitution dates from an Act which diminished the royal power so little, and from the rule of a king whose prerogatives were so great.

The first of these rights, that of summoning, proroguing, and dissolving parliament was limited generally by the clause in the Bill of Rights that, for the redress of grievances and the amending of the laws, 'parliaments ought to be held frequently'; and, more specifically by the Triennial Act of 1694.[1] This latter statute was modified by an Act of 1696,[2] the year of the Jacobite Assassination Plot, which enacted that parliament should not determine by the death of the sovereign, but might sit for six months thereafter. These were the legislative measures which ensured for parliament a permanent place in the constitution, and so must be regarded as the most important element in the Revolution settlement.

It is in these measures, and in the debates to which they gave rise, that we can detect the most striking characteristic of parliament, namely, the gradual adaptation of a medieval institution to more modern needs. Of this process, the starting-point was the widely held opinion that annual parliaments were of remote antiquity, an opinion apparently confirmed by those statutes of Edward III which required that the legislature should be summoned once a year, or more often if need be. As in so much else, the statesmen and politicians of William's reign had in view the lessons to be deduced from the more recent past, and here they were influenced by two sets of precedents; first, the Long Parliaments of Charles I and Charles II; and, second, the facts that, after the Oxford Parliament of March 1681, no parliament was summoned by Charles, and that James was without a legislature after November 1685. Now these two sets of precedents pointed in different directions and were of differ-

[1] 6–7 W. and M., c. 2. *Documents*, no. 51.
[2] 7–8 Wm. III, c. 15. *Documents*, no. 52.

ent degrees of consequence; for, while the two Long Parliaments, by their inordinate length, appeared to violate the ancient parliamentary constitution, the conduct of the later Stuarts appeared to abolish it altogether. Only by experience and experiment could there be devised a satisfactory solution of this, the fundamental problem in the English constitution.

These two sets of precedents were kept constantly in mind during the later part of the seventeenth century and the earlier part of the eighteenth. In regard to the first, it was generally held that the two Long Parliaments had completely changed in character during their lives, and that, before their dissolution, they had become arbitrary and unrepresentative. A standing parliament was therefore considered as dangerous as a standing army. But here is one of the many instances where we are better able than contemporaries to assess an important stage in historical evolution; our best qualification for understanding the seventeenth century is that we do not live in it. We can now see how these two legislatures reflected a transformation in the functions of the House of Commons. In medieval times the Commons might well meet annually, or more often, because their sessions were short and their province limited; the same was still true, though to a less extent, in the sixteenth century; but, by Stuart times, the Commons were encroaching on all the prerogatives of the crown, except foreign policy; their status, with reference to the Lords, was changing; and, most of all, they were now seen to be organic institutions, capable of growing up, in spite of assiduous attempts to clip and control them. In a formal sense these two parliaments had ceased to be 'representative'; nevertheless, in some remarkable way, they evidenced a development which transcended and even anticipated the course of national evolution, a phenomenon clearly perceived by possibly only one contemporary, that great rake the second duke of Buckingham. In a speech[1] to the Lords in 1677, containing so many unpalatable truths that he was sent to the Tower, the duke said:

I have often wondered how it should come to pass that this House of Commons . . . should be less respectful to your lordships . . . than any House of Commons that were ever chosen in England; and yet, if the matter be a little enquired into, the reason of it will plainly

[1] *Documents*, no. 49.

appear. For, my Lords, the very nature of the House of Commons is changed. They do not think now that they are an assembly that are to return to their own homes and become private men again (as by the laws of the land and the ancient constitution of parliaments they ought to be) but they look upon themselves as a standing senate, and as a number of men picked out to be legislators for the rest of their lives. And if that be the case, my Lords, they have reason to believe themselves our equals. But, my Lords, it is a dangerous thing to try new experiments in a government.

Buckingham was right. The parliament, of which he was such a colourful member, ended its nearly eighteen years of existence by formulating most of the principles afterwards embodied in the Revolution settlement; so there seemed no limit to what a House of Commons might do if only it sat long enough. For a full exercise of its fast-increasing powers it needed a certain duration of tenure, short parliaments being characteristic of those more limited assemblies which had served the purposes of earlier times.

But the other set of precedents was of more immediate importance. How could parliament ensure that it would be summoned frequently or regularly? In 1664 a Triennial Act had provided that there should not be more than three years' interval between parliaments, but nothing was said about their length. Charles II had violated this statute; and James II had seemed likely to follow his brother's example. Meanwhile, this Act remained on the statute book, but the Revolution legislators practically ignored it. As early as 1689 they had set themselves to devising means of ensuring that parliament would not be dispensed with; here indeed was their most urgent task. In the first draft[1] of their Bill for this purpose, it was enacted that, ten months and twenty days after a dissolution, if no warrant came from Their Majesties, the lord chancellor should issue writs of summons to the peers; failing such action, the peers were to meet on the fortieth day after the date[2] when parliament ought to have met. So too, if no writs had been issued to the sheriffs, they were to cause elections to be made in boroughs and counties. Failing the sheriffs, the freeholders

[1] *H.M.C. Rep.* xii, app. 6, *MSS. of House of Lords, 1689–90*, 364, 17 Dec. 1689.

[2] Presumably the date as determined by the Triennial Act of 1664. For this Act see *Documents*, no. 48.

might lawfully meet, and choose one of their number to act as 'sheriff of elections'. A lord chancellor neglecting his duties under this Bill was to incur the penalties of the statute of provisors and praemunire,[1] and a sheriff guilty of similar negligence was to forfeit what was then the enormous sum of £1,000. This Bill dropped at the prorogation of 27 January 1690; its terms are here recited because they show, as nothing else could, how the Commons were striving to obtain definite guarantees for the regular summoning of parliament. But the Triennial Act, as finally assented to on 22 December 1694, merely enacted that parliament should be summoned at least once in three years; to this was added a new proviso—that its life should not last more than three years.

As William was in the habit of keeping his word, there never was any doubt about the frequent summoning of parliaments in his reign; indeed, the longest intermission between them was a period of ten months;[2] and the fact that this was much criticized at the time shows how England was becoming habituated to the regular summoning of one parliament after the dissolution of another. Contemporaries were more impressed by the limitation in the length of its life; indeed, this Triennial Act was hailed as the beginning of a golden age in politics,[3] because the electorates would now have more frequent and regular opportunities for passing judgement on the conduct of their representatives. But this enthusiasm speedily waned. Some thought that triennial or more frequent elections endangered family influence in the constituencies, by encouraging outsiders to intervene; as elections were more frequent, more money had to be spent on them, thereby debauching the people and prejudicing trade; electors, it was thought by some, might prefer to return an old member, provided he had an office, for this alone ensured that he could spend money on his re-election. The fact that parliaments now had a definite maximum life may also have encouraged a greater amount of management and preparation in the constituencies, and in this way the nation probably became more politically minded; indeed, it was said that, in consequence of the Act, a permanent faction was maintained in every county and borough.[4] In this closer

[1] 16 Ric. II, c. 5.

[2] *Supra*, 457.

[3] *Burnet*, iv. 239.

[4] Ibid. 455.

correlation between Westminster and the electorates, those party distinctions which were just beginning to divide the House may have been gradually extended to the constituencies.

The measure also had some influence on the evolution of party politics. It was regarded as the alternative to the abortive Place Bills favoured by the Tories; and, like the Septennial Act, it came down to the Commons from the Lords. In the one case, the Upper House took the initiative in curtailing the tenure of the Lower; in the other case, they took the initiative in extending it, in this way maintaining the Commons in their seats for a longer period than that for which they had been originally returned. Accordingly, the Tories of 1716 could argue, with some justification, that the Septennial Act was a breach of trust with the nation, and that it threatened a return to those Long Parliaments which had so profoundly altered the constitution; hence the Triennial Act, opposed by many Tories in 1694, was acclaimed by nearly all of them in 1716 as one of the sacred things in the constitution, and so one more was added to the popular rights demanded by a new Toryism. But the Whigs, whose development showed greater continuity, were justified in a measure which gave longer life and therefore greater power to parliament; and this, not merely because 1715 was a year of crisis and rebellion, but because the accession of George I implied that, in effect, much of the surviving prerogative would pass to the Commons. There must, for instance, be more continuity in foreign policy than was possible in a succession of short parliaments. This difficulty had been obviated in William's reign by the fact that the king retained supreme direction of foreign affairs; short parliaments, in the closing years of his reign, did not greatly matter, so far as our external relations were concerned; but it was otherwise under the Hanoverians, when a ministry, actually responsible as much to the Commons as to the crown, was beginning to take the place of groups of officials responsible only to the king. So the Triennial Act, like the attempts to exclude placemen from the Commons, had to be abandoned, the one because it was found inadvisable, the other because deemed impracticable, two examples of how our constitution has been built up by the method of trial and error.

In regard to the second element in William's prerogative,

the right to dismiss judges, their independence was an axiom implicit in the Revolution settlement, and a clause securing their tenure had just missed inclusion in the Bill of Rights. Before the matter was finally set at rest by the Act of Settlement, it was apparently within the power of the king to remove a judge as he might remove a secretary of state; moreover, in 1692 William vetoed a Bill intended to provide a safeguard against royal dismissal. But, from the beginning, he completely respected the independence of the judges. He tried to interfere with the lord chancellor's right of appointment to legal offices;[1] but not once did he show displeasure at the opinions or conduct of a judge. Events proved that the threat to judicial independence might come from a source nearly as formidable as the throne, namely, the House of Lords; and it was in this reign that the distinction between Westminster Hall and the Upper House was first clearly vindicated, in a case not in itself important, but involving momentous issues.

This was the curious and complicated case of Charles Knollys, earl of Banbury, an earldom which Charles I had created by letters patent. The son of the first earl had sat and voted in the Lords, until it was discovered that he had received no writ of summons; so it appeared that his son, Charles Knollys, was a peer, but not a lord of parliament. Only by ending this ambiguity could he claim full parliamentary privilege, which, at that time, was so ample as to ensure for the lords of parliament almost complete immunity from the consequences of a capital crime. So, as if to put this matter to the test, Knollys committed murder in 1692, and then petitioned the Lords to be admitted as earl of Banbury, so that he might be tried by his peers. He had judged rightly. At his arraignment before Holt in King's Bench he put in a special plea that, as a peer, he could not be indicted there; and, as the judges were convinced, from the evidence produced, that the accused was earl of Banbury, they quashed the indictment and released him on bail. Meanwhile, the Lords acted with some irregularity in regard to the claim before them. They refused to consult thereon with the judges; and, in spite of opposition, they took it upon themselves to reject Knollys's claim to the earldom.[2] There then

[1] *Hardwicke State Papers*, ii. 426–7, Somers to the king, 27 Mar. 1693.

[2] *L.J.* xv, 17 Jan. 1693 and 11 Apr. 1694.

followed a period in which Knollys was suspended, as it were, between two courts—House of Lords and King's Bench—both of which refused to put him on trial, a period of suspense in which the earl (having also committed bigamy) was engaged with another tribunal, the High Court of Delegates, which had the difficult task of deciding between his two 'wives'.[1]

The deadlock might have continued, had not the irrepressible Knollys petitioned the king, in 1697, that he should be formally recognized as earl of Banbury, a petition which the king referred to the Lords. As they were now probably aware of their initial mistake, the Lords, in a vindictive mood, were anxious to vent their spleen on others; so they summoned Holt and his colleagues before them to answer for their conduct. The defence of the lord chief justice was based on two contentions; first, that his judgement in King's Bench could always be questioned by appeal. As one responsible for that judgement, he refused to give his reasons in any place other than his own court. 'I am not', he said, 'to be arraigned for what I do judicially.' His second contention was that the Lords had treated Knollys's claim to the earldom as an original cause, whereas they could properly entertain it only by way of appeal. The Upper House, Holt contended, was not entitled to try a matter of fact—in this case, whether or not Knollys was earl of Banbury—such a matter being beneath the dignity of a supreme court; moreover, if the Lords insisted on trying an original cause, the subject's right of appeal would be lost. These were courageous words, and their speaker was very nearly committed to the Tower.[2] As for Knollys, the cause of all the trouble, a contemporary noted that 'he remains untried to this day', a failure of justice which nevertheless helped to ensure the establishment of two essential principles; namely, that although, after the Act of Settlement, a judge may be removed by an address from both Houses, he is not obliged to explain or justify his judgements to either of them; and that the function of the House of Lords is that of a supreme court, its province limited to those cases that come to it by appeal.

[1] *P.R.O. Court of Delegates*, 212, no. 494, *countess of Banbury* v. *earl of Banbury*.

[2] The proceedings will be found in *State Trials*, xii. 1157–1208, and *English Reports*, xc. 1191 sqq., and xci. 904 sqq.

The above case helps also to explain why the judges, when consulted, were always so unwilling to express an opinion about the proceedings of either House, or about what is now called constitutional law. In the case just cited, there was a clear distinction between Knollys's earldom, which was as triable at law as his estates, and the right of the Lords to petition the king to summon him to be of their body, which was no concern of Westminster Hall. Led by Holt, the judges insisted that, as their province was limited to common and statute law, they could not be drawn into any pronouncement on what they conceived to be outside these domains. So, in 1689, they declined to pronounce on the social contract, because it was not mentioned in their books;[1] and most of them adopted the same attitude in regard to the crown's alleged right to declare forfeit a grant of incorporation.[2] This action of the judges implied that, in their view, there was no distinction between 'constitutional' and common or statute law, since the former was comprised in the latter; hence one of the distinctive characteristics of the British constitution, that it is governed by no laws more 'fundamental' than others, all the laws being equally fundamental.

The third right exercised by William—that of appointing to high offices of state—was acquiesced in, but not always willingly. In 1689 the Commons, admitting that their main function was to give advice, disclaimed any right to make recommendations for the filling of the higher executive posts;[3] but two years' experience of the conduct of the naval war caused them in November 1691 to discuss a proposal that the House should appoint to the higher naval commands;[4] and the royal choice of commissioners of the Admiralty was objected to on the ground that so few of them had naval experience.[5] So too with the army. The infamous conduct of Solms at Steenkirk prompted an address by the Lords that only British subjects should be appointed to the supreme military posts,[6] an address which William ignored. As regards civil places, high office in William's reign still meant high office connected with the royal household, or the privy council, or the administration of the

[1] *Supra*, 226. [2] *Supra*, 61–62.

[3] *Grey*, ix. 473.

[4] Report of F. Bonnet, 6/16 Nov. 1691 in *Ranke*, vi.

[5] *Grey*, x. 274. [6] *L.J.* xv, 18 Feb. 1693.

law, a fact which helped the king to retain his right of appointment, since there still remained a certain personal element in the relation of these offices with the crown. The long process whereby that personal element has been diminished dates from William's reign; for the modern minister, though still one of His Majesty's ministers, and though he still receives the seals of office from the sovereign, is mainly the creation of new administrative needs, of which, in this period, the most important were economic and financial. In December 1695 a member of the House of Commons declared that, while we might do without a king, we could not do without trade;[1] accordingly, early in the next year the council of Trade and Plantations came into existence, the ancestor of the Board of Trade and the Colonial Office. A few years earlier, the chancellor of the Exchequer, from an obscure official responsible only to the Treasury, suddenly became a minister, responsible to parliament and nation. Here was the beginning of a development, not anticipated by the Bill of Rights, and (by its exclusion of office holders) repudiated by the Act of Settlement, a development which can be directly associated with the strain imposed by William's war. With this extension of government (as distinct from royal) control, and the consequent creation of new departments, there has been effected a transformation, not only in the character of the House of Commons, but even in our conception of the functions of the state. The state, whose duties are primarily to defend from external enemies and to suppress internal enemies, has been succeeded by the state which not only rules, but provides for an increasingly large number of human needs. But whether new department is but old king writ large is one of the debatable questions of modern politics.

William vetoed five public Bills, of which four were important measures. In chronological order these were: the Bill establishing the salaries and tenure of judges;[2] the first version of the Triennial Act;[3] a Place Bill, or Bill for free and impartial proceedings in Parliament;[4] and a Bill for regulating elections.[5] This use of the veto aroused considerable criticism, but the fiction was adopted of imputing its exercise to evil councillors,

[1] *H.M.C. Rep. MSS. of marquis of Downshire*, i. 597, 13 Dec. 1695.

[2] 24 Feb. 1692; *supra*, 359–60.

[3] 14 Mar. 1693; *supra*, 387.

[4] 25 Jan. 1694; *supra*, 391.

[5] 10 Apr. 1696.

so diverting attack from the king himself; who was also saved, by a majority vote, from the imputation that his conduct showed ignorance of the English constitution.[1] In the fourth instance, the rejected Bill would have imposed on all knights of the shire a territorial qualification of £500 per annum, and on all burgesses a similar qualification of £200. The city of London and several boroughs protested, as this would have excluded many substantial merchants who, it was thought, were at least as well qualified to sit in parliament as ignorant squires, concerned mainly with enforcement of the game laws. William may have been influenced by such protests. It is notable that all these measures eventually passed into law; but only the first, that relating to the judges, was to prove permanent. William did not exercise the veto after 1696, though on several occasions he may have wished that he could do so, as on the presentation of the Bill for annulling grants of Irish forfeitures, which was tacked to a money Bill.[2] By his moderate exercise of this right William preserved it for his successor, whose use of it showed even greater restraint.

It was in his power to make war and peace that William's prerogative differed most obviously from that of the modern constitutional sovereign. Two things helped to confirm him in this right—the facts that the Revolution settlement implied a European war, and, even more, that he had a much better knowledge of Europe and European affairs than any English statesman. But the length and cost of his war, together with the king's engaging in two unfortunate partition treaties, caused both Houses to be much more critical of this right, though their feelings were assuaged to some extent by the king's communication to them of copies of some of the treaties whereby England was committed abroad. In this connexion, the Lords made an interesting proposal in March 1701, during their discussion of the partition treaties. They suggested[3] that, in all matters of such moment, the king should act only on the advice of his natural-born subjects, and that for this purpose he should create a council of trustworthy persons, for discussion of all affairs of importance, both at home and abroad. This was a clear hint that the king must no longer conduct foreign affairs

[1] *C.J.* xi, 27 Jan. 1694.

[2] *Supra*, 451.

[3] *L.J.* xvi, 20 Mar. 1701.

on his own, or with the advice only of such foreigners as Portland. It was unfortunate that the Commons were not invited to join in this address. But, on their side, the Commons were making it abundantly clear, by their impeachments, that ministers who merely registered the royal decrees in the sealing of treaties were doing so at very great risk. Thus, by the end of the reign, it was evident that this part of the prerogative was being tacitly surrendered; and the circumstance that William was followed in succession by a woman and by a foreigner unable to speak English helped to ensure that, in regard to foreign policy, parliament could not be ignored.

It was by means of his moderate and reasonable use of such a vast prerogative that Willliam helped to secure for the crown a permanent place in the British constitution. This is all the more remarkable as he was by nature autocratic and headstrong; but his great self-control kept these instincts within bounds. Almost unfettered by the letter of the constitution, he nevertheless respected its spirit.

The House of Lords[1] in William's reign consisted of more than 150 members, as contrasted with barely sixty at the beginning of the century, a difference which provides evidence of the large number of Stuart creations, James I having been responsible for no less than sixty-two. There was a strong Whig element in William's House of Lords, increased by addition of the newly appointed bishops; but on the other hand, neither the debates nor the divisions in the Upper House were usually conducted on what could be called party lines. Always conscious of their historical priority to the Commons, aware of their closer personal contact with the sovereign, and proud of the part which they had played in national history, the Lords in this period were more than usually insistent on their rights; but the comparative absence of faction or strong party spirit among them helps to account for their emergence, notably at the Revolution and in the international crisis of 1701, as a senate rather than a branch of the legislature. It was in their numerous disputes with the Commons that clear expression was given to this exalted conception of their rights.

These disputes sometimes resulted in refusal to co-operate

[1] Reference may be made to A. S. Turberville, *The House of Lords in the Reign of William III.*

with the Commons in matters where national interests were obviously concerned. Thus, in December 1692, when the whole conduct of the war was under review, they refused to join with the Lower House in an address to the king, a refusal which evoked an emphatic protest from a minority, which urged that the king himself had expressed a desire for such advice from parliament, and had communicated to both Houses papers relating to the conduct of the war.[1] Even in finance there was disagreement. While it was recognized that the Commons controlled the purse, the principle was not always easy of application; for example, in 1689 when the Lords introduced into a money Bill a clause reducing the rate on goods imported for re-export, an occasion when the Upper House claimed the right to diminish the rate of tax granted by the Commons, if such action was for the benefit of trade, 'of which the Lords conceive that they are equal and competent judges'.[2] In 1693 they claimed that, regarding the Poll Bill of the previous year, they had good precedents for assessing themselves; but they surrendered this claim, in order to allow a Money Bill to pass, asserting at the same time their right to amend or abate Bills of Supply.[3] So too, in 1697, they claimed the right to add an amendment, imposing a pecuniary fine for infraction, to a Bill forbidding the importation of wrought silks, a penalty which they refused to regard as charging money on the subject, since the subject could avoid the penalty by not breaking the law.[4] All this showed how the Lords might try to invade even the financial preserves of the Commons. More serious differences were the prolonged deadlock, in the earlier years of the reign, over the Trial of Treasons Bill, and the bitter quarrels over the impeachments in 1701. The Lords were attempting the difficult task of keeping the Commons in their place.

On their side, the Commons were not clear what was their place. That they should be completely detached from the administration was the opinion of the Tories; but there was less certainty on the question whether or not they might exercise executive powers. In its distrust of crown officials and its increasing disquiet at the conduct of the war the House at times seems to be feeling its way, anxious to extend its control

[1] *L.J.* xv, 7 Dec. 1692.
[2] Ibid. xiv, 27 July 1689.
[3] Ibid. xv, 20 Jan. 1693.
[4] Ibid. xvi, 12 Mar. 1697.

by creating bodies responsible to the Commons alone, even though the functions of these bodies might overlap those of existing institutions responsible to the crown. The first example was seen in 1689, when an Act[1] was passed for the enforcement of more adequate measures in the suppression of unlawful export of wool. By this statute, the Commons appointed their own commissioners, who were given executive powers likely to bring them into conflict with the Customs commissioners. The institution of this supplementary board appears to have been welcomed by the cloth merchants, who suffered from the smuggling of wool;[2] but, on the other hand, the Treasury naturally objected to the payment of commissioners not under their control.[3] The second of such extra-constitutional bodies appointed by the Commons—again by statute[4]—was the committee for examining and stating the public accounts, which, as a source of information, provided the House with an alternative to the Treasury itself, and served to expose many of the opportunities whereby the executive could ensure support by places and pensions. A third body instituted on the initiative of the Commons was the council of Trade and Plantations, the origin of which can be attributed to the alarm of parliament and nation at the serious losses of ships and cargoes in the war, and to a realization of the need for investigation and co-ordination of our resources at home and in the plantations, as well as for a better-planned direction of our overseas trade. The demand for such a body was regarded by the supporters of the Court as a serious encroachment on the prerogative; and, but for the changed attitude to William occasioned by the Assassination Plot of 1696, the terms of the commission might well have implied such encroachment. Eventually, the functions of the new council were limited to inquiry and advice, their recommendations being submitted to king in council, and their findings were often embodied in legislation.[5] It is impossible to

[1] 1 W. and M., c. 32. For this see R. M. Lees, 'Constitutional Importance of the Commissioners for Wool, 1689' in *Economica*, xiii (1933).

[2] *Cal. Tr. Bks.* xiv, 1698–9, 180–1, Nov. 1699. Petition from the cloth merchants.

[3] Ibid. 85; 23 May 1699.

[4] 2 W. and M., sess. 2, c. 11. Also *supra*, 341.

[5] *Supra*, 305–7. Also *Documents*, no. 207. For the resolutions of the Commons, see *C.J.* xi, 31 Jan. 1696. It had originally been proposed to establish this body

distinguish any clear party principle in all of these three instances; what they show, however, is that dissatisfaction with the conduct of the executive was so great as to prompt the Commons to invade its domains.

Members of both Houses enjoyed distinctive privileges; the fact that those of the Lords were even more numerous than those of the Commons helps to explain the animosity with which the Lower usually regarded the Upper House. Like church and crown the peers diffused around themselves an atmosphere of immunity and exemption, their virtues and abilities being second only to those of crowned heads. Some of their rights were inherent in the status of peerage; others were derived from privilege of parliament; by the grant of a written 'protection' a lord of parliament might confer on others some of the privileges which he himself enjoyed. All this was characteristic of a theocratic society, dominated by a hierarchy of birth; it was natural, therefore, that the peers were prominent among those who insisted on the death penalty for atheism,[1] and were warm supporters of the numerous measures intended to penalize debauchery among the lower classes.

Parliamentary privilege, as exercised by members of either House, was so extensive as to have serious social consequences. When pleaded, it might suspend judicial proceedings indefinitely;[2] it extended to the solicitors and attorneys acting for peers, though this was withdrawn by resolution of the Lords in 1697.[3] In practice, freedom from arrest for debt was the most important privilege enjoyed by members of both Houses and their servants, since it applied during sessions and for forty days before and after sessions. Hence, a debt might be so long evaded that, by pleading a statute of limitations, it could eventually be wiped out. Privilege might be waived by permission of either House; or it might even be granted to an

by statute, but the proposal was negatived. See also R. M. Lees, 'Parliament and the Proposal for a Council of Trade, 1695–6,' in *E.H.R.* liv (1939).

[1] e.g. the Atheism and Blasphemy Bill, imposing the death penalty for atheism, and making the offence incapable of pardon or reprieve. This passed the Lords in Jan. 1678, but was laid aside by the Commons. *H.M.C. Rep.* ix, app. pt. 2. *MSS of House of Lords*, 98.

[2] For examples see *L.J.* xv, 12 Jan. 1692, report from committee of privileges, and *C.J.* xii, 10 Feb. 1699.

[3] *L.J.* xvi, 24 Mar. 1697.

outsider, as when in 1701 the Lords conceded it to sir John Dillon, who had a divorce petition before the Lords, but could not afford to prosecute it, because of debts contracted by his wife after her elopement.[1] The written 'protection', which might be issued by a member of either House, was so valuable that it was sometimes sold[2] or forged.[3] One of the peers, lord Morley and Mounteagle, used this right as a means of raising around him a body of retainers, reminiscent of the old days of livery and maintenance. Sixty persons were said to enjoy his lordship's protection; and at his headquarters in Hornby it was unsafe for a sheriff's officer to attempt an arrest without Morley's approval. His town, as an informal place of sanctuary, was nicknamed Whitefriars, and his men were called the Blackguards.[4] Extremely sensitive, like his fellow peers, about his reputation, he brought an action of *Scandalum Magnatum* for £1,000 against one who said that he was no peer. He was really the last of the barons.

It is to their credit that, in William's reign, both Houses showed some self-denial by limitation of their privileges. A standing order of the Lords took away privilege of parliament from peers' sons, noblewomen, and peers' widows, 'saving their peerage'; and the widow of a peer marrying a commoner was declared to forfeit her rights of peerage altogether.[5] The Lords also, while retaining 'protections',[6] limited their number, as well as instituting a register of all that were issued.[7] In this matter of protections, the Commons went farther; for, in 1690, they declared them void, and resolved that no more should be issued;[8] moreover, in 1699 they withdrew privilege from office-holding members in respect of anything done in the execution of their office.[9] The culmination of this process came in 1701 with the Act[10] which limited parliamentary privilege, so that it became more difficult to use it as a means of evading payment of debt. Generally, in these matters, the Commons, particularly

[1] *L.J.* xvi, 1 Apr. 1701. [2] Ibid., 15 Jan. 1697.

[3] *C.J.* x, 17 Jan. 1690; *H.M.C. Rep.* xiii, app. pt. 5, 27–28.

[4] Ibid. xiv, app. pt. 6 (*MSS. of House of Lords*), 7 sqq., 4 Jan. 1692.

[5] *L.J.* xv, 21 Feb. 1693.

[6] As late as 1725 a peer (the earl of Suffolk) was committed to the Tower for abusing this privilege. *Cobbett*, viii. 414.

[7] *L.J.* xv, 21 Nov. 1692. [8] *C.J.* x, 23 Jan. 1690.

[9] Ibid. xiii, 28 Nov. 1699. [10] 12–13 Wm. III, c. 3. *Supra*, 467–8.

where there was a Tory majority, appear to have been more sensitive to public opinion than were the Lords, whose privileges were derived not only from office but from birth.

Like the Lords, the Commons insisted on the absolute privacy of their proceedings, and maintained what amounted to a censorship of the press. In 1690 they condemned as a 'false and scandalous libel' a pamphlet giving a list of those who had voted against offering the crown to William and Mary,[1] and they resolved that no newsletter writer should presume to meddle with the debates or proceedings of the House.[2] For his comments on the financing of Exchequer Bills, the editor of that enterprising newspaper *The Flying Post* was taken into custody. Charles Blount's *King William and Queen Mary Conquerors*, which claimed that these sovereigns owed their crowns to conquest, was ordered to be burned by the common hangman, and the press censor Edmund Bohun was imprisoned and dismissed from his office for licensing the book. Another manifesto, maintaining the same thesis, had the advertisement of public incineration, namely, a pastoral letter by Burnet. The bishop must have ruefully contrasted this attitude with the reception given in 1679 to the first volume of his *History of the Reformation in England*, when he had been thanked by both Houses, and requested to continue the great work. Molyneux's *Case of Ireland Stated*[3] and at least one pamphlet on the Darien disaster were among the many expressions of opinion that incurred the anathema of the Commons. The Lords were particularly severe on the publication of anything reflecting on one of their own order. For printing a paper reflecting on lord Grey of Werk a printer was committed to the Gatehouse and fined £100;[4] and an oilman who made outspoken remarks about lord Morley was 'attached'.[5]

Regulation of its rights and privileges was accompanied by the attempts of parliament to reform the procedure at elections. For this purpose, three Bills were passed in 1696. The first of these, which was designed to check the increasing cost of elections, forbade, under penalties, the giving of money or bribes to electors;[6] the second, intended to diminish double or false

[1] *C.J.* x, 2 May 1690.
[2] Ibid. xi, 22 Dec. 1694.
[3] Ibid. xii, 27 June 1698, and *supra*, 9.
[4] *L.J.* xiv, 8 Mar. 1689.
[5] Ibid., 30 July 1689.
[6] 7–8 Wm. III, c. 4.

returns, enacted that returns on a franchise contrary to the last determination of the Commons were to be adjudged invalid.[1] The third Act[2] instituted a limit of forty days between the issue and the return of the writ. Public notice was to be given of the time and place of the election at least four days before the event, and no unnecessary adjournment was to be allowed. No person under twenty-one was allowed to vote. This was probably the most comprehensive measure yet enacted for limiting abuses at elections, but it does not appear to have proved effective; equally ineffective was the attempt to prevent revenue officers from interfering in elections.[3]

In making their choice, the electorates were influenced by a great variety of motives, ranging from the extremes of the bribery that might be practised by a wealthy 'carpet bagger' to the almost hereditary claims of a landed family in the neighbourhood.[4] On at least one occasion, namely, in the fiercely contested election of January 1701, the crown was said to have sent agents to several boroughs known to have previously returned Tories in order to bribe them to return Whigs, a practice which led to complaint in the House.[5] In a different category were those cases where it was expedient to secure the return of some important administrative official, such as lord Ranelagh, paymaster of the forces, holder of an Irish peerage. In 1695 Ranelagh was without a seat, so he addressed himself to secretary Shrewsbury, who first solicited the earl of Bath for one of the Cornish boroughs, and eventually induced lord Tankerville to nominate him as one of the burgesses for Chichester.[6] An increasing number of boroughs was coming to be 'managed' in this way, sometimes on a large scale; and it was to the 'managers' that the secretary of state or the candidate himself would apply. Sometimes this pressure assumed a more primitive form. Thus at Chippenham when it appeared, early in 1695, that a general election was imminent, a number of gentry in the neighbourhood, on behalf of the sitting members, threatened to withdraw their work and custom from the borough

[1] 7–8 Wm. III, c. 7.

[2] 7–8 Wm. III, c. 25.

[3] *Supra*, 466.

[4] For this see *supra*, 124–5.

[5] Tallard to Louis XIV, 3 Feb. 1701 in *Baschet*, 187.

[6] The correspondence will be found in *Add. MS.* 40771 (Vernon Papers), ff. 75–87. Also f. 325 for nomination to a Cornish borough in 1698.

if these persons were unseated.[1] Often, the mere presence of a great personage or official at an election would serve the purpose; as in 1701 at Winchester, when the appearance of no less than three dukes at the hustings was followed by the return of the candidates for whom they expressed approval. In the same election, at Huntingdon, a peer and other persons, armed with swords and clubs, assaulted the Recorder and all who voted the wrong way, an incident which caused the Commons to pass a resolution that, for any peer or lord lieutenant to meddle in elections was an infringement of the rights and privileges of the House. A more insidious influence was that which a landlord or lord of the manor might exercise over his tenants; most straightforward of all was the application of public funds, by a receiver of revenue, for the purpose of bribing electors. All these examples,[2] selected from instances in the year 1701, show that, so far as elections were concerned, the eighteenth century had dawned.

It can well be understood that foreign observers were at a loss to understand how a body of men, returned to Westminster by such a variety of methods, not all of them creditable, could have exercised such influence, not only in England, but in Europe. No one could predict what a House of Commons might do, a factor which often defeated the most ingenious manœuvres of Court managers and the most subtle calculations of foreign diplomats. We may even wonder how such an oddly constituted body of men came, on so many occasions, to group itself into two fairly well-defined parties, especially as party doctrines appear to have had little influence, in the greater part of William's reign, on the choice made by electors. Possibly the quarrelsomeness, for which Englishmen were notorious at this time, may have helped to create a dualism as soon as the members had been long enough in each other's company; it needed only an important event to divide an irritable assembly into two fiercely opposed camps. But these frequent groupings, which might be precipitated by any question of the hour, provided Commons and nation with that experience from which party principle and discipline were being evolved.

In spite of innumerable outposts, and unwillingness to accept party labels, two main combatants can be distinguished before

[1] *C.J.* xi, 5 Jan. 1695.

[2] Ibid. xiii, 15 Feb. 1701.

the end of the seventeenth century, the Whigs and the Tories. In the last years of Charles II's reign the Whigs could claim to represent all who valued national independence (then bound up with Protestantism); parliamentary government; toleration for all but Roman Catholics; ministerial responsibility and the social contract. In contrast, their opponents were still shackled by the absurdities which Filmer had fastened to the Old Testament, and were bedevilled by analogies from a long series of crowned and anointed personages, most of them ruffians, to whom obedience was due, even to the point of martyrdom. The first set-back to this doctrine was the affair of the Seven Bishops, who, had they suffered martyrdom in the cause of Passive Obedience, would have died, not for obedience, but for disobedience. But, before that level of absurdity had been reached, the Whigs had offered an alternative. The great lesson which they deduced from the execution of Charles I—the most important political event of the century—was the futility, and even the impossibility, of enforcing personal responsibility on the king; to destroy him was the supreme confession of clumsiness and failure. Charles had been put to death on the assumption that he had done wrong; his successors were doing much more wrong. The popular profession of willingness to endure martyrdom in such circumstances seemed to the Whigs a helpless, obsolete attitude; so they suggested a novel device. For his public acts of state, as distinct from his private deeds, the king needed a minister; and, so long as the king had the initiative, the minister might shelter himself under the cloak of the royal command. It was in order to deprive the minister of this shelter that the Whigs revived the old lawyers' fiction: *The king can do no wrong*. This maxim had at first meant little more than that, for every wrong, the subject has a remedy in the king's courts; it was now applied to matters of state in such a way that the fictive innocence of the king was postulated in order to ensure the responsibility of the minister. On the white screen of royal innocence could be measured, in shades of grey and black, the guilt of ministerial accomplices; and as this responsibility could be enforced only by impeachment, the Whig doctrine implied the regular meeting of parliament. Kings would go on being bad, but with this difference, that their advisers, thinking of the block, exile, or imprisonment, would hesitate to share in their misconduct, knowing that the measure of royal innocence was the measure of ministerial guilt. In this way, so far as his acts of state were concerned, the king would be sterilized.

The maxim had never been a part of Tory or Divine Right theory, for the Tories had always admitted that the king can do wrong, and they had insisted on his responsibility; but, as for wrongs to the subject, the only escape was martyrdom, and as for royal responsibility, that was to God alone. Charles II, who was intelligent enough to understand the meaning of the Whig principle, shielded Danby from its application by giving him a full pardon, and leaving him for his own safety in the Tower; he naturally preferred the halo with which the Tories surrounded the throne to the vacuum in which the Whigs would have enveloped it. But, just as in nature it is difficult to create an absolute vacuum, so in English history, the process of completely extracting responsibility from the king's person proved difficult of achievement; and so it is not surprising that a long time elapsed, including the reign of George III, before the process was completed. This is now one of the few basic things in the British constitution, so implicit and fundamental that it is not even mentioned in the constitutional documents commonly known to the historian, though it is well known to the lawyers, and its application to the subject in litigation has recently (1945) had to be modified.

A political party may lose its appeal in proportion as its doctrines come to be accepted as commonplaces. This happened to a slight extent with the Whigs in the seventeenth century, as it happened to a great extent with the Liberals in the twentieth. In the course of William's reign the Tories, abandoning for the most part the Divine Right and Non-Resistance millstones by which their necks were encumbered, quietly appropriated the Whig lifebelts which alone ensured survival in the raging seas of royal iniquity; and in 1701 they tried to enforce the principle that the king can do no wrong. The situation then, in regard to Somers, Halifax, and Orford, was almost identical with that of Danby more than twenty years before. In both cases the king had used a minister or ministers for negotiation with a foreign power; in one case to obtain money, in the other to effect a partition of the Spanish empire.

In both, it was clear that, so far as there was wrongdoing, it was the king's. But neither the Whigs of 1678 nor the Tories of 1701 breathed a word against the king; the ministers alone must be called to account. On 16 April 1701 the Tory House of Commons made the first clear demonstration of the oblique consequences of the principle; for, in their address to the king,[1] they expressed satisfaction that he had not entered into the partition treaties without the advice of his English councillors (as a matter of fact, he had practically ignored them). The address then repudiated the allegations of the three ministers that His Majesty had entered into the treaties without their advice. The fiction was thus pushed as far as falsehood.

It is true that in 1715, when, in their turn, Tory lords were impeached by Whigs, the former sought to shelter themselves behind the cloak of royal responsibility, so reverting, for a time, to their old doctrine that the king can do wrong. But meanwhile, this address of 1701 was one of the most important pronouncements of the reign, for it showed that the Tories were gradually adopting one of the fundamental positions of the Whigs, and in this way the principle of ministerial responsibility came to be elevated above party strife. That doctrine, inseparable from parliamentary sovereignty, was an essential element in the legacy of the seventeenth century to modern times.

It was in the means for its enforcement that parliament revealed a characteristic which distinguishes it from other legislatures, namely, its functions as a high court. By Bill of attainder or by process of impeachment both Houses joined in the task of dealing with exalted offenders, and the king himself was head of this judicial body. All this helped to confer on parliament a dignity and finality such as no mere debating society could ever have achieved; for the responsibility of the minister, inseparably linked with the fictive innocence of the crown, could be readily established within doors, without resort to Westminster Hall. That public opinion is now strong enough to provide this safeguard is evidence of our political advance.

This book has attempted, in its references to society and institutions, to connect the development of English civilization

[1] *C.J.* xiii, Ap. 16, 1701.

with the gradual and peaceful adaptation of medieval survivals; in illustration of this development, the examples of crown and parliament may be cited. In parliament, even as late as the end of the seventeenth century, the Lords, in this little distinguishable from the feudal magnates, still exercised personal privileges which we would consider social abuses; while the Commons were returned by methods, few of which would be commended by the political theorist of today. In both Houses there were thus traces of a perverted medievalism. Nevertheless, parliament had now become permanent and national, directing the state through its first European war, and committing it to another, in which the foundations of world supremacy were to be laid. A similar process of adaptation can be seen in the changed place assigned to the crown in our constitution; and, in the functions now performed by the king, it is possible to detect the sublimated relics of ancient party aspiration. On the one hand, the old Whig, applying his common law maxim to the prerogative, would acclaim in the sovereign such absolute detachment from party distinction and political initiative as to make public wrongdoing impossible; on the other hand, the old Tory, his religion transmuted into a sentiment, would applaud in the same sovereign a human link, binding together a great commonwealth of free nations, a ruler far more potent than any Divine Right king. Thus the monarchy is the most remarkable of all these survivals because, while its powers are still regulated by a medieval fiction, it has been adapted to conditions undreamt-of in the past.

XVIII

THE DAWN OF THE EIGHTEENTH CENTURY

THE periods which for convenience we call the seventeenth and eighteenth centuries were divided, not by the year 1700, but by an indeterminate frontier stretching across that landmark. In order to indicate some of the characteristic features of that frontier, selection is here made mainly from the years 1690–1710, and the following groups of subjects have been chosen for summary treatment: (1) Censorship, Patronage, and Journalism; (2) Science and Deism; (3) Social Reform Movements; (4) Rival views about man and society—Mandeville, Shaftesbury, and Locke.

1. CENSORSHIP, PATRONAGE, AND JOURNALISM

Until 1695 (with a brief interval) the Press was subject to the Licensing Act of 1663, which had organized a system of censorship, derived from Star Chamber practice, whereby books, in accordance with their subject, were licensed by the lord chancellor, the archbishop of Canterbury, or one of the secretaries of state. Written permission was signalized by the word *Licensed*, usually appearing on the blank page facing the title-page. The phrase *With Allowance* was used wherever the permission was verbal. *Published by Authority* implied almost a command to publish. As well as this, all books had to be entered in Stationers' Hall, and a new official had been created, namely, the surveyor of imprimery, whose duty it was to enforce the Act of 1663 and search for unlicensed books and printing presses. This official worked in conjunction with Stationers' Hall. Between 1663 and 1688 the surveyor was the famous (or notorious) sir Roger L'Estrange,[1] who, with Henry Care, conducted in James's reign intensive literary propaganda, not of a high level, on behalf of the royal policy. L'Estrange, who was given wide powers of entry and search, was respon-

[1] For a full account see G. Kitchin, *Sir Roger L'Estrange*.

sible for bringing many printers and authors to trial and conviction.

L'Estrange's successors, Fraser and Bohun, held office for very short periods, both being removed for licensing books which gave cause for public offence—the first for permitting the publication of a book maintaining that Gauden, not Charles I, was the author of *Eikon Basilike*, the other for licensing Blount's *King William and Queen Mary Conquerors*. In this way the censorship was discredited, and the Licensing Act, together with the surveyor, came to an end in 1695.

This has usually been hailed as a triumph for the freedom of the Press, and even as evidence of greater enlightenment after the Revolution. But contemporaries did not think so. Hitherto the publication of political news had been the monopoly of the *London Gazette*, and the mere publication of such news by an unauthorized person might lead to prosecution, because the Press still remained subject to the law of libel, and in the late seventeenth century that law extended very far. In 1704 Holt declared that any criticism of the government constituted seditious libel;[1] accordingly, the editors of newspapers had to be very careful about their political comments. Even thus, in 1698 and in 1701 Bills were introduced into parliament for the restoration of the licensing system, but they were not proceeded with,[2] possibly because by that time newspapers had become securely established. But there still remains the question: why was the Licensing Act allowed to lapse? In April 1695 the Commons sent to the Lords a Bill for continuing certain Acts. From the list they omitted the Licensing Act; by an amendment, the Lords restored it. This led to the usual dispute; and, at a conference, the Commons gave their reasons. In the statement[3] of these, there is not a word about freedom of the Press, but a great deal about the monopoly of the Stationers' Company. It was alleged that, by the necessity of entry in the Company's registers, the publication of many 'innocent' books was delayed; moreover foreign books, which could be imported only into London, were detained for long periods at the Custom House until the Company sent its searcher. Still more, the

[1] In *Rex* v. *Tutchin*.

[2] *MSS. of House of Lords*, new series, iii, 1697–9, 271 sqq., and *L.J.* xvii, 24 Jan. 1702.

[3] *L.J.* xv, 18 Apr. 1695.

Stationers monopolized the printing of several classical authors, and so scholars had often to be content with imperfect texts; even the printing trade was hampered by the restriction of employment to those who were free of the Stationers; and the smiths who made the iron-work for presses could not do so without giving notice to the Company. The Lords accepted these arguments, adduced not in favour of freedom, but against an older kind of 'freedom', and so the Licensing Act lapsed.

The censorship had been in abeyance for six years after 1679, a fact which helps to account for the great volume of pamphlet literature inspired by the Popish Plot and the Exclusion controversy. Within three years of the abolition of the censorship, there was evidence of change in regard to one form of opinion, namely religious opinion. This was evidenced by an Act of 1697–8,[1] for the suppression of blasphemy and profaneness, which enacted that anyone brought up as a Christian who, by writing or speaking, denied that any one of the persons of the Trinity was God, should, for a first offence, be deprived of his office or employment; for a second offence, the penalty was three years' imprisonment. Now, the impressive thing about this Act is the moderation of its penalties, so strikingly contrasted with those which, only a few years before, had been proposed in the legislature,[2] and contrasted even more strongly with those which were still enforced for religious disbelief in France and Scotland. This indeed may be cited as evidence of the advance achieved by England of the Revolution; for, while there was still a strict control over political opinion, it was now recognized that the harsh repression of religious scepticism might do more harm than good. For a first offence, an atheist was merely deprived of his office; whereas, in Europe generally the penalty was death. Thenceforward, in England, Christianity did not have to depend for its truth on the gallows.

A similar change, following closely on the abolition of the censorship, can be traced in public opinion.[3] The reaction

[1] 9 Wm. III, c. 35.

[2] *Supra*, 501 n. 1.

[3] For this see A. Beljame, *Le Public et les hommes de lettres, 1660–1714*. This book, as valuable for the student of history as for the student of literature, was first published in 1881. An English translation appeared in 1948; and in 1954 it was reproduced, with an introduction by B. Dobrée.

against the Stuarts was accompanied by reaction from the type of drama which they had popularized, and men must have realized the injustice of a system which penalized independence and permitted indecency. This change was to prove one of the formative influences in post-Revolution literature, for writers speedily realized that they had abundant scope in the broad provinces between the seditious and the salacious. This greater freedom (provided they refrained from criticism of the government) may have encouraged them to consider their readers more carefully; indeed, after about 1695, one can begin to think in terms of a reading public, kept closely in view by such writers as Defoe, Addison, and Steele. Moreover, the new lenience in regard to religious opinion helped to encourage writings of a philosophic, or semi-philosophic kind, and so accounts for the spread of Deism, and systems based on Natural Religion.[1] Orthodoxy may have suffered, but humanity benefited. Had the censorship survived, it would have experienced difficulty with writers, such as Mandeville and Swift, who resorted to allegory; of these, the first would have been banned and prosecuted as soon as his meaning was understood. So the lapse of the system at least removed a clog on literary output, and induced the writer to think in terms of a tribunal more final and exacting than any imposed by the state.

In an age when one of the functions of the state was to control or repress, and of the nobility to direct or encourage, the patron, whether king or duke, was the complement of the censor. Together, the two institutions were intended to ensure that inspiration was both sponsored and regulated. For poet, dramatist, and artist, patronage was often a matter of economic necessity; on the other side, by giving public and discriminating encouragement, a great man might add to his prestige.

The English kings of the seventeenth century were munificent patrons of pictorial art; portraiture was the one interest shared by the sovereigns of that period, and their encouragement, in succession, of such foreign artists as Van Dyck, Lely, and Kneller has given to posterity a record, not only of the royal lineaments, but of the notables, male and female, who thronged their Courts. To Van Dyck, we owe a depiction of the somewhat melancholy dignity of Charles I, to which the

[1] *Infra*, 528–30.

hauteur and assurance of his consort serve as a foil; and the young Charles and James were caught by the artist while still in the bloom of boyhood. Then, in 1641, the prince of Orange, coming to England for the hand of Mary Stuart, brought in his train the Dutchman Peter Lely, who perpetuated on canvas those languishing, somewhat unintelligent-looking beauties, who made such insistent demands on the fickle allegiance and the public money of Charles. A rival soon appeared. Godfrey Kneller was introduced to English society in 1675; and, while Lely was painting Charles in 1678, Monmouth presented the young German artist, who soon took Lely's place as fashionable Court painter. James proved such an assiduous patron, and commissioned so many portraits of the royal family, that Kneller claimed to perceive in the features of the Pretender evidence of his authenticity. The same appreciation of his art was shown by William and, later, by Anne. The galleries of Windsor and Hampton Court, as well as the National Portrait Gallery and many private collections, attest the unbroken and discriminating patronage of art exercised by a series of sharply contrasted sovereigns.

This proved a factor of notable consequence in the evolution of English society. Noble families, and the wealthy in general, followed the royal example; before the end of the century, many private collections of importance were being formed. The Grand Tour helped to enlarge these treasures and to familiarize the educated traveller with the masterpieces of European galleries. England became an art-loving as well as a music-loving nation.

In pictorial art, there was no native English talent comparable with that shown in music. It may be that, as music had always had the support of the church, its traditions were not completely broken by the Reformation; whereas, pictorial art and ornamentation were regarded by the early Protestants as relics of popery. Alternatively, it is possible that painting flourishes best where there are close-packed civic communities, such as in Renaissance Italy, or fifteenth-century Flanders, or seventeenth-century Holland; by contrast, England was for long primarily agricultural; and, outside London, the towns were unlikely to include men who either practised or encouraged art. Nevertheless, there was some native talent and even a hint of great things to come. Francis Place, a Yorkshire amateur, executed a number of topographical drawings, some of them lightly tinted, all of them depicting scenes in his county.[1] He failed to be convincing with his rocks—a notorious stumbling-block to many later artists; but, here and there, he anticipates Paul Sandby and the early English water-colour school. This is noticeable in his 'Ouse Bridge, York' and his 'South-East side of Richmond Castle', in both of which he showed a sense of architecture in the setting of a lightly suggested landscape. More notable was his contemporary Mary Beale, a protégé of Lely's. Those of her portraits that are preserved in the British Museum are mostly of members of her family, and so have a certain sameness of feature; but, none the less, these exquisite miniatures in red chalk show a delicacy and perception which confirm the view that this talented woman was among the earliest of the great school of British portraitists.

Of musical achievement in England there was a wider and deeper basis, for church and king had long encouraged a high standard of performance, well maintained by a succession of organists and choirmasters, who either excelled in composition, or produced sons who did. There was also public appreciation; indeed, in the later years of the century there was an awareness of how the choral services of the church, particularly those of the cathedrals, were exercising a profound influence on the formation of musical taste; and it was freely admitted by several preachers that the singing of the psalms and listening to the voluntaries might have an effect as good as that of the sermon.[2] Already, however, there had occurred what appeared to be a disastrous break in this tradition, namely, the Puritan expulsion of music from the church. But, outside the church, the Puritans encouraged music. Opera in England dates, not from the Restoration, but from the Commonwealth. This came about indirectly. Davenant was astute enough to realize that a Puritan audience would welcome a musical play, so long as it was not called a play; this is why he styled his *Cruelty of the*

[1] A considerable number of Place's drawings will be found in the Print Room of the British Museum.

[2] Two sermons in praise of church music, preached in 1693 and 1700, will be found in *Bodl. G. Pamph.* 2960.

Spaniards in Peru (1658) an 'entertainment', and that sufficed.[1] Accordingly, in Commonwealth England there was inaugurated a movement similar to that afterwards exemplified in the Germany of Bach, the Italy of Vivaldi, the France of Couperin, a movement which encouraged the composer, usually a church organist or musician, to devote part of his efforts to secular themes. The Commonwealth was therefore a formative period in English music because a new direction was given to the art. After all, the Puritans included such music lovers as Milton, Bunyan, and Cromwell himself.

As the saints drove music from the church, so Charles II restored it to the church. But with a difference.[2] Neither the king nor his Court had any appreciation of the devotional; but they liked a simple, easily-remembered tune, or the fruity voice of a tenor soloist, or a well-matched melody for strings. So in 1663 Charles sent to France Pelham Humfrey, one of the choir-boys of the Chapel Royal, in order to study French models. This royal appreciation of foreign ideals, together with the large amount of talent available, particularly among the choir-boys and organists, helped to create what sir Hubert Parry described as 'one of the most interesting and unfortunate phenomena' in the history of this art, in so far as it was hectic, self-contained, having few links with the past, and creating no tradition for the future. But, even since Parry's time, there has been a keener appreciation of this period of English music, in proportion as unpublished compositions have been brought to light, and acquaintance with them diffused by means of broadcasting; indeed, in this way there has been some re-adjustment of values, for we are gradually realizing the enormous amount of talent, even genius, hidden away in the works of English composers hitherto regarded as obscure. Whatever may be one's opinion of the merits of the later Stuarts, there can be no doubt about the merits of their composers and musicians.

Of these, at least two were men of genius. John Blow (1649–1708) began as one of the children of the Chapel Royal, and at

[1] Percy A. Scholes, *The Puritans in Music*, provides the best account of this subject.

[2] For this see C. H. H. Parry, *The Music of the Seventeenth Century* (Oxford History of Music, vol. iii), ch. 7.

the age of twenty-one he was organist of Westminster Abbey, a post which he held for two periods, his pupil Purcell acting in that capacity during the interval (1680–95). He was also organist of the Chapel Royal and master of the choristers; like Bach, he was famous in his own day mainly as an organist. Best known for his numerous anthems and service settings, including the *Salvator Mundi* and *O Lord God of my Salvation*, he turned his hand to a secular subject in his *Venus and Adonis*, a masque which contains some of the finest instrumental music of the century. He has long been overshadowed by Henry Purcell who also began as a chorister. In 1677 he was appointed composer-in-ordinary to the king. His music was popular then, and that popularity has steadily increased, a fact to be accounted for, not only by its intrinsic quality, but by its wide range, for it included many anthems and services, the odes on St. Cecilia's Day, the musical settings of several plays and operas, of which the greatest was *Dido and Aeneas*. He conferred equal distinction on secular and sacred themes, and even his most popular tunes retained some of the integrity of the old church music. So when Handel settled in England he found a high level of musical appreciation and achievement in the country of his adoption.

Thus, both in pictorial art and in music, the patronage of church and king proved a formative influence of the highest consequence; and, but for the encouragement that came from these sources, the level of achievement would almost certainly have been lower. In these two spheres of imaginative expression, there was at that time a certain element of selectivity, since both painting and musical composition were thought to require a certain minimum of technical competence or training, without which nothing could be done. But it was very different in literature, because anyone can write; accordingly, in this sphere, the patronage system may have done harm, by encouraging bad writers and diverting the aims of good ones; still worse, many of Dryden's contemporaries wrote, not because they had something to say, but because they were expected to say something. In this way, the most personal and intimate of all forms of self-expression was, as it were, socialized; and as England became more purposeful and self-conscious, the public life, dominating every other interest, brought even poetry within its orbit, so that the couplet became a counterpart of the repartee, and verse an elegant form of polite conversation. But there was one poet. Dryden might have applied to himself what he said of Shakespeare:[1] 'he is always great when some great occasion is presented to him'. Such an occasion had been presented in 1666, the year of the Great Fire and the Four Days' Battle with the Dutch, when, in his *Annus Mirabilis*, he was inspired to write a miniature epic, having as its undercurrent the emergence of the nation from the perils of Plague, Fire, and War, an undercurrent which seems to weave its way among the stanzas like the ebb and flow of the sea. Then there was another great occasion in 1681, when England was just beginning to recover from the hysteria of the Popish Plot. All that was needed was healthy laughter, the ability to see even one's own follies in perspective. Dryden performed that great national service in his *Absalom and Achitophel*. But the poet-laureateship and increasing dependence on patrons eventually proved his undoing. Having changed his religion in James's reign, he produced his *Hind and Panther* in defence of his new faith and his new master. No production ever lent itself more easily to ridicule, and that ridicule was supplied by Charles Montagu and Matthew Prior in *The Town and Country Mouse*.

Dryden's adulation of patrons was noted by contemporaries. In this respect the women writers emulated and even outdid the men. Mrs. Manley, dedicating *The Royal Mischief* to the duke of Devonshire, claimed that, under his aegis, she was immune from the critics: 'the honour of Your Grace's approbation will be security for me that none of sense will condemn what you seemed to approve.' Not to be outdone, her sister pioneer Mrs. Trotter dedicated her *Fatal Friendship* to the princess Anne, with this admission—'permit me to decline your encomium . . . best expressed in an awful silence'. Somewhat more discriminating patrons were Somers and Montagu, both of whom encouraged the young Addison, for whom in 1698 a Treasury grant of £200 was obtained in order to enable him to travel abroad. For such noblemen as the duke of Newcastle, the earls of Orrery, Dorset, and Mulgrave, association with polite literature added a certain renown to their status; with the decline of the system, the man of letters had to take his chance with the most fickle of all patrons—the public.

[1] *Essays of Dramatic Poesy* (ed. W. P. Ker), 79.

It was to the public, and not even the educated public, that journalism appealed; its great development, in the years after the treaty of Ryswick, may be connected not only with the lapse of the censorship, but with that process, evidenced in the last years of William's reign, whereby people became more interested in questions of the hour. Another factor favouring journalism was the vogue of the essay, already exemplified so brilliantly by Dryden. This has some historical significance; for, while the theologian usually speaks, as it were, in the indicative; the secular essayist, thinking not so much of truth as of opinion, may favour what might be called a subjunctive mode of thought; and so may offer us, instead of a single dogma, a set of alternative interpretations. This transition from priest to layman is thus not only one of subject matter, but of literary expression; and, on the eve of the eighteenth century, Englishmen were revelling in the discovery that there might be a great many different solutions to an apparently simple problem. In other words, a mentality was in process of creation which, in essence, was tolerant; and, of all the fruits of civilization, tolerance is that which has deepest roots.

Illustration of this contention must therefore come from humble sources—not from the plays, or poems or learned treatises which, after all, were the work mainly of men brought up on traditional standards, and were known only to a small minority; it must come from the newspapers and popular journals, many of which penetrated below stairs. This more tolerant spirit can be seen in what was obviously a new feature adopted by several journals, such as the *London Mercury*, when answers, some half serious, others merely facetious, were given to questions, presumably submitted by readers. Occasionally the answer may have suggested a point of view very different from any in the mind of the questioner. For example, the problem: 'whether cock-fighting and bear-baiting be not unlawful for Christians?' received this unexpected answer: 'Christianity teaches us the deepest compassion and tenderness of nature, and this even to irrational creatures. Delight in suffering of animals is cruelty.'[1] Doctrinal orthodoxy was slowly giving way to common humanity.

Some of this literature was so ephemeral that we know of it

[1] The *London Mercury*, no. 14, 25 Mar. 1692.

only indirectly, through references in the newspapers. In 1700 *The Post Man*[1] advertised a serial publication, entitled *The Art of Living*, which apparently consisted of short essays, some dealing with popular prejudices or superstitions, others maintaining a somewhat startling paradox. One of these, entitled 'The learned differ', summarized the conflicting opinions given by experts at Hertford Assizes on the death of Mary Stout;[2] another discoursed on the curious situation that might arise from princes marrying by proxy those whom they had never seen. Mostly, the titles of these short essays suggest some entirely novel attitude of mind; 'in praise of the toothache', 'in praise of poverty', 'on being unmarried by Act of Parliament', 'in defence of a mean birth', 'a defence of speedy marrying after death', 'proving there's nothing new under the sun', and so on. The technique of popular journalism was coming into existence; and from it, even the humblest were learning that there are usually two sides to a question. Even more, a new and human element was penetrating into literature. The editor of the official *London Gazette* must have been anonymous and absolutely impersonal to his readers; indeed, it was essential that it should be so; and the same was true of most newspapers. But in the newer journals, the editor had a personality, whether genuine or fictive, of which his readers were made conscious. Every week he came forward with some new discovery or hypothesis; his personal reaction to events could be followed closely from his regular commentaries; to his readers, he became a genuine, though anonymous human being. With his unfailing solution for every conceivable conundrum, or his ready answer to every question from readers, whether real or imaginary, the editor became a Father Counsellor to thousands who had access to no other source of opinion or advice.

Many of these journals were short-lived; some because they had been launched in order to meet a demand created by the war, such as that for a knowledge of European geography; others because they fell on evil days. Those that survived usually had a remarkable variety of topic. An example is the *Gentlemen's Journal*, the first number of which appeared in January 1692, a miscellany consisting of news, history, philosophy, poetry, music, and translations. The editor announced

[1] *The Post Man*, 13–15 Aug. 1700.

[2] *Supra*, 102.

that, in spite of the name, the magazine was intended also for women; 'they will not need to blush'. For those interested in science there was an article on 'the nature of dryness and moistness', followed by 'enigmatic' verses and a review of a recent volume of Temple's Memoirs. The editor expressed the hope that serving soldiers and sailors would send him an account of their experiences, and the number concluded with a new song set to music by Purcell. All this shows that a reading public was coming into existence, demanding neither the technical nor the erudite, but something combining enjoyment, whether literary or musical, with the stimulation of interest and curiosity.

Nor was all of this literature intended to be merely ephemeral. In 1698 a bookseller in Little Britain was producing 'sixpennies' on such subjects as these: angling, fowling, painting, bee-keeping, cooking, and 'how to live on 2*d.* a day'. These practical manuals, enlightened by *A spark from the Altar*, *The whole duty of the Sabbath*, and the (inevitable) funeral sermon provided the first series of cheap, popular books published in England. In the same year, a rival bookseller brought out a series for the more historical-minded at 1*s.* each. This included an account of the kings of England from the Conquest; a history of Scotland and a history of Ireland; a biography of Drake, a history of earthquakes from the Creation, and *The English Empire in America, with pictures of the strange creatures Therein*, a title which suggests that English opinion was being prepared for Dr. Johnson's description of America as a place where emigrants (mostly convicts) immersed themselves and their posterity in surroundings of unrelieved barbarism.[1] As these manuals were not likely to be taken by learned libraries, they have probably perished.[2]

In this new journalism by far the greatest figure was Defoe. As a none-too-successful tradesman in his earlier years, encumbered with a wife and six children, he acquired a practical experience of life such as was unknown to contemporary writers; and so, on most of the questions of the hour, he could speak from an unusual angle—that of the common man. A Dissenter, he had no university connexion; a courageous individualist,

[1] *Boswell's Johnson*, ed. Birkbeck Hill, v. 78.

[2] The author knows of these manuals only through advertisements in the newspapers, and has not been able to trace any of them.

he knew more of the pillory than of the patron. This unique position called for a new technique. Perceiving that an author's books are usually read only by those who share his views, and that the plain statement of a minority opinion would bring on him a storm of abuse, or something worse, he adopted an oblique approach—he penetrated into the enemy camp in disguise. The disguise usually consisted of sarcasm and irony, by means of which he presented the enemy case with just enough fidelity to make it look genuine, and just enough exaggeration to make it ridiculous. But even he sometimes failed to mix the ingredients in the right proportion, as witness his *Shortest Way with the Dissenters* (1702), in which he suggested a settlement of the problem by wholesale hanging. Some readers regarded the book as comparable with the bible; others thought that its author should be made a bishop; many earnest-minded churchmen welcomed this expression of their heart-felt convictions in what appeared to be a devotional work. The fury of such readers can be imagined when it was discovered that the book was a hoax. The result was Defoe's appearance in the pillory, but the cheers and health-drinking by the sympathetic crowd proved that an odd pair of twins had come into the world—journalism and tolerance.

It was in the weekly *Review*,[1] begun in February 1704 when he was in prison, that Defoe established his reputation as a great journalist, and revealed the enormous possibilities of the Press as an agent in social reform. No other writer had shown such an acute awareness of those things which contemporaries condoned and we condemn. Among many examples are his vigorous condemnation of the wreckers of the south coast, who not merely stole the cargoes of wrecked ships, but murdered the sailors, or left them to drown;[2] there was also his criticism of the system of debtor's prisons, indeed of the whole principle of imprisonment for debt.[3] Defoe was probably the first Englishman to realize the social and economic background of crime, much of which he attributed to sheer want: 'Give me not poverty lest I steal'; 'Necessity is the parent of crime'.[4] His

[1] In this paragraph I have quoted from the extracts in W. L. Payne (ed.), *The Best of Defoe's Review, an Anthology*.

[2] Ibid. 190–4.

[3] Ibid. 119–21.

[4] Ibid. 269–71.

attitude to social problems was, therefore, not only more humanitarian, it was more penetrating than that of his age. Characteristic also of this intelligent journalism was his pride in Britain. Against those who decried its soil and climate, he contended that in no other country was there such variety of product and pasture; both, especially in the production of wool, essential elements in English prosperity.[1] Of trade he said many shrewd things. Everyone recognized its importance, but social convention still decreed that connexion with retail trade implied something mean and even dishonourable, an attitude which has long persisted. Lastly, Defoe was one of the few contemporaries who realized the full significance of the Union of 1707. For him, it meant the creation of a new and united nation; so he deplored alike the resentments that lingered in the north, as well as the hostility and contempt so often expressed in the south. Writers may roughly be classified according as they encourage people in their beliefs or shock people out of them. Defoe was of the latter class, which, at that time, had need of courage as well as of independence.

2. Science and Deism

Many people were also shocked out of their opinions by the scientists, though, in this case, the process was longer and more subtle. Intellectual activity in the later seventeenth century might be loosely distinguished according as it was directed to scholarly pursuits of a traditional kind; or according as it was concerned with those investigations into natural phenomena which gradually transformed men's ideas of the world and of the universe. In these spheres, English achievement was immense; and in both, though otherwise so different, there was the same practical or concrete element, so characteristic of English mentality. The first of these, scholarship, was fostered not only by the universities, but by great libraries, such as the Bodleian, the libraries of the Inns of Court, of Lambeth Palace, of private collectors, such as sir Robert Bruce Cotton; there were also many state papers in the Tower, already reduced to some kind of order by the labours of Prynne; and at Westminster there were the archives of the Exchequer, recently explored by Selden, and soon to be investigated by Madox. In William's

[1] W. L. Payne (ed.), *The Best of Defoe's Review, an Anthology*, 272.

reign, Thomas Rymer was busily engaged, with the help of a small government grant, on the collection of material for his monumental *Foedera*; in a more private and academic capacity, Thomas Hearne was producing a large number of medieval texts, while Henry Dodwell was applying to ancient history some of the canons of criticism recognized today. If there was little of what would now be called history writing, there was nevertheless much preparation for it, since the vast resources of material were being examined, and made more easily available. In this enterprise the churchmen played a notable part. Atterbury and Wake engaged in a heated dispute over the medieval antecedents of Convocation; Edmund Gibson produced in 1695 a translation, with additions, of Camden's *Britannia*; and the non-juror George Hickes, who devoted himself to the compilation of a grammar and dictionary of the ancient Scandinavian languages, perpetuated the tradition of Anglo-Saxon scholarship already inaugurated by Spelman.[1]

In this type of scholarship there was no obviously scientific element, save in the fact that, as it was concerned mainly with the interpretation of originals, critical standards were being applied, where formerly legend or tradition had prevailed. But, in another class of scholar, the antiquaries, the link with science is more obvious; for these men, notably Ashmole, Plot, Thoroton, Aubrey, and Thoresby, were essentially observers and topographers, who included what we call botany and geology among their interests at a time when these subjects, so far from being specialized, were considered to be within the province of every intelligent observer. The ardent explorers of those ruins, which the Reformation had done so much to create, were also keenly interested in plants and fossils; so their explorations of a dead past served to illuminate a living present. This great band of men, few of them having any academic connexion, all of them the continuators of Camden and Leland, were concerned mainly with the discovery of England; inevitably, interest in armorial bearings and tombstone inscriptions was deflected to those natural objects whose mystery invited the scrutiny of the inquiring mind. Of this evolution from antiquary to scientist sir Hans Sloane provided a good example. In 1687 he went out to Jamaica as physician to its new governor, the duke of

[1] For this see D. C. Douglas, *English Scholars, 1660–1730*.

Albemarle, and made notes of his observations in several of the West Indian islands.[1] As an antiquary, he recorded customs and folk-lore, including the songs sung by the negroes in the plantations; as a scientist, he kept a daily record of the weather, and preserved innumerable plants for examination.

Sloane, afterwards to prove such a distinguished and generous figure in English life, was only one of a large number of physicians who were applying their trained intelligence to the investigation of natural or human phenomena. Thoroton, the antiquary of Nottinghamshire, was a country doctor, who announced that, as he made his livelihood by preserving the living, so he would find his hobby in preserving the dead; another physician was John Woodward, whose examination of fossils led to some of the earliest theories regarding the strata of the earth's crust. Of the same profession was Nehemiah Grew, one of the first to explore the cellular tissue of plants and the phenomenon of pigmentation: there was also Richard Morton, whose field was tuberculosis, in which he diagnosed the characteristic cough of the consumptive, still known as Morton's Sign; and, lastly, Sydenham, a great medical pioneer, who studied his patients as much as his books.

These last three—Grew, Morton, and Sydenham—had also this in common that, as nonconformists or low churchmen, they had been debarred by the Act of Uniformity (1661) from a career in the church. In this indirect way, even intolerance had promoted the cause of science. The same is true of John Ray,[2] the greatest naturalist of the century. At first a lecturer in Greek and mathematics at Trinity College, Cambridge, he combined these studies with botanical excursions in the neighbourhood of Cambridge, the results of which were incorporated in his *Catalogus Plantarum* (1660), in which he enumerated and described about 600 species. He resigned his fellowship rather than comply with the Act of 1661, and thereafter he devoted himself to the work of botanical classification, conducted in England and on the continent. It is noteworthy that he also recorded local customs and antiquities. He was

[1] Published in 1707 as *A Voyage to the Islands Madeira, Barbados, Nevis, St. Christopher and Jamaica.*

[2] For Ray see S. H. Vines and F. W. Oliver, *Makers of Modern Botany*, and C. E. Raven, *John Ray.*

probably the first, before Linnaeus, to insist on the necessity for exact terminology in the description of natural objects; as well as this he perceived the many affinities between animal and vegetable life; indeed, it was with Ray that natural history became established as a scientific pursuit, instead of as the hobby of antiquary or topographer.

It is characteristic of the great diversity of intellectual activity in this period that even a cursory reference to its scholarship and antiquarianism has, by a not unnatural sequence, led to science. After all, the pinnacles of Newton and Boyle, and the heights achieved in mathematics and astronomy by such men as Halley, Hooke, and Flamsteed, have obscured this substratum of diffused scientific inquiry and interest. One might almost expect this of an age when the whole field of knowledge was open to men of intelligence and initiative, with results which place England of the later seventeenth century on an intellectual level even higher than that of Renaissance Italy. Here our concern is not with these achievements,[1] but with some of their historical consequences. As the Italian Renaissance was followed by a wave of scepticism and anti-clericalism, so the scientific movement in England was accompanied by a more critical attitude to the clergy and a readjustment of belief. For a time, there was a sharp conflict of loyalties. Did the truths of revealed religion stand or fall by the failure or success of the new science? Did the theory of gravitation disprove the old cosmogony? Now Newton was a Christian first and a scientist afterwards; he would have regarded with horror any suggestion that his discoveries discredited the teachings of Christianity. But, to lesser men, it appeared that Christianity was dependent on the supernatural, and that the Newtonian system undermined the religious foundations on which society was built. In this way were brought together three things, namely, the revolutionary significance of the scientific movement; the desire of the scientists to be free from the imputation of infidelity; and increasing disquietude, among churchmen and laymen alike, regarding the possibility of a reconciliation between the new physics and the old bible. This unusual conjunction precipitated a conflict not unlike that produced in the

[1] For a good, general account see H. Butterfield, *The Origins of Modern Science*.

nineteenth century by Darwin's theory of evolution; and the solution was to prove of as great consequence in the development of English civilization.

The conflict had its centre in the Royal Society. As a comparative new-comer, this institution owed much of its position to the patronage of Charles II, and to the fact that prince Rupert had been a fellow; but, on the other hand, its object, investigation of natural phenomena, was abhorrent to many of the clergy; while its methods, experiment and field research, were frowned upon by the scholars, who soiled their hands only with dusty books. Such prejudices had to be disproved or lived down. Accordingly, its first historian, bishop Sprat, claiming that the Society was 'a general bank and free port of the world',[1] commended it on the ground that most of its members were gentlemen (this had been denied by some critics). Hitherto, according to Sprat, the cause of knowledge had suffered from the fact that, as students were mostly indigent, they usually had to sacrifice learning to a livelihood; also they thought of truth as something taught by an authoritative master to submissive pupils. Both of these disadvantages were, it was claimed, avoided by the concourse of a body of men, few of whom had to earn a living, and all of whom were on equal terms. This was a shrewd thrust at the universities. Nor was this all. In the bishop's opinion, England had unique advantages which served to make her the spearhead for the advancement of knowledge. One of these was 'the noble and inquisitive genius of our merchants'.[2] They lived honourably, not meanly, in foreign parts, conversing freely, and learning from all. Of this intellectual curiosity, the Royal Society was the embodiment.

But the forces ranged on the other side were even stronger. They were assisted by two hatreds—hatred of the Puritans, who for long had been connected with encouragement of science, as well as with revolutionary schemes for university reform; and hatred of Hobbes, who also had criticized the universities and, still worse, was under the imputation of atheism. By his rejection of revelation and the supernatural, Hobbes, so far from making converts, had greatly strengthened the case of his adversaries, who now insisted more than ever

[1] T. Sprat, *History of the Royal Society* (2nd ed. 1701), 64.
[2] Ibid. 88.

on the extra-natural character of Christianity. This the Royal Society had to keep in mind, so it was thought inexpedient that Hobbes should be a fellow; moreover, the fact that he claimed to have squared the circle provided good, ostensible ground for excluding him altogether. So both the theologians and the mathematicians were placated; and, with this demonstration that religion and science were quite compatible, the Society would gladly have offered an honorary fellowship to the Almighty.[1] For a time, indeed, among educated men and even within the Royal Society, revelation had the better of research. Some of the Cambridge Platonists resorted to spirit-rapping as a means of fortifying their faith; and, at a time when the uneducated were ceasing to believe in witches, the last defence in England of belief in witchcraft was produced by Joseph Glanvill, a fellow of the Royal Society.[2] In Scotland, this incongruity was to be found within the covers of one book. In 1683 George Sinclair, professor of mathematics in Glasgow, published his *Natural Philosophy Improved by New Experiments*. This book, consisting mainly of accounts of investigations in hydrostatics, and in the air at the bottom of mines, ended with an appendix entitled: 'A true relation of an evil spirit that troubled a man's family for many days'. In England opinion was fortunately well in advance of Glanvill; in Scotland it was just abreast of Sinclair, so witch-hunting lasted longer in the north.

Such a vigorous intellectual ferment obviously could not last for long. The supernatural and the scientific which, even today, sometimes share the same uneasy bed, are best kept apart. A middle way was bound to be forthcoming to end both the acute antagonism and the unnatural union between these two extremes. The solution was called Deism. It was not new, but the name was; and, from this time onwards, for a new set of beliefs to flourish, some name, preferably ending in -ism is essential; indeed, much of the subjective life of the English-speaking peoples is expressed in -isms, which serve to denote

[1] I am indebted for this simile and for much of the earlier part of the above paragraph to a brilliant essay by R. F. Jones, 'The Background of the Attack on Science . . .', in *Pope and his Contemporaries*, ed. J. L. Clifford and L. Lande.

[2] Joseph Glanvill, *Saducismus Triumphatus*, 1666.

opinion as an alternative to creed, a situation possible only in those countries where either there is no infallible church, or the established church is tolerant. The new opinion was clearly formulated by John Toland, in whose education English culture had played no part. Born in the north of Ireland of a Roman Catholic family, he was a Protestant at the age of sixteen, and his education at Scottish universities was completed at Leyden. He was thus a convert and a cosmopolitan, whose travels had familiarized him with the extremes of obscurantism and scepticism. In 1696 appeared his *Christianity Not Mysterious*. It began with a daring pronouncement on the social basis which sometimes underlies orthodoxy—the fact that even intelligent men were unwilling to admit divergence from an established faith, either because of the law, or from fear of ostracism. He then claimed that it was absurd to base religious belief on obvious contradictions of nature; as for 'transubstantiation' and 'ubiquity', these he denounced as 'eastern ordures received into this western sink'.[1] Revelation, he claimed, could be regarded as no more than a primitive device for imparting information; the doctrines of the Gospel were, he thought, quite compatible with reason. Deism therefore, so far from being an attack on religion, merely claimed to establish it on a basis different from that commonly accepted.

As an alternative to the recognized creeds, the movement assumed different forms, all having a rationalist approach. It was associated with an increasing distrust of the hierarchy, and even a feeling that a priest, so far from being a good exponent of Christianity, may be its worst enemy. 'Priestcraft is the curse of all religions', declared a writer in 1702.[2] But it is important that, unlike France or Italy, England was never greatly influenced by anti-clericalism, because the English clergy, so far from being a separate caste, fitted intimately into the social order of things; and their influence in the parish was second only to that of the squire. It was partly for this reason that scepticism was seldom aggressive, or joined with ridicule; on the contrary, doubts about formal religion came to be entertained by an increasingly large number of thoughtful men, who found in 'natural religion' a more genuine expression of the

[1] J. Toland, *Christianity Not Mysterious*, preface.

[2] E. Hickeringill, *Priestcraft, its Character and Consequences*.

instinct of reverence. From this there resulted a new discovery,[1] that human misery and misfortune, so far from being punishments sent by God, are usually caused by deviation from right reason, or by giving way to passion. Happiness was elevated to supremacy as the chief aim of life; virtue, it was now thought, did not necessarily entail misery, nor sin enjoyment. So, by the dawn of the eighteenth century, a conception of society, based on reason and the pursuit of happiness, was in process of formulation; an alternative to the older orthodoxy, which limited complete happiness to the future world, and insisted on right beliefs in this. From such a changed conception of the role of Providence in human life, there naturally followed ideas of progress, since God was no longer thought of as the sole architect of man's fate.

But meanwhile, an alternative had been offered, namely, pietism or evangelicism, which, beginning as a crusade to penalize the vices of the poor, broadened out into a movement for human betterment, of which the more remote repercussions remained long perceptible. These were among the streams contributing to the broadening river of eighteenth-century English life.

3. Social Reform Movements

Throughout the later seventeenth century in both England and Scotland the one point of agreement between Crown, Lords, and Commons was the necessity for legislation to suppress sabbath-breaking, profaneness, and debauchery; indeed, in moments of tension, the legislature sometimes found relief by adding one more decree to an already overburdened moral code. The legislation of Charles II's reign was the most fruitful in such measures; and in no other period has there been such solicitude for the morality of the lower classes, or such determination to penalize their vices. But example seems to have outweighed prohibition; for, after the Revolution, Englishmen awoke to the fact that their metropolis was one of the most disorderly and dissipated cities in Europe, and that Restoration drama was the most obscene thing of its kind in the history of literature. 'A thick gloominess hath overspread our horizon, and our light looks like the evening of the world'—such was the

[1] R. L. *An Enquiry into Happiness* (3rd ed. 1717).

announcement made in the prospectus[1] issued by a Society for the reformation of Manners in 1692.

The establishment of such societies is the most notable social change in the last decade of the seventeenth century. One of the earliest[2] of these was a body of churchmen, formed in 1692, who agreed to invite their friends (of the church of England) to give information to the justices of all breaches of the moral code that came to their notice; and, for this purpose, to make use of informers, whose names were to be withheld from the convicted persons. So numerous were the laws dealing with profaneness and vice, that a printed compendium[3] was issued for the use of magistrates, clergy, and private persons, together with copies of the most recent proclamations on the subject. Zeal was stimulated by emphasis on the widely held opinion that popery favoured debauchery, because of the (alleged) ease with which absolution or indulgence might be obtained.[4] By 1698 the Dissenters had joined the Anglicans in this campaign, but at first it was thought that their support concealed a design for undermining the church.[5]

The simplest expression of the new movement might be no more than a visit by the justices and churchwardens to the public houses during the hours of divine service, in order to seize all who were found tippling there at that 'close' time; or it might be an elaborate organization for helping the magistrates with information about sabbath-breaking or keeping disorderly houses. The volunteers in this moral guard were given full instructions how to proceed. Thus, on Sundays, bakers in the streets with their baskets, barbers with their pots and periwig boxes, vendors standing by their stalls or open booths—all these were good game, each of whom, on conviction, would have to pay 5*s.*; but the amateur policemen were to exercise discretion, in cases of necessity or mercy, and were not to report those vendors who opened the doors of their cellars, since they might do so for light or ventilation.[6] Black lists of

[1] *Proposals for a National Reformation of Manners*, in *Bodl. Firth E. 25*, no. 8.

[2] *A Vindication of the Late Undertaking* . . ., 1692, in *Firth E. 22.*

[3] *A Help to a National Reformation* (1700), in *Bodl. Pamph.* 234.

[4] *A Specimen of a Declaration against Debauchery* . . ., in *Bodl. Pamph.* 190, no. 25.

[5] *Letters Illustrative of the Reign of William III*, ed. G. P. R. James, ii. 128, July 1698.

[6] *A Help to a National Reformation.*

offenders were drawn up and circulated. Such societies increased rapidly in the last years of the century, spreading to the provinces, Scotland,[1] Ireland, and the Plantations,[2] thus providing one of the earliest examples of organized effort for a social purpose. A specimen agreement for such bodies, 'where there are three or four pious persons', arranged for weekly meetings, at which controversial points of religion were to be avoided, invitation to friends to join in the movement, encouragement and help to officers of the law in the discovery of disorderly houses, consultation with lawyers wherever there was doubt about a prosecution, and constant prayer for the reformation of the nation in general.[3]

By the end of the reign these societies, which included all denominations, had the approval of the bishops, and it was known that the king was sympathetic. The cause was recommended in advice given to parliamentary candidates,[4] and was included in the Legion Memorial among the many desirable things that the Tory House of Commons had neglected. A great tradition had been set going. One of the first of queen Anne's proclamations[5] was not merely for the punishing of vice and immorality, but for 'the promotion of piety and virtue'; with her royal example, and that of her immediate predecessor, debauchery became less fashionable, and to that extent the Jacobite cause lost ground. A movement which had begun merely as an attempt to penalize tippling and sabbath-breaking among the humblest, had expanded into a nationwide reformation, thus creating an atmosphere of pietism and constraint which afterwards ensured the success of the Wesleyan and Evangelical movements. The aridity of the old theology was giving way to the fertile pastures of reformed manners and good morals.

While it is easy to recognize the narrowness of the movement as it at first took shape, it is difficult to measure its breadth as it gradually extended to the religious and social life of the nation; for it proved to be the precursor of a long series of

[1] *Domestic Details of sir David Hume*, 70–71.
[2] C. Bridenbaugh, *Cities in the Wilderness*, 229.
[3] These details are from *A Help to a National Reformation*, already cited.
[4] *The Elector's Right Asserted*, 1701, in *Bodl. Pamph.* 240, no. 21.
[5] *Steele*, i, no. 4814, 26 Mar. 1702.

concerted movements, whereby public opinion was brought to bear on what, each in its turn, was seen to be a deep-seated evil in our civilization. Moral reform led inevitably to social reform, and as England became less religious, she became more Christian. Meanwhile, in the period here considered, certain achievements can be recorded. One of these was the demonstration of how success may ultimately reward the sustained efforts of small groups of men; here indeed was a proof of what can be done by patient, active minorities. Another achievement was the bringing together of church and sect in a common crusade of humanity. Great institutions also owe their origin to the movement. In 1696 there was founded, by a small number of private persons, the Society for the Propagation of Christian Knowledge, a branch of which was established in 1701 as the Society for the Propagation of the Gospel in Foreign Parts. The first of these, in addition to the circulation of bibles and tracts, helped to found a large number of charity schools, and in this way did much to promote the education of the poor; the second extended its missionary work to the negroes in the Plantations. The discovery, in this scientific age, that the poor man and the black man have souls is comparable in its importance with the discovery of the theory of gravitation.

The influence of the movement can also be traced in two other spheres—in schemes for the betterment of humanity, and in a change whereby literature came to depend for its inspiration more on sentiment than on obscenity. Of the first, the schemes for social betterment, examples are the charitable projects that were launched, such as for the families of sailors,[1] or for widows.[2] It would be rash to assume that these schemes were always successful, or even that their promoters were honest, but at least they were based on the likelihood of public response; and they show that people were beginning to interest themselves directly in relieving the lot of less fortunate members of society. At the same time, attention was focused on the innumerable hospitals and charitable trusts which, like many survivals from the past, were often diverted from their original purpose, so that trustees and managers juggled with the rents and leases in order to benefit themselves. In 1701 the House

[1] *Supra*, 331.

[2] 'The Friendly Society for Widows', *Cal. S.P. Dom. 1697–8*, 337.

of Commons appointed a committee to investigate such abuses, which reported in favour of surveys of the lands constituting the endowments of these trusts, and the institution of a standard method of letting and leasing the lands. It was resolved that the lord chancellor, on application from the justices or from Quarter Sessions might issue a commission to the justices for investigation into complaints regarding the administration of such endowments, and it was even suggested that one-half of the funds should be applied to the benefit of the poor, while the other half was to be given to distressed seamen and their widows.[1]

There were also concrete plans for social reform. At that time, the Isle of Man was considered so undeveloped as to offer a good field for experiment; accordingly, a scheme was suggested to its suzerain, the earl of Derby.[2] The proposal was that, in every village of the island, a 'matronable' woman should be delegated to teach girls to spin, read, and do needlework. In order to make the inhabitants more 'civilized', a start was to be made with the children who, in the hour before divine service, were to be instructed in the Scriptures by the parson—an early proposal for a Sunday school. After the service, the whole village was to dine in a public booth, to which the better sort were to send provisions, in order that the poor might be entertained; after the meal, there were to be reading and 'laudable conversation'; in other words, some kind of parish hall was in view. Immigration into the island was to be promoted, and couples encouraged to marry before the age of twenty-five, when, if the husband was not in a trade, he was to be assigned 100 acres. For these objects a corporation was to be formed and a town to be erected where all having 1,000 acres or £600 stock in the company were each to build a house. There was to be a public workhouse and a public register; in the administration of the law, only murder, blasphemy, and rebellion were to be punished by death. This was one of the most advanced of all the social schemes propounded in the seventeenth century.

The second, the literary repercussions of the movement, may have been helped by the facts that, as early as 1682, the dramatist Sotherne was introducing virtuous women on the

[1] *C.J.* xiii, 9 Apr. 1701.

[2] *H.M.C. Rep.* xiv, app. pt. 4, *MSS. of lord Kenyon*, 430 sqq.

stage, and Tonson the bookseller produced a number of serious books, including a translation of Virgil and (in 1688) an edition of *Paradise Lost.*[1] This reaction came to a head with the publication of the *Short View of the Immorality and Prophaneness of the English Stage* (1698) by the non-juring Jeremy Collier. The reception given to his book should be contrasted with that accorded, earlier in the century, to a similar attack on the stage—the *Histriomastix* of William Prynne. Collier's argument was reinforced by many sermons, such as those of Tillotson, against immorality; and indeed there were some who would have abolished the stage altogether. Fortunately, it was preserved, but there had already begun a movement which substituted sentiment for indecency, a change which had been noticed about the year 1696, when Colley Cibber produced a bad play with a good purpose—his *Love's Last Shift.*[2] The word 'sensible' was now coming to be used in its eighteenth-century connotation—almost the converse of that of today—for it implied sensitiveness, and denoted a refined type of being, receptive only of exalted thoughts and moved only by noble passions. It was fitting that this new sentimentalism should be expressed mainly by women, two of whom were writing for the stage in William's reign.[3] These were Catherine Trotter and Mary Manley, whose dramas, because of their 'sensibility', may have made a special appeal to the female sex. Both writers were not only creating a place (still somewhat controversial) for women in literature, but were starting the vogue of the 'sensible' young lady, destined to a very long life, in spite of her liability to swoon on the slightest provocation.

But (so difficult is it to get at true origins) even these pioneers had been anticipated by another woman, Mrs. Aphra Behn, the first professional woman writer in England, known to many readers and theatregoers of the Restoration as the author of novels and plays. As she had to make a living in the England of Charles II, she adopted titles for her compositions which often suggested a libertinism that was not fully confirmed by their

[1] A. Beljame, op. cit. (1954 ed.), ch. 3.

[2] For this see J. W. Krutch, *Comedy and Conscience after the Restoration*, ch. viii.

[3] Joyce M. Horner, *The English Women Novelists and their Connection with the Feminist Movement 1688–1797*, in Smith College Studies in Modern Languages, vol. xi.

subject-matter; for Mrs. Behn was really (so far as we know) a virtuous person; and, for a time at least, this feminine compromise seems to have worked. Humanity and 'sensibility' were clearly revealed in her most famous creation, Oroonoko, the royal slave, whose tragedy at the hands of brutal slave masters she so feelingly depicted. Oroonoko, according to Mrs. Behn, although nominally a savage, was handsome, noble, and generous; devoid of the sophistication of polite society, but qualified to excel in it. 'He knew almost as much as if he had read much';[1] he had heard of, and admired the Romans; he spoke English, French, and Spanish; he knew enough of English history to deplore the death of Charles I (Mrs. Behn was an enthusiastic admirer of the Stuarts). 'He had nothing of barbarity in his nature', and acquaintance with him would have proved that wit is not limited to the whites, who indeed would have had reason to be ashamed by comparison with such a noble representative of a race which they exploited and despised. It is not surprising that such a shrewd connoisseur as Charles II was interested in him; so also were many readers in post-Revolution England, who witnessed Sotherne's dramatized version on the stage (1696).

Here was an expression, not only of a new humanitarianism, but of an important discovery—that certain beings, for long supposed to be our inferiors, were really possessed of such genuine qualities as to provide an object lesson for civilized men. A woman had proclaimed that a negro was capable of exalted sentiments; soon, in the conduct of their moral crusade, the respectable, by contact with the disreputable, must have realized that even the lower classes are human, a discovery which, in spite of some scepticism, continued to gather force in the next century. Throughout that century, in western Europe, there was an awareness that civilization had reached a peak, beyond which there must be decline or revolution; to avert which evils, recourse must be had to origins, to the fundamental, uncorrupted bases of the nation or race. In such a quest it was inevitable that comparison should be made with imaginary representatives of those peoples who, it was assumed, still retained their primitive virtues, since by contrast with their

[1] *Oroonoko*, in the 1722 edition of Mrs. Behn's novels, I. 86. For good comment see A. Beljame, op. cit. v. ch. 2, pt. i.

straightforward humanity, one could register the contortions and aberrations of sophisticated and degenerate men. For this purpose, Montesquieu chose a Persian; Frederick the Great (in a spirit of raillery) selected a Chinaman; Rousseau, less exotic in his taste, found what he wanted in the inhabitants of Corsica and Poland; Dr. Johnson showed judicious conservatism in his preference for an Ethiopian. In the seventeenth century a woman had started it all with a Negro. So, by the end of that century, the Scarlet Woman, at long last, had made her protesting exit over the remains, not of broken hearts, but of lost souls; and her place was taken, in silent dignity, by Natural Man, the embodiment of those sterling qualities which civilization was now striving to regain.

4. Rival Views about Man and Society: Mandeville, Shaftesbury, and Locke

The natural creatures in which inquiring minds were now becoming interested did not consist only of the human species; for civilized society was becoming so self-conscious that humbler forms of corporate organization came to be studied with avidity, and with some disconcerting results. For long, the communal life of bees had fascinated poets and moralists, both of whom agreed in commending the industry, the organization, and even the public spirit of the hive, which seemed to prefigure the sociability and co-operation on which the human state is built. But it was Hobbes who first disturbed this agreeable analogy by his criticism that the beehive was a stable community, not because its inhabitants were so human, but because they were so inhuman; for, unlike men, they are not prompted by competition for honour or gain; their individual good is identical with the common good; as they are devoid of reason, they fail to see defects in the organization of their common business; and, as they are without speech, as we know it, no one member can hope to persuade the others that black is white. All that the beehive proves, according to Hobbes, is how much more precarious is organized human society, since men have so many vices from which bees are free. But this doctrine, so flattering to apian prestige, was upset in 1705 by another philosopher, Bernard Mandeville (1670–1733), a Dutch physician who settled in England late in the seventeenth century. His investigations showed that the hives had degenerated sadly from the homogeneity and simplicity of Hobbes's day. There were two contrasted types. One was poor, unenterprising, and honest; so honest, indeed, that a bishop acted as treasurer; but, in these backward hives, the bees were of such low mentality that they were prepared to swallow the doctrine of Non Resistance. The other hives were rich, powerful, and aggressive, having an unlimited supply of cheap workers; organizations directed by expert, progressive management, intent on exploiting for the common good not the virtues of the bees, but their weaknesses and even their vices. Here incidentally we have a comparison, from an unusual point of view, of the England of 1685 with that of 1705. The upshot of it all was that, whatever doubts remained about the morality of bees,[1] there was none about the immorality of their two commentators, Hobbes and Mandeville, each in turn the bogey man of his century. And here was the moral of it all:

> Fools only strive
> To make a great and honest hive.
> T'enjoy the world's conveniences,
> Be fam'd in war, yet live in ease,
> Without great vices, is a vain
> Eutopia seated in the brain.
> Fraud, luxury and pride must live,
> While we the benefits receive;
> Hunger 's a dreadful Plague, no doubt,
> Yet who digests or thrives without?

'If originality consists in not being anticipated, then no one was ever original.'[2] Many predecessors had contributed to the intellectual outlook of Mandeville, author of *The Fable of the Bees*, including Erasmus, Montaigne, Hobbes, Spinoza, La Rochefoucauld, and Bayle; indeed, all the anti-idealist opinions of these writers were fused together in order to present a view of human society which, however repugnant, has some kind of consistency, in the sense that a liquid distilled from many

[1] This old problem has at last (1954) been settled by scientific research at Rothamsted, which shows that bees are not by nature industrious, but are activated by the 'dope' exuded from the queen. Dr. C. Butler, *The World of the Honeybee*.

[2] This quotation is from page cxii of Mr. F. B. Kaye's introduction to his scholarly edition of *The Fable of the Bees*.

disagreeable ingredients may have clarity and uniformity. Pursuit of the paradox may have led him farther than he had intended to go, so that he was obliged to disclaim any hostility to virtue or preference for sin; furthermore, his system was based not on evil, but on something very different, namely vice; the first dangerous to society from its strength, the second useful to the statesman from its weakness. At first his parable had attracted little attention, because after all it was only a parable, and in doggerel at that. But when, in 1714, he re-issued it with explanatory comments, the book was presented as a public nuisance by the Middlesex grand jury.

In these comments, and in such essays as that *On Charity and Charity Schools*, and in his *Search into the Nature of Society*, this unusual author expounded the principles which, in his opinion, best accounted for the wealth and greatness of a state. These principles were based on assumptions about the nature of man and his environment. His environment was obviously bad, for it includes water which drowns, fire which destroys, insects and reptiles which poison; the fruits of the earth are gathered only after toil—here Mandeville is obviously selective. As for civilized man, he prides himself on his virtues and his superiority over the animal creation. But his nature remains essentially animal, concealed beneath qualities which are labelled virtues. Of these qualities, according to Mandeville, courage arises merely from horror of shame; religion from fear and humility; honour (non-existent in the lower classes) is a quality hereditary in noble families, like the gout, and is inflamed by the reading of romances; prosperity is based on fraud; diligence is known only by its absence in children and servants; charity is a device for soothing our susceptibilities; pity is a frailty, like anger or pride; good breeding consists in flattering the vanity or hypocrisy of others whom we know to be either fools or knaves. 'To be at once well-bred and sincere is a contradiction.' So the civilized man of Mandeville is the natural man of Hobbes decked out with a periwig and gold lace.

The bees contributing to the hive were very unevenly rewarded, those who had laboured most receiving least; but this was an essential principle of apian as of human economy, discontent being precluded by the fact that the unlucky ones had no idea of the felicity enjoyed by their more fortunate brethren.

By stirring up emulation among the workers, they would outdo each other in supplying still more honey to the drones; the more workers, the more honey, and the greater the renown of the hive. If, on the other hand, the workers were educated above their station, as by charity schools, they would naturally cease to be workers, and the bottom would fall out of the system. Private vices, by the management of a dexterous statesman, might thus be turned into public benefits; for, as all society is based on selfishness, skilled direction can utilize human weaknesses in order to increase the wealth, and with it the power of the state. Hence, luxury and waste can be defended because they create work for others; war is a natural expression of human pugnacity, in which personal sacrifice is imposed only on the poor, who have this disability, that they can rise no higher, and this comfort, that, while their superiors have their ups and downs, they can sink no lower. The cells of the honeycomb as of the state are held together by the adhesive wax of self-interest, which prompts us to tolerate the vices of others so that our own will not be exposed.

The cynic may often express a disagreeable whole truth; much more acceptable is the agreeable half-truth, especially if its expression be pompous or authoritative. Mandeville had in mind a purveyor of what he considered agreeable half-truths, namely, the third earl of Shaftesbury, author of a collection of essays, known as *The Characteristics*, first published in their entirety in 1711, but including items of an earlier date.

The name Shaftesbury recalls some matters of interest to the student of history. As grandson of the first earl, the author of *The Characteristics*[1] had to live down the evil things in that great statesman's career; but, on the other hand, he perpetuated the idealism and optimism which had inspired the better elements in the activities of Charles's chancellor, just as he anticipated the benevolent humanity of his descendant, the philanthropist earl of the nineteenth century. Another matter of interest about him was his health. He died in 1713 at the age of forty-two. A man of vigorous intellectual life, he was debarred from a public career by tuberculosis and asthma, disabilities which obliged him to regulate his life by a strict régime. Now, it is undeniable

[1] A good modern edition is that, edited in two volumes, by J. M. Robertson.

that the health of a writer may influence, and even determine, the character of his output; one might go farther and claim that, from about this period onwards, it is possible to distinguish the contribution made to English life and letters by men who, though of different temperaments, had this in common, that they were obliged, by some physical infirmity, to stand aside from the turmoil of everyday life, and to view that life with a detachment not so easily attainable by more robust contemporaries. Mandeville was aware of this when he suggested[1] that the mild, benevolent Shaftesbury believed himself virtuous because, through ill health, his passions were dormant. In this way, it is perhaps possible to speak of the beginnings of a valetudinarian tradition, represented (to take eighteenth-century England alone) by such writers as Addison, Pope, Gray, Cowper, and Gibbon, all of them characterized by a detached attitude, occasionally degenerating into the selfish, the querulous, or, as with Pope, the waspish. Of these writers, it was probably Addison who had the greatest influence on his contemporaries. Today we find him tepid, or insipid; but, to his first readers, accustomed to the hot condiments of religious or political controversy, he must have brought something infinitely cool and refreshing.

The seventeenth century, with its tense religious and political experience, was in need of the corrective that could best be provided by such a spectator as Shaftesbury. His early education had been supervised by Locke, the friend and physician of the family, an education completed in Holland, where Pierre Bayle had popularized an attitude of liberal scepticism. Like Locke, Shaftesbury wrote for the educated man, as much as for the professed metaphysician; he thought of himself as a moralist, rather than a philosopher, and his importance lies in this, that he outlined a system of ethics, vague it is true, but entirely independent of religion or the supernatural. As with Locke also, his teaching had as much influence in France as in England; and only his style, diffuse and involved, has prevented a wider knowledge of his writings.

In his analysis of human character, he starts from the current conception of bodily 'humours', which connected temperament with the quantitative proportion in the body of the four

[1] Mandeville, *Fable of the Bees* (ed. F. B. Kaye), 332.

chemical elements. These humours, he says, must have 'vent'; the heterogeneous particles in the mind must be thrown out by 'fermentation'.[1] Accordingly, 'bad' humours find their outlet in 'enthusiasm', that is, religious strife, for which the only antidote is 'good' humour, the foundation of true piety and religion. Most of the great religious reformers, according to Shaftesbury, were 'enthusiasts', who, as worshippers of a deity even more irritable and vindictive than themselves, had encouraged a 'snappish' spirit, thereby creating sects, intent on tearing each other 'tooth and nail'. To worship a vengeful, implacable deity is therefore likely to breed the same qualities in the worshipper. Translating this into modern terms, it appears that Shaftesbury connected the excesses of religious life, not with erroneous doctrines, but with something abundantly evidenced by his contemporaries, namely, a costive habit of body and a quarrelsome disposition of mind. From this unusual beginning he claimed that the true 'theist' is he who believes that everything is ordered for the best; while the perfect 'atheist' is one who, rejecting this divine and benevolent principle, believes that life is governed by chance.[2]

It was in his 'Enquiry concerning Virtue or Merit'[3] that he expressed most clearly his ethical principles. He set himself to formulate a system which would make a man 'honest in the dark', a system working independently of the fear of either hell or the police. It is not certain that he succeeded in this difficult task. But he was an optimist. He claimed that everyone had a natural sense of right and wrong, a 'moral sense', capable of development by worship of a deity who embodied, in their supreme form, the qualities of justice and goodness.[4] At this point a certain aesthetic element intervened. Virtue he defined as 'the love of order and beauty in society',[5] a definition more likely to be accepted by a Platonist than by a Christian, because it has relevance only for such exclusive civilizations as that of Athens in the age of Pericles, or England in the age of Whig magnates and aristocratic connoisseurs. But his principle was expanded into a message of wider import, for Shaftesbury was concerned not only with sociability, but with human happiness.

[1] Shaftesbury, *Characteristics*, ed. J. M. Robertson, i. 12–13.
[2] Ibid. 240.
[3] Ibid. 237 sqq.
[4] Ibid. 262.
[5] Ibid. 278.

He based happiness not on right doctrines, but on right affections—right in reference to oneself and one's fellow men; 'to have the natural affections such as love, complacency, good will, and a sympathy with the kind or species, is to have the chief power and means of enjoyment'.[1] Happiness was thus linked with benignity (the *bienfaisance* of his contemporary Fontenelle); a natural and kind affection was the best corrective to ill humour and unsociability. Only by sharing with others could human happiness be achieved. Shaftesbury's ethics amount, therefore, to no more than his belief that character may be developed and felicity enjoyed by the encouragement of those social and friendly feelings which, as they are practised in the family, may with advantage be extended to the state.

Critics have found it easy to expose the somewhat vague idealism which permeated the *Characteristics*. But, to the student of the seventeenth century, these badly written essays have an interest to be found nowhere else, because, as in a mirror, they reveal the deformities of that age; its crudities, its literalism, the still-glowing embers of fanaticism and hate. These things could be seen best by one who stood somewhat apart. But Shaftesbury has more than a negative importance. He bridged, as did no one else, those two contrasted periods of English life which, in the absence of any better terminology, we are obliged to designate the seventeenth and eighteenth centuries; the one heated by struggle and effort, the other, mellowed by a sense of achievement, having a civilization exclusive and selfish, it is true, but abounding in those social amenities and aesthetic enjoyments, which could be appreciated to the full so long as England remained an island, and the 'poor' could be taken for granted. Shaftesbury had a formula for human happiness, not altogether new, but in desperate need of reassertion. Like the Greeks, he found it, not in rigid adherence to principle or doctrine, but in the simple, essentially human affections, shared with others; in a sense of balance and proportion; in the harmonious adaptation of man to his environment. The Augustan Age proved that England was ready for such an interpretation of life.

From all this it may be surmised that by the dawn of the eighteenth century many of the asperities of English life and

[1] Shaftesbury, *Characteristics*, i. 292.

thought were in process of mitigation; and, moreover, after years of struggle and experiment, the Revolution had provided a constitution which, whatever its defects, had this merit, that it worked. At last men were becoming proficient in what, after all, is not a science, but an art, the art of living together in society. Of that art, John Locke was the greatest exponent. His style, devoid of the subtle charm of Hobbes, as of the irony of Defoe, is so simple and straightforward that his books can be read with understanding and appreciation by any educated person; indeed, it is this clearness and unpretentiousness of expression, so eloquent of sincerity and conviction, that has won for him a place among the philosophers comparable with that of Plato. Abroad, Locke's reputation was even greater than at home; for he was accepted as the almost official exponent of a state of society, happily achieved in England, and earnestly longed for by the idealists of less fortunate lands. To few thinkers has such a tribute been accorded.

Like Descartes, he rejected the preconceptions of the past. Thought he regarded as the product of sensory experience; what we call original ideas arise, in his view, from the observations of the senses, actuated by the operations of the mind. The mind has power to repeat, compare, and unite simple ideas, so creating complex ideas, and this an infinite extent. His *Essay concerning humane Understanding* (1690), in which these principles are maintained, would thus be consistent with the modern theory which regards the brain as a mechanism, composed of innumerable electric cells, each responsive to some stimulus from without. To contemporaries, Locke's psychology must have seemed new or revolutionary, since it rejected innate ideas, and connected the subjective, not with the supernatural, but with the perceptive.

In *Some thoughts concerning Education* (1693) he made an essay in applied psychology. He condemned harshness and cruelty; 'people should be accustomed from their cradles to be tender to all sensible creatures'. History, as taught to the young, was often no more than a record of fighting and killing; conquerors, in the fashion set by historians, were lauded in proportion to the butcheries they had committed. All this may nowadays seem trite, but it has not always been trite. More novel was Locke's opinion about children's questions. In his view, these should be taken seriously, for 'children are travellers newly arrived in a strange country; we should therefore make conscience not to deceive them'. More, he thought, might be learned from the unexpected questions of a child than from the discourse of men 'who walk in a road', according to their prejudices or borrowed notions. In other words, a child may be illiterate, but, unlike so many literate men, he has not yet parted with his intellectual honesty. This was not so trite. In the practical work of educating the young, Locke favoured the use of mechanical devices, by which it might appear that a game was being played. He commended for older pupils the study of Greek, law, accountancy, and shorthand; as regards Latin, he thought that writing of Latin verses was overdone. About music he was doubtful, since so few reach that stage where their performances are likely to give pleasure.

In his *Letter concerning Toleration* (1690) he maintained that no peace was possible so long as men believed that dominion was founded on grace, and that religion should be propagated by force. The clergy, he considered, should be limited to their ecclesiastical duties, because church and state are separate. This separation was indeed an English achievement, and dates from the Revolution.[1] Locke, an intensely religious man, had no great regard for the hierarchy; and he noted how quickly the churchmen changed their doctrines according to royal needs or behests. Generally, he would extend toleration to all who are tolerant. He would therefore have excluded not only atheists (everyone agreed in this), but also those who are guilty of antisocial conduct or opinion; also those whose allegiance is primarily to some foreign power, or whose integrity is vitiated by a dangerous principle, such as that faith need not be kept with heretics. This was the most convincing theory of toleration that had yet been enunciated; convincing, because it claimed that toleration is a social virtue, to be denied only to those whose principles or conduct are antisocial. The Toleration Act of 1689, however limited it may seem to us, was based on this social foundation.

Best known of all are his two treatises *On Government* (1690). Of these, the first is a criticism, one might even say a demolition of Filmer's *Patriarcha*. In the seventeenth century pedigree

[1] *Supra*, 238–9.

came second in importance only to divine intention; so an institution which united the two was strong indeed. They were united in hereditary, anointed monarchy. According to Filmer there had been a donation of sovereignty to Adam, and all lawful kings held their title by direct descent from him. To this, Filmer's critic objected that the dominion granted to Adam was not of the regal type, for it was shared with the rest of mankind; moreover, Adam was a poor sort of king, since he had to work for his living. God had given him, not a sceptre, but a spade. Locke had no difficulty in removing the father of mankind from his place at the top of the list of divine-right monarchs.

The second treatise is of wider import. Its account of the origin of society and the contract was given sharper outline by contrast with the doctrines of Hobbes, who had wilfully deprived natural man of his natural goodness, and had deposed natural law (*jus naturale*) from its high position as an ideal towards which men aspire, degrading it into natural license, which men must live down. Natural man and natural law had therefore to be restored to the respectability which they had enjoyed before Hobbes interfered with them. According to Locke, man in the state of nature is not necessarily at war, and he may even have good qualities; in such a primitive condition, all things are held in common. But, unfortunately, it is a precarious state, since some men by their industry add to their possessions, so creating envy among less industrious neighbours. Hence, in the state of nature, private property is engendered; and, in order to safeguard it, some kind of civil society must be instituted. Implicit in this is the theory that labour is the origin and justification of property. Such a view could not have commended itself to eighteenth-century landlords, who obviously had not acquired their property by labour; hence, it was in their interests to defend private property on semi-religious grounds, not unlike those on which the old kingship itself had been based. So the divine right of kings was succeeded by the divine right of property owners. In practice, therefore, the labour or 'natural right' theory of property was relegated to academic discussion; but the other part of Locke's theory, that one of the main functions of the state is to protect property, was eagerly welcomed. In this way, Locke had the singular felicity of accommodating both those who wanted a more satisfactory justification of property, and those who sought for security in the enjoyment of what they already possessed.

Of more permanent importance was his identification of law with freedom. There had been wide acceptance of Hobbes's opinion that law was inhibition or restraint; but, to Locke, law was the direction of a free and intelligent people towards its proper interests; instituted, not to abolish or restrain, but to preserve and enlarge. To many of Locke's contemporaries this may have seemed strange, since, in their experience, man-made laws were often harsh and oppressive. But the common lawyers, exponents of a jurisprudence whose origins were lost in the mists of antiquity, were convinced that English law was the bulwark of English liberty; and alone, among all the legal systems of the civilized world, the common law was identified with both the genius and the freedom of a race. Hence Locke's association of law with liberty was neither paradoxical nor fanciful, and was soon to be reaffirmed by Rousseau, the most deeply intuitive of those thinkers who preceded the French Revolution. From Bracton and Coke to Blackstone and Bentham English law, by its response, however tardy, to new needs and circumstances, has maintained a continuity to be found in no other of our institutions, a continuity perpetuated by the settlers on the American continent, for whom it provided the inspiration of a new and independent state.

The art of living together in society is one of the most difficult of all arts, and history is strewn with the wreckage of failures to achieve it. To us, the Revolution of 1688 and the establishment of a Protestant, maritime state may well seem remote, as the thought of Locke may seem trite or commonplace; the first to be taken for granted, the second in danger of depreciation, because anyone can understand it. We may have outgrown these things, but nevertheless they have determined the evolution of Anglo-Saxon civilization in two hemispheres, maintained by communities which are as ready to defend their liberties as they are unwilling to enforce them on others. This voluntary element, this aversion from proselytism and propaganda, this spirit of live and let live is our most precious heritage from the seventeenth century. That its exponents still survive the threats of intolerance and repression is the distinctive achievement which unites the English-speaking world.

INDEX